The Making of the Magdalen

The Making of the Magdalen

PREACHING AND POPULAR DEVOTION
IN THE LATER MIDDLE AGES

Katherine Ludwig Jansen

PRINCETON UNIVERSITY PRESS
PRINCETON, NEW JERSEY

SECOND PRINTING, AND FIRST PAPERBACK PRINTING, 2001
PAPERBACK ISBN 0-691-08987-6

THE LIBRARY OF CONGRESS HAS CATALOGED THE CLOTH EDITION
OF THIS BOOK AS FOLLOWS

JANSEN, KATHERINE LUDWIG.
THE MAKING OF THE MAGDALEN : PREACHING AND POPULAR DEVOTION IN THE
LATER MIDDLE AGES
/ KATHERINE LUDWIG JANSEN.
P. CM.
INCLUDES BIBLIOGRAPHICAL REFERENCES AND INDEX.
ISBN 0-691-05850-4 (ALK. PAPER)
1. MARY MAGDALENE, SAINT—CULT—ITALY—HISTORY—MIDDLE AGES, 600–1500.
2. MARY MAGDALENE, SAINT—CULT—FRANCE—PROVENCE—HISTORY—MIDDLE AGES,
600–1500.   3. SPIRITUAL LIFE—HISTORY OF DOCTRINES—MIDDLE AGES, 600–1500.
4. PREACHING—ITALY—HISTORY—MIDDLE AGES, 600–1500.
5. PREACHING—FRANCE—PROVENCE—HISTORY—MIDDLE AGES, 600–1500.
6. CHRISTIAN HAGIOGRAPHY—HISTORY AND CRITICISM.   7. WOMEN IN
CHRISTIANITY—ITALY—HISTORY—TO 1500.   8. WOMEN IN
CHRISTIANITY—FRANCE—PROVENCE—HISTORY—TO 1500.   9. ITALY—CHURCH
HISTORY—475–1400.   10. ITALY—CHURCH HISTORY—15TH CENTURY.
11. PROVENCE (FRANCE)—CHURCH HISTORY.   I. TITLE.

BS2485.J36   1999   274'.05 21—dc21   99-045174

BRITISH LIBRARY CATALOGING-IN-PUBLICATION DATA IS AVAILABLE

THIS BOOK HAS BEEN COMPOSED IN GALLIARD

PRINTED ON ACID-FREE PAPER. ∞

WWW.PUP.PRINCETON.EDU

PRINTED IN THE UNITED STATES OF AMERICA

3 5 7 9 10 8 6 4 2

Contents

PART IV: RESPONSES

List of Illustrations

Acknowledgments

I have incurred many debts to both institutions and individuals during the research and writing of this book. It is a delight at last to give credit where credit is due.

Many libraries and archives granted me access to their collections during the course of my research. I am grateful to the archivists of the Archivio di Stato in Florence and Naples, as well as the Archivum Generale Ordinis Praedicatorum, Rome. Most of my time was spent in libraries, however, and I would be remiss if I did not express my gratitude to the directors and librarians of the Biblioteca Antoniana in Padua, the Biblioteca Nazionale Centrale in Florence, the Biblioteca Nazionale Marciana in Venice, the Biblioteca Nazionale Vittorio Emanuele III in Naples, the Library of the Sacro Convento in Assisi, the British Library, the Library of Balliol College in Oxford, the Library of St. John's College in Cambridge, and the Index of Christian Art in Princeton. But it was in the libraries of Rome where this project really took wing: my thanks go to the Biblioteca Angelica, the Biblioteca Casanatense, and the Biblioteca Vallicelliana, as well as the libraries of the École Française and the Biblioteca Herziana. The Library of the American Academy in Rome became a second home and its superb staff a second family to me. But at the heart of my research lies the incomparable collection of sermon manuscripts housed in the Biblioteca Apostolica Vaticana. I regard myself as having been privileged to have worked in the Vatican Library during the prefecture of Fr. Leonard Boyle.

This book had its genesis as a doctoral thesis which enjoyed the beneficence of many institutions including the Fulbright-Hays Fellowship to Rome, the Gladys Krieble Delmas Foundation Research Grant, the American Historical Association's Bernadotte E. Schmitt Research Grant, Princeton University's Harold E. Dodds Fellowship, and the Mellon Foundation's Post-Enrollment Fellowship. The Rome Prize from the American Academy in Rome allowed me to complete the dissertation in the splendor of the refurbished villa atop the Gianicolo. Caroline Bruzelius, Pina Pasquantonio, and the entire Academy staff made it a memorable year that I will always cherish. The dissertation prize from Princeton University's Department of History, which released me from a semester's teaching, as well as a summer grant from Catholic University's Research Fund, allowed me to transform the dissertation into a book. Finally, a fellowship from the National Endowment for the Humanities aided immeasurably in preparing the manuscript for publication. I wish to thank all these institutions and the people who represent them for their financial munificence.

I have been extremely fortunate to have been a student of some of the most remarkable historians in the profession. As an undergraduate, Penny Johnson and Norman Cantor, gifted teachers both, first introduced me to and encouraged me to pursue the study of the Middle Ages. Caroline Walker Bynum, Giles Constable, and John Fleming opened up the vistas in graduate school. Peter Brown's gentle but persistent nudges have saved me time and again from indulging in my own worst analytical and rhetorical strategies. His work on the not uncomplicated relations of sanctity and society has inspired my own. Finally, I wish to thank Bill Jordan, my advisor, who supported me from the moment I arrived at Princeton. He has been extremely generous in giving his time and assistance to me over the years. I am fortunate to have been his student and to count him now as my friend.

A group of people read this manuscript (in part and in full) in various drafts and stages of its preparation. I would like to thank Peter Brown, Natalie Davis, Peter Dougherty, David Hall, Penny Johnson, Bill Jordan, Pamela Ludwig-Dreyfuss, Ann Matter, Marla Stone, and Brigitta van Rheinberg for their perceptive comments, criticism, and sage advice. I am indebted above all to Nicole Bériou who read the chapters focusing on sermons. I am grateful for her friendship and her generous help with this study. Her bibliographic suggestions and scrupulous readings, along with the blue pencil of copy editor Bill Laznovsky saved me from many errors. Those that still remain are mine alone.

In addition to close readings, the content of this book has been enriched enormously by conversations with many people who have either supplied me with pertinent information, asked the telling questions, or provided hospitality and friendship when needed most. They include Fr. Louis-Jacques Bataillon, Uta Blumenthal, Brenda Bolton, David d'Avray, Suzanne Briod, Dana Calbi, Giovanna Casagrande, Tracy Ehrlich, Jonathan Elukin, Julia Fischer, DJ Ford, Fr. Reginald Foster, Julian Gardner, Mario Geymonat, Giovanna Gronda, Martha Hodes, Nicholas Horsfall, Diane Owen Hughes, Beverly Kienzle, Lester Little, Alison Morgan, Larry Poos, Louise Rice, and Roberto Rusconi. My friends at Princeton, my fellow fellows at the American Academy in Rome, and my colleagues in the department of history at CUA will recognize their presence in these pages as well.

My family's interest in and enthusiasm for my project has not waned since the day I began. To their credit, not one of them ever asked when I would finish. I acknowledge with gratitude the support of my parents, Janine Lowell and Allan Ludwig, along with his wife, Gwen Akin. My Mom, especially, deserves credit for proofreading my book manuscript not once but twice. My godparents, Susan Minot Woody and Melvin Woody, have been models to me throughout my life. My brother Adam's talent and skill in his own craft have been an inspiration to me. Randy, Raphaelino, and now Sophia have provided needed distractions and brought pure joy at critical junctures over the last few years. Though we live 3,000 miles apart, 7,000 miles during much of the research and writing of this book, my sister Pammy has been the voice of sanity and reason, and most important of all, my best friend through thick and thin.

My final words of gratitude are reserved for Massimo. It was he who held the ladder while I photographed in Bergamo; it was he who searched the dark streets of Cusiano for the butcher-sacristan so that we could illuminate the frescoes in the parish church; it was he who twice scaled La Saint-Baume with me; and it was he whose teeth chattered with mine that midsummer's day when it snowed on us in Pontresina. It was also he who helped me track down errant references, and it was he who patiently corrected every page of this manuscript. This book is now as much his as it is mine. It is to him that I dedicate it.

Abbreviations

AASS	*Acta Sanctorum*
AFP	*Archivum Fratrum Praedicatorum*
AGOP	Archivum Generale Ordinis Praedicatorum
BAV	Biblioteca Apostolica Vaticana
BHL	*Bibliotheca Hagiographica Latina*
BRDU	*Bollettino r. deputazione di storia patria per l'Umbria*
BS	*Bibliotheca Sanctorum*
Casanat.	Biblioteca Casanatense
CCCM	*Corpus Christianorum, Continuatio Mediaevalis*
CCSL	*Corpus Christianorum, Series Latina*
CSCO	*Corpus Scriptorum Christianorum Orientalium*
CSEL	*Corpus Scriptorum Ecclesiasticorum Latinorum*
DBI	*Dizionario biografico degli italiani*
DHGE	*Dictionnaire d'histoire et de géographie ecclésiastique*
DIP	*Dizionario degli istituti di perfezione*
DS	*Dictionnaire de spiritualité, ascétique et mystique, doctrine et histoire*
DTC	*Dictionnaire de théologie catholique*
Flor. Naz.	Biblioteca Nazionale Centrale (Florence)
Marc.	Biblioteca Nazionale Marciana (Venice)
MEFRM	*Mélanges de l'École Française de Rome. Moyen Âge*
Nap. Naz.	Biblioteca Nazionale Vittorio Emanuele III (Naples)
O.E.S.A.	Ordinis Eremitarum Sancti Augustini
O.F.M.	Ordinis Fratrum Minorum
O.P.	Ordinis Praedicatorum
PG	*Patrologiae Cursus Completus: Series Graeca*, ed. J.-P. Migne
PL	*Patrologiae Cursus Completus: Series Latina*, ed. J.-P. Migne
RLS	*Repertorium der lateinischen Sermones des Mittelalters für die Zeit von 1150–1350*, ed. J. B. Schneyer
Scriptores	*Scriptores Ordinis Praedicatorum Medii Aevi*, ed. Thomas Kaeppeli, O. P.
SC	*Sources Chrétiennes*

A Note on Transcription, Translation, and Names

*I*n the interests of saving space, when quoting from a source, I give an English translation in the body of the text, while the Latin (only of manuscript sources and incunabula) has been consigned to the footnotes. I have not standardized spellings; I have, however, modernized punctuation. All translations are my own unless indicated otherwise.

For the most part I render the names of preachers in the vernacular (rather than the Latin) according to their place of origin. Thus I name Remigio de' Girolami rather than Remigius de Girolamis Florentinus. I retain the Latin name either when a preacher is commonly known by that name (e.g., Jacobus de Voragine) or when his place of origin is obscure or unknown. The primary exception to this rule is when a name has been anglicized by tradition; Antonio da Padova, for example, is rendered as Anthony of Padua.

The Making of the
Magdalen

Introduction

*I*n mid-fifteenth-century Mantua, on the day on which "the church re-
cites the gospel about Mary Magdalen," a member of the noble Coppini family ducked into church while awaiting the birth of his child. There
he heard a sermon preached. The aim of any sermon was (and continues
to be) twofold: it was meant both to teach and animate the Christian faith.
In Quattrocento Mantua the preaching seems to have been particularly effective: Signor Coppini returned home so moved by the words of the
preacher that he decided to christen his newly born daughter Maddalena.[1]

Signor Coppini's response to the Magdalen sermon illustrates forcefully
the capacity of medieval preaching to influence the lives of the laity. In this
case the preacher's words induced contrition and inspired an act of devotion—the naming of a child—in honor of Saint Mary Magdalen. This book
examines the development of the cult of Mary Magdalen both through the
lens of medieval preaching, and the responses of those who heard the friars' sermons.[2] In a broader sense this is a study of later medieval religious
culture, which uses the figure of the Magdalen to open up the richly symbolic world of the later Middle Ages. Structured around questions of origins, transmission, and reception, the task of this book is to explain why,
by the later medieval period, Mary Magdalen had become the most popular female saint after the Virgin Mary. Toward that end, this study unpacks
the social meanings of the Magdalen to demonstrate how sanctity functioned in the later Middle Ages.

Why the later Middle Ages? I concentrate on the later medieval period
because it was the era when devotion to Mary Magdalen was at its height
in the Mediterranean regions of Provence and Italy. It is a fact first observed
forty years ago by Victor Saxer, doyen of modern critical studies on the

---

[1] G. Michele Piò, *Delle vite degli huomini illustri di S. Domenico. Libri Quatro. Ove
compendiosamente si tratta de i santi, beati, & beate, & altri di segnalata bontà dell'Ordine
de' Predicatori* (Bologna: Sebastiano Bonomi, 1620), 439.

[2] I use the word cult in its strictest sense to mean acts of reverential devotion or homage
paid to a holy person or saint.

saint.[3] Saxer, however, was interested primarily in the history of the cult of the Magdalen in the High Middle Ages, particularly in northern France. My study picks up chronologically and geographically where Saxer's effectively ends.

The thirteenth century, then, is my starting point, a point that coincides neatly with the growth of a concerted campaign to bring preaching to the people in the later Middle Ages. Not that preaching had been absent from medieval life prior to that point, but on 11 November 1215, at the first plenary session of the Fourth Lateran Council, Canon 10, *inter caetera,* decreed:

> Among the various things that are conducive to the salvation of the Christian people, the nourishment of God's word is recognized to be especially necessary, since just as the body is fed with material food so the soul is fed with spiritual food. . . . It often happens that bishops by themselves are not sufficient to minister the word of God to the people . . . . We therefore decree by this general constitution that bishops are to appoint suitable men to carry out with profit this duty of sacred preaching, men who are powerful in word and deed and who will visit with care the peoples entrusted to them in place of the bishops, since these by themselves are unable to do it, and will build them up by word and example. . . . We therefore order that there be appointed . . . coadjutors and cooperators not only in the office of preaching but also in hearing confessions and enjoining penances and in other matters which are conducive to the salvation of souls.[4]

The immediate and primary beneficiaries of this canon were the nascent mendicant orders of Saint Francis and Saint Dominic. They were the persons mighty in "word and deed" who, in the event, were sent out into the world to fulfill the "duty of sacred preaching."[5] It is their sermon collec-

---

[3] *Le culte de Marie-Madeleine en occident des origines à la fin du moyen-âge,* 2 vols. (Cahiers d'archéologie et d'histoire, 3) (Auxerre-Paris: Publications de la Société des Fouilles Archéologiques et des Monuments Historiques de l'Yonne-Librairie Clavreuil, 1959), 224.

[4] The Latin text of the council is found in *Conciliorum oecumenicorum decreta,* ed. G. Alberigo, C. Leonardi, et al. (Centro di Documentazione Istituto per le Scienze Religiose— Bologna) (Rome: Herder, 1962), 215–16. I use the English translation (with facing page Latin) in *Decrees of the Ecumenical Councils,* 2 vols., trans. Norman Tanner (Washington, D.C.: Sheed and Ward, 1990), vol. 1, 239–40.

[5] The literature on mendicant preaching is vast; see especially A. Lecoy de la Marche, *La chaire française au Moyen Age spécialement au XIIIe siècle* (Paris: Librairie Renouard, 1886); Johannes Baptist Schneyer, *Geschichte der katholischen Predigt* (Freiburg im Breisgau: Seelsorge, 1969); Carlo Delcorno, *La predicazione nell'età comunale* (Florence: Sansoni, 1974), 22–35; Delcorno, "Origini della predicazione francescana," in *Francesco d'Assisi e francescanesimo dal 1216 al 1226* (Atti dei convegni della società internazionale di Studi Francescani, vol. 6), (Assisi: Typografia Porziuncola, 1977), 127–60; Delcorno, "Rassegna di studi sulla predicazione medievale e umanistica (1970–80)," *Lettere Italiane* 33 (1981): 235–76; Jean Longère, *La prédication médiévale* (Paris: Études Augustiniennes, 1983); D. L. d'Avray, *The Preaching of the Friars: Sermons Diffused from Paris before 1300* (Oxford:

tions, dating from the later thirteenth century, that survive in manuscript in libraries throughout Europe, and which serve as the source for much of my analysis.[6]

I pursue my themes until the close of the Middle Ages, about 1500, or more precisely to 1517, the textbook date marking the advent of the Reformation. It would have been arbitrary to select a date prior to the early sixteenth century to end this study as the themes considered in late medieval sermons on the Magdalen were remarkably consistent over time. This is not to say that a sermon by Anthony of Padua could be mistaken for one by Bernardino da Siena. Clearly certain points were amplified and elaborated differently, and in greater detail in the fifteenth century than they were in the thirteenth; but as we shall see, the essential content and message of medieval *de sanctis* sermons did not change drastically until the Reformation, when preachers were confronted by the Protestant challenge to the cult of the saints.

Pursuing the subject of preaching on and response to Mary Magdalen into the later period has an additional advantage: by the later Middle Ages, when lay literacy was on the rise, we can begin to see more clearly lay responses to sermons on the saints.[7] It is from the fourteenth century onwards that we have letters, spiritual autobiographies, commonplace books, *ricordanze,* and the like that reveal what the saints, particularly Mary Magdalen, meant to the laity, both men and women.

The geographical focus of this book is Italy and its axis with Provence, but with an eye always on concomitant developments throughout western Christendom. Provence is important for the study of the progress of the

---

Oxford University Press, 1985); Zelina Zafarana, "La predicazione francescana," and "Predicazione francescana ai laici," both now collected in *Da Gregorio VII a Bernardino da Siena,* ed. O. Capitani, C. Leonardi, et al. (Quaderni del Centro per il collegamento degli studi medievali e umanistici nell'Università di Perugia) (Florence: La Nuova Italia, 1987); Hervé Martin, *Le métier de prédicateur en France septentrionale à la fin du Moyen Age 1350–1520* (Paris: Cerf, 1988); Augustine Thompson, O.P., *Revival Preachers and Politics in Thirteenth-Century Italy: The Great Devotion of 1233* (Oxford: Clarendon Press, 1992); Fr. Louis-Jacques Bataillon, *La prédication au XIIIe siècle en France et Italie. Etudes et documents* (Aldershot, England: Variorum, 1993); and Nicole Bériou and D. L. d'Avray, *Modern Questions about Medieval Sermons: Essays on Marriage, Death, History and Sanctity* (Biblioteca di Medioevo Latino, 11) (Spoleto: Centro italiano di studi sull'alto medioevo, 1995).

[6] Johannes Baptist Schneyer has cataloged mendicant sermon collections (along with others) up to the mid-fourteenth century in *Repertorium der lateinischen Sermones des Mittelalters für die Zeit von 1150–1350* (Beiträge zur Geschichte der Philosophie und Theologie des Mittelalters 43), 11 vols. (Münster-Westfalen: Aschendorffsche, 1969–90). Hereafter it is abbreviated as *RLS.*

[7] For this topic, see M. B. Parkes, "The Literacy of the Laity," in *The Medieval World,* ed. David Daiches and Anthony Thorlby (London: Aldus Books, 1973), 555–77, and M. T. Clanchy, *From Memory to Written Record: England 1066–1307* (Oxford: Blackwell, 1993; 2d ed.).

cult of Mary Magdalen in the later Middle Ages because in 1279 the saint's relics were (re)discovered there at the church of Saint-Maximin. The guiding hand behind the discovery was the Angevin prince, Charles of Salerno, heir apparent to the county of Provence. Equally important for our purposes was that in 1289, when Charles became Count of Provence, he also inherited the throne of the Kingdom of Naples. Through Charles II and the mendicant orders Magdalen devotion was imported into southern Italy.

Italy is important to any understanding of the success of the cult of Saint Mary Magdalen in the later medieval period, not only because of Angevin rule of the South, but because of its high concentration of mendicant friars, the greatest disseminators of the Magdalen cult in Christendom. It was in central Italy that the Franciscans and Dominicans both clustered heavily, establishing themselves by founding convents, priories, and *studia* in cities such as Assisi, Florence, and Bologna.[8] Both orders were envisioned as preaching orders from their inception: Francis and his early followers were authorized to preach penance, provided that they did not speak on arcane matters of theology; Dominic's order was instituted with the express mission of preaching against heresy. The words of the friars fell on fertile ground, particularly in central Italian urban centers where newly found wealth among the bourgeoisie was cause for a certain amount of spiritual discomfort. The penitential fervor stirred up by the sermons of the friars— in which Mary Magdalen served as a figurehead for the preaching of penance—seems to have provided just the appropriate salve city dwellers required to assuage their anxious consciences and enrich their spiritual lives.

I examine the transmission of the medieval cult of the Magdalen through preaching, mainly mendicant preaching, drawn for the most part from unpublished sermon manuscripts.[9] Sermon literature is the centerpiece of my research because sermons were the mass media of the day. They were a mediating culture between the institutional authority of the church and its lay audience.[10] Sermons were the crossroads, as it were, the point at which the transmission of ideas and their reception often intersected. And it was

---

[8] For the early Franciscan foundations, see Luigi Pellegrini, *Insediamenti francescani nell'Italia del Duecento* (Rome: Ed. Laurentianum, 1984) and John Moorman, *Medieval Franciscan Houses* (St. Bonaventure, NY: Franciscan Institute, 1983). For good general histories of the orders, see John Moorman, *A History of the Franciscan Order from Its Origins to the Year 1517* (Oxford: Clarendon Press, 1968) and William A. Hinnebusch, O.P., *The History of the Dominican Order*, 2 vols. (Staten Island, NY: Alba House, 1966–73).

[9] Nicole Bériou based her study of the Magdalen on sermons as well. Her study was confined to thirteenth-century Parisian sermons, however. See "La Madeleine dans les sermons parisiens du XIIIe siècle," in *MEFRM* 104/1 (1992): 269–340.

[10] See Peter Burke, *Popular Culture in Early Modern Europe* (New York: New York University Press, 1978), 70–71.

there, in sermons, that we find a web of social meanings actively being rehearsed, contested, and redefined. Sermons were not always, as is commonly assumed, some sort of monolithic institutional discourse imposed from on high on the passive lay subject. They could be, in Bakhtin's terms, dialogical in that it is not just the institutional voice, or the preacher's voice, that is contained in them; frequently, if we listen carefully, the voice of the audience can also be discerned.[11] Preachers were attentive to the concerns of their audiences, and some sermons reflect an interchange of ideas between the friar and his congregation.[12] Sermons, therefore, had the ability both to shape popular opinion and to reflect it. Consequently, they were, as one scholar long ago suggested, "the surest index of the prevailing religious feeling of their age."[13]

People listened and responded to the preaching of the friars. We have already noted Signor Coppini's reaction to a Magdalen sermon; it should be noted that his was in no way a unique or isolated response to medieval preaching. In her spiritual autobiography, the Poor Clare, Camilla Battista da Varano, relates how when she was only eight or ten years old she heard a sermon that changed the course of her life. Writing to her spiritual director in 1491, she recollected that his sermon on that day in 1466 was the beginning of her conversion to the religious life:

> Know, my sweet and beloved father, that all my spiritual life had its origin, beginning and foundation in you and no other. . . . Know, my Father, that when you preached at Camerino the last time, I could not have been more than eight or ten years old. . . . On Good Friday I wanted to hear you preach. Blessed indeed was that holy sermon of yours to which, thanks to the holy spirit, I listened not only with attention, but wholly rapt in it, almost outside myself. . . . At the close of your sermon, you made an exhortation to the people to weep over the passion of Christ, asking every one of them, at least on Fridays, to meditate on the passion, and to shed a little tear in memory. You affirmed that nothing else would be more pleasing to God, or more profitable to our souls. These holy words . . . from your lips, made such an impression on my tender heart . . . and were impressed in such a way in my mind and in my heart that I never forgot them. . . . When I was a bit older, I made a vow

---

[11] See Mikhail M. Bakhtin, *The Dialogic Imagination,* ed. Michael Holquist, trans. Caryl Emerson and Michael Holquist (Austin: University of Texas Press, 1981), particularly 272–79.

[12] I am thinking especially of the Dominican preacher Giordano da Pisa. See chapter 3 for Giordano's incorporation of his congregation's questions into his sermon.

[13] Mark Pattison, "Tendencies of Religious Thought in England, 1688–1750," in Pattison, *Essays and Reviews* (London, 1860; 2d ed.), 267, cited in David d'Avray, *Death and the Prince: Memorial Preaching before 1350* (Oxford: Clarendon Press, 1994), 203. Pattison was arguing, however, that sermons only reflect popular opinion.

to God to shed at least one tear every Friday, out of love for the passion of Christ. And so began my spiritual life, as you intended it.[14]

The course of Camilla Battista's life changed because of a sermon, but we should not assume that all sermons had such consequential effects. In the ordinary way they served to instruct the laity in religious belief and practice. Or as Bernardino da Siena, a great practitioner of the genre, remarked to his congregation:

> What would become of this world, I mean of the Christian faith, if there were no preaching? . . . How ever shouldst thou have known what sin is, if not from preaching? What wouldst thou know of hell, if there were no preaching? What wouldst thou know of any good work, or how thou shouldst perform it, if not from preaching, or what wouldst thou know of the glories of Heaven?[15]

One cannot possibly imagine a less disinterested source than Bernardino; nevertheless, sermons do get us closer than theological treatises and other learned discourses to the religious message imparted to the plain people of medieval Europe. They were also the vehicle which transported the contents of the gospels to ordinary people. Margery Kempe learned most of what she knew about her faith from sermons, as her autobiography reveals. Margery recounts that she was often reproved for "conversing about scripture, which she learned in sermons and by talking with clerks."[16]

By the end of the Middle Ages sermons were not just heard, they were also read, having entered the canon of devotional literature of the later medieval period. Sometimes a literate lay person would transcribe a sermon heard *viva voce* into a commonplace book for future reflection, but equally, lay people of certain means owned books of sermon collections.[17] As we might expect, monasteries and friaries owned sermon collections, tools of the trade, as it were; but so did female houses, a clear sign that sermons were read and reflected on as devotional material.[18]

---

[14] Beata Camilla Battista da Varano, *La vita spirituale* in *Le opere spirituali*, ed. Giacomo Boccanera (Jesi: Scuola Tipografica Francescana, 1958), 9–11. As Camilla Battista was unsure whether she was eight or ten years old at the time, the sermon was preached either in 1466 or 1468.

[15] Translated in Ray C. Petry, *No Uncertain Sound: Sermons that Shaped the Pulpit Tradition* (Philadelphia: Westminster Press, 1948), 270.

[16] *The Book of Margery Kempe*, ed. B. A. Windeatt (New York: Penguin, 1985), 65.

[17] For an example of a lay person transcribing a sermon for personal reflection, in this case a Magdalen sermon, see Zelina Zafarana, "Per la storia religiosa nel Quattrocento. Una raccolta privata di prediche," now collected in *Da Gregorio VII a Bernardino da Siena*, particularly 283 and 312–16. Zafarana called his notebook a "personal *summula* of the Christian faith." The fifteenth-century Lady Peryne Clanbowe is one example drawn out of many lay people who owned books of sermons. See Anne Clark Bartlett, *Male Authors, Female Readers: Representation and Subjectivity in Middle English Devotional Literature* (Ithaca, NY: Cornell University Press, 1995), 12.

[18] See, for example, the library inventory of the Clarissan convent of Monteluce in *Memor-*

Consideration of reading habits inevitably raises questions of reception. How does a listener or reader receive a text, in this case a sermon? Reading (or listening), as Anne Clark Bartlett, among others, has argued, "can never represent the unproblematic transmission of a fixed message into the ready mind of a reader, no matter how pious and receptive."[19] Rather, these acts are "always a process of negotiation" between, as another literary scholar suggests, "the *culturally activated* text and the *culturally activated* reader, an interaction structured by the material, social, ideological, and institutional relationships in which *both* texts and readers are inescapably inscribed."[20] Medieval audiences, then, were no mere passive receptacles into which preachers poured their sermons. Medieval audiences—readers, listeners, and spectators—clearly responded to the messages they received. Consequently, another goal of this study is to uncover audience response to the preachers' Magdalen.

Evidence for investigating audience response includes, among other sources, letter collections, spiritual autobiographies, naming practices, testamentary bequests, artistic commissions, ecclesiastical endowments, and hagiography. The time has long since past when scholars had to mount elaborate *apologiae* for using hagiography as a historical source; nonetheless, a word or two about how I employ medieval writings on the saints seems appropriate here. There is no question that hagiography, like sermons, influenced the spiritual and devotional lives of the people of the Middle Ages. There are countless examples of medieval people whose religious lives were significantly altered after having encountered a particular saint's life. The conversion of Waldes after hearing a jongleur recount the life of Saint Alexis, or Giovanni Colombini's spontaneous conversion upon hearing the *vita* of Saint Mary of Egypt are just two celebrated examples of hagiography's powers of persuasion. Of course not everybody responded so dramatically to the lives of the saints; most people used the saints' *vitae* merely as aids to inspire their spiritual lives. Many lay people owned collections of saints' lives; others, such as Isabel Bourchier, countess of Eu, commissioned them for their personal devotional reading.[21] Still others

---

iale di Monteluce. Cronaca del monastero delle clarisse di Perugia dal 1448 al 1838, intro. by Ugolino Nicolini (S. Maria degli Angeli [Assisi]: Edizioni Porziuncola, 1983), Katherine Gill, "Women and the Production of Religious Literature in the Vernacular, 1300–1500," in *Creative Women in Medieval and Early Modern Italy*, ed. E. Ann Matter and John Coakley (Philadelphia: University of Pennsylvania Press, 1994), 64–104, and Roberto Rusconi's comments in "Women Religious in Late Medieval Italy: New Sources and Directions," in *Women and Religion in Medieval and Renaissance Italy* (Chicago: University of Chicago Press, 1996), 313. For comparison, see David N. Bell, *What Nuns Read: Books and Libraries in Medieval English Nunneries* (Kalamazoo, MI: Cistercian Publications, 1995).

[19] Bartlett, *Male Authors, Female Readers*, 2–3.

[20] Tony Bennett, "Texts, Readers, Reading Formations," *Journal of the Midwest Modern Language Association* 16 (1983): 12, cited in Bartlett, *Male Authors, Female Readers*, 2–3.

[21] For her devotion to Mary Magdalen, see chapter 9.

had saints' lives read to them, as did Cecily of York who seems to have preferred hearing about active female saints. At her mid-day meal she enjoyed
listening to "holy matter" including the lives of Saint Mary Magdalen and
Saint Catherine of Siena, or the Revelations of Saint Birgitta of Sweden.[22]

Within the genre of hagiography itself the impact of the lives of the saints
can also be detected. It is a commonplace in the scholarship to remark that
writings about the saints often reflect other writings about the saints in
both form and content. Conventions, stock images, and models are all part
and parcel of the hagiographer's craft. Emphasis on the hagiographer and
his craft, however, obscures the importance of the subject's contribution
to the text. Recent scholarship on medieval hagiography, focusing particularly on the lives of later medieval holy women and their confessor-biog-
raphers, has begun to address this problem. By shifting attention to the female subject's personal relationship with her hagiographer, often her
confessor, we see holy women begin to emerge from subject status into individual agents who actively contributed to and shaped the texts—the
vitae—eventually written about them.[23] I am not suggesting that hagiography is a transparent window reflecting women's experience, or that it is
unmediated; I am suggesting, rather, that later medieval *vitae* can be read
as collaborative efforts between the hagiographer and his subject. Reading
in this way allows *vitae* to be used as signposts of audience response to both
hagiographic and homiletic themes. Therefore, when the *vita* of Margaret
of Cortona proclaims that she was much influenced by Mary Magdalen, we
should not dismiss the statement as a hagiographical topos, or her hagiog-

---

[22] *Orders and Rules of the Princess Cecill, Mother of King Edward IV* in *A Collection of
Ordinances and Regulations for the Government of the Royal Household, made in divers
reigns. From King Edward III, to King William and Queen Mary.* (Society of Antiquaries
of London) (London: J. Nichols, 1790), 37, cited in Bartlett, *Male Authors, Female
Readers,* 11.

[23] See Sofia Boesch Gajano and Odile Redon, "La *Legenda Maior* di Raimondo da Capua,
costruzione di una santa," in *Atti del simposio internazionale Cateriniano-Bernardiniano*
(Siena 17–20 April 1980), ed. Domenico Maffei and Paolo Nardi (Siena: Accademia senese
degli Intronati, 1982), 15–35; Anna Benvenuti Papi, "Padri Spirituali," now collected in *In
castro poenitentiae,* 205–46 (originally published as "Devozioni private e guide di coscienze
femminili nella Firenze del Due-Trecento," *Ricerche storiche* 16 [1986]: 565–601); John
Coakley, "Gender and Authority of Friars: The Significance of Holy Women for Thirteenth-
Century Franciscans and Dominicans," *Church History* 60 (1991): 445–60 and "Friars as
Confidants of Holy Women in Medieval Dominican Hagiography," in *Images of Sainthood in
Medieval Europe* (Ithaca, NY: Cornell University Press, 1991), 222–46; Elizabeth Alvilda
Petroff, "Male Confessors and Female Penitents: Possibilities for Dialogue," in *Body and Soul:
Essays on Medieval Women and Mysticism* (Oxford: Oxford University Press, 1994), 139–60;
and Catherine M. Mooney, "The Authorial Role of Brother A. in the Composition of Angela
of Foligno's Revelations," in *Creative Women in Medieval and Early Modern Italy: A Religious
and Artistic Renaissance,* ed. E. Ann Matter and John Coakley (Philadelphia: University of
Pennsylvania Press, 1994), 34–63.

rapher's flight of fancy; rather, we must take seriously the possibility that Margaret's devotion to Mary Magdalen was a defining feature of her spiritual life.

My work on Mary Magdalen in the later medieval period examines the meanings of both the ecclesiastical and lay contributions to the development of her cult. In this way my study departs from the work of my colleagues and predecessors in the field. The first serious study of the historical figure of Mary Magdalen emerged from the new field of textual criticism developed by humanist scholars in the early modern period. In 1517, the French Dominican scholar Jacques Lefèvre d'Étaples fueled acrimonious debate when he concluded in his treatise, *De Maria Magdalena*, that no evidence supported the venerable Gregorian claim that Mary Magdalen was indeed one and the same person as Luke's sinner and Mary of Bethany. John Fisher, Bishop of Rochester, rose to refute this sacrilege and defend the Roman Church's position on Magdalenian unity.[24] By the next century that controversy had died down, only to be replaced by another one when Jean de Launoy in his *De commentitio Lazari et Maximini, Magdalenae et Marthae in Provinciam appulsu* (1641) poured scorn on the beloved provençal legends which claimed Mary Magdalen had evangelized southern Gaul. He dismissed them as nothing more than pious nonsense. Outraged local scholars rushed to the defense of the legends, publishing tomes with titles such as *Ratio vindicatrix calumniae contra negantem adventum Lazari, Magdalenae et Marthae in Provinciam* (1644) and *Le triomphe de la Madeleine en la créance et vénération de ses reliques en Provence* (1647).[25] It was not until two centuries later, however, when the Sulpician father E.-M. Faillon produced *Monuments inédits sur l'apostolat de Sainte Marie Madeleine en Provence* (1848) that an elaborate *apologia* of the provençal claims was mounted in a style that twentieth-century scholars would recognize as something akin to modern scholarship.[26] Faillon's two volumes are still useful (if used with due caution) since they gather together in one place hundreds of documents dispersed throughout libraries and archives of Europe. All of Faillon's erudition, research, and documentation

[24] Jacobus Faber Stapulensis, *De Maria Magdalena, et triduo Christi disceptatio* (Paris: Henri Estienne, 1517). On Lefèvre, see Eugene Rice, "The Humanist Idea of Christian Antiquity: Lefèvre d'Étaples and His Circle," *Studies in the Renaissance* 9 (1962): 126–60. On the debate, see Anselm Hufstader, "Lefèvre d'Étaples and the Magdalen," in *Studies in the Renaissance* 16 (1969): 31–60. For the Gregorian Magdalen, see chapter 1.

[25] *Ratio:* F. Michel Jourdain (Aix, 1644) and *Triomphe:* J. B. Guesnay (n.p., 1647). For this debate, see Michel Feuillas, "La controverse Magdalénienne au milieu du XVIIe siècle. Ripostes provençales à Jean de Launoy," in *Marie Madeleine dans la mystique, les arts et les lettres,* ed. Eve Duperray (Paris: Beauchesne, 1989), 89–109.

[26] E.-M. Faillon, *Monuments inédits sur l'apostolat de Sainte Marie-Madeleine en Provence et sur les autres apôtres de cette contrée, Saint Lazare, Saint Maximin, Sainte Marthe,* 2 vols. (Paris: J.-P. Migne, 1859).

did not hold up to more exacting methods of scholarship, however. By the late nineteenth century, the tough-minded Louis Duchesne concluded that despite Faillon's protestations to the contrary, Magdalen veneration had come to Provence no earlier than the mid-eleventh century.[27]

In this century, the Magdalen emerged from the realm of regional and confessional debate to draw the attention of modern critical scholarship from a wide array of disciplines. Beginning in 1937 Hans Hansel published a body of work focusing on the textual histories and transmission of the medieval Magdalen legends.[28] Helen Meredith Garth's *Saint Mary Magdalen in Mediaeval Literature*[29] set its sights a bit broader and attempted to synthesize the medieval literature on the saint. Marjorie Malvern's *Venus in Sackcloth*,[30] a quirky survey of the figure of the Magdalen in literature and art, covered some two millennia of Magdalenian history.

Recently scholars of early Christianity, particularly feminist scholars, have taken up the case of Mary Magdalen in an effort to demonstrate the presence of authoritative female leaders in the early Christian church. Elisabeth Schüssler Fiorenza, Ben Witherington III, Carla Ricci, and Karen King have fixed on the historical Magdalen of the gospels as a means of spotlighting the important role of women in the primitive church.[31]

In the field of art history, Marga Janssen laid the groundwork for research on the medieval iconography of the saint in the West.[32] An important exhibition, *La Maddalena fra sacro e profano,* mounted at Florence's Pitti Palace in 1986, brought together for the first time a vast collection of

---

[27] L. Duchesne, "La légende de Sainte Marie-Madeleine," *Annales du Midi* 5 (1893): 1–33, reprinted in *Fastes épiscopaux de l'ancienne Gaule* (Paris: Albert Fontemoing, 1907).

[28] See, in particular, Hans Hansel, *Die Maria-Magdalena-Legende. Eine Quellen Untersuchung* (*Greifswalder Beiträge zur Literatur und Stilforschung,* 16/1) (Greifswald: Hans Dallmeyer, 1937).

[29] *Saint Mary Magdalene in Mediaeval Literature* (Baltimore: Johns Hopkins Press, 1950).

[30] *Venus in Sackcloth: The Magdalen's Origins and Metamorphoses* (Carbondale, IL: Southern Illinois University Press, 1975).

[31] Fiorenza, "Feminist Theology as a Critical Theology of Liberation," *Theological Studies* 36 (1975): 605–26 and *In Memory of Her: A Feminist Theological Reconstruction of Christian Origins* (New York: Crossroad, 1983); Witherington, *Women and the Genesis of Christianity* (Cambridge: Cambridge University Press, 1990); Ricci, *Maria di Magdala e le molte altre. Donne sul cammino di Gesù* (Naples: D'Auria, 1991), now translated as *Mary Magdalen and Many Others: Women Who Followed Jesus* (Minneapolis, MN: Fortress Press, 1994); and King, "Prophetic Power and Women's Authority: The Case of the *Gospel of Mary* (Magdalene)," in *Women Preachers and Prophets through Two Millennia of Christianity,* ed. Beverly Mayne Kienzle and Pamela J. Walker (Berkeley: University of California Press, 1998), 21–41.

[32] Marga Janssen, *Maria Magdalena in der abendländischen Kunst. Ikonographie der Heiligen von den Anfängen bis ins 16. Jahrhundert* (Inaugural diss., Freiburg im Breisgau, 1961) and "Maria Magdalena," in *Lexikon der christlichen Ikonographie,* 8 vols. (Rome: Herder, 1968–76), vol. 7 (1974), 516–41.

visual evidence that demonstrated both the continuity and change in representing the saint from early Christianity to the present.[33]

But the most important work on the saint, indeed the source on the cult of the Magdalen, is Monsignor Victor Saxer's *Le culte de Marie-Madeleine en occident des origines à la fin du moyen-âge*.[34] Written in 1959, it remains the most valuable piece of scholarship on the cult of Mary Magdalen in the West, chiefly for its work on the liturgy, which has not been superseded.

When I began work on the Magdalen for my doctoral dissertation, from which this study has descended, the only recent major contribution to the field was a collection of conference essays entitled, *Marie Madeleine dans la mystique, les arts et les lettres*.[35] Its essays, by no means centered on the medieval period, ranged far and wide in their subject matter moving easily from Petrarch to Georges de La Tour to Le Corbusier. It was a portend, however: the 1990s would usher in a flurry of scholarship dedicated to Mary Magdalen. Lilia Sebastiani's *Tra/Sfigurazione*[36] was published in 1992 as was the École Française de Rome's volume of essays on the medieval Magdalen, containing important contributions by Nicole Bériou and Jacques Dalarun, among others.[37] Susan Haskins' *Mary Magdalen: Myth and Metaphor* appeared at the end of 1993.[38] Haskins was trained as an art historian, Sebastiani as a moral theologian; nevertheless they approach the Magdalen similarly. Both books are big synthetic surveys, based on published texts, that encompass both the Roman and the Orthodox Churches from early Christianity to the present. While revising my book for publication two more monographs appeared. The first examines the late medieval German legends; the second is a study produced in France of the figure of Mary Magdalen in medieval literature.[39] The field of Magdalen studies has

[33] The catalog of the exhibition is *La Maddalena tra sacro e profano,* ed. Marilena Mosco (Milan: Mondadori, 1986). My discussion has centered on full-length studies; articles worth mentioning are Sarah Wilk's excellent study of fifteenth-century Florentine imagery, "The Cult of Mary Magdalen in Fifteenth-Century Florence and Its Iconography," *Studi Medievali*, 3d series, 26 (1985) II: 685–98, and Victor Saxer's almost annual contributions to the field, many of which are listed in the bibliography.

[34] The full citation is at n. 3.

[35] The full citation is at n. 25.

[36] *Tra/Sfigurazione: Il personaggio evangelico di Maria di Magdala e il mito della peccatrice redenta nella tradizione occidentale* (Brescia: Queriniana, 1992).

[37] *La Madeleine (VIIIe–XIIIe siècle), MEFRM* 104/1 (1992).

[38] *Mary Magdalen: Myth and Metaphor* (London: HarperCollins, 1993). In addition to all this activity, a doctoral thesis by Raymond Clemens, *The Establishment of the Cult of Mary Magdalen in Provence, 1279–1543* (Ph.D. diss., Columbia University, 1997), has also been completed.

[39] M. Boxler, "*Ich bin ein Predigerin und Appostlorin.*" *Die deutschen Maria Magdalena-Legenden des Mittelalters (1300–1550). Untersuchungen und Texte* (Deutsche Literatur von den Anfängen bis 1700, 22) (Berne: Peter Lang, 1996) and E. Pinto-Mathieu, *Marie-Madeleine dans la littérature du Moyen-Age* (Paris: Beauchesne, 1997).

hardly had time to fallow in recent years; the 1990s seem to be the true era of "Magdalenian fermentation."[40]

Why should scholars of the 1990s have developed such a great interest in Mary Magdalen? Doubtless much of the credit is due to the development over the past twenty years or so of a coherent body of feminist scholarship that has made the study of women a legitimate (and vital) field of historical investigation. Its offspring, the more recent fields that examine the cultural construction of gender and sexuality, have further contributed new ways of thinking critically about topics traditionally associated with women's studies. Apart from the institutionalization of new critical disciplines within academe, the study of saints and their cults, which came of age in the 1980s, is also a contributing factor to the rise in the Magdalen's scholarly popularity. The pathbreaking work of scholars such as Peter Brown, Caroline Walker Bynum, and André Vauchez laid the groundwork for all subsequent studies of sainthood, particularly sanctity in the medieval period.[41]

The present study has been influenced by and contributes to these scholarly fields and traditions, as a survey of its contents demonstrates. The overall argument of the book is cumulative: though the chapters are structured around different themes, nevertheless they are interwoven to give a complete picture of the late medieval cult of the Magdalen, its symbolic meanings, and the uses of sanctity in the Middle Ages.

Chapter 1 is an introductory chapter that presents in a synthetic manner a survey of the legacy of early Christian, late antique, and early medieval texts that shaped the image of the Magdalen inherited by the later medieval period. It documents the rise of the cult of the Magdalen in the Middle Ages and introduces a number of themes and arguments that run throughout the book. As I hope this book will be read by scholars and non-scholars alike, this chapter is intended primarily for the reader who has no prior grounding in Magdalenian scholarship.[42] For the specialist, this chapter frames and analyzes familiar texts in a fresh way. That is, the texts presented here are examined according to the demands of the communities that pro-

---

[40] The phrase is Victor Saxer's in "Maria Maddalena," *BS*, vol. 8 (1967), 1089.

[41] See Peter Brown, *The Cult of the Saints: Its Rise and Function in Latin Christianity* (Chicago: University of Chicago Press, 1981); Caroline Walker Bynum, *Holy Feast, Holy Fast: The Religious Significance of Food to Medieval Women* (Berkeley: University of California Press, 1987); and André Vauchez, *La sainteté en occident aux derniers siècles du Moyen Age d'après les procès de canonisation et les documents hagiographiques* (Bibliothèque des Écoles Française d'Athénes et de Rome, fasc. 241) (Rome: l'École Française de Rome, 1981) at last translated as *Sainthood in the Later Middle Ages,* trans. Jean Birrell (Cambridge: Cambridge University Press, 1997).

[42] Toward that end, and where possible, my footnotes have included references to published English translations.

duced them. This method focuses on literary artifacts as products of community need and desire, an approach that emphasizes the social and ideological pressures informing the creation of texts.

The study is then divided into four parts. The chapters in Part One treat the mendicant friars' deep identification with the Magdalen.[43] In chapter 2 I examine how and why they used her as a symbol of the *vita apostolica*, their own way of living in the world. In contrast to chapter 1, this chapter tightens the frame, moving directly into the heart of medieval Magdalen devotion. It also contributes to a contemporary debate about whether or not women can preach in the Catholic tradition. Chapters 3 and 4 analyze the mendicants' construction of the Magdalen as a symbol of the active and contemplative lives. Chapter 3 has a dual focus: like the first chapter, it has a broad frame that serves first to chart the history of lay religiosity in the Middle Ages, and second to show how by the thirteenth century, Mary Magdalen was being preached as a symbol embodying the active life of the laity. Chapter 4 shows how Mary Magdalen's scriptural and legendary *personae* were fused to produce a contemplative mystic. Taken together, the chapters in Part One suggest that through the process of symbolic gender reversal the mendicants identified themselves with the faithful and humble Magdalen in opposition to the institutional church, as symbolized by Peter, prince of the apostles, who faithlessly had denied Christ.

The chapters in Part Two trace the evolution of the Magdalen from Luke's nameless sinner to the symbol of *luxuria* in medieval sermons. I argue that preachers and moralists of the later Middle Ages invented a Magdalen to address philosophical and social exigencies: the nature of Woman, the care and custody of women, and the ever-increasing problem of prostitution. Through recourse to the symbol of the Magdalen these chapters disclose medieval gender discourse in the making.

Part Three analyzes the Magdalen as the unrivaled symbol of penance in the later Middle Ages. I tie the Magdalen's fortunes as penitential symbol to the rise of penitential devotion in both its sacramental form—the four-fold obligation enshrined at the Fourth Lateran Council in 1215—and as it was expressed in the penitential spirituality of the laity. This section demonstrates not only how Mary Magdalen became the medieval model of penitence, but more important, it shows how she became the paradigmatic symbol of hope for all sinners in the later Middle Ages, explaining much of her universal appeal.

The study concludes by turning from the preachers to their audiences in an effort to uncover the public's reception of the saint. It is the task of Part Four to distinguish how the preachers' symbolic Magdalen was received

---

[43] I have used the writings of members of the Franciscan, Dominican, and Augustinian orders.

and understood by their congregations; in other words, to disclose audience response to the saint.

Who precisely made up the audience of those reading and listening to sermons? Ideally, and most probably in reality too, they were people from all stations in life, as a glance at the list of those targeted by Humbert of Romans in his handbook for preachers makes abundantly clear.[44] Thus both men and women, nobles and peasants, prostitutes and impending saints, all comprised the audiences of the preachers. Consequently, in Part Four, the chapters on reception, I examine both the responses to preaching on the Magdalen of lay people and those now venerated as saints. I include the responses of holy people to the Magdalen, especially the views of lay saints—those who were not priest, monk, or nun—because they were an important and visible presence in the later Middle Ages. They were fully integrated members of late medieval society, particularly Italian society. It would thus constitute a bizarre disservice to the period to remove their views from my analysis just because they themselves have subsequently entered the ranks of the blessed.[45]

Chapter 8 looks at responses to the scriptural saint while chapter 9 examines responses to the legendary saint. Both chapters reveal some rather "uncanonical" responses indicating a laity actively involved in shaping images of the Magdalen for their own ends. Chapter 10 pursues this theme further and discloses a Magdalen in the making—a mother and virgin—whose image was shaped by the Virgin Mary, but whose construction was very much a creation of the needs of the laity. Each chapter uses gender as a category of analysis to argue that although Mary Magdalen was an important symbol for both men and women, their understanding of her religious meaning was by no means the same: a gendered response can be discerned. Chapter 11 examines a royal response to the saint. It argues that behind Angevin devotion to the saint lay a politics of piety that reflected the new dynasty's need for a saintly protector. Moreover, the chapter demonstrates that those families in southern Italy whose acts of veneration of the saint were most public were those who had the most to gain from associating themselves with the parvenu house of Anjou in Italy.

Ultimately, this book illuminates the complexity of the medieval symbolic economy and how it functioned in the later Middle Ages. More spe-

<hr />

[44] "De modo prompte cudendi sermones," in *De eruditione praedicatorum,* ed. Marguerin de La Bigne in *Maxima bibliotheca veterum patrum* (Lyons: Anissonius, 1677), vol. 25, 456–567.

[45] On the rise of lay saints in later medieval society, see André Vauchez, *The Laity in the Middle Ages,* trans. Margery J. Schneider (Notre Dame: University of Notre Dame Press, 1993) and Donald Weinstein and Rudolph Bell, *Saints and Society: The Two Worlds of Western Christendom, 1000–1700* (Chicago: University of Chicago Press, 1982).

cifically, it explains the importance of devotion to Saint Mary Magdalen in the later medieval period. It shows why Mary Magdalen (after the Virgin Mary) was the most important female saint of the period and how her cult exemplified, reflected, and refracted some of the most important social issues, theological questions, and pressing politics of the later Middle Ages.

ONE

"In Memory of Her": From History to Legend

Amen I say to you, wherever in the whole world
this gospel is preached, this also that she has done
shall be told in memory of her.
(Matt. 26:13; Mark 14:9)

On 9 December 1279 an ancient sarcophagus in the crypt of the church of Saint-Maximin near Aix-en-Provence was opened and its contents inspected. The authorities convened by Charles, Prince of Salerno, examined and duly confirmed that the relics contained in the tomb were those of Saint Mary Magdalen who, it was popularly believed, had evangelized southern Gaul. The Dominican Bernard Gui, a somewhat belated witness to the events, described in his chronicle how marvelous signs accompanied the opening of the sarcophagus. Beyond the sweet fragrance ("as if an apothecary shop of sweet spices had been opened") that normally issued from saints' relics upon discovery, a further sign authenticated the finding: a tender green shoot was found growing from the Magdalen's tongue.[1] A sign, however, is of little value without an interpretation, and that was duly supplied by Philippe Cabassole, chancellor of the Kingdom of Naples, when in 1355 he described the *inventio* (discovery) in his *Historical Book of Blessed Mary Magdalen*. He suggested that the small palm frond issuing from the saint's tongue signified that as *apostolorum apostola*,

---

[1] *Flores chronicorum seu catalogus pontificum Romanorum* (ca. 1311–31), cited in E.-M. Faillon, *Monuments inédits sur l'apostolat de Sainte Marie-Madeleine en Provence . . .* , 2 vols. (Paris: J.-P. Migne, 1859), vol. 2, 777–78; *BHL* 5506. The date of Bernard's text is supplied by Thomas Kaeppeli, *Scriptores,* vol. 1, 212. Portions of this chapter have been published as "Maria Magdalena: Apostolorum Apostola," in *Women Preachers and Prophets through Two Millennia of Christianity,* ed. Beverly Mayne Kienzle and Pamela J. Walker (Berkeley: University of California Press, 1998), 57–96.

apostle of the apostles, Mary Magdalen had announced to the other apostles that Christ had risen from the dead and that subsequently she had preached to the pagans.[2]

I have chosen to begin with the Angevin prince's discovery of the saint's relics in Provence, and the interpretation of that event by one of the dynasty's apologists, because the text quite neatly encapsulates a number of the themes that are the concern of this book. First, it reveals some of the legendary aspects of the saint's life—her apostolate and subsequent burial in Provence. Those elements, as we shall see, had been fabricated by the canons of Vézelay to shore up their claim that they possessed Mary Magdalen's relics. Second, it emphasizes a particularly medieval title—apostle of the apostles—under which Mary Magdalen was venerated in the later medieval period. It is a title that is inspired by scripture, though not found there. The gospels identify Mary Magdalen as the first witness of the resurrection whom the risen Christ entrusts to announce the good news to the apostles, but this title seems to have emerged in the twelfth century. Third, it reveals the not uncomplicated association of sanctity and politics that so characterized the Middle Ages. The text underscores the house of Anjou's proprietary relationship to the saint by emphasizing that Charles of Salerno presided over the discovery of Mary Magdalen's relics in his father's comital territory of Provence. Miraculous signs had revealed her earthly remains to be genuine. One of the signs pointed to the saint's missionary activities in Provence when as apostle of the apostles she had converted the pagan Gauls to Christianity. Thus this was not just any garden-variety missionary who had evangelized Provence but rather it was Mary Magdalen, an intimate of the Lord Jesus Christ. The provençal discovery, therefore, allied the beloved disciple of Jesus (now glorified in heaven but whose powerful relics still remained in Provence) with the parvenu Angevin dynasty and its ambitions of empire. With Charles of Salerno's serendipitous discovery, Mary Magdalen became both an Angevin patron and the protector of Provence.

This heady mix of politics and sanctity was by no means uncommon in the Middle Ages as this chapter demonstrates. It also shows how the historical record yielded a legendary saint whom the Middle Ages and subsequent generations venerated as Mary Magdalen, but doubtless a figure all but unrecognizable to her companions of the early Christian church.

Since this chapter intends to set the stage for the subject of this book—

---

[2] *Libellus hystorialis Mariae beatissimae Magdalenae,* cited in Faillon, *Monuments,* vol. 2, 792; *BHL* 5509. For the most recent commentary on this text, see Victor Saxer, "Philippe Cabassole et son *Libellus hystorialis Marie beatissime Magdalene.* Préliminaires à une édition du *Libellus,*" in *L'État Angevin: Pouvoir, culture et société entre XIIIe et XIVe siècle* (Collection de l'École Française de Rome, 245) (Rome: École Française de Rome, 1998), 193–204.

the social meaning of late medieval devotion to the Magdalen—much (but not all) of what follows is a synthetic presentation of both the early Christian and early medieval sources treating the saint. To those who are acquainted with the rise of the cult of Mary Magdalen at Vézelay, this material will already be familiar through the studies of Helen Meredith Garth, Victor Saxer, Marjorie Malvern, Susan Haskins, and other scholars.[3] But to those who are coming to the subject for the first time, in addition to scripture it will be useful to review the writings of the fathers of the church, the early liturgical sources, the establishment of the pilgrimage site at Vézelay, and the growth of legendary material all of which served to elaborate various aspects of Mary Magdalen's life which the gospels had passed over in silence.

What's in a Name?

Before the nominalists of the later medieval period cast doubt on philosophical realism, most medieval thinkers believed that names and things were intimately related. That is, they presumed that a name prophesied the thing or person it denoted. Texts such as Isidore of Seville's *Etymologies* guided the reader not just to a history of the word in question, but to its very ontological essence. Medieval commentators inevitably began their treatment of a holy person with a *praesagium nominis,* a prophecy from the name.[4] We shall do likewise.

In the last decade of the fourth century, drawing on the work of Philo and Origen, Saint Jerome wrote a treatise entitled, *On the Interpretation of Hebrew Names,*[5] that ambitiously set out to explicate the meanings of all the names mentioned in the Bible. His interpretations were cited throughout the Middle Ages. In his chapter on the gospel of Mark he noted: "Most people think that Mary is to be interpreted as 'they illuminate me' or 'illuminator' or 'myrrh of the sea,' but it does not seem at all likely to me. It is better that we say . . . a 'drop of the sea' or 'bitter sea.'"[6] It was believed

---

[3] Helen Meredith Garth, *Saint Mary Magdalene in Mediaeval Literature* (Baltimore: Johns Hopkins Press, 1950); Victor Saxer, *Le culte de Marie-Madeleine en occident des origines à la fin du moyen-âge.* 2 vols. (Cahiers d'archéologie et d'histoire, 3) (Auxerre-Paris: Publications de la Société des Fouilles Archéologiques et des Monuments Historiques de l'Yonne-Librairie Clavreuil, 1959); Marjorie Malvern, *Venus in Sackcloth: The Magdalen's Origins and Metamorphoses* (Carbondale, IL: Southern Illinois University Press, 1975); and Susan Haskins, *Mary Magdalen: Myth and Metaphor* (London: HarperCollins, 1993). See my introduction for a historiographical overview of the subject.

[4] See, for example, Jacobus de Voragine's entries in the *Golden Legend,* trans. William Granger Ryan, 2 vols. (Princeton: Princeton University Press, 1993).

[5] *Liber interpretationis hebraicorum nominum* in *S. Hieronymi presbyteri opera (Pars I: Opera Exegetica), CCSL* 72 (1959), 57–161.

[6] *Liber interpr.* (Matt.), 137; cf. ibid. (Ex.), 76.

that the Christian name Mary derived from the Hebrew name Miriam, therefore the two names were interpreted similarly. Miriam, of course, was Moses' sister and a prophet who features prominently in the Hebrew bible.[7] Nominally, then, Mary Magdalen was linked both to Miriam the Hebrew prophet and to the Virgin Mary, to say nothing of the five other scriptural Marys.

Her surname, however, set her apart. The name Magdalen was assumed to refer to Magdala, her native city on the west bank of the sea of Galilee.[8] The place name Magdala was believed to derive from the Hebrew word for tower (*migdol* or *migdal*); Magdalene was the latinized adjectival form of the word meaning of or from the tower.[9] Significantly, Mary Magdalen, as distinct from all the other scriptural Marys, was identified by her place of origin rather than one of the more common designations for women. The usual method was to identify a woman by reference to a man: Mary of James was James's mother, while Mary Cleopas was the wife of Cleopas, one of Jesus' followers. Since Mary Magdalen was identified only by her city it is possible that she was living some sort of independent life.[10] Our source for that life is contained in the New Testament, the gospels of the evangelists Matthew, Mark, Luke, and John.

The Gospels

Any account of Mary Magdalen's life must begin with the New Testament, the oldest historical source documenting the existence of this faithful follower of the teacher, Jesus of Nazareth.[11] All told, the four gospels contain just twelve references to this woman, only one of which is independent of the passion and resurrection narratives. Luke 8:2–3 reports that

---

[7] See Num. 12:1, 12:4–5; 12:10; 12:15; and 20:1 as well as Ex. 15:20 and Deut. 24:9. The Hebrew name Miriam, derives possibly from the Egyptian *mr'* (to be loved) or from *rà a* (to see, the seer). See Carla Ricci, *Mary Magdalen and Many Others: Women Who Followed Jesus* (Minneapolis, MN: Fortress Press, 1994), 129–30.

[8] Ricci, ibid.

[9] Jerome, *Liber interpr.* (Matt.), 137. Jerome used this interpretation of the Magdalen's name when writing to Principia: "Mary of Magdala, called 'of the tower' because of her earnestness and ardent faith, was privileged to see the rising Christ first even before the apostles." *Ep. CXXVII (Ad Principiam)*, in *CSEL* 56 (1918), 149; in *Select Letters of St. Jerome*, trans. F. A. Wright (New York: G. P. Putnam's Sons, 1933), 450–51.

[10] See Lilia Sebastiani, *Tra/Sfigurazione: Il personaggio evangelico di Maria di Magdala e il mito della peccatrice redenta nella tradizione occidentale* (Brescia: Queriniana, 1992), 41, and Françoise Bovon, "Le privilège pascal de Marie-Madeleine," in *Révélations et Écritures: Nouveau Testament et littérature apocryphe chrétienne* (Geneva: Éditions Labor et Fides, 1993), 216, n. 3, for which I thank Beverly Kienzle for the reference.

[11] For studies focusing on Mary Magdalen's role in the early church, see the work of Fiorenza, Witherington, Ricci, and King cited in the introduction.

"Mary who is called Magdalen" was the woman from whom Jesus cast out seven demons. After he did so, Mary from Magdala along with Joanna, Susanna, and "many others" became one of Jesus' steadfast disciples, ministering to him from her own financial resources (Luke 8:3).

As the drama of the passion unfolds, however, the gospels assign a more prominent position to this devoted disciple. Her presence is recorded at the crucifixion (Matt. 27:56; Mark 15:40; John 19:25), and is noted again at the entombment (Matt. 27:61; Mark 15:47), and yet again on Easter Sunday among Jesus' female disciples who return to the sepulcher to anoint his body with sweet spices (Matt. 28:1; Mark 16:1; Luke 24:10; John 20:1).

In the gospel of Mark, generally agreed by scholars to be the oldest of the gospel accounts, the evangelist includes Mary Magdalen among the three Marys who arrive at the tomb early on Easter morning to perform the ritual anointing of the body. There, they are informed by an angel that Jesus of Nazareth has risen. Although the angel invites them to spread the good news among the other disciples, the angelic apparition has startled them too much to do so. The evangelist then recounts that Mary Magdalen received the paschal privilege of seeing the risen Christ first, before all others: Jesus "appeared first to Mary Magdalen, out of whom he had cast seven devils." After she had seen him with her own eyes she reported the good news of the resurrection to the other disciples, "and they, when they had heard that he was alive, and had been seen of her, believed not" (Mark 16:9–10).

In Matthew's version of the events of Easter morning, Mary Magdalen and "the other Mary" go to the tomb, find it empty, and are greeted by an angel who tells them that the savior has risen. He bids them give the good news to the other disciples. They hasten to do so and on the way are met by the risen Christ, who himself entrusts them to tell the disciples that they shall see him in Galilee (Matt 28:1–10). Thus in Matthew's account, the first appearance of the risen Christ is to Mary Magdalen and an indeterminate "other Mary." Nevertheless, in both the accounts of Mark and Matthew, Mary Magdalen is among the first witnesses of Christ's resurrection.

Luke's recounting of the Easter morning events differs from the other two synoptic reports. According to Luke 24:10–11, upon arriving at Jesus' empty tomb on Easter morning, Mary Magdalen was among a group of women advised by two radiant angels that Christ had risen. She and the other women brought these tidings back to the apostles who greeted their words as "idle tales." Subsequently, in Luke's telling, Christ shows himself first not to the women, or to the eleven apostles, but to two of his disciples journeying to the village of Emmaus (Luke 28: 13–15).

The final version of the Easter narrative, found in the penultimate chapter of John whose gospel is believed to post-date the synoptic texts, differs not so much in content from Mark and Matthew's accounts, but rather in its emphasis on Mary Magdalen's encounter with the risen Christ. It is the most extended treatment of Mary Magdalen in any of the four gospels. In John's narrative, Mary Magdalen arrives at the sepulcher, discovers it empty, and hastens off to tell Peter and John that Jesus' body has been removed. They return with her to the tomb, are duly bewildered to find it empty, but do not choose to linger graveside. By contrast, the faithful Magdalen remains, standing vigil and weeping at the tomb. Peering into the empty sepulcher her eyes fall on two angels who ask her why she is weeping. Upon responding, a man she assumes to be the gardener approaches and repeats the angels' question, adding, "Whom seekest thou?" She explains that she is weeping because the body of her lord has been removed from the tomb. The man then calls out her name: "Mary." At last, recognizing her lord, she turns toward him and addresses him using the Hebrew word "rabboni" (master). Although Jesus rebuffs her touch, nonetheless he charges her with the duty of bearing the good news of his resurrection to the other disciples. The last we know of Jesus' devoted disciple from Galilee is that "Mary Magdalen came and told the disciples that she had seen the Lord and that he had spoken these things unto her" (John 20: 1–18).

According to scripture, then, Mary Magdalen is the woman whom Christ heals of demonic possession, who becomes one of his loyal disciples, who ministers to him during his lifetime, who stands beneath the cross at his crucifixion, who is present at his burial, who brings ointments to the tomb after his death, who is the first person (in three of the four accounts) to witness the risen Christ, and is the person on whom he bestows the honor of announcing the good news to the other disciples (in three of the four accounts). Thus she was doubly blessed: not only was she first to witness one of the central tenets of the Christian faith—the resurrection—she also received the paschal privilege of announcing it.

The *Acts of the Apostles,* the fifth book of the New Testament generally attributed to Luke, contains one last rather vague reference that should be construed as including Mary Magdalen. After Christ's ascension from the Mount of Olives, the apostles return to Jerusalem and gather in an upper room along with "the women, and Mary the mother of Jesus" for prayer and supplication (Acts 1:12–13). Given that Luke's gospel had previously placed the Magdalen in a group of undifferentiated women (only to identify her subsequently), we can conclude that as one of Jesus' most faithful followers she was among the women in this group who received the gift of tongues at Pentecost.[12]

---

[12] Cf. Luke 23:49, 55–56; 24:1–9. Only in 24:10 does Luke name some of the women: Mary Magdalen, Joanna, and Mary the mother of James. Medieval writers, as we shall see, concluded that Mary Magdalen was one of the women referred to in *Acts.*

The Gnostic Gospels

It is worth noting that the books contained in the New Testament are not unique early Christian witnesses to the life, teaching, and deeds of Jesus and his disciples.[13] When, in the mid-second century, the authority of Matthew, Mark, Luke, and John was established, alternative gospels, those authored by gnostic Christians, were already in circulation. Gnosticism is a blanket-term comprising a number of second-century Christian sects such as the Valentinians and the Marcionites. What all had in common was the belief in *gnosis,* a Greek word meaning knowing or knowledge, that implies revealed knowledge or insight as distinct from empirical knowledge. *Gnosis* could be revealed knowledge of God, the universe, the destiny of humankind, or oneself. To receive *gnosis* was, in effect, to receive the ability to redeem one's spiritual aspect. Gnosticism, with its emphasis on personal inspiration, inevitably came into conflict with the institutional church whose insistence on tradition and hierarchy allowed the gnostic sects no quarter. By the early Middle Ages the Church had succeeded in suppressing most of the gnostic sects. Indeed, it succeeded so well that until the discovery of a cache of Coptic texts at Nag Hammadi in Upper Egypt in 1945–46 (which yielded 52 gnostic texts), most of what was known about gnosticism came from the poison pens of its persecutors.[14]

There are three gnostic gospels in which Mary Magdalen features prominently: the *Pistis Sophia* and the *Gospel of Mary,* both of which have been known since the eighteenth and nineteenth centuries, respectively, and the *Gospel of Philip,* which was among those gnostic texts found at Nag Hammadi.[15]

---

[13] In what follows I am dealing with the gnostic gospels rather than the apocryphal books of the New Testament which aimed to fill in the details of Christ's childhood, the Virgin Mary's life, and Christ's Harrowing of Hell. The only apocryphal gospel in which the portrayal of Mary Magdalen departs from or adds significantly to the books in the New Testament is the fourth-century *Gospel of Nicodemus* (also known as the *Acts of Pilate*). Here, Mary Magdalen proclaims at Christ's burial "Who shall make this known unto all the world? I will go alone to Rome unto Caesar: I will show him what evil Pilate hath done, consenting unto the wicked Jews." See Montague Rhodes James, *The Apocryphal New Testament* (Oxford: Clarendon Press, 1924), 117. Here James notes that the legend of the Magdalen's voyage to Rome is also to be found in Byzantine chronicles and "other late documents." See now the updated, *The Apocryphal New Testament,* ed. J. K. Elliott (Oxford: Oxford University Press, 1993).

[14] For the fascinating account of the discovery at Nag Hammadi, and an astute analysis of the contents of the gnostic material, see Elaine Pagels, *The Gnostic Gospels* (New York: Random House, 1979).

[15] In the overview that follows I am indebted to Haskins, *Mary Magdalen,* 33–57, and Sebastiani, *Tra/Sfigurazione,* 63–75. Malvern, *Venus,* also analyzes the gnostic texts, 30–56. For a full treatment of Mary Magdalen in gnostic literature, see Antti Marjanen, *The Woman Jesus Loved: Mary Magdalene in the Nag Hammadi Library and Related Documents* (Leiden: E. J. Brill, 1996).

In the oldest of these texts, the *Gospel of Mary* (the only gospel—canonical, apocryphal, or gnostic—to be named for a woman), Mary Magdalen is both a prophet and the moral conscience of the disciples.[16] She exhorts the other apostles to act on the Lord's precepts and reveals a vision in which Christ extols her constancy of faith. As much as this was a commendation of the Magdalen's unwavering faith, it was also an implicit rebuke to Peter, who had not only denied Christ three times in the course of one evening, but had even gone so far as to dismiss the Magdalen's announcement of the resurrection as "idle tales." Irked perhaps at the lengthy recitation of her vision, Andrew challenges its authenticity while Peter asks: "Did he really speak with a woman without our knowledge (and) not openly? Are we to turn about and all listen to her? Did he prefer her to us?" Their verbal assault reduces the Magdalen to tears. Order is restored to the group only when Levi (read: Matthew) comes to her defense, reprimanding the others by observing that if the savior rendered her worthy, who were they to reject her? She, whom "he loved more than us."[17]

In the *Pistis Sophia*, a third-century gnostic text that takes the form of a dialogue between the risen savior and his disciples, Mary Magdalen's privileged place as Jesus' special interlocutor is preserved. Jesus compliments her thus: "Excellent, Maria. Thou are blessed beyond all women upon the earth. . . . Speak openly and do not fear. I will reveal all things that thou seekest."[18] Again, as in the *Gospel of Mary*, the Magdalen is commended above the others, because it is she, not the other apostles, who through divine *gnosis* perceives the mysteries of the faith more perfectly. Indeed, because of her deep spiritual understanding, Mary Magdalen monopolizes much of the discussion (asking 39 of the 46 questions),[19] much to the irritation of Peter, who twice breaks in complaining, "My Lord, we are not able to suffer this woman who takes the opportunity from us, and does not allow anyone of us to speak, but she speaks many times."[20] Though Peter's pointed interventions do not prompt tears as they did in the *Gospel of Mary*, they do provoke this response: "I am afraid of Peter, for he threatens me and he hates our race [sex]."[21]

---

[16] *The Gospel of Mary*, trans. George W. MacRae and R. McL. Wilson in *The Nag Hammadi Library in English* (hereafter *NHL*), ed. James M. Robinson (New York: Harper San Francisco, 1990; 3d rev. ed.), 523–27. For an insightful discussion of this text and its implications for women's leadership, see Karen King, "Prophetic Power and Women's Authority: The Case of the *Gospel of Mary* (Magdalene)," in *Women Preachers and Prophets*, 21–41.

[17] *Gospel of Mary*, *NHL*, 526–27.

[18] *Pistis Sophia*, ed. Carl Schmidt, trans. Violet Macdermot (*Nag Hammadi Studies*, vol. 9) (Leiden: E. J. Brill, 1978), bk. 1, chap. 20, 28–29.

[19] Bovon, "Le privilège," 223.

[20] *Pistis Sophia*, 58. Cf: ibid., 377: "My Lord, let the women cease to question, that we also may question."

[21] *Pistis Sophia*, 162.

The theme of the Magdalen's more perfect *gnosis* and the jealous rivalry it engenders among the male apostles reaches a fevered pitch in the *Gospel of Philip,* written in the latter half of the third century.[22] Here, however, the Magdalen's position as Christ's favorite is more italicized than ever because of the sexual language and imagery employed in the text.

> And the companion of the [. . .] Mary Magdalene. [loved] her more than [all] the disciples [and used to] kiss her [often] on her [. . .]. The rest of [the disciples . . .]. They said to him, "Why do you love her more than all of us?"[23]

A scholar of early Christianity has labeled this a "perplexing" passage,[24] as indeed it is on first glance. But if we scrutinize what precedes it, namely, an explication of the kiss between the perfect, the passage becomes a bit less opaque. The kiss between those who have attained *gnosis* is thus explained:

> For it is by a kiss that the perfect conceive and give birth. For this reason we also kiss one another. We receive conception for the grace which is in one another.[25]

In other words: those who have attained *gnosis* are able to exchange kisses that contain grace. As one scholar of Gnosticism has explained it: "It is in this context that Jesus' kissing Mary ought to be understood. The Logos lives in those whom he has kissed, hence the disciples' jealousy, for they are not yet worthy of the kiss."[26] But such a mystical reading does not attempt to make sense of the overtly sexual imagery with which the passage is suffused. Some scholars have argued that this imagery alludes to a tenet of gnostic theology that posits a mystical bridal chamber where, in a sacrament of communion, male and female will eventually reunite for all time. From this union will come the perfection of humankind. It is an allegorical reading: Mary Magdalen and Jesus represent the Logos and the Spirit, Adam and Eve, male and female.

I would suggest yet another interpretation that reads on both a mystical and literal level. Jesus' kiss is a gift of grace, of gnosis or visionary understanding—bestowed on Mary Magdalen not despite her sex but precisely because of her sex. Conventional wisdom held that as a woman she was already inclined toward intuitive rather than acquired understanding. The apostles objected to this preferential treatment not only because they were

---

[22] *Gospel of Philip,* trans. Wesley W. Isenberg in *NHL,* 139–60.

[23] Ibid., 148.

[24] Jorunn Jacobsen Buckley, "'The Holy Spirit is a Double Name': Holy Spirit, Mary, and Sophia in the *Gospel of Philip,*" in *Images of the Feminine in Gnosticism,* ed. Karen King (Philadelphia: Fortress Press, 1988), 215.

[25] *Gospel of Philip,* 145.

[26] Buckley, ibid., 216.

unable to understand the mystical nature of the kiss, but also because they understood all too well that their sex, their maleness, precluded such privileged and sexually charged treatment. As Karen King has observed, "Prophecy is sometimes understood as the penetration of the body by a spirit, and thus was sometimes conceived and expressed in sexual terms. As a consequence of a system of heterosexual gender symbolization in which the penetrator is symbolically male and the penetrated is symbolically feminine, the penetrated body of the prophet could be understood to be either feminine or feminized."[27] In the monotheistic tradition where God is gendered male and a heterosexual perspective is assumed, the disciples took offense at the Magdalen's preferential treatment because their sex precluded them from receiving similar treatment.

What cannot go without remarking is the anxiety present in the early Christian community as revealed through and personified in the figure of the Magdalen. The tensions that bubble under the surface of the New Testament reach a rolling boil in the gnostic gospels. Elaine Pagels has argued that such tensions reveal a problem with political implications: the crux of the matter was whether or not prophetic gifts translated into authority within the orthodox Church. The dilemma was whether leadership in the Church, following the gnostics, would be charismatic, personal, visionary, and prophetic, or would it operate through tradition and apostolic authority handed down from generation to generation, from bishop to bishop?[28] There is, however, another dimension to the problem: gender. When we take gender into consideration the problem becomes even more complex. Now the issue becomes: would ecclesiastical authority be based on feminine principles of vision, prophecy, and spiritual understanding (*sapientia*), as embodied by Mary Magdalen to whom Christ had appeared first and whom he had charged to announce the good news of the resurrection? Or would it be vested in the male principles of apostolic tradition, hierarchy and acquired knowledge (*scientia*) as represented by Peter, the rock upon whom Christ had built the Church, bestowed the keys of the kingdom of heaven, and granted the powers to bind and loose (Matt. 16:18–19)?

Already, in the New Testament, Peter and the other disciples were beginning to reject the authority of the female prophetic tradition, notably dismissing the Magdalen's announcement of the resurrection as "idle talk." Those words of course are significant: idle talk was the normative mode of both labeling and dismissing female speech. The competition between

---

[27] "Prophetic Power and Authority," in ibid., 30–31.

[28] Pagels, *The Gnostic Gospels,* 13–14. This was part of Saint Paul's dilemma at Corinth (1 Cor. 11: 34–35) on which see Antoinette Clark Wire, *Corinthian Women Prophets: A Reconstruction through Paul's Rhetoric* (Minneapolis, MN: Fortress Press, 1990).

Mary and Peter intensifies in the gnostic gospels because, as Pagels has shown, the Magdalen represents the gnostic bid for leadership in the Christian community that challenged the episcopal authority of Peter's successors.[29] When, in the *Pistis Sophia*, Mary Magdalen expresses her fear of Peter who threatens her, it is a poignantly prophetic statement. The institutional Church did more than threaten gnostic Christianity—it suppressed it entirely. Yet the problem of female ecclesiastical leadership, whose authority derives from spiritually attained knowledge as distinct from knowledge acquired from tradition, did not die with Gnosticism, nor did it move outside the church into heresy; it remained a paradox at the very heart of Christian experience, and the figure of the Magdalen embodied it. We shall confront this problem again in its later medieval form in the next chapter.

The Patristic Writers

When the fathers of the Church turned their attention to Mary Magdalen the occasion was usually a commentary on scripture. They adverted to her most frequently when considering her role as herald of the resurrection. One of the earliest meditations on Mary Magdalen's paschal role is in a commentary on *The Song of Songs* once attributed to Hippolytus, bishop and martyr of Rome (d. ca. 235).[30] The author suggests that the Shulammite, or Bride of the *Canticles*, who was seeking her beloved (Cant. 3:1) in the garden, prefigured typologically Mary and Martha who sought Christ in the sepulcher. He explains that the women represent the Synagogue and in that capacity reveal the good news as apostles to the apostles (*quae apostoli ad-apostolos*) sent by Christ. He maintains:

> Lest the female apostles doubt the angels, Christ himself came to them so that the women would be apostles of Christ and by their obedience rectify the sin of the ancient Eve . . . Therefore the women announced the good news to the apostles. . . . That the women not appear liars but rather truth-bearers . . . Christ showed himself to the (male) apostles and said to them: . . . "It is I who appeared to these women and I who wanted to send them to you as apostles."[31]

Three items should be noted in this passage. First is that two women share the role as first witness. Mary is not identified as Mary Magdalen, but given her pairing with Martha it seems possible that Hippolytus was asso-

---

[29] Pagels, ibid., 14. See also Elisabeth Schüssler Fiorenza, *In Memory of Her*, 294–315.

[30] Paul-Marie Guillaume, "Marie-Madeleine," in *DS* 10 (1980), 559–75.

[31] *CSCO* 264 (1965), 43–49. The commentary survived only in Georgian. The Latin edition is a translation made from the Georgian by Gérard Garitte.

ciating Mary Magdalen with Mary of Bethany, an identification which, as we shall see, eventually becomes routine. The second item to note is that the author seems compelled to have his Christ defend the words of women against the skepticism of the apostles echoing gender-related tensions we have already witnessed in the early Church. Finally, the author's vocabulary should be noted: he refers to the women as apostles.

According to the gospels and the commentaries on them, Mary Magdalen, Martha and Mary, "the other Mary," and of course the three Marys, all played a role in the history of salvation. The lack of specificity about to whom—precisely—Christ had first shown himself and whom—precisely— he had designated to proclaim the good news of his resurrection was not of course due to exegetical incompetence. Imprecision arose from the daunting task of trying to reconcile the evangelists' (apparently) inconsistent Easter narratives. A further difficulty with which the commentators had to contend was the "muddle of Marys"[32] that populates the gospels. Christ's immediate circle of female followers, in addition to the Virgin Mary, consisted of at least five other women called Mary: Mary mother of James the less and Joses, the "other Mary," Mary of Bethany, Mary Cleopas, and of course Mary Magdalen.[33] Theoretically, the place-name Magdala should have been enough to distinguish at least one Mary from the next; in practice it was not quite so simple. At one point Ambrose, clearly suffering the deleterious effects of an overdose of scriptural Marys, suggested that there were two Mary Magdalens. In an act of exegetical exasperation (possibly following Eusebius), he remarked:

> Some of the women are not aware [of the resurrection], others are. . . . One Mary of Magdala does not know according to John, the other Mary Magdalen knows according to Matthew; the same woman cannot know it at first and then not know it. Therefore if there were many Marys, there were perhaps many Magdalens, because the latter is a surname, the former a placename.[34]

One might assume that the Virgin Mary, by virtue of her unique and exalted status as mother of Christ, stood apart from the exegetical difficulties posed by a surfeit of Marys and Magdalens. This was not the case, however. The Alexandrine method of textual analysis tended to produce a cer-

---

[32] It is Marina Warner's phrase. *Alone of All Her Sex: The Myth and the Cult of the Virgin Mary* (New York: Vintage Books, 1983), 344.

[33] Mary mother of James the less and Joses (Mark: 15:40, 47; 16:1); the "other Mary" at the tomb (Matt. 27:61; 28:1); Mary of Bethany (Luke 10: 39–42 and John 11:1–45; 12:1– 8); Mary Cleopas (John 19:25) and Mary of Magdala (Matt. 27:56, 61; 28:1; Mark 15:40, 47; 16:1,9; Luke 8:2; 24:10; John 19:25; 20:1–18); Ricci, *Mary Magdalen*, 62–63.

[34] *Expositio evangelii secundam Lucam,* Lib. X, *CSEL* 32 (1902), 513–14. Eusebius had already developed the idea in *Quaestiones ad Marinum, PG* 22, 947.

tain amount of ambiguity in relation to Marian identity. The elaborate literary conceit employed by these commentators sometimes identified the Virgin as the Church, sometimes the Magdalen as the Church, and all three as brides of Christ. Consequently, the *personae* of the Virgin Mary and Mary Magdalen were not as entirely distinct as their individual biographies might suggest. Although Augustine had defined a clear division of labor in the history of redemption—one woman had brought Christ into the world while another had proclaimed the news of his resurrection; nevertheless such clarity did not always obtain, particularly in the East.[35] In a discourse traditionally attributed to Cyril of Jerusalem, the author claimed that the Virgin herself had told him that "I am Mary Magdalen because the name of the village wherein I was born was Magdala. My name is Mary of Cleopa[s]. I am Mary of James the son of Joseph the carpenter."[36] Thus in one fell swoop the Virgin Mary assumed the identities of three other scriptural Marys, all witnesses to the crucifixion.

A later Coptic text, the apocryphal *Book of the Resurrection of Christ*, ascribed to the Apostle Bartholomew, exacerbates the confusion. Here the Virgin Mary appropriates the role of herald that the evangelist John (20:16–18) had explicitly assigned to the Magdalen:

[The] Savior came before them . . . and he cried out . . . "Thou Mary, the mother of the Son of God." And Mary, who understood the meaning turned herself and said, "Rabonnei" . . . And the Savior said unto her, "Go thou unto My brethren, and tell them that I have risen from the dead." . . . Mary said unto her Son, "Jesus, my Lord, and my only Son, bless Thou me . . . if indeed Thou wilt not allow me to touch Thee."[37]

Here the Virgin literally takes the words—"Rabboni"—out of Mary Magdalen's mouth. Evidently she had also received the *noli me tangere* admonition and then been dispatched to bear the news of the resurrection to the apostles. In the West this sequence of events in the Iohannine resurrection drama always retained Jesus and Mary Magdalen as the central protagonists.

Ephrem the Syrian's hymns also tended to fuse together the *personae* of

---

[35] *Sermo 232, SC* 116 (1966), 262.

[36] A Coptic text cited in James, *The Apocryphal New Testament,* 87. See also E. A. Wallis Budge, *Miscellaneous Coptic Texts in the Dialect of Upper Egypt* (Oxford: Oxford University Press, 1915), 630.

[37] E. A. Wallis Budge, *Coptic Apocrypha in the Dialect of Upper Egypt* (Oxford: Horace Hart, 1913), 221–24. James, *The Apocryphal New Testament,* 186, dates the text between the fifth and seventh centuries. See also Ciro Giannelli, "Témoignages patristiques grecs en faveur d'une apparition du Christ ressuscité a la Vierge Marie," *Revue des Études Byzantines* (Mélanges Martin Jugie) 11 (1953): 106–19, who notes that Chrysostom also gave this privilege to the Virgin Mary.

the Virgin and the Magdalen. Robert Murray has suggested that this penchant for mingling the Virgin Mary's identity with those of the other Marys reflected a strong eastern, particularly Syrian, devotion to the Virgin. Essentially it was a form of praise to endow the Virgin Mary with all the important female roles and laudable attributes of women who figured in the gospels.[38] M. R. James poured scorn on this Eastern tradition, acidly dismissing it as "the reckless identification of the Virgin Mary with all the other Maries of the gospels" which was "typical of the disregard of history" of this genre.[39] Whether or not we find this tendency as offensive as James evidently did, it cannot be dismissed as a Coptic eccentricity. In the next chapter we shall encounter these problems again in the Latin West of the later Middle Ages when we look at how medieval preachers treated the problem of Christ's first appearance on Easter morning. It was important for salvation history to argue that Mary Magdalen, a sinner, had been the first witness of the resurrection; nevertheless there were those whose loyalties to the mother of Christ obliged them to carry on the eastern tradition of the Virgin Mary's first witness of the risen Christ, endowing her with all female glory, including the Magdalen's. On the other hand, in chapter 10, we shall see how the glorified Magdalen of the later medieval period was remade in the image of the Virgin Mary, borrowing many of her attributes, including virginity and motherhood.

As distinct from eastern writers, a theme that preoccupied the Latin fathers was Mary Magdalen's compensatory role in salvation history, that is, her role as a counterweight to Eve. Although it was probably the fourth-century bishop Hilary of Poitiers who introduced this theme into western exegesis, Augustine's analogy based on likeness is emblematic of such a style of interpretation. He argued in an Easter homily that just as "humanity's fall was occasioned by womankind, humanity's restoration was accomplished through womankind, since a virgin brought forth Christ and a woman announced that he had risen from the dead." And in a celebrated statement he suggested: *per feminam mors, per feminam vita* (through a woman death, through a woman life).[40] By bearing the news of the resurrection, Mary Magdalen, who symbolized the female sex, restored the order of creation that original sin and its consequences had destroyed. In other words, she helped to bring about salvific symmetry. The formulation was this: both Mary Magdalen and the Virgin Mary represented the new Eve, paralleling Christ's role as the new Adam. In her capacity as the new Eve, the Virgin brought salvation into the world by giving birth to Jesus

---

[38] *Symbols of Church and Kingdom* (Cambridge: Cambridge University Press, 1975), 146–48, 329–31. See also Giannelli, "Témoignages," 106–19.

[39] James, *The Apocryphal New Testament,* 88 and 186.

[40] Augustine, *Sermo 232, SC* 116 (1966), 262.

Christ while the Magdalen as the new Eve proclaimed that salvation was at hand when she announced his resurrection.

In theory it would seem that the Latin fathers had bestowed an honor on the Magdalen by positioning her as *co-redemptrix* in salvation history, but in practice it was not always the case. For unlike the Virgin Mary, Mary Magdalen was frequently sullied by Eve's original sin. Here is how Ambrose formulated the problem:

> Mary worshipped Christ, and so was sent to the apostles as the first herald of the resurrection, dissolving the hereditary link of the female sex and immense sin. The Lord performs this through a mystery: since where sin had once abounded now grace super-abounded (Romans 5:20). And rightly a woman was sent to the men so that she who had first announced sin to man, would be the first to announce the grace of God.[41]

Although Ambrose does not directly identify Mary Magdalen as a sinner, he implies her sin first by the fact of her sex. Because she is female she is implicated in original sin. His quotation of Saint Paul on the merits of grace is also revealing. Essentially he argues that grace now suffuses Mary Magdalen where sin once abided. Similitude called for a female sinner to rectify the sin of Eve, the first female sinner. Because it was a charge for which the immaculate Virgin was ill-suited, the responsibility fell to Mary Magdalen whose reputation was now stained by Eve's sin.[42]

Ultimately there was discussion, but no real consensus about Magdalenian identity in the late antique period. Instead she remained rather ill-defined: sometimes a sinner, sometimes the herald of the resurrection, sometimes both. But this was about to change. In the late sixth century Pope Gregory the Great transformed the Magdalen's identity, producing the familiar saint whom subsequent centuries would venerate as Mary Magdalen.

The Composite Saint

On 21 September 591 Pope Gregory the Great preached a homily in the basilica of San Clemente in Rome that established a new Magdalen for western Christendom.[43] In his thirty-third homily that took as its theme the gospel pericope Luke 7:36–50, Gregory proclaimed: "We believe that

---

[41] *De spiritu sancto,* Lib. III, *CSEL* 79 (1964), 181.

[42] As we shall see, sermons of the later Middle Ages frequently used the text of Romans 5:20 to remind audiences of Mary Magdalen's sins now forgiven.

[43] The *PL* provides the day and month, Victor Saxer proposes the year in "Les origines du culte de Marie-Madeleine en Occident," in *Marie Madeleine dans la mystique, les arts et les lettres* (Actes du Colloque international Avignon 20–21–22 juillet 1988), ed. Eve Duperray (Paris: Beauchesne, 1989), 33–47.

this woman [Mary Magdalen] whom Luke calls a female sinner, whom John calls Mary, is the same Mary from whom Mark says seven demons were cast out."[44] In other words, Gregory collapsed into one individual the identities of three distinct women described in the gospels. First was the unnamed female sinner who, unbidden, entered the banquet of Simon the Pharisee where Jesus was reclining. In a memorable and dramatic conversion she washed the Lord's feet with her tears, dried them with her hair, and anointed them with her perfumed oils (Luke 7:37–50). Second was Mary of Bethany, sister of Martha, at whose beckoning Jesus raised Lazarus from the dead (John 11:1–45; 12:1–8). Third was the demonically possessed Mary Magdalen, whom Jesus had healed of her affliction and who then became his devoted disciple (Mark 16:9).

By appropriating the identity of Luke's sinner, Gregory the Great's Magdalen inherited a sinful past; by assuming the character of Mary of Bethany, the Magdalen acquired siblings (Martha and Lazarus) and became associated with the contemplative life. It was an audacious but not capricious piece of exegesis. Gregory was evidently responding to questions about Magdalenian identity, which, as we have seen, was already the subject of not a little confusion.

Why did Gregory append the identity of Luke's sinner to the figure of Mary Magdalen? At least four reasons can be posited. The first is textual proximity in Luke's gospel. The narrative of the unnamed sinner who makes her conversion at Jesus' feet closes out chapter 7 of Luke's testimony. "Mary called Magdalen" makes her appearance in the second verse of chapter 8; perhaps for this reason, it has been suggested, the two women's identities were combined.[45] Textual proximity aside, by the time Gregory the Great was pondering the Magdalen question, the biblical city of Magdala had acquired a reputation of depravity and godlessness, a fact that presumably contributed to Mary Magdalen's link with sin.[46] Yet a third reason is that John 11:1–2, sounding much like Luke's anonymous sinner, identifies the woman who anointed Christ and dried his feet with her hair as Mary of Bethany, sister of Martha and Lazarus. (The evangelist goes on to describe this anointing in John 12:1–8.) Fourth and most important was that Gregory the Great's preferred method of exegesis was by recourse to the tropological sense of the text, or its moral sense. He maintained that the seven demons with which Mary Magdalen had been beset before her encounter with Jesus were to be understood not only literally but also morally as the seven deadly sins.[47] Thus Mary Magdalen's demons,

---

[44] *Homilia 33* in *Homiliarum in evangelia*, Lib. II, *PL* 76, 1239.

[45] Haskins, *Mary Magdalen*, 19.

[46] Ricci, *Mary Magdalen*, 130.

[47] "What is designated by the seven demons except the universal sins? Since all time is

the wages of sin, were both the effect and outward manifestation of her sinful life. Her transgression was deemed to be sexual, since most medieval thinkers assumed that "all feminine sin was expressed sexually."[48] Coupled to that assumption was the certainty that unbridled sexuality led irrevocably to prostitution. Thus, by means of a potent combination of implication, insinuation, and ideology Jesus' loyal disciple became a penitent prostitute.[49]

But the Magdalen's metamorphosis was not yet complete. As will be recalled, Gregory added a contemplative component to her persona as well. In the passage cited above, Gregory identifies Mary Magdalen as the woman "whom John calls Mary." In another homily he illuminates this identification by telling his audience that after she had abandoned her wicked ways "she sat at the feet of Jesus, and listened to the words of his mouth."[50] Sitting at the feet of the master or teacher was the traditional position of the disciple or student. But the contemplative Mary sitting at the feet of the Lord listening to his word is a Lucan not a Iohannine image. In Luke 10:39 the evangelist describes Jesus' visit to the home of Martha and Mary of Bethany. Anxious Martha, preoccupied with serving the Lord, complains that Mary is of no help, having seated herself at Jesus' feet. The Lord gently rebukes his hostess reminding her that "Mary has chosen the better part which shall not be taken from her" (Luke 10: 38–42). The better part, Christian commentators made clear, was the contemplative life.

John's gospel, on the other hand, describes two of Jesus' visits to Bethany. On the first occasion, the raising of Lazarus, John observes that Mary and Martha of Bethany were the dead man's sisters, and that Mary was the woman who "anointed the Lord with ointment" (John 11:1–3).[51] On Jesus' second visit, six days before Passover, "they made him a supper there; and Martha served" (John 12:2–3). The description of Martha serving implicitly recalls the Lucan text in which contemplative Mary has seated herself at Christ's feet. As such we have arrived at Gregory's contemplative Magdalen, "the woman John calls Mary."[52]

Gregory the Great's Magdalen was a multifaceted figure whose pious

---

comprehended in seven days, totality is rightly signified in the seventh number. Mary had seven demons because she was filled with the totality of vices." *Homilia 33*, in ibid.

[48] Ruth Mazo Karras, "Holy Harlots: Prostitute Saints in Medieval Legend," *Journal of the History of Sexuality* 1/1 (1990): 30.

[49] I examine this transformation in depth in chapters 5 and 6.

[50] The homily was given at the Lateran in the week after Easter. *Homilia 25*, in ibid., 1196. Cf. his letter to Gregoria in which he associates the female sinner and the contemplative quite clearly. *Ep. 22, Registrum Epistularum Libri I-VII, Reg. II, CCSL* 140 (1982), 473.

[51] Neither Matthew 26:6–13 nor Mark 14:3–9 name Mary as the anointer at Bethany; she is identified only as a woman bearing an alabaster of precious ointment. As we have seen, Luke's anointing scene takes place in the home of the Pharisee and is performed by a female sinner (Luke 7:36–50).

[52] The Magdalen's contemplative aspect is examined in chapter 4.

ministry to Christ, witnessing of the risen savior, heralding of the resurrection, and contemplative nature rendered her worthy of veneration. But most important to Gregory was the Magdalen's symbolic aspect as an exemplar of "hope and repentance" for all sinners. This aspect of her persona of course derived from her identification as Luke's repentant sinner whose sins were forgiven by the Lord.[53] Gregory's composite saint ordained the agenda of Magdalen veneration for the entire Middle Ages and well beyond. So great was the pontiff's authority that the Roman Church accepted his Magdalen for almost fourteen hundred years, until the liturgical calendar reform of 1969.[54]

The Cult

When we move beyond the gospel and its attendant exegetical literature to evidence of the Magdalen's developing cult in the West, liturgical calendars are among the earliest documentary sources. Bede's martyrology (ca. 720) is the first piece of evidence of the Magdalen's cult in the West. It notes July 22d as the date on which her feast should be celebrated.[55] In terms of liturgical celebration, prayers for the Magdalen's feast-day are found as early as the ninth century, but a complete mass dedicated to the saint (with introit, gradual, offertory, communion, and lessons) does not appear until the eleventh or twelfth centuries, at about the same time that offices in her honor appear.[56]

Physical signs of her cult appear on the western landscape in the tenth century: a church in Exeter, England, claimed a relic of the saint and in Halberstadt, Germany, an altar was dedicated in her honor.[57] But it was not until the eleventh century—the century Saxer has dubbed one of "Magdalenian fermentation"[58]—that signs of devotion to the Magdalen began to accumulate en masse. Most important of all was the implemen-

---

[53] *Hom.* 25, in ibid., 1196. This is the subject of chapter 7.

[54] The Greek Church never accepted the Gregorian conflation. Its liturgical calendar marked separate feasts for distinct women: June 4 for Mary of Bethany while Mary Magdalen was celebrated variously on June 30, July 22, and August 4. See Victor Saxer, "Les saintes Marie Madeleine et Marie de Béthanie dans la tradition liturgique et homilétique orientale," *Revue des sciences religieuses* 32 (1958): 1–37. For a Latin-Greek Orthodox encounter on this issue see, Andrew Jotischky, "Gerard of Nazareth, Mary Magdalene and Latin Relations with the Greek Orthodox," *Levant* 29 (1997): 217–25. I thank Jim Powell for this reference.

[55] Saxer, *Le culte,* 40–41. Various feasts were kept for the saint in the East, particularly in Constantinople and Ephesus, prior to the eighth century. See Saxer, "Maria Maddalena," *BS* 8, 1078–88. For the cult in Anglo-Saxon England, see Veronica Ortenberg, "Le culte de Sainte Marie Madeleine dans l'Angleterre Anglo-Saxonne," *MEFRM* 104/1 (1992): 13–35.

[56] Saxer, ibid., 1091–92.

[57] Ibid., 1088–89.

[58] Ibid., 1089.

tation of Mary Magdalen's cult at Vézelay, the great Romanesque church in Burgundy, founded in the ninth century and originally dedicated to the Virgin Mary. The new patron of the church is first attested in a papal document dated 27 April 1050, during the tenure of Abbot Geoffrey. Under his leadership the abbey was reformed and brought into the orbit of Cluny, but more important for our purposes, it was under Abbot Geoffrey that the abbey church began claiming possession of Mary Magdalen's relics. From that time onward, Vézelay became a pilgrimage destination. In 1058, a papal bull of Pope Stephen recognized Vézelay's claims, bolstering the business of the newly booming pilgrimage site.

The presence of the Magdalen's relics helped the sanctuary at Vézelay become so important that Bernard of Clairvaux preached the second crusade there in 1146, and pious Louis IX made four visits, even attending the *elevatio* of her relics in 1267, at which time he received some of them for his personal collection.[59]

It should be noted that Vézelay was well positioned along one of the main pilgrimage routes that brought the faithful from Germany and the East down to the shrine of Santiago de Compostela. After stopping at Vézelay to venerate the relics of the Magdalen, one could then proceed further south and worship at the shrine of Saint Leonard, patron saint of prisoners, before continuing on to Santiago. The popular sanctuaries of Saint Martin at Tours and Saint Foy at Conques would not have been difficult side-trips from the road leading from Vézelay to Compostela.[60]

Hagiography

The final body of evidence relating to the rise of Magdalen veneration in the West is the hagiographical or legendary material. Among the earliest

---

[59] Saxer, *Le culte*, 186: Louis IX's four visits were as follows: in 1244; in 1248 before leaving on the seventh crusade; in 1267 upon the *elevatio* of the relics, the occasion on which he received some of them; and in 1270 before his last crusade. Salimbene describes the king's visit in 1248 in his *Cronica*, ed. Giuseppe Scalia, 2 vols. (Bari: Giuseppe Laterza & Figli, 1966) (Scrittori d'Italia series, vols. 232–33), vol. 1, 323. The *Cronica* is dated 1285–87. For Louis IX's piety, see William C. Jordan, *Louis IX and the Challenge of the Crusade: A Study in Rulership* (Princeton: Princeton University Press, 1979), and most recently, Jacques Le Goff, *St. Louis* (Paris: Gallimard, 1996).

[60] The literature on pilgrimage is vast: two useful works are Pierre-André Sigal, *Les marcheurs de Dieu, pèlerinages et pèlerins au Moyen Age* (Paris: A. Colin, 1974) and Jonathan Sumption, *Pilgrimage: An Image of Mediaeval Religion* (Totowa, NJ: Rowan and Littlefield, 1975). For Saint Leonard, see Michael E. Goodich, *Violence and Miracle in the Fourteenth Century: Private Grief and Public Salvation* (Chicago: University of Chicago Press, 1995), 137–41; for Saint Martin, see Sharon Farmer, *Communities of Saint Martin: Legend and Ritual in Medieval Tours* (Ithaca, NY: Cornell University Press, 1991); and for Saint Foy and the shrine's miracle register, see *The Book of Saint Foy*, ed. Pamela Sheingorn (Philadelphia: University of Pennsylvania, 1995).

hagiographical accounts of Christian saints are the passions written to preserve the heroic deaths of the early Christian martyrs. When, after the third century, widespread persecution of Christians ceased, a new type of saint—the confessor saint—emerged in the martyr's stead. Some of the earliest examples of this new saint were the eremitical saints of Egypt, Syria, and Palestine. These hermits withdrew to the desert to live ascetical lives of contemplative solitude. Persecution, however, remained a leitmotif in the narrative accounts of their lives. But this persecution was self-imposed, taking the form of harsh asceticism. A memorable typology emerged to distinguish the martyr from the confessor saint: a red martyr was baptized in blood, while a white martyr suffered the agonies of spiritual martyrdom. In addition, a new literary genre, the saint's *vita,* or life, evolved to accommodate the dimensions of the new spiritual martyr: the *vita* emphasized the heroic life rather than the heroic death of the saint. It also came to serve a variety of functions. *Vitae* were written to enhance what was already known about the saint, and as Stephen Wilson has observed: "Lives were written to stimulate devotion and provide examples of piety; . . . [and] to further the interests of particular groups or institutions."[61] The various *vitae* of Mary Magdalen illustrate each of these points.

Mary Magdalen's first *vita,* known now as the *vita eremitica,* is a hagiographic text of ninth-century southern Italian provenance, possibly from the pen of a Cassianite monk.[62] It is believed to have been imported to the West by Greek monks fleeing Byzantium. The *vita eremitica* assimilates Mary Magdalen's biography to the *vita* of Saint Mary of Egypt, one of a number of ascetical female sinner-saints whose lives were included in the *vitae patrum,* a popular collection of legends about the eastern desert saints.[63] The *vita eremitica* narrates how after the ascension of the Lord

---

[61] *Saints and Their Cults: Studies in Religious Sociology, Folklore and History* (Cambridge: Cambridge University Press, 1983), 16.

[62] *BHL* 5453–56. Hans Hansel, *Die Maria-Magdalena-Legende. Eine Quellen-Untersuchung,* (*Greifswalder Beiträge zur Literatur und Stilforschung,* vol. 16) (Greifswald: Hans Dallmeyer, 1937) sorts out the tangled web of Magdalen legends. The *vita eremitica* was thought in the Middle Ages to have been written by Josephus Flavius. One version has been printed in Jean Misrahi, "A Vita Sanctae Mariae Magdalenae (*BHL* 5456) in an Eleventh-Century Manuscript," *Speculum* 18 (1943): 335–39. The other three (5453–55) are transcribed in J. E. Cross, "Mary Magdalen in the *Old English Martyrology:* The Earliest Extant 'Narrat Josephus' Variant of Her Legend," *Speculum* 53 (1978): 16–25. An interpolated version has been printed more recently in Guy Lobrichon, "Le dossier magdalénien aux XIe–XIIe siècle," *MEFRM* 104/1 (1992): 177–80.

[63] *PL* 73 contains a Latin version of the *vitae patrum.* Benedicta Ward's *Harlots of the Desert: A Study of Repentance in Early Monastic Sources* (Kalamazoo, MI: Cistercian Publications, 1987) focuses on the female sinner-saints. Contrary to popular belief, not all the female desert saints were ex-prostitutes. In the Migne version, four out of eleven *vitae* are lives of repentant women. A recent translation of Mary of Egypt's life is included in *Holy Women of Byzantium: Ten Saints' Lives in English Translation,* ed. Alice-Mary Talbot, trans. Maria Kouli (Washington, D.C.: Dumbarton Oaks, 1996), 65–93. For a very good analysis

Mary Magdalen fled to the solitude of the desert and for thirty years lived as a hermit without food or clothing. This *vita* was rapidly transmitted to the rest of Europe; it was known in England, for example, by the middle of the ninth century.[64] The conflation with Mary of Egypt's biography is significant: Mary of Egypt had been a prostitute before her penitential conversion.

Though not technically a piece of hagiography, the *vita evangelica,* a homily once attributed to Odo of Cluny, is nonetheless an important text in the legendary cycle because it is the first attempt to combine into one narrative sequence all the gospel passages relating to Mary Magdalen's life. That is, it creates one coherent *vita* out of all the scriptural passages pertaining to Mary Magdalen, Mary of Bethany, and Luke's unnamed sinner. Colorful fictional embellishments are a mark of the *vita evangelica,* a late ninth- or early tenth-century sermon issuing from the environs of Cluny.[65]

The Magdalen's *vita* was further enhanced in the eleventh century to account for the presence of her relics in Burgundy. A pious fiction began circulating that narrated how a monk called Badilus was sent to Provence in 749 to rescue Mary Magdalen's imperiled relics from Saracen invaders. The monk found the area in ruins, but the saint unharmed. He was also granted a vision of the saint who informed him not to fear since his mission had been ordained by God. The next day, in a classic *furtum sacrum,* as this sort of holy theft has been described, Badilus spirited Mary Magdalen's bones off to Burgundy.[66]

If a holy theft brought the saint's relics to Vézelay, it might well be asked how they had come to rest in Provence in the first place. Another legend, the *vita apostolica,* conveniently explained that feat.[67] It claimed that as vic-

---

of the lives of the desert saints, see Alison Goddard Elliott, *Roads to Paradise: Reading the Lives of the Early Saints* (Hanover, NH: University Press of New England, 1987).

[64] It was, apparently, the source for the Mary Magdalen entry in the *Old English Martyrology,* which dates to the first half of the ninth century. See Cross, "Mary Magdalen in the *Old English Martyrology,* 20, and Ortenberg, "Le culte," 17.

[65] *BHL* 5439 in *PL* 133, 713–21. See V. Saxer, "Un manuscrit décembré du sermon d'Eudes de Cluny sur Ste. Marie-Madeleine," *Scriptorium* 8 (1954): 119–23, and Dominique Iogna-Prat, "'Bienheureuse polysémie.' La Madeleine du *Sermo in veneratione Sanctae Mariae Magdalenae* attribué à Odon de Cluny (Xe siècle)," in *Marie Madeleine,* ed. Duperray, 21–31, and an expanded version, "La Madeleine du *Sermo in veneratione Sanctae Mariae Magdalenae* attribué à Odon de Cluny," in *MEFRM* 104/1 (1992): 37–70.

[66] *Translatio posterior, BHL* 5491. Guy Lobrichon, "Le dossier magdalénien," has produced an edition of this *vita,* 169–77. The anonymous author's Carolingian chronology was a bit skewed; he says the event took place in 749 under Louis the Pious. For thefts of relics, see Patrick J. Geary, *Furta Sacra: Thefts of Relics in the Central Middle Ages* (Princeton: Princeton University Press, 1978).

[67] *BHL* 5443–49. Guy Lobrichon, "Le dossier magdalénien," ibid., has made an edition of this *vita,* 164–69.

tims of early Christian persecutions, Mary Magdalen and a cohort of Christ's disciples were set adrift at sea. Providentially, they washed ashore in Marseilles where they evangelized the pagan Gauls. Mary Magdalen preached in Aix-en-Provence, converting the city to Christianity. Afterwards, those new Christians proclaimed her colleague Maximin their first bishop. It was not long before the *vita eremitica* and the *vita apostolica* were stitched together to form what is now known as the *vita apostolico-eremitica*.[68] It related how, after an apostolic career preaching and saving pagan souls in Gaul, Mary Magdalen retired to a cave where she lived out the rest of her life in ascetical contemplation. When she died she was buried at the church of Saint-Maximin in Provence, from whence the Burgundian monk Badilus allegedly robbed her body approximately seven hundred years later.

These legends supported Vézelay's claims to possessing Mary Magdalen's relics. The possession of relics was important for two fundamental reasons. First, the relics and the miraculous power they contained attracted pilgrims to Burgundy, bringing prestige, not to mention the lucrative pilgrimage trade, to the region. Second, with the arrival of the Magdalen's relics, Burgundy now had a powerful protector since it was popularly believed that a saint was bound by a reciprocal arrangement to protect the region in which his or her relics resided. In return for protection, the local community paid respect to the saint in the form of supplications, ex votos, feasts, offices, and church decoration.[69] But there was something more important beyond the benefits of prestige, profit, and protection. By claiming Mary Magdalen's relics, Vézelay was forging a link to apostolic Christianity. Vézelay was not alone in so doing; it seems to have been part of a European phenomenon that began in the ninth century when Compostela began proclaiming that Saint James had preached and been martyred there, and wily Italian merchants, in a celebrated *furtum sacrum,* smuggled the body of Saint Mark out of Alexandria in a barrel of pork, translating it to its present quarters in Venice. Neither of these locations of course had had contact with any of the twelve disciples; nor for that matter had France or England, two other regions that both began forging links to apostolic Christianity. Given that the whereabouts of the twelve were largely accounted for, the next best thing was to claim a relationship with a New Testament figure, preferably someone close to Jesus, or failing that, someone

[68] *BHL* 5443–48. Saxer has gathered the Vézelay documents in a volume entitled, *Le dossier vézelien de Marie-Madeleine. Invention et translation des reliques en 1265–1267. Contribution à histoire du culte de la sainte à l'apogée du Moyen Age* (*Subsidia hagiographica,* n. 57) (Brussels: Société des Bollandistes, 1975).

[69] For the punishment meted out to relics and saints that failed to protect their clients, see Patrick Geary, "The Humiliation of the Saints," and "Coercion of Saints in Medieval Religious Practice," now reprinted in Patrick J. Geary, *Living with the Dead in the Middle Ages* (Ithaca, NY: Cornell University Press, 1994), 95–115 and 116–24.

who had been associated with such a figure. Thus, in the ninth century, the monastery of Saint-Denis in Paris began to claim that it was founded and Paris evangelized by Saint Denis, convert and student of Saint Paul.[70] At about the same time that Vézelay began to promote the Magdalen legends, Limoges claimed to possess the relics of Saint Martial who, popular belief maintained, had been baptized by Christ, and who had been present at the last supper and the ascension.[71] Two centuries later the abbey church at Glastonbury declared that it had been founded by Joseph of Arimathaea, one of Christ's disciples. In this context, Richard Landes has observed that "the cult of an apostolic saint who knew Christ in the flesh should appeal to an anxious audience; with trust and devotion to the saint, one could assure oneself of favor and salvation." It is in this same context of fashioning bonds to apostolic Christianity that the translation of Mary Magdalen's relics to Vézelay must be understood.[72]

A relic, however, was only as important as its last miracle. Fortunately for Vézelay the legendary Magdalen performed many miracles during her lifetime and after her death. She is associated with spectacular cures, assistance with matters of fertility and childbirth, the liberation of prisoners, and the raising of the dead, all of which were appended to her *vita*. Jacobus de Voragine (d. 1298), the Dominican author of the *Golden Legend*, the most celebrated medieval collection of saints' lives, drew on these miracle stories as well as various legends to construct his own *vita* of Mary Magdalen.[73] Although probably intended as a reference tool for preachers,

---

[70] For the Saint Denis legends, Paris, and their relationship to the Capetian dynasty, see the suggestive article by Gabrielle M. Spiegel, "The Cult of St. Denis and Capetian Kingship," in *Saints and Their Cults,* ed. Wilson, 141–68.

[71] For the cult of Saint Martial at Limoges, see Richard Landes, *Relics, Apocalypse, and the Deceits of History: Ademar of Chabannes, 989–1034* (Cambridge, MA: Harvard University Press, 1995).

[72] E. Delaruelle has noted in passing the rise in devotion to the apostles after the eleventh century in "Dévotion populaire et hérésie au Moyen Ages," in *Hérésies et sociétés dans l'Europe pré-industrielle 11e-18e siècles,* ed. Jacques Le Goff (Paris: Mouton & Co., 1968), 149. See also Landes, *Relics,* 315. A study of the emergence of apostolic cults in the West would be of great value in understanding the religious culture of the early and central Middle Ages.

[73] A critical edition of the *Golden Legend* has recently appeared: Iacopo da Varazze, *Legenda Aurea,* ed. Giovanni Paolo Maggioni (Florence: Sismel, Edizioni del Galluzzo, 1998). The standard Latin edition is Jacobus de Voragine, *Legenda aurea vulgo historia lombardica dicta,* ed. Th. Graesse. I have used the second edition (Leipzig: Carolus Ramming, 1850). The most recent English translation is the *Golden Legend,* trans. William Granger Ryan, 2 vols. (Princeton: Princeton University Press, 1993). The entry on Mary Magdalen is in vol. 1, 374–83. It is worth noting that the *Golden Legend* was neither the first, nor the only thirteenth-century compendium of saints' lives. Earlier legendaries, also Dominican, are by Jean de Mailly, *Abbreviatio in gestis et miraculis sanctorum* (after 1225), trans. Antoine Dondaine, O.P. as *Gestes et miracles des saints* (*Bibliothèque d'Histoire Dominicaine,* vol. 1) (Paris: Cerf, 1947), a source for both Jacobus de Voragine and Vincent of Beauvais; and

the compendium soon outstripped its original purpose and became a best-selling devotional work. The *Golden Legend* survives in over seven hundred Latin manuscripts and more than one hundred and fifty editions from the first century of printing. By the fifteenth century it had been translated into most vernaculars, including Dutch and Czech.[74] The Magdalen of legend was thus widely disseminated through popular devotional literature and the sermons that drew upon it.

Given his affection for the Dominican Order whose members were both consummate preachers and compilers of saints' lives alike, it is more than likely that the pious Angevin prince, Charles of Salerno, became familiar with Mary Magdalen's legendary career in Provence exactly through those means of transmission. It is also possible that he first learned of Mary Magdalen's apostolate in Provence at his mother's knee, as Beatrice herself was provençale, and the heiress to the county of Provence.[75] Learning of the saint's apostolate in Provence is one thing; concluding against all evidence to the contrary that her relics remained buried in Provence was quite another. Nonetheless he did so and in 1279 Charles miraculously discovered Mary Magdalen's relics in the crypt of the church of Saint-Maximin in the county of Provence, his own backyard, as it were. On May 5 of the following year, with great pomp and ceremony and in the presence of the archbishops of Narbonne, Arles, and Aix, among other ecclesiastical and

---

Bartholomew of Trent, *Epilogus in gesta sanctorum* (ca. 1244) now published in *Bartolomeo da Trento. Domenicano e agiografo medievale,* ed. Domenico Gobbi (Trent: Grafiche Artigianelli, 1990). The Dominican Vincent of Beauvais's *Speculum historiale* (bk. 4 of *Speculum Maioris*) (Graz: Akademische Druck- und Verlagsanstalt, 1965; repr. of Douai, 1624), though not a legendary but a world history first published in 1244, also contains much material on the lives of the saints. Popular fourteenth-century legendaries which rivaled, but did not supersede, the success of the *Golden Legend* are those by the Dominican Pietro Calo da Chioggia, *Legendae de sanctis* (ca. 1340), on which see A. Poncelet, "Le légendier de Pierre Calo," *Analecta Bollandiana* 29 (1910): 5–116, and Pietro de' Natali, *Catalogus sanctorum et gestorum eorum ex diversis et multis voluminibus collectus,* completed in 1372, and first printed at Vicenza in 1493. It was reprinted at least ten times during the first half of the sixteenth century.

[74] For the numbers, see Barbara Fleith, "Legenda aurea: destination, utilisateurs, propagation. L'histoire de la diffusion du légendier au XIIIe siècle," in *Raccolte di vite di sante dal XIII al XVIII secolo,* ed. Sofia Boesch Gajano (Fasano di Brindisi: Schena, 1990), 42–43. For the legendary, see Alain Boureau, *La Legende dorée: Le système narratif de Jacques de Voragine (†1298)* (Paris: Cerf, 1984) and Sherry Reames, *The Legenda Aurea: A Reexamination of Its Paradoxical History* (Madison, WI: University of Wisconsin Press, 1985).

[75] Victor Saxer has commented that "on aimerait savoir d'où était venue au prince angevin l'idée que le corps de la sainte reposait à Saint-Maximin et non à Vézélay à quelles sources il avait puisé sa dévotion Magdalénienne." *Le culte,* 263. Charles's devotion to the Dominicans and Mary Magdalen is discussed at length in chapter 11. There is no monograph on Charles II; for now, see A. Nitschke, "Carlo II d'Angiò" in *DBI* 20 (1977), 227–35.

noble dignitaries, the saint's relics were translated to appropriately opulent reliquaries. Mary Magdalen's head was placed in a golden reliquary studded with precious gems, while her body was placed in a separate but equally precious vessel. Contemporary chroniclers such as the Franciscan friar Salimbene, not to mention the somewhat later Dominican historians Ptolomy of Lucca and Bernard Gui, whose account of the second provençal *inventio* opened this chapter, attested to the prince's discovery of the saint's relics.[76]

Charles's personal piety and his particular devotion to Mary Magdalen are without doubt genuine. Yet it is likely that reasons beyond pious personal devotion prompted Charles to rediscover the body of Saint Mary Magdalen, thereby associating his name with hers. For it must be remembered that at the same time that the prince discovered the saint in his family's comital territory of Provence, his father, Charles of Anjou, was otherwise occupied in founding an Angevin empire in the Mediterranean. Although his imperial ambitions were on a much grander scale, his territory at the time included Anjou, Maine, Provence, and Forcalquier. But his most recent and most prized acquisition, made through the conquest of the Hohenstaufen in 1266, was the *Regno,* which included most of the Italian peninsula south of Rome, and for the moment the island of Sicily.[77] Though Runciman's assessment that Charles I's "piety was in its way genuine, but it chiefly took the form of a belief that he was the chosen instrument of God" is clearly overstated, it nonetheless makes the point that religious matters were not always foremost in his thoughts.[78] As such, it fell to his son, Charles, Prince of Salerno, to associate the Angevins with a saintly protector. Feeling the anxiety of influence, the upstart house of Anjou, a cadet branch of the Capetian kings of France (Charles I of Anjou was Louis IX's youngest brother), may well have felt the need for a patron

[76] Salimbene's account can be found in his *Cronica,* vol. 2, 761. He, unlike the other chroniclers, dates the *inventio* to 1283. The accounts of Ptolomy of Lucca and Bernard Gui are in Faillon, *Monuments,* vol. 2, 775–84. Faillon published all the reports of Charles of Salerno's *inventio* and *translatio* from the major ecclesiastical histories of the period in *Monuments,* vol. 2, 775–800.

[77] For Charles I of Anjou, see Peter Herde, *Karl I von Anjou* (Stuttgart: W. Kohlhammer, 1979). See also Jean Dunabin, *Charles I of Anjou: Power, Kingship and State-Making in Thirteenth-Century Europe* (London: Longman, 1998). For the Angevins in Italy, see Édouard Jordan, *Les origines de la domination angevine en Italie* (Paris: A. Picard, 1909); Emile-Guillaume Léonard, *Les Angevins de Naples* (Paris: Presses Universitaires de France, 1954); G. M. Monti, *La dominazione angioina in Piemonte* (Turin: Casale Monf., 1930); and most recently, the collected essays from a 1995 conference, *L'État Angevin: Pouvoir, culture et société entre XIIIe et XIVe siècle.* (Collection de l'École Française de Rome, 245) (Rome: l'École Française de Rome, 1998).

[78] Steven Runciman, *The Sicilian Vespers: A History of the Mediterranean World in the Later Thirteenth Century* (Cambridge: Cambridge University Press, 1958; Canto ed., 1992), 72.

saint. Who better for a new and ambitious dynasty to ally itself with than an intimate of the Lord who had brought Christianity to the heart of the Angevin empire and whose remains (and therefore intercessory powers) still resided there? Just as Saint Denis had served to authenticate the rule of the Capetian kings in northern France, now Saint Mary Magdalen would protect and legitimate the house of Anjou in the Mediterranean.[79]

In 1295, fifteen years after the *inventio*, Charles II, now king of Naples and count of Provence, installed the Dominican Order as caretakers of Saint Mary Magdalen's shrine at the church of Saint-Maximin. By 1315 they had produced the *Book of Miracles of Saint Mary Magdalen*, documenting all the miraculous intercessions and cures the saint had brought about at her provençal sanctuary.[80] That the final miracle recorded in the book displayed the powerlessness of Vézelay's relics was certainly no narrative accident: the intent of the provençal register was to celebrate Provence's triumphant link to Mary Magdalen's intercessory powers, while simultaneously underscoring the decline of Burgundy as a reliable locus of the miraculous.

Some years later, the Dominicans at Saint-Maximin, eager to publicize the origins of their royal foundation in Provence, fabricated a more divinely inspired version of Charles's discovery of Mary Magdalen's relics. This legend described how in the year 1279, on the vigil of the feast of Saint Mary Magdalen, a desperate Charles of Salerno, taken prisoner during the War of the Sicilian Vespers, threw himself on the mercy of his patron saint. That

---

[79] It is not unrelated that in 1300, three years after Philip the Fair gilded the Capetian family tree by successfully promoting the cause for the canonization of Louis IX, Charles II opened the canonization proceedings for his son Louis of Toulouse (d. 1297). On the subject of political sanctity, particularly as a dynastic initiative, see André Vauchez, *La sainteté en occident aux derniers siècles du Moyen Age d'après les procès de canonisation et les documents hagiographiques* (Bibliothèque des Écoles Française d'Athénes et de Rome, fasc. 241) (Rome: l'École Française de Rome, 1981), 264–72, now translated as *Sainthood in the Later Middle Ages* (Cambridge: Cambridge University Press, 1997). The Angevin family saint was pronounced by John XXII in 1317, proving that the Angevins too could engage in the politics of sanctity. In *La Sainteté*, 266n. 255, Vauchez argues that Charles "exploited" both his son and Mary Magdalen for political ends. On Louis of Toulouse, also called Louis of Anjou, see M.-H. Laurent, *Le culte de S. Louis d'Anjou à Marseille au XIVe siècle* (*Temi e Testi*, 2) (Rome: Ed. di Storia e Letteratura, 1954). For other Angevin saints, see Gábor Klaniczay, "The Cults of Dynastic Saints in Central Europe: Fourteenth-Century Angevins and Luxemburgs," in *The Uses of Supernatural Power: The Transformation of Popular Religion in Medieval and Early-Modern Europe* (Princeton: Princeton University Press, 1990), 111–28.

[80] For a transcription of the recently recovered book of miracles, see Jacqueline Sclafer, "Iohannes Gobi Senior OP. *Liber Miraculorum B. Mariae Magdalenae*," *AFP* 63 (1993): 114–206. See also Bernard Montagnes, "Saint-Maximin, foyer d'une création hagiographique. Le *Liber miraculorum beate Marie Magdalene* (1315)," in *Marie-Madeleine*, ed. Eve Duperray, 49–69, and Raymond Clemens, "The Establishment of the Cult of Mary Magdalen in Provence, 1279–1543" (Ph.D. diss., Columbia University, 1997).

night when the Magdalen appeared to him in a vision, the prince implored her to liberate him from his prison cell in Barcelona. Moments later Charles found himself miraculously transported to Narbonne. In return for his divine deliverance, the Magdalen ordered the prince to go to Saint-Maximin to recover her earthly remains that were not resting at Vézelay as legends claimed. Her relics would be readily identifiable by means of an ancient label (preserved in a wooden casing) which would read: "Here lies the body of blessed Mary Magdalen." In addition, she told the prince that he would discover the following important relics: the *noli me tangere,* the piece of flesh still adhering to her skull that marked the spot where the risen Christ had touched her when he appeared to her in the garden on Easter morning; an amphora containing bits of blood-soaked earth that she had collected from beneath the cross at Calvary; her hair now turned to ashes; and finally a green shoot growing from her tongue. She then instructed the prince to make the discovery known to all Christendom so as to increase devotion at her provençal shrine. She further ordered that Charles build a new church in her honor and a convent where the Order of Preachers were to be installed. She selected the Dominican friars to care for her shrine because, in her view, they were following in her footsteps as the new apostles of Christ. Finally she requested that the *translatio* of her relics be celebrated annually and that an office be established for that feast.

Bound in manuscript to the *Book of Miracles of Saint Mary Magdalen,* the *Dominican Legend* was written sometime after 1458, a century and a half after the incidents it purports to describe. Its purpose was to make manifest the divine concatenation of events that ineluctably linked together Saint Mary Magdalen, first an intimate of the Lord Jesus Christ, then the apostle of Provence; the Angevin dynasty, rulers of Provence and the Kingdom of Naples and devotees of the saint; and the Dominican Order, the great preachers of the day and the new evangelists of southern France whose convent was founded by royalty and protected by the saint.[81] Thus history, assisted by legend, bound sanctity to politics. What was missing, however, was historical accuracy. Although there is little doubt that in 1279 Charles of Salerno discovered some relics that he believed belonged to Saint Mary Magdalen, he did not receive the vision directing him to do so while held prisoner in an Aragonese prison cell. The War of the Sicilian Vespers did not occur until 1282 and Charles was not taken prisoner until 1284, a problematic five years after the discovery date of her relics.

But then historical accuracy was not the point of hagiographical legend.

[81] For a transcription of the legend and commentary, see Bernard Montagnes, O.P., *Marie Madeleine et l'ordre des prêcheurs* (Marseilles: Atelier Sainte-Catherine, 1984). See also Montagnes, "La Légende Dominicaine de Marie-Madeleine à Saint-Maximin," *Mémoires de l'Académie de Vaucluse,* 7th series, 6 (1985): 73–86.

The essence of writings on the saints was to be "ethically rather than factually true," as Alison Goddard Elliott has observed.[82] Moreover, hagiography was meant to edify as well as to serve the interests of specific "textual communities," to use Brian Stock's phrase.[83] We have seen texts do just that. The Gnostics devised their "knowing" Magdalen; Gregory the Great, responding to vexing questions about Magdalenian identity, preached a composite saint; the eremitical monks of southern Italy made of the Magdalen a contemplative ascetic; Vézelay created a patron who had evangelized Gaul; the Angevin dynasty cultivated relations with a protector whose relics watched out for the welfare of the house of Anjou; and the Dominicans of Provence constructed a Magdalen whose miracles at their shrine outshone all those effected at Vézelay, and whose patronage had divinely established them as the new apostles of Christianity.

This overview of sources for the history of the cult of Mary Magdalen has revealed how by the mid-fifteenth century the historical Mary Magdalen had been transformed into a legendary miracle-worker and patron saint. We have also seen how through the process of accretion and the pressures of the interests of textual communities the centuries enhanced the Magdalen's biography and shaped her persona accordingly. Further, we have seen how the fraught issue of authority within the Church—visionary or institutional—emerged as a gendered issue incarnated in the figures Mary Magdalen and Peter. This problem, though ignited by Gnosticism, was not inherently a gnostic problem. It was a Christian problem, one that burned at the core of Christian identity. For the moment it will suffice to say that the type of problematic visionary authority embodied by the Magdalen did not vanish with Gnosticism. In the next chapter, and again in chapters 6 and 9, we shall see how later medieval discussions that focused on Mary Magdalen's apostolic authority continued to reveal tensions concerning this matter in the Christian church. The problems that the figures Peter and Mary Magdalen represented would continue; but the later medieval period found ingenious strategies to finesse them.

In the preceding pages I have discussed various genres of later medieval sources, many of them Dominican, that take up the subject of Mary Magdalen. They include Bernard Gui's chronicles, Jacobus de Voragine's *Golden Legend,* the Dominican-authored *Book of Miracles of Saint Mary Magdalen,* and the *Dominican Legend,* which narrated the foundation of

---

[82] *Roads to Paradise,* 6.

[83] *The Implications of Literacy: Written Language and Models of Interpretation in the Eleventh and Twelfth Centuries* (Princeton: Princeton University Press, 1983), 90. I use the phrase a bit differently than Stock had intended, although, still in "a descriptive rather than technical sense." In using the phrase I wish to invoke the text's audience, which puts pressure on the text, infusing and structuring it with the group's common interests.

the royal convent of Saint-Maximin in Provence. So many Dominican sources might lead to the conclusion that the Order of Preachers was cultivating a special relationship with Saint Mary Magdalen. And so it was. But so were the Franciscan and Augustinian orders. In the next three chapters we will examine how the mendicant orders from the thirteenth century onward fashioned their own Magdalen, and through the process of symbolic gender reversal modeled themselves closely on her apostolic mission, contemplative aspect, and unwavering faith. It is to this Magdalen—the mendicant Magdalen—that we now turn.

PART ONE

The Mendicant Magdalen

TWO

The Vita Apostolica

Holy are they who in the course of
contemplation likewise return to action.
Saint Anthony of Padua[1]

In 1274, at the Second Council of Lyons, Pope Gregory X rebuked the
secular clergy for their persistent attacks on the mendicant orders:

> If you lived as they live and studied as they study, you would have the same
> success. They perform, at the same time, the roles of Mary and Martha. Like
> Mary they sit at the feet of the Lord, and like Martha they do everything to
> serve him.[2]

The women whom the pope summoned to the defense of the friars were
the sisters of Bethany described in Luke 10:38–42. That passage narrates
how agitated Martha scurried around the hearth attending to domestic
chores while her sister Mary sat absorbed in contemplation at Jesus' feet.
In the medieval metaphorical vocabulary Martha and Mary were long-
established symbolic types who represented, respectively, the active and
contemplative lives.[3] Martha stood for the active life of busy engagement
in the world while Mary symbolized the contemplative life, a life which
began with contemplation but aspired to mystical communion with the
Lord.[4]

---

[1] Cited in Jacobus Heerinckx, O.F.M., "Vita activa et vita contemplativa secundum S.
Antonium Patavinum," *Apostolicum* 1 (1932): 7. This chapter contains material originally
published as "Maria Magdalena: Apostolorum Apostola," in *Women Preachers and Prophets
through Two Millennia of Christianity,* ed. Beverly Mayne Kienzle and Pamela J. Walker
(Berkeley: University of California Press, 1998), 57–96.

[2] Cited in John Moorman, *A History of the Franciscan Order from Its Origins to the Year
1517* (Oxford: Clarendon Press, 1968), 177–78.

[3] The active and contemplative lives were also represented by the pairs Leah and Rachel
and Peter and John, among others.

[4] For studies of these entwined notions, see Dom Cuthbert Butler, *Western Mysticism: The*

The pope's characterization of the mendicants as both Marthas and Marys is the subject of the next three chapters. That is, the chapters in this unit examine how the mendicant vision of the mixed and apostolic life—the life that bound together action and contemplation, the lives of Martha and Mary with the twine of apostolic poverty, itinerancy, and vocation—came to inform the friars' preaching about Saint Mary Magdalen. Furthermore, Part One taken as a whole suggests that although the friars' apostolic Magdalen was constructed for public consumption and disseminated in sermons, perhaps more revealingly, the new image of the saint doubled back to become a paradigm for fashioning mendicant identity in the late medieval period. As terms are important to the ensuing discussion, let us first establish what the mendicant friars meant when they used the phrase *vita mixta,* the mixed life of action and contemplation.

When Dominic of Guzman and Francis of Assisi, the celebrated founders of the Dominican and Franciscan Orders, answered their religious vocations in the early decades of the thirteenth century, both took up active preaching ministries in the world. Dominic and his early followers waged preaching campaigns against the Cathars in southern France, while Francis aimed at converting Christians through practicing evangelical poverty and preaching repentance. Both are remembered for their lives of action. What is often forgotten, however, is that both Francis and Dominic were proponents of the *vita mixta.* As their visions of the active life of preaching were not altogether identical, so we should not expect their notions of the contemplative life to be entirely commensurate. Where Dominic stressed the restorative powers of meditative prayer and study, Francis preferred withdrawal from the world into mystical retreat.[5] These differences notwithstanding, when their followers used the phrase *vita mixta* they were signifying the union of the active and contemplative lives. When conjoined by the adhesives of vocation and mission, absolute poverty, itiner-

---

Teaching of Augustine, Gregory and Bernard on Contemplation and the Contemplative Life (New York: Harper Torchbooks, 1966; 2d rev. ed., 157–99), and Mary Elizabeth Mason O.S.B., *Active Life and Contemplative Life: A Study of the Concepts from Plato to the Present* (Milwaukee, WI: Marquette University Press, 1961), a gentle corrective to Butler. See also Giles Constable, "The Interpretation of Mary and Martha," in *Three Studies in Medieval Religious and Social Thought* (Cambridge: Cambridge University Press, 1995), 1–141.

[5] For Dominic's positions of prayer in his *de modo orandi,* see the miniatures in MS BAV Ross. 3, ff. 6r–13r. For analysis, see Jean-Claude Schmitt, "Entre le texte et l'image: les gestes de la prière de Saint Dominique," in *Persons in Groups,* ed. R. Trexler (Binghamton, NY: Medieval and Renaissance Texts and Studies, 1985), 195–220, and William Hood, "St. Dominic's Manners of Praying: Gestures in Fra Angelico's Cell Frescoes at S. Marco," *Art Bulletin* 68 (1986): 195–206. Francis had many sites of eremitical retreat throughout Umbria, Tuscany, and Lazio, among them the Eremo delle Carceri outside Assisi (Umbria), the romitorio di Fontecolombo (Lazio), Lago Trasimeno (Umbria), and La Verna (Tuscany), where he received the stigmata.

ancy, and obedience it became what we now recognize as the mixed and apostolic life, the life modeled on the early disciples of Jesus as depicted in the *Acts of the Apostles*.[6] Having been called to their mission, the friars were expected to discharge the duties of Martha in the world, although it was also assumed that they would refresh themselves from time to time in the contemplation of Mary. Or, as the great Dominican teacher Remigio de' Girolami (d. 1319) understood the friars' mission: "It is necessary, just as Gregory says, that preachers absorb in contemplation what they pour out in preaching."[7]

The mixed life, then, as most commonly understood, was the life synthesized from the active and contemplative. The mendicants considered this third way—their form of life—the best life. Bernardino da Siena (d. 1444), one of the brightest lights of the Franciscan Observant Reform, noted that it was the life Saint Francis had chosen in following Christ: "Having first the knowledge of nature through the active life, comes the knowledge of glory through the contemplative life; from these two lives comes a third, namely the mixed life which comprises both God and man."[8] It is not surprising that the mendicant orders considered this mode

---

[6] M.-H. Vicaire, O.P., *L'imitation des apôtres: moines, chanoines et mendiants IVe–XIIIe siècles* (Paris: Cerf, 1963), 74–76.

[7] He is paraphrasing Gregory the Great: "Oportet enim sicut dicit Gregorius quod predicatores in contemplationem sorbeant quod in predicationem effundunt." MS Flor. Naz. Conv. Sopp. D. 1. 937, f. 228v; *RLS* 5: 802. For Remigio, see *Scriptores*, vol. 3 (1980), 297–302, and Charles T. Davis, "Remigio de' Girolami O.P. (d. 1319) lector of S. Maria Novella in Florence," in *Le scuole degli ordini mendicanti (secoli XIII–XIV)* (Convegni del Centro di studi sulla spiritualità medievale XVII) (Todi: Accademia Tudertina, 1978), 283–304.

In the fourteenth-century *Meditations on the Life of Christ,* whose authorship some scholars attribute to the Franciscan Giovanni de Caulibus, we find a more refined version of the mixed life. The author turns to the writings of Bernard of Clairvaux to formulate a definition of this new type of life that his order, and those of other mendicants, embodied. He argues that there are two parts of the active life, but the parts are not contiguous; they are interrupted by the contemplative life. He suggests that the first part of the active life is the one spent in prayer, study, and charity, while the second part is concerned with the salvation of others and pertains to the sphere of prelates and preachers. The contemplative life is the life that intervenes between the two active parts and is, as traditionally defined, a life that is characterized by leisured repose and solitude conducive to contemplation of sacred things. A recent Latin edition that endorses the authorship of Giovanni de Caulibus is *Meditaciones vitae Christi olim S. Bonaventuro attributae,* ed. M. Stallings-Taney, *CCCM* 153 (1997). I cite the English translation: *Meditations on the Life of Christ: An Illustrated Manuscript of the Fourteenth Century.* Trans. and ed. Isa Ragusa and Rosalie B. Green (Princeton: Princeton University Press, 1961), 246–90.

[8] Bernardino: *Sermone XLIV* in *Le prediche volgari,* ed. Piero Bargellini (Milan: Rizzoli & Co., 1936), 1056. Remigio de' Girolami, the Thomist master of the *studium* at Santa Maria Novella, did not teach that the mixed life was the best life, however. In a Magdalen sermon quoting Aristotle's *Ethics* he preached: "Bona est vita activa quae ista prius habuit in suorum distributione. Sed melior est activa simul et contemplativa quae habuit in predicatione. Sicut

of life to be the best form of life. What is surprising, given the evangelical facts of her life, is that the friars believed that it was the form of life Mary Magdalen had followed. The celebrated Dominican preacher Giovanni da San Gimignano (d. ca. 1333) preached thus on the Magdalen's mixed life:

> There is also a third life composed from each one. And this is considered the best because it embraces each of them . . . and the Magdalen selected the best life for herself because sometimes, as it were, she was active and she ministered to him [Christ], washing his feet, both ministering to him on the journey and pouring out her precious oils on him. . . . She was also a contemplative, as it were, when she was meditating, listening to his words. This was an admirable life made best through the exercise of both lives.[9]

This chapter examines how the friars in their hagiography and public preaching transformed Mary Magdalen, Jesus' devoted disciple, into the *apostolorum apostola,* apostle of the apostles. It also proposes a gendered understanding as to the reasons that lay behind the mendicants' choice of fashioning their own role and identity in the later medieval world after that of a first-century female disciple of the Lord.

The Apostolate

In the eleventh century, probably in relation to the development of Mary Magdalen's cult at Vézelay, a legend known now as the *vita apostolica* began circulating in the West. It described the evangelization of Gaul by Mary Magdalen and her companions.[10] It narrated that when the first wave of Christian persecutions began, Mary Magdalen and her cohort, which included her sister Martha, her brother Lazarus, their servant Marcella, and Maximin (one of the seventy-two disciples), were expelled from Palestine. They were thrust into a rudderless boat and cast adrift at sea. By divine providence they washed ashore in Provence where they dispersed to preach the new Christian faith. Maximin and Mary Magdalen acted as missionaries first in Marseilles, then in Aix-en-Provence, while Martha evangelized

---

patet in legenda. . . . Sed optima est contemplativa gloriosa . . . Philosophus in .x. Eth." MS Flor. Naz. Conv. Sopp. D. 1. 937, f. 228v.

[9] "Est quoque tertia vita ex utraque composita. Et hec potest digna optima ut pote utramque conplectens . . . et hanc optimam vitam elegit sibi Magdalena quia et interdum tamquam activa ei ministrabat scilicet pedes lavando et in itinerem ministrando et unguenta preciosa ipsum efundendo. . . . Et tamquam contemplativa verba illius audiens cogitabat. . . . Haec mira fuit vita . . . optima facta est per exercitium utriusque vite." BAV MS Barb. lat. 513, f. 99r; *RLS* 3: 377. For Giovanni, see *Scriptores,* vol. 2 (1975), 539–43.

[10] *BHL* 5443–49. See Saxer, "Maria Maddalena," *BS* 8 (1967), 1093–94. Guy Lobrichon, "Le dossier," in *MEFRM* 104/1 (1992), 164–69, has made an edition of this *vita.*

Tarascon. Lazarus remained in Marseilles where he was raised to the episcopal see.

By the twelfth century these legendary events were considered the biographical facts of Mary Magdalen's life. An anonymous Cistercian author (once believed to be Rabanus Maurus) drew on the *vita apostolica* to describe Mary Magdalen's preaching activities in Gaul. He linked them explicitly to her role as herald in salvation history:

> [She] preached to the unbelievers and confirmed the believers in their faith. . . . Who among the apostles clung so firmly to the Lord? . . . It was fitting, then, that just as she had been chosen to be the *apostle* of Christ's resurrection and the prophet of his ascension, so also she became an evangelist for believers throughout the world. . . .[11]

The Cistercian was of course referring to the moment in John 20:17 when Christ bestowed on the Magdalen the paschal privilege of bearing the news of his resurrection to the other disciples, connecting it explicitly to her apostolate in Gaul.

The *vita apostolica* very quickly became *materia praedicabilis,* preaching material, that enlivened sermons. The Benedictine Abbot Geoffrey of Vendôme (d. 1132) remarked that the Magdalen preached and testified to the truth of the resurrection until the end of her days. His account drew on the *vita apostolica* narrating how after the ascension the "venerable disciple of the truth" saying farewell to her country, for the love of her Creator, undertook the joy of exile" and ended her days preaching.[12]

Inevitably some clever author came along and spliced together the *vita eremitica* and the *vita apostolica,* the two most important versions of her *vita,* and came up with what scholars now somewhat ponderously call the *vita apostolico-eremitica.*[13] This, together with the homily from Cluny and various miracle stories, eventually formed the patchwork *vita* that Jacobus de Voragine included in the *Golden Legend.*[14] The *Golden Legend* in turn

[11] The emphasis is mine. *PL* 112, 1494–95; It has been translated as *The Life of Saint Mary Magdalen and Her Sister Martha,* trans. David Mycoff. (Cistercian Studies Series, vol. 108) (Kalamazoo, MI: Cistercian Publications, 1989), 96. Henceforth I cite Mycoff's version. For commentary on this *vita,* see Victor Saxer, "'La vie de sainte Marie-Madeleine' attribuée au pseudo-Raban Maur, oeuvre claravalienne du XIIe siècle," in: *Mélanges Saint Bernard* (XXIVe Congrès de l'Association bourguignonne de Sociétés savantes [VIIIe centenaire de la mort de S. Bernard]) (Dijon: Marlier, 1953), 408–21.

[12] *PL* 157, 273–74. Jacques Dalarun has examined Geoffrey of Vendôme's writings on the Magdalen in the context of those by contemporaries, Marbode of Rennes and Hildebert de Lavardin, in "La Madeleine dans l'Ouest de la France au tournant des XIe–XIIe siècles," in *MEFRM* 104/1 (1992): 71–119.

[13] *Vita apostolico-eremitica* (*BHL* 5443–48). Edition in Lobrichon, "Le Dossier," 164–69. Splicing: in eleventh-century Italy, according to Mycoff, *Life,* 6.

[14] For the Cluny sermon, see chapter 1. The *vita evangelico-apostolica* (*BHL* 5450) fuses together the Cluny homily (*BHL* 5439) with the *vita apostolico-eremitica* (*BHL* 5443–48).

provided material for preachers to compose their sermons, as Carlo Delcorno has demonstrated.[15] The infusion of Magdalenian lore into sermons not only helped to enliven them, it also provided the raw material for late medieval preachers' conceptualization of the Magdalen's apostolate, founded as it was on her preaching career.

It might well be asked at this point how all this talk of a female apostle preaching and behaving just like any other early Christian missionary fitted in with the Pauline injunction that women should not deign to teach (I Tim. 2:12). Awkwardly, is the only appropriate reply. Just at the time that the image of the apostolic Magdalen became a commonplace in the preachers' homiletic vocabulary, a debate emerged—not coincidentally—that turned on the question of whether or not women were allowed to preach. Responses to that question of course informed and reverberated throughout much of what was then preached about Mary Magdalen's apostolate.

The Debate

In the fourth century, citing Paul as his authority, Ambrose had interpreted the words *noli me tangere* (the phrase that the risen Christ uses in John 20:17 to forbid Mary Magdalen's touch) to mean that women were forbidden to teach in church.[16] Ambrose's interpretation still obtained in the twelfth century: Peter Comestor (d. ca. 1179) and Peter the Chanter (d. 1197), Parisian masters both, taught that the moral sense of the *noli* was a prohibition against women preaching and administering the sacraments.[17] This moral interpretation also found its way into the mid-twelfth-century *Glossa ordinaria*. Echoing Ambrosian speech and sentiment, it declared that women were not to undertake important things (such as teaching in church), but consult those who were more perfect.[18]

Gratian's *Decretum* (ca. 1140), which compiled centuries of ecclesiastical tradition into canon law, forbade women to handle sacred objects, vest-

---

[15] Carlo Delcorno, "Il racconto agiografico nella predicazione dei secoli XIII–XV," in *Agiografia nell'occidente cristiano secoli XIII–XV*. Atti dei Convegni Lincei 48 (Rome: Accademia Nazionale dei Lincei, 1980), 79–114, and Delcorno, "La *Legenda Aurea* e la narrativa dei Predicatori," in *Jacopo da Varagine*. Atti del I Convegno di Studi (1985), ed. Giovanni Farris and Benedetto Tino Delfino (Varazze: Centro Studi Jacopo da Varagine, 1987), 27–49.

[16] *Expositio evangelii secundam Lucam*, Lib. X, CSEL 32 (1902), 519.

[17] Michel Lauwers, "*Noli me tangere:* Marie Madeleine, Marie d'Oignies et les pénitentes du XIIIe siècle," *MEFRM* 104/1 (1992): 244n. 183. See also Philippe Buc, "Vox Clamantis in Deserto? Pierre le Chantre et la prédication laïque," *Revue Mabillon*, n.s. 4, 65 (1993): 5–47.

[18] *Biblia sacra cum glossa interlineari ordinaria*, cited in Lauwers, "*Noli*," 244.

ments, and incense. It also prohibited them from carrying the consecrated host to the sick, and teaching, even if the woman in question was *docta et sancta,* learned and holy.[19] Pope Innocent III, well versed in canon law and the moral theology with which it was suffused, expressed similar views in a letter to two Spanish bishops dated 11 December 1210:

> Recently certain news has been intimated to us, about which we marvel greatly, that abbesses . . . give blessings to their own nuns, and they also hear confessions of sins, and, reading the gospel, they presume to preach in public. This thing is inharmonious as well as absurd, and not to be tolerated by us. For that reason, by means of our discretion from apostolic writing, we order that it be done no longer, and by apostolic authority to check it more firmly, for, although the Blessed Virgin Mary surpassed in dignity and in excellence all the Apostles, nevertheless, it was not to her but to them that the Lord entrusted the keys to the kingdom of heaven.[20]

Twenty-four years later Gregory IX cited this letter in full in his *Decretals* which themselves had the force of law. Elsewhere he acted to prevent women from entering the sanctuary, serving at mass, reading the gospel in public, acting as confessor, and preaching.[21] Contemporaneously, in the *Summa Theologiae,* Thomas Aquinas (d. 1274) adduced an argument against women's witness of the resurrection, arguing that "it is preaching which makes this witness public and preaching is not a woman's function." Paul and Ambrose are his authorities, but the Roman legal tradition which legislated against women giving public witness informed his judgment as well.[22]

---

[19] Baptize: *Decreti tertia pars de consecratione,* dist. IV, C. XX; Sacred objects and vestments: *Decreti prima pars,* dist. XXIII, C. XXIV–XXV, and cf. *tertia pars,* dist. I, C. XLI; Host: *Decreti tertia pars,* dist. II, C. XXIX; Docta et Sancta: *Decreti prima pars,* dist. XXIII, C. XXIX, and cf. *tertia pars,* dist. IV, C. XX, *Decretum magistri Gratiani,* in *Corpus iuris canonici,* ed. Aemilius Friedberg, 2 vols. (Graz: Akademische Druck- und Verlagsanstalt, 1959), vol. 1. Cited in Lauwers, "*Noli,*" 244, nn. 184–86. Lauwers also reminds us that all these interdictions have their origins in late antiquity. Gratian himself cites the authority of the Fourth Council of Carthage, but in fact they originated in the *Statuta ecclesiae antiqua,* a fifth-century document drawing on third- and fourth-century sources. For Gratian's view of the condition of women, see René Metz, "Recherches sur la condition de la femme selon Gratien," in *Studia Gratiana* (*Collectanea Stephan Kuttner,* II) 12 (1967): 379–96.

[20] Ep. 187, *PL* 216, 356. I use the translation of E. Ann Matter, "Innocent III and the Keys to the Kingdom of Heaven," in *Women Priests: A Catholic Commentary on the Vatican Declaration,* ed. Leonard and Arlene Swidler (New York: Paulist Press, 1977), 145–51. The abbess in question ruled the Cistercian house of Las Huelgas.

[21] Lib. V, tit. XXXVIII, *De poenitentiis,* cap. X, *Decretalium Collectiones,* in *Corpus iuris canonici,* ed. Aemilius Friedberg (Graz: Akademische Druck- und Verlagsanstalt, 1959), vol. 2. See also Lauwers, "*Noli,*" 245.

[22] *Tertia pars, The Resurrection of the Lord* (3a. 53–59,) *Summa Theologiae,* ed. Blackfriars (Latin text and English translation), 60 vols. (London: McGraw-Hill Book Co., 1965–), vol.

The *quodlibetal* tracts of the period, which took up the question of whether or not women could preach, added yet another dimension to the debate. Although such mid-thirteenth century masters as Gauthier de Château-Thierry and the Franciscan Eustache d'Arras parted ways on detail, both agreed that female saints such as Mary Magdalen, Catherine, Lucy, and Cecilia had preached by divine dispensation, and in extraordinary circumstances because the early Church was bereft of preachers.[23] The logic of the argument was this: because their mandate issued from the Holy Spirit these women had been exempted from the Pauline prohibition. Henry of Ghent argued similarly in his late thirteenth-century *Summa quaestionum* when he asked "whether a woman has the power to teach religious knowledge." (It should be noted that his notion of teaching comprises preaching as well.)[24]

As was to be expected, manuals for preachers forbade women to discharge the office of preaching. In his *De eruditione praedicatorum* the retired Dominican master general Humbert of Romans (d. 1277) advanced four compelling reasons for banning women from the pulpit: "(1) women are lacking in sense, . . . (2) are bound by a subject condition, . . . (3) if they preach, they provoke lust, just as the *Glossa* [*ordinaria*] says, and finally, (4) in memory of the foolishness of the first woman, Bernard said 'she taught [just] once and subverted the whole world.'"[25]

In addition, sermons themselves often contained admonishments about women preaching. In a sermon given on 11 April 1305 the Dominican firebrand Giordano da Pisa (d. 1311) declared: "Not everyone is granted the office of preaching, which is above all forbidden to women altogether and forever."[26]

Inquisitor's manuals and treatises refuting heresy likewise condemned

---

55 (1974), ed. C. Thomas Moore, O.P., 36–41. See also E. Ann Matter, "Innocent III," 148.

[23] Both texts are cited in Nicole Bériou, "La Madeleine dans les sermons parisiens du XIIIe siècle," *MEFRM* 104/1 (1992): nn. 106–7. She discusses them further in "The Right of Women to Give Religious Instruction in the Thirteenth Century," in *Women Preachers,* 134–45.

[24] See the *questio* by Henry of Ghent, edited by Alcuin Blamires and C. W. Marx, "Woman Not to Preach: A Disputation in British Library MS Harley 31," *Journal of Medieval Latin* 3 (1993): 34–63, and Alcuin Blamires, "Women and Preaching in Medieval Orthodoxy, Heresy and Saints' Lives," *Viator* 26 (1995): 139.

[25] *De persona praedicatoris* (chap. 12) in *De eruditione praedicatorum,* in *Opera de vita regularis,* ed. Joachim Joseph Berthier, O.P., 2 vols. (Rome: Typ. A. Befani, 1888–89), vol. 2, 406. On Humbert, see Edward Tracy Brett, *Humbert of Romans: His Life and Views of Thirteenth Century Society* (Toronto: Pontifical Institute of Medieval Studies, 1984).

[26] Giordano da Pisa (da Rivalto), *Prediche sulla Genesi recitate in Firenze nel 1304,* ed. Domenico Moreni (Florence: Magheri, 1830), 175. For Giordano, see Carlo Delcorno, *Giordano da Pisa e l'antica predicazione volgare* (Florence: Leo S. Olschki, 1975).

female preaching. In his treatise against the Waldensians and Cathars (ca. 1241), the Dominican inquisitor Moneta da Cremona railed against Waldensian women who justified their claims to the pulpit by appealing to the Magdalen's role as herald of Christ's resurrection. He argued in response that Mary Magdalen had not preached but merely announced the good news to the apostles.[27] The late fourteenth-century anonymous disputation attacking the Lollard Walter Brut's position on female preaching conceded Mary Magdalen's role as preacher in Marseilles, but nonetheless concluded that women, even if they have "the grace of wisdom and learning" can share it only by teaching in private.[28]

Concerns about heresy (and the concomitant belief that the women of these sects preached) forced the issue of women's preaching into the foreground of academic debate. Thus the debate about Mary Magdalen's apostolic career "was not merely an academic matter," a tediously pedantic exercise in disputation; rather, it was formulated as a response to heretical teachings of the period. The controversy was also no doubt informed by contemporary events occurring at Vézelay and Saint-Maximin. Recall that in 1265 the saint's relics were again displayed for verification in Burgundy, and fourteen years later, in 1279, Charles of Salerno discovered conversely that Mary Magdalen's relics had never left Provence. Both of these events were rooted firmly in the belief that Mary Magdalen had preached the gospel in southern Gaul.[29]

The Defense

One might assume that given all the sanctions against women preaching—from the unassailable authority of Saint Paul, to Parisian masters, to the *Glossa ordinaria,* to canon law, to the *quodlibet* debates, and finally to preaching manuals and sermons themselves—sensible preachers would not have bothered incorporating Mary Magdalen's problematic preaching apostolate in Gaul into their sermons. Surprisingly, this is not what happened at all: Mary Magdalen's apostolate in Provence became a popular motif in medieval preaching and, diffused as it was by the liturgy and sermons, it provided the inspiration for representation in various other cultural forms. Fresco cycles depicted her missionary activities among the pagans in Marseilles, *laude* sung the praises of her preaching, and sacred plays represented her as a preacher, going so far as to re-create the words of her

---

[27] Beverly Mayne Kienzle, "The Prostitute-Preacher: Patterns of Polemic against Medieval Waldensian Women Preachers," in *Women Preachers,* 99–113.

[28] Translated in *Women Defamed and Women Defended: An Anthology of Medieval Texts,* ed. Alcuin Blamires, Karen Pratt, and C. W. Marx (Oxford: Clarendon Press, 1992), 255.

[29] For the quotation, see Blamires, "Women and Preaching," 144, who argues similarly.

sermons. Before examining these sources, let us analyze what late medieval preachers, particularly friars, were preaching about the *apostolorum apostola,* apostle of the apostles.

The Penitent Herald

Preachers took Mary Magdalen's mission in Provence to be a natural consequence of her mandate from Christ to announce the news of his resurrection. But this event raised an important question: that is, Why had Christ designated Mary Magdalen as the first witness of the resurrection? In good scholastic fashion, Bonaventura (d. 1274) proposed four reasons: "(1) because she loved more ardently than the rest, (2) to show that he had come for sinners, (3) in order to condemn human pride, and (4) to instill faith."[30]

Some preachers, following Jerome, argued that Christ had made female apostles in order to shame the complacent male apostles, a line of argument implicit in Bonaventura's third reason.[31] Others, following Augustine, explained the episode in terms of gender similitude—it was necessary for a woman to atone for the sin of the first woman.[32] But in the later medieval period, more often than not, preachers explained the episode in terms of the Magdalen's great penance, an event implied in Bonaventura's second reason. Christ himself had proclaimed that he had come not for the righteous but for sinners; consequently he had shown his resurrection first to a former sinner. The Dominican preacher Ugo da Prato Florido (d. 1322) exemplified this view when he preached: "great was the consolation to the woman who was at first a sinner because the first apparition of the Lord's resurrection was manifested to her."[33] Anthony of Padua (d. 1231) expressed the same view when he represented the episode. He described the first witness only as a "penitent soul."[34] Another Franciscan, Servasanto da Faenza (d. ca. 1300), tells us that the Lord wanted to show

[30] *Commentarius in evangelium S. Lucae* in *S. Bonaventurae S.R.E. Episcopi Cardinalis Opera Omnia,* 10 vols., ed. PP. Collegii S. Bonaventurae (Quaracchi: Typ. Collegii S. Bonaventurae, 1882–1902), vol. 7 (1895), 590.

[31] *Commentariorum in Sophoniam prophetam,* in *Commentarii in prophetas minores, CCSL* 76 (1970), 655. Significantly, Jerome made this argument in the prologue that enumerated female worthies in the pagan world, the Hebrew bible, and the New Testament. The prologue was addressed to Paula and Eustochium, his own loyal disciples.

[32] *Sermo 232* in *SC* 116 (1966), 262.

[33] "Magna fuit consolatio mulieri que primo peccatrix fuit quod illi facta fuerit prima resurrectionis dominice apparatio vel representatio." *Sermones de sanctis per annum* (Paris: O. Petit, 1542), 249. For Ugo, see André Rayez, "Hugues de Prato," *DS* 7/1 (1969), 893–94.

[34] *In Pascha Domini* in *S. Antonii Pat. Sermones dominicales et in solemnitatibus quos mss. saeculi XIII codicibus qui Patavii servantur,* ed. Antonius Maria Locatelli (Padua: Societas S. Antonii Patavini, 1895), 128. For Saint Anthony, see G. Sabatelli, "Antonio da Padova, santo," *DBI* 3 (1961), 561–68.

himself first to Mary Magdalen—a sinner—to demonstrate that he had died for the sake of sinners. In the *Arbor vitae crucifixae Jesu,* a mystical treatise written in 1304, drawn possibly from sermons preached in 1302–4, the Spiritual Franciscan Ubertino da Casale (d. after 1329) asserted: "[Jesus] then, moreover, chose the Magdalen, a former sinner, to announce the glory of his resurrection to the beloved disciples."[35] The pleasing narrative symmetry of such an explanation, combined with the increasing importance of penance in the later Middle Ages, accounts for the popularity of such an interpretation with the preachers.

Mary Magdalen or the Virgin Mary?

Another question that emerged from the focus on the Magdalen's role as first witness of the resurrection, one that distinguished late medieval sermons—particularly Easter sermons—from their late antique predecessors, was the vexing problem of why the risen Christ had not appeared first to his mother.[36] As Marian devotion grew ever stronger in the later Middle Ages this indeed became a burning issue not only for the preachers but their audience. In the twelfth century, Eadmer of Canterbury (d. 1128) dealt with the problem effortlessly enough when, continuing the late antique tradition of awarding the Virgin Mary with all female honorific titles, he dubbed her *apostolorum apostola* and *evangelistarum evangelista.*[37] But the haphazard award of titles did not erase the disconcerting fact that scripture did not record that Jesus first appeared to his mother after the resurrection. Giordano da Pisa gave voice to the problem in a sermon when he repeated a question that he had evidently been asked by a follower: "Why

[35] *Servasanto:* "Voluit primo apparere beate Marie Magdalene ut ostenderet se esse mortuum pro peccatoribus." MS Antoniana 490, f. 102r. Although many of Servasanto's sermons were published as Bonaventura's, *Sancti Bonaventurae ex ordine Minorum S.R.E. Episcopi Card. Albanen. eximii Ecclesiae Doctoris Operum Tomus. III. Sermones de Tempore ac de Sanctis complectens* (Rome: Vatican Typographia, 1596), this was not one of them. See V. Gamboso, "I sermoni festivi di Servasanto da Faenza nel codice 490 dell'Antoniana," *Il Santo* 13/1 (1973): 55–56. See also *Siboto:* "Voluit autem suam resurrectionem primo omnium manifestare ei que peccatrix extiterat ut daret intelligi quia passus est et resurrexit pro peccatoribus." MS BAV Vat. lat. 6005, f. 113r. For Siboto, see *Scriptores,* vol. 3 (1980), 338–40. *Ubertino da Casale:* "Nunc etiam ad nunciandum sue resurrectionis gloriam ipsismet dilectis discipulis magdalenam quondam peccatricem elegit," *Arbor vitae,* bk. 4, chap. 29, unpaginated. Cf: Ubertino: "Quante enim pietatis fuit: & consolationis ad peccatores devotos: quod primo apparere voluit magdalene. Et ut huius pietatis exprimeretur affectio. . . . Vide quia qui propter peccatores mortuus est: peccatoribus sue resurrectionis gloriam conquisivit. Unde & huic principali peccatrici primo apparuit," Ibid. For Ubertino, see Frédégard Callaey, *L'idéalisme franciscain spirituel au XIVe siècle. Étude sur Ubertin de Casale* (Louvain: Bureau du Recueil, 1911).

[36] For the late antique tradition in the East that cast the Virgin Mary as the first witness, see my discussion in chapter 1.

[37] In *De quatuor virtutibus quae fuerunt in Beata Maria ejusque sublimitate, PL* 159, 582.

did [Christ] . . . not show himself first to his mother?"[38] There was no stock response, nor was there a party line; preachers had to follow their own inclinations on this matter. Some, despite scriptural evidence to the contrary, maintained the conviction that Christ had indeed first shown himself to his mother. Servasanto da Faenza preached that "the Magdalen saw his resurrection first, after the appearance to his mother, about which fact," he adds regretfully, "the gospels are silent."[39] In a sermon for the Easter vigil, the Dominican Jacobus de Voragine, more famous perhaps as the compiler of the *Golden Legend,* but also a celebrated preacher, pursued such logic to its end and constructed an elaborate apologia for the Virgin in the Easter drama. He argued that there was no reason for her to go to the tomb along with the other Marys because she knew already that her son's body was not there, that he had risen. Furthermore, the pious must believe that he had appeared to her before all others for three reasons: (1) On account of authority: because the venerable doctor of the church Sedulius had said so; (2) on authority of custom: The pope always celebrates the first station on Easter Day at Santa Maria Maggiore commemorating that Christ appeared first to his mother, and (3) on account of the moral reason: For God commanded 'Honor thy Father and thy Mother.' The Genoese preacher further explained that it hardly would have been honorable had Christ first shown himself to everyone else and then deigned finally to darken the doorstep of his "disconsolate mother."[40]

Popular devotional literature also inclined toward this view. In his vernacular version of the life of Mary Magdalen the Dominican Domenico Cavalca (d. 1342) narrated how Christ, having tarried too long in the task of harrowing hell, appeared to his mother in the company of those he had liberated from limbo. Jesus reassures his anxious mother that his wounds

---

[38] *Sermo 88, Quaresimale Fiorentino 1305–1306,* ed. Carlo Delcorno (Florence: Sansoni, 1974), 420.

[39] "Quintus est quia post resurrectionem suam primo Magdalena apparuit; videlicet post apparitionem matris de cuius apparitionem evangelie tacent." MS Antoniana 490, f. 102r. Bernardino da Siena argued similarly in *Giorno di Pasqua* in *Prediche della settimana santa. Firenze 1425,* ed. Marco Bartoli (Milan: Figlie di San Paolo, 1995), 242.

[40] "Primo per auctoritatem. Sedulius enim magnus & antiquus doctor ecclesiae, agens de Christi apparitione dicit. . . . Secundo per ecclesiae romanae antiquam & probatam consuetudinem. Summus enim pontifex ad S. Mariam maiorem in die Pasche primam stationem celebrat, per hoc inveniens ad beatam Mariam primam factam fuisse apparitionem. Tertio per quandam moralem rationem. Deus enim praecepit. Honora patrem & matrem. Sed si esset aliquis filius in ultra marinis partibus constitutus, de quo mater intellexisset quod mortuus esset, & tandem sanus rediens personas extraneas visitaret, & ad matrem tribulatam ultimo accederet, iste bonus filius non esset, nec matrem honorasset. Sic etiam Christus matrem non multum honorasse videretur, si prius alios de sua resurrectione laetificasset, & tandem matri desolatae apparuisset." *Sermones Quadragesimales eximii Doctoris, Fratris Iacobi de Voragine, Ordinis Praedicatorum, quondam Archiepiscopi Ianuensis* (Venice: Iohannes Baptista Somaschus, 1571), 209. For Jacobus de Voragine, see Ernest C. Richardson, *Materials for a Life of Jacopo da Varagine* (New York: H. W. Wilson, 1935).

no longer pained him, and presents none other than John the Baptist along with Adam and Eve to console her. After narrating this marvelous event, the author, like Servasanto, expresses a few misgivings. "I am blythe to think that she had this overwhelming consolation of sight and understanding . . . but I do not affirm it, because, for all I know, it is not to be found so in the Scriptures; but I delight to think that she should receive full consolation from her blessed Son."[41]

The Augustinian friar Jordanus of Quedlinburg (d. 1380) had no qualms about such a view. He maintained that the Virgin Mary knew of Christ's resurrection and therefore had no need to look for the living among the dead. Furthermore, he preached: "It must be believed that the risen Christ appeared first to her although scripture is silent on this matter."[42] Such thinking provided the Franciscan Rosary with the justification for incorporating this meta-scriptural visit to the Madonna among the joyful mysteries of the Virgin.[43]

Contested though it was, this was not the prevailing opinion in late me-

---

[41] Domenico Cavalca, *Vite de' santi padri*, ed. Bartolomeo Sorio and A. Racheli (Milan: l'Ufficio Generale di Commissioni ed Annunzi, n.d.), 383. There is an incomplete English translation attributed to "Pseudo-Cavalca," *The Life of Saint Mary Magdalen Translated from the Italian of an Unknown Fourteenth Century Writer*, trans. Valentina Hawtrey (London: John Lane, The Bodley Head, 1904), 283–86. I cite the translation as *The Life*. In the introduction, Vernon Lee suggests that this text comes from a Franciscan provenance, in my view an unconvincing argument. I would incline more to Carlo Delcorno's view which attributes such *vitae* to Cavalca or at least to his "bottega." See his "Cavalca, Domenico," in *DBI* 22 (1979), 577–86.

The *Meditations on the Life of Christ*, narrates a touching reunion of mother and son in which the Virgin examines her son's wounds and asks poignantly whether they still caused him pain. After an intimate conversation, Jesus asks permission to console the distraught Magdalen. "'My blessed Son, go in peace and console her,'" said the Virgin, "'for she loves you very much and grieves . . . at your death; and remember to come back to me,' and embracing Him, she let Him go." *Meditations*, 362.

[42] "Credendum est enim quod resurgens christus primo ei apparavit licet scriptura hoc taceat." *Sermo 255*, in *Opus postillarum et sermonum Iordani de tempore* (Strasbourg, 1483), unpaginated.

[43] Giovanni da Capistrano is credited with the "Corona Francescana." See *Chronica Fratris Nicolai Glassberger, O.F.M, obs.* in *Analecta Franciscana* 2 (1887): 34, and Leone Bracaloni O.F.M., "Origine, evoluzione ed affermazione della Corona Francescana Mariana," *Studi Francescani* (1932): 274. The Franciscan Rosary was one of the traditions invoked to explain Pope John Paul II's statement on Easter Monday 1994 when he shocked thousands of pilgrims gathered in Saint Peter's square remarking: "Even if the gospels do not speak of it there is the conviction that the first announcement [of the risen Christ] was made to the Madonna." This pronouncement apparently caused so much agitation among the faithful that the pope, in his next public address two days later, reversed himself saying: "The first person to whom the risen Christ appeared was Mary Magdalen," *La Repubblica*, 7 April 1994, 22. Be that as it may, three years later he made a similar declaration about the Virgin Mary. On 21 May 1997 he told an audience of pilgrims that the Madonna was probably the first to see the risen Christ. Marco Politi, "Giovanni Paolo II corregge i Vangeli. 'Fu Maria la prima a vedere Cristo risorto,'" *La Repubblica*, 22 May 1997, 1, 25.

dieval sermons: most preachers hastened to defend the view found in scripture that Mary Magdalen was indeed the first witness of the resurrection.
Iohannes de Biblia (d. ca. 1338), a Dominican preacher active in Bologna,
disputed with no less an authority than Ambrose when he argued (citing Augustine) that the Lord showed himself immediately after the resurrection to
Mary Magdalen, alone. Iohannes maintained that despite Ambrose's arguments to the contrary, Jesus had not yet shown himself to the disciples or to
his mother.[44] In an *ad status* sermon directed to all women, Humbert of
Romans hoped to put the matter to rest once and for all when he maintained
that Christ appeared first to one woman: namely, Mary Magdalen.[45] The famous crusade preacher Eudes de Châteauroux (d. 1273), Cardinal-bishop
of Tusculum (Frascati), preached to the Orvietans that the "Lord privileged
Mary Magdalen above the rest of the apostles and even the Blessed Virgin
because he appeared to her first and so quickly." Her second privilege was
the office which the Lord entrusted to no other. Eudes referred to her as
both *apostola* and *praedicatrix veritatis,* preacher of the truth.[46]

Apostolorum Apostola

It is virtually impossible to discern the origins or exact provenance of the
phrase *apostolorum apostola.* I have found no reference to the title earlier
than the twelfth century by which time it had already passed into common
currency.[47] Consequently, I suspect that the appellation may have emerged
in the wake of the *vita apostolica,* the *vita* issuing from Vézelay that recounted the Magdalen's apostolate in Gaul. Many of the twelfth-century
writers who use the title *apostolorum apostola,* in fact, had some relation to
Vézelay's mother house, Cluny. Abbot Hugh of Semur (d. 1109), under

[44] "Non se manifestaverat dominus adhuc discipulis nec ipsi genitrici. Ambrosius tamen
quarto *de virginibus* dicit eum primo matri apparuisse per hec verba: 'Vidit Maria
resurrectionem domini et prima vidit,' et statim adiungit 'vidit et Maria Magdalena quamvis
adhuc ista nutaret.'" MS BAV Borgh. 24, f. 63r; *RLS* 3: 91. For Iohannes, see *Scriptores,* vol.
2 (1975), 385–86.

[45] "Item tempore resurrectionis, primo apparuit mulieri, scilicet, Magdalenae." *De modo
prompte cudendi sermones* in *De eruditione praedicatorum,* Lib. II, ed. Marguerin de La Bigne
in *Maxima bibliotheca veterum patrum* (Lyons: Anissonius, 1677), vol. 25, 503.

[46] "In hoc eam privilegiavit dominus pre ceteris apostolis et etiam beata virgine quod
primo ei apparuit et quod tam cito. Secundum privilegium eius est quod de officio alicuius
mulieris vel etiam alicuius alterius personae non legimus dominum tantum se commendasse."
MS AGOP XIV.35, f. 181r; *RLS* 4: 947. Johannes Baptista Pitra printed excerpts of this
sermon in *Analecta novissima. Spicilegii solesmensis altera continuatio,* 2 vols. (Frascati: Typus
Tusculanus, 1883), vol. 2, 341–42. For the title *predicatrix veritatis,* see his sermon edited
by Bériou, "La Madeleine," 336. For Eudes, see Marie-Madeleine Lebreton, "Eudes de
Châteauroux," *DS* 4 (1960), 1675–78.

[47] I exclude from consideration the text attributed to Hippolytus of Rome examined in
chapter 1 because the Latin version is modern, made from a Georgian text.

whom Cluny flourished, brought devotion to the apostolic Magdalen to that great monastic foundation. In a letter of instruction for the nuns of Marcigny he refers to the Magdalen as the sinner who was so glorified that she was worthy to be called *apostolorum apostola* of the resurrection.[48]

It is interesting to note that the two great adversaries of the twelfth century, Peter Abelard (d. 1142) and Bernard of Clairvaux (d. 1153), while unable to agree on most everything else, concurred at least in bestowing the title apostle of the apostles on Mary Magdalen.[49]

Significantly, the first western pictorial representations of Mary Magdalen discharging her duty as *apostolorum apostola* also date from the twelfth century. The St. Albans Psalter (1120–30), made possibly for Christina of Markyate, depicts Mary Magdalen heralding the good news to eleven rather wide-eyed apostles (Fig. 1).[50] The twelfth century is also the period when hymns begin to employ the designation *apostolorum apostola* for Mary Magdalen. Of twelve Magdalen hymns that use the phrase, two are datable to either the eleventh or twelfth century, two more are from the twelfth century proper, and the rest are from the later medieval centuries.[51]

By the thirteenth century Mary Magdalen sermons and hagiography used the title *apostolorum apostola* almost reflexively to describe the saint's role in the resurrection drama. The title was even used by men such as Innocent III who, as we have seen, had no truck with the notion of women

[48] *Commonitorium ad successores suos pro sanctimonialibus Marciniacensibus, PL* 159, 952. The first mention of Mary Magdalen's feast at Cluny is found in the "Customary of Bernard," written about 1063. It combined three readings from Gregory the Great's 33d homily. The first known martyrology from Cluny, that written for the nuns of Marcigny-sur-Loire between 1087/89 and 1095 also mentioned the feast. Finally, the second lectionary of Cluny, dated about 1100, attests that the feast had grown in importance: there were now twelve readings from Gregory's 33d homily. Dominique Iogna-Prat, "La Madeleine du *Sermo in veneratione Sanctae Mariae Magdalenae* attribué à Odon de Cluny," *MEFRM* 104/1 (1992): 37–67, 40.

[49] Abelard used the title in a sermon that drew a comparison between the honor bestowed on women at Passover in the Old Testament (Miriam) and at Easter in the New Testament (Mary Magdalen). *Sermo 13, PL* 178, 485. The association of Miriam and Mary Magdalen was not unusual; Miriam, tambourine in hand, makes an appearance in the Magdalen Chapel in the lower church at Assisi as well. Abelard also uses the title in the plural to refer to the three Marys. See Letter 6, "On the Origin of Nuns," the pertinent passage translated in Blamires et al., *Women Defamed,* 234. Bernard of Clairvaux also used the title in the plural—*apostolae apostolorum*—for the three Marys. *Sermo 75, PL* 183, 1148.

[50] I treat this visual motif more fully in chapter 9. For the psalter, see Otto Pächt, C. R. Dodwell, and Francis Wormald, *The St. Albans Psalter (Albani Psalter)* (London: The Warburg Institute, 1960), 5. For the dating of the MS, see R. M. Thomson quoted in *The Life of Christina of Markyate,* ed. C. H. Talbot (Oxford: Clarendon Press, 1959; reprint 1987), v. For a listing of Magdalenian iconography, see Marga Anstett-Janssen, "Maria Magdalena," in *Lexikon der christlichen Ikonographie,* 8 vols. (Rome: Herder, 1968–76), vol. 7 (1974), 516–41.

[51] Joseph Szövérffy, "*Peccatrix quondam femina:* A Survey of the Mary Magdalen Hymns," *Traditio* 19 (1963): 79–146.

Figure 1. *Apostolorum Apostola* (1120–30). Mary Magdalen preaches the good news of the resurrection to the apostles. Her right index finger is pointed upwards in the traditional preaching gesture. Miniature from the *St. Albans Psalter*, Dombibliothek, Hildesheim. (Photo: Dombibliothek, Hildesheim)

wielding any form of sacerdotal authority.[52] The title *apostolorum apostola* is too ubiquitous in medieval texts to list its every appearance; it shall suffice to say that it is found in the works of most later medieval preachers, popes, hagiographers, and moralists including Jacques de Vitry, Honorius III, Gregory IX, Franco Sacchetti, Catherine of Siena, Remigio de' Girolami, Ubertino da Casale, Boninus Mombritius, and Antonino Pierozzi, among many others.

The compilers of medieval legendaries ensured that those who drew from their compendia were aware of this honorific title. In his compendium of *vitae* Bartholomew of Trent O.P. (d. 1251) abstracted for preachers what he considered to be the most salient points in the individual lives of the saints. He regarded the title *apostolorum apostola* as so important that in his brief Magdalen entry he twice drew his reader's attention to the fact that Christ had made her apostle of the apostles. It is indeed the closing remark of his account.[53]

Nunciare (to announce) was most often the verb that described the Magdalen's mission to the apostles; when it came to describing what she did among the pagans of Marseilles, however, *praedicare* (to preach) was the verb of choice. Some preachers such as Humbert of Romans and the

---

[52] "Et facta est apostolorum apostola per quam dominus resurrectionis sue gaudium nunciavit." MS BAV Arch. Cap. S. Petri D. 211, f. 78r. This sermon, the *incipit* of which is: *Rogabat Jesum quidam phariseus ut manducaret cum illo,* is not included in either of the two sixteenth-century editions of the *Opera Omnia,* nor is it found in Migne, *PL* 217, which is based largely on the two earlier editions. Nor does Schneyer include it in the *RLS.* B. Hauréau, however, published a partial transcript of it from a damaged MS in *Notices et extraits de quelques manuscrits latins de la Bibliothèque Nationale,* 2 vols. (Paris: C. Klincksieck, 1890), vol. 1, 173–79. My edition of the full sermon is forthcoming. My essay on this sermon, "Innocent III and the Literature of Confession," will be published in *Innocent III: Urbs et Orbis.*

[53] "Primo ei resurgens Christus apparuit et apostolorum apostola[m] fecit." MS BAV Barb. lat. 2300, f. 18r. The *Epilogus in gesta sanctorum* (ca. 1244) was a compendium for preachers constituted mainly of Italian and Dominican saints. See G. Abbate, "Il *Liber Epilogorum* di fra Bartolomeo da Trento," in *Miscellanea Pio Paschini* I (Rome: Facultas theologica pontificii athenaei lateranensis, 1948–49), 269–92.

"Preacher and herald of faith," "privileged preacher," "doctor," "doctor of the apostles," "messenger," "witness of truth," "originator," and "school of wisdom" were among the other related titles that preachers used to designate this honor. *Praedicatrix et annunciatrix fidei:* Matteo d'Aquasparta, MS Assisi 682, 193r; *praedicatrix privilegiata:* Remigio de' Girolami, MS Flor. Naz. Conv. Sopp. D. 1. 937, f. 232r; *doctrix:* Iohannes de Biblia, MS BAV Borgh. 24, f. 61r and *doctrix apostolorum:* Siboto, MS BAV Vat. lat. 6005, f. 112v; *magistra:* Iohannes de Biblia, ibid.; *prenuncia:* Sermo 105 in *Sermones thesauri novi de sanctis* (Strasbourg: Martinus Flach, 1488), unpaginated; *testis veritatis:* Siboto, MS BAV Vat. lat. 6005, f. 112v; *seminatrix:* anonymous, MS British Library, Add. 15682, f. 108r; *sapientiae schola:* Bernardino da Siena, *Sermo XLVI, Opera Omnia,* vol. 3 (1956), 438. Similar titles show up in hymns: *Marsiliae apostola, vitae praedicatrix,* and *testis crucis Christi;* see Szövérffy, "*Peccatrix,*" 92.

Augustinian Alberto da Padova (d. 1282) upheld the view found in the *quodlibets* that indeed Mary Magdalen had preached after the ascension, but it was only by special privilege.[54] Iohannes de Biblia held the same opinion but tried to normalize her preaching by placing it in its historical context. He observed that there were women prophets among the Jews, as there were sibyls among the pagans.[55] Giovanni da San Gimignano, mindful of the Pauline injunction, observed that "one reads that after Pentecost [Mary Magdalen] preached as an apostle to the people. But then it was prohibited to other women by the Apostle saying, 'Let women keep quiet in Church.'"[56] The Dominican historian Vincent of Beauvais (d. 1264) found an ingenious solution to the problem: he maintained that upon hearing the news of the Apostle's pronouncement the saint retired immediately from her apostolic career and gave herself over entirely to a life of penance and contemplation.[57]

Caution did not mark the majority of preached narratives of the Magdalen's apostolic career, however. Most preachers presented this episode in the saint's life without disclaimers or qualifications. An anonymous Franciscan from Marseilles remarked that thanks to her preaching the men and women of Marseilles were converted, and by her "mediation many more were saved than damned."[58] Although the canonist Huguccio had taught that women were not to ascend the pulpit, nonetheless that is just where

---

[54] *Humbert of Romans:* "Ipsa tamen ex privilegio singulari hoc est officium executa. Predicavit enim Marsilie gentibus . . . sicut dicit historia." *Liber de eruditione praedicatorum,* ed. Simon Tugwell, O.P. (Oxford: Oxford University Press, forthcoming). I am indebted to Fr. Tugwell for providing me with his working edition of the text. *Alberto da Padova:* "Facta est autem Maria Magdalena resurrectionis Christi praenuncia, & verborum ipsius relatrix, cum tamen apostolus prohibeat mulierem docere & predicare. Quod speciale privilegium merita gratiarum beatae Mariae Magdalenae accumulant." *Evangelia totius anni dominicalia* (Turin: Antonius Ranotus, 1529), 172.

[55] "Licet enim secundum legem comunem mulieri docere non permittat apostolus, ex speciali tamen privilegio doctoris officium ei commisit spiritus sanctus. Unde etiam in populo iudeorum alique mulieres prophetie spiritum et officium habuerunt et apud gentiles sibelle . . . extiterunt." MS BAV Borgh. 24, f. 63v.

[56] "Unde post pentecostem legitur tanquam apostola populis pradicasse. Quod tunc aliis mulieribus ab apostolo prohibetur dicente (1 Cor. 14) 'Mulieres in ecclesia taceantur.'" MS BAV Barb. lat. 513, f. 98v.

[57] "Sancta Maria Magdalena cum diutius verbum Dei predicasset, maximeque cum ad eius notitiam pervenisset quod Apostolus 'mulieres in ecclesiis tacere precepisset,' contemplationi arctius vacare desiderans, monente Domino, ad eremum asperrimum se contulit." *Speculum Historiale* (vol. 4 of *Speculum Maioris*) (Graz: Akademische Druck- und Verlagsanstalt, 1965; reprint of Douai, 1624), bk. 9, chap. 102, 359.

[58] "Massilia conversa sua predicatione ubi possimus dicere quod quo tempore homines et mulieres de Massilia sunt salvati mediantibus suis meritis. Sunt salvati et sic incomparabiliter plures quam dampnavit." MS BAV Borgh. 138, f. 145v; *RLS* 9:96. I am grateful to Fr. L.-J. Bataillon for bringing this manuscript to my attention.

later medieval artists envisioned Mary Magdalen preaching.[59] In a very damaged fresco from the church of Sant'Antonio di Ranverso (near Turin) the Magdalen is shown in a pulpit striking the traditional preaching position, right hand raised, index finger pointing upwards (Fig. 2). In Francesco Laurana's altar made for La Vieille Major in Marseilles, the saint performs the *computio digitorum,* another preaching gesture that indicates the orator's enumeration of arguments presented (Fig. 3).[60]

Two of the most interesting examples of this motif that I have found come from a fifteenth-century ecclesiastical vestment of German provenance, now in Lübeck. The cope, presumably worn by a priest or prelate on the feast of the Magdalen, is embroidered with ten scenes from Mary Magdalen's life. Three of them represent her preaching; two of them depict her in a pulpit (Fig. 4). One of these scenes shows her preaching to the pagans of Marseilles, a crowd that includes the ruler and his consort. The other scene, however, is a *rara avis.* It is placed in a narrative sequence on the left side of the vestment, the side that portrays the saint's life in Palestine. (The right side portrays her mission in Gaul.) It follows directly on the scene representing Mary Magdalen's announcement of the good news to the other apostles. The scene in question portrays Mary Magdalen in a pulpit preaching the new faith to a mixed group that includes women and Jews. The Jews are recognizable by their beards and funnel hats, iconography that identified Jews as such in the later medieval period (Fig. 5).[61]

[59] See Buc, "Vox," 15n. 31.

[60] The fresco is one of the few extant scenes from a late Trecento narrative cycle in a chapel dedicated to the saint. The painter has been tentatively identified as Pietro da Milano. See Enrico Castelnuovo, "Appunti per la storia della pittura gotica in Piemonte," *Arte Antica e Moderna* 13–16 (1961): 97–111. He reproduces some of the frescoes as figs. 33b, 34a, 34b, 35a, and 35b. The predella of the altar of Saint Lazarus was commissioned with the permission of King René of Anjou in 1477 and depicts the life of Mary Magdalen and her brother Lazarus. One of the bas-reliefs represents Mary Magdalen in the pulpit preaching to the citizens of Marseilles. See the catalog *Le roi René en son temps (1382–1481)* (Aix-en-Provence: Musée Granet-Palais de Malte, 1981), 158–62. Colette Deremble, "Les premiers cycles d'images consacrées à Marie Madeleine," in *MEFRM* 104/1 (1992): 187–208, mentions that the stained glass sequence of Mary Magdalen's life at Auxerre (dating from the second quarter of the thirteenth century), represents the saint in a pulpit, making it the earliest representation of this scene. For an early sixteenth-century Flemish example of the Magdalen in a rustic pulpit, now in the Johnson Collection in Philadelphia, see Jeanne Tombu, "Un triptyque du maitre de la légende de Marie-Madeleine," *Gazette des Beaux Arts* 15/1 (1927): 299–311. For preaching gestures, see Roberto Rusconi, "'Forma apostolorum': L'immagine del predicatore nei movimenti religiosi francesi ed italiani dei secc. XII e XIII," *Cristianesimo nella Storia* 6 (1985): 513–42.

[61] For a description of the vestment, see W. Mannowsky, *Der Danziger Paramentenschatz: Kirchliche Gewänder und Stickereien aus der Marienkirche,* 5 vols. (Berlin: Brandussche Verlagsbuchhandlung, 1932), vol. 1, 18–19. The only other example of Mary Magdalen preaching to the Jews of which I am aware is again German, and reproduced as the frontispiece in Boxler, *Ich bin ein Predigerin und Appostlorin.*

Figure 2. *Mary Magdalen Preaches in a Pulpit* (late 14th c.). Mary Magdalen preaches to the pagans of Marseilles from a pulpit. Damaged fresco attributed to Pietro da Milano, Church of Sant'Antonio di Ranverso, Buttigliera Alta (Piedmont). (Photo: Author)

Figure 3. *Mary Magdalen Preaches in a Pulpit* (1481). Mary Magdalen preaches to the pagans of Marseilles from a pulpit. Relief by Francesco Laurana, Lazarus Altar, Church of La Vieille Major, Marseilles. (Photo: Herziana)

Far more common than the pulpit imagery, however, was the image of the newly arrived missionary in Provence who spontaneously begins to preach from a portico of an ancient temple. A fifteenth-century fresco from the church of San Domenico in Spoleto exemplifies this motif. Here Mary Magdalen is shown giving her benediction to the people of Marseilles; a pagan idol can be seen enshrined in the background temple (Fig. 6).[62]

---

[62] Of the four early stained glass cycles of her life in France, the Magdalen's preaching apostolate is represented at Notre Dame at Semur-en-Auxois (1225–30) and Auxerre (1230). See Deremble, "Les premiers cycles:" 202–4; Virginia Chieffo Raguin, *Stained Glass in Thirteenth-Century Burgundy* (Princeton: Princeton University Press, 1982), reproduces the scene from Semur as fig. 136. Of four fifteenth-century German stained glass windows, this motif can be found in the earliest at Lübeck. See Marga Janssen, *Maria Magdalena in der abendländischen Kunst. Ikonographie der Heiligen von den Anfängen bis ins 16. Jahrhundert* (Inaugural diss., Freiburg im Breisgau, 1961), 276.

Of the thirteen later medieval fresco cycles (14th–15th c.) that represent scenes from the saint's legend, six of them depict her preaching apostolate. (That number may have been larger as some of the frescoes at S. Lorenzo Maggiore [Naples] and S. Maria Maddalena [Bergamo] have been lost.) The cycles that depict this scene are: (1) Cappella Pipino (early 14th c.), S. Pietro a Maiella, Naples; (2) S. Maria Maddalena (ca. 1370), Bolzano; (3) Cappella della Maddalena (1392–95), S. Antonio di Ranverso, Buttigliera Alta (prov. Turin); (4) Cappella della Maddalena (ca. 1400), S. Domenico, Spoleto; (5) S. Maria Maddalena (1470–97), Cusiano (Trentino); and (6) S. Maria (1495), Pontresina (Engadine). For reference, the other cycles are: Cappella della Maddalena (ca. 1295–1300), S. Lorenzo

Figure 4. *German Ecclesiastical Vestment* (first half of 15th c.). Cope embroidered with ten scenes from the life of Mary Magdalen. St. Annen Museum/Museum für Kunst und Kulturgeschichte der Hansestadt, Lübeck. (Photo: Herziana)

Figure 5. *Mary Magdalen Preaches to the Jews*. Detail of Fig. 4. (Photo: Herziana)

Figure 6. *Mary Magdalen Blesses the Pagans of Marseilles* (ca. 1400). Fresco from Cappella della Maddalena, Church of S. Domenico, Spoleto. (Photo: Hutzel Collection, by permission of the Getty Research Institute, Research Library)

Maggiore, Naples; Cappella Brancaccio (1308–09), S. Domenico Maggiore, Naples; Cappella della Maddalena (ca. 1312), Basilica of S. Francesco, Assisi; Cappella del Podestà (ca. 1322), Bargello, Florence; Cappella Rinuccini (1360–70), S. Croce, Florence; S. Maria Maddalena (mid 14th c.), Bergamo; and Oratorio di S. Maria Maddalena (early 15th c.), S. Maria del Belverde, Cetona (Siena). For Magdalenian iconography in Italy, see George Kaftal, *Iconography of the Saints,* 4 vols. (Florence: Sansoni, 1965–86).

So far as the scene is depicted in manuscripts, Janssen, ibid., finds the preaching scene in four later German examples. Another example is MS British Library Add. 15682, a late fourteenth-century German devotional book containing the Magdalen legend, sermons, and hymns in her honor. See fig. 7. Presumably her preaching was illustrated in the *Leggendario Ungherese* that originally contained 16 scenes of her life, half of which have been lost. See n. 72.

Two final examples of this scene must be mentioned. The earliest painted example of her

Not only did preachers credit the Magdalen with the office of preaching, some of them even went so far as to argue that she had earned the right to wear the golden aureola, the crown normally reserved for preachers. In his *questio* on the subject of women preaching, the Franciscan Eustache d'Arras suggested that Mary Magdalen merited the celestial crown of preaching because she had converted many people to faith in Christ.[63] François de Meyronnes (d. 1328) crowned the Magdalen with the golden coronet for having disseminated the seed of the word in the whole realm of Marseilles, and having converted the Prince and his wife, and most of Provence, to the faith of Christ. He maintained furthermore that she had earned the quadruple crown; one tier of which was golden—the one reserved for the learned (*doctoribus*). "Because wisdom is noted in gold according to Gregory, and she taught wisdom and knowledge of the Christian faith."[64] He made no mention whatsoever of the Apostle's injunction, or that she undertook her ministry by special privilege. In the normal way, the aureola was represented as a triple honor deriving from excellent deeds. Hugh of Ripelin (d. 1268), prior of the Dominican convent at Strasbourg, explained the triple crown in this way:

> whence it is clear that the aureola is due to virgins, martyrs and preachers. Martyrs conquer the world, virgins the flesh, and preachers the devil whom they not only expel from themselves but also from the hearts of others.[65]

---

preaching apostolate is one of eight scenes that make up the cycle in the Magdalen Master panel painting (ca. 1280). See fig. 40. Finally, a late-fifteenth-century example by Ronzen in the Musée du Vieux Marseille, Marseilles. It is reproduced as the frontispiece of Duperray, *Marie Madeleine*. The exhibition, *La Maddalena tra sacro e profano*, at the Palazzo Pitti in Florence in 1986, did not pursue this visual aspect of Mary Magdalen's *vita*. For the catalog, see *La Maddalena tra sacro e profano*, ed. Marilena Mosco (Milan: Mondadori, 1986).

For the chapel at Spoleto, see Roberto Quirino, "Un argomento di pittura spoletina fra tre e quattrocento: Il Maestro dei Cavalari," *Esercizi: Arte, Musica, Spettacolo* 5 (1982): 20–33.

[63] Cited in Blamires, "Women and Preaching," 148.

[64] "Et dicitur quod habuit quadruplicem coronam. . . . Secundo coronam auream quam datur doctoribus unde in auro notatur sapientia secundum Gregorium et ipsa docuit sapientiam et scientiam fidei christiane. De qua corona dicitur ecclesiasti." *Sermones de laudibus sanctorum* (Venice: Pelegrinus de Pasqualibus, 1493), 79–80. For François, see Heribert Rossmann, "François de Meyronnes," in *DS* 10 (1980), 1155–61. In his exposition on the book of Daniel, Hugh of Saint-Cher maintained that doctors and preachers received the double celestial prize of the *aurea* and *aureola* in *Prima pars huius operis continens textum biblie cum postilla domini hugonis cardinalis librorum infra signatorum*, 7 vols. (Basel: Johann Amerbach, 1498–1502), vol. 5, unpaginated. Nicole Bériou very kindly supplied me with this reference.

[65] "Unde patet quod virginibus, martyribus et predicatoribus debet aureola. Martyres enim vincunt mundum; virgines carnem; predicatores diabolum quem non solum de se sed etiam eum expellunt de cordibus aliorum." MS Balliol 230, f. 97r. For Hugh, see *Scriptores*, vol. 2 (1975), 260–69.

In a miniature from a fourteenth-century German manuscript, the Magdalen is shown wearing the triple crown, the crown reserved for martyrs, virgins, and preachers (Fig. 7).[66]

Although a century and a half separated them, Guillaume Peyraut (d. 1271) and Nicolas of Dinkelsbühl (d. 1433) both preached that Saint Catherine of Alexandria wore the triple aureola as well.[67] Catherine, like Mary Magdalen, was often represented in her missionary guise. What linked the two was that both were regarded as learned women who had converted pagans to Christianity: Catherine by her public disputation with the philosophers, the Magdalen by her preaching. Such images were disseminated widely. David d'Avray points out in relation to Saint Catherine that since her feast-day was a solemn feast—a holiday on which work stopped—the laity would have encountered the model of the female intellectual saint in her feast-day sermon. The same would have obtained for the feast-day of the Magdalen.[68]

Frequently the two saints are found paired in Trecento and Quattrocento religious painting. A polyptych by Simone Martini made for the Dominican monastery of Santa Caterina in Pisa exemplifies this relationship (Fig. 8). Here Mary Magdalen and Catherine are each paired with saints

[66] MS British Library, Add. 15682, f. 144r. For the significance of the triple aureola, see Antonio Volpato, "Il tema agiografico della triplice aureola nei secoli XIII–XV," in *Culto dei santi, istituzioni e classi sociali in età preindustriale,* eds. Sofia Boesch Gajano and Lucia Sebastiani (L'Aquila: L. U. Japadre, 1984), 509–26. See also his "*Corona aurea* e *corona aureola:* ordini e meriti nella ecclesiologia medioevale," in *Bollettino dell'Istituto Storico Italiano per il Medio Evo* 91 (1984): 115–82.

[67] Volpato, "Il tema," 514, 521 n. 18. Despite the calendar reform of 1969, Catherine of Alexandria was and still is venerated as the patron saint of scholars, male and female. For images of Catherine and other medieval *beate* preaching, see Roberto Rusconi, "Women's Sermons at the End of the Middle Ages: Texts from the Blessed and Images of the Saints," in *Women Preachers,* 173–95.

[68] "Katherine of Alexandria and Mass Communication in Germany: Woman as Intellectual," in N. Bériou and D. L. d'Avray, *Modern Questions about Medieval Sermons: Essays on Marriage, Death, History and Sanctity* (Biblioteca di Medioevo Latino, 11) (Spoleto: Centro italiano di studi sull'alto medioevo, 1995), 402. I am grateful to David d'Avray for sharing this essay with me prior to its publication.

Mary Magdalen's feast became an obligation in Oxford in 1222 and in Paris around 1268. For Oxford, see Garth, *Saint Mary Magdalene,* 89; for Paris, see Bériou, "Marie-Madeleine," 274 n. 13. See also C. R. Cheney, "Rules for the Observance of Feast-Days in Medieval England," *Bulletin of the Institute of Historical Research* 34 (1961): 117–47. In a letter dated 27 June 1228, Gregory IX urged the prelates and clergy of Germany to celebrate the Magdalen with a solemn feast. See André Simon, *L'ordre des pénitentes de Ste Marie-Madeleine en Allemagene au XIIIme siècle* (Thèse) (Fribourg: Imprimerie et Librairie de l'oeuvre de Saint-Paul, 1918), 26. Haskins lists a number of retributive punishments "meted out" to those who failed to honor Mary Magdalen properly on her feast-day. One poor peasant was struck by lightning, two women were whipped, and the town of Béziers was attacked by crusaders; in *Mary Magdalen,* 135.

Figure 7. *Mary Magdalen Wearing the Triple Crown* (14th c.). The triple crown is composed of the crowns reserved for martyrs, virgins, and preachers. Miniature from a German devotional manuscript, British Library, London. (Photo: The British Library)

Figure 8. *Mary Magdalen, Catherine of Alexandria, and Dominican Saints flank the Virgin and Child* (1319). The Dominican polyptych is dedicated to the theme of preaching. Simone Martini (ex Convento di S. Caterina), Museo Nazionale di S. Matteo, Pisa. (Photo: Author)

from the Order of Preachers. The confessor-preachers Saints Dominic, John the Evangelist, and Mary Magdalen adore the Madonna and child from her right, while the martyr-preachers Catherine of Alexandria, John the Baptist, and Peter Martyr flank her left.[69] The Dominican Order, founded on the twin pillars of erudition and service, showed particular devotion to these two saintly preacher-intellectuals whose *vitae* revealed similarities to their own conception of mission. Given that the Order of Preachers saw something of themselves in Mary Magdalen, we are now in a better position to understand why in 1297, at the General Chapter of Venice, the order claimed Mary Magdalen as its patron.[70]

[69] Enzo Carli, *Il Museo di Pisa* (Pisa: Pacini, 1974), 51–52. Color plates of the Magdalen and Catherine are reproduced as Figs. XI and XII. He argues that the polyptych was completed by 1319 and precedes a similar one made by Martini for the Dominicans in Orvieto in 1320. See also Joanna Cannon, "Simone Martini, The Dominicans and the Early Sienese Polyptych," *Journal of the Warburg and Courtauld Institutes* 45 (1982): 69–93. Although this fine article argues that the altarpiece stressed the theme of teaching and preaching, it does not connect the Magdalen to this mission.

[70] See William R. Bonniwell, *A History of the Dominican Liturgy 1215–1945* (New York: Joseph F. Wagner, 1945; 2d. ed.), 220; Daniel-Antonin Mortier, *Histoire des maîtres gén-*

Like any other early-Christian missionary Mary Magdalen was affronted by pagan superstition and attempted to destroy it root and branch. Servasanto da Faenza directed those preaching from his model collection to "say how for two years she preached in Marseilles and how the idols were destroyed." The Polish Dominican Peregrinus de Oppeln (d. ca. 1322) observed that Mary Magdalen's preaching was so effective that afterwards the people of Marseilles destroyed all the idols in their city and built many churches.[71] In the *Leggendario Ungherese*, a lavishly illustrated catalogue of saints' lives made for an Angevin prince, a caped-crusader Magdalen is shown destroying the idols, while in a fresco cycle from a *disciplinati* church dedicated to the saint in Bergamo others zealously do her bidding (Figs. 9 and 10).[72]

éraux de l'ordre des frères prêcheurs, 7 vols. (Paris: Alphonse Picard et fils, 1903–14), vol. 2 (1904), 345. Mortier concedes that there is no official decree proclaiming the saint as patron of the order; however, in their liturgical calendar the following words can be found: *Sanctae Mariae Magdalenae Protectricis Ordinis Nostri*. He observes: "Le corps de Madeleine est sous la garde des Prêcheurs, l'ordre des Prêcheurs, sous la garde de Madeleine." The royal convent at Saint-Maximin still remembers the Magdalen as *apostolorum apostola*. In the old chapel (now used for conferences) there is a fresco by Jean Martin-Roch that depicts Mary Magdalen announcing the good news to the new apostles, the Dominican Order. It dates from 1940–41.

The great Dominican convent at Pisa that produced the likes of Domenico Cavalca and Giordano da Pisa was under the patronage of Santa Catarina. For its history, see *Cronica antiqua conventus sanctae Catharinae de Pisis*, ed. Francesco Bonaini in *Archivio storico italiano*, ser. I, 6/2 (1845): 399–593.

[71] *Servasanto:* "Sed dic quomodo per duo annos predicavit in Marsilia et quomodo destructa sunt omnia ydola." MS Antoniana 490, f. 103r. *Peregrinus:* "Tunc in civitate et in terra sua omnia ydola destruentes multas ecclesias eo struxerunt." MS BAV Pal. lat. 465, f. 156r; *RLS* 4: 147. For Peregrinus, see *Scriptores*, vol. 3 (1980), 211–12.

There was a chapel beside la Vieille Major in Marseilles dedicated to Mary Magdalen which commemorated her evangelization. It was supposedly built on the ruined temple of Diana of Ephesus (against whom Saint Paul preached in Acts 19: 23–40). At this church the canons recited a little "cantinella" in Provençal during a procession that went from la Vieille Major to the chapel at vespers on Easter. It commemorated her role as apostle of the apostles:

Verse 14:
En prêchant les louanges du Christ,
Elle convertissait les païens
Et arracha Marseille à l'erreur
Ceux qui l'entendaient prêcher
Se convertissaient avec amour.

Bernard Laluque, *Marseille fut-elle evangelisée par une femme?* (Marseilles: Le Comité du Vieux Marseille, 1986), 350, 368.

[72] MS BAV Vat. lat. 8541, f. 103v. For the legendary, see *Heiligenleben. Ungarisches Legendarium Cod. Vat. lat. 8541* (Facsimile edition and commentary) (Zurich: Belser, 1990); *Bergamo: Pittura a Bergamo dal romanico al neoclassicismo*, ed. Mina Gregori (Milan: Silvana Ed. d'Arte, 991), 9, 74, 226; *I pittori bergamaschi dal XIII al XIX secolo*, 13 vols. (Bergamo: Bolis, 1975–92), vol. 1 (1975); *Le origini*, ed. Miklós Boskovits, 408–14. My thanks to Lester Little who unearthed the Bergamo references.

Figure 9. *Destruction of the Idols in Marseilles* (1333–43). Miniature from the *Leggendario Ungherese*, Biblioteca Apostolica Vaticana, Città del Vaticano. (Photo: Biblioteca Apostolica Vaticana)

Figure 10. *Destruction of the Idols in Marseilles* (late 14th c.). Fresco by Lombard Master, Palazzo della Ragione, Bergamo (ex Disciplinati Church of S. Maria Maddalena.) (Photo: Author)

After preaching the new religion, destroying pagan idols, and confirming people in the faith, an early Christian missionary usually baptized people. Mary Magdalen, contrary to canon law, engaged in this activity as well. The hagiographer Pietro de' Natali's (d. 1400) legend described how after destroying the pagan temples, the Magdalen performed the rite of baptism.[73] The church of Saint Maurice in Angers preserves the font in which she was believed to have baptized the ancient rulers of Provence. It was piously donated by René (d. 1480), the Angevin king of Provence.[74]

Along with artifacts and objects, the liturgy too would have reminded the faithful of the Magdalen's designation as *apostolorum apostola* since the

[73] "Omniaque idolorum templa destruens cum omni populo baptisma suscepit." *Catalogus sanctorum* (Venice: Nicolaus de Frankfordia, 1516), 257. Thomas Aquinas argued that in a case of necessity a woman could baptize if no man could be found. See Kari Elisabeth Børresen, *Subordination and Equivalence: The Nature and Role of Woman in Augustine and Thomas Aquinas,* trans. Charles H. Talbot (Washington, D.C.: University Press of America, 1981), 39.

[74] Laluque, *Marseille,* 404.

credo was recited on her feast-day, the only woman to merit this honor other than the Virgin Mary.[75] The antiphon "*O apostolorum apostola*" would have been yet another reminder.[76] Humbert of Romans assumed that the canonesses to whom he directed one of his *ad status* sermons were familiar with this antiphon. He reminded them that "it must be noted that once there were not only prophets, but also prophetesses . . . and not only apostles but apostlesses, as is sung about the Magdalen."[77]

Another musical form of praise, *laude,* also sung of the apostolic Magdalen. One from Cortona chanted:

> So he made her his disciple
> as scripture recounts and tells.
> Then she stood as an apostle in his stead
> in order to preach his gospel.[78]

Sacred drama also celebrated the *apostolorum apostola*. In one, *Rappresentazione di S. Maria Maddalena,* Maximin, arriving in Marseilles with the Magdalen, surveys the pagan temple, the portico, and the icon enshrined inside. He then beseeches the saint: "And you Mary, you who are so eloquent, would you preach to these people first?" Rising to the challenge, Mary Magdalen preaches:

> O benighted people, O ignorant people,
> O people mired in error and sin . . .

She concludes with this rousing finale:

> Leave your pagan sect now
> which is full of every false error.
> And come to the true and holy faith
> which saves everyone who believes.[79]

[75] Josef A. Jungmann, *The Mass of the Roman Rite,* 2 vols. (New York: Benziger, 1950–55), vol. 1, 470n. 55. According to Jungmann, some medieval liturgists advised that the *credo* be said on Mary Magdalen's feast-day on account of her title *apostolorum apostola*. It was recited for all feasts of the Lord from Christmas through Pentecost, the feasts of the Virgin Mary, the feasts of the apostles, All Saints, and All Souls.

[76] *Analecta hymnica medii aevi,* ed. Guido Maria Dreves, 55 vols. (Leipzig: Fues's Verlag, 1886–1922), vol. 1, 161n. 171. At the convent for repentant prostitutes dedicated to Mary Magdalen in Avignon, according to the statutes of 1367, the antiphon was sung daily after Matins, mass, and Vespers. See P. Pansier, *L'oeuvre des repenties à Avignon du XIIIe au XVIIIe siècle* (Paris and Avignon: Honoré Champion and J. Roumanille, 1910), 114.

[77] "Notandum quod sicut olim fuerunt non solum prophetae, sed etiam prophetisse . . . et non solum Apostoli, sed & Apostolae, ut cantatur de Magdalena." *De eruditione praedicatorum,* in *Maxima biblioteca,* 483–84.

[78] *Lauda* 40 in *Laude cortonesi dal secolo XIII al XV,* (Biblioteca della rivista di storia e letteratura religiosa. Studi e testi, vol. 5), ed. Giorgio Varanini *et al.* (Florence: Leo S. Olschki, 1981), 280.

[79] *Sacre rappresentazioni dei secoli XIV, XV e XVI,* ed. Alessandro d'Ancona, 3 vols. (Florence: Successori le Monnier, 1872), vol. 1, 404.

Devotional literature took up the theme of the Magdalen's apostolate and elaborated it. The *Golden Legend*—not mentioning a word about special dispensation—narrated that when she began to preach to the pagans "all who heard her were in admiration at her beauty, her eloquence, and the sweetness of her message . . . and no wonder, that the mouth which had pressed such pious and beautiful kisses on the Savior's feet should breathe forth the perfume of the word of God more profusely than others could."[80] Cavalca's *vita* told of her evangelization of Gaul, but also narrated how the Magdalen preached the faith even during Christ's lifetime. She preached the doctrine of the Lord so sweetly to the tenants of her estates that the people all wept for devotion, and they began to cry with one voice, saying: "Magdalen, do not leave us, for now we will be more faithful and better servants than ever before."[81] But their cries went unheeded. She left them; and like the other apostles she sold all she had and gave the profits to the poor. Servasanto da Faenza remarked the parallel between the Friars Minor, the Magdalen, and the other apostles observing that all, having been called to their apostolic vocation, renounced the world and themselves.[82]

Not only was she called to a vocation, as Servasanto made plain, it was also believed that she had received a mission to preach since she had been present when the holy spirit descended at Pentecost. A fourteenth-century German devotional book, referring to the *Acts of the Apostles,* maintained that "the pious Magdalen, apostle of the apostles, being on the same day and at the same time in the room with the others, was filled with the gift of the same holy spirit."[83] An Italian legend narrated that when the holy spirit descended it was "in the form of tongues afire and it infused all who were present including the Madonna, the disciples, and the dear hostesses Martha and the Magdalen and the rest."[84] The founder and first prior of the convent of San Domenico in Naples, and the man who received Thomas Aquinas into the order, Tommaso Agni da Lentini (d. 1277), preached that after the ascension of the Lord, she and the other disciples

[80] *Golden Legend,* vol. 1, 376–77.

[81] *The Life,* 100–102; *Vita,* 348.

[82] "Et hac vocatione vocati sunt apostoli (Matt. 4) . . . Hac vocatione sunt vocati fratres minores qui relinquerunt mundum et se ipsos. Hac vocatione vocavit Magdalenam." MS Antoniana 490, f. 101r.

[83] "Eodem die et eadem hora pia Magdalena apostolorum apostola existens in cella horum beatorum replebatur dono eiusdem spiritus sancti; cum tali ac tanta graciarum habundancia sicut ceteri apostoli a domino honorati postquam igitur electa cristi discipula largo sancti spiritus." MS British Library, Add. 15682, ff. 101r–101v.

[84] *Il Libro di Lazero & Martha & Magdalena* (Florence: Francesco Buonaccorsi, 1490), unpaginated. Among other sources, the Dominican hagiographer Bartholomew of Trent in his *Epilogus in gesta sanctorum* said that Mary Magdalen "received the holy spirit along with the others." MS BAV Barb. lat. 2300, f. 18r. See also Geoffrey of Vendôme, *PL* 157, 273–74, and Mycoff, *Life,* 84.

took up many works including praying, teaching, and converting men to the faith of Christ.[85] Thus it was believed that she had discharged her office admirably, converting many pagans to Christianity.

But there was more. Every friar was quick to underscore how she, a rich heiress, had obeyed Christ's commandments about evangelical poverty found in Matt. 19:21, a foundational text for the mendicant version of the *vita apostolica*. The Augustinian preacher and papal apologist Agostino d'Ancona (d. 1328) observed that just as she had once heartlessly squandered her patrimony on frivolities, frittering it away on entertainers and actors rather than the poor and needy; now, after her conversion, she disposed of all her worldly things among the poor. A Quattrocento fresco cycle in Cusiano is the text's visual analogue. It shows the saint and her siblings distributing their worldly goods to the needy (Fig. 11).[86]

According to its moral interpretation, Mary Magdalen's act of anointing Christ's feet signified similarly. Her ascetical existence at La Sainte-Baume, the subject of chapter 4, further linked her to absolute poverty: having renounced the world, she retained nothing, not even a stitch of clothing. Our Franciscan from Marseilles observed that she was naked, solitary, and famished in her desert abode.[87] Naked, except for a decorous covering of her own hair, she followed the naked Christ up to and even after his crucifixion.

To the Cross

The Magdalen's fidelity at the cross, suffused as it was in virtuous perseverance, was deeply admired by the mendicant orders. Her fidelity to the Lord was expressed throughout his life and italicized after his death, when she alone stood weeping at the sepulcher after all the other disciples had abandoned him (John 20: 10–11). Eudes de Châteauroux used the occasion of the Magdalen's feast to preach on the theme of the fortitude of women, suggesting that women unlike men showed strength and perse-

---

[85] "Nam post ascensionem domini cum discipulis multos sustinuit labores . . . in orando in docendo et convertendo homines ad fidem christi. Sicut patet in legenda." MS Vat. lat. 4691, f. 114v; not listed in *RLS*. For Tommaso Agni da Lentini, see *Scriptores,* vol. 4, 325–28.

[86] "Fuit crudelis et insensibilis cum ipsa divicias sibi a patre eius relictas non pauperibus et indigentibus sed ioculatoribus et hystrionibus largiretur." MS Angelica 158, f. 122r and: "omnia temporalia inter pauperes dispensavit." Ibid., f. 122v. Significantly he concludes the sentence thus: "Et omnes divicias sibi a patre relictas post ascensionem domini ad pedes apostolorum posuit qui patres pauperum erant per Christum constituti." As such, Mary Magdalen gave both to the poor and to the fathers of the poor—the apostles established by Christ. For Agostino, see B. Ministeri, "Agostino d'Ancona (Agostino Triumfo)," *DBI* 1 (1960), 475–78. For the fresco cycle, see Quirino Bezzi, "Gli affreschi di Giovanni e Battista Baschenis di Averaria nella chiesa di S. Maria Maddelena di Cusiano," *Studi Trentini* 49 (1970): 358–71.

[87] "Nuda, solitaria et famelica." MS BAV Borgh. 138, f. 145v.

Figure 11. *Mary Magdalen, Martha, and Lazarus Distribute Their Worldly Goods to the Needy* (1470–97). Fresco by Giovanni and Battista Baschenis de Averaria in the Church of S. Maria Maddalena, Cusiano (prov. Trentino). (Photo: Fototeca del Servizio Beni Culturali della Provincia Autonoma di Trento)

verance. (His is also an interesting comment on the state of the Cistercian Order in the thirteenth century.) He preached:

> So today as men are withdrawing from the Lord through sin, women stand manfully with the Lord against the Devil. They are spiritual Amazons. . . . We see many men who have left the Cistercian Order, but women rarely seem to

leave the order. Accordingly [we can say] women are more upstanding and stronger than men, just like this blessed saint.[88]

Eudes' gendered language is significant. He represents Cistercian nuns as Amazons, virile women, a mode of representation that male writers of the Middle Ages often employed to describe holy women. As Caroline Bynum has pointed out, male writers often employed the language of gender inversion to describe female spirituality but more frequently did so in descriptions of their own interior spiritual lives.[89] Following this logic, I would like to suggest that the mendicant orders—not just the sainted founder of the Friars Minor—in an effort to distance themselves from what they viewed as the decadence of the established religious orders, employed narrative strategies of symbolic gender reversal that served to highlight the differences between themselves and the ecclesiastical hierarchy.[90] Significantly the difference was gendered female. Many of the mendicant virtues such as poverty, humility, and obedience were qualities that medieval society already long associated with the female sex. Witness only the notion of poverty: in the Franciscan lexicon poverty was enfleshed as Lady Poverty, the beloved spouse of Saint Francis himself. In the stories the friars told about themselves they emphasized their possession of and association with "womanly" virtues, most of which Mary Magdalen was made to exemplify.

The account of Saint Dominic's mission in the south of France is instructive. A Cistercian delegation, having been sent by Innocent III to preach against the Cathars in the Midi, had met with little success. The reason was apparent to both Diego, bishop of Osma, and his assistant, Dominic, at that time a canon regular. The opulence and finery of the Cistercian prelates spoke louder about the arrogance, wealth, and power of the Church than any sermon could do to convince otherwise. As one of the earliest of Dominic's *vitae* recounts: on the advice of the bishop, the legates "abandoned all their splendid horses and clothes and accoutrements, and adopted evangelical poverty, so that their deeds would demonstrate the

---

[88] Bériou has transcribed this sermon in the appendix of "La Madeleine," 331–37.

[89] See Caroline Walker Bynum, "Jesus as Mother and Abbot as Mother: Some Themes in Twelfth-Century Cistercian Writing," in *Jesus as Mother: Studies in the Spirituality of the High Middle Ages* (Berkeley: University of California Press, 1982), 110–69, and "Women's Stories, Women's Symbols: A Critique of Victor Turner's Theory of Liminality," in *Fragmentation and Redemption: Essays on Gender and the Human Body in Medieval Religion* (New York: Zone Books, 1991), 27–51. In the latter, a cogent critique of Victor Turner, she argues that medieval women's narratives did not engage in symbolic gender reversal; rather, women emphasized gender continuity in their stories.

[90] For the gender inversion in Saint Francis narratives, see Bynum, "Women's Stories," 34–35, and Victor Turner, *The Ritual Process: Structure and Anti-Structure* (Chicago: Aldine, 1969), 131–65.

faith of Christ as well as their words."[91] Clearly, when it came time to found his own order, Dominic took his cue from the bishop of Osma. As distinct from the Cistercians and the institutional Church they represented, Dominic and his preachers would be humble, poor, and obedient, a feminine anti-type to the masculinized Church. Through the language and process of symbolic inversion, Dominic found a system to renounce power, prestige, and authority, but at the same time articulate the virtues of poverty, humility, and inspiration. Symbolic disempowerment allowed the mendicants to construct an identity, gendered female, which was in and of itself a powerful critique of the wealthy and masculinized institutional Church represented by Saint Peter.[92] It was not irrelevant that faithless Peter had three times denied Christ; Mary Magdalen, on the other hand, had been the embodiment of fidelity to the Lord, when she alone stood weeping at his tomb. The mendicants identified particularly with her as Christ's beloved and most faithful disciple, to say nothing of her office of apostle of the apostles.

With the emergence of the new mendicant orders in the thirteenth century, the inspirational element in the Church—gendered female—had reasserted itself, reviving the ancient question of what to do with those whose spiritual authority was distinctly non-institutional. In the previous chapter we saw one manifestation of this problem: the visionary Gnostics symbolized by Mary Magdalen challenged the apostolic authority of the Church represented by Peter. The Gnostics were suppressed; their challenge to the Church was not. Now here it was again, in a rather different thirteenth-century form: the Magdalen-identified friars were presenting a clear challenge to the institutional authority of Peter. The friars, unlike the Gnostics, however, found a way to incorporate themselves and their charismatic (read: female) brand of authority into the body of the Church while simultaneously remaining separate and apart: the solution was an oath of obedience to the Church hierarchy. Humble submission, a female-inflected gesture epitomized by Mary Magdalen's submission to Jesus in the house of the Pharisee, was the key. In the event, the friars, through symbolic gen-

---

[91] Jean de Mailly, *The Life of St. Dominic,* in *Early Dominicans: Selected Writings,* ed. Simon Tugwell, O.P. (New York: Paulist Press, 1982), 54.

[92] As is well known, the mendicant orders, particularly the Franciscans, rejected the capitalistic ethos of medieval society. Like women who were meant to remain paradigms of virtue, so too the friars, who embraced evangelical poverty, became the vessels of conscience of bourgeois medieval Italy. Ironically, in so doing, the friars profited handsomely from testamentary bequests. Samuel K. Cohn Jr. has found: "The five mendicant orders—all creations of the early Duecento—constituted throughout this period the major monastic beneficiaries of the Sienese testators." *Death and Property in Siena, 1205–1800: Strategies for the Afterlife* (Baltimore: Johns Hopkins University Press, 1988), 33.

der inversion, were able to distance themselves from the hierarchy while remaining obedient to the masculine authority of the Church. The late medieval challenge to the Church, though similar, was not identical to the late antique dispute about inspirational versus institutional leadership; nonetheless, it is significant that in both cases Mary Magdalen was the symbol of that challenge.

Perhaps the most arresting piece of evidence supporting the friars' identification with the humble Magdalen is to be found in the lower church of San Francesco at Assisi.[93] Teobaldo Pontano, bishop of Assisi and himself a member of the Friars Minor, commissioned the giottesque Mary Magdalen chapel, completed about 1312. Along with scenes from the life of Mary Magdalen, in a departure from tradition, Pontano had two distinct donor portraits painted in his chapel. In one portrait, Pontano is represented in his resplendent episcopal vestments genuflecting, head bowed respectfully, at the feet of Saint Rufino, Assisi's first bishop (Fig. 12). In the other portrait, Pontano, garbed in his humble brown friar's habit, is represented at the feet of Saint Mary Magdalen (Fig. 13). Evidently, Bishop Pontano identified with Saint Rufino when discharging his episcopal office; as a humble friar, however, Fra Teobaldo associated himself with Mary Magdalen.

Similarly, when the friars evoked Mary Magdalen in their sermons they were representing at once their identification with the saint and their own submissive and obedient relationship to the Church. Giovanni da San Gimignano lauded the Magdalen's submission to authority when he preached about the moment at the Pharisee's banquet when she covered the feet of the Lord with kisses:

> The Magdalen exhibited obedience to Christ because she kissed his feet. Thus her kisses were kisses of devotion and holiness. Likewise, the kiss to the foot is a sign of veneration. Thus a person kisses the foot of the pope. And so did the Magdalen, out of reverence and humility, not kissing his mouth like a wife, or his hand, like a daughter, but his feet like a servant.[94]

The friars made similar gestures of humble obedience. In lieu of a vow of stability Francis and Dominic had each sworn allegiance to the papacy. Indeed, the opening passage of Francis's Rule of 1221 states: "Brother Fran-

---

[93] For the chapel, see Lorraine C. Schwartz, *The Fresco Decoration of the Magdalen Chapel in the Basilica of St. Francis at Assisi* (Ph.D. diss., University of Indiana, 1980). I further discuss this iconography in chap. 10.

[94] "Exhibuit Magdalena Christo obsequium de labiis suis quia obsculabatur pedes eius . . . Sic ista obscula Magdalenae erant obscula devotionis et sanctitatis. Item est obsculum venerationis ad pedes. Sic homo obsculatur pedem papae. . . . Et sic Magdalena obsculata est ex reverentia et humilitate non os ut sponsa non manum ut filia sed pedes ut ancila." MS BAV Barb lat. 513, f. 101r; *RLS* 3: 378.

Figure 12. *Bishop Teobaldo Pontano and Bishop Rufino* (ca. 1312). Donor portrait. Fresco attributed to School of Giotto from Cappella della Maddalena, Lower Church of the Basilica of S. Francesco, Assisi. (Photo: Anderson, reproduced by permission of Alinari/Art Resource, N.Y.)

Figure 13. *Friar Teobaldo Pontano and Mary Magdalen* (ca. 1312). Donor portrait. Fresco attributed to School of Giotto from Cappella della Maddalena, Lower Church of the Basilica of S. Francesco, Assisi. (Photo: Anderson, reproduced by permission of Alinari/Art Resource, N.Y.)

cis and whosoever shall be head of this *religio* shall promise obedience and reverence to the lord pope Innocent and his successors."[95] Moreover, the friars humbly obeyed the bishops, those in direct Petrine succession to the pope. They preached in a city only after having obtained episcopal consent.

Even though the mendicants took no vow of stability, they wished to be known for their perseverance, yet another quality which the faithful Magdalen embodied. Agostino d'Ancona lauded the Magdalen's courage and constancy when he preached "*O admirabilis audacio*" o admirable courage. He noted that unlike the other disciples, she never abandoned Christ, neither in life nor in death. "Whence Gregory talks about her constancy: the other disciples left the sepulcher, but she did not."[96] Mary Magdalen's perfect devotion to Christ was famously in evidence at the Crucifixion. John 19:25 had narrated that she, the Virgin Mary, and Mary Cleopas stood faithfully beneath the cross. In stark contrast, the disciples, particularly Peter, had already denied or abandoned the Lord (John 18: 17–27). From these events Innocent III construed the Magdalen's constancy remarking that "when, having abandoned Christ, the disciples fled, Mary followed Christ right up to the cross."[97] Giovanni da San Gimignano commented that she, unlike the others, followed Christ as a true lover, extending as much love to him suffering and dying as she had in life. She did not abandon him at the Passion—naked and crucified—as did the disciples, who fled when faced with adversity. He drew the analogy of the vine: "When full of fruit it is visited frequently and cared for, but when empty it is abandoned."[98] Mary Magdalen exemplified the virtue of constancy just as the mendicant friars aspired to do. They would follow the Magdalen—not faithless Peter—*usque ad crucem*, up to the cross, suffering and weeping along with her at the sight of the crucified Lord. In the *Paradiso*, Dante represented Saint Francis and Lady Poverty at the foot of the cross alongside Mary Magdalen.[99]

Another image that resonated deeply with the mendicants was the figure of the distraught Magdalen clinging desperately to the cross. They identified profoundly with her compassion for the suffering Christ. As is well known, this sort of emotional, impassioned piety, centering on the humanity and suffering of Jesus, had emerged from the writings of Anselm of

---

[95] Cited in Moorman, *The History*, 16.

[96] "Quia post eius conversionem ex quo incepit Christo adherere numquam eum dimisit, nec in vita nec in morte. Unde de eius constancia dicit Gregorius 'recedentibus discipulis a monumento, ipsa non recedebat.'" MS Angelica 158, f. 122v.

[97] *Sermo 23*, *PL* 217, 561.

[98] "Sicut accidit de vinea que plena fructibus bene visitatur et custoditur sed vacua derelinquitur." MS BAV Barb. lat. 513, f. 98v.

[99] Canto XI, *Paradiso*, 52–81, *The Divine Comedy*. Charles S. Singleton (Italian Text, trans., commentary), Bollingen Series LXXX (Princeton: Princeton University Press, 1975), 122–23.

Canterbury and Bernard of Clairvaux a century earlier. By the late thirteenth century, the mendicant friars, particularly the Franciscans, had so associated themselves with this sort of ardent spirituality through the *imitatio Christi* that it is often characterized as Franciscan piety. The *Meditations on the Life of Christ,* of Franciscan provenance, is the quintessence of this affective Bernardine piety. It relies on the reader's reserves of imagination and empathy. Intended as a contemplative primer for a Poor Clare, the text continuously exhorts its reader to witness the life of Christ and meditate on the events, as if present as an eyewitness. It teaches: "Your soul should be in all places and deeds just as if you were present there in body." As for the Magdalen's anointing of Christ's feet, it suggests: "Watch her carefully and meditate particularly on her devotion."[100] Thus the first step in spiritual ascent was to empathize deeply with the human sufferings of Jesus and all those who surrounded him.

The Franciscan cardinal Matteo d'Aquasparta (d. 1302) preached similarly when he suggested that the Virgin Mary, Mary Cleopas, and Mary Magdalen standing at the foot of the cross were themselves crucified by the compassionate agony they felt at the Crucifixion.[101] Another Franciscan, François de Meyronnes, awarded Mary Magdalen the quadruple tiara. It will be remembered that one coronet—that of precious gemstones—was destined for martyrs. François argued that indeed Mary Magdalen was herself a martyr because she had been "impaled by the sword of the death of Christ."[102] Eudes de Châteauroux preached simply that the Magdalen was a martyr on account of her compassion.[103]

Such themes reverberated also in Bonaventura's meditative prayer, *Arbor vitae:*

O my God, good Jesus,
although I am in every way without merit and unworthy,
grant to me,
who did not merit to be present at these events
in the body,
that I may ponder them faithfully
in my mind
and experience toward you,

---

[100] *Meditations,* 364, 172.

[101] "Stabat utique paciens compaciens morienti commoriens crucifixo crucifixa." MS Assisi 682, f. 192v; *RLS* 4: 78. For Matteo, see Alexandre-Jean Gondras, "Matthieu d'Aquasparta," *DS* 10 (1980), 799–802.

[102] "Quia gladiata gladio mortis christi." *Sermones de laudibus,* 79.

[103] Bériou, "La Madeleine," 336.

my God crucified and put to death for me,
that feeling of compassion
which your innocent mother and
the penitent Magdalen experienced
at the very hour of your passion.[104]

This very same spirit permeates Ubertino da Casale's *Arbor vitae,* but with a marked difference. Whereas Bonaventura prayed to participate in the "feeling of compassion" of the Virgin Mary and the Magdalen, Ubertino actually achieved it. In an extraordinary passage he describes how Jesus made him a participant in the passion. He narrates how he was "now the sinner Magdalen, now his bride, now brother and disciple John, now the pious woman lamenting him, now the good thief nailed to the cross," and then, finally, "innocent Jesus himself, on the wood of the cross crying out and dying in pain."[105]

The Spiritual Franciscan poet Jacopone da Todi (d. 1306) succeeded in imagining himself into the *vita Christi* as Mary Magdalen. He wrote in the Magdalen's voice versifying her compassion in a *lauda* composed for Good Friday:

And I sad Magdalen,
threw myself at his feet
where I made a great gain
where I purged my sins.
Nail me to his feet
and never let me rise again.[106]

Although it has been argued that this sort of identification with the passion is particularly Franciscan, the Friars Minor did not hold a monopoly on it. Cavalca's Mary Magdalen flung herself at the foot of the cross crying out in grief: "Oh, most blessed cross! Would I had been in Thy stead, and that my Lord had been crucified in mine arms, my hands nailed against His, and that the lance which pierced His heart had passed even into mine, so that I had died with Him, and thus neither in life nor death ever de-

---

[104] Bonaventura, *Bonaventure: The Soul's Journey into God, The Tree of Life, The Life of St. Francis,* trans. Ewert Cousins (New York: Paulist Press, 1978), 158.

[105] "Tandem iuxta sue passionis supplicia sic me transformative sibi faciebat assistere: ut nunc mihi viderer magdalena peccatrix: nunc quedam ab ipso electa sponsa: nunc frater & discipulus electus ioannes ille: nunc pia mulier lamentans que ipsum genuit nunc latro dexter sibi confixus: nunc ipse purus iesus in ligno crucis clamans: et in dolore expirans." *Arbor vitae,* prologus, bk. 1, chap. 1, unpaginated.

[106] Cited in Haskins, *Mary Magdalen,* 202. The translation is mine.

parted from Him."[107] The Observant Dominican Savonarola's (d. 1498) *laude* of the Quattrocento echo the same emotions.[108]

In essence, these meditative prayers, treatises, sermons, *laude,* and hagiography proposed that one make oneself a martyr of compassion, just as Matteo d'Aquasparta, François de Meyronnes, and Eudes de Châteauroux preached the Magdalen had done. As such, I would like to suggest that alongside the *imitatio Christi* in which one became *as if* Christ, as both Saints Francis and Catherine of Siena had done, their bodies inscribed with the wounds of the stigmata, there existed another, more humble, affective model of piety or sanctity: the *imitatio Magdalenae*.[109] Now, through imagination and empathy, weeping and compassion, one could become a second Magdalen at the foot of the cross. Affective piety was above all emotional piety, and of that there was no greater example than Mary Magdalen. The *imitatio Magdalenae* was perhaps a lesser rung on the ladder of pious devotional practice, but then it was also more attainable for the average Christian penitent. After all, not everyone was cut from the same cloth as Saint Francis of Assisi or Saint Catherine of Siena. The devotee, rather than take on the wounds of Christ himself, instead, through deep compassion, partook of the Magdalen's grief, sorrow, and emotional suffering at the foot of the cross. The *imitatio Magdalenae* was, in the event, a more humble model of spiritual devotion, but as a Riminese panel demonstrates, the two *imitationes* could exist side by side beneath the cross (Fig. 14).[110]

Italian religious art, finding this motif irresistible, represented all sorts of people beneath the cross, just as the devotional treatises instructed. Saint Francis is most frequently represented at Jesus' feet with the Magdalen, but examples abound of *beati* and patrons (both religious and lay) kneeling

---

[107] *The Life,* 236–37.

[108] O Cross, make a place for me
   and take my limbs,
   so that my heart and soul may
   burn with your holy fire.

Cited and translated by Patrick Macey, "*Infiamma il mio cor:* Savonarolan *Laude* by and for Dominican Nuns in Tuscany," in *The Crannied Wall: Women, Religion and the Arts in Early Modern Europe,* ed. Craig A. Monson (Ann Arbor, MI: University of Michigan Press, 1992), 169. Possibly the most dramatic visual representation of the Magdalen at the foot of the cross was made by Masaccio in 1426 for a private chapel in the Carmine in Pisa, a Carmelite church. Now called the Pisa polyptych, it was the upper portion of an altarpiece (now dismembered), depicting the Virgin, John the Evangelist, and the Magdalen at the foot of the cross. The Magdalen kneels, her back toward the viewer, her arms thrown up above her head in a gesture of lamentation. It now hangs in the Galleria Nazionale di Capodimonte in Naples.

[109] The phrase is Macey's, "*Infiamma,*" 179.

[110] Vatican Pinocateca, no. 54. See Raimond Van Marle, *The Development of the Italian Schools of Painting,* 28 vols. (The Hague: Martinus Nijhoff, 1924), vol. 4 (1924), 294.

Figure 14. *Saint Francis and Mary Magdalen beneath the Cross* (first half of 14th c.). Panel painting, School of Rimini, Vatican Museums, Pinacoteca. (Photo: Musei Vaticani)

with the Magdalen at the foot of the cross. In a panel painting by Jacopo di Paolo, an uncharacteristically composed Magdalen is shown gesturing toward a kneeling *beata* (presumably the donor). Mary Magdalen appears to be introducing her disciple to compassionate meditation on the Crucifixion (Fig. 15).[111]

---

[111] The Crucifixion scene is of the Bolognese School and dates to about 1400. Van Marle called Jacopo di Paolo the "most vulgar" of the Bolognese painters of the Trecento. See Fern Rusk Shapley, *Paintings from the Samuel H. Kress Collection: Italian Schools,* 3 vols. (London: Phaidon Press, 1966), vol. 1 (XII–XV c.), 72.

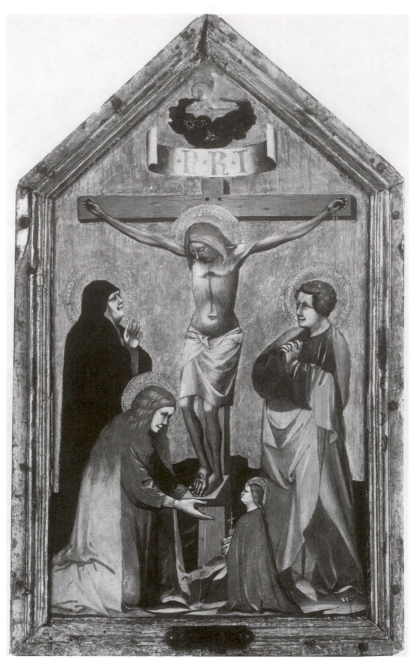

Figure 15. *Mary Magdalen and Beata beneath the Cross* (1400). Panel painting by Jacopo di Paolo, Vanderbilt University Fine Arts Gallery, Nashville. (Photo: Vanderbilt University Fine Arts Gallery)

Figure 16. *Mary Magdalen at Christ's Feet* (second half of 13th c.). Detail of painted crucifix by Sienese Master, Galleria dell'Accademia, Florence. (Photo: Soprintendenza per i beni artistici e storici delle provincie di Firenze e Pistoia)

Identification with the grieving Magdalen became so strong indeed that her image frequently became superfluous in devotional pictures. Saint Francis occupies the Magdalen's traditional place in countless altarpieces, panel paintings, and frescoes.[112] And although this imagery is decidedly more Franciscan than Dominican, nevertheless there are numerous examples of Dominic and Dominicans either praying at or embracing the foot of the crucified Christ. The Dominican artists were, however, more

[112] There are endless examples. See Evelyn Sandburg Vavalà, *La croce dipinta italiana e l'iconografia della passione* (Verona: Apollo, 1929), figs. 518, 522, 525, 529, 533, 536, and 550. For the influence of Franciscan spirituality on artistic representation, see Daniel Russo, "Saint François, le Franciscains et les représentations du Christ sur la croix en Ombrie au XIIIe siècle. Recherches sur la formation d'une image et sur une sensibilité au Moyen Age," *MEFRM* 96/2 (1984): 647–717. For mendicant identification with the Magdalen in art, see also Russo's "Entre le Christ et Marie: la Madeleine dans l'art italien des XIIIe–XVe siècles," in *Marie Madeleine,* ed. Duperray, 173–90, and Sarah Wilk, "The Cult of Mary Magdalen in Fifteenth-Century Florence and Its Iconography," *Studi Medievali,* 3d series, 26 (1985) II: 685–98.

circumspect than their Franciscan counterparts. Although the Dominicans did not hesitate to place themselves beneath the cross, rarely are they found fervently clutching it as do Mary Magdalen and Francis. Most often the members of the Order of Preachers are found in acts of contemplative prayer. The miniatures illustrating Saint Dominic's *de modo orandi* are one example of this genre.[113]

Nonetheless, Catherine of Siena, a Dominican tertiary, urged her spiritual daughters to throw themselves at the foot of the cross as Mary Magdalen had done. Catherine exhorted Monna Mellina of Lucca to run "with the dear loving Magdalen to the most sweet venerable cross" where Catherine herself would be waiting. To Monna Agnesa Malavolti she wrote that the Magdalen "embraced the cross. Indeed, in order to see her Master, she was bathed in blood."[114] A painted Trecento crucifix from Siena shows a tiny Magdalen adoring the copious blood flowing from Christ's feet. Another painted crucifix hanging in the apse of the church of San Francesco at Arezzo, represents Francis in a similar position (Figs. 16 and 17). The figures show a remarkable affinity. In both, they practically bathe in the blood that symbolized Christ's human suffering and his great sacrifice. To adore it, to immerse oneself in it, was to partake at once in his sufferings and to be cleansed of sin.

Ultimately the mendicant strategy of fashioning themselves as faithful Magdalens was a spectacular success. By the late thirteenth century Pope Gregory X was invoking Magdalenian imagery to laud the mixed and apostolic lives of the mendicant friars, while artists and patrons so associated the friars with constancy and compassionate piety that the saint's likeness was no longer even required beneath the cross. A Dominic or Francis in her stead was enough to conjure the notion of her fierce fidelity to the Lord.

In contrast to the loquaciousness of the friars, a Trecento panel painting attributed to Antonio Veneziano captures wordlessly the essence of the mendicant Magdalen's mixed and apostolic life (Fig. 18). The scarlet-clad Mary Magdalen, her long hair unbound and cascading around her shoulders, holds in one hand a book, in the other, an alabaster vase. In the hands

[113] MS BAV Ross. 3, ff.6r–13r. For bibliography, see n. 5, this chapter. William Hood has reproduced a fine Trecento example of a Dominican beneath the cross in *Fra Angelico at San Marco* (New Haven: Yale University Press, 1993), fig. 189.

[114] *Le lettere di S. Caterina da Siena,* ed. Niccolò Tommaseo, 4 vols. (Florence: G. Barbèra, 1860), vol. 1, ep. 61 (To Monna Agnesa Malavolti), and vol. 2, ep. 164 (To Monna Mellina). *The Letters of St. Catherine of Siena,* vol. 1 (4 projected), trans. Suzanne Noffke, O.P. (Medieval & Renaissance Texts & Studies, vol. 52) (Binghamton, New York: Center for Medieval and Renaissance Studies, 1988). See letters 2 and 58.

Figure 17. *Saint Francis at Christ's Feet* (13th c.). Detail of painted crucifix attributed to Margarito d'Arezzo, Basilica of S. Francesco, Arezzo. (Photo: Author)

Figure 18. *The Mixed Life: Mary Magdalen with Book and Vase* (late 14th c.). Panel painting attributed to Antonio Veneziano, Vatican Museums, Pinacoteca. (Photo: Musei Vaticani)

of the evangelists and the Twelve, a book normally symbolized the New Testament. In the hands of others it usually represented the saint's reputation for great learning. I would like to argue that in this case the book is inscribed with both meanings. First, it represents Mary Magdalen's reputation for great learning and wisdom acquired at Bethany when she sat at the feet of the Lord, and later when she was chosen to witness and announce the good news of the resurrection. Her codex furthermore represents the gospel, which at Pentecost she too had been sent to preach. The book, then, simultaneously evokes her learning, her vocation, and her apostolic preaching mission. The friars would have immediately recognized the symbolism of the book as the office of preaching refreshed by the solitude of contemplative study.[115]

What purpose, other than being her standard attribute, does the vase serve in this context? I would suggest that in relation to the book it carries another meaning: here, it points to Mary Magdalen's active ministry, apart from her preaching apostolate. Read according to its literal sense, the vase held her aromatic ointment for anointing the body of Jesus; but read according to its mystical sense, the vase contained Mary Magdalen's *opera misericordiae*, her good works, symbols of the active life of charity discharged for the sake of Christ's poor. By the fourteenth century, Mary Magdalen's iconographic emblems bound together the elements of the mixed and apostolic life. The book signified contemplation and its fruits, apostolic preaching; the vase, on the other hand, provided a metaphorical link to Mary Magdalen's active life of charity, the subject of the next chapter.

---

[115] Vatican Pinocateca no. 19. For the panel, see Wolfgang Fritz Volbach, *Il Trecento Firenze e Siena*, trans. Francesca Pomarici (Catalogo della Pinacoteca Vaticana), 4 vols. (Vatican City: Libreria Editrice Vaticana, 1987), vol. 2, 17–18. Some scholars, including F. Zeri, attribute the panel to Cenni di Francesco. Others examples of the Magdalen holding both vase and book are an anonymous early-fourteenth-century fresco in the church of Santa Maria Maddalena in Alatri (Lazio) and in the predella of the fourteenth-century altarpiece by Giovanni del Biondo in the Cappella Tosinghi-Spinelli in the church of Santa Croce, Florence. For color reproductions, see A. Dono, *Storia dell'affresco in Alatri* (Rome: Istituto Poligrafico e Zecca dello Stato, 1980), fig. 4 and *Il complesso monumentale di Santa Croce*, ed. Umberto Baldini and Bruno Nardini (Florence: Nardini Editore, 1983), 250.

The Magdalen holds a book in the stained glass windows at Chartres and Semur. See Deremble, "Les Premiers," 197 and 203. Two southern Italian frescoes represent the Magdalen holding a book. The first, from the thirteenth century, at the Dominican convent of Sant'Anna in Nocera, shows Saints Catherine and Mary Magdalen flanking the Madonna and child; each saint holds a codex. See Gerardo Ruggiero, "Il monastero di Sant' Anna di Nocera: dalla fondazione al Concilio di Trento," *Memorie Domenicane*, n.s., 20 (1989): 5–166, figs. 5 and 8. The second, a damaged fresco in the Magdalen cycle in the Cappella Pipino at the church of San Pietro a Maiella in Naples, shows the saint, book in hand, preaching to the pagans in Marseilles. To my knowledge this image has not been published. On the chapel, see Ferdinando Bologna, *I pittori alla corte angioina di Napoli 1266–1414* (Rome: Ugo Bozzi, 1969), 313–17.

THREE

The Vita Activa

I have never understood that any could attain to the
contemplative life, however complete it be, without first
passing through the active life.
(Domenico Cavalca)[1]

A t the beginning of the thirteenth century, Pope Innocent III
preached an Easter sermon in the basilica of Santa Maria Maggiore
in Rome that took as its theme the gospel pericope, "Mary Magdalen,
Mary of James, and Salome bought aromatic oils." (Mark 16:1)[2] In the
course of his sermon, the pontiff instructed his congregation (on this occasion made up largely of the laity) that the three Marys who had come to
the sepulcher early on Easter morning each represented an order within the
Christian Church, the mystical body of Christ. That body was made up of
the laity, represented by Mary Magdalen; monastics, symbolized by Mary
of James; and the secular clergy, for whom Salome stood. Expanding his
mystical explanation, the pope further explained that the life of a lay person was active and secular; the life of a religious was contemplative and spir-

---

[1] For Cavalca, see chapter 1, n. 42. *The Life,* 86.

[2] Medieval sermons usually took the day's gospel reading as their theme; on Easter the
reading then as now came from Mark 16. Giuseppe Scuppa, *I sermoni di Innocenzo III* (Tesi
di laurea, Pontificia Universitas Lateranensis, 1961), 91–92, suggests that most of Innocent's
sermons were composed between 1202 and 1204. Following the Roman ordinal of this
period, the Easter Sermon would have been preached at Santa Maria Maggiore. See Stephen
Van Dijk, O.F.M., *The Ordinal of the Papal Court from Innocent III to Boniface VIII and
Related Documents,* completed by Joan Hazelden Walker (Spicilegium Friburgense, vol. 22)
(Fribourg: The University Press, 1975), 288. This particular sermon was not included in
J.-P. Migne's edition of the sermons in the *PL* 217: 309–688. Francesco Segna edited and
published it as a pamphlet dedicated to Pope Leo XIII entitled *Tertius sermo in die sancto
Paschae* (Rome: Typ. Iuvenum Artificum a S. Josepho, 1903), unpaginated. John C. Moore
has published a transcription of this sermon and an English translation in "The Sermons of
Pope Innocent III," *Römische Historische Mitteilungen* 36 (1994): 81–142.

itual; while the life of the clergy was mixed, that is, a combination of the active and contemplative.[3]

Innocent was proposing a new model of Christian society, one that threatened to replace the venerable model that considered Martha and Mary as symbolic types representing, respectively, the active and contemplative modes of life. By the end of the late twelfth century such a neat dichotomous model no longer adequately served to describe the orders and modes of life contained within the Church. When Lothario de' Conti di Segni ascended the papal throne as Innocent III in 1198, he was heir to a great spiritual reawakening that had over the course of the century transformed the Church. The Augustinian and Premonstratensian canons had revived the mixed form of life and were attracting record numbers of converts, men and women, who wanted to take up that life.[4] Now in the early decades of the thirteenth century the friars were doing similarly. As such, a three-tiered paradigm was necessary to reflect a new ecclesiastical reality.[5] This is not to say, however, that Innocent III had invented one *ex nihilo*. In 999, during the great period of monastic reform inspired by Cluny, the abbot of Saint-Benoît-sur-Loire wrote:

Among the Christians of both sexes, we know that there exist three orders and three degrees, so to speak. Although none of the three is exempt from sin, the

___

[3] "Tres istae mulieres designant tres vitas: laicalem, regularem et clericalem. Vita laicorum est activa, et saecularis; vita religiosa est contemplativa et spiritualis; vita vero clericorum quasi mixta est et communis quia partim est saecularis in quantum divina ministrat." Segna, *Sermo Tertius,* unpaginated. Given the emphasis on the active life in this sermon, we can presume that the laity was expected to be in attendance. Innocent sometimes preached in the vernacular to the laity (although no texts survive), as the dedicatory letter of his sermon collection shows, *PL* 217, 312. For the mystical sense of scripture, see H. Caplan, "The Four Senses of Scriptural Interpretation and the Medieval Theory of Preaching," *Speculum* 4 (1929): 282–90.

[4] The bibliography on the renewal of religious life in the twelfth century is enormous. See, among other works, Marie-Dominique Chenu, *Nature, Man, and Society in the Twelfth Century: Essays on New Theological Perspectives in the Latin West,* ed. and trans. Jerome Taylor and Lester Little (Chicago: University of Chicago Press, 1968), 219–30; Lester Little, *Religious Poverty and the Profit Economy in Medieval Europe* (Ithaca, NY: Cornell University Press, 1978); Caroline Walker Bynum, "The Spirituality of Regular Canons in the Twelfth Century," in *Jesus as Mother: Studies in Spirituality of the High Middle Ages* (Berkeley: University of California Press, 1982), 22–58; and the essays in *Renaissance and Renewal in the Twelfth Century,* ed. Robert L. Benson and Giles Constable (Cambridge, MA: Harvard University Press, 1982).

[5] As is well known, the feudal model of society was also a hierarchical arrangement of those who worked (*laboratores*), those who fought (*bellatores*), and those who prayed (*oratores*). This tripartite model of medieval society was made famous by Georges Duby in *The Three Orders: Feudal Society Imagined,* trans. Arthur Goldhammer (Chicago: University of Chicago Press, 1980).

first is good, the second better, the third excellent. . . . The first is that of the laity, the second that of the clergy, the third that of the monks.[6]

According to Abbo of Fleury's model, the Church consisted of three orders: the laity, the clergy, and the monks, this last occupying the most exalted position in the hierarchy. Innocent appropriated this model, but modified it ever so slightly in the process. In his scheme, the clergy, the representatives of the mixed life of action and contemplation, assumed the uppermost position in the hierarchy. Subtle as this shift appears, it is in fact a radical transformation of the Church's vision of itself. No longer did the regular life, the monastic life, reign supreme at the top of the hierarchy. It had been displaced by a life that drew equally from action and contemplation. But there is something more at stake than the triumph of the mixed life: this new hierarchy of the orders of Christian society also reveals an esteem for the active life of the laity. In establishing the priority of the mixed life, drawing as it did from the well of the active life, Innocent III endowed the life of the laity with an unprecedented amount of dignity and prestige hitherto unexpected or imagined. Indeed, the late twelfth century marks the beginning of a period of efflorescence for the Christian laity.

This chapter discusses the active life of the laity in the late medieval church and Mary Magdalen as an emblem of that life. Of course Martha still remained the paradigmatic symbol of the active life; nonetheless, preachers also appealed to the active ministry of the Magdalen when exhorting the laity to take up that life.[7] I have already argued that the friars put one aspect of the Magdalen to work in fashioning a social identity for themselves. Let us now see how they drafted her into service as a mirror for the laity.

The Laity

The religious life of the laity in the medieval period begins to come into focus first in the eleventh century, at the time of the Gregorian reform when the Pataria, a group of lay people drawn mainly from the middle and lower classes, began to impress on the clergy their own religious convictions and aspirations. Their campaign began with an assault on the corruption of the Milanese church. They railed against widespread nicolaitism

---

[6] Cited by André Vauchez, *The Laity in the Middle Ages: Religious Beliefs and Devotional Practices,* trans. Margery J. Schneider (Notre Dame, IN: University of Notre Dame Press, 1993), 41.

[7] It has been suggested recently that through her act of anointing Christ—a pious work of mercy—Mary Magdalen became irrevocably associated with the active life, even overshadowing her sister Martha. See Bériou, "La Madeleine," 298, and Lauwers, "*Noli me tangere,*" 230.

and voiced loud demands that the worldly clergy return to apostolic simplicity. To rally support for their cause, the Patarenes preached, engaged in public disputations, organized processions, and, if necessity required, prepared to spill their own blood in martyrdom. Their reforming zeal won them a large measure of support from Rome particularly from Gregory VII and Cardinal Peter Damian.[8]

Expressions of lay piety began to emerge elsewhere in Europe by the last quarter of the twelfth century. In Lyons, the Waldensians were choosing to live in voluntary poverty while dedicating themselves to evangelical preaching. Their leader, an ex-merchant and no Latin scholar, had the gospels translated into the vernacular, an act which won him no friends in Rome.[9] In Liège, women whom their contemporaries called simply *mulieres sanctae,* holy women, were also choosing a life of voluntary poverty. Rather than depend on alms, these women supported themselves by the fruit of their own labor. Although spontaneous communities emerged, the beguines resisted strict enclosure and permanent monastic vows.[10]

It is noteworthy that both the Waldensians and the beguines, among the most important lay religious movements in the Middle Ages, arose in urban centers. Italy, thanks both to the commercial revolution and the communal movement, was the most highly urbanized, not to mention one of the wealthiest areas in western Europe in this period—fertile ground for the seeds of lay religious initiatives. First among the new religious movements to take root in Italy were the Humiliati who, like the Patarenes, emerged in Lombardy. Not confined to Milan, they eventually were found in many of the urban centers of central and northern Italy. Essentially, they were pious lay people, drawn mainly from the artisan classes (the wool trade

[8] On the Patarenes, see H.E.J. Cowdrey, "The Papacy, the Patarenes and the Church of Milan," *Transactions of the Royal Historical Society,* 5th series, 18 (1968): 25–48.

[9] Herbert Grundmann first saw the connections between various heretical groups, women's religious movements, and the mendicant orders in the twelfth and thirteenth centuries. Grundmann's work, first published in 1935 (1961; 2d ed.), has finally been translated into English by Steven Rowan as *Religious Movements in the Middle Ages* (Notre Dame, IN: University of Notre Dame Press, 1995).

[10] Ernest W. McDonnell, *The Beguines and Beghards in Medieval Culture, with Special Emphasis on the Belgian Scene* (New Brunswick, NJ: Rutgers University Press, 1954); Brenda Bolton, "Mulieres Sanctae," *Studies in Church History* 10 (1973): 77–95, reprinted in *Women in Medieval Society,* ed. Susan M. Stuard (Philadelphia: University of Pennsylvania Press, 1976), 141–58; Bolton, "Vitae Matrum: A Further Aspect of the Frauenfrage," in *Medieval Women,* ed. Derek Baker (Oxford: Basil Blackwell, 1978), 253–73; Jean-Claude Schmitt, *Mort d'une hérésie: L'Église et les clercs face aux béguines et aux béghards du Rhin supérieur du XIVe au XVe siècle* (Paris: Mouton, 1978); and Walter Simons, "The Beguine Movement in Southern Low Countries: A Reassessment," *Bulletin de l'Institut historique belge de Rome* 59 (1989): 63–105.

being the livelihood of many), who were concerned to be in the world but
not of it. The Humiliati, so called because of the humble undyed woolen
garments they wore, sought to live a simple but common religious life
within the bonds of family and society. They lived by their own labor and
in voluntary poverty.[11] Jacques de Vitry, a contemporary and champion of
many lay religious movements of the period, lauded the Humiliati for living sober lives and showing the greatest example of humility in their own
words and deeds.[12]

Unlike the Waldensians they were not beggars; but like them the Humiliati claimed a vocation to preach which brought ecclesiastical censure
down upon their heads in 1184. Soon after his election, however, Innocent III issued a safe-passage of sorts, a decree exhorting new religious
groups to return to the Church. By the year 1200 the leaders of the Humiliati approached Innocent for direction, and the next year the pope approved their *propositum*, or statement of intent. That document provided
for a separate third order of the Humiliati, one especially instituted for lay
people. By the next century, the lay order had produced a *beata* of its own,
the saintly Aldobrandesca of Siena (d. 1309).[13]

Innocent III's act of reconciling the Humiliati to the Church was part
and parcel of the pastoral revolution that characterized his eighteen-year
pontificate. At the heart of this revolution lay his concern for the spiritual
welfare of the laity. Innocent's renewed emphasis on pastoral preaching and
his insistence on annual confession and communion; his tracts on marriage,
alms-giving, and charity; his foundation of the hospital of Santo Spirito to
deal with the problems of poverty and child-abandonment; his proposal for
rescuing prostitutes, to say nothing about his distress about the progress
of Catharism (which culminated in the terrible Crusade of 1209) are all

---

[11] See *Sulle tracce degli Umiliati*, ed. Maria Pia Alberzoni et al. (Milan: Vita e Pensiero,
1997). Brenda Bolton brought the Humiliati to the attention of English-speaking audiences
in a series of articles: "Innocent III's treatment of the Humiliati," in *Studies in Church History*
8 (1972): 73–82; "Tradition and Temerity: Papal Attitudes to Deviants, 1159–1216," in
Studies in Church History 9 (1972): 79–91; "The Poverty of the Humiliati," *Franziskanische
Forschungen* 27 (1975): 52–59; and "Sources for the early history of the Humiliati," in
Studies in Church History 11 (1975): 125–33, the last three now collected in Bolton,
Innocent III: Studies on Papal Authority and Pastoral Care (Aldershot: Variorum, 1995).
Forthcoming is Frances Andrews, *The Early Humiliati: The Development of an Order c. 1176–
1270* (Cambridge: Cambridge University Press).

[12] *The Historia Occidentalis of Jacques de Vitry*, ed. John Frederick Hinnebusch, O.P.
(Spicilegium Friburgense, vol. 17) (Fribourg: The University Press, 1972), 144–45.

[13] For Innocent III and the Humiliati, see the articles by Bolton cited in n. 11. A Latin
vita of Aldobrandesca of Siena can be found in AASS 26 April. Elizabeth Petroff has translated
a sixteenth-century summary of the fourteenth-century Italian *vita* in *Consolation of the
Blessed* (New York: Alta Gaia Society, 1979), 166–78.

manifestations of his profound concern for the spiritual well-being of lay people.[14]

Yet another indicator of his concern for the religious life of the laity is the case of Omobono of Cremona (d. 1197), the first non-royal lay person ever to be officially canonized. He became a saint in 1199: it was Innocent's gift to the laity—a model of piety to which they too could aspire. In his bull of canonization, *Quia pietas,* Innocent III declared that the Cremonese merchant merited sainthood because of his charity and great piety; he was also, not uncoincidentally, the implacable enemy of heresy. According to André Vauchez, Omobono's recent biographer, Innocent believed that the new saint "incarnated the penitential ideal, which was presented as a privileged way for laypeople to attain salvation."[15] Let us now examine the "penitential ideal," the privileged way of life Innocent III proposed for the laity. We shall do so through the figure of Mary Magdalen, another lens for the laity through which that ideal was refracted.

The Penitential Life

The penitential way of life in the Middle Ages was a broad complex of ideas including repentance, conversion, expiation, self-mortification, and acts of charity, not infrequently held together by the bond of voluntary poverty. Like the tableau of the three Marys at the tomb, it is often difficult to dis-

[14] The Latin texts of Canon 10, *inter caetera,* and Canon 21, *omnis utriusque sexus,* are in *Conciliorum Oecumenicorum Decreta,* ed. G. Alberigo, C. Leonardi, et al. (Centro di Documentazione Istituto per le Scienze Religiose—Bologna) (Rome: Herder, 1962), 215–16 and 221; in English as *Decrees of the Ecumenical Councils,* 2 vols., trans. Norman P. Tanner (Washington, D.C.: Sheed and Ward, 1990), vol. 1, 239–40, 245. Innocent's tracts on marriage (*De quadripartita.specie nuptiarum*), alms-giving (*Libellus de elemosyna*), and charity (*Encomium charitatis*) are in *PL* 217: 745–62, 921–68. For his concerns about charity, alms, and poverty, see Bolton, "Hearts not Purses: Innocent III's Attitude to Social Welfare," 123–45 and "Received in His Name: Rome's Busy Baby Box," 153–67, both now collected in Bolton, *Innocent III.* For his proposal on rehabilitating prostitutes through marriage, see *Ep.* 112 in *Die Register Innocenz' III,* vol. 1: *Pontifikatsjahr 1198–99,* ed. O. Hageneder and A. Haidacher (Graz-Cologne: Hermann Böhlaus Nachf., 1964, 169–70). See also Michele Maccarrone's collected essays on Innocent III, *Studi su Innocenzo III* (Italia Sacra, vol. XVII) (Padua: Antenore, 1972). For the crusade against the Cathars, see Joseph Strayer, *The Albigensian Crusade* (Ann Arbor, MI: University of Michigan Press, 1992). For Innocent's education at Paris which John W. Baldwin suggests may have profoundly shaped his thinking on pastoral issues, see *Masters, Preachers, and Merchants: The Social Views of Peter the Chanter and His Circle.* 2 vols. (Princeton: Princeton University Press, 1970).

[15] "Homebon de Crémon (†1197), marchand et saint," in *Les laïcs au Moyen Age. Pratiques et expériences religieuses* (Paris: Cerf, 1987), chap. 6, which unfortunately was dropped from the English edition of this volume, *The Laity in the Middle Ages.*

criminate one penitential form of life from the next because they are so closely related; nevertheless we can begin to distinguish some of the various strands that make up the penitential tapestry if we examine the preachers' use of Mary Magdalen as symbol of that life.[16]

Conversion was the first step along the path of a penitential life, and Mary Magdalen was regarded as the model of conversion given her tearful repentance at the Lord's feet in the house of Simon the Pharisee. So preached Ubertino da Casale as recorded in the *Arbor vitae*. Ubertino suggested that the three Marys at the sepulcher represented the three states of the soul.[17] Mary Magdalen in this scheme represented not the perfected state of the soul, contemplation, but the humble beginner—the converted sinner. The Augustinian friar Jordanus of Quedlinburg proposed a different interpretation of the three Marys. He regarded them as representing the three states of salvation. In his view Mary Magdalen represented the penitent state, the first milestone on the road to salvation.[18]

Fundamentally the penitential life was related to the sacrament of penance, particularly to the third part of the sacrament: satisfaction. It was generally agreed by thirteenth-century theologians that satisfaction was the payment of the temporal punishment for the offense committed against God by sin. Such a technical definition, however, does not attempt to bridge the chasm between the sacrament of penance and the life of a penitent. But Peter Lombard, in his discussion of the constituent parts of penance, moves a bit closer toward that goal. He suggests that each part of penance expressed itself in a different mode. Satisfaction, in his view, was expressed in action.[19] Therefore we may understand that conversion to the life of a penitent, characterized by active works of expiation, was the mode of life medieval preachers intended for the laity.

[16] I am distinguishing between fulfilling the obligations of a penitential life expressed frequently through prayer, charity, and asceticism, and sacramental penance (contrition, confession, satisfaction, and absolution), a subject that I discuss fully in chapter 7.

[17] "Sed primo videamus triplicem statum animae per has triplices mulieres mystice designatum scilicet Conversionis, Conversationis, Consumationis. Primus est status in magdalena designatus . . . quia erat peccatrix." *Arbor vitae*, bk. 3, chap. 23, unpaginated.

[18] "Quantum ad primum sciendum quod tres sunt status hominum salvandorum quorum quilibet querit Christum . . . scilicet incipientium, proficientium, perfectorum. Sive penitentium, activorum et contemplativorum. Et hi tres status signantur per tres Marias que querebant dominum. Status penitentium signatur in Maria Magdalena que famosa peccatrix fuerat et penituit. Et licet alibi ipsam accipiatur vita contemplativa ut tamen Marcus de ea hic loquitur inter penitentes reputatur." *Sermo 258, Opus postillarum et sermonum Iordani de tempore* (Strasbourg, 1483), unpaginated. Thomas Aquinas held a similar view; see *Summa Theologiae* IIa-IIae, 24, 9 cited in Mason, *Active Life*, 99.

[19] Peter Lombard, *Sentences*, bk. IV, d. 16, c. 6, n. 2, p. 336 (Grottaferrata: Collegio S. Bonaventurae, 1981), quoted by Pierre Adnes, "Pénitence," *DS* vol. 12.1 (1984), 971.

Significantly, a new lay movement—a movement of penitents—emerged in northern and central Italy in the first quarter of the thirteenth century. As in the case of the beguines, women were at the forefront of this phenomenon. And a phenomenon it appeared to be, particularly to contemporaries. John the Spaniard, who taught at Bologna in the mid-thirteenth century, described the movement as one of "female penitents [*pynzocarae*] who just recently arose from the dust."[20] Less organized, less easily defined, and less studied than other lay movements of the period, this particular penitential movement expressed itself in a multiplicity of religious forms.[21] Mario Sensi has summed up the institutional forms of this life as "the cenobitic life of moderately cloistered communities; the eremitical life of solitary oblates, recluses, and hermits, whether within the city or outside its walls; and the penitential life followed by women in their own homes."[22] In central Italy, uncloistered communities of penitent women not uncommonly put themselves under the patronage of the Magdalen. In Umbria alone, such late-thirteenth-century communities existed in Spoleto, Monteluco, Foligno, and Trevi.[23] Though the institutional forms may have varied, charity—either receiving or distributing it—was central to the life of a penitent.

---

[20] "Pynzocarae quae de pulvere nuperrime surrexerunt," cited by Gilles Gérard Meersseman, *Ordo fraternitatis: Confraternite e pietà dei laici nel Medioevo* (Italia Sacra, 24–26) (Rome: Herder, 1977), 374–75. The *pinzochere* were the Italian analogue to the northern beguine movement. See the entry "Pinzochere," by Romana Guarnieri in *DIP* 6 (1980), 1721–49. The movement of pinzochere should be distinguished from the official third order of penitents and confraternities affiliated with the mendicant orders. For these, see the essays by Meersseman, collected in ibid. and recently, Daniel E. Bornstein, *The Bianchi of 1399: Popular Devotion in Late Medieval Italy* (Ithaca, NY: Cornell University Press, 1993).

[21] Most of the scholarship on lay penitents in Italy has been done in the last few decades, on a local level, by a group of dedicated Italian scholars. Since their work has not been much translated, and is often published in hard-to-find journals and conference proceedings, it has not received much recognition in the English-speaking world. With the publication of *Women and Religion in Medieval and Renaissance Italy,* ed. Daniel Bornstein and Roberto Rusconi, trans. Margery J. Schneider (Chicago: University of Chicago Press, 1996), this situation should change. This volume translates essays by Antonio Rigon, Mario Sensi, and Anna Benvenuti, among others, all important scholars of the medieval penitential movement in Italy. The great omission, however, is Giovanna Casagrande of the University of Perugia, whose careful work in Umbrian archives has contributed substantially to the historiography of this field. See the ample bibliography of her own essays listed in her recent book, *Religiosità penitenziale e città al tempo dei comuni* (Rome: Istituto Storico dei Cappuccini, 1995). See also Katherine Gill, "Open Monasteries for Women in Late Medieval and Early Modern Italy: Two Roman Examples," in *The Crannied Wall: Women, Religion, and the Arts in Early Modern Europe,* ed. Craig A. Monson (Ann Arbor, MI: The University of Michigan Press, 1992), 15–47, one of the few English-language scholars working in this field.

[22] "Anchoresses and Penitents in Thirteenth- and Fourteenth-Century Umbria," in *Women and Religion,* 57.

[23] Sensi, ibid., 68, 78n. 63.

Works of Mercy

Medieval Lenten sermons emphasized the theme of charity because, among other reasons, it was the time of year that preachers could expect the laity to be in regular attendance at the sermon. Jacobus de Voragine used the occasion of a Lenten sermon to establish Mary Magdalen's active life of charity for his audience:

> She and Martha fed him, she brought him ointment, she and many other women ministered to him out of their own resources, she received him as a guest, she dressed him in the cotton of purity and the ruby-red of charity, she visited him in his time of trouble, and stood next to the cross with his mother and her sister Mary Cleopas, and she was among those at his tomb.[24]

In effect, Jacobus de Voragine was suggesting that Mary Magdalen's active life of service to Christ was tantamount to performing the seven corporal works of mercy. His proposal, though interesting, is in fact quite similar to what Innocent III had suggested earlier in the century. Drawing inspiration from the oil-filled alabasters that the Marys bore to the tomb, Innocent III's Easter sermon may have established the motif of the active Magdalen and her works of mercy:

> The laity [Mary Magdalen] ought to buy the six types of fragrances necessary for anointing him [Christ]. They are the six works of piety which Christ will commend according to the [last] Judgment when he says to those standing at his right side: "I was hungry and you fed me; I was thirsty and you quenched my thirst; I was a stranger and you gave me hospitality; I was naked and you clothed me, I was sick and you visited me; I was imprisoned and you came to me." (Matt. 25: 35–36)[25]

What he calls works of piety are also known as the corporal works of mercy, not quite, in Innocent's time, codified at seven.[26] A generation later, Easter

[24] "Ipsa enim ipsum pavit. Fecerunt ei coenam ibi, & Martha ministrabat. Maria ergo accepit libram unguenti &c. Cum illo erant aliquae mulieres curatae scilicet Maria Magdalena & aliae multae quae ministrabant ei de facultatibus suis. Ipsa eum hospitio recepit. . . . Ipsa bysso puritatis & purpura charitatis eum induit. . . . Ipsa eum in tribulatione positum visitavit, & associavit. Stabant iuxtra [*sic*] crucem Iesu mater eius, & soror matris eius: Maria Cleophae & Maria Magdalenae. Ipsa eius sepulturae interfuit." Sermo II (*Quinta feria quintae hebdomadae Quadragesimae*), in *Sermones Quadragesimales,* 163.

[25] "Laici quidem sex emere debent species aromaticas ad suum efficiendum unguentum, id est sex opera pietatis, quae Christus in iudicio commendabit cum dicet his qui a dextris eius assistent: 'Esurivi et dedistis mihi manducare; sitivi et dedistis mihi bibere; hospes eram et collegistis me; nudus et operuistis me; infirmus et visitastis me; in carcere eram et venistis ad me' (Matt. 25:35–36)." Segna, *Tertius Sermo,* unpaginated.

[26] See Irénée Noye, "Miséricorde (oeuvre de)," *DS* 10 (1980), 1327–49. Until the twelfth century the traditional number was six, taken from Matt. 25: 35–36. At the end of the twelfth century burying the dead was added taken from Tob. 12: 13. See especially ibid., 1341–42.

sermons would disclose the addition of the seventh and final work of mercy. In his Easter sermon on precisely the same theme, Hugh of Saint-Cher (d. 1263), the Dominican provincial of France who finished his career as titular cardinal of Santa Sabina in Rome, appended the seventh with this explanation: "I was dead and you buried me. This is found in the *Book of Tobias*, not in the gospels. Christ himself indicated as many fragrant spices of mercy."[27]

Each Christian order was required to fulfill certain obligations towards the mystical body of Christ, the Church. Those who followed Mary of James, monks bound by a monastic rule, were to anoint Christ's head, his divinity, with prayer and contemplation. Those who followed Salome, the clergy, cared for the body of Jesus, his Church, with word and deed. And finally, those who followed the Magdalen, the laity, were to anoint Christ's feet, the poor of the world, with the oil of charity, the seven works of mercy. Visual evidence also reveals the Magdalen's ministry of good works. Her most common attribute is an alabaster jar. Given a literal reading, it was a jar containing ointments to anoint the body of Christ. But read mystically, it was a vase which contained precious aromatic oils, her metaphorical works of mercy, with which as the representative of the laity she tended to Christ's poor.

A century after Innocent's Easter sermon, in the early fourteenth century when the Dominican Giordano da Pisa was preaching in Florence, we find that the conception of the active life for the laity has expanded considerably. Evidently responding to questions members of his audience had posed about the relative merits of the active life, the friar confessed: "Many come to me and ask: 'Fra Giordano, which is better: fasting and saying the "Our Father" or collecting indulgences on pilgrimages? Or which is better: giving alms or serving the hospitals?' Everyone asks questions of this kind."[28] After mulling it over the friar replied:

> This life has many parts: the active life is giving food to the poor, clothing them, quenching their thirst, visiting the sick and those incarcerated, and such things; and giving alms, and fasting, and wearing a hairshirt, and practicing abstinence, and such works. The active life is also marriage, managing the family, governing it and teaching the commandments of God, ruling and direct-

---

[27] "Mortuus et sepelistis me. Hoc invenitur in *Tobia* quia in evangelio non est. Quantum autem sint odorifera ista aromata ipse Christus ostendit." MS Angelica 1057, f. 50v; not listed in *RLS*. For Hugh of Saint-Cher, see E. Mangenot, "Hughes de Saint-Cher," in *DTC* 7.1 (1922), 219–39.

[28] This sermon was published in pamphlet form by P. Zanotti, *La vita attiva e contemplativa predica di frate Giordano* (Verona: Tipografo Vescovile, 1831), 13. In the same year it was also published in *Prediche del Beato Fra Giordano da Rivalto dell'ordine dei Predicatori. Recitate in Firenze dal MCCCIII al MCCCVI*, ed. D. Moreni, 2 vols. (Florence: Magheri, 1831), vol. 1, 180–89.

ing people, and also defending the faith against infidels. The active life is also building bridges and hospitals, serving the sick and going on pilgrimage. Preaching is also a part of the active life.[29]

Giordano's vision of the active life of the laity is breathtakingly inclusive, consisting of the traditional corporal works of mercy. It also included performing penitential works of satisfaction, governing the family and society justly, contributing to the common weal, defending the faith, and naturally enough for one so engaged, preaching.

The homiletic message that the life of the laity should entail *opera misericordiae,* works of mercy, did not fall on deaf ears in the Italian communes. Many of the *popolo,* those of the merchant and artisan classes who made up the core of the preachers' audiences, wanted both to live penitential lives of good works, and to come to the aid of the commune through charity. Thus the goals of the penitential life fused imperceptibly with the values of civic religion in an attempt to remedy the many social problems—poverty, leprosy, child-abandonment, prostitution—all of which were magnified in the urban setting of the medieval city.[30] Penitential confraternities of lay people assisted the commune by providing necessary social services such as burying the dead and giving comfort to those condemned to die.[31] Other confraternities, such as one dedicated to Mary Magdalen in Borgo Sansepolcro, devoted themselves to rehabilitating repentant prostitutes.[32] Individual initiative supported community efforts. The testament of Francesco di Marco Datini (d. 1410), the merchant of Prato, discloses that at the end of his life he bequeathed a large part of his fortune to succor the poor of his native city, while 1,000 florins went to the hospital of Santa Maria Nuova in Florence to found a hospital for foundlings. It is revealing that in his later years Francesco was no stranger to mendicant sermons.[33]

Mary Magdalen's metaphorical works of mercy for Christ inspired oth-

---

[29] *La vita attiva,* 13–14.

[30] See John Henderson, *Piety and Charity in Late Medieval Florence* (Oxford: Oxford University Press, 1994).

[31] For confraternities, see Henderson, *Piety,* and Ronald F. E. Weissman, *Ritual Brotherhood in Renaissance Florence* (New York: Academic Press, 1982).

[32] James Banker, *Death in the Community: Memorialization and Confraternities in an Italian Commune in the late Middle Ages* (Athens, GA: University of Georgia Press, 1988), 23n. 23. I discuss the founding of communities for repentant prostitutes in chapter 6.

[33] That foundation became the Ospedale degli Innocenti. On Francesco Datini, see Iris Origo, *The Merchant of Prato: Francesco di Marco Datini* (New York: Knopf, 1957). On Datini's bequest, see Philip Gavitt, *Charity and Children in Renaissance Florence: The Ospedale degli Innocenti, 1410–1536* (Ann Arbor, MI: University of Michigan, 1990). On testamentary bequests as expressions of personal piety, see Samuel K. Cohn Jr. *The Cult of Remembrance and the Black Death: Six Renaissance Cities in Central Italy* (Baltimore: Johns Hopkins University Press, 1992).

ers to perform good works in her name. Victor Saxer has pointed out that Alpine hospices under Mary Magdalen's patronage emerged in this period. Their mission was to assist pilgrims and travelers.[34] The Order of Saint John (the Hospitallers) also recognized Mary Magdalen as the patron of hospices: at their headquarters in Jerusalem they founded a hospice in her name to care for female pilgrims.[35] More numerous, however, were hospital dedications made to the saint. Fra Giordano's references to building hospitals and serving the sick (made in the context of a sermon on Mary Magdalen's feast-day) are, therefore, of more than just intrinsic interest. Roberta Gilchrist has observed in respect to medieval England that "Mary Magdalen was linked to healing through the episodes of anointing [and] her special place at the resurrection"; consequently she "became a popular saint for the dedications of hospitals."[36] In England alone sixty-three hospitals were dedicated to Mary Magdalen. Seven of them were founded by members of the laity. In the twelfth century William le Gros founded Newton and Holderness, both in Yorkshire, and Robert de Waterwill (Wateville) founded Sandon (Surrey). While in the thirteenth century, Roger de Merlay established Catchburn (Northumberland), W. Heriz founded Gonalston (Nottinghamshire), and John de Waren, Earl of Surrey, instituted Saint Mary Magdalen at Thetford (Norfolk). By 1344, Ann Boteler had founded a Magdalen hospital in Little Torrington (Devonshire).[37] In

---

[34] *Le culte,* 213, 225–26.

[35] Sally Thompson, *Women Religious: The Founding of English Nunneries after the Norman Conquest* (Oxford: Clarendon Press, 1991), 50.

[36] Roberta Gilchrist, *Gender and Material Culture: The Archeology of Religious Women* (York: Routledge, 1994), 187.

[37] Following Clay, the counties are listed according to their traditional designations. *Twelfth Century* (20 foundations): Reading (Berkshire); Stourbridge (Cambridgeshire); Barnstaple (Devonshire); Witton Gilbert (Durham); Colchester (Essex); Gloucester (Gloucestershire); Southampton (outside the walls) (Hampshire); Winchester (outside the walls) (Hampshire); Preston in Amounderness (Lancashire); Partney (Lincolnshire); Lynn or Gaywood (Norfolk); Norwich (Sprowston) (Norfolk); Newcastle-upon-Tyne (outside the walls) (Northumberland); Crowmarsh in Bensington (Oxfordshire); Holloway or Lyncomb (Somerset); Ipswich (Suffolk); Coventry (Spon) (Warwickshire); Broughton nr. Malton (Yorkshire); Hedon or Newton Garth (Yorkshire); and Killingwoldgrove (Yorkshire). *Thirteenth Century* (25 foundations); Dunstable (Bedfordshire); Newbury (Berkshire); Wallingford or Newnham (Berkshire); Ely (Cambridgeshire); Bridport or Allington (Dorset); Alton (Hampshire); Andover (Hampshire); Baldock (Hertfordshire); Hertford (outside the walls) (Hertfordshire); Dartford (Kent); Mile End of Stepney (Middlesex); Thetford (Norfolk); Bamborough (Northumberland); Catchburn nr. Morpeth (Northumberland); Bawtry (outside the walls) (Nottinghamshire); Gonalston (Nottinghamshire); Southwell (Nottinghamshire); Glastonbury (Somerset); Langport (Somerset); Bramber (Bidlington) (Sussex); Chichester (outside Eastgate) (Sussex); Hemsworth (in Burn) (Sussex); Malmesbury by Burton (Wiltshire); Pontrefact (Yorkshire); and Newenham (either Warwickshire or Glouc.) *Fourteenth Century* (14 foundations): Luton (Bedfordshire); Abingdon (outside the walls) (Berkshire); Spondon or Locko (Derbyshire); Teignmouth near Teignton (Devonshire); Little Torrington (Devonshire); Shaftesbury (Dorset); Durham (Durham); Berwick-on-Tweed (Northumberland); Capelford by Norham

France, nine hospitals were dedicated to the saint in the same period. A layman Robert Fitz Erneis founded the hospital of Saint Mary Magdalen at Saint-Samson-en-Auge; while the Burgundian Magdalen hospitals of Dijon and Beaune each received testamentary bequests from Richard de Montbéliard in 1333. Four years later Richard's widow Isabeau left a pious bequest to the Mary Magdalen hospital in Dijon.[38]

In thirteenth-century Italy Magdalen hospitals appear in the rolls of the *decime,* the records of tithes collected for the Church. They are found throughout the peninsula: Gubbio, Perugia, Mantua, Pavia, Modena, Alatri, Ferentino, Veroli, San Severo, Lucca, Volterra, Siena, and Rome were just some of the cities that founded such institutions in the name of the saint.[39]

(Northumberland); Wooler (Northumberland); Eye (outside the walls) (Suffolk); Wilton (Wiltshire); Sherburn-in-Elmet (Yorkshire); and Skipton (Yorkshire). *Fifteenth Century* (2 foundations): Liskeard (Cornwall) and Norwich, Fybridge Gate (Norfolk). *Sixteenth Century* (1 foundation): Gorleston (Suffolk). Rotha Mary Clay, *The Mediaeval Hospitals of England* (London: Frank Cass & Co., 1909; repr. 1966), Appendices, 278–337. See also Saxer, *Le culte,* 121–22, 135–36, 146, 256, and Gilchrist, *Contemplation,* 220.

[38] *Twelfth century:* Aigueperse, Boulogne, and Rouen (Normandy). At Rouen there were 27 *sorores* who acted as nursing sisters. See Penelope Johnson, *Equal in Monastic Profession: Religious Women in Medieval France* (Chicago: University of Chicago Press, 1991), 53n. 149. *Thirteenth century:* Beauvais (Champagne); Saint-Samson-en-Auge (Normandy); Aiguines (sur le Verdon); and Aix (Provence). *Fourteenth century:* Dijon (Burgundy) and Beaune (Burgundy). *Thirteenth-century Lowlands:* Huy and Bruges. Saxer, *Le culte,* 108, 117, 128, 143, 201, 204, 254, 257. This list of foundations and those that follow are meant to be suggestive rather than exhaustive.

[39] *Gubbio* (1333): *Rationes. Umbria I,* items: 3111, 2924, 3212; *Perugia* (1333): Ibid., item: 1306; *Mantua: Rationes. Lombardia et Pedemontium,* item: 1306 (1295–98); *Pavia:* Ibid., item: 301 (1321–24); *Modena: Aemilia. Le Decime,* item: 311; *Alatri: Latium. Rationes,* items: 1108 (1328–29) and 1552 (1333–35); *Ferentino:* Ibid., items: 2328, 2423, 2499, 2578; *Veroli:* Ibid., items: 1841, 1971; *San Severo: Rationes ... Apulia, Lucania, Calabria,* item: 5281 (1325); *Lucca: Tuscia I,* items: 4391, 4917 (1276–77); *Tuscia II. Le Decime,* item: 4074. *Volterra:* The hospital in Volterra (1346) is listed in the *fondo diplomatico* of the ASF, but not in the *decime,* at least not as a hospital. (There is a Santa Maria Magdalena in Volterra but it is listed as a church not as a hospital: vol. 2, Tuscia, item: 3074 [dec. 1302–3]. This is one of the many problems associated with the *decime:* church-related institutions were not categorized as precisely as contemporary historians would like. Moreover, the *decime* are far from a complete listing of all Italian religious foundations in the Middle Ages.) *Siena: I necrologi di San Domenico in Camporegio,* ed. M.-H. Laurent, in *Fontes vitae S. Catharinae Senensis Historici,* ed. M.-H. Laurent and Franciscus Valli (Florence: Sansoni, 1937), vol. 20, v, notes that in 1221 Suor Emilia and Rainieri Rustichini dei Piccolomini donated the Hospital of Saint Mary Magdalen located outside of the Porta S. Maurizio to the Dominican Order. *Rome:* The hospital in Rome was called S. Maria Magdalena in Burgo, and was located "prope muros civitatis Leoniae," near the walls of the Leonine city. See Christian Huelsen, *Le chiese di Roma nel Medio Evo* (Florence: Leo S. Olschki, 1927), 378. It is probably the church on which Cola di Rienzo had an angel painted before he left Rome. See *Life of Cola di Rienzo,* trans. John Wright (Toronto: Pontifical Institute of Mediaeval Studies, 1975), 125.

Some of the hospitals named above were probably leprosaria, hospitals dedicated to treating leprosy. Through her relation to Lazarus whom the Middle Ages conflated with the leprous beggar in Luke 16:20, Mary Magdalen became a patron of leper hospitals as well.[40] The charitable work of aiding lepers, in remembrance of the Magdalen's works of mercy, inspired the titular dedications of leper hospitals to the saint. The leprosarium at Rivo Torto, at the foot of Assisi, where Saint Francis spent his early years of conversion nursing lepers, was dedicated to the Magdalen, as were Santa Maria Maddalena in Terracina (Lazio), Santa Maria Maddalena de' leprosi in Aversa (Campania), and Santa Maria Maddalena dei Malsani (unwell) on the outskirts of Prato (Tuscany). The foundation in Rome, called Santa Maria Maddalena *extra urbem* (now Monte Mario), founded in 1278, changed its name in the sixteenth century to San Lazzaro de' Leprosi, but its function, the care of lepers, remained the same. All are foundations dating from the thirteenth and fourteenth centuries.[41]

Many female penitents engaged in acts of charity working in leper hospitals or other hospices. Before founding her community in Liège, Mary of Oignies and her husband worked in a leprosarium. Two of the most well known third-order penitents of the later medieval period, Margaret of Cortona (d. 1297) and Catherine of Siena (d. 1380), expressed their piety by charitably tending to the sick and dying in the hospitals of Tuscany. Lesser known women did likewise, perhaps responding to the duties of the active life that preachers outlined for them in Magdalen sermons.[42] The Augus-

---

[40] An alternative name for leper hospital in Italian is *lazzaretto*. Leprosy is frequently called the disease of Saint Lazarus.

[41] *Assisi: Speculum perfectionis (minus)*, ed. Marino Bigaroni, O.F.M. (Pubblicazioni della biblioteca Francescana, Chiesa Nuova, vol. 3) (Assisi: Edizioni Porziuncola, 1983), 13. Bigaroni suggests that this hospital had a double dedication to Mary Magdalen and to Lazarus. A leprosarium called Santa Maria Maddalena de Archis shows up in the Assisi documents that Fr. Cenci has painstakingly gathered. It is difficult to ascertain whether this is the same hospital. See the Trecento and Quattrocento entries in Cesare Cenci, O.F.M., *Documentazione di vita assisana 1300–1448* (Spicilegium Bonaventurianum, vols. 10–12) (Grottaferrata: Collegium S. Bonaventurae ad Claras Aquas, 1974), 69, 175, 179, 183, 279, 294, 770. *Terracina:* Saxer, *Le culte*, 217; *Prato:* Ruggero Nuti, "Lo spedale del Ponte Petrino e la sua chiesa" (3-part article), in: *Archivio Storico Pratese* 5(4) an. 10, fasc. IV, 152–58; 5(5) an. 11, fasc. I, 17–25; 5(5) an. 11, fasc. II, 81–88; and Francesco Guerrieri, *La chiesa dello spedale del Ponte Petrino* (Prato, n.d.). *Aversa:* Matteo Camera, *Annali delle due Sicilie: Dall'origine e fondazione della monarchia fino a tutto il regno dell'augusto sovrano Carlo III. Borbone*, 2 vols. (Naples: Dalla Stamperia e Cartiere del Fibreno, 1806), vol. 2, 184. *Rome:* Huelsen, *Le chiese di Roma*, 379. It is also quite possible that of the many hospital dedications to the saint found in the *decime*, some are leprosaria but are not categorized as such. Michel Lauwers found three leper hospitals dedicated to the saint in and around Liège at Namur, Huy, and Liège itself. See "*Noli*," 209–68, 216.

[42] Anna Benvenuti, "Mendicant Friars and Female Pinzochere in Tuscany: From Social Marginality to Models of Sanctity," in *Women and Religion*, 100n. 24, mentions Ubaldesca of Calcinaia, Aldobrandesca of Siena, and Tessa of Florence who also worked in hospitals. She

tinian Jacopo Capocci da Viterbo (d. 1308), archbishop of Benevento and Naples, reminded the women in his earshot that "although the Magdalen had the leisure of sacred contemplation; nevertheless she performed pious works." Therefore, he exhorted his female followers: "you Christian women, according to the example of Mary Magdalen, don't be lazy!"[43]

Expedient as the active life was deemed to be, it nonetheless brought with it anxiety and solicitude. No further proof was needed than the Lord's chastening words to Martha: "Martha, Martha, you are worried and distracted by many things." (Luke 10:41) Giordano da Pisa elaborated: "There can be no active life without agitation. . . . For how much trouble is there in marriage and the household and in other things? It is not even possible to say." Glossing the passage "only one is necessary" (Luke 10:42), Giordano further explained that the works of the active life such as fasting, sackcloth, pilgrimages, marriage, and serving hospitals are not as important for one's salvation as is contemplation.[44] Furthermore, he argued, "in the active life one can commit mortal sin in many ways." Giordano adduced the penitential practice of pilgrimage (a expiatory work of the active life) as a trap awaiting the unwary:

> A man is going on pilgrimage to Santiago and before he arrives he falls into one mortal sin, or perhaps two, and then three or maybe more. Now, what kind of pilgrimage is this? . . . Therefore, I advise no one to go on these trips and pilgrimages, or to Saint Gall; since there is more danger than benefit. People go here and there mistaking their feet for God. You are deceived: this is not the way. Pulling yourself together, contemplating the creator, weeping about your sins, and the misery of your neighbor, is better than any trips you could ever make.[45]

Aldobrandino Cavalcanti (d. 1279), prior of the Dominican convent of Santa Maria Novella in Florence, preached likewise: "The one who easily

---

furthermore notes that "female involvement in hospital activities was very common and merits more detailed study."

[43] "Magdalena quae licet haberet otium sacre contemplationis tamen exercebat negotium pium. Et vos igitur Christiane mulieres exemplo Magdalene non sitis otiose!" MS BAV Arch. Cap. S. Petri D. 213, cols. 363–64; not listed in *RLS*. I thank Fr. L.-J. Bataillon for bringing this autograph MS to my attention. For Jacopo da Viterbo, see H. X. Arquillière, "Jacques de Viterbo," in *DTC* 6 (1947), 305–09.

[44] *La vita attiva*, 16. The similarities to Jerome's letter to Eustochium (Ep. 22) should be noted. It should further be noted that Giordano's contemporary and colleague at Pisa, Domenico Cavalca, was engaged in translating that letter into Italian as a devotional text for the laity. It has been published along with his translation of Gregory the Great's *Dialogues* as *Volgarizzamento del dialogo di San Gregorio e dell'epistola di S. Girolamo ad Eustochio*, ed. G. Bottari (Milano: G. Silvestri, 1840).

[45] Ibid., 16.

evades traps on earth is the one who has his mind in heaven."[46] Domenico Cavalca came to the defense of the active life of the laity only to conclude: "If only those of the contemplative life were saved, few indeed would have salvation. Nevertheless it is the best life; but the active life is of greater use."[47]

The active life, then, was good because expedient, but not without its drawbacks and dangers, as the preachers made plain. Though it paled in comparison to the contemplative life, the active life had never before been so esteemed as it was in the later medieval period. In large measure its revaluation was brought about by Innocent III's great concern for the spiritual welfare of the laity, but the friars in collaboration with a willing laity also contributed to its transformation. In the previous chapter we examined the process by which the image of Mary Magdalen was pressed into service to represent the friars' mixed and apostolic life; in this one we have seen how the friars appropriated her image to serve as a mirror for the life of the laity. Admired as the active life came to be in the later medieval period, most people, even Domenico Cavalca, a champion of the active life, had to concede that the contemplative life was more noble.[48] Let us now contemplate that more noble life and its great exemplar, Mary Magdalen.

[46] "Facile evadit laqueos in terris qui mentem habet in celis." MS BAV Borgh. 175, f. 29v; *RLS* 1: 343. For Aldobrandino, see A. Paravicini Bagliani, "Cavalcanti, Aldobrandino," *DBI* 22 (1979), 601–3.

[47] *The Life*, 95.

[48] *I frutti della lingua*, ed. G. Bottari (Rome: Antonio de' Rossi, 1754), 182. He notes in both texts that the active precedes the contemplative life: *The Life*, 95 and *Frutti*, 183. Daniel Lesnick, *Preaching in Medieval Florence: The Social World of Franciscan and Dominican Spirituality* (Athens, GA: University of Georgia Press, 1989), 101, suggests that Cavalca transformed his sermons into his celebrated devotional treatises for the laity.

FOUR

The Vita Contemplativa

Mary has chosen the better part.
(Luke, 10:42)

M ary Magdalen's contemplative life began at Bethany—at Jesus' feet—where rapt, she sat listening intently to his every word. The Lord had commended Mary for her choice of contemplation over action with these words: "Mary has chosen the better part which shall not be taken from her" (Luke, 10:42).[1] Giordano da Pisa and other preachers took the relative clause in that sentence to mean that the active life, while good, was fleeting; the contemplative life, on the other hand, would endure throughout eternity.[2] This chapter examines how preachers used Mary Magdalen as the symbol of the "better part," transforming her in the process from Jesus' attentive student into a veritable medieval mystic. It also explains why the new mendicant orders identified deeply with the image of the contemplative and mystical Magdalen.

Spiritual Concentration

It seems a tautology to state that the object of the contemplative life is contemplation. But like action, contemplation has many components. At its most elementary it consists of empathetic meditation on the life, passion, and resurrection of Jesus. It also comprises listening intently to sermons or the words of holy people, introspection, reflective acts of prayer, and *lectio divina,* meditative reading. These are parts of acquired or ordinary contemplation, the lower rungs on the contemplative ladder. The end toward

---

[1] Medieval preachers, following Gregory the Great, were of course assuming that Mary Magdalen and Mary of Bethany were one and the same person. See my discussion of the Gregorian composite saint in chapter 1.

[2] *La vita attiva,* 17.

which the contemplative aspires is mystical union, an infused or extraordinary state in which the enlightened soul attains a personal knowledge of the divine. Supernatural states such as trances, levitation, ecstasies, visions, and revelations sometimes accompany mystical experience but are not a crucial constituent of it.[3] The *vitae* of Mary Magdalen demonstrate that eventually she scaled the heights of mystical contemplation, but it all began in a humble novitiate at the feet of the Lord at Bethany.

The Augustinian Agostino d'Ancona commented that "blessed Magdalen was drawn by contemplation of the divine word even there, in the house of Martha her sister, where sitting at the feet of the Lord, she listened to his word."[4] Aldobrandino Cavalcanti emphasized that Mary's seated position denoted her contemplative state, her repose of mind, while other preachers focused on the spiritual meal of the divine word upon which Mary feasted.[5] Jacopo Capocci da Viterbo was not alone in noticing that while Martha labored to feed Christ corporally, Mary was being fed spiritually by the word of the Lord.[6] And in a pithy maxim, Agostino d'Ancona summed up his approval of her spiritual repast thus: "Nourishing the mind is better than nourishing the stomach."[7] Thus the novice contemplative partook of a spiritual feast at the Lord's feet.[8]

---

[3] The distinction between infused or extraordinary contemplation, and acquired or ordinary contemplation, was first drawn by Denis the Carthusian in the fifteenth century. See Butler, *Western Mysticism*, 213–17.

[4] "Beata Maria Magdalena fuit tracta divinorum verborum contemplatione et hoc in domo Marthe sororis eius in qua domo Maria Magdalena sedens secus pedes domini audiebat verbum eius." MS Angelica 158, f. 122v; *RLS* 1: 126.

[5] "Quia activa in labore corporis et contemplativa in occio mentis est. John XI. Maria domi sedebat. Gloriosa Maria sedet quia in Christo mentis requies fruitur." MS BAV Borgh. 175, f. 29v; *RLS* 1: 343.

[6] "Quia eloquentia divina est refectio et repletio mentis de hoc effectu repletionis dixit Augustinus in Omelia evangeliorum de Martha & Maria . . . Laborabat illa vacabat ista. Illa erogabat haec implebatur et post intenta erat Martha quando pascetur dominum; intenta erat Martha quando pascetur a domino." MS BAV Arch. Cap. S. Petri D. 213, col. 363; not in *RLS*. Cf. Matteo d'Aquasparta, MS Assisi 682, ff. 194v–195r: "Martha ministrabat sed Maria vacabat. Martha occupabatur sed Maria contemplabatur et contemplando iocondabatur. Martha pascebat dominum. Maria pascebatur a domino."

[7] "Maior est refectio mentis quam ventris." MS Angelica 158, f. 122v.

[8] Although a popular symbol in sermons and exegetical literature, it is worth mentioning that Mary of Bethany, the contemplative, was not a theme that inspired visual artists or their patrons. One of the few examples, completed about 1370, is found in Giovanni da Milano's Magdalen cycle in the Rinuccini Chapel at Santa Croce, the Franciscan church in Florence. Mary sits with her back toward Martha, attentively absorbed by the master's teachings. For the chapel decoration, see Mina Gregori, *Giovanni da Milano in Santa Croce* (Valmorea: Comune di Valmorea, 1980). For other medieval examples of this scene, see Jane Couchman, "Action and Passio: The Iconography of the Scene of Christ at the Home of Mary and Martha," *Studi Medievali*, 3d series, 26/2 (1985): 711–19. A medieval example that she does not include, however, comes from a Florentine predella of the life of Mary Magdalen now in

As one who had received instruction directly from the master himself, the Magdalen was regarded as a model student, at least in the view of the Franciscan Matteo d'Aquasparta. In the first of his Magdalen sermons he used the contemplative Magdalen as an example of scholarly comportment, presumably in contrast to the imperfect examples he had encountered during his teaching career at the universities of Paris and Bologna. The text is worth citing in full. He maintained:

> We have here in Mary the ordered example of study for which three things are required: [First], the leisure of repose without distraction. This is signified by sitting, rather than students who are wandering about and running hither and thither. Second is her humility of mind, without vain display, since it is noted that she sat at the Lord's feet. This is contrary to the presumptuous and the proud who, immediately when they know something, despise all the others, and reject the positions of their elders. Third is her diligence of attention since it is understood in the act of listening. This is contrary to those who want to speak rather than listen, or those who want to be masters rather than students. The master is the one to whom you ought to listen. Christ is in his *cathedra* in heaven and his school is on earth; his scholars are his members. For he himself teaches human knowledge. Whence I believe that if scholars would first consult the master through prayer they would profit more than by consulting any teacher.[9]

It is clear that the audience for this sermon was male: men in holy orders, probably university men engaged in pursuing their higher degrees in theology. By the fifteenth century, two English colleges dedicated to the Magdalen were founded in order to house university men: one at Oxford and one at Cambridge.[10]

---

the Stoclet Collection in Brussels. It has been attributed to both the Master of the Fabriano Altarpiece and Giovanni da Milano. It is reproduced in Richard Offner with Klara Steinweg, *A Critical and Historical Corpus of Florentine Painting* (New York: College of Fine Arts, New York University, 1930–; repr. Florence: Giunti Gruppo Editoriale), III.5 (1947), pl. XLVI (1).

[9] "Ecce igitur habens in Maria exemplum studi[i] ordinatum ad quod tria requiruntur scilicet ocium quietis sine distractione. Hoc significatur in sessione contra discurrentes et vagos scolares. . . . 2. Humilitas mentis sine ostensione quod denotatur quia sedebat secus pedes, contra presumptuosos et superbos qui statim quando sciunt omnes alios contempnunt, positiones maiorum contempnunt. . . . 3. Diligentia attencionis quia intellegitur in auditu . . . contra eos qui aut volunt loqui quam audiant aut volunt fieri magistri quam fiant discipuli. . . . Magister autem quem debes audire Christus est, eius cathedra in celo est et scola eius in terra et scolares eius membra eius. Ipse enim qui docet hominem scientiam. Unde puto quod si scolares primum magistrum consulerent per orationem multo magis proficient quam per lectorem." MS Assisi 682, f. 193v; *RLS* 4: 78.

[10] Magdalene College in Cambridge was originally founded in 1427 as a hospice for Benedictine monks. It was refounded and dedicated to the saint in the 1540s by the Lord Chancellor, Lord Audley. It has been suggested that Audley chose the patron because his own

But women too were expected to use the Magdalen as a contemplative guide. The Franciscan Bertrand de la Tour (d. 1332), who ended his career as Cardinal-bishop of Tusculum (Frascati), took the occasion of a Magdalen sermon to point out to his auditors that Mary said very little, because a female religious should not be garrulous.[11] Given the common belief about her scandalous past, it would seem that Mary Magdalen was a rather unlikely candidate to become a model for cloistered women. But contrary to all expectations she became just that as preachers transformed her into a mirror for contemplative nuns. The Dominican Guillaume Peyraut told his auditors that the Magdalen's feast was celebrated by everyone, but especially by enclosed nuns who lead the contemplative life of which Mary is the example and mirror.[12]

Convents of Benedictine, Premonstratensian, and Cistercian nuns were founded under the spiritual patronage of the Magdalen throughout much of Europe and the Latin Middle East by the mid-twelfth century.[13] In that century, England led the way with six foundations at Davington (Kent), Kynewaldgraves (Yorkshire), Bristol (Gloucestershire), Sewardsley (Northamptonshire), Wintney (Hampshire), and Ickleton (Cambridgeshire).[14]

---

name was contained in the dedication: "M-AUDLY-N," as contemporaries spelled the saint's name. See the concluding note in Christopher N. L. Brooke, "The Dedications of Cambridge Colleges and their Chapels," in *Medieval Cambridge: Essays in the Pre-Reformation University,* ed. Patrick Zutshi (Woodbridge: Boydell Press, 1993), 7–20. Magdalene College, Oxford, was founded by William Waynflete, Lord Chancellor of Henry VI in 1458. For a further discussion of Waynflete, see chap. 9.

11 "Et adverte quod Maria pauci dicebat . . . quod religiosa et contemplativa non debet esse garula." MS Antoniana 208, f. 332r; *RLS* 1: 1216. The *explicit* says: "Episcopus Salernitensis," which might indicate that the sermons were compiled ca. 1320, when he still was, or at least remembered as, archbishop of Salerno. For Bertrand, see J. Goyens, "Bertrand de la Tour," in *DHGE* 8 (1935), 1084. On the sin of garrulousness, see Carla Casagrande and Silvana Vecchio, *I peccati della lingua: Disciplina ed etica della parola nella cultura medievale* (Rome: Istituto della Enciclopedia Italiana, 1987), 150–55 and 425–40.

12 "Sed specialiter a claustralibus, qui contemplativam ducunt vitam, quorum Maria exemplar est et speculum." Some of his sermons were published under the name of Guillaume d'Auvergne. See Guillaume d'Auvergne, *Opera Omnia,* 2 vols. (Paris-Orléans: Ludovicus Billaine and F. Hotot, 1674), vol. 2, 437. For Guillaume Peyraut, see Philippe Delhaye, "Guillaume Peyraut," *DS* 6 (1967), 1229–34.

13 The literature on women's monasticism is quite large, see among other studies: Bruce L. Venarde, *Women's Monasticism and Medieval Society: Nunneries in France and England, 890–1215* (Ithaca, NY: Cornell University Press, 1997); Penelope Johnson, *Equal in Monastic Profession: Religious Women in Medieval France* (Chicago: University of Chicago Press, 1991); Sally Thompson, *Women Religious: The Founding of English Nunneries after the Norman Conquest* (Oxford: Clarendon Press, 1991); Sharon Elkins, *Holy Women of Twelfth-Century England* (Chapel Hill: University of North Carolina Press, 1988); and Catherine Boyd, *A Cistercian Nunnery in Mediaeval Italy: The Story of Rifreddo in Saluzzo, 1220–1300* (Cambridge: Harvard University Press, 1943).

14 *Twelfth-century England:* Davington (Daunton) (Kent) was a Benedictine priory founded

The convent at Bristol had a female benefactor: it was founded by Eva, widow of Robert Fitz Harding, who may even have become the prioress of her nunnery.[15] In the same century, there were three foundations in France, one each at Orleans, Rouen, and Etrun. In addition, one community of Norbertine women was founded in Anvers and another near Prague. Nor was the German Empire or the Holy Land bereft of convents of contemplative Magdalens.[16]

The earliest notice for an Italian foundation is in Norman Sicily. A document of 1151 records Roger II's endowment of lands near Sciacca to Adelicia, abbess of the Benedictine convent of Saint Mary Magdalen near Corleone in the diocese of Palermo.[17] Another early foundation for Bene-

---

in 1153 by Fulke of Newenham; Kynewaldgraves was founded before 1169; Bristol ca. 1170–73; Sewardsley (Northamptonshire), a convent of Cistercians, was founded ca. 1173–88 by Richard of Lester. *Thirteenth century:* Wintney (Hampshire) was a Cistercian house founded ca. 1200 by Richard Holte (de Hereard) along with his wife, Christine, daughter of Thomas Cobreth; Remsted (Kent) was a priory of Benedictine nuns founded ca. 1229–31 by Richard, archbishop of Canterbury; Whistones (Worcester), a Cistercian convent, was founded by bishop Gautier of Cantilupe and dedicated in 1255. Saxer, *Le culte,* 135–36, 146, 196–97. On the nuns of Whistones, referred to in royal close rolls in 1241 as both "the white sisters of Worcester" and the "sisters of penance" of Worcester, see Sally Thompson, *Women Religious,* 199–200. Gilchrist, *Gender and Material Culture,* 129, adds the Benedictine convent at Ickleton (Cambridgeshire). Neither this list, nor any that follows, pretends to be an exhaustive listing of foundations made in the name of Mary Magdalen in the Middle Ages. For the sake of comparison, it should be noted that in the period 1151–1216 Alison Binns has found 18 English monastic church dedications to Mary Magdalen for male houses. Mary Magdalen was the fifth most popular titular saint for English monastic foundations in that period, tied for that honor with Saints James and John the Evangelist. Binns found 6 Benedictine dedications; 4 Cluniac; 7 Augustinian; and 1 Premonstratensian. The Virgin Mary is the only female saint to exceed the Magdalen in number of monastic dedications; indeed, she is the most popular titular of all. See A. Binns, *Dedications of Monastic Houses in England and Wales, 1066–1216* (Woodbridge, England: Boydell Press, 1989), 18, 34–38.

[15] Thompson suggests that Eva's foundation may have originally been a hospital which only later became a convent. See *Women Religious,* 45–46.

[16] *France:* Orléans, a Fontevrist foundation, was founded ca. 1113. Rouen was a Cistercian abbey called Sainte-Marie-Madeleine de Bival, which records two foundation dates: 1128 and 1154. Etrun was founded in 1142. Abbess Marie obtained apostolic protection for the convent. Monteux (Provence) was a convent of Benedictines founded in 1354 by Jean Blanqui of Avignon. *Low Countries:* The priory was founded in Anvers in 1135. *Bohemia:* This abbey of Premonstratensian nuns had a double dedication to Saints Wenceslas and Mary Magdalen. It was founded by Blessed Hroznata ca. 1196–1202 at Chotesov, in the diocese of Prague. *German Empire:* Albert de Kevernbourg founded a convent at Magdebourg, consecrated in 1231. *Latin Kingdom:* A convent of Benedictines was founded in Jerusalem by 1092; in Nicosia (Cyprus) by 1192; a Cistercian convent in Tripoli; and by 1223 a convent in Acre. See Jacques de Vitry, *Historia Occidentalis,* Appendix C, 268. The other references are from Saxer, *Le culte,* 116–17, 119, 122, 145, 219, 246, with the exception of Orléans which is from Johnson, *Equal in Monastic Profession,* 268. Again, it is worth stating that these lists do not pretend to be exhaustive.

[17] Lynn Townsend White Jr., *Latin Monasticism in Norman Sicily* (Cambridge, MA:

dictine women was in 1162, at Subiaco, where Saint Benedict himself had formed his first community of monks. The new foundation was made near the cave where Chelidonia of Abruzzo had spent most of her life, possibly in imitation of the legendary Magdalen.[18]

By the next century, however, Italy had far outstripped the rest of Europe in its establishment of cloistered communities of women dedicated to Mary Magdalen; in the thirteenth and early fourteenth centuries Benedictine and Cistercian convents were founded throughout the peninsula: in Urbania, Verona, Alexandria, Recanati, San Severo, Castellaneta, Marta, Chieti, Florence, and Perugia.[19] Likewise for the more recent reformed orders. The blessed Santuccia Carabotti of Gubbio (d. 1305), who by the time of her death had founded a monastic congregation which included some twenty foundations, seems to have had a special fondness for Saint Mary Magdalen. In fact, over one-quarter of the convents in her congregations were named for the saint.[20]

Medieval Academy of America, 1938), 158–59. It was subject to Monreale in 1177; this was confirmed by the pope in 1183.

[18] *Monasticon Italiae I: Roma e Lazio,* ed. Filippo Caraffa (Centro Storico Benedettino Italiano) (Cesena: Badia di Santa Maria del Monte, 1981), 174 n. 227: This monastery bore a double dedication to Saint Mary Magdalen and Saint Chelidonia (d. 1162).

[19] The Benedictine abbey of *Urbania* (Marche) was founded in 1200; the Benedictine convent of *Verona* (Veneto) was founded in 1211; the penitents of *Alessandria* (Piedmont) received a papal privilege in 1247; a convent at *Recanati* (Marche), near Ancona, was founded before 1249; the Benedictine convent of *San Severo,* near Foggia (Apulia), was founded before 1258; the Benedictine convent at *Castellaneta,* near Taranto (Apulia), was founded by the testamentary bequest of one Magister Nicolas in 1283; Pope Nicolas IV gave an indulgence to the convent of Saint Mary Magdalen on the island of *Marta,* in Bolsena (Lazio) in 1290. They claimed that Count Gherado of Burgundy brought relics of their patron to the island in the year 751(!); a Cistercian convent was founded in *Chieti* (Abruzzo) before 1309 while *Florence* (Tuscany) had its Cistercian convent of nuns at Cestello in Borgo Pinti by 1325; and finally, Perugia (Umbria) founded a Benedictine convent in the fourteenth century. For Urbania, Verona, Alessandria, Recanati, and Chieti, see Saxer, *Le culte,* 215–17, 262. For San Severo and Castellaneta, see *Monasticon Italiae III: Puglia e Basilicata,* ed. Giovanni Lundardi, Hubert Houben, and Giovanni Spinelli (Centro Storico Benedettino Italiano) (Cesena: Badia di Santa Maria del Monte, 1986), 48n. 91 and 97n. 281. For Marta, see *Monasticon Italiae I: Roma e Lazio,* 148n. 130. For Florence, see Alison Luchs, *Cestello: A Cistercian Church of the Florentine Renaissance* (New York: Garland, 1977). For Perugia, see Giovanna Casagrande, *Religiosità penitenziale e città al tempo dei comuni* (Rome: Istituto Storico dei Cappuccini, 1995), 233.

[20] Don Leandro Novelli dell'abbazia de Cesena, "Due documenti inediti relativi alle monache benedettine dette 'Santucce,'" *Benedictina* 22 (1975): 237–42. The convents were: Perugia (1262), Cagli (1270), Cortona (1270), Urbino (1270), Borgo Sansepolcro (1271), and Massa di Cerbone (by 1305). For an introduction to Santuccia's reforming enterprise, see Katherine Gill, "*Scandala:* Controversies Concerning *Clausura* and Women's Religious Communities in Late Medieval Italy," in *Christendom and Its Discontents: Exclusion, Persecution and Rebellion, 1000–1500,* ed. Scott Waugh and Peter D. Diehl (Cambridge: Cambridge University Press, 1996), 177–203. For *Borgo Sansepolcro* (Tuscany), see James R.

The mendicant orders were no less dedicated in founding contemplative convents in honor of the Magdalen. In 1286, thirty years after the Order of Hermits of Saint Augustine was formally organized, the first convent of Augustinian nuns was founded in Orvieto and dedicated to Mary Magdalen. Other communities of female contemplatives associated with the friars soon emerged. In the diocese of Spoleto alone eleven mendicant-associated convents were dedicated to Mary Magdalen during the thirteenth and fourteenth centuries. No other female saint, not even the Virgin Mary who was commemorated with ten foundations in the diocese, could claim so many titular honors.[21] Outside of the Spoleto valley, female contemplative foundations emerged at Siena, Atri, Città di Castello, Forlì, Perugia, Borgo Sansepolcro, and San Gimignano, among other central Italian cities.[22]

A document dated 20 February 1334 from the convent at San Gimignano provides a glimpse of the material and spiritual life of such nuns. A certain Monna di Rufo di Petroio received a privilege from John, cardinal-deacon of Saint Theodore and legate to the holy see, to build a monastery complex including a church, altar, bell tower, residence, cemetery, and other necessities. The twelve nuns, of whom seven are named, followed the Augustinian rule. The abbess and enclosed nuns were able to select

---

Banker, *Death in the Community: Memorialization and Confraternities in an Italian Commune in the Late Middle Ages* (Athens, GA: University of Georgia Press, 1998), 30–31, 151. By 1271 the Santucce had moved to new quarters and another group of nuns occupied the old monastery of Santa Maria Maddalena.

[21] The foundations were at Cascia (today Santa Rita), Gualdo Cattaneo ('de Mercatali'), Montefalco, Monte Martano, Norcia, Paterno, Rupino, Spello, two at Spoleto ('de Capati' and 'de Colleluce'), and Trevi. See S. Nessi, "Le *religiosae mulieres*," in *Il processo di canonizzazione di Chiara da Montefalco,* ed. Enrico Menestò (Quaderni del Centro per il collegamento degli studi medievali e umanistici nell'Università di Perugia, 14) (Florence: La Nuova Italia Editrice, 1984), 546–55.

[22] *Augustinian foundations:* For the foundations in Orvieto (Umbria) and Siena (Tuscany) in 1339, see David Gutiérrez, O.S.A., *The Augustinians in the Middle Ages, 1256–1356* (History of the Order of St. Augustine, vol. 1, part 1) (Villanova, PA: Augustinian Historical Institute, 1984), 203, 207. (Siena had earlier founded Santa Marta [1328], also an Augustinian convent, ibid.) *Franciscan affiliations:* For *Atri* (Abruzzo) in 1324, see *Aprutium-Molisium. Le decime,* items 3129 and 3368. They were evidently an order of Poor Clares who had at one point been under interdiction and excommunication. For *Città di Castello* (Umbria), see Casagrande, *Religiosità,* 296, which she lists (with a question mark) as a convent of Poor Clares. *Dominicans:* For *Forlì* (Emilia-Romagna) in 1303, see J. Quetif and J. Echard, *Scriptores Ordinis Praedicatorum,* 3 vols. (Paris: J.-B.-C. Ballard & N. Simant, 1719–1934), vol. 1, vii, who list this as a house of Dominican nuns. *Unknown affiliations:* In *Perugia,* a third Mary Magdalen dedication (13th c.), see Casagrande, *Religiosità,* 233, and *Borgo Sansepolcro;* Banker, *Death,* 155, mentions a "monastery of the sisters of Santa Maria Maddalena in Borghetto." The *decime,* of course, list many Mary Magdalen foundations; it is for the most part impossible to distinguish between male and female houses.

their own priest or suitable confessor. Their complex was dedicated to Saint Mary Magdalen.[23]

Preachers intended that the contemplative Magdalen serve both cloistered nuns and ordinary women alike. Toward this end they stressed her great wisdom acquired through listening to the word of the Lord. Nicolas de Hanappes (d. 1291), a Dominican who ended his career as cardinal-bishop of Ostia and patriarch of Jerusalem, named Mary Magdalen under the rubric, *De sapientia mulierum* (*On the wisdom of women*), in his book of *exempla*.[24] Giovanni da San Gimignano, prior of the Dominican convent in Siena, contrasted the Magdalen's wisdom with the foolishness of Eve. The imprudent woman, he argued, opens her ears to the words of lechers like the serpent—the devil—whereas the wise woman, as exemplified by Mary Magdalen, closes her ears to such types and opens them only for the word of God.[25] Persuading certain women to listen to the word of God was no easy matter, at least according to Humbert of Romans. According to the Dominican master general, some women "are not devoted to the word of God, but rather when they are in church, they just talk, say their prayers, genuflect before images, [and] take holy water. They can hardly be persuaded to go now and then to the preaching." For these ordinary women

[23] ASF, *Diplomatico normale, San Gimignano, agostiniane, pergamene 20 Feb. 1334:* "Ad laudem omnipotentis dei et beate Marie Magdalene ac pro salute anime tue facere construi et hedificari unum monasterium monialium inclusarum sub vocabulo ipsius sancte et regula beati Augustini in quo possint et esse debeant duodecim moniales et una Abbatissa . . . Quare nobis humiliter supplicasti ut construi et hedificari faciendi Monasterium ipsum in loco predicto cum ecclesia, altari, campanili, domibus et aliis necessariis officinis ac cimiterio in quo abbatissa, moniales, servitores, et servitrices dicti monasterii qui et que fuerint pro tempore valeant sepelliri. Necnon recipiendi ex nunc dilictas in domino Blaxiam filiam Cursi, Palmam et Ciciliam sorores filias fratris Jacobi, Elisabecht[am] filiam Gerardi et Bartholomeam filiam de Frontis de Sancto Gemmiano ac Johannam filiam Viviani de Petrolo puellas dicte diocese que çelo devotionis accense . . . Quibus Abbatisse et monialibus liceant et possint sibi eligere huiusmodi sacerdotem sive confexorem ydoneum." The monastery flourished until 1570. See Diana Norman, "The Case of the *Beata* Simona: Iconography, Hagiography and Misogyny in Three Paintings by Taddeo di Bartolo," *Art History* 18 (1995): 154–84. She identifies Monna di Rufo di Petroio as Beata Simona. Unlike many a female community which often suffered financial hardship, this one seems to have been prospered. In 1456, Benozzo Gozzoli painted an altarpiece of an enthroned Madonna and child, flanked by Mary Magdalen and Martha for them. It is now in the Museo Civico and illustrated in Raimond Van Marle, *The Development of the Italian Schools of Painting,* 28 vols. (The Hague: Martinus Nijhoff, 1924–36), vol. 11 (1929), 183–84, fig. 118.

[24] *Exempla sacrae scripturae ordinata secundum alphabetum* (n.p., 1473), unpaginated. It was once attributed to Bonaventura and published under his name. For Nicolas, see André Duval, "Nicolas de Hanappes," *DS* 11 (1982), 283–84.

[25] "Fuit sagacitas sapientie. Eva enim fuit mulier stulta que aperuit aures serpenti, dyabolo, sicut faciunt mulieres que aperiunt aures lecatoribus . . . Sed mulier sapiens claudit aures ad verba lecatoris et aperit ad verba dei. Sic fecit Magdalena . . . que sedens secus pedes domini audiebat verbum illius." MS BAV Barb. lat. 513, f. 98r; *RLS* 3: 377.

who participated in the rituals of the faith without much reflecting on their deeper meaning, Humbert urged upon them "the example of the Magdalen, who sitting at the feet of the Lord listened to his word."[26]

Thus preachers turned to Luke's image of Mary Magdalen, "absorbed in listening and attending to words of the Lord,"[27] to promote devotion to the contemplative aspect of the saint. There was, however, another source for this image. Legends also transmitted the image of the contemplative saint, but that representation differed quite markedly from the one found in scripture. In her *vitae* Mary Magdalen became a type of desert saint, a hermit, who, hungering in spirit, retired to the wilderness to devote herself entirely to the mystical contemplation of God.[28]

The Mystical Magdalen

As we have seen previously, the legend of the eremitical Magdalen, a conflation with the *vita* of Mary of Egypt, began circulating in Europe prior to the mid-ninth century. Honorius Augustodunensis (d. 1137), whose Magdalen homily made up a part of his *Speculum ecclesiae*, drew on the *vita eremitica* to enliven his sermon. In his account of her life, after receiving the holy spirit with the other disciples, Mary Magdalen withdrew to the desert where she lived out the rest of her years in solitary reclusion.[29] Honorius's description of her eremitical life is rather laconic; the *vita eremitica* provided more detail. It narrated that Mary Magdalen secluded herself in a grotto for thirty years, taking no earthly fare; she did, however, receive spiritual refreshment at the canonical hours when angels sent by the Lord transported her into the ether where they nourished her with divine sustenance.

Although this legend gained widespread currency throughout Europe, the eremitical facts of her life were not accepted unanimously. A contemporary of Honorius Augustodunensis, an anonymous Cistercian, who in

---

[26] "Item quaedam sunt ita indevotae ad verbum Dei, quod quando sunt in Ecclesia, in qua praedicatur, modo loquuntur, modo dicunt orationes suas, modo stant coram imaginibus suis flexis genibus, modo accipiunt aquam benedictam, & vix possunt induci interdum, ut appropinquent ad praedicantem relictis locis consuetis. . . . Exemplum de Magdalena, quae sedens secus pedes Domini audiebat verbum illius." *De eruditione praedicatorum* in *Maxima bibliotheca*, 506.

[27] "Absorta audiendo et attendendo Maria verbis domini." François de Meyronnes, *Sermones de laudibus sanctorum*, 79.

[28] It should be noted that some such as Cavalca say that she retired to the desert to do penance. Others such as Jacobus de Voragine say that it was for the sake of contemplation. Still others say it was for both reasons. Intense asceticism and mystical ecstasy are of course frequently intertwined, as was well known in the Middle Ages.

[29] *PL* 172, 981.

the early twelfth century wrote a *vita* once ascribed to Rabanus Maurus, dismissed the *vita eremitica* with this withering piece of source criticism:

> The rest of the tale—that after the ascension of the Savior she immediately fled to the Arabian desert; that she remained there without any clothing in a cave; and that she saw no man afterwards until she was visited by I know not what priest, from whom she begged a garment, and other such stuff—is false and a fabrication of storytellers drawn out of the accounts of the Penitent of Egypt [Mary of Egypt]. And these tale-spinners convict themselves of falsehood from the very beginning of their story, for they ascribe their account to Josephus, that most learned historian, though Josephus never mentions anything about Mary Magdalen in his books.[30]

The Cistercian's most severe censure was directed at the episode that scholars acknowledge was a direct "borrowing" from the *vita* of Mary of Egypt. But he was not entirely convinced of the angelic episode either. He suggests that it too was "an apocryphal story," but then retreats from such an exacting position by proposing that "if this is understood in a mystical sense, it is not completely unbelievable, for it is a fact that admits no doubt that she was quite often refreshed by the sight of angels, aided by their services, and delighted by their conversation."[31] Nevertheless, he is the only writer known to me who expressed any sort of skepticism in relation to Mary Magdalen's angelically assisted mystical life. By the thirteenth century most hagiographers and preachers embraced the story wholeheartedly, even using the language of mysticism to describe the events in the wilderness. Thus Agostino d'Ancona told his audience that "Mary Magdalen was rapt by the jubilation of angels."[32]

What made the figure of the eremitical Magdalen, secluded in her grotto and attended by angels, such an attractive figure to medieval preachers? I would like to argue that it is all of a piece of the mendicant identification with the saint that we examined earlier in respect to the symbol of the apostolic Magdalen. As will be recalled, the apostolic or mixed life, the life of the friars, drew equally from the wells of contemplation and action. The contemplative life was the life that spiritually restored the preachers so that they could better discharge their active ministries in the world. All too often, however, the duties of office were so burdensome that no time remained for such solitary refreshment.

The case of the Dominican Raymond of Peñafort (d. 1275) is revealing. Sometime in the period between 1231 and 1236 while he was serving as papal penitentiary to Gregory IX, Raymond wrote a letter to the prioress

---

[30] Mycoff, *Life*, 98.
[31] Ibid.
[32] "Maria Magdalena fuit rapta ab angelorum iubilatione." MS Angelica 158, f. 122v.

of the convent of Dominican contemplatives in Bologna asking to be remembered in her prayers. Here is Raymond's wistful supplication:

> Living, as I do, in the whirlwind of the court, I am hardly ever able to reach,
> or, to be quite honest, even to see from afar, the tranquility of contempla-
> tion. . . . So it is a great joy and an enormous comfort to me to feel how I am
> helped by your prayers. I often think of this service which you and your sis-
> ters do for me, sitting as you do at the Lord's feet with Mary, enjoying the
> delights of your spouse, our Lord Jesus Christ, contemplating the face of him
> whom the angels desire to look upon. So when all is going well for you with
> your spouse in the secrecy of your chamber, do not forget, in your mutual un-
> interrupted love, to pray for me and beg alms for me in my poverty and
> need.[33]

Clearly, Raymond was longing to sit at the feet of the Lord with Mary
but, given his manifold obligations at the papal court, he was compelled to
live the life of Martha. The Catalan friar's experience was not unique. As
John Coakley has pointed out, since the friars were frequently unable to
attend to their own interior lives, they often devoted themselves to recording the contemplative lives of the visionary women whom they served as
confessors.[34] Women, of course, were forbidden from holding clerical office; but nevertheless, as Caroline Bynum has vividly demonstrated, they
developed an authoritative voice in the later medieval Church through
their active interior lives which were recorded for posterity in the form of
vitae.[35] The friars, their confidants and chaplains, were fascinated by the
women's supernatural knowledge received frequently in the form of visions. Though the friars regarded such mystical gifts as signs of holiness,
they were assisted in this belief by the tenets of medieval medicine that suggested that female inspiration could be explained by sex differences. Sci-
entific discourse, based on the ancient theory of humors, maintained that
physiologically women were composed of cold and wet properties. Ex-
trapolating from biology, medieval thinkers claimed women's cold and wet

---

[33] *Early Dominicans: Selected Writings,* ed. Simon Tugwell (New York: Paulist Press, 1982), 409.

[34] "Friars as Confidants of Holy Women in Medieval Dominican Hagiography," in *Images of Sainthood in Medieval Europe,* ed. Renate Blumenfeld-Kosinski and Timea Szell (Ithaca, NY: Cornell University Press, 1991), 222–46; id., "Gender and the Authority of the Friars: The Significance of Holy Women for Thirteenth-Century Franciscans and Dominicans," *Church History* 60 (1991): 445–60; and id., "Friars, Sanctity, and Gender: Mendicant Encounters with Saints, 1250–1325," in *Medieval Masculinities: Regarding Men in the Middle Ages,* ed. Clare A. Lees (Minneapolis, MN: University of Minnesota Press, 1994), 91–110.

[35] Bynum, *Holy Feast and Holy Fast: The Religious Significance of Food to Medieval Women* (Berkeley: University of California Press, 1987).

natures disposed them toward infused knowledge: inspiration, mysticism, revelations, and visions.[36] Men, on the other hand, being constitutionally hot and dry, were considered more rational creatures and therefore inclined to acquired learning, by the traditional means of study and education. Therefore, in the very restricted context of mystical perfection, being male and in clerical orders was a distinct disadvantage.[37] We have encountered this distinction earlier: recall that in the gnostic *Gospel of Mary* Mary Magdalen is the visionary, while Peter and the other apostles merely look on in wonder and envy at her prophetic gifts. But here of course the similarity ends; whereas in the gnostic text the apostles attack the veracity of the Magdalen's visionary experience, by the late medieval period the friars were reporting in lavish detail her mystical experiences.

Both biology and priestly office conspired to distance the friars from engaging in the sort of mystical life for which they achingly yearned and which the eremitical Magdalen practiced daily at the seven canonical hours. By attending to the details of that life in their sermons, the preachers were able to refresh themselves vicariously in the restorative waters of contemplation. By recording it, speaking it, and preaching it, the friars were willing themselves into the contemplative life.

Thus it is not surprising that the preachers relished describing the forbidding and desolate spot that Mary Magdalen, avid for contemplation, had chosen for reclusion. It was called variously an *aspirum heremum, rupes, spelunca, desertum,* or *antrum,* words meaning desert or cave, all medieval shorthand for denoting "the wilderness." The Franciscan Servasanto da Faenza was by no means alone when he described the place as bereft of even the slightest natural consolation: there were no streams, no trees, not even any grass.[38] Salimbene (d. 1288), the loquacious Franciscan chronicler who had actually been to the Magdalen's provençal grotto on pilgrimage, described the region as being "secluded, uninhabitable and deserted."[39] Interestingly, although the *vita eremitica* began circulating as early as the ninth century, the precise localization of this southern French

---

[36] For the elaboration of medieval gender theory from sexual difference, see Joan Cadden, *Meanings of Sex Differences in the Middle Ages: Medicine, Science, and Culture* (Cambridge: Cambridge University Press, 1993).

[37] For this theme in fourteenth-century Umbrian and Tuscan hagiography, see Catherine Marie Mooney, *Women's Visions, Men's Words: The Portrayal of Holy Women and Men in Fourteenth-Century Italian Hagiography* (Ph.D. diss., Yale University, 1991).

[38] "In quo quidem loco, nec aquarum fluenta, nec arbor, nec herbarum solacia." MS Antoniana 490, f. 100v; not listed in *RLS.*

[39] Salimbene de Adam, *Cronica,* ed. Giuseppe Scalia, 2 vols. (Scrittori d'Italia series, vols. 232–33) (Bari: Giuseppe Laterza & Figli, 1966), vol. 1, 962. *The Chronicle of Salimbene de Adam,* trans. Joseph L. Baird, Giuseppe Baglivi, and John Robert Kane (Medieval & Renaissance Texts & Studies, vol. 40) (Binghamton, NY: Medieval & Renaissance Texts & Studies, 1986).

desert did not occur in legendary and homiletic material until the twelfth century.[40] Even then it was usually unnamed and reckoned in relation to Marseilles. Bertrand de la Tour referred to it as being in the *deserto marsiliense,* in the Marseillaise desert, while Jean de Mailly situated it fourteen miles from Marseilles.[41]

The saint's mystical rapture in the desert wilderness was frequently the culmination of a Magdalen sermon. The Franciscan provincial Luca da Padova (d. 1287) closed one of his sermons preaching how the Magdalen's life of ascetical contemplation fulfilled the laws of *ordo in contrarium,* order through opposition. Before her conversion she was a base sinner, afterwards she was so precious that angels elevated her to the heavens. Moreover, one was to understand that she was not only elevated intellectually, but also corporeally. Likewise, before her conversion she dressed herself in soft and expensive finery, but afterwards no material clothing touched her at all. Finally, in regard to her alimentary habits, when she was a sinner she was accustomed to sup on delicacies, now she was refreshed by celestial fare, having rejected all carnal nourishment.[42]

Pietro de' Natali in his *Catalogus sanctorum,* observed that such privations signified that Christ wished to satisfy the Magdalen not with earthly banquets but heavenly meals.[43] Preachers and hagiographers linked the divine meals that Jesus had prepared for Mary at Bethany with the angelic sustenance he offered her in the desert. Fasting, as was known in the Middle Ages, often induced mystical experiences and accompanying supernatural states such as levitation. Domenico Cavalca cited the Magdalen's mystical levitation as an "example of spiritual concentration," one of many types of prayer he analyzed in his *Frutti della lingua.* He remarked that those thus engaged are frequently rapt in the ecstasy of the mind and lose sensation; others, "through the force of an enraptured heart also levitate the body

---

[40] Saxer, "Maria Maddalena," *BS* 8 (1967), 1092.

[41] *Sermo* 217, in *Sermones Bertrandi de tempore et de sanctis. Una cum quadragesimali epistolari* (Strasbourg: Georg Husner, [ca. 1500]), unpaginated. The Dominican hagiographer Jean de Mailly reckoned it as "fere .xiiii. milibus a Marsilia." MS BAV Vat. lat. 1198, ff. 69v–70v. Salimbene estimates the site as being fifteen miles from Marseilles, *Cronica,* vol. 1, 962.

[42] "Primo enim cum hominibus ut peccatrix vilissima conversabatur. Sed postmodum ab angelis vero praeciosissima ad celestia ellevabatur. . . . corpus eius quia non tamen intelectualiter sed etiam sensibiliter corpore ellevabat. Item quae prius mollibus et praeciosis vestimentis induebatur, iam nullo materiali vestimento tegebat[ur]. Item quae delicatis cibis utebatur, iam celesti cibo reficiebatur, omni refectione carnali abiecta." MS Antoniana 466, f. 270v; *RLS* 4: 95.

[43] "Ut sic daretur intelligi: quod non terrenis dapibus sed epulis tantum celestibus eam Christus disposuerat satiare. . . . Sic que saciata nullis aliis corporalibus alimentis indigebat." *Catalogus sanctorum,* 257–58.

above the ground, as did Thomas Aquinas, Saint Anselm and the Magdalen."[44] Margaret of Cortona also levitated, possibly in a mimetic act of self-identification with the Magdalen's "spiritual concentration." Fra Giunta, her biographer, who did not hesitate to cast Margaret as a second Magdalen, related many stories of her levitation, including one in which she experienced the ecstasy of mystical marriage. After crowning her with a diadem, and placing a ring on her finger, Jesus directed his angels to bestow her with the same gift of contemplation as he had given the Magdalen.[45]

The motif of the Magdalen's desert retreat was not confined to hagiography and sermons. It also found expression in the liturgy. By the fourteenth century, hymns not uncommonly praised the desert saint. One for the office of lauds sung:

> Rejoice daughter of the highest king
> who is conveyed outside
> the cave at the seven hours.[46]

One of Savonarola's two *laude* dedicated to the Magdalen sang of the contemplative saint in her grotto, suspended in the air by angels. He encouraged his audience to join her at the forbidding mountain with sweet songs and a serene mind:

> Up to that harsh mountain,
> where the Magdalen contemplates,
>
> Let us go with sweet songs
> and a pure and serene mind
>
> She is suspended in the air
> in the sweet Nazarene face.[47]

If writers exulted in imagining the Magdalen's mystical ecstasies in the desert, painters did so all the more. Almost every late medieval Italian fresco cycle of her *vita* included at least one scene representing her anchoritic withdrawal from the world, something that cannot be said about

---

[44] *Racconti esemplari di predicatori del Due e Trecento,* ed. Giorgio Varanini and Guido Baldassarri, 3 vols. (Rome: Salerno Ed., 1993), vol. 3, 141.

[45] Cited in Haskins, *Mary Magdalen,* 187.

[46] This was one of three hymns found appended to Bernardino's sermon, *Feria Quinta,* in *Opera Omnia,* vol. 3 (1956), 441n. 64. It was used popularly as well; it was published as a chapbook called *Sette gaudi di Santa Maria Maddalena* (n.p., n.d.). One of these is preserved in the Capponi collection in the BAV: Capponi V.686. int. 64. Other hymns using this motif are listed in Szövérffy, "'Peccatrix quondam femina,'" 103, 141.

[47] These are stanzas 1, 2, and 9 of the *lauda* which can be found in Patrick Macey, "*Infiamma il mio cor,*" 161–89. I have modified his translation.

any other episode in her life, either scriptural or legendary.[48] To take Angevin Naples as just one example, in the three churches that contain late-thirteenth- to early-fourteenth-century fresco cycles dedicated to the saint, all three include a scene of desert reclusion, Pietro Cavallini's in the Dominican church of San Domenico Maggiore perhaps being the finest example (Fig. 19).[49] Many cycles such as the one at the church of San Domenico in Spoleto represent her angelic levitation, probably borrowing the iconography from the Assumption of the Virgin Mary (Fig. 20).[50] It must be stressed, however, that such iconography was not restricted to fresco cycles of her *vita;* it is also found in individual "portrait" frescoes, altarpieces, panel and predella paintings, and in manuscript decoration. A devotional book, written in Latin but of German provenance, shows the Magdalen clothed in nothing more than her mane of hair, borne aloft by a fiery-red group of angels (Fig. 21).[51]

It is worth pausing for a moment to examine this image which so italicizes the Magdalen's naked body beneath that mane of abundant hair. Her hair and nakedness were not inconsequential in contributing to the success of this motif in both its literary and visual forms. From time immemorial female hair—loose, unbound, and uncovered—was associated with sexuality. It is revealing that in both her pre- and post-conversion lives Mary Magdalen's most predominant physical attribute was her copious and flowing hair. When she was a sexual sinner Mary Magdalen entered the house of the Pharisee, wept at the feet of the Lord, and dried them with her hair. It is significant that at the moment of her conversion her hair—the sym-

[48] For the locations of the painted cycles of her life, see chapter 2, n. 63. Of the thirteen later medieval fresco cycles representing the life of Mary Magdalen only two do not make reference to this episode in her life. The first is the Magdalen chapel at Sant'Antonio di Ranverso. Since most of this damaged cycle is lost, presumably it too contained a scene referring to her eremitic reclusion. Only Giovanni da Milano's Rinuccini chapel in Santa Croce in Florence does not witness this event. Out of five scenes, four are gospel scenes and only one is a legendary scene: the Marseilles miracle. Perhaps since he had already included the contemplative scene at Bethany (a rarity), the artist did not feel obliged to make reference to the legendary contemplative as well. For the chapel, see n. 8.

[49] All three churches—San Lorenzo Maggiore, San Domenico Maggiore, and San Pietro a Maiella—were directly or indirectly patronized or connected to the Angevins, a subject further discussed in chapter 11. For the decoration of the three chapels, see Ferdinando Bologna, *I pittori alla corte angioina di Napoli 1266–1414* (Rome: Ugo Bozzi, 1969), 94–97, 115–46, 311–20.

[50] For further examples of this motif, see *La Maddalena fra sacro e profano*, 31–64, 218–27. For the chapel, see chapter 2, n. 62.

[51] The fourteenth-century MS from which this miniature is taken is a devotional book dedicated to Mary Magdalen. It contains a version of her legend, miracles, five sermons, antiphons, and hymns. The MS was copied in Germany by Bertholdus Heyder. It is now in the British Library, MS Add. 15682, f. 105r. The scene is also found in the Magdalen Master panel (fig. 40), the *Leggendario Ungherese*, MS BAV Vat. lat. 8541, f. 103v, and Botticelli's predella for his *Trinity*, discussed in chapter 6.

Figure 19. *The Desert Saint in Her Grotto* (1308). Fresco by Pietro Cavallini, Brancaccio Chapel, Church of S. Domenico Maggiore, Naples. (Photo: I.C.C.D., Rome)

Figure 20. *Angelic Levitation* (ca. 1400). A priest witnesses Mary Magdalen's angelic levitation. Fresco from Cappella della Maddalena, Church of S. Domenico, Spoleto. (Photo: Hutzel Collection, by permission of the Getty Research Institute, Research Library)

bol of her sexual sin—became the emblem of her penitence. Such multivalent symbolism informed representation of her post-conversion life at La Sainte-Baume as well. According to legend, after years of reclusion and harsh penitence in the desert, her clothes had fallen away and her hair had grown to cover her nakedness. On one level, of course, representations of the Magdalen's nakedness could be construed as her post-conversion condition of innocence and purity. But given her prior association with sins of the flesh, medieval depictions of the hair-covered and naked Magdalen did more than evoke images of edenic innocence: they also pointed back to the

Figure 21. *Angelic Levitation* (14th c.). Miniature from a German devotional manuscript, British Library, London. (Photo: The British Library)

sexual aspect of her nudity, a reminder of her past as a sexual sinner. It should never be forgotten that Mary Magdalen was known in the medieval world as the *Beata peccatrix,* the holy sinner, a title that simultaneously evoked both sin and sanctity. Suggestive images of the naked, eremitical, hair-clad Magdalen functioned similarly. Her nakedness was at once innocent and seductive. Her mane of hair served as a veil of modesty, but nonetheless invoked female sexuality. Medieval artists, their patrons, preachers, and moralists were all seduced by the rich paradox contained in such a symbol, which no doubt contributed to making the eremitical Magdalen one of the most enduring images of the Middle Ages.

The hermit-saint also recalled images of John the Baptist. The Magdalen and the Baptist were frequently paired off together in medieval art by virtue of their association with the desert.[52] Roberta Gilchrist further reminds us that the Christian notion of "rebirth through baptism and repentance" also linked these two saints in an association of ideas.[53] Perhaps this nexus explains the city of Florence's devotion to the Magdalen. The Baptist was (and still is) Florence's patron saint, but the Magdalen was frequently paired with him in Tuscan art. Indeed, in Florence's Cappella della Maddalena in the Palazzo del Podestà the south wall is frescoed with the life of the Magdalen, the north wall with scenes from the Baptist's life.[54]

Significantly, both saints were also regarded as prophets. The anonymous Cistercian hagiographer called her the prophet of Christ's ascension, arguing:

> She witnessed the ascension on the mountain; just as she announced to the apostles the first event as soon as it had taken place . . . she showed she was equal to John the Baptist in being more than a prophet. . . . Her deeds are equal to his, write the four evangelists.[55]

[52] An early fourteenth-century Florentine triptych epitomizes this relationship. The central panel is an enthroned Madonna surrounded by saints. The left wing is divided into two registers: the upper portion is occupied by John the Baptist in the desert; the lower part by the hirsute Magdalen, captured in an act of contemplative prayer. Offner and Steinweg, *Corpus* III.7 (1967), fig. 29.

[53] Roberta Gilchrist, *Contemplation and Action: The Other Monasticism* (London: Leicester University Press, 1995), 216.

[54] See Giovanni Poggi, *Il Duomo di Firenze* (Berlin: Bruno Cassirer, 1909), 99–100, fig. 71, for a trecento polyptych illustrating Florence's patron saints. The hermits Mary Magdalen and John the Baptist are among them. For the Magdalen chapel in the Palazzo del Podestà, see Janis Elliott, "The Judgement of the Commune: The Frescoes of the Magdalen Chapel in Florence," *Zeitschrift für Kunstgeschichte* 61 (1998): 509–19, who notes that there are two scenes of the life of the Baptist in the Magdalen chapel. Tuscany did not have a monopoly on the visual pairing of the two saints, however. Among numerous examples, see the fourteenth-century hair-clad saints in the baptistery in Parma, for example. For a color reproduction, see *Battistero di Parma,* 2 vols. (Milan: Franco Maria Ricci, 1992–93), texts by G. Duby, G. Romano, C. Frugoni, and J. Le Goff, vol. 2, 160. For a discussion of the possible political implications of this pairing, see chap. 11, nn. 48–51.

[55] Prophetess: Mycoff, *Life,* 84–85, 96. Among others who associate Mary Magdalen with

The popularity of the Magdalen's eremitical model of sanctity was assisted in the fourteenth century by the great success of Cavalca's *Vite de' santi padri,* a *volgarizzamento* of the *Vitae patrum,* made for the devotional needs of the laity. Written in Italian, it included a *vita* of Mary Magdalen in the section on the *Vitae matrum,* the lives of the desert mothers.[56] Cavalca's translation of this and other eremitical lives no doubt also aided the popularity of all the desert saints in this period including saints Honophrius, Anthony Abbot, and Jerome.[57]

---

prophecy are: Rabanus Maurus: *PL* 111, 84; Peter Abelard: *PL* 178, 485; Iohannes de Biblia, MS BAV Borgh. 24, f. 63v; and Humbert of Romans, *De eruditione praedicatorum,* Lib. II, 483–84. The themes of prophecy and penance continued to inspire visual representations of both of these saints. Donatello's wooden sculpture of the Magdalen made for the baptistery in Florence, to say nothing of his similar figure of John the Baptist made for the Frari in Venice, were influenced by this eremitical model of sanctity, which was being preached by Antonino Pierozzi in Florence at precisely the time when the sculptor undertook these commissions in the mid-Quattrocento. There is no documentation regarding the commission of the Magdalen. John Pope-Hennessy, *Donatello Sculptor* (New York: Abbeville, 1993), 276–77, gives the Magdalen a date of 1454, the year when Donatello returned from Padua. Wilk, "The Cult of Mary Magdalen," proposes Antonino's preaching as inspiration for Donatello's Mary Magdalen, 685–98. The John the Baptist was made in 1438 for the Frari in Venice. The church is Franciscan; the commission was made by the Florentine *scuola* (confraternity), explaining the presence of the only work by Donatello in Venice. Rona Goffen, *Piety and Patronage in Renaissance Venice: Bellini, Titian and the Franciscans* (New Haven: Yale University Press, 1986), 26. Another Baptist, made for the Duomo in Siena and dated about 1457, also bears a striking resemblance to the Magdalen. It is illustrated in Pope-Hennessy, *Donatello,* figs. 287 and 288. For other examples of wooden penitents from the same period and provenance, see *La Maddalena tra sacro e profano,* 48–52.

[56] For an introduction to and a reading of the lives of some of the desert saints, see Alison Goddard Elliott, *Roads to Paradise.* For the diffusion of this eremitical model of sanctity in medieval Italy, see Carlo Delcorno, "Le *Vitae patrum* nella letteratura religiosa medievale (secc. XIII–XV)," *Lettere Italiane* 2 (1991): 187–207, and the conference proceedings in the volume entitled, *Eremitismo nel francescanesimo medievale.* (Atti del XVII convegno della Società Internazionale di Studi Francescani, Assisi, 12–14 ottobre 1989.) (Perugia: Università degli Studi di Perugia, Centro di Studi Francescani, 1991), particularly the essays by Giovanna Casagrande, "Forme di vita religiosa femminile solitaria in Italia centrale," 51–94; Edith Pásztor, "Ideali dell'eremitismo femminile in Europa tra i secoli XII–XV," 129–64; and Daniel Russo, "L'iconographie de l'érémitisme en Italie à la fin du Moyen Age (XIIIe–XVe siècles)," 187–207. See also Anna Benvenuti Papi, "Donne religiose nella Firenze del Due-Trecento," *'In castro poenitentiae': santità e società femminile nell'Italia medievale* (Rome: Herder, 1990), 593–634.

[57] For the eremitical Jerome, see Eugene Rice, *Saint Jerome in the Renaissance* (Baltimore: Johns Hopkins University Press, 1985). Chiara Frugoni has argued that Cavalca's translation of the *Vitae patrum* made at the Dominican house of Santa Caterina in Pisa was the source for Buffalmacco's visual representation of the *Vitae patrum* at the Camposanto in the same city. See her "Altri luoghi, cercando il paradiso (Il ciclo di Buffalmacco nel Camposanto di Pisa e la committenza domenicana)," *Annali della Scuola Normale Superiore di Pisa* (Classe di Lettere e Filosofia) ser. III, vol. XVIII/4 (1988): 1557–1643. The late-fourteenth-century frescoes depicting the lives of the hermits by Leonardo da Besozzo and Perrinetto da Benevento at the Augustinian church of San Giovanni a Carbonara in Naples are also probably

Whether or not they intended to do so, hagiographers, artists, and preachers were creating a prescriptive literature when they described in detail the Magdalen's eremitical retreat into the wilderness. In this regard the preaching of Bernardino da Siena is paradigmatic. His recipe for such a life (found in a Magdalen sermon) included these redolent ingredients: the solitude of wild animals, anonymity, nakedness except for the cover of one's own hair, a body so thin that flesh clings to the bones, no human food, heavenly marriage, the ground for one's bed, and an awareness that the whole world has been abandoned and forgotten, all of which induce a wondrous intoxication of the mind.[58] Many an impending holy person tried to live according to such a program. Margaret of Cortona seems to have intended to imitate the Magdalen's eremitical life but was dissuaded in a vision by Christ himself who told her: "Even though it is not your destiny to live in the desert (because deserts are not adapted to our times), you can live in solitude in your land *as if* you lived in the desert places."[59] Many holy women engaged in "urban eremitism," either living in cells just outside the city walls, or locked away in seclusion in the family *palazzo,* as did noblewomen Filippa Mareri (d. 1236) in Rieti and Umiliana de' Cerchi (d. 1246) in Florence, both early *beatae* associated with the Franciscan order.

Whether they practiced metaphorical eremitism or actual eremitism, the Magdalen became a patron to anchorites and hermits. The ascetical women at Ankerwyke in Buckinghamshire dedicated their foundation to Mary Magdalen, and on their official seal, the image which represented them in the world, they inscribed a timber-framed and thatched roof hermitage.[60] On the continent women did similarly. In the early twelfth century, in the black forest of Thuringia, a solitary called Pauline built first a wooden, then a stone chapel dedicated to the Magdalen at her retreat in the wilderness. Eadmer of Canterbury reported two recluses living near the oratory of Saint Mary Magdalen in Lyons; one of them, Adelaide, experienced visions and levitated just as her patron saint had done.[61] Solitary reclusion seems to have been favored by women more than men in the Middle Ages. In England, for example, Ann K. Warren has found that out of 780 anchorites who lived in the period between 1100 and 1539, women outnumbered

---

indebted to the wide diffusion of Cavalca's translation of the *Vitae patrum.* See also Ellen Callman, "Thebaid Studies," *Antichità Viva* 14 (1975): 3–22.

[58] *Feria quinta post dominicam de passione, De Sanctissima Magdalena* (Sermo 46), *S. Bernardini Senensis Opera Omnia,* 9 vols. (Quaracchi: Collegium S. Bonaventurae, 1950–65), vol. 3 (1956), 436. In the same sermon Bernardino mentions the Magdalen's levitation, 434.

[59] AASS, Feb. vol. 3, par. 46, 312. Emphasis is my own.

[60] Gilchrist, *Contemplation,* 136.

[61] Saxer, *Le culte,* 110 and 120. He also mentions two male hermits of the same period: Adjuteur of Tiron and Girard of Vienne, 113 and 126.

men by more than 2 to 1.[62] The numbers for central Italy are even more striking. In Perugia, in the year 1277, the commune first doled out charity to 20 female and 2 male recluses, and then again a few weeks later to 36 female anchoresses and 8 male anchorites. In 1290 charitable assistance was received by 56 sisters and 12 brothers.[63] These small communities of female recluses frequently put themselves under the patronage of Mary Magdalen. In the Spoleto valley alone, for example, thirteen communities of penitents were founded within the last decade of the thirteenth century. Mary Magdalen is the only saint who patronized more than one community: one in Monteluco (1294), the other, Santa Maria Maddalena "de Capatis" on Monte Çiçiano (1300).[64]

In Tuscany, hermitages at Pisa, Cortona, Chiusi, and Lucca took Mary Magdalen as their patron.[65] The one at Lucca was notable for its double dedication to Saints Mary Magdalen and Francis of Assisi. Contemplation was the theme that linked them. Both saints experienced mystical ecstasies culminating in angelically assisted unions with Christ. It did not go unnoticed by preachers and painters that Francis received the stigmata at the rocky sanctuary of La Verna high in the Tuscan hills, while celestial care was bestowed on Mary Magdalen on a similar *altissimo monte saxoso* (high and rocky mountain), reckoned by Salimbene to be so high above sea level that three of Bologna's Asinelli towers placed end to end could not reach it.[66] Accordingly, it was entirely possible that the Franciscan theologian and preacher François de Meyronnes, a native of neighboring Digne, knew

[62] Ann K. Warren, *Anchorites and Their Patrons in Medieval England* (Berkeley: University of California Press, 1985), 18–20.

[63] Sensi, "Anchoresses and Penitents in Thirteenth- and Fourteenth-Century Umbria," in *Women and Religion,* 57, 64. For the year 1290 he is citing the work of Giovanna Casagrande, 76n. 56.

[64] Sensi, "Anchoresses," 78n. 63. Saint Catherine of Alexandria also receives two, but one of them is a double dedication under the title "Santa Caterina and Santa Croce de Colle floris." It should be noted that two of the foundations listed by Sensi (Montefalco and de Capati) are listed by Nessi as convents. See n. 21. For *Monteluco* (1300), a hermitage of female recluses near Spoleto, see also Giovanna Casagrande, "Movimenti religiosi umbri e Chiara da Montefalco," in *Chiara da Montefalco e il suo tempo,* 61.

[65] *Pisa:* Casagrande, *Religiosità,* 44. *Rationes Decimarum Tuscia,* vols. I (1274–80) and II (1295–1304). The Tuscan *decime* are the only ones that list hermitages separately from churches or monasteries. It is likely that there were others throughout Italy, but just not listed as such. The exact dedications of the *hermitoria* are as follows: *Cortona: Heremus/Ecclesia,* item 2846 (vol. II, 1302–3); *Chiusi: Heremus Sanctae Mariae Magdalenae Montis Carcianesi,* items 2768 (vol. I, 1275–76) and 2814 (vol. I, 1276–77); *Lucca: S. Maria Magdalena de Chifenti* Titolare: S. Maria Maddalena e S. Francesco, item 5073 (1260); *Hermitorium de Iunceto* Titolare: S. Maria Magdalena, item 5133 (1260); and *Hermitorium S. Maria Magdalena Vallisbone de Versilia,* items 3835 (vol. I, 1275–76) and 4429, and 3854 (vol. II, 1302–3).

[66] Salimbene, *Cronica,* vol. 2, 762–63. In his day, the Magdalen's cave had already become a noted pilgrimage site.

firsthand the physical layout of the Magdalen's grotto. He associates the two grottoes in the first of his three Magdalen sermons. While considering the Magdalen's contemplative hideaway which he refers to as "that mountain," it occurs to him that Francis prayed on the mountain of *alverna,* because the saint was known to say that "the spirit of the lord is found in solitary places."[67] This textual linking of the Magdalen and Francis in their rocky retreats finds an iconographical analogue in a panel painting made in 1307 by Giuliano da Rimini for a confraternity of women in Urbania. The central image is a Madonna and child who are flanked by various saints. The saints filling the bottom register are female saints; on the top from left to right are Saints Francis, John the Baptist, John the Evangelist, and Mary Magdalen (Fig. 22). Francis, on the far left, is shown at La Verna receiving the stigmata from a seraphim, while Mary Magdalen is shown in her cave at La Sainte-Baume communing with an angel (Figs. 23 and 24).[68]

At Fontecolombo, the hermitage near Rieti where in 1221 Francis retreated to write the rule for the order, there was, even in his time, a small chapel on the mountainside dedicated to Mary Magdalen.[69] Francis himself did not shrink from representing the eremitical life of which he was occasionally able to partake as the life of Mary Magdalen. In his rule for anchorites (ca. 1223–24) he suggests that those who want to undertake the eremitical life should group themselves into clusters of threes and fours. Two should take the part of mothers who care for at least one son. The two mothers should lead the life of Martha, while the others take up the life of Mary in individual cells where they can devote themselves to meditation and prayer.[70]

Writers of Franciscan devotional literature fancied their founder a second Magdalen. In one late-thirteenth- to early-fourteenth-century tract, the anonymous author claims that Francis, after having had a vision of the naked Christ on the cross, "yearned to serve Christ 'til the end, naked fol-

---

[67] "Spiritus domini in locis solitariis." *Sermones de laudibus sanctorum,* 79.

[68] The painting is in the Isabella Stewart Gardner Museum (Boston). See Philip Hendy, *The Isabella Stewart Gardner Museum: Catalogue of the Exhibited Paintings and Drawings* (Boston: Trustees of the Museum, 1931), 175–78. See also the predella of the Rinuccini altarpiece by Giovanni del Biondo (1379) in which an enthroned Madonna and child are flanked by (*r–l*) Saint Francis, John the Baptist, John the Evangelist, and Mary Magdalen. The predella painting of Francis is of the stigmatization at La Verna, the Magdalen's corresponding image is of her angelic levitation in a grotto outside Marseilles. For a color plate, see *Il complesso monumentale di Santa Croce,* 252.

[69] Later fourteenth-century frescoes in the Magdalen chapel at Fontecolombo include one of the hair-clad Magdalen attended by angels.

[70] *De religiosa habitione in eremo* in *Opuscula S. Francisci et scripta S. Clarae Assisiensium,* ed. Ioannes M. Boccali, O.F.M. and Luciano Canonici, O.F.M. (Biblioteca Francescana, Chiesa Nuova, vol. 1) (Assisi: Ed. Porziuncola, 1978), 160. Boccali's n. 3 on this text explicitly states that half of the manuscripts say *Mariae Magdalenae* instead of simply *Mariae.*

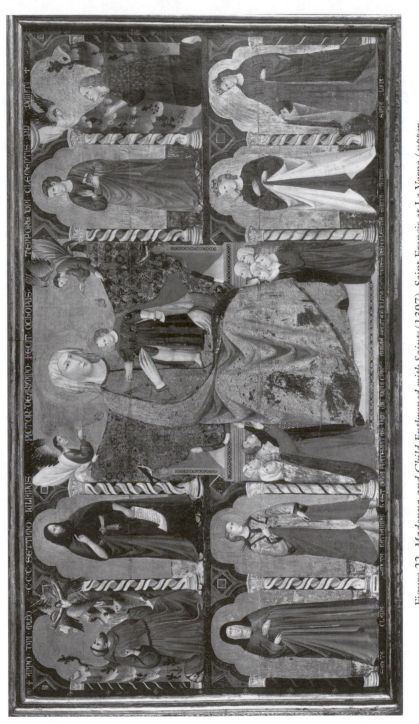

Figure 22. *Madonna and Child Enthroned with Saints* (1307). Saint Francis at La Verna (*upper left*) and Mary Magdalen at La Sainte-Baume (*upper right*). Panel painting made for a female confraternity (represented at the Virgin's feet) by Giuliano da Rimini, Isabella Stewart Gardner Museum, Boston. (Photo: Isabella Stewart Gardner Museum)

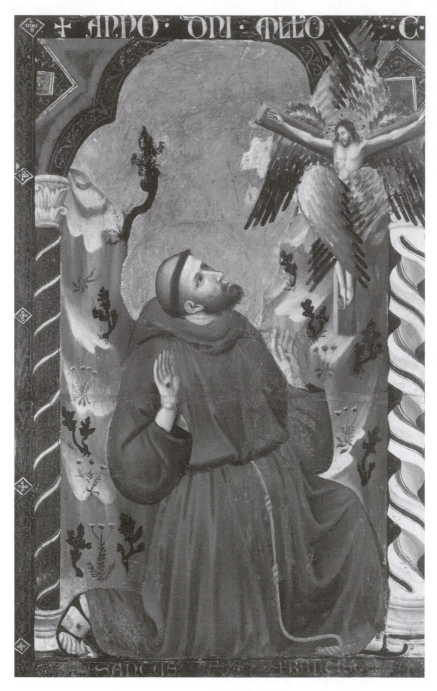

Figure 23. *Saint Francis at La Verna*. Detail of Fig. 22.

Figure 24. *Mary Magdalen at La Sainte-Baume*. Detail of Fig. 22.

lowing the naked one, far removed from the world and unknown to all people, just like one reads about Mary Magdalen and many other saints; to wit, he offered himself up to death, by preaching of the faith and by witnessing Jesus Christ to the Saracens and the other infidels, and by suffering every harsh torment."[71] These few sentences provide a wealth of information about mendicant *mentalité*. Mary Magdalen is invoked as the example whom Francis followed in following Christ. Following in her footsteps, he became a contemplative recluse, as well as the naked follower of Christ, preaching and suffering for the faith.

These last three chapters have shown how through recourse to symbolic gender reversal the mendicant friars not only cast themselves, but were considered by others to be new Magdalens, particularly in their capacity as inheritors of the apostolic life. They have also shown how the friars recommended the Magdalen as a model to both the laity and women under monasticism. The friars did so because they identified closely with Mary Magdalen's special relationship with Christ, her active mission in the world, her retreat into contemplative mysticism, and her unwavering devotion to the Lord. Nevertheless, there were limits to such self-identification and modeling: the friars by no means identified with every aspect of her life. Indeed, in the next two chapters we will examine how the preachers distanced themselves from the Magdalen's vanity and sexuality, subjects which alternatively fascinated and repelled them. As much as they manipulated symbolic language to identify with the apostolic Magdalen, so they also used the language of gender to denounce her perceived weaknesses. In the chapters that follow we will examine how and why the friars used the symbol of the Magdalen to attack the vanity, folly, and sexual licentiousness ascribed to all women. In the name of social amelioration the preachers attempted to control and subjugate the female sex through the symbol of Mary Magdalen.

[71] *Vita del povero et humile servo de Dio Francesco,* ed. Marino Bigaroni (Biblioteca Francescana, Chiesa Nuova, vol. 4) (Assisi: Ed. Porziuncola, 1985), 6.

PART TWO

The Wages of Sin

FIVE

"Vanity of Vanities, All Is Vanity"

(Eccl. 1: 2)

On the eve of the Lenten season of 1497 and again in 1498, Girolamo Savonarola exhorted the citizens of Florence to rise up and cast their vanities onto a burning pyre. In one fire-and-brimstone sermon he thundered:

> O lustful ones, dress yourselves in hair-cloth and do that penance which you need! . . . O you who have your houses full of vanities and pictures and indecent things and evil books . . . bring them to me to make a bonfire or a sacrifice to God. And you, mothers, who adorn your daughters with so much vanity and extravagance and fancy hair ornaments, bring all these things to us to throw into the fire, so that, when the wrath of God comes, He will not find them in your houses.[1]

Savonarola's bonfire of vanities and the incendiary prophetic sermons that provoked them are well known, if not notorious; they are not, however, unprecedented in the history of preaching. Three-quarters of a century earlier, Bernardino da Siena, after a week of impassioned Lenten preaching, incited those Florentines gathered in the piazza of Santa Croce to burn their vanities with the rallying cry, "to the fire!"[2] One and a half centuries

---

[1] Translated by G. M. Puccia in Ray C. Petry, *No Uncertain Sound: Sermons that Shaped the Pulpit Tradition* (Philadelphia: Westminster Press, 1948), 299. For his works, see *Edizione Nazionale delle Opere di Girolamo Savonarola*, 24 vols. (Rome: A. Belardetti, 1955–). A good introduction to Savonarola and his times is Donald Weinstein, *Savonarola and Florence: Prophecy and Patriotism in the Renaissance* (Princeton: Princeton University Press, 1970).

[2] Bernardino da Siena, *Le prediche volgari*, ed. Ciro Cannarozzi, O.F.M. (Quaresimale Firenze 1424) 2 vols. (Pistoia: Cav. Alberto Pacinotti & Co., 1934), vol. 2, 87. For Bernardino's other vernacular sermon cycles, see *Le prediche volgari*, ed. C. Cannarozzi (Quaresimale Firenze 1425), 3 vols. (Florence: Libreria Editrice Fiorentina, 1940); *Le prediche volgari*, ed. C. Cannarozzi (Predicazione, Siena 1425), 2 vols. (Florence: E. Rinaldi, 1958); and *Prediche volgari sul Campo di Siena 1427*, ed. Carlo Delcorno (Milan: Rusconi, 1989), a critical edition

earlier, another famous Franciscan preacher, Berthold of Regensburg (d. 1272), recommended the fire for female vanities. Counseling husbands to take the upper hand in such matters he preached:

> Thou art a man after all, and bearest a sword, yet thou art easily conquered with a distaff. Take courage, and pluck up heart and tear it [her veil] from her head, even though four or ten hairs should come away with it, and cast it into the fire! Do thus not thrice or four times only; and presently she will forebear. It is fitting that the man should be the woman's lord and master.[3]

The particular objects of reprimand in a medieval sermon condemning vanity were, naturally enough, subject to change according to circumstances and audience; the one element that usually remained constant in such sermons was the preacher's appeal to sinners to take Mary Magdalen as an example. They were exhorted to purge themselves of the vanities, curiosities, and superfluities of this world as she had done. Or as Bernardino da Siena had counseled: "Following the example of the most holy Magdalen, let fruitless and empty profane love be transformed into the fullness of sacred love."[4]

Medieval preachers regarded the pre-conversion Magdalen as the symbol of vanity, a venial sin; but more often, she represented vanity's dire consequence, *luxuria,* one of the seven deadly sins. This symbolic representation invited preachers and moralists to develop their views on the nature of women, or what critics in our own day would refer to as issues of sex and gender. Thus the aim of this chapter is to use sermon literature as a point of departure revealing medieval gender ideology in the making. This chapter also lays the groundwork for the discussion of prostitution that follows in chapter 6.

Vanity, lust, prostitution: how did these things pertain to the sketchy facts of Mary Magdalen's life as recorded in the gospels? In a word: they did not. The two chapters in this section argue that preachers made them conform to the rather vague biographical facts of her life in order to address exigent questions about the nature of Woman, women's place in society, the need for female protection, and the problem of prostitution. In

---

of the Sienese cycle of 1427 that supersedes P. Bargellini, *Le prediche volgari* (Milan: Rizzoli & Co., 1936). Near the end of his life, with an eye on posterity, Bernardino translated his vernacular sermons into Latin and inserted learned references throughout. These are the sermons edited by the Franciscan fathers in S. Bernardini Senensis, *Opera Omnia,* 9 vols. (Quaracchi: Collegio S. Bonaventurae, 1950–65).

[3] Translated by G. G. Coulton in Petry, *No Uncertain Sound,* 213. For Berthold of Regensburg, see Frank G. Banta, "Berthold von Regensburg," in *Die deutsche Literatur des Mittelalters, Verfasserlexikon,* 8 vols. (Berlin: Walter de Gruyter, 1978–), vol. 1, 817–23.

[4] *Sermo 46,* in *Opera Omnia,* vol. 2 (1950), 73.

other words, preachers and moralists invented a Magdalen in order to address what they perceived to be a woman-problem.

"There Was a Sinner in the City" (Luke 7:36)

In the gospel of Luke (7:36–50), the evangelist describes an event in the life of Christ, the medieval interpretation of which continues even today to imbue the reputation of Saint Mary Magdalen. This passage narrates simply that an unnamed female sinner, carrying an alabaster jar of ointment, entered the house of Simon the Pharisee where Jesus was dining. Standing behind him, she bathed his feet in her tears, dried them with her hair, and then anointed them with her oils. The Vulgate referred to the woman in question simply as *peccatrix*, female sinner. Western Christendom identified this woman as Mary Magdalen.

Why did medieval exegetes sully Mary Magdalen's good name by identifying her with this unnamed and unknown sinner? Three reasons can be posited. First is that in Luke's subsequent chapter (8:2), Mary Magdalen is named as one of Christ's female followers, the one from whom Christ cast out seven devils. The second reason, again, perfectly sensible, is that the other three gospels refer to an anointing of Christ at Bethany. In both Matthew (26:6–7) and Mark (14:3), the anointing is performed by a woman (though not called a sinner); but rather than minister to his feet, she pours her oils on the Lord's head. In these two accounts, the proprietor of the house is called Simon the Leper, creating room for confusion with Luke's Simon the Pharisee. The narrative of John 12: 1–3 is similar to the synoptic representations of the anointing but differs in regard to two significant points. The anointing still takes place at Bethany with the woman anointing Christ's feet and drying them with her hair, but in this telling Jesus is the guest of Martha, and the woman doing the anointing is called Mary. The third reason for Mary Magdalen's identification as the female sinner is the famous Gregorian conflation of Marys, encountered earlier, which constituted Saint Mary Magdalen out of three disparate scriptural figures, including Luke's unnamed sinner. Moreover, in that very same homily, Gregory had allegorized Mary of Magdala's seven demons as the seven capital sins. In so doing, the pontiff transformed Mary of Magdala's demonic possession into a disease of the soul caused by sin. Consequently her physical symptoms became outward signs of the sinful sickness afflicting her soul. Henceforth she was known as *peccatrix*.[5]

---

[5] *Homilia 33*, in *XL Homiliarum in evangelia*, Lib. II, *PL* 76, 1239. For the history of the seven capital sins, see Morton Bloomfield, *The Seven Deadly Sins: An Introduction to the History of a Religious Concept with Special Reference to English Literature* (East Lansing, MI: Michigan State College Press, 1952).

What then was the sin of the unnamed sinner? Although the evangelist did not specify the sin of his *peccatrix,* nonetheless there was no doubt in the minds of medieval exegetes that hers was a sexual sin, a sin of the flesh. Sins of the flesh were not all sexual in nature of course—gluttony was a sin of the flesh—but a woman's sin was inevitably construed as one involving sexuality. Sexual sins such as the public display of one's body, fornication, and prostitution were categories of sin primarily reserved for women.[6] The perception that the Magdalen had sinned sexually was reinforced by another episode in the New Testament, the story of the woman taken in adultery as related in John 8:3–11. She too was an unnamed sinner whom Christ had defended and then blessed, commanding her to sin no more. Mary Magdalen was rarely mistaken for this woman but sermons stressed their likeness. In a sermon focusing on the Magdalen's pre-conversion life, the Franciscan preacher Luca da Padova recited verbatim the draconian Mosaic law that decreed the stoning of adulteresses (John 8:5).[7] As such the two unnamed sinners were, if not conflated, at least popularly associated with each other.

In the chapters in Part One we examined how preachers and hagiographers filled in the missing details on the canvas of the Magdalen's post-ascension life; they did likewise for her pre-conversion *vita.* The scriptural silences gave license to flights of the imagination, and the lacunae were filled up with resourcefulness and brio. Cavalca shamelessly proclaimed his technique of elaborating Mary Magdalen's pre-conversion life thus:

> It delights me to tell of the Magdalen, and what she did at this time according to my fancy. The truth remains stable in its place, and by the grace of God, I hold no opinion, nor believe any other than what is taught by the holy mother Church; and those thoughts of mine that are not affirmed by the Church, I do not affirm at all. But it rejoices and delights me to be imagining such things to the profit of this our mother the Church.[8]

Since it was widely accepted that Mary Magdalen was Luke's sinner, hagiographers and preachers undertook to explain why she had descended into the depths of moral turpitude. To do so, medieval writers turned first to the Magdalen's youth to uncover the reasons why she had surrendered to the temptations of sin.

---

[6] See Ruth Mazo Karras, "Holy Harlots: Prostitute Saints in Medieval Legend," *Journal of the History of Sexuality* 1/1 (1990): 3–32.

[7] "Unde signatur in muliere illa Jo .viii. que fuit deprehensa in adulterio et moyses sive lex moysii 'mandavit [nobis] huius[modi] lapidare.'" MS Antoniana 466, f. 268v; *RLS* 4: 95.

[8] Domenico Cavalca, *Vite de' santi padri,* ed. Bartolomeo Sorio and A. Racheli (Milan: l'Ufficio Generale di Commissioni ed Annunzi, n.d.), 355. *The Life of Saint Mary Magdalen. Translated from the Italian of an Unknown Fourteenth Century Writer.* Trans. Valentina Hawtrey (London: John Lane, The Bodley Head, 1904), 137.

Wealth, Freedom, and Beauty

Although preachers and hagiographers disagreed frequently about certain pieces of biographical data pertaining to Mary Magdalen's life, they were all in agreement about her lineage. As Humbert of Romans phrased it: she descended from *stirpe regia,* royal stock, a point he made sure to italicize in his sermon directed at noble women.[9] The early tenth-century sermon from Cluny, examined earlier, claimed not only that the Magdalen was of distinguished bloodlines but also, according to the laws of inheritance of her times, an heiress.[10] The twelfth-century Cistercian text, also previously examined, elaborated the Magdalen's *vita* narrating that her mother was called Eucharia and came from the royal house of Israel, while her father Theophilus descended from noble satraps and was the governor of Syria and its surrounding maritime territories.[11] Moreover, Theophilus "was later moved to become a disciple of Christ by his teaching, and renouncing his worldly power, followed humbly in his footsteps."[12] As for siblings, the Magdalen had two: Martha, the Lord's active hostess, and Lazarus, whom Christ, out of compassion for the two distraught sisters, had raised from the dead. Their patrimony included a portion of Jerusalem over which Lazarus was lord, Bethany, Martha's domain, and the *castellum* of Magdala from which Mary took her name.[13]

As the proprietor of Magdala, Mary Magdalen received rents and owned

[9] *Stirpe regia:* from Humbert of Romans sermon, *de sancta Maria Magdalena,* in Simon Tugwell's critical edition, *De eruditione predicatorum* (Oxford: Oxford University Press, forthcoming). For Humbert's *ad status* sermon to noble women, see Humbert of Romans, *De eruditione praedicatorum,* in *Maxima bibliotheca,* vol. 25, ed. Marguerin de la Bigne (Lyons: Anissonius, 1677), 504.

[10] *PL* 133, 714. Hagiography and sermons are all in agreement on this point. André Vauchez has argued that in the later Middle Ages the preponderant number of saints in non-Mediterranean Europe were of royal lineage. See A. Vauchez, *La sainteté en occident aux derniers siècles du Moyen Age d'après les procès de canonisation et les documents hagiographiques* (Bibliothèque des Écoles Française d'Athénes et de Rome, fasc. 241) (Rome: l'École Française de Rome, 1981), 209–15. See also Vauchez, "*Beata Stirps:* Sainteté et lignage en occident aux XIIIe et XIVe siècles," in *Famille et parenté dans l'occident médiéval (Collection de l'École Française de Rome,* 30 [1977]), ed. Georges Duby and Jacques Le Goff, 397–401.

[11] There is general agreement on the name Eucharia. Theophilus is also known as Syrus, probably a confusion with his nationality. See, for example, Jacobus de Voragine, *Golden Legend,* trans. William Granger Ryan, 2 vols. (Princeton: Princeton University Press, 1993), vol. 1, 375.

[12] *PL* 172, 1433. *The Life of Saint Mary Magdalen and Her Sister Martha,* trans. David Mycoff (Cistercian Studies Series, 108) (Kalamazoo, MI: Cistercian Publications, 1989), 28–29. This is the *vita* once attributed to Rabanus Maurus.

[13] See, for example, Jacobus de Voragine, *Golden Legend,* vol. 1, 375, and Pietro de' Natali, *Catalogus sanctorum* (Venice: Nicolaus de Frankfordia, 1516), 257.

slaves, as Cavalca's *vita* narrated.[14] By all accounts and keeping with her noble station, she was wealthy. According to mendicant preachers (who in theory had rejected all individual and corporate wealth), love of riches was the source of all evil. The author of the *Thesaurus Novus* taught in a Mary Magdalen sermon that wealth was no protection against sin because riches cause gluttony. Carnal concupiscence, it was argued further, was one consequence of gluttony. Thus riches led inevitably to carnal sin. Preachers did not hesitate to hold Mary Magdalen's affluence accountable for her dissolute way of life.[15]

Another great difficulty with wealth, preachers argued, was that it allowed too much time for idleness, time that the wily devil booked with sinful appointments. The *Thesaurus Novus* in the same Magdalen sermon, preached that indolence taught much wickedness, and quoting Seneca it solemnly concluded: "Leisure is the burial of an active person."[16] Prescriptive tracts recommended that women occupy themselves with spinning, needlework, and weaving, otherwise the devil would make work for idle hands. Charity was also an appropriate way to fill up those potentially dangerous hours of leisure.[17] The Magdalen, however, engaged in none of these recommended activities; therefore, it was argued, she created congenial circumstances for the seductions of the devil.

Another condition of the Magdalen's pre-conversion life which allowed her, in the preachers' view, to sink to the depths of depravity was the unfettered liberty she enjoyed. She was an autonomous woman, under the control of no man.[18] According to some versions of her legend, her father had died prematurely and her brother Lazarus, consumed by his military career, had no time to look out for his sister's welfare. Without male supervision she fell into the clutches of the devil.[19] Other legends suggest that Mary Magdalen was the jilted bride left standing at the altar at Cana when John the Evangelist received his calling from Christ. Still others tell

[14] Cavalca, *Vita*, 348; *Life*, 101.

[15] "Si eris dives non eris immunis a peccato. Nam divitie causant gulam ex qua sequitur carnalis concupiscentia." *Sermo 102*, in *Sermones Thesauri Novi de sanctis* (Strasbourg: Martinus Flach, 1488), unpaginated; *RLS* 5: 275–83.

[16] "Multam maliciam docuit ociositas. Sen. Ocium est vivi hominis sepultura." Ibid.

[17] See Carla Casagrande, "The Protected Woman," trans. Clarissa Botsford, in *Silences of the Middle Ages*, ed. Christiane Klapisch-Zuber (*A History of Women in the West*, vol. 2) (Cambridge, MA: Belknap Press of Harvard University Press, 1992), 96–97.

[18] This condition would have been anomalous in late medieval Tuscany. David Herlihy and Christiane Klapisch-Zuber, using the Tuscan Catasto of 1427, report that 97% of 25-year-old women were either married or widowed. They further argued that nearly 90% of 15-year-old girls were married. David Herlihy and Christiane Klapisch-Zuber, *Tuscans and Their Families: A Study of the Florentine Catasto of 1427* (New Haven: Yale University Press, 1985), 215.

[19] Jacobus de Voragine, *Golden Legend*, vol. 1, 375.

a different story: the Magdalen ran off to the fleshpots of Jerusalem after fleeing a husband in Magdala.[20]

Whichever legend one chose to believe, the unshakable fact still remained that the Magdalen was outside the realm of male supervision, a grave danger to a young woman's moral development. In the view of medieval moralists, female nature more naturally inclined toward sin. Without male wisdom to guide her, they argued, a woman was easily seduced into wickedness. This was the line taken by the author of the *Thesaurus Novus* in regard to the saint: "She was a free woman [and] feared no one. Gregory the Great says: 'Where there is no fear of a censor, the seducer beckons more easily.' Thus there is no advantage to women being left in liberty, following their own will." He concluded his analysis of the Magdalen's situation by citing Saint Paul's injunction that women submit themselves to their husbands (Eph. 5:22).[21]

Those comments, laconic and schematic as they are, illustrate how medieval gender discourse was constructed. Supported by authorities such as Aristotle, the Hebrew bible, Saint Paul, and Saint Augustine, it effectively naturalized the female sex into a condition of inferiority. As is well known, women were regarded as the fragile sex: not only were their bodies weaker, so correspondingly, it was argued, were their intellectual capacities and powers of moral discrimination. Indeed, by recourse to Aristotle, whose theories about the sexes had entered the medieval intellectual economy, a Giles of Rome (d. 1316) could argue: "The soul matches the constitution of the body; women's bodies are limp and unstable, and so women are unstable and unsteady in desire and will."[22] Isidore of Seville's etymology of *mulier* (woman) suggested that the word derived from *mollitia* which

---

[20] Cavalca, citing Jerome, suggested that Mary Magdalen was the betrothed of John the Evangelist: "I like to think that the Magdalen was the spouse of John, not affirming it . . . I am glad and blythe that St. Jerome should say so." *Vita*, 329; *Life*, 2–3. In 1449 King René gave to the cathedral of Angers the amphora from Cana in which Jesus changed water to wine. He acquired it from nuns of Marseilles who told him that Mary Magdalen had brought it with her from Judea. See Jacques Levron, *Le bon roi René* (n.p.: Arthaud, 1972), 154. Others vehemently rejected the tradition of her betrothal to the Evangelist. Jacobus de Voragine dismissed it stating that it was a "false and frivolous" tale; *Golden Legend*, vol. 1, 382. Honorius Augustodunensis suggested she ran away from an unnamed husband in Magdala, *PL* 172, 979. Still other hagiographers suggested that her life of sin began as youthful folly; for example, the Cistercian *vita*, *PL* 112, 1434; *The Life*, 30.

[21] "Libera enim fuit neminem timuit. Gregorius. Ubi non timetur reprehensor securius accedit temptator. Ideo non est proficuum mulieribus ut relinquantur in earum libertate et propria voluntate." *Sermo 102, Sermones Thesauri*, unpaginated. Giovanni da San Gimignano also identifies her freedom—"*facultas libertatis*"—as a reason for her sin. MS BAV Barb. lat. 513, f. 99v; *RLS* 3: 378.

[22] Cited in C. Casagrande, "The Protected Woman," 87. For Giles of Rome, see F. del Punta, S. Donati, and C. Luna, "Egidio Romano," *DBI* 42 (1993), 319–41.

could mean softness, weakness, or wantonness.[23] Thus women's soft, weak bodies echoed in form their irrational, emotional, morally inferior natures. Or as the Aristotelian-inspired Dominican Aldobrandino da Toscanella (d. after 1293) preached: "Woman is, just as the Philosopher maintains in *On Animals,* a defective male. Whence one says *mulier* because of *mollis.* And indeed she [Mary Magdalen] was truly weak because she did not resist those things bearing down on her, but rather she flung herself willingly at them."[24]

If pagan philosophy was not adequate proof of the natural inferiority of women, preachers could always turn to the Hebrew bible, a veritable gold mine of evidence cataloging women's failings and frailties. Resorting to essentialist theory, Eve was invoked time and again to prove female disability. Giovanni da San Gimignano maintained in a Magdalen sermon that when the devil approached Adam and Eve, he went not to the man who was stronger, but to the woman who was more apt to be seduced.[25] The preaching king, Robert of Naples (d. 1343), explained in one of his Magdalen sermons that a woman frequently runs into adversity because "she is incautious and because she does not believe all that she sees and hears according to reason. Because she is malleable, she is inclined easily either from evil to good, or from good to evil. . . . Hence, because of her inconstancy of mind, the first woman, Eve, trusted at once in the instigations of the devil."[26]

As we saw in the *Thesaurus Novus* sermon, medieval preachers often quoted the epistles of Saint Paul, offering as they did an infallible source of women's fallibility. Medieval theologians and preachers found Pauline arguments particularly irresistible since they rested on an incontrovertible and hierarchical celestial principle. The apostle had summarized divine law

---

[23] Isidore of Seville, *Isidori Hispalensis Episcopi Etymologiarum sive Originum,* ed. W. M. Lindsay, 2 vols. (Oxford: Clarendon Press, 1911), vol. 2, Lib. XI. ii. 18.

[24] "Mulier sicut vult philosophus est mas occasionatus in libro *de animalibus.* Unde dicitur mulier quia mollis. Et vere mollis fuit ipsa quia opprimentibus se non resistebat sed se voluntarie ingerebat." MS BAV Chig. C. IV. 99, f. 36r; not listed in *RLS.* For Aldobrandino da Toscanella, see *Scriptores,* vol. 1 (1970), 40–46. Aristotle's notorious formulation can be found in *Generation of Animals,* trans. A. L. Peck (Loeb Classical Library) (Cambridge, MA: Harvard University Press, 1943), II, iii, 175.

[25] "Unde volens dyabolus primos parentes inducere ad peccandum non a viro incepit qui erat fortior sed a muliere que erat fragilior et ideo labilior." MS BAV Barb. lat. 513, ff. 99r–99v; *RLS* 3: 378.

[26] "Primo inquam est mulier naturaliter incurrens inadvertentiam ex levitate etc. Sexus enim mulieris incautus et mollis est ut dixit Chrysostomus super Mattheum. Incautus quidem quia non omnia que videt et audit cum ratione considerat. Mollis quia facile flectatur vel de malo ad bonum vel de bono ad malum. . . . Hinc est quod prima mulier Eva ex levitate et inadvertentia diabolo suggerenti cito credidit." MS Marc. lat. Cl. III. 76 (2101), f. 89r; *RLS* 5: 227.

in this way: "But I would have you know, that the head of every man is Christ; and the head of the woman is the man; and the head of Christ is God" (I Cor. 11:3). Berthold of Regensburg, as we saw earlier, alluded to these words when he encouraged husbands to take charge of their vain and disorderly wives, while countless medieval preachers and theologians reiterated these words in regard to the pre-conversion Mary Magdalen, who, freed from male custody, had subverted the divinely ordained hierarchy.

As was to be expected, the fathers of the Church also took a dim view of female independence. Preachers endlessly quoted Augustine on the subject of female custody. Here is Jacobus de Voragine in a Lenten sermon for the Thursday before Palm Sunday:

> Indeed since Woman is weaker and Man stronger, so with regard to Woman four restraints must be applied as Augustine says in *de decem chordis*. They are: fear of God, vigilant male protection, modesty and embarrassment in the world, and fear of the public laws, which condemn adulterous women. And Augustine adds: therefore because Woman is weaker greater restraint must be used.[27]

Thus it was deemed necessary for masculine reason to take custody of feminine folly, but particularly so when female foolishness was coupled with great beauty. Medieval preachers frequently invoked Proverbs 11:22 to argue that foolish beauty was no better than a pig with a golden ring through its snout, since beauty (unaccompanied by reason) would sink itself in the filth of carnal sin, much like a pig wallows in mud. Each combination of beauty/unattractiveness and wisdom/foolishness was analyzed by the preachers for its relative dangers. According to the Franciscan Luca da Bitonto (d. 13th c.), beauty and wisdom were the winning combination because wisdom kept a woman out of trouble. The next best combination was unattractiveness coupled with foolishness since no one harasses an unattractive woman. "But when a woman is beautiful and foolish then it is a danger because the beautiful woman is indeed harassed by many people, and since she is foolish, she doesn't know how to protect herself."[28]

---

[27] "Quia enim mulier magis fragilis est et homo magis virilis, ideo circa mulierem quatuor custodiae sunt adhibendae. Sicut dicit Augustinus libro *de decem chordis* quae sunt timor Dei, diligens custodia viri, verecundia, et confusio mundi, et terror legum publicarum, quae uxores fornicarias condemnant . . . Et subdit Augustinus: Ideo mulieri adhibenda est maior custodia, quia in ea est maior infirmitas." *Sermones Quadragesimales* (Venice: Iohannes Baptista Somaschus, 1571), 162. Luca da Bitonto had read his Augustine, too. In his Lenten sermon for the same day, he preached: "Quia mulier est homine magis fragilis et infirma ideo sibi debetur maior custodia." MS Casanat. 17, f. 67r; not in *RLS*. Cf. Ubertino da Casale, *Arbor vitae* (Venice: De Bonettis de Papa, 1485), Lib. 3, cap. 22, unpaginated.

[28] "Mulier pulcher [*sic*] et fatua. Sicut enim sus habens circulum aureum in lutum se immerget, sic mulier habens pulchritudinem carnalia se immerget. Nam quando mulier est pulcra et sapiens non est periculum quia sapientia se conservat. Nec si est turpis et fatua nemo

Preachers and hagiographers may have been discreetly silent about the Magdalen's intellectual failings,[29] but they were anything but reserved when it came to singing the praises of her legendary beauty.

Domenico Cavalca gushed that "she was the most beautiful woman that could be found in the world, excepting the Virgin Mary."[30] The Magdalen's Cistercian biographer wrote this panegyric on her beauty:

> Now Mary, from the time she became a woman, shone in loveliness and bodily beauty: handsome, well-proportioned, attractive in face, her hair a marvel, sweet in mind, decorous and gracious in speech, her complexion a mixture of roses and the whiteness of lilies. All graces shone in her form and beauty, so much so that she was said to be a masterwork of God.[31]

Ubertino da Casale observed that the Magdalen was in mortal danger because she was beautiful, rich, and lived under the control of no one. Bernardino da Siena added yet another danger to this combustible mixture: "if a fourth item is added, i.e., fickleness or foolishness, then may God help her!"[32] Heaven help the fragile woman, her powers of ratiocination and moral scruple enfeebled by her sex, when cursed by the quadruple threat of wealth, freedom, beauty, and foolishness. The Cistercian author explained how the Magdalen's marvelous beauty, combined with her great wealth, put her at risk:

> But because outward beauty is rarely allied to chastity, and an affluence of possessions may often be an enemy to continence, when she became a young woman, abounding in delights and rejoicing in a noble heart, she, as is usual at that age, followed after the pleasures of the flesh. Vigorous youth, attractive shape, and many riches enervate good conduct; a beautiful body and a heart inclined to pleasure breathe forth false sweetness and profane love; nobility of blood, grace of speech and many possessions destroy the heart's pru-

---

eam molestat. Sed quando est pulcra et fatua tunc est periculum quia enim pulcra sollicitatur a multis. Et quia fatua custodire se nescit." MS Casanat. 17, f. 67r. For Luca, see Pierre Péano, "Luc de Bitonto," *DS* 9 (1976), 1121–22. Jacobus de Voragine preaches almost verbatim the same passage, *Sermones Quadragesimales*, 161–62. Cf. Giovanni da San Gimignano, MS BAV Barb. lat. 513, f. 99v.

[29] Most hagiographers passed over the question of the Magdalen's intelligence in silence, but at least two deemed it necessary to comment on her intellectual prowess. Cavalca says she was a great intellect but marred by evil desires; *Vita*, 329; *Life*, 1. The anonymous Cistercian says she and her siblings were intelligent and literate in Hebrew letters. *Vita*, *PL* 112, 1433; *Life*, 29.

[30] *Life*, 1; *Vita*, 329.

[31] *Life*, 30; *Vita*, *PL* 112, 1433–34.

[32] "Nam pulchra fuit: dives fuit: et sub nullius potestate extitit." *Arbor vitae*, Lib. 3, cap. 22, unpaginated. Bernardino: *Opera Omnia*, vol. 3 (1956), 419.

dence; in short, the hotness of youth, the desires of the flesh, the weakness of the sex all turn one away from bodily chastity.[33]

The Cistercian was patient with the Magdalen's shortcomings; Bernardino da Siena was not. Using the swinish image from Proverbs 11:22, he preached that like that pig with the golden ring through its snout, so was the Magdalen before tumbling headlong into the muck of *luxuria*.[34] What then did the golden ring signify? It was the preachers' symbol of vanity, a vice that seduced women in particular since their inherently weak natures rendered them unable to resist its siren call.[35]

Vanity

The history of vanity has yet to be written, but if one were to pursue its tracks in the historical record, one would do well to begin by reading through legal codes of the ancient world. Both Solon and Augustus, no doubt reacting to economic pressures, tried to outlaw vanity by enacting sumptuary laws regulating extravagance in fashion and behavior.[36] A close reading of the Hebrew bible would provide further insight into the ancient meaning of vanity and its social implications. One need turn only to the pages of *Ecclesiastes* to grasp the all-encompassing sense of the word that obtained in ancient Judaism. As for Christianity, one would do well to cast an eye over the epistles of Saint Paul. He set the tone for Christian society when he wrote that women ought to "adorn themselves in modest apparel, with shamefacedness and sobriety; not with braided hair, or gold, or pearls, or costly array" (1 Tim 2:9). The vanity of the world, as represented by precious metals, jewels, and modish hairstyles, he starkly contrasted against simple modesty, the symbol of Christian virtue.

Many early Christian writers also expounded on the subject of vanity. The author of the *Didascalia,* the apostolic constitutions of the third century, Clement of Alexandria, Cyprian, Jerome, and John Chrysostom, to name just a few, all contributed to the anti-vanity discourse.[37] In his *de*

---

[33] *Life,* 30; *Vita, PL* 112, 1434.

[34] Ibid.

[35] Berthold of Regensburg preached that women "go to church more readily than men, and ye pray more readily than men, and come to hear preaching and to earn indulgences more readily than men; and many of you would be saved but for his [the devil's] one snare, which is called vain glory and empty honor." Translated in Petry, *No Uncertain Sound,* 212.

[36] For a brief introduction to sumptuary laws in the ancient world, see Sarah B. Pomeroy, *Goddesses, Whores, Wives, and Slaves: Women in Classical Antiquity* (New York: Schocken Books, 1975), 46, 57, 63, 131, 182.

[37] See Gábor Klaniczay, "Fashionable Beards and Heretic Rags," in *The Uses of Supernatural Power: The Transformation of Popular Religion in Medieval and Early-Modern Europe,* trans. Susan Singerman (Princeton: Princeton University Press, 1990), 57.

cultu feminarum, Tertullian narrowed his sights to address the problem of female vanity, arguing among other things, that vanities such as makeup, jewelry, and precious dyes were invented by fallen angels and granted to sinful women, the daughters of Eve.[38]

Such, in a nutshell, is the tradition that medieval preachers inherited.[39] They themselves made a significant contribution to the discourse by personalizing it: they employed the Magdalen as their great symbol. In his thirty-third homily, Gregory the Great established the theme on which all subsequent preachers played variations. Following the law of *contrappasso,* he argued that because the Magdalen (in fact, Luke's anonymous *peccatrix*) had made satisfaction for her sins with her eyes, hair, mouth, and oils, therefore she must have used them for wicked purposes in the past. The subject of the Magdalen's vanities itself became a vanity, as it were, inasmuch as besotted medieval writers spent endless hours lingering on detailed descriptions of them. They suggested that her eyes which now wept bitter tears of contrition once had sinned by batting their eyelashes, casting sidelong glances here and there, and gazing at trifles.[40] The Magdalen's mouth, which now humbly kissed the Lord's feet, had once given lascivious kisses to lovers, eaten delicacies, sung silly songs, recited love poems and little nonsense ditties, all the while laughing in jest.[41] Her oils, which she now offered as a tribute to the Lord, she had used once to perfume herself in the service of lust.[42]

---

[38] Translated as "The Apparel of Women," in Tertullian, *Disciplinary, Moral and Ascetical Works,* trans. Edwin A. Quain, S.J. (The Fathers of the Church, vol. 40) (New York: The Fathers of the Church, 1959), 119. He devotes chapter 8 to male vanity.

[39] For medieval preachers on vanity see: A. Lecoy de la Marche, *La chaire française au Moyen Age* (Paris: Librairie Renouard, 1886), 428–49; Thomas M. Izbicki, "Pyres of Vanities: Mendicant Preaching on the Vanity of Women and Its Lay Audience," in *De ore Domini: Preacher and Word in the Middle Ages,* ed. Thomas Amos et al. (Studies in Medieval Culture, vol. 27) (Kalamazoo, MI: Medieval Institute Publications, 1989), 211–34; Marie-Anne Polo de Beaulieu, "La condamnation des soins de beauté par les prédicateurs du Moyen Age (XIIIème–XVème siècles)," in *Les soins de beauté. Moyen Age début des temps modernes* (Actes du IIIe Colloque International, Grasse [26–28 April 1985]) (Nice: Centre d'Études Médiévales de Nice, 1987), 297–310; and Diane Owen Hughes, "Regulating Women's Fashion," in *Silences of the Middle Ages,* ed. Christiane Klapisch-Zuber, *A History of Women in the West,* vol. 2, 136–58.

[40] For her eyes, see Bernardino da Siena, *Le prediche volgari* (Quaresimale del 1425 [Firenze]), vol. 3, 182, and Servasanto da Faenza: "[Mulieres] offendunt enim Christum in oculorum nucibus respiciendo inhoneste." MS Antoniana 490, 101r; not listed in *RLS.*

[41] Bernardino da Siena, ibid.; Remigio de' Girolami: "Prius os ad oscula venerea nunc ad oscula sancta pedum Christi," MS Flor. Naz. Conv. Sopp. D. 1. 937, f. 232r; *RLS* 5: 806, and Peregrinus de Oppeln: "Ore etiam superbe locuta fuerat et indisciplinate," MS BAV Pal. lat. 465, f. 154v; *RLS* 4: 147.

[42] A Franciscan preacher now known only as Pseudo-Anthony of Padua concocted an elaborate metaphorical history of the Magdalen's sinful oils imagining that first she gathered the herbs of sin, then ground them up in her thoughts, and finally cooked them in her heart, aflame with depraved desires. He preached: "Et illud unguentum peccatorum haec mulier

But it was her hair above all else that drew the most exorbitant commentary. Preachers argued that her abundant hair that now served humbly to dry Christ's feet had once been curled, crimped, and bedecked with ribbons and knots for the sinful purpose of attracting suitors.[43] Giordano da Pisa scolded Florentine women for their excesses by telling them that the poor were suffering while they blithely continued to adorn their heads with decoration costing the princely sum of two hundred gold florins. It was an obscenity in his view, and the reason why the city was tormented by so many afflictions. He urged women to take the Magdalen as their example and make satisfaction for their vanities. He fulminated:

> One woman will put one hundred florins' worth of gold on her head for decoration's sake. Now what is this? And the poor do not even have clothes to cover themselves, nor anything to eat: and that sack of dung holds one hundred or two hundred gold florins on her head in ornamentation, and the unlucky husbands consent to it, and they lose their souls too. They should make laws and proclamations about such vanity, if they were the sort of men they ought to be. Do not marvel that these superfluities which women are engaging in is one of the reasons for the destruction of this city, because God abominates and holds contemptible excesses and superfluities. And therefore the Magdalen . . . made satisfaction. And this is shown when she made a lovely white kerchief of her hair to wash those blessed feet of Christ.[44]

Because hair was associated with female sexuality, and because it was regarded as a superfluity,[45] but also because preachers believed that upper-class women (in imitation of prostitutes) were spending vast amounts of time and money on their own elaborate hairstyles and ornaments, the Magdalen's copious hair provoked endless tirades from the pulpit. Combs, hair-

---

prius confecerat per hunc modum. Primo namque collegit herbas peccatorum, quae copiose inveniuntur in horto mundi, collegit dico per sensus: per vagationes visus, auditus, et sic de aliis sensibus, deinde trivit per modum pulmenti cogitationes ipsius, deinde in olla cordis sui igne pravi desiderii coquit, quo facto inungitur, dum, scilicet opus exterius prodit, in tantum aliquando, quod malus odor peccati diffunditur per hanc domum. . . . Sed hoc unguentum factum fuit ad corporis lasciviam vel delectationem, sicut debuit fieri ad salutem animae." *Sancti Francisci Assisiatis, minorum Patriarchae nec non S. Antonii Paduani, eiusdem ordinis, Opera Omnia* (bk. 2), ed. Iohannes de la Haye (Stadt am Hof: Ioannes Gastl, 1739), 123.

[43] Cf. Servasanto da Faenza who says that the Magdalen offended Christ: "In capillorum cultibus crispando, frixiando," ibid., and Innocent III: "Mulier haec olim capillos composuerat ad decorem et crines crispaverat ad ornatum, circumvolvens illos variis ligaturis, circumvolutionibus eos ligans ut intuentium in se provocaret affectus." MS BAV Arch. Cap. S. Petri D. 211, 79v; not listed in *RLS*.

[44] *Racconti esemplari di predicatori del Due e Trecento,* ed. Giorgio Varanini and Guido Baldassarri, 3 vols. (Rome: Salerno Ed., 1993), vol. 2, 375–76.

[45] Ugo da Prato Florido: "Capilli enim corporis superfluitates sunt per quos bona temporalia designantur." MS Vall. C. 80, f. 56v.

pieces, trains, and other decorations were routinely condemned as diabolical inventions.[46] Bernardino da Siena even used the occasion of a Magdalen sermon to condemn hair coloring. He accused the saint (whom medieval artists had anachronistically envisioned as blond) of bleaching her hair and sun-drying it to make it even more golden.[47] Preachers also warned, using Absalom as their example, that too much concern about one's hair could be lethal. Listeners were reminded that vain Absalom's hair had been his undoing: his abundant locks, having gotten entangled in the boughs of an oak tree, suspended him there until his enemies found him hanging helplessly and shot him through with darts.[48]

Though preachers indulged their fantasies about the Magdalen's vanities, they never wandered too far from the parameters that Gregory the Great had established for them. Now and then, preachers added another vanity or two to the list. Agostino d'Ancona, for example, accused the Magdalen of squandering her fortune on jesters and actors, while Remigio de' Girolami suggested that she had also sinned with her ears, nose, and feet.[49] For the most part, however, preachers adhered to the Gregorian canon of Magdalenian vanities.

Late medieval dramatists, on the other hand, had no such scruples. From the rather modest Gregorian catalog of vanities, they imagined that the Magdalen had given her entire life over to vain pleasures. They represented her as having dedicated herself to a spiritually shallow life of games, songs, dancing, and merry-making of every sort.[50] A play of the early sixteenth century represented a Magdalen consumed by vanities, much to the consternation of pious Martha who had come to beseech her sister to hear

[46] Lecoy de la Marche, *La chaire,* 439–40, and Hughes, "Regulating Women's Fashion," 145.

[47] *Le prediche volgari* (Quaresimale del 1425 [Firenze]), vol. 3, 182. Tommaso Agni da Lentini also preached about the Magdalen's tinted hair; see MS Vat. lat. 4691, f. 114r; not listed in *RLS*. Haskins reminds us that treatises on beauty, such as that of Firenzuola, directed that beautiful hair was considered "fine and blonde, similar to gold or honey or to the rays of brilliant sunshine." She also cites a seventeenth-century description of how Venetian women lightened their hair by sitting in the sun. See *Mary Magdalen,* 247–48.

[48] 2 Sam. 14: 25–26 and 18: 9–15. Cf. Ugo da Prato Florido: "Absalon . . . et postea per capillos suspensus interfectus fuit," ibid.; *Thesaurus Novus:* "Nam non bene successit absaloni," *Sermo 103, Sermons Thesauri,* unpaginated; Luca da Padova, MS Antoniana 466, f. 268v; *RLS* 4: 94.

[49] Agostino: "Fuit crudelis et insensibilis cum ipsa divicias sibi a patre eius relictas non pauperibus et indigentibus sed ioculatoribus et hystrionibus largiretur." MS Angelica 158, f. 122r; *RLS* 1: 126. Remigio: "Prius aures ad verba carnalia et mundana nunc ad verba spiritualia et divina. Prius nares ad odores florum et unguentorum nunc odores morum. . . . Prius pedes ad discursus vagos, nunc ad accessus devotos ad Christum. Denique totum corpus ad luxuriam nunc ad sanctimoniam. Unde Gregorius in Omelia." MS Flor. Naz. Conv. Sopp. D. 1. 937, f. 232r.

[50] For a good resumé of such scenes in medieval drama, see Haskins, *Mary Magdalen,* 163–68.

Jesus' preaching. Mary Magdalen, preoccupied with party preparations, sharply dismissed her sister's request with this rebuff: "Since I am busy with the entertainment and the party, having prepared songs, music and dancing, I would like you to leave immediately."[51]

Dancing came in for particular condemnation by medieval preachers. Jacques de Vitry (d. 1240), the preacher's preacher, inveighed against all forms of it in his sermons. He likened women's songs and dances to a demonic liturgy: "The woman who leads the chorus is the chaplain of the devil; those who respond are her priests."[52] Another preacher censured the innocent round thus: "It is a dance whose center is the devil and all lean toward the sinister side."[53]

According to the preachers Mary Magdalen's pre-conversion behavior—including her dancing—was to be condemned not imitated. But clearly there were those who thought otherwise, as an incident of 1249 recorded in the episcopal visitation register of Eudes Rigaud reveals. Upon visiting the priory of Villarceaux, where twenty-three nuns and three lay sisters were in residence, Eudes was dismayed to find the sisters living a rather disorderly life, not unlike the life of the pre-conversion Magdalen. In a disciplinary letter to the priory Eudes warned:

> We decree that no more saffron shall be placed on the veils, that the hair be not arrayed in vain curls, nor shall silver or metaled belts, or the skins of divers and wild animals be worn, nor shall the hair be allowed to grow down below the ears. Item, we forbid you to continue the farcical performances which have been your practice at the feast of the Innocents and of the Blessed Mary Magdalen, to dress up in worldly costumes, or to dance with each other or with lay folk.[54]

The unruly sisters of Villarceaux clearly associated vanity, frivolity, and dancing with the feast-day of Mary Magdalen, despite the preachers' persistent and escalating condemnations. Indeed, dancing became so associated with the Magdalen that by the early modern period choreographed dances were even named in her honor.[55] Though an early sixteenth-

---

[51] "Un miracolo di Santa Maria Maddalena," in Alessandro d'Ancona, *Sacre rappresentazioni dei secoli XIV, XV e XVI*, 3 vols. (Florence: Successori le Monnier, 1872), vol. 1, 395. Cf. "Conversione di Maria Maddalena e resurrezione di Lazzaro" (anon., 15th c.), in *Le sacre rappresentazioni italiane. Raccolta di testi dal secolo XIII al secolo XVI* (N.p.: Bompiani, 1942), 257. For an introduction to medieval drama, see Karl Young, *The Drama of the Medieval Church*, 2 vols. (Oxford: Clarendon Press, 1933; repr. 1951).

[52] Cited in C. Casagrande, "The Protected Woman," 85.

[53] Cited in Lecoy de la Marche, *La chaire*, 447n. 2.

[54] *The Register of Eudes of Rouen*, trans. Sydney M. Brown, ed. Jeremiah F. O'Sullivan (New York: Columbia University Press, 1964), 49–50.

[55] See H. Colin Slim, "Music and Dancing with Mary Magdalen in a Laura Vestalis," in *The Crannied Wall: Women, Religion, and the Arts in Early Modern Europe*, ed. Craig A. Monson (Ann Arbor, MI: University of Michigan Press, 1992), 139–60.

century engraving of Lucas van Leyden is now entitled "The Dance of the Magdalen," it is bereft of dancing; what it does depict is the worldliness that characterized the Magdalen's pre-conversion life. Out for a *passaggiata* in the countryside, on the arm of a male companion, the Magdalen is surrounded by amorous couples, scenes of the hunt, music-making, and general profane revelry.[56]

Although a popular theme in sermons and sacred drama of the Middle Ages, and unlike the baroque period, the Magdalen's vanities were not well represented in medieval art. In only two Italian fresco cycles is her voluptuous pre-conversion life depicted, and then, with reserve. In an early Quattrocento cycle in her eponymous church in the vineyards just outside Bolzano, she is shown dressed to the nines, a revealing skirt slit thigh-high while the neckline and hem of her garment drip with furs. She is accompanied by a foppish suitor, also dressed à la mode. On her right, a troubled Martha seems to be speaking words of rebuke (Fig. 25).[57] In Cusiano, she is shown in all her splendid finery, surrounded by male admirers, while a banderole beneath her feet explains in the vernacular: "How Mary Magdalen was in her castle where she gave herself to the pomp and vanity of the world" (Fig. 26).[58] A fifteenth-century German ecclesiastical vestment, embroidered with episodes from her life, also contained this scene envisioned in a unique way. Here, a seated Mary Magdalen, resplendent in sumptuous garments and an ostentatious headdress, is encircled by animal-headed suitors who obsequiously hold a mirror so that she can inspect her appearance (Fig. 27).[59] The theatricality of the scene suggests that its representation was influenced by sacred plays which, as we have seen, elaborated this episode of her life.

The pleasures that vanity brought were alas ephemeral, unlike those offered in the heavenly kingdom. The fourteenth-century Dominican preacher Siboto underscored this theme in his fourth Magdalen sermon. He preached against the world and its transitory delights thus:

> The first desert is this world. According to Isaiah 40: "I am a voice crying out in the desert." This desert abounds in transitory and lethal things. . . . These

---

[56] Both the Uffizi and the British Museum own examples of this engraving dated 1519. It is reproduced in both *La Maddalena tra sacro e profano,* ed. Marilena Mosco (Milan: Mondadori, 1986), 257, and in Haskins *Mary Magdalen,* fig. 24.

[57] The cycle is reproduced in Helmut Stampfer's booklet on the church, *La chiesa di Santa Maddalena presso Bolzano* (Bolzano, 1988).

[58] The cycle dates from 1470 to 1497 and is attributed to the brothers Giovanni and Battista Baschenis di Averaria. For the frescoes, see Quirino Bezzi, "Gli affreschi di Giovanni e Battista Baschenis di Averaria nella chiesa di S. Maria Maddalena di Cusiano," *Studi Trentini* 49 (1970): 358–71.

[59] For the vestment, see chap. 2, n. 61. The animal-headed suitors were presumably represented as such because of the lust that Mary Magdalen's beauty had aroused in them, effectively reducing them to beasts.

Figure 25. *Vanity: The Pre-Conversion Magdalen* (early 15th c.). Martha rebukes her sister Mary. Fresco from the Church of S. Maria Maddalena, Bolzano. (Photo: Author)

pleasures consist in the works of the flesh, in beautiful clothing, and makeup, but they are delights one must flee and loathe.[60]

Preachers regarded expensive finery, eye makeup, hair dye, rouge, trains, jewels, and ornaments as follies, or worse. Vanity was a lethal distraction because it diverted attention from the most exigent of problems: the salvation of the soul. But preachers also suggested that vanity threatened the here and now. According to late medieval preachers, the most pressing problem associated with vanity was that the damage done was not restricted to the one who luxuriated in its pleasures; the fabric of society itself was threatened by a preoccupation with vanities. First, vanity hurt the poor because all the money that should have gone to their succor was frittered away on unnecessary luxuries.[61] Second, it enriched the Jews because it en-

[60] "Primum desertum dicitur mundus iste. Iuxta illud Ys .xl. 'Ego vox clamantis in deserto.' Istud desertum habet delitias in deserto transitorias et mortiferas . . . Iste delitie consistunt in operibus carnis, in pulcris vestibus et ornatu faciei, sed iste delitie sunt fugiende et detestande." MS BAV Vat. lat. 6005, f. 113v; not listed in *RLS*. For Siboto, see F. J. Worstbrock, "Siboto," *Die deutsche Literatur des Mittelalters*, 8 vols. (Berlin: Walter de Gruyter, 1978–), vol. 8 (1992), 1138–40.

[61] Bernardino da Siena devotes chapter 4 of *Sermo 46* (a Lenten sermon) to this theme in *Opera Omnia*, vol. 2 (1950), 81.

Figure 26. *Vanity: The Pre-Conversion Magdalen* (1470–97). Mary Magdalen and suitors. Fresco by Giovanni and Battista Baschenis de Averaria in the Church of S. Maria Maddalena, Cusiano (prov. Trentino). (Photo: Fototeca del Servizio Beni Culturali della Provincia Autonoma di Trento)

Figure 27. *The Symbol of Vanity* (first half of 15th c.). Mary Magdalen surrounded by animal-headed suitors. Detail of Fig. 4. (Photo: Herziana)

couraged usury. Since the cost of luxury goods was so high, families would be forced to take out usurious loans to buy them, or so the anti-Jewish argument ran.[62] Third, vanity injured society because men, unable to marry and maintain a wife and family in the sumptuous style they were accustomed to expect, turned instead to sodomy.[63] Fourth, it was a drain on the financial resources of a city, particularly if that city was at war. It was not coincidental that a sumptuary law regulating fashion and table was enacted in the Angevin Kingdom of Naples during the protracted war with Aragon following the Sicilian Vespers. Fittingly, the law was decreed to go into effect 22 July 1290, the feast-day of Mary Magdalen.[64]

Though vanity was considered a venial sin by most theologians,[65] it was nonetheless considered a henchman to the mortal sin of pride. Tertullian had argued that the application of makeup was in some sense a criticism of God's handiwork: "Surely they are finding fault when they try to perfect and add to His work, taking these their additions, of course from a rival artist. This rival artist is the Devil."[66] The devil had fallen from grace through pride, and by resorting to the diabolical trickery of makeup, women too sinned against God through pride. In medieval treatises on the virtues and vices, vanity can often be located in the chapter on pride, as in the Dominican preacher Stephen of Bourbon's *De superbia et eius speciebus*.[67]

More often, however, vanity allied itself with *luxuria*, another capital sin, defined by the theologians as an inordinate craving for carnal pleasure. It

---

[62] See Diane Owen Hughes, "Distinguishing Signs: Ear-rings, Jews, and Franciscan Rhetoric in the Italian Renaissance City," *Past and Present* 112 (1986): 24–25, 28. See also Hughes, "Regulating," 146.

[63] Richard Trexler, *Public Life in Renaissance Florence* (New York: Academic Press, 1980), 380–81.

[64] Giuseppe del Giudice, *Una legge suntuaria inedita del 1290* (Naples: Tipografia della Regia Università, 1887). The law was decreed by the vice-regents for Charles II, Mary Magdalen's devoted follower. For analyses of Italian sumptuary laws of this period, see Diane Owen Hughes, "Sumptuary Law and Social Relations in Renaissance Italy," in *Disputes and Settlements: Law and Human Relations in the West*, ed. John Bossy (Cambridge: Cambridge University Press, 1983), 69–99, and James Brundage, "Sumptuary Laws and Prostitution in Late Medieval Italy," *Journal of Medieval History* 13 (1987): 343–55, now collected in *Sex, Law and Marriage in the Middle Ages* (Aldershot: Variorum, 1993).

[65] Thomas Aquinas argued that if women adorn themselves out of vanity rather than lust they do not always sin mortally. *Summa Theologiae*, Blackfriars edition, vol. 44 (*Parts of Temperance*), 2a 2ae. q.169, a.2, 236–37 In the later medieval period this distinction did not always obtain. See Izbicki, "Pyres," 219–23.

[66] *The Apparel of Women*, 136.

[67] In *Le traité des sept dons du saint esprit*, composed around 1250–61 and edited in A. Lecoy de la Marche, *Anecdotes historiques, légendes et apologues tirés du recueil inédit de E. de Bourbon* (Paris: Librairie Renouard, H. Loones, 1877).

was believed that women, due to their cold and wet biological natures, were particularly prone to this sin. As such, it was inevitably personified as a woman.[68] Preachers argued that women, indulging in vanity, deceived men into becoming fornicators. The argument usually went like this: Women's makeup, fancy hairstyles, jewelry, perfumes, and fine clothing— artifices all—were nothing but traps designed to ensnare naive and gullible men. "Dressed like a whore ready for ensnaring souls," a phrase from Prov. 7:10, was quoted endlessly in Mary Magdalen sermons. Jacobus de Voragine, in a Lenten sermon that took as its theme the Magdalen's conversion, preached that beauty is a liar because it deceives many. He compared female beauty to burning embers, a shining sword, a beautiful apple, each one a deception for unwary young men. When touched the embers burn, the sword wounds, and the apple reveals its worm-infested core.[69] An early modern English commentator was more gruesomely succinct. For him, fashionable women were "painted coffins with rotten bones."[70] Jean Gobi the Younger, a Dominican at Saint-Maximin, summed up the sentiments of many when he concluded his essay on women with these words: "Woman is a deceiver of men."[71] *Luxuria* was born, at least in the late Middle Ages, from an excess of just about anything. Giacomo della Marca (d. 1476) argued that touching, regarding, smelling, caressing, and singing could all engender *luxuria*.[72] *Luxuria*, then, was very easily brought into this world; the problem was that it was not so easily extinguished. Like the potential damage wrought by a piece of burning ember, a whole city (to say nothing of its inhabitants, lay and clerical alike) could be consumed by the sins of one *luxuriosa*. This is what Eudes de Châteauroux preached in a Magdalen sermon:

[68] For the medieval discourse concerning women and *luxuria*, see Mario Pilosu, *La donna, la lussuria e la chiesa nel Medioevo* (Genoa: ECIG, 1989). For the personification of the virtues and the vices, see Adolf Katzenellenbogen, *Allegories of the Virtues and Vices in Medieval Art: From Early Christian Times to the Thirteenth Century*, trans. Alan J. P. Crick (New York: W. W. Norton and Co., 1964; first published by The Warburg Institute, University of London, 1939). For an example of vainglory represented as a woman (being crushed under the foot of John the Evangelist along with Pride and Avarice), see Giovanni del Biondo, *Saint John the Evangelist* (Uffizi, Florence), reproduced as fig. 71 in Millard Meiss, *Painting in Florence and Siena after the Black Death: The Arts, Religion, and Society in the Mid-Fourteenth Century* (Princeton: Princeton University Press, 1951).

[69] "Vana est pulchritudo. Est enim vana: quia cito transit. Et est fallax quia multos decipit. Pulchritudo enim mulieris est sicut carbo fulgidus: est sicut gladius splendidus; est sicut pomum pulchrum, plenum vermibus. Pueri igitur videntes carbones fulgentes eos tangunt, et comburuntur, videntes gladios splendentes eos accipiunt et vulnerantur, videntes poma pulchra exterius et interius faetida, eligunt et decipiuntur." *Sermones Quadragesimales*, 162.

[70] Joseph Swetnam, cited in Hughes, "Regulating," 143–44n. 10.

[71] Polo de Beaulieu, "La condamnation," 304.

[72] *Sermo 4*, in *Sermones Dominicales*, ed. Renato Lioi, O.F.M., 4 vols. (Falconera M.: Biblioteca Francescana, 1978), vol. 1, 109.

O how blackened was that ember: namely, the Blessed Magdalen since she had been blackened by the sin of *luxuria*. That lighted ember set her whole neighborhood afire, indeed fire is increased from a scintilla. Sometimes, in fact, a lighted ember flames, and even burns down an entire great city. Indeed, it was not enough to set fire to the city of Magdala—her native city—unless she could burn down that city and, possibly, the holy city of Jerusalem. Whence Luke 7 says: "There was in the city a sinner." And just as it is not enough to burn down enemy villages and cities, unless both the monasteries and holy places burn which are in them; so it follows that it was not enough for her to inflame lay and poor people with the fire of her lust unless she could ruin clerics and religious too.[73]

Medieval preachers believed that one peccadillo attracted another, and then another, until finally the hapless sinner was delivered into the arms of mortal sin itself. The Franciscan Jean de La Rochelle (d. 1245) argued that "a sinner adds sin to sin."[74] Thus a dalliance with vanity, in the preachers' view, would lead ineluctably to an affair with *luxuria* and possibly worse. Jacques de Vitry represented the chain of events this way: a virgin gazing in the mirror

> smiles to see if this makes her more beautiful. . . . She lowers her eyes; is she more pleasing with her eyes wide open? She pulls her dress to one side to reveal bare skin, loosens her sash to reveal her cleavage. Her body is still home, but in God's eyes she is already in a brothel, trussed up like a whore preparing to ensnare the souls of men.[75]

We may regard this *exemplum* as polemical overstatement; medieval people did not. From time immemorial vanity and bodily adornment were regarded as signs of harlotry. For Bernardino da Siena the semiotic system was crystal clear: "Whorish appearance is the sign of whorish character."[76] There was no arguing with such logic. If you dressed like a whore and acted like a whore you were considered a whore. Medieval preachers took it as

---

[73] "O quot denigravit iste carbo: id est Beata Magdalena quoniam peccato luxurie erat denigrata. Iste carbo succensus totam suam viciniam inflammabat a scintilla enim ignis augetur. Aliquando enim unus carbo succensus totam unam magnam civitatem inflammat et comburit. Enim non suffecit incendere opidum de quo erat id est Magdalum nisi et ipsam civitatem combureret et fortassis sanctam civitatem Ierusalem. Unde dicitur Luca .vii. Erat quaedam mulier in civitate peccatrix et sicut non suffecit inimicis comburere villulas nisi et civitates comburant et monasteria et loca sancta que in eis sunt. Sic talibus non suffecit igne luxurie sue incendere laicos et pauperes nisi clericos et religiosos comburant." MS AGOP XIV. 35, f. 182r; *RLS* 4: 948.

[74] "Peccator peccatum peccato addidit." MS Angelica 823, f. 154r; *RLS* 3: 141. For Jean, see Ignace Brady, "Jean de La Rochelle," *DS* 8 (1974), 599–602.

[75] Cited by C. Casagrande, "The Protected Woman," 93.

[76] *Sermo 44*, in *Opera Omnia*, vol. 2 (1950), 50.

axiomatic that Mary Magdalen had been a prostitute before her penitential conversion at the house of Simon the Pharisee. Her *vita,* padded with
hagiographers' fantasies about her youthful vanity, vanity's notorious link
with *luxuria,* and her identification as Luke's *peccatrix,* provided preachers with unassailable evidence that Mary Magdalen indeed had been a
whore. The image of her sordid past, how the friars capitalized on it, and
to what ends medieval society used it, is the focus of the next chapter.

SIX

"There Was a Sinner in the City"

(Luke 7:36)

A Franciscan preacher from Marseilles, embroidering the prophet Jeremiah (Jer. 3:3), suggested in a Mary Magdalen sermon that "a
prostitute is someone who keeps herself from no one, offers herself to
everyone, and sells herself for a moderate price."[1] His explanation is very
close indeed to the canon law definition that defined a prostitute in both
legal and moral terms. Drawing on Roman law, a woman was considered
a prostitute if she offered her body in return for remuneration.[2] But canon
law, suffused as it was in moral theology, also regarded a woman as a prostitute if she made any sort of public display of herself, exhibited lust in any
way, or if she simulated love.[3] Consequently, in the minds of most medieval
commentators the sin of *luxuria,* or lust, was inextricably bound up with
prostitution.

This chapter examines the reasons why Mary Magdalen was tarred with
the brush of *luxuria* and consigned to the brothel. It shows how Mary

---

[1] "Frons meretricis est que nulli se prohibet, omnibus se offert, et modico pretio se
vendit." MS BAV Vat. Borgh. 138, f. 150r; *RLS* 9:99. A selected list of studies on medieval
prostitution includes: James A. Brundage, "Prostitution in the Medieval Canon Law," *Signs*
1/4 (1976): 825–45; E. Pavan, "Police des moeurs, société et politique à Venise à la fin du
moyen âge," *Revue historique* 264 (1980): 241–88; Richard Trexler, "La prostitution
florentine au XVe siècle: patronages et clientèles," *Annales E.S.C.* 6 (1981): 983–1015.
Translated as "Florentine Prostitution in the Fifteenth Century: Patrons and Clients," in
Trexler, *The Women of Renaissance Florence,* vol. 2 of *Power and Dependence in Renaissance
Florence,* 3 vols. (Asheville, NC: Pegasus Press, 1993), 31–65.; Leah Lydia Otis, *Prostitution
in Medieval Society: The History of an Urban Institution in Languedoc* (Chicago: University
of Chicago Press, 1985); Jacques Rossiaud, *Medieval Prostitution,* trans. Lydia G. Cochrane
(Oxford: Basil Blackwell, 1988); Ruth Mazo Karras, "Holy Harlots: Prostitute Saints in
Medieval Legend," *Journal of the History of Sexuality* 1/1 (1990): 3–32; Maria Serena Mazzi,
Prostitute e lenoni nella Firenze del Quattrocento (Milan: Mondadori, 1991); and Karras,
Common Women: Prostitution and Sexuality in Medieval England (Oxford: Oxford University
Press, 1996).

[2] Brundage, "Prostitution," 825–27.

[3] Ibid., 827.

Magdalen, suffused as she was deemed to be in the sin of *luxuria,* was deployed by preachers and moralists to initiate a discussion about the perils of prostitution. Sermons for the Magdalen's feast-day and penitential Lenten sermons featuring the pre-conversion saint gave the preachers a platform to discuss the problem of prostitution, one of the many social ills that afflicted medieval society.

A no less important aim of this chapter is to examine the solution to the problem of prostitution proposed by the preachers. Friars such as the Augustinian Simone Fidati da Cascia founded refuges for reformed prostitutes while the sermons of his fellow friars inspired concerned citizens to action. The later medieval period saw the emergence of the convent for *convertite,* penitent prostitutes, an institution founded in the name of Christian charity, the mission of which was to offer an alternative life to those prostitutes who repented their wicked ways. These convents, in fact, served also as custodial institutions, where women were protected from the worst instincts of their own "nature." Most commonly, such institutions were placed under the protection of Mary Magdalen, the patron saint of repentant prostitutes. In the previous chapter we examined Mary Magdalen's dalliance with vanity and its link to *luxuria.* Now we must turn to *luxuria*'s notorious relation to prostitution.

Luxuria[4]

Identified as Luke's sinner, but lacking scriptural evidence about the specific nature of her transgression, preachers and hagiographers attributed the usual female sins of vanity and *luxuria* to Mary Magdalen. Once tainted by *luxuria,* however, all it took was a leap of the imagination to transform the female sinner (*peccatrix*) into a prostitute (*meretrix*).[5] Let us now examine some of the more imaginative leaps that preachers made in their efforts to cast Mary Magdalen as a whore.

James Brundage has pointed out that canon law considered promiscuity a crucial component in the legal definition of prostitution.[6] Preachers rep-

---

[4] I use the evocative Latin term rather than the English word "lust," which in its current usage is too one-dimensional, focusing solely on libidinous desire. For a discussion of female sinner-saints and their association with *luxuria,* see Erhard Dorn, *Der Sündige Heilige in der Legende des Mittelalters* (Munich: Wilhelm Fink, 1967).

[5] Not everyone accepted that Mary Magdalen had been a common whore. Cavalca suggested, "I know well that the Magdalen had that sin in her heart, but I cannot believe that she yielded to it, as many will have it said; but her brazen ways and the other sins that she committed were quite enough to render her infamous." *Vita,* 330; *Life,* 9. And in a jab at the women of his own period he added: "If they had lived in the Magdalen's time they too would have been called prostitutes." Ibid. (My trans.)

[6] Ibid., 827.

resented the Magdalen as a promiscuous woman: she was a captive of *luxuria,* a victim of an "extraordinary sexual appetite."[7] According to the tenets of medieval science, women, on account of the cold and wet humors that characterized their physical makeup, possessed insatiable sexual appetites.[8] Apparently, Mary Magdalen was no exception. Allusions to her promiscuity were reiterated almost as many times as she herself was deemed to have been promiscuous. Preachers suggested that the adverb *ecce* attested her promiscuity. Ubertino da Casale claimed: "The evangelist shows the great number and magnitude of sins in relation to the sinner in the demonstrative adverb: *ecce mulier* because it signifies astonishment at her excess."[9] Giovanni da San Gimignano noted that just as a writer is not regarded a writer on account of one text, nor was the Magdalen called a sinner for one sin—it was because of the repetition of it.[10] The Dominican historian and preacher Martin of Troppau (d. 1278) agreed: "When one says sinner it is not because of one act, but because it has been repeated many times."[11] Ugo da Prato Florido noted that the word *peccatrix* designates the frequent repetition of the same sin and someone who has complied wickedly with everyone. And just in case the nature of the wickedness remained unclear he followed it up with a quotation from Jeremiah (3:1): "You are a fornicator with many lovers."[12]

Preachers argued that the Magdalen's endless repetition of vices ac-

---

[7] Antonino Pierozzi of Florence, *Summa theologica,* as cited in Mazzi, *Prostitute,* 79.

[8] See Joan Cadden, *Meanings of Sex Difference in the Middle Ages: Medicine, Science, and Culture* (Cambridge: Cambridge University Press, 1993). In the thirteenth century, Hugh of Saint-Cher identified avarice as the chief sin of men; fornication as the sin to which women were most inclined, see Haskins, *Mary Magdalen,* 430n. 50. See also Dorn, *Der Sündige Heilige,* 104–14.

[9] "Ostendit autem evangelista in peccatrice peccatorum multitudinem et magnitudinem in adverbio demonstrativo. 'Ecce mulier:' quod notat admirationem excessus." *Arbor vitae,* bk. 3, chap. 22, unpaginated. Bernardino da Siena, citing Ubertino, says the same thing, *Opera Omnia,* vol. 3 (1956), 418. Ugo da Prato Florido says: "Nam ecce est adverbium demonstrandi et interdum aliquid magnum demonstrat ut in Ysaias: Ecce virgo concipiet. . . . Sic facit hic: Ecce ergo mulier plena peccatis." MS Vall. C. 80, f. 56r–56v; not listed in *RLS.*

[10] "Non enim propter unum peccatum dicebatur peccatrix. Sicut nec per unam litteram quam homo scribat dicitur scriptor. Sed propter multa peccata dicitur peccatrix. Et notandum quod Magdalenam in multa peccata cadere fecerunt." MS BAV Barb. lat. 513, f. 99v; *RLS* 3: 378.

[11] "Cum dicit peccatrix quod non fuit ex actu uno sed actum peccati pluries iterando." *Sermo CXXLIII,* in *Sermones Martini Ordinis Praedicatorum penitentiarii domini pape de tempore et de sanctis super epistolas et evangelia cum promptuario exemplorum* (Strasbourg, 1488), unpaginated. For Martin, see André Duval, "Martin de Troppau," *DS* 10 (1980), 964–65.

[12] "Designat etiam peccatrix eiusdem mali actibus frequentem iterationem. Non enim dicitur peccatrix que solum semel vel solum cum uno male agit. Sed peccatrix dicitur que cum omnibus male facere est parata. . . . 'Tu es fornicata cum amatoribus multis.' Et sic patet culpa." MS Vall. C. 80, f. 56v.

counted for the loss of her name. (Recall that in Luke 7:36 she is called only *peccatrix*.)[13] According to a Franciscan known now only as Pseudo-Anthony of Padua, Mary Magdalen lost her name "because so long as sinners remain in sin, they have been deleted from the book of God."[14] Though she had lost her name, nevertheless no sinner was more famous than she. Eudes de Châteauroux likened Mary Magdalen's notoriety to that of a king in his own country. The sovereign's proper name was subsumed under the title "king" and everyone recognized him as such. By analogy, such was the case with the Magdalen. Everyone knew her as *peccatrix*.[15]

The notion that she was known by everyone reveals the very public character of her sin, yet another piece of circumstantial evidence indicating that indeed she had been a notorious prostitute. We noted earlier that Roman law tradition had considered any woman a prostitute who had put her body on display; the jurist Hostiensis (d. 1271) glossed the definition further by asserting that one must also take into consideration public notoriety.[16] Matteo d'Aquasparta's preaching reflected this modification: he remarked that Mary Magdalen was "a public and notorious woman." Aldobrandino Cavalcanti was even more adamant calling her a *"famosissima peccatrix,"* a most notorious sinner, while Innocent III referred to her as a "public prostitute available to everyone," because the whole city knew of her sin.[17]

The fact that she had conducted her sordid business in the city further signified the public nature of her sin.[18] Ugo da Prato Florido preached that

[13] For example: Agostino d'Ancona: "In tantum ut iam proprio nomine perdito peccatrix appellaretur." MS Angelica 158, f. 122r; *RLS* 1: 126. Cf: Aldobrandino da Toscanella, MS Angelica 812, f. 66r; *RLS* 1: 252; Jean de La Rochelle, MS Angelica 823, f. 154r; *RLS* 3:141 and Giovanni da San Gimignano, MS BAV Barb. lat. 513, f. 97r; *RLS* 3: 337, et al.

[14] "Nota non ponitur hic nomen, quia peccatores quamdiu sunt in peccato, de libro Domini sunt deleti." *Sancti Francisci Assisiatis, minorum Patriarchae nec non S. Antonii Paduani, eiusdem ordinis, Opera Omnia* (bk. 2), ed. Iohannes de la Haye, (Stadt am Hof: Ioannes Gastl, 1739), 12.

[15] "Sic rex non nominatur nomine proprio in regno suo sed nomine communi quia notorium est quis est rex in terra illa. Unde per antonomasiam intelligitur quis sit rex. Sic cum ista nominatur peccatrix in civitate per antonomasiam." MS AGOP XIV. 35, f. 188r; *RLS* 4: 950.

[16] Brundage, "Prostitution," 827.

[17] Matteo d'Aquasparta: MS Assisi 682, f. 197r; *RLS* 4: 79. See also Friar Ludovicus, MS Marc. lat. fondo antico 91 (1775), f. 16v; *RLS* 4:15; Aldobrandino Cavalcanti: MS BAV Borgh. 175, f. 28r; *RLS* 1:340 and Innocent III: "Magnum plane quia peccatrix erat, id est publica meretrix exposita universis; manifestum autem quia peccatrix erat in civitate, id est cuius peccatum tota civitas agnoscebat." MS BAV Arch. Cap. S. Petri D. 211, f. 79r; not in *RLS*.

[18] Preachers such as Aldobrandino da Toscanella accused the Magdalen of shamelessly conducting her business in the city, a place of sin: "fuit in ea defectus pudoris quia in civitate peccatrix ubi loca sunt peccatricum." MS BAV Chig. C. IV. 99, f. 36r.

she sinned openly in the city rather than locked away in her house while Eudes de Châteauroux told his audience that the Magdalen, who had once stood outside, sometimes in the marketplaces, sometimes in the public squares (as do prostitutes soliciting business), now was installed in heaven among the angels.[19]

Some preachers, recalling the days of public penance, argued that Mary Magdalen's satisfaction, made at the Lord's feet, was only congruent since public sin called for public penance. The Franciscan Iohannes de Castello summed up such sentiments thus: "She came into the banquet so that she who had sinned publicly might do public penance."[20] Others remarked the fitting congruity that the Magdalenian legends offered. Commenting on her eremitical retirement to the wilderness of Provence, it was frequently observed that she remained there for thirty years unknown to anyone; this, in contrast to her former notoriety.

Innocent III, in one of his two sermons for the Magdalen's feast-day, used the episode of Mary Magdalen's public penance to preach on the Lord's infinite kindness. Recalling the scene of the Magdalen's conversion at the Lord's feet, and using himself as a foil, he taught:

> I am the type, for instance, who if a prostitute wanted to touch me . . . I would immediately repel her with a kick, as if I might be fouled by contact with her. Not so, not so, He who came to call not the righteous but sinners.[21]

Aside from Innocent's splendid rhetoric, the passage discloses the conceit which most often described the problem of prostitution; namely that it was a potential pollutant to both body and society.[22] The sin of fornication was infectious: it harmed not just the prostitute but all who employed her services. After all, a prostitute does not sin alone, argued the preachers. Thus Mary Magdalen had compounded her sin by implicating others in it. Accordingly, the friar from Marseilles maintained that the Magdalen's

---

[19] Ugo: "Non in domo et clavi peccabat sed in civitate manifeste." MS Vall. C. 80, f. 56v. Cf: Siboto: "Peccabat enim non in occulto sed in publico." MS BAV Vat. lat. 6005, f. 113r and Eudes de Châteauroux: "Steterat nunc foris, nunc in plateis, nunc iuxta angelos insidiens." MS AGOP, XIV. 35, f. 189r.

[20] "Venit in convivio ut que publice peccaverat publice peniteret." MS Assisi 470, f. 494r; RLS 3:725.

[21] "Qualis forsan sum ego quem si publica meretrix tangere vellet . . . statim eam calce repellerem tanquam ex ipsius contactu fedarer. Non sic, non sic fecit ille qui non venit vocare iustos sed peccatores." MS BAV Arch. Cap. S. Petri D. 211, f. 79r.

[22] Prostitution imperiled the soul, but it also endangered the purity of society. By engaging in prostitution one could unwittingly violate racial taboos or the degrees of consanguinity. Eudes cites the Hebrew sanctions against intermingling in his discussion of Mary Magdalen and prostitutes: "Et filiis Israel inhibentur ne conceptam gentibus conubia miscent (Deut. 7)." MS AGOP XIV. 35, f. 189r. See Mary Douglas, *Purity and Danger: An Analysis of the Concepts of Pollution and Taboo* (London: Ark Paperbacks, 1985; repr.).

sins were more dangerous than most: her carnal sins defiled others and led them to mortal *culpa* and eternal damnation.[23] Iohannes de Castello served up a memorable metaphor on the same theme. In his version, Mary Magdalen symbolized the devil's saucepan in which she sautéed as many sinners as fell into her clutches. This vessel, he concluded, contaminated the many people who came into contact with it.[24]

The metaphor of *luxuria* as a form of pollution or contagious disease, found in both the works of Innocent III and Iohannes de Castello, is a leit-motif that runs throughout medieval literature. Preachers considered *luxuria* a sickness of the soul, indeed of the most infectious sort. Eudes de Châteauroux regarded it the most contagious of all sins. He preached:

> Thus whoever defiles himself with a lustful person envelops himself in lust. . . . For whoever will have touched a sinner will be polluted by her. For sin is a contagious disease and especially so is the sin of *luxuria*.[25]

Not coincidentally, theologians and preachers also regarded leprosy as a disease of the soul.[26] They moralized it, suggesting that the outward skin disorder was merely a manifestation of the inner sickness of the spirit, a soul deemed to be aflame with lust. The fourteenth-century Franciscan preacher, Nicolas d'Hacqueville, associated the two diseases of the soul. In the second of his Mary Magdalen sermons, after quoting Jeremiah on fornication (Jer. 3:1), he turned to II Kings 5: 1–14 and told lepers (sinners) to wash themselves thoroughly in the waters of the Jordan (the waters of

---

[23] "Sed qui peccat ita ut peccatum suum personam secundam transeat, peccat magis periculose quia peccatum ad plures extendit et sic peccavit Maria Magdalena. Quia peccata sua carnalia ad multas personas secundas transivit quas omnes et ad culpam mortalem et ad dampnationem eternalem quantum in se fuit perduxit." MS BAV Borgh. lat. 138, ff. 144v–145r; *RLS* 9: 96.

This is not the conventional theological position. Most preachers, following the theologians, drew a distinction between spiritual and carnal sins. They argued that a carnal sin (of the body) was less easy to resist, and therefore venial. A spiritual sin derived from the will and reason; therefore it was more culpable. A carnal sin was a sin against the body; a spiritual sin was a sin against God. See, for example, Giovanni da San Gimignano's lengthy disquisition on the subject, MS BAV Barb. lat. 513, f. 99v.

[24] "Talis lebes fuit Magdalena que ardore succensa libidinis multum exhibuit et in eam tot dyabolus coxit cibos quot peccatores in eius amore succendit . . . hoc lebes multos suo contactu polluit." MS Assisi 470, f. 494v; *RLS* 3: 726.

[25] "Sic qui communicat luxurioso induet luxuriam . . . Qui enim tetigerit peccatricem inquinabitur ab ea. Peccatum enim est morbus contagiosus et maxime peccatum luxurie." MS AGOP, XIV. 35, f. 182r; *RLS* 4: 948.

[26] For a study of leprosy in medieval society and literature, see Saul N. Brody, *The Disease of the Soul: Leprosy in Medieval Literature* (Ithaca, NY: Cornell University Press, 1974). For sermons to lepers, see Nicole Bériou and François-Olivier Touati, *Voluntate dei leprosus: les lépreux entre conversion et exclusion aux XIIème et XIIIème siècles* (Spoleto: Centro italiano di studi sull'alto medioevo, 1991).

confession). By so doing their flesh would be restored and they would be returned to a state of purity.[27]

Women, particularly prostitutes, were believed to be the primary transmitters of leprosy. Arnauld de Verniolles of Pamiers, whose testimony appears in Jacques Fournier's inquisitorial record, bears witness to this popular belief when he recalled his days in Toulouse: "One day I 'did it' with a prostitute. And after I had perpetrated this sin my face began to swell. I was terrified and thought I had caught leprosy."[28]

Popular belief and sophisticated metaphors connected prostitutes and therefore Mary Magdalen to leprosy, but so did some of her friends, relations, and forerunners. We saw in an earlier chapter that exegetes claimed that the prophetess Miriam, sister of Moses, prefigured Mary Magdalen. Significantly, Miriam had been afflicted and then miraculously cured of leprosy. Moreover, Matthew's telling of the Magdalen's conversion (26:6) transformed the host Simon the Pharisee into Simon the Leper. Finally, Lazarus, Martha and Mary's brother, was frequently conflated with the leprous beggar called Lazarus in Luke 16:20.

Yet another reason why Mary Magdalen *meretrix* was associated with lepers is that medieval society, ever vigilant of defilement and impurity, and therefore intolerant of difference, physically separated and regulated lepers and prostitutes at the margins of civil society.[29] The two groups were tol-

---

[27] "'Tu autem fornicata es cum amatoribus multis' . . . Reg. .v. dixit Eliseus ad Nahaman qui leprosus erat. Vade et lavare te septies in Jordane et recipiet caro tua sanitatem et mundaberis . . . Nahaman significat peccatorem quia leprosus erat." MS BAV Vat. lat. 1251, f. 16v; *RLS* 4: 137. For Nicolas, see Pierre Péano, "Nicolas d'Hacqueville," in *DS* 11 (1982), 283.

[28] Emmanuel Le Roy Ladurie, *Montaillou: The Promised Land of Error,* trans. Barbara Bray (New York: Vintage, 1979), 145. For women and leprosy, see Danielle Jacquart and Claude Thomasset, *Sexuality and Medicine in the Middle Ages,* trans. Matthew Adamson (Princeton: Princeton University Press, 1988), 177–93.

[29] In 1284 a statute from Pisa ordered: "We do not permit the diseased or the leprous in the city of Pisa, indeed we will have them expelled from the city." Similar bans can be found in the statutes of Florence, Siena, Lucca, and San Gimignano; see Ruggero Nuti, "Lo spedale del Ponte Petrino e la sua chiesa," *Archivio Storico Pratese* 5 (4): an. 10, fasc. IV, 152–58. Roberta Gilchrist, in her work on varieties of female monasticism in medieval England, finds a leper house dedicated to Mary Magdalen outside the city walls at Bootham, York, and a leprosarium outside the Magdalen gate in Norwich. See *Contemplation and Action: The Other Monasticism* (London: Leicester University Press, 1995), 40, 222. Presumably the hospitals dedicated to Mary Magdalen listed in Clay, *The Medieval Hospitals of England,* 279–324 as "without [the walls]" were leper hospitals. They are: Abingdon (Berkshire); Southampton (Hampshire); Winchester (Hampshire); Hertford (Hertfordshire); Newcastle-upon-Tyne (Northumberland); Bawtry (Nottinghamshire); Eye (Suffolk); and Chichester without Eastgate (Sussex). Following Clay, the counties are listed according to their traditional designations. For the regulation of prostitution at society's margins, see Otis, *Prostitution,* 77–88.

erated, but just. Town councils literally legislated their marginalization at the edges of cities, keeping them quarantined, as it were, from the healthy body politic. Humbert of Romans sharply reminded prostitutes of their impure moral condition when he compared brothels to toilets containing the foulest of filth.[30] Lepers were told similarly.

In England, Mary Magdalen was the supreme patron of lepers. Indeed, the "'Maudlin-house' was almost synonymous with leper hospital," while the phrase "mawdlyn lands" often denoted the site of a leper colony. The fear of infection explains why British leper houses, as well as those on the continent, were almost always outside the city gates and generally went by the designation "without the walls." We have already noted the many thirteenth- and fourteenth-century leper hospitals dedicated to the saint in Italy. It is now worth noting that at least three of those dedicated to Mary Magdalen were "without the walls." Among them was the Magdalen foundation outside Assisi's walls where Saint Francis spent the early period of his conversion working charitably for the welfare of the inmates at Rivo Torto. Others scattered throughout the peninsula were Santa Maria Maddalena *extra urbem* (now Monte Mario) in Rome and Santa Maddalena de' Malsani (unwell) on the outskirts of Prato (Tuscany).[31] As is only fitting, Jean Gobi the Elder's record of miracles from Saint-Maximin relates that

---

[30] *Ad mulieres malas corpore sive meretrices,* in *De eruditione praedicatorum,* in *Maxima bibliotheca,* ed. Marguerin de la Bigne (Lyons: Anissonius, 1677), vol. 25, 506. Medieval justification of the need for prostitution in society used precisely this metaphor. Augustine (*de ordine,* II, IV, 12) had argued, "Remove prostitutes from human affairs and you will unsettle everything on account of lusts." In the Middle Ages this text was glossed thus: "The public woman is in society what a bilge is in a [ship at] sea and the sewer pit in a palace. Remove this sewer and the entire palace will be contaminated." The gloss was believed to have been written by Augustine. Both texts cited in Rossiaud, *Medieval Prostitution,* 80–81.

[31] For England, see Clay, *Medieval Hospitals,* 252. For Assisi, see *Speculum Perfectionis (minus),* ed. Marino Bigaroni, O.F.M. [Pubblicazioni della biblioteca Francescana, Chiesa Nuova, vol. 3] (Assisi: Edizioni Porziuncola, 1983), 13 where it is suggested that this hospital bore a double dedication to Mary Magdalen and to Lazarus. There is another leprosarium called Santa Maria Maddalena de Archis listed in the Trecento and Quattrocento entries in Cesare Cenci, O.F.M., *Documentazione di vita assisana 1300–1448* [Spicilegium Bonaventurianum vols. 10–12] (Grottaferrata: Collegium S. Bonaventurae ad Claras Aquas, 1974), vol. 1, 69, 175, 179, 183, 279, 294; vol. 2, 770. For Rome, see Christian Huelsen, *Le chiese di Roma nel medio evo* (Florence: Leo Olschki, 1927), 379. For Prato, see Ruggero Nuti, "Lo spedale del Ponte Petrino e la sua chiesa" (3 part article) in: *Archivio Storico Pratese* 5(4) an. 10, fasc. IV: 152, 158; 5(5) an. 11, fasc. I: 17, 25; 5(5) an. 11, fasc. II: 81, 88 and Francesco Guerrieri, *La chiesa dello spedale del Ponte Petrino* (Prato, n.d.). For sanitary reasons Venice placed its *lazzaretto,* now called San Lazzaro degli Armeni, on one of the islands in the lagoon. It should be noted that the *decime* do not distinguish leprosaria from other ecclesiastical foundations.

the Magdalen healed a certain Jacobus, a citizen of Amalfi, of the disfiguring disease.[32]

As is well known, Jews too suffered segregation, regulation, ostracism, and worse. Preachers linked them to prostitution through money-lending. They argued that Jews profited from the wages of *luxuria* because usury increased alongside the demand for luxury items. After 1215, churchmen urged that Jews, like prostitutes, wear distinguishing signs on their clothing.[33] Late medieval statutes forbade Jews, prostitutes, and lepers from handling bread, fish, or meat, unless of course they bought it first.[34] Likewise, both prostitutes and Jews were compelled to participate in civic celebrations and festivals, willing or not. In Trecento Perugia the citizens, preparing for a battle against Arezzo, organized a competition "of whores with their skirts raised up to their belts."[35] Similarly, in fifteenth-century Florence, on the feast-day of Mary Magdalen, a race of prostitutes and young men was held in the courtyard of the commune's *podestà*.

Thus medieval society moralized, marginalized, and regulated its Jews, lepers, and prostitutes.[36] They were not outlawed, but in both body and

---

[32] Jacqueline Sclafer, "Iohannes Gobi Senior OP, 'Liber Miraculorum B. Mariae Magdalenae,'" in *AFP* 63 (1993): 198–200.

[33] See, for example, Diane Owen Hughes, "Distinguishing Signs: Ear-rings, Jews and Franciscan Rhetoric in the Italian Renaissance City," *Past and Present* 112 (1986): 30, 24. Among the many things Hughes argues in this suggestive article is that the signs Jewish women were forced to wear on their clothing were frequently identical to those legislated for prostitutes. Earrings, especially, served as the distinguishing sign Jewish women were compelled to wear in Italian cities in the later Middle Ages. Giacomo della Marca had preached that earrings are what "Jewish women wear in place of circumcision, so that they can be distinguished from other women." In one Sienese triptych (now in the Musée du Petit Palais, Avignon), Angelo Puccinelli of Lucca (active in Tuscany 1380–1407) puts golden hoops in the ears of the Magdalen, suggesting at once her Jewishness and the impurity of her former life. Reproduced in Hughes, "Ear-rings," fig. 5. I would add furthermore that when preachers cited Jeremiah on Israel's faithlessness in Magdalen sermons, they would have evoked simultaneously her Hebrew origins and her dissolute past.

[34] The 1293 statutes of the city of Salon stated that neither Jews, prostitutes, nor lepers could touch the goods; those from Avignon, on the other hand, mention only Jews and prostitutes. Cited in Pilosu, *La Donna*, 81.

[35] Mazzi, *Prostitute*, 186. She also cites examples of prostitutes forced to exhibit themselves in Foligno and Brescia in the course of celebrations. Prostitutes also participated in festivals in Lucca, Rome, and Florence; ibid., 186–87. For the Florentine example and others, see Richard Trexler, "'Correre la Terre': Collective Insults in the Late Middle Ages," *MEFRM* 96 (1984): 845–902.

[36] See R. I. Moore, *The Formation of a Persecuting Society: Power and Deviance in Western Europe, 950–1250* (Oxford: Blackwell, 1987) who argues that the social exclusion of certain groups marked as "others" was both a hallmark and symptom of the emerging states in the Middle Ages.

spirit they were marked for social exclusion: they were considered exiles. Theoretically, at least, all of these groups could be reintegrated into the Christian body social through conversion. This is the theme of Bertrand de la Tour's *ad status* sermon to prostitutes that begins with the exhortation: "Return, return, Shulammite" (Cant. 6:13). He encouraged prostitutes to leave their place of moral exile and return to the Church: "Consider the brothel a place of exile," he admonished. It is also the theme of Humbert of Romans' sermon to prostitutes.[37] In preaching on the evils of prostitution the preachers transformed Mary Magdalen into a powerful example of the rehabilitated prostitute who had successfully reentered the Christian community. The great prostitute had become a great saint.

What incentive did preachers offer to women to renounce their occupations? Ultimately, they offered the hope of salvation; but it came at a price. Repentant prostitutes, or *convertite,* by entering refuges established for their welfare, exchanged civil surveillance for moral regulation. Recall that women needed protection from their own natures; fallen women even more. In effect, though asylums offered social assistance, they also functioned, as we shall see, as instruments of social control.

Convents for Repentant Women

The preaching campaign to rehabilitate prostitutes seems to have begun in France in the early twelfth century.[38] Robert of Arbrissel's entourage is known to have included notorious women: significantly one of the four houses of his Augustinian monastic foundation at Fontevrault, was dedi-

---

[37] "Considera locum prostibuli locum exilii." MS BAV Arch. Cap. S. Petri G. 48, f. 31v; *RLS* 8: 71. The *ad status* sermon collection manuscript in which this sermon is found is attributed to "Arbor." Having surveyed the incipits, I believe these sermons can be attributed to Bertrand de la Tour. Humbert of Romans: *Ad mulieres malas corpore sive meretrices* in *De eruditione praedicatorum,* in *Maxima bibliotheca,* 506.

[38] A very good summary of the medieval initiatives to redeem prostitutes is given by A. Martínez Cuesta, "Maddalene," in *DIP* 5 (1978), 801–12. The important monographs in the field are: P. Pansier, *L'oeuvre des repenties à Avignon du XIIIe au XVIIIe siècle* (Paris and Avignon: Honoré Champion and J. Roumanille, 1910); André Simon, *L'ordre des pénitentes de Ste Marie-Madeleine en Allemagne au XIIIme siècle.* (Thèse) (Fribourg: Imprimerie et Librairie de l'oeuvre de Saint-Paul: 1918); Leah Lydia Otis, "Prostitution and Repentance in Late Medieval Perpignan," in *Women of the Medieval World,* ed. J. Kirshner and S. F. Wemple (Oxford: Basil Blackwell, 1985), 137–60; and Sherrill Cohen, *The Evolution of Women's Asylums since 1500: From Refuges for Ex-Prostitutes to Shelters for Battered Women* (Oxford: Oxford University Press, 1992). Although Cohen's study is not concerned with the Middle Ages *per se,* her first chapter provides useful background information. In the pages that follow, I am indebted to the theoretical framework she employs for analyzing such institutions.

cated to Saint Mary Magdalen.[39] A short time later, around 1115 or so, the charismatic preacher, Henry of Le Mans (eventually condemned as a heretic) exhorted the prostitutes of Le Mans to give up their wicked ways, strip themselves naked, and "burn their dresses and hairlocks in front of everyone." Thereafter, "all the street-girls were given a piece of material costing four solidi, hardly enough to cover their nakedness, then, on Henry's demand, the young men of the town married them all."[40] On 29 April 1198 Innocent III, proposed a similar plan to the Christian faithful:

> Among works of charity . . . not least is that of recalling a person erring from his mistaken path, particularly to invite women living voluptuously and selling themselves indifferently to whomever into the society of legitimate marriage, so that they may live chastely. We decree that for everyone who will extract public women from the whorehouses and marry them, because they do so, their sins shall be remitted.[41]

Evidently, his word fell upon fertile soil. Fulk of Neuilly, after a successful preaching campaign in Paris, married off a number of repentant prostitutes. As for the rest, he founded a monastic institution for them known as Saint-Antoine des Champs.[42] Again in Paris, in 1225, Guillaume d'Auvergne established the Filles-Dieu under the Augustinian rule. The South followed suit shortly thereafter: convents for repentant women were founded in Avignon circa 1257, in Marseilles around 1272 by a layman

---

[39] The usual attribution is: Notre Dame for nuns, Saint John the Evangelist for monks, Saint Mary Magdalen for penitents, and Saint Lazarus for lepers. Jacques Dalarun has argued that despite numerous citations in the scholarly literature, there is no medieval evidence supporting the theory that the convent dedicated to the Magdalen segregated the repentant prostitutes from the rest of Arbrissel's followers. This view seems to have originated in the seventeenth century. See his "Robert d'Arbrissel et les Femmes," *Annales E.S.C.* 39/5 (1984): 1144.

[40] Cited in G. Klaniczay, "Fashionable Beards and Heretic Rags," in *The Uses of Supernatural Power,* 72.

[41] *Die Register Innocenz' III,* ed. O. Hageneder and A. Haidacher (Graz-Cologne: Böhlaus, 1964), vol. 1, Ep. 112, 169–70. Brundage says that Innocent was simply following the twelfth-century canonist Rolandus who became Alexander III. See "Prostitution," 843.

[42] *The Historia Occidentalis of Jacques de Vitry,* ed. John Frederick Hinnebusch, O.P. (Spicilegium Friburgense, vol. 17) (Fribourg: The University Press Fribourg, 1972), 99–100. Hinnebusch says that *Saint-Antoine des Champs* was founded in 1198 and in 1208 adopted the Cistercian rule. The convent was suppressed in 1791; today the Hôpital Saint-Antoine occupies the site. See *Historia,* 100n. 3. Simon and Cuesta give 1204 as the year the Cistercian rule was adopted. Other scholars put the foundation date at 1197, ante-dating Innocent's letter. In any event, both men, having studied with Peter the Chanter, were infused with similar ideas. For their pastoral education, see John W. Baldwin, *Masters, Preachers and Merchants: The Social Views of Peter the Chanter and His Circle,* 2 vols. (Princeton: Princeton University Press, 1970).

called Bertrand, Aix-en-Provence (13th c.), Toulouse (ca. 1300), Carcas-sonne (ca. 1310), Narbonne (ca. 1321), Montpellier (ca. 1328), while Limoux made a foundation in the fourteenth century.[43] In the neighboring Kingdom of Majorca, the queen had founded a Magdalen convent for ex-prostitutes circa 1316.[44] Although most of these institutions were dedicated to Mary Magdalen, and most followed the Augustinian rule, they did not constitute an order.

In Germany, on the other hand, an actual order of penitent women, called the *Sorores Poenitentes Beatae Mariae Magdalenae* emerged in the second quarter of the thirteenth century.[45] Their origins are told in a chronicle of Colmar which narrates that Rudolph of Worms, entrusted with a preaching mission, encountered a group of prostitutes at a crossroads. As he approached them they cried out to him: "Oh sir, we are without resources and cannot find any other way of subsisting. Give us just a little bread and water and we will do whatever you wish."[46] He found husbands for some, and to others he offered the convent life. Thus were the humble origins of the Penitent Sisters of Blessed Mary Magdalen, which Gregory IX affirmed with papal approbation and the rule of Saint Benedict.[47] During the course of the thirteenth century they would establish more than forty convents throughout Germany, the Low Countries, and Bohemia.[48]

Unlike in Germany, the Italian situation was less organized and more spontaneous. The foundation of refuges for repentant prostitutes in Italy was usually a matter of private initiative. Sometimes preachers themselves made foundations, other times they provided the inspiration for charitable beneficence. The flagellant company of Santa Maria Magdalena in Borgo

---

[43] Here I am following Cuesta, "Maddalene," 802–4; Saxer, *Le culte*, 212, 249–51, and Simon, *L'ordre*, 6–7.

[44] Otis, "Prostitution and Repentance," 149.

[45] André Simon's thesis, *L'ordre des pénitentes de Ste Marie-Madeleine*, is still the exemplary study. This order is also known in private documents as the *Ordo Magdalenitarum, Albae Dominae de Ordine Poenitentium, Dames Blanches*, or the *Weissfrauen*. Simon, *L'ordre*, 10.

[46] Cited in Simon, *L'ordre*, 15.

[47] Originally they followed the Benedictine rule and Cistercian constitutions. By 1232 they were given the Augustinian rule and the constitutions of San Sisto, those followed by the Dominican nuns in Rome. They were absorbed into the Dominican Order for two years, 1286–88. See Simon, ibid., 26–31, 85–94.

[48] Simon notes that the order was a great favorite of Hugh of Saint-Cher who was papal legate in Germany in 1251–53. He bestowed on them many privileges and indulgences. By this time, however, the sisters drew mainly from the ranks of the upper classes rather than repentant prostitutes. Ibid., 53–55. In Prague, a celebrated house of prostitutes known in both Latin and Czech as "Venice," was closed down by one of the friars' preaching campaigns. In its place arose "Jerusalem," with a chapel dedicated to Mary Magdalen. See Christopher Ocker, *Johannes Klenkok: A Friar's Life, c. 1310–1374* (Philadelphia: American Philosophical Society, 1993): 90. My thanks to Bill Jordan for this reference.

Sansepolcro, for example, regarded the conversion of prostitutes as one of its charitable activities.[49] Both Aldobrandesca of Siena and Agnes of Montepulciano worked to reform prostitutes in their native cities.[50] In 1240, in response to a Dominican preaching campaign in the city of Pisa, an institution called the *Sorores Repentite Hospitalis S. Marie Magdalene de Spina* was founded as a home for repentant prostitutes, or *convertite*.[51] In 1243 a convent for *convertite* was founded in Viterbo, by mid-century Bologna and Messina could each claim their own,[52] and in 1257 Santa Maria Maddalena la Penitente in Florence's Borgo Pinti district had been established.[53] In 1255, Alexander IV charged Juan of Toledo, titular cardinal of San Lorenzo in Lucina, to establish a house for *convertite* in Rome in the church of Santa Maria sopra Minerva.[54] By the early fourteenth century, Genoa had established a convent and Pisa yet another one, of which Domenico Cavalca was appointed confessor in 1329.[55] Meanwhile in Florence, the sermons of Simone Fidati da Cascia had so inspired the members of the *Compagnia di Santa Maria delle Laude di Santo Spirito,* a confraternity associated with that Augustinian church, that by 1338 they had founded yet another refuge for ex-prostitutes: Sant'Elisabetta delle Convertite. Venice followed suit in 1353.[56]

[49] See James Banker, *Death in the Community: Memorialization and Confraternities in an Italian Commune in the Late Middle Ages* (Athens, GA: University of Georgia Press, 1988), 263n. 23.

[50] See Elizabeth Petroff, *Consolation of the Blessed* (New York: Alta Gaia, 1979), 173, 200.

[51] I thank Mary Martin McLaughlin for supplying me with this reference from the *spedali* and *diplomatico* fondi in the ASP. The hospital was suppressed by Nicolas IV on 27 August 1290.

[52] Cuesta, "Maddalene," 805–6. For Bologna, see Gabriella Zarri, "I monasteri femminili a Bologna tra il XIII e il XVII secolo," *Atti e Memorie. n.s. Deputazione di storia patria per le province di Romagna*, 24 (1973): 133–224.

[53] *Convertite* resided here until 1321 when it passed to Cistercian nuns. The foundation of the convent on 28 March 1256 was made appropriately in the Borgo Pinti (*Penitenti*), located in the parish of San Pier Maggiore, outside the city walls. See Alison Luchs, *Cestello: A Cistercian Church of the Florentine Renaissance* (New York: Garland, 1977), 128 n. 7.

[54] Simon, *L'ordre*, 7, where it should be noted that the pontiff employs the metaphor of pollution to discuss prostitution. Because the church of Santa Maria sopra Minerva had in the meantime been given to the Dominicans, the Cistercian cardinal moved the *convertite* to San Pancrazio where they were given the Cistercian rule. It was confirmed by Alexander IV on 1 Dec. 1255.

[55] The convent at Genoa was called *hospitio* or *monasterium repentite*. See Carlo Marchesani and Giorgio Sperati, *Ospedali genovesi nel medioevo* (Atti della Società Ligure di Storia Patria, n.s., 21 (95)—Fasc. I) (Genoa: Società Ligure di Storia Patria, 1981), 248–50. The convent founded in Pisa on 17 March 1308 was called *monasterium S. Marie, S. Marthe et S. Marie Magdalene* or *monasterium dominarum de misericordia (de repentitis)*. It was most commonly called Santa Marta. I am grateful to Mary Martin McLaughlin for this information from the ASP, *spedali, diplomatico S. Marta,* and *corporazioni religiose soppresse* fondi.

[56] The clearest account of the foundation of this convent is G. Bacchi, "Il monastero di 'S. Elisabetta delle Convertite' di Firenze," *Bollettino Storico Agostiniano*, vol. 7/5 (1931):

In the mid-fourteenth-century Kingdom of Naples, Queen Sancia founded two convents for *convertite* in response, evidently, to a growing problem in the *Regno*. In 1304, the Angevin registers reveal that Charles II had ordered "that prostitutes and other people of notorious reputation leave" the principal piazza of the port district of Naples. Charles's son and heir, Robert the Wise, expelled the prostitutes from the piazza of San Gennaro near the monastery of San Severino.[57] His secretary Niccolò d'Alife complained that "dishonest women" lived in his neighborhood too. Clearly the Neapolitan situation had gotten out of hand. Consequently, in 1342 pious Queen Sancia, Robert's wife, founded the convent of Santa Maria Maddalena in Naples for repentant prostitutes. In a bull of 21 November 1342, acknowledging the foundation and putting it under papal protection, Clement VI noted that there were already 340 sisters, the abbess included. The pontiff remarks, furthermore, that of that number some have expressly professed the rule and also vowed chastity, poverty, obedience, and perpetual enclosure.[58] Such an extraordinary number of women wishing to enter the convent explains why within the same year the queen founded another institution for *convertite,* this one under the patronage of Saint Mary of Egypt, another great penitent prostitute.[59] Sancia took a lifelong interest in both of these institutions endowing them generously in her will.[60]

Life in the convent was not without difficulties. Turning from documentary sources to literary evidence, an anonymous Franciscan chronicler reports that the Neapolitan sisters, oppressed by their newly found purity and seized by demonic impulse, could not resist returning to the sordidness of their former lives. Sancia, at wit's end, turned to her Franciscan confessor Philip of Aix. His eloquent preaching inspired the recidivists to withdraw from carnal attractions and do fervent penance.[61] Evidently there was nothing so effective as a good sermon.

145–47. It is continued in *BSA* 7/9 (1931): 234–38; *BSA* 8/4 (1932): 150–52; and *BSA* 8/6 (1932): 182–83. For Venice: Haskins, *Mary Magdalen,* 287.

[57] Charles II: Reg. Car. an. 1304 lit. C. fol. 139v; Robert: Reg. Rob. an. 1314 lit. A. fol. 142v. Matteo Camera cites the destroyed Angevin registers in *Annali delle due Sicilie,* vol. 2, 228–29.

[58] *Bullarium Franciscanum,* ed. Conrad Eubel, O.F.M. (Rome: Typus Vaticanis, 1902), vol. 6 (1902), 96–97.

[59] If the numbers are to be credited, the exorbitant number combined with Clement VI's observation that only some of the women had professed the rule and taken vows, suggests that it was not expected that all women would become cloistered nuns. Rather, these twin institutions may have operated also as halfway houses for marginal women. This is certainly the way refuges for *convertite* functioned in the early modern period. On this point, see Cohen, *The Evolution,* 61–80, and Otis, "Prostitution and Repentance," 151.

[60] *Bullarium Franciscanum,* vol. 6 (1902), 176.

[61] *Chronica XXIV generalium Ordinis Minorum,* in *Analecta Franciscana* 3 (1897), 567.

Such disorderly conduct on the part of the Neapolitan *convertite* confirmed everything that medieval gender ideology claimed about women: they were unstable, easily seduced, and predisposed toward sexual sin. Therefore, it was necessary for them to be subject to male surveillance and guidance at all times. Statutes from medieval *convertite* convents sanctioned this view. The statutes from Sancia's foundations have not survived; nevertheless, we do have constitutions from the same period from a convent in Avignon.[62] In addition, Leah Otis has published some notarial documents relating to the refuge of Saint Mary Magdalen in Perpignan,[63] a convent probably founded by Sancia's mother, Queen Esclaramonde. These documents disclose glimpses of refuge life in Avignon and Perpignan in all their similarities and differences. They also reveal medieval gender discourse at full throttle.

The second article of the constitutions of the *Domus sororum repentitarum beate Magdalene de Miraculis* in Avignon (first redacted 1376) demonstrates clearly how gender ideology informed social institutions:

> We decree and ordain that from this moment on, there will be received in the said monastery only young women of the age of twenty-five years who in their youth were lustful, and who by their beauty and formliness could still be prompted by worldly fragility and inclined to worldly voluptuous pleasures and to attract men to the same totally.[64]

The founders invoked the familiar concatenation of female beauty, youth, lust, weakness, temptation, and seductive powers to justify the need for their institution and whom they would admit. After a short trial period, the sisters, only about fifteen in number, would decide whether or not to admit the prospective novice to their ranks. The novice, having been received into the convent, could bring only money, clothing, and items deemed necessary for her entrance by the governess, prioress, confessor, and chaplain.[65]

Just like in any other monastic rule, clothing and speech were highly regulated, but for the *convertite* of Avignon, especially so. In contrast to the costly finery the women had worn in their former lives, the sisters' habits were meant to be uniform and loose-fitting, of "white wool cloth neither

---

[62] They are reproduced in Pansier, *L'oeuvre*, 107–24.

[63] Otis, "Prostitution and Repentance," 137–60.

[64] Translated in Rossiaud, *Medieval Prostitution*, 202. He has provided partial translations of the fifteenth-century French translation. I use his translations when I can, otherwise I translate from the Latin in Pansier, *L'oeuvre*, who published the statutes in full. Haskins, *Mary Magdalen*, cites the sixteenth-century historian Francesco Sansovino who himself sounds much like a statute: "Here live quite a large number of women, and all very beautiful because only those who are very beautiful are accepted; so as not, after repenting, to fall back into sin through their beauty, which attracts the desires of others, they devote themselves with marvelous order to diverse occupations," 287–88.

[65] Pansier, *L'oeuvre*, 108.

delicate nor precious." Unlike Dominican nuns of the period, they were not allowed fur linings for their mantles.[66] Nor were they to sleep naked (or with each other), crimes punishable by a diet of bread and water.[67] Clothing (or the lack thereof), as we have already seen, was a system of signs that admitted no ambiguity. "Decent widows" were the model after which the sisters of Mary Magdalen were veiled, exhibiting "nothing curious or precious. So that by exterior honesty their intrinsic purity can shine through to be an example of good life."[68]

Speech too was carefully regulated, in Avignon possibly more than usual. Preachers characterized female speech as "flighty and garrulous," and the statutes regarding conversation reflect this view.[69] The sisters were encouraged to engage in humble and modest conversation and refrain from "pleasurable, proud, wandering and idle" words.[70] Their words were meant to encourage one another to do penance and perform charitable works for the community. As we saw in an earlier chapter, the sisters were meant to raise their voices together in the antiphon "*O Apostolorum Apostola*" after Matins, mass, and Vespers.[71]

As distinct from Perpignan, the physical layout of the Avignon convent emphasized both community and cloister. In Avignon the women slept in dormitories in which they were not allowed to eat or drink, while at Perpignan the sisters had private bedrooms with adjacent dining nooks.[72] The nuns at Avignon were strictly enclosed. In Perpignan there was no *clausura*, indeed the institution of the *questa*, the collection of alms by pairs of itinerant sisters for the upkeep of the convent, militated against the possibility of strict enclosure.[73]

Uncloistered women, as preachers and moralists reminded time and again, were at risk as an event from the convent of Mary Magdalen in Perpignan reveals. On 21 November 1394, Sister Antonia Richa, who had been called on the carpet during a chapter meeting, confessed to the prioress that "by my sin, while outside the present convent, I conceived and gave birth to a daughter, whose name is Johana, who is the daughter of Berengar Cavenelles, beneficed priest in the church of St. James."[74] We

---

[66] Rossiaud, *Medieval Prostitution*, 203. Cf. The Constitutions of San Sisto (Rome) cited in Simon, *L'ordre*, 146.

[67] Pansier, *L'oeuvre*, 117. As we have seen previously, the idea of nakedness conjured notions of *luxuria* rather than edenic innocence for the authors of the statutes.

[68] Rossiaud, ibid., 203.

[69] "Vaga et garrula." See, for example, Luca da Padova, MS Antoniana, 466, f. 265r; *RLS* 4: 94.

[70] Rossiaud, *Medieval Prostitution*, 203.

[71] Pansier, *L'oeuvre*, 114.

[72] Avignon: Rossiaud, *Medieval Prostitution*, 204; Perpignan: Otis, "Prostitution and Repentance," 151–52.

[73] Pansier, ibid., 113, and Otis, ibid., 152.

[74] Otis, ibid., 152.

have heard enough from late medieval preachers to know who would have been blamed for this unfortunate episode.

Gender Discourse, the *Pala delle Convertite,* and the *Golden Legend*

Medieval gender discourse, arguing as it did for the necessity of controlling, guiding, subjecting, and supervising women, even contributed to the construction of the Magdalen's *vita,* which found its most well known and popular form in Jacobus de Voragine's *Golden Legend.* Significantly, this "canonical" text of the Magdalen's *vita* was redacted at roughly the same time that female custodial institutions began to emerge. The notion of social and moral control that characterizes such institutions found its counterpart in the leitmotif of clerical control that runs through Jacobus de Voragine's Magdalen legend. I would like to illustrate this conjunction of gender ideology, hagiography, and social institution through recourse to the *Pala delle Convertite,* an altarpiece commissioned for the *convertite* of Florence and painted by Sandro Botticelli and his workshop in the 1490s.[75] Designed as an aid for contemplation, it is in every sense a didactic tool. The representations of the Magdalen, for the most part culled from the *Golden Legend,* encapsulate precisely the penitential path to salvation that the converted prostitute was meant to follow. At every moment along the way her actions were circumscribed and authorized by male sacerdotal authority. Simone Fidati da Cascia, the eloquent preacher-founder of the monastery, could not have improved on the sentiments embodied in this painting.

The central portion of the altarpiece represents the Trinity flanked by the eremites John the Baptist and Mary Magdalen, a prophetic pair we have previously encountered.[76] As a good confessor might do, the Baptist, his face turned toward the viewer, extends his right arm toward the center, indicating the Trinity, the object of contemplation for the nuns. The ascetic Magdalen, gaunt and drawn, her former beauty having vanished due to years of austere penance, stands in profile, her hands raised in prayer, her gaze fixed on the triune God. She is the model whom the nuns are to imitate.

The predella is more revealing. The first scene, a rarity in Magdalenian iconography depicts the Magdalen's presence at Christ's preaching (Fig.

---

[75] See Ronald Lightbown, *Sandro Botticelli.* 2 vols. (London: Paul Elek, 1978), vol. 2 (*Complete Catalogue*), 75–78. It is reasonable to assume that since the *Compagnia di Santa Maria delle Laude* seems to have paid for the altarpiece (the *convertite* did not) they also commissioned its subject matter.

[76] The figures in the foreground are Tobias and the angel Raphael.

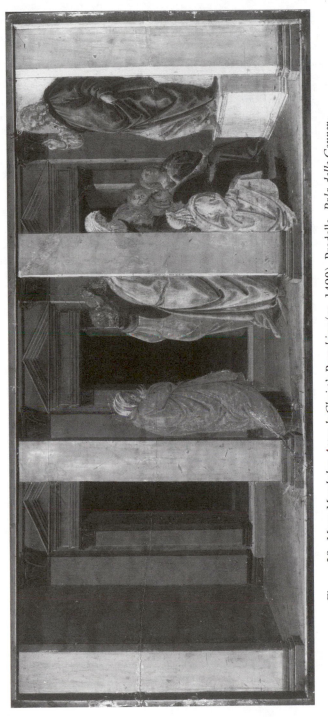

Figure 28. *Mary Magdalen Attends Christ's Preaching* (ca. 1490). Predella, *Pala delle Convertite*, Sandro Botticelli, ex Convent Church of Sant'Elisabetta, Florence. John G. Johnson Collection, Philadelphia Museum of Art. (Photo: Philadelphia Museum of Art)

28). This scene does not come from the *Golden Legend,* but is found in contemporary sacred drama, often staged by preachers.[77] It is significant that this episode was included in this altarpiece, made for this particular audience, since as will be recalled, the monastery for converted Magdalens was founded in the wake of a preaching campaign in Florence. Perhaps the nuns were meant to think of their founder-preacher Simone Fidati when they contemplated the preaching Christ, and of themselves when they meditated on the attentive but silent Magdalen.

The next panel shows the Magdalen's conversion at the house of Simon the Pharisee (Fig. 29). Christ is shown giving absolution to the sinner at his feet. In the next chapter we will examine how preachers interpreted this moment as the Magdalen's confession; for now it will suffice to say that it was another episode whose meaning was abundantly clear to the *convertite.* At the house in Avignon confession was required on all solemn feasts, and if no such feast occurred, at least once a month. During Advent and Lent confession was expected once a week.[78] Since 1215 confession had been the centerpiece of sacramental penance; but it was also, as many scholars have argued recently, a means of social control.[79]

Botticelli next shows the *noli me tangere,* the moment in the garden when, after the resurrection, the Magdalen recognizes her master, the risen Christ, and rushes to embrace him (Fig. 30). This is also the moment when Christ entrusts her to tell his disciples that he has risen and makes her his *apostolorum apostola,* an image we have already analyzed. It is of course an extremely common image in medieval art, but its presence here was meant to remind the nuns of women's role in salvation history. Eve had brought death to the world, but through paschal privilege, the Magdalen had brought the good news of life everlasting. Christ's first appearance was to a converted prostitute as a reminder that he had come to the world not for the righteous but for sinners. Through an arch we see the wilds of Provence

---

[77] See, for example, the sacred play of 1516 reproduced in *Sacre rappresentazioni dei secoli XIV, XV e XVI,* ed. Alessandro d'Ancona, 3 vols. (Florence: Successori le Monnier, 1872), vol. 1, 395–99. Martha beseeches her sister to come hear Jesus' preaching, promising that he is handsome and eloquent. The Magdalen finally relents, and at the conclusion of his sermon on penance she makes a teary-eyed confession.

[78] Pansier, *L'oeuvre,* 119–20.

[79] See particularly the essays by Nicole Bériou, "Autour de Latran IV (1215): La naissance de la confession moderne et sa diffusion"; Jacques Berlioz, "Images de la confession dans la prédication au début au XIVe siècle. L'exemple de l'Alphabetum Narrationum d'Arnold de Liège"; and Hervé Martin, "Confession et contrôle social à la fin du moyen âge," collected in *Pratiques de la confession. Des pères du désert à Vatican II* (Paris: Cerf, 1983), 73–136, and Roberto Rusconi, "De la prédication à la confession: transmission et contrôle de modèles de comportment au XIIIe siècle," in *Faire Croire: Modalités de la diffusion et de la réception des messages religieux du XIIe–XVe siècle* (Collection de l'École Française de Rome, 51) (Rome: l'École Française de Rome, 1981), 67–85.

Figure 29. *Conversion of Mary Magdalen* (ca. 1490). Predella, *Pala delle Convertite*, Sandro Botticelli, ex Convent Church of Sant'Elisabetta, Florence. John G. Johnson Collection, Philadelphia Museum of Art. (Photo: Philadelphia Museum of Art)

Figure 30. *Noli me tangere* (ca. 1490). Predella, *Pala delle Convertite*, Sandro Botticelli, ex Convent Church of Sant'Elisabetta, Florence. John G. Johnson Collection, Philadelphia Museum of Art. (Photo: Philadelphia Museum of Art)

where the Magdalen, after the ascension, would bear the good news. Significantly, what we do not see in this rendering is an image of the Magdalen preaching to the pagans.

A related and apposite episode from the *Golden Legend,* not represented here either (but included in fuller cycles of the saint's life), is the Marseilles miracle, the conversion narrative of the pagan provençal ruler and his wife who are unable to conceive a child.[80] The ruler, skeptical of the new faith, demands to know whether or not the saint can prove the faith she preaches, to which she responds: "I am ready indeed to defend it, because my faith is strengthened by the daily miracles and preaching of my teacher Peter, who presides in Rome!"[81] Driving a hard bargain, the ruler offers to convert on the condition that she intervene to grant them a son. The Magdalen accepts, intercedes on their behalf, and soon the ruler's wife is pregnant. Not content with this miracle, the ruler decides to go to Rome in order to "find out whether what Magdalen preached about Christ was the truth."[82] The couple embark for Italy, but only after a series of tragedies does the ruler finally arrive in Rome, where he is received by Saint Peter who escorts him to Jerusalem, guides him to the holy places, and for two years instructs him in the faith.[83]

I would suggest that this episode is yet another strand of the gender ideology that we have already seen woven throughout the Magdalen's *vita.* Though the Magdalen may have been *apostolorum apostola,* it was never to be forgotten that Peter, prince of the apostles, represented the authority of the institutional Church. This view is epitomized in a late fourteenth-century fresco in her eponymous church in Pontresina (Fig. 31). Here, the artist illustrates the provençal ruler's reception at the papal court. The ruler and his companions genuflect at the feet of Saint Peter who is represented *in cathedra* giving his benediction. The enthroned Saint Peter is surrounded by a retinue that includes a bishop and (anachronistically) two cardinals, one of whom holds the papal tiara. Thus Peter, in the midst of this Magdalen cycle, is depicted with all the symbols representing the power of ecclesiastical office. It is a potent reminder that the Magdalen, though deemed a great preacher and miracle worker in her own right, was not to be regarded as an ecclesiastical authority. The artist at Pontresina, following the *Golden Legend,* made the point that though Mary Magdalen may have preached and converted pagan souls, nonetheless she bowed to Rome and Saint Peter when it came to explicating the intricacies of the faith. The

---

[80] Jacobus de Voragine, *Golden Legend,* trans. William Granger Ryan (Princeton: Princeton University Press, 1993), vol. 1, 377–80. For discussion of this episode as a fertility miracle, see chapter 10.

[81] Ibid., vol. 1, 377.

[82] Ibid.

[83] Ibid., 377–79.

Figure 31. *Saint Peter Receives the Pilgrim from Marseilles at the Papal Court* (1495). Fresco from Church of S. Maria, Pontresina (Engadine). (Photo: Foto Flury)

later Middle Ages, then, resolved the Peter-Magdalen tension by acknowledging Mary Magdalen's apostolic mission but yoked it to her humble submission to Peter.[84]

---

[84] The friction between the prince of the apostles and the *apostolorum apostola* is preserved as a theme in sacred drama of the late medieval period. A German play has Peter, incredulous at the Magdalen's news of the Resurrection, threatening her with a beating and taunting

The final panel of the predella of the *Pala delle Convertite,* a double subject, shows first the eremitical Magdalen in her grotto caught in the act of angelic levitation, and second, her final communion (Fig. 32). Both episodes are narrated in the *Golden Legend.*[85] The first, the Magdalen's levitation, is a subject familiar from chapter 4. Here it bears remarking that the mystical contemplation that this scene represents was the ideal aim for the contemplative *convertite* of Sant'Elisabetta. Moreover, it will be remembered that the Magdalen's mystical elevation occurred at the seven canonical hours, the daily office that nuns themselves were bound to keep. What is compelling about the depiction of this scene in prose and in visual media is the presence of the priest. Peregrinus de Oppeln, "borrowing" from the *Golden Legend,* narrates the episode in this way:

> A certain priest, desiring to live the solitary life, placed his cell nearby to hers at a distance of twelve furlongs. Then on a certain day he saw that angels were lifting blessed Mary Magdalen into the ether. Wanting to know if his eyes deceived him, he approached the spot. Because he had already come a stone's throw away, and could go no further, invoking the name of Christ, he cried out: "I swear to you on the name of the living God that if you are human or some other rational creature who lives in that cave, answer me!" Mary Magdalen responded, "Come closer and I will tell you." Then he came to her and she said, "Have you heard in the gospels of Mary Magdalen, that notorious female sinner who washed the feet of the savior with her tears?" To which the priest replied, "I have heard. Nevertheless, more than thirty years have passed since this was done." "I am," she said, "that woman who has remained unknown for thirty years. And just as you saw yesterday, so every day, I have merited to hear angelic songs."[86]

---

her: "Hurry home and mind your spinning! It is a sin and a shame that females run all over the countryside." Cited in Marjorie Malvern, *Venus in Sackcloth: The Magdalen's Origins and Metamorphoses.* (Carbondale, IL: Southern Illinois University Press, 1975), 38. In a fifteenth-century Italian play from Pordenone, the apostles chide the announcement of the three Marys thus: "Women always have a hammer in their heads that makes their brains spin 'round." In Vincenzo de Bartholomaeis, *Laude drammatiche e rappresentazioni sacre,* 3 vols. (Florence: Felice le Monnier, 1943), vol. 3, 300.

[85] *Golden Legend,* vol. 1, 380–81.

[86] "Sacerdos quidam solitariam vitam agere cupiens ad .xii. stadia loco eidem vicinam sibi cellam locavit. Unde quadam die vidit quod angeli beatam Mariam Magdalenam in ethera sublevabant. Volens autem sacerdos huius visionis veritatem agnoscere ibidem accesit. Sed cum ad unius lapidis ictum iam venisset ulterius accedere non potuit, sed invocato nomine Christi clamavit. 'Adiuro te per nomen deum vivum [*sic*] ut si homo es vel alique creatura rationalis que in ista spelunca habitas mihi respondeas.' Maria Magdalena respondit 'Accede proprius et dicam tibi.' Cumque ad illam venisset ait, 'Audisti ex evangelio de Maria Magdalena, de illa famosa muliere peccatrice que pedes salvatoris cum lacrimis lavit.' Cui sacerdos, 'Audivi. Et tamen plus sunt quam xxx anni evoluti quod hoc factum est.' 'Ego' inquit 'sum illa que per xxx annos incognita permansit. Et sicut heri vidisti sic diebus singulis cantus angelicos audire auribus promerui.'" MS BAV Pal. lat. 465, f. 155r; *RLS* 4: 147.

Figure 32. *Angelic Levitation and Final Communion* (ca. 1490). Predella, *Pala delle Convertite*, Sandro Botticelli, ex Convent Church of Sant'Elisabetta, Florence. John G. Johnson Collection, Philadelphia Museum of Art. (Photo: Philadelphia Museum of Art)

It is a curious narrative device, one that is entirely superfluous except when one remembers the important role that male confessors played in the history of female spirituality. In many ways their role was to report and authenticate female mystical experience. I would suggest that is precisely the service the peeping priest executes in this narrative sequence. His "clerical gaze" is the seal legitimating the Magdalen's mystical experience, reporting as he does her presence and visions to Saint Maximin. He is a regular presence in both the literary and visual representation of the scene, as in the fresco cycle from San Domenico, Spoleto (Fig. 20). Any visions the *convertite* of Sant'Elisabetta may have experienced would have to have been legitimated through the agency of male sacerdotal authority.

The final episode narrated in the predella is the Magdalen's communion. In the next chapter we will examine the Magdalen's penitential link with communion; here it is enough to point out that *convertite* were allowed to partake of the Eucharist, according to the advice and arrangement of their confessors.[87] Women may have been visionaries, prophets, and holy, as was the Magdalen, but the feast of the Eucharist was still administered by men. The central symbol of Christian communion was mediated and authorized by male authority. The predella of the altarpiece reminded the nuns of Sant' Elisabetta that the ultimate act of communion entailed submission to male authority. The representation of the obedient and reverent Magdalen, taking communion from the hand of the bishop-priest, served to place women's visionary experience in its proper submissive perspective.

There has been some discussion among art historians as to whether or not this altarpiece is indeed the *Pala delle Convertite* because no historical description of the painting has been found, and because Saint Elizabeth herself is not represented in the painting.[88] However, when we consider that the convent was named after Sant'Elisabetta only because the site occupied the preexisting hospital of Saint Elizabeth of Hungary, the argument loses much of its force.[89] When we further consider that the convent's coat of arms depicted an alabaster of oil on which the word *convertite* was inscribed, we must acknowledge that Mary Magdalen was its true patron.[90] If not in name, then in spirit, the convent's protector was Mary Magdalen, a converted prostitute, whose biography was laced at critical junctures with the interventions of male sacerdotal authority and female

[87] Pansier, *L'oeuvre*, 119.

[88] Lightbown, *Sandro Botticelli*, vol. 1 (*Life and Work*), 110 (though he is wrong to identify the *convertite* of Sant'Elisabetta with the German order of penitents).

[89] As G. Bacchi explains, "Some wonder why a saint who was never a penitent is its patron. The existing hospice carried the title of S. Elisabetta, so did the oratory, then transformed into a church for nuns." In "Il Monastero di 'Sant'Elisabetta delle Convertite' di Firenze," *BSA* 7/5 (1931): 146.

[90] Lightbown, ibid.

submission to that authority. It was both a fact of life and an object of meditation for the *convertite* of Sant'Elisabetta.[91]

The chapters in this section have suggested that preachers and moralists invented a woman called Mary Magdalen in order to preach on the evils of vanity, *luxuria*, prostitution, and the frailties of women. They have further argued that charitable institutions—refuges for converted prostitutes—which had as their aim the amelioration of society, served also as instruments of social control—particularly of disorderly and unruly female sexuality.

Late medieval preachers and those to whom they preached believed that the twin vices of vanity and *luxuria* and their dire consequences threatened to tear asunder the moral fabric of society. Dante, a student of the Dominican master Remigio de' Girolami, echoes the preachers' chorus in the *Divine Comedy* when Cacciaguida laments Florence's innocence lost:

> There was no necklace,
> No coronal,
> No embroidered gowns,
> No girdle that was more to be looked at than the person.[92]

Savonarola maintained similar convictions about Florentine society; his apocalyptic sermons convinced others of this view. Circa 1497, one of his followers commissioned a painting on this theme from Botticelli (Fig. 33).[93] The painting represents a beautiful, prostrate Magdalen clinging to the foot of the cross; on the right is an angel about to smite some sort of

---

[91] An instructive comparison (with possible gender implications) is to the devotional panel of 1514, made by Ambrogio d'Asti, now in the Museo Nazionale di S. Matteo in Pisa. It shows an enthroned Christ flanked by Mary and Martha. Mary, on Christ's left, her right arm raised, anoints the Lord's head, pouring oil from a golden cup. It is an extraordinary devotional image and in the words of one scholar, "One of the rare instances in the visual arts where Mary Magdalen is raised from her customary servile position at Christ's feet, to assume a role of authority and perform a ritual which, even in our own day, would be conducted by a man." Ruth Wilkins Sullivan, "Mary Magdalen Anointing Christ's Head: A Rare Devotional Image," *Arte Cristiana* 78 (1990): 320. As the catalog entry reveals that the panel was in the church of the Dominican nuns of San Domenico in Pisa, it is tempting to speculate that this devotional image of female religious authority was commissioned by the nuns themselves.

[92] Dante Alighieri, *Paradiso*, XV, 99–102, *The Divine Comedy*, ed. Charles S. Singleton (Italian Text, Trans., Commentary) (Bollingen Series LXXX) (Princeton: Princeton University Press, 1975), 168–69.

[93] Lightbown, ibid., 130–33. For Savonarola and this panel painting, see Ronald M. Steinburg, *Fra Girolamo Savonarola, Florentine Art, and Renaissance Historiography* (Athens, OH: Ohio University Press, 1977), 69–77.

Figure 33. *Mystic Crucifixion* (ca. 1497). Panel painting, Sandro Botticelli. In this apocalyptic panel Mary Magdalen symbolizes the city of Florence repenting of her sinful ways. Fogg Art Museum, Cambridge, Mass. (Photo: Fogg Art Museum, Harvard University Art Museums)

animal he holds by the tail. In the background on Christ's left, a terrible sky threatens blackness, smoke, and firebrands, all symbols of imminent divine punishment. On his right, the city of Florence bathes in the light of God the protector enthroned above. Critics agree unanimously that the prostrate Magdalen personifies the city of Florence, which Pius II had punningly called the meretricious city.[94] The message of the picture is clear. Only through repentance and the casting off of vanity, *luxuria,* and all her evil ways, could the whorish Magdalen/Florence save her soul from perdition.

Botticelli's painting contains a message of hope, as did Savonarola's sermons. Ultimately, when we strip away the shrill threats, the bonfires, and the inflamed rhetoric, we find that beneath the fire-and-brimstone lay a message of hope and liberation. The closing lines of a sermon by the anonymous author whom the Middle Ages believed to be Saint Augustine neatly encapsulate this message. They assert: "And lest anyone despair, take the sinner Mary, lady of luxury, mother of vainglory, sister of Martha and Lazarus as an example, who afterwards was worthy to be called apostle of the apostles."[95] Of course one had first to repent, but ultimately salvation was at hand. The entwined themes of penance and hope are the subject of the next chapter.

[94] "La città mercatrice, ma che dico, meretrice," cited by Trexler, "La Prostitution," 983.
[95] Pseudo-Augustine, *PL* 40, 1298.

PART THREE

Do Penance

SEVEN

The Exemplar
of Perfect Penance[1]

The Historical Background

In November of 1215, Pope Innocent III assembled 3 patriarchs, 412 bishops, and more than 800 priors and abbots at the Fourth Lateran Council. Among many other matters, they acted to reformulate penitential theology. Canon twenty-one, *omnis utriusque sexus*, was the result. It decreed that in order to participate in holy communion, every member of the Church was obliged to make annual confession of his or her sins. To this obligation was added the necessity of fulfilling the penance or satisfaction imposed by one's priest. The sanction ordered excommunication and forbade Christian burial to those who did not comply.[2]

Henry Charles Lea called this canon "perhaps the most important legislative act in the history of the Church."[3] Hyperbole was not an unknown weapon in Lea's rhetorical arsenal; in this case, however, he did not overstate the point. The inclusion of confession in the penitential obligation of contrition, satisfaction, and absolution irrevocably changed the way the sacrament was conceived, understood, and performed.[4] It is important to

---

[1] Portions of an earlier draft of this chapter were published as "Mary Magdalen and the Mendicants: The Preaching of Penance in the Late Middle Ages," *Journal of Medieval History* 21/1 (1995): 1–25.

[2] The participants are listed by M.-H. Vicaire, O.P., *Saint Dominic and His Times*, trans. Kathleen Pond (Green Bay, WI: Alt Publishing, 1964), 191. For the text of the entire council, see G. Alberigo, C. Leonardi, et al., *Conciliorum oecumenicorum decreta* (Centro di Documentazione Istituto per le Scienze Religiose—Bologna) (Rome: Herder, 1962). Latin and English translation in *Decrees of the Ecumenical Councils*, trans. Norman Tanner, 2 vols., (Washington, D.C.: Sheed and Ward), 1990.

[3] *A History of Auricular Confession and Indulgences in the Latin Church*, 3 vols. (Philadelphia: Lea Bros. & Co., 1896), vol. 1, 230.

[4] On penance, see Lea, *A History*; Oscar D. Watkins, *A History of Penance*, 2 vols. (London: Longmans, Green, Co., 1920); Émile Amann, "Pénitence-Repentir," in *DTC* 12

understand, nonetheless, that the Lateran Council by no means created compulsory confession *ex nihilo*—theologians had approved it and episcopal statutes required it long before the thirteenth century—but now the annual obligation was supported by the full weight of papal and conciliar authority.[5]

This new emphasis on sacramental penance made itself felt in society not only through the institutionalization of confession, but also in the penitential fever, or wave of evangelical penance that was being preached popularly in the streets.[6] Although high theological matters were theoretically off-limits to those untrained in such things, the general theme of repentance provided the early friars with ample subject matter on which to preach.[7] This was particularly true for the Franciscans, whose founder actively scorned scholastic enterprise and favored extemporaneous sermons on the theme of repentance.[8] According to his earliest biographer, the leitmotif of penitential preaching that runs throughout Francis's *vita* began during his period of conversion. He experienced an epiphany while listening to a priest explain how the Lord had sent his disciples out into the world, instructing them to take neither money, bread, nor staff, but to preach penance and the Kingdom of God.[9] Upon hearing this passage, Francis exclaimed, "This is what I wish, this is what I seek, this is what I long to do with all my heart!"[10] The evidence suggests that he fulfilled his

---

(1933), 722–48; A. Michel, "Pénitence du IVe concile du Latran à la réforme," *DTC* 12 (1933), 947–1050; Bernard Poschmann, *Penance and the Anointing of the Sick*, trans. Francis Courtney, S.J. (New York: Herder and Herder, 1964); Joseph A. Spitzig, *Sacramental Penance in the Twelfth and Thirteenth Centuries* (Washington, D.C.: Catholic University of America Press, 1947); Cyrille Vogel, ed., *Le pécheur et la pénitence au moyen âge* (Paris: Cerf, 1969; 2d ed., 1982); Gianfranco Garancini, "Persona, peccato, penitenza. Studi sulla disciplina penitenziale nell'alto medio evo," *Rivista di storia del diritto italiano* 47 (1974): 19–87; and Thomas Tentler, *Sin and Confession on the Eve of the Reformation* (Princeton: Princeton University Press, 1977).

[5] Lea, *A History,* 227–28.

[6] A good starting point (and bibliography) for the notion of evangelical penance is André Vauchez, "Pénitents au moyen âge," *DS* 12 (1984), 1010–23.

[7] In 1199, in a letter to the Christian faithful, Innocent III argued that only those trained to do so could preach on the sacraments and the *arcana* of the faith. Ep. 132 (141) in *Die Register Innocenz' III* (Pontifikatsjahr, 1199–1200), ed. O. Hageneder, W. Maleszek, A. Strnad (Rome-Vienna: Verlag der Oesterreichischen Akademie der Wissenschaften, 1979), vol. 2, 271–75.

[8] In 1212, when Francis and his disciples went to Rome to seek Innocent III's approval of their order, the pope gave them permission to preach provided that they preached only repentance. Thomas of Celano, *Vita prima*, 33 (hereafter *I Cel.*), trans. Placid Hermann in *St. Francis of Assisi: Writings and Early Biographies: English Omnibus of the Sources for the Life of St. Francis*, ed. Marion A. Habig (Chicago: Franciscan Herald Press, 1983; 4th rev. ed.). Cf. *Legenda trium sociorum*, 25 (hereafter *3 Soc.*), trans. Nesta de Robeck in ibid.

[9] Matt. 10:9–10; Luke 9:2–3, 10:4; Mark 6:8.

[10] *I Cel.* 9.

desire; most accounts of his life remark his zeal for preaching penance.[11] In a letter which dates nearly to the end of his life, Francis continued to emphasize the importance of penance, exhorting the superiors of the Friars Minor: "In all your sermons you shall tell the people of the need to do penance, impressing on them that no one can be saved unless he receives the Body and Blood of our Lord."[12] But by 1226, the year of Francis's death, Franciscan preaching had changed; it had become more learned in order to refute heresy and evangelize more effectively. Erudition did not dilute the message of repentance that lay at the heart of mendicant preaching, however. Over time the friars' sermons became more sophisticated and refined, but a penitential message beat always at their heart.

This was equally true for the Order of Preachers. Unlike his Franciscan counterpart, Dominic had always promoted erudition in his order, but the mission of preaching penance was neither forgotten nor ignored. A century after the death of the order's founder, the Dominican translator Domenico Cavalca, in his tract on preaching, argued that an apostolic life was predicated on the preaching of repentance. "Those who are the successors of Christ and of the apostles, such as prelates, religious, and priests, are obliged to preach the gospel, and to call people to penance: they cannot keep quiet without committing a grave sin."[13]

This chapter suggests that the concomitant emergence of mendicant preaching, and the Fourth Lateran Council's reformulation of the sacrament of penance, inspired a new wave of devotion to Saint Mary Magdalen. Popular enthusiasm for the saint, in evidence since the eleventh century, in turn, helped to diffuse the late medieval cult of penance. The texts of 22 July sermons—Mary Magdalen's feast-day—are crucial to our understanding of this phenomenon. They are the site on which the friars worked out the practical implications of the Council's penitential theology.[14] The sermons invite questions. How did the preachers understand the meaning of sacramental penance? How did they elaborate it? What was entailed in its practice? Sermons also provide a measure of audience response. By lis-

---

[11] Cf. *I Cel.* 10; *3 Soc.* 8.

[12] This letter, from a unique Latin codex in the Guarnacci Library in Volterra, is translated in *St. Francis of Assisi*, ed. Habig, 113.

[13] *Frutti della lingua* (Rome: Antonio de' Rossi, 1754), 214.

[14] An explosion of preachers' manuals appeared to aid confessors in their duties; my discussion, however, is limited for the most part to sermons. For a valuable list of *summae* and manuals, see the index of Pierre Michaud-Quantin, *Sommes de casuistique et manuels de confession au moyen âge (XII–XVI siècles)* (Analecta Mediaevalia Namurcensia, 13) (Louvain: Nauwelaerts, 1962). For an overview of the literature, see Tentler, *Sin and Confession*, 28–53. See also Leonard E. Boyle, "The Summa for Confessors as a Genre and Its Religious Intent," in *The Pursuit of Holiness in Late Medieval and Renaissance Religion (Studies in Medieval and Renaissance Thought)*, ed. Charles Trinkhaus and Heiko A. Oberman (Leiden: E. J. Brill, 1974), 126–30.

tening closely, we can occasionally eavesdrop on the conversions between preacher and penitent. Thus we can ask how the ordinary Christian understood and performed the fourfold obligation of penance. Before we turn to the preachers, let us first examine briefly the sacrament of penance as it developed in the faculties of theology in the medieval universities.

The Theology of Penance

By the time we reach the early thirteenth century, the theology of penance and its attendant penitential system had undergone a radical transformation of which *omnis utriusque sexus* is perhaps the most celebrated example. Theologians such as Peter Abelard, Peter Lombard, Thomas Aquinas, and Duns Scotus were the prime movers of change. Here, a thumbnail sketch of those changes must suffice. In sum, the severe late antique system of public penance and tariffed penances—pilgrimages, vigils, fasting, and the like—was all but replaced by a milder practice in the form of private penance.[15] Thomas Tentler has identified four factors in penitential practice and theology that occurred between the ninth and thirteenth centuries to account for such a change: (1) penances were diminished and made discretional (i.e., independent of canonical decree); (2) contrition came to supersede penitential exercises; (3) private confession, already widely accepted, was pronounced compulsory by the canon *omnis utriusque sexus;* and (4) the role of sacerdotal authority in the fourth and final part of the sacrament was more fully defined and elaborated.[16]

Of these four factors, items 2 and 4 require further explanation. What the emphasis on contrition meant practically was that remorse about one's sins almost replaced expiatory works of satisfaction. Perfect sorrow was tantamount to the forgiveness of sins, and tears were the visible symbol of contrition. The eleventh-century reformer Peter Damian maintained that "tears which are from God rise up to the divine tribunal and plead immediately, trusting in the certain remission of our sins."[17] The notion of the primacy of contrition derives principally from Abelard's teachings, particularly his arguments about the ethic of pure intent, and his identification of sin with intention. "Works, in fact, should be called good or bad only

---

[15] For a good introduction to the early medieval penitential system, see Vogel, *Le pécheur.* For a view that argues against the thesis that the older penitential system disappeared after 1215, see Mary Claire Mansfield, *Public Penance in Northern France in the Thirteenth Century* (Ph.D. diss., University of California, Berkeley, 1989) and Mansfield, *The Humiliation of Sinners: Public Penance in Thirteenth-Century France* (Ithaca, NY: Cornell University Press, 1995).

[16] *Sin and Confession,* 16.

[17] *PL* 145, 308.

on account of the intention of the agent," he argued.[18] His theology influenced the Victorines, Alain de Lille, Gratian, and Peter Lombard, among others. These theologians established a distinction between the *culpa* (the guilt which signified the sinner's fall from grace and the possibility of eternal damnation) and the *pena* (the temporal punishment due, which could be mitigated in purgatory),[19] both of which resulted from sin. The *pena*, theologians more or less agreed, could be remitted by good works, penitential exercises, prayers, or, in sum, the proper performance of the satisfaction imposed by the priest. The celebrated preacher and hagiographer Jacques de Vitry, in an *ad status* sermon directed at married couples, narrated a vivid biography of the *pena* as it was expunged through proper penance: "Contrition changes the *pena* of hell into the *pena* of purgatory; confession into temporal *pena*, fitting satisfaction into nothing. In contrition the sin dies, in confession it is removed from the house, in satisfaction it is buried."[20]

How the *culpa* was forgiven, on the other hand, was far from clear. Peter Lombard argued that the *culpa* was absolved through perfect contrition infused by God; the Thomists claimed that remission of the *culpa* depended on the collaboration of the perfectly contrite penitent and the priest's absolution; and the Scotists maintained that only sacerdotal absolution expiated the *culpa*.[21]

Exemplum Perfecte Penitentie

Why did Mary Magdalen become the exemplar of perfect penance rather than any of the other saints, the Virgin Mary, or indeed Christ himself? Giordano da Pisa posed this rhetorical question in a sermon preached on Thursday, 22 July 1305 at the church of Santa Maria Maddalena Oltrarno in Florence. The friar discards the possibility of Christ or his mother as penitential models, arguing that their purity precluded sin and subsequent contrition; therefore, they were less than suitable exemplars. What, then, about the rest of the saints? Giordano, not surprisingly, explains that while there

---

[18] *Ethics*, ed. D. E. Luscombe (Oxford: Oxford University Press, 1971), 42–44, 45, 54–56.

[19] For the development of the notion of purgatory in the Middle Ages, see Jacques Le Goff, *The Birth of Purgatory*, trans. Arthur Goldhammer (Chicago: University of Chicago Press, 1984).

[20] Cited in Michel Lauwers, "*Noli me tangere:* Marie Madeleine, Marie d'Oignies et les pénitentes du XIIIe siècle," *MEFRM* 104/1 (1992): 223n. 66.

[21] My discussion of absolution is indebted to Bernard Poschmann, *Penance and the Anointing of the Sick*, 169–74; Tentler, *Sin and Confession*, 22–27; and Mansfield, *Public Penance*, 45–46.

are other examples of penitent saints such as Peter, Paul, and Mary the Egyptian, Mary Magdalen is the highest and most perfect example of penance.[22] The others pale in comparison. Indeed, these other saintly sinners often frequent Mary Magdalen sermons as if they were some sort of celestial supporting cast. Peter weeping over having denied Christ; Paul lamenting his pre-conversion persecution of the early Christians; Mary the Egyptian's bodily mortification for having been a prostitute; David's sorrow about adultery committed; Matthew's remorse about his former occupation as publican; and the Good Thief's repentance on the cross were all familiar images in the medieval vocabulary of repentance.[23]

Nor were these penitents confined solely to rhetoric. Pictorial representation employed them, too. The fresco cycle in the Magdalen Chapel in the basilica of San Francesco in Assisi is a visual analogue of the friars' sermons.[24] The upper narrative register of the chapel illustrates episodes from Mary Magdalen's *vita*. This narrative band is visually sustained by a lower register that features portraits of the penitents Peter, Matthew, Paul, David, Miriam, and Mary the Egyptian, among others. In the lower church at Assisi, as in mendicant sermons, they are the supporting players to Mary Magdalen's star turn as *exemplum perfecte penitentie,* the example of perfect penance.[25]

There was some danger, however, in using penitents as models of comportment. Ludovicus, a Franciscan preacher, seems to have encountered such a difficulty. In the text of his Mary Magdalen sermon, he reports that there was always the possibility that obstinate parishioners, when asked why they had fallen into sin, would retort, "Don't the saints sin?" But the good friar anticipated the reply and circumvented the difficulty by citing an *exemplum*. Saint Ambrose, it seems, had rebuked a certain emperor for having asked, "Didn't David sin?" "If you have followed him erring," replied

---

[22] *Prediche del Beato Fra Giordano da Rivalto dell'ordine dei Predicatori. Recitate in Firenze dal MCCCIII al MCCCVI* (ed., D. Moreni), 2 vols. (Florence: Magheri, 1831), vol. 1, 181–82.

[23] This flexible cast of characters appears in the Mary Magdalen sermons of Gregory the Great, *Hom. 25, Homiliarum in evangelia,* Lib. II, *PL* 76, 1196; Peregrinus de Oppeln, MS BAV Pal. lat. 465, f. 156v; not in *RLS;* Anonymous of Marseilles, MS BAV Vat. Borgh. 138, f. 146r; *RLS* 9: 97; and Innocent III, MS BAV Arch. Cap. S. Petri D. 211, f. 78r; not in *RLS,* among others.

[24] For the patronage and "authorship" of the chapel, see Lorraine Schwartz, *The Fresco Decoration of the Magdalen Chapel in the Basilica of St. Francis of Assisi* (Ph.D. diss., Indiana University, 1980), and her "Patronage and Franciscan Iconography in the Magdalen Chapel at Assisi," *The Burlington Magazine* 133 (1991): 32–36. Although she deals with the iconography of the chapel, she does not vigorously pursue the theme of penance. For instance, she does not identify the figures of Matthew and Miriam as penitents. There is no reason for their inclusion in the iconographical program except as examples of penitents.

[25] Matteo d'Aquasparta, MS Assisi 682, f. 194v; *RLS* 4: 78.

the saint, "also follow him practicing penance." The emperor was duly impressed: "Pricked by conscience, he converted immediately to penance."[26] It was to be hoped that any impertinent penitents would do likewise.

Friar Ludovicus's difficulties aside, the model of the penitent saint was a persuasive symbol in the friars' discourse of repentance. The very notion that sinners could become saints was an attractive idea to those who had lived less than holy lives. Thus it was fitting for preachers to hold up a penitent as a model to which sinners could aspire. And who more appropriate than the famous sinner Mary Magdalen? Indeed, Berthold of Regensburg called the feast-day of the Magdalen, "the feast of Sinners," while Eudes de Châteauroux assumed the Magdalen's voice and exhorted: "Sinners ought to rejoice and celebrate me." According to Agostino d'Ancona, it was entirely fitting that one who had once—by her example—led people away from the path of God, inducing them to sin, now after her conversion, led them to penance.[27]

Medieval preachers were great proponents of teaching through *exempla*. Thus, what better *exemplum* of penance than a great sinner transformed through penitence into a great saint? Sinners were expected to identify with the Magdalen's sins and her tears. Relying on his auditors' powers of empathy, an anonymous Franciscan from Marseilles preached:

> Indeed the human heart is naturally affectionate. So if we see someone weeping, we weep with him. . . . And so, when regarding Mary Magdalen we see her anxious, sorrowful and tearful, we too should be anxious, sorrowful and tearful along with her. If indeed you are a sinner, she gives you an example of weeping so that you will weep with her.[28]

---

[26] "Hic aliqui convertunt in excusationem obstinationis cum quaeritur a quibusdam cur iaceant in peccatis. Respondent 'Nonne sancti peccaverunt?' Posset illis dici quod Ambrosius dixit cuidam imperatori. Legitur in quodam libro Ambrosii quod reprehendebat quondam imperatorem et cum respondisset 'Nonne David peccavit?' dicebat Beatus Ambrosius 'si secutus es errantem sequere et penitentem.' Et ad hoc verbum statim est compunctus et ad penitentiam conversus." MS Marc. Lat. fondo antico 91 (1775), f. 16v; *RLS* 4: 15. Schneyer attributes the sermons in this MS to Saint Louis of Toulouse. After careful examination of this MS, I found no evidence—internal or external—to support this attribution. Schneyer, *RLS* 4: 117.

[27] Berthold of Regensburg: "Per totum annum aliquociens celebramus festa sanctorum set hodie celebramus festum peccatorum et quomodo ad hoc peccator ut festum suum celebret." MS BAV Pal. lat. 138, f. 102r; *RLS* 1: 159; Jacques de Vitry used the same phrase for the feast: "Hodie igitur festum peccatorum." See the sermon edited in Lauwers, "*Noli me tangere*," 261. Eudes de Châteauroux: "et ideo peccatores debent gaudere et festum agere de me." MS AGOP XIV. 35, f. 182r; *RLS* 4: 948 Agostino d'Ancona: "Quia sicut ipsa ante eius conversionem exemplo suorum peccatorum multos proximos a via dei averterat et ad peccatum induxerat. Ita post eius conversionem exemplo sue sanctitatis multos ad penitentiam revocavit." MS Angelica 158, f. 123r; *RLS* 1: 126.

[28] "Cor enim humanum est naturaliter pium et ideo si videmus plorantem aliquem

People were meant to participate in her sorrow, weeping empathetically with her over their own sins.

Beatissima Peccatrix

The most common title for Mary Magdalen in medieval sermons is *beata peccatrix*[29] (blessed sinner), an evocative phrase rich in paradox. It suggests both sanctity and sin, two states or conditions which characterized Mary Magdalen's *vita* in hagiography and sermons. Simply put, in her pre-conversion life she was a sinner; after her conversion at the house of the Pharisee, she became a saint. These events, in the normal way, are circumscribed by the narrative pattern of history: they are events that happened in time, and are reported in chronological sequence. The beauty of the phrase *beata peccatrix* is its ability to collapse the borders of time and narrative to summon the two phases of her life simultaneously. It was a useful rhetorical device for preachers and moralizers in that it served always to remind ordinary Christians that Saint Mary Magdalen, who was now glorified in heaven, had once been a *famosa peccatrix*.[30]

In good medieval fashion—through the notion that "contrary cures contrary"—the *peccatrix* was able to add *beata* to her title by transforming her seven vices into seven virtues through penance. Indeed, the Dominican Guy d'Evreux (d. ca. 1290) suggests the suitability of such a theme for preaching in one of his seven Magdalen sermon sketches for his *summa sermonum*.[31] Infused by the love of God, the Magdalen's marvelous penance extracted her from the sordidness of sin and installed her in the heavens at the side of the Lord and his "princes."[32] At the outset we asked why Mary Magdalen became the paradigmatic penitential saint. We have seen it was because she was regarded as the greatest of sinners, but also the greatest of penitents. Now we must examine her penance, the performance of which transformed her from sinner to saint.

---

ploramus cum illo. . . . Et quia respiciendo Mariam Magdalenam videmus eam anxiam, dolorosam, et lacrimosam, debemus anxiari, dolore, lacrimari cum ea. Si enim peccator es tribuit tibi ad plorandum exemplum ut plores cum ea." Anonymous of Marseilles, MS BAV Borgh. 138, f. 144v; *RLS* 9: 96.

[29] *Beatissima Peccatrix:* Jean de La Rochelle, MS Angelica 823, f. 154r; *RLS* 3: 141; *Santa Peccatrix:* Pseudo-Anthony of Padua, *Sancti Francisci Assisiatis, minorum Patriarchae nec non S. Antonii Paduani, eiusdem ordinis, Opera Omnia,* ed. Iohannes de la Haye (Pedepontus [Stadt am Hof]: Ioannes Gastl, 1739) (bk. 2), 12; *Beata Peccatrix:* Berthold of Regensburg, MS BAV Pal. lat. 138, f. 102r; *Sermo 107, Sermones thesauri novi de sanctis* (Strasbourg: Martinus Flach, 1488), unpaginated.

[30] Friar Ludovicus, MS Marc. lat. fondo. antico 91 (1775), f. 16v.

[31] MS BAV Borgh. 66, f. 174r; *RLS* 2: 491. For Guy d'Evreux, see *Scriptores,* vol. 2 (1975), 71–73.

[32] Friar Ludovicus: "Ut sedeat cum principibus et solium gloriae teneat." MS Marc. lat. fondo antico 91 (1775), f. 16v.

Penitentia

Contrition

We have seen how the theologians defined penance, but what did it mean for the medieval preacher and his flock? Giordano da Pisa framed this rhetorical question for his listeners: "What is penance?" The answer? "Sorrowing about sin."[33] Penance was, in other words, contrition, the first step of the penitential obligation as enshrined by the theologians. For medieval people—preacher and penitent alike—"tears were the witnesses of sorrow."[34]

Not coincidentally, tears were one of the Magdalen's most salient attributes, and their efficacy was emphasized repeatedly in medieval sermons. According to the evangelists, she was preternaturally disposed toward weeping. She wept at the house of the Pharisee, bathing Christ's feet with her tears; she wept at the tomb of her dead brother Lazarus; and she most famously wept outside Jesus' tomb, causing the risen Christ to ask, "Woman, why are you weeping?"[35] Scriptural witness was enough for medieval preachers to cast her as the lachrymose exemplar of contrition.[36] Nicolas d'Hacqueville uses the figure of the Magdalen to explore the theme of contrition in a lovely 22 July sermon. He begins by imagining himself empathetically into the banquet at the house of Simon the Pharisee: "If I had come to the feet of the Lord with blessed Mary Magdalen, I would have flooded those feet with the tears of contrition."[37]

Pain, too, suffused the state of contrition, and tears were its manifestation. Jacobus de Voragine, in the fourth of his five sermons dedicated to the Magdalen, explicated the mysterious workings of divine love. Employ-

---

[33] *Prediche del Beato Fra Giordano*, vol. 1, 181.

[34] "Lacrime enim testes dolores sunt." Iohannes de Biblia quoting Augustine's *de penitentia*, MS BAV Borgh. 24, f. 61v; *RLS* 3: 91. For the symbolic significance of tears, see Pierre Adnes, "Larmes," *DS* 9 (1976): 287–303. For a discussion of tears as a speech act, see Peter Burke, *The Historical Anthropology of Early Modern Italy* (Cambridge: Cambridge University Press, 1987), 9.

[35] Luke 7: 36–50; John 11: 1–44 and 20: 11–18.

[36] Medieval preachers and hagiographers were so effective in identifying the Magdalen with tears (water) that in the early thirteenth century the water carriers' guild donated to Chartres cathedral a stained glass window depicting an episode from the *vita* of the saint. See Nicole Bériou, "La Madeleine dans les sermons parisiens du XIIIe siècle," *MEFRM* 104/1 (1992): 282n. 42.

The Magdalen became so identified with tears that in the mid-sixteenth century John Stephen of Calcar, who collaborated with Vesalius at Padua, fashioned a didactic woodcut of a skeleton, hands raised to eyes, caught in the act of weeping. It was entitled "The Weeping Magdalen" and was included in *de humani corporis fabrica*. It is reproduced in A. Hyatt Mayor, *Prints and People: A Social History of Printed Pictures* (New York: Metropolitan Museum of Art, 1971). Thanks to my father for bringing this to my attention.

[37] "Si ad pedes domini cum beata Maria Magdalena venissem eosque lacrimis irrigassem conpunctionis." MS BAV Vat. lat. 1251, f. 16r; *RLS* 4: 137.

ing an Augustinian metaphor, he observed that tears are the witnesses of pain, which like arrows wound the heart of the sinner. Therefore, he argued, the Lord, through his great love, had shot the arrow of pain into the mind of Mary Magdalen, the evidence of which was her tears of contrition.[38]

Bitterness also characterized contrition. This was apposite in the case of the Magdalen, given that her first name, Maria, was thought to have derived from the words *stella maris,* star of the sea.[39] Nicolas d'Hacqueville repeats this etymological interpretation remarking that "Maria is interpreted as the star of the sea. By the sea which is bitter I understand the bitterness that a penitent must have when she thinks about her sins."[40] He similarly scrutinizes her surname:

> Through Magdala a penitent is signified. Magdala is interpreted as the almond, food for the sick, thus penance is food for penitents. Note that two elements make up an almond: the exterior shell which is bitter, by which the bitterness of penance is signified. The sweetness, the consolation of penance, is represented within, in the kernel.[41]

The Dominican Jacobus de Lausanne (d. 1321) continues the conceit of using medicinal language to speak about penance. His therapeutic notions are based on techniques of catharsis rather than the administering of medicaments, the penitential regime as Nicolas represented it. In a Magdalen sermon that employs an extraordinary amount of bestiary imagery, Jacobus compares the penitent to a stork who, having gorged on too many snakes and toads, must drink bitter seawater to prick and goad its intestines into vomiting up the superfluity. In the same way, a penitent must drink the bitter potion of contrition to purge the soul of sin.[42]

---

[38] "Amor Dei fecit in ea mentis sagitta doloris. Et hoc patet per lachrymas quas effudit, quia ut patet per Augustinum. Lacrymae sunt testes doloris, quibus quasi sagittis cor peccatoris vulneratur." *Sermo 4, Sermones Aurei de praecipuis sanctorum festis quae in ecclesia celebrantur, a vetustate et in numeris prope mendis repurgati* (Mainz: Petrus Cholinus, 1616), 260.

[39] The Virgin Mary's name was also the object of the same etymological reflections. Interpretative lists of biblical names were frequently appended to thirteenth-century manuscript bibles. I thank Nicole Bériou for clarifying this point.

[40] "Maria interpretatur stella maris. Per mare quod amarum est intelligo amaritudinem quam debet habere penitens quando cogitat de peccatis suis." MS BAV Vat. lat. 1251, f. 114r–14v; *RLS* 4: 136. Cf. Jacobus de Voragine, *Golden Legend,* trans. William Granger, 2 vols. (Princeton: Princeton University Press, 1993), vol. 1, 374–75.

[41] "Similiter per Magdalam penitens significatur. Magdala interpretatur admigdalum quod est cibus infirmorum. Ita est penitentia cibus penitentium. Nota in admigdalo duo sunt. Cortex exterior qui amara est per quam amaritudo penitentie significatur. Interius in nucleo est dulcedo per quod consolatio designatur." MS BAV Vat. lat. 1251, f. 14v.

[42] "Ita legitur de ciconia qui serpentes comedit et bufones et cum sentit se gravata nimia replecione aquam maris igitur incorporat quae mordet et purgit intestina et sic emittit super-

If we further pursue the tracks of the Magdalen's tears, we find that they are so abundant and so imbued with meaning that there is some difficulty in separating one teardrop from the next. Here, it is enough to indicate that tears, for medieval preachers, were a multi-vocal symbol. As we have seen, they represented the state of contrition—sorrowful, painful, and bitter. But they could also denote woman per se, since they were a form of water, an archetypal emblem gendered female. Simultaneously they could signify baptism and rebirth in that they washed away sin.[43]

Anima mea liquefacta est (Cant. 5:6) suited the theme of the Magdalen and her tears; not surprisingly the preachers appropriated it frequently. Tears represented the state of liquefaction, which in turn symbolized the state of contrition of the soul. The Franciscan Guibert de Tournai (d. 1284) remarked of Mary Magdalen that she had been reduced entirely to liquid and tears through the effect of devotion.[44]

The preachers contrasted the image of liquefaction, representing the state of contrition, to the condition of sin, characterized by frigidity, sterility, and obduracy.[45] The metaphor "hardhearted" was entirely familiar to medieval preachers. Citing Job 41: 24, Aldobrandino Cavalcanti argued that through the *culpa* of sin, the heart is hardened just like a stone.[46] Spiritual hardness or frigidity, however, could be overcome by heat, the divine infusion of *caritas,* ardent love. Through the application of *caritas,* hardness dissolved into liquid.[47] Just as the Magdalen transformed her vices to virtues through the tears of sorrow, she converted frigidity to ardor; barrenness to fertility; obduracy to liquid tears.

---

fluum quo gravabatur. Sicut prima infirma propter nimia replecionem peccatorum debet bibere amaram contritionem." MS BAV Vat. lat. 1250 P. II, f. 68v; *RLS* 3: 565. For Jacobus de Lausanne, see *Scriptores,* vol. 2 (1975), 323–29.

[43] For woman, see Lilia Sebastiani, *Tra/Sfigurazione: Il personaggio evangelico di Maria di Magdala e il mito della peccatrice redenta nella tradizione occidentale* (Brescia: Queriniana, 1992), 60–62. For baptism, see Mircea Eliade, *Images and Symbols: Studies in Religious Symbolism,* trans. Philip Mairet (New York: Sheed and Ward, 1961), 155–57.

[44] "Tota liquefacta et tota in lacrimis per devotionis affectum." MS Angelica 819, f. 286r; *RLS* 2: 129. For Guibert, see Baudouin d'Amsterdam, "Guibert de Tournai," *DS* 6 (1965), 1139–46.

[45] *Frigidity:* Aldobrandino da Toscanella, MS Angelica 812, f. 66r; *RLS* 1: 252; *Sterility:* Iohannes de Biblia, MS BAV Borgh. 24, f. 57v; *Obduracy:* Aldobrandino Cavalcanti, MS BAV Borgh. 175, f. 27v; *RLS* 1: 340.

[46] "Per culpam eius cor hominis induratur et obstinatur. Job. 41. Cor eius indurabitur quasi lapis." MS BAV Borgh. 175, f. 27v.

[47] Hardness could also be liquefied by love, and subsequently take another form. Iohannes de Castello, preaching on the theme of *Erunt lebetes quasi phiale* (Zach. 14:20), in a vivid metaphor says that the Magdalen was placed in the furnace of love for liquefaction. She then assumed the form of another vase, the vase of election: "Patet in Magdalena posuit enim eam in fornacem amoris ut ibi liquefieri et alterius vasis formas assumeret." MS Assisi, 470, f. 495r; *RLS* 3: 726.

In another variation on this theme, Eudes de Châteauroux represents the Magdalen as a fountain in the middle of the Church from which thirsty sinners can drink and wash away their sins.

> The Orvietans would celebrate if a fountain erupted in the middle of the city, just as the sons of Israel were delighted when water surged abundantly from the rock struck twice by Moses. In this way the people would also drink. . . . And so all the thirsty sinners desirous of being washed from sin, ought to rejoice about this, that the Lord made blessed Mary Magdalen, as it were, an over-flowing fountain in the middle of his Church in which sinners are able to wash away their sins.[48]

His conceit is Moses striking the rock that burst forth with abundant waters (Num. 20: 11). In Eudes' scenario, the Magdalen's hardened heart, symbolized by the stone, was shattered by a blow, the word of the Lord. Upon her conversion she became a fountain both for herself and the benefit of other sinners.[49]

Significantly, women, according to the tenets of medieval science, were categorized by the property of wetness or liquefaction. In the fourteenth century, the Benedictine Pierre Bersuire, in his aptly named moralized encyclopedia, *Reductorium,* remarked that "woman by her nature is very pliant and wet. And thus because of the abundance of fluids is more readily accustomed to shed tears."[50] In biological terms women were more disposed to weep; in symbolic terms they were more inclined to enter the salvific state of contrition. The Magdalen's tearful contrition italicized this notion and created a symbolic link between medieval science and theology.

---

[48] "Urbevetani enim magnum festum agerent, si fons in medio ipsius civitatis erumperet, sicut filii Israel gavisi sunt quando egresse sunt aque largissime de silice percusso bis a Moyse, ita ut et populus biberet. . . . Sic et omnes peccatores salutem animarum sitientes et desiderantes ablui a peccatis, gaudere debent super hoc quod dominus fecit beatam Mariam Magdalenam velut fontem redundantissimum in medio ecclesie sue in quo possint peccatores abluere sordes suas." MS AGOP XIV. 35, f. 180r; *RLS* 4: 947. Although Pitra edited this sermon in *Analecta novissima spicilegii solesmensis altera continuato,* 2 vols. (Frascati: Typus Tusculanus, 1883), vol. 2, 341–42, I prefer to cite the MS. The Pitra edition excised a great portion of the sermon, and is not entirely reliable.

[49] "Tunc ista beata planxit peccata sua ad dominum est conversa. Et in die illa facta est ipsa fons. Patens et sibi et aliis. Tunc enim dominus percussit cor eius quod erat induratum quasi lapis et quasi malleatoris incus verbo suo." MS AGOP XIV. 35, f. 180v. This passage is not found in Pitra's edition. Ugo da Prato Florido invokes a similar image regarding the Magdalen's attribute, the alabaster: "Alabastrum unguenti est cor plenum contritionis. Quia sicut unguentum vulnera sanat ita contritio peccata delet quod minutatim frangi debet ad pedes Christi et evacuari. Id est coram sacerdote qui est vicarius Christi." MS Vall. C. 80, f. 56v; not in *RLS*.

[50] *Foemina* in *Reductorium* (Anvers, 1609), cited in Lauwers, "*Noli me tangere,*" 256. For Bersuire, see *Dictionnaire des lettres françaises. Le Moyen Age* (Paris: Fayard, 1992), 1161–62.

Eudes' image of Mary Magdalen as a fountain, then, functioned similarly. If sinners could symbolically drink of salvation and wash away their sins in the liquefaction of the female saint, it was possible, then, that all women, who biologically inclined toward liquefaction, carried symbolically the promise of conversion and exemplarity.

The physiology of the female body made women more disposed than men toward penitential liquefaction. (This is not the first time we have seen how medieval notions of the body unexpectedly privileged the female body in the religious sphere. It will be recalled that women, because of their cold and wet humors, were more inclined toward mystical revelations and visions.) Medieval science in the service of theology, then, explains why Mary Magdalen, a woman, rather than Peter or Paul, penitents both, became the exemplar of perfect penance.

Tears, of course, had functions other than liquefaction in the medieval symbolic economy. As Eudes implied in the passage cited above they also served as baptismal water washing away the stain of sin, and restoring the contrite weeper to the condition of purity and innocence. In his fifth sermon on the Magdalen, based on a passage from the *Song of Songs,* Eudes assumed the voice of the saint and announced: "I am black but beautiful [Cant. 1: 5] . . . because I was blackened and deformed by a multitude of sins, God both remade me and adorned me with the beauty of virtues and grace."[51] And now, speaking in his own voice, he continued: "This woman was both cleaned and purified and changed from blackness into whiteness through the effusion of tears and through the fire of love. For we do not read in the canon of scripture about such an effusion of tears of anyone else other than she who bathed the feet of the Lord with her tears."[52]

The Magdalen's sin was transformed into purity through the symbolic cleansing of her river of tears. Jacobus de Voragine maintained that the Magdalen's tears of contrition produced a cleansing tantamount to purgation of all sin, a serene conscience, and finally, the suppression of all her sins.[53] Where then did confession fit into such a formulation? As we have already seen, the Fourth Lateran Council added confession to the sacramental definition of penance, an act predicated on the mustering of proper

---

[51] "Nigra sum sed formosa [Cant. 1: 5] . . . quia denigrata fui et deformata multitudine peccatorum et deus reformavit me et formosam fecit decore virtutum et gratiarum." MS AGOP XIV. 35, ff. 181v–182r; *RLS* 4: 98.

[52] "Hec mundata fuit et purificata et a nigretudine in candorem mutata. Per profluvium lacrimarum et per ignem caritatis. Non enim legimus in canone scripture de tanto profluvio lacrimarum alicuius sicut istius que lacrimis rigavit pedes domini." MS AGOP XIV. 35, f. 183r.

[53] "Quae quidem lachrymae tres magnas efficacias habuerunt. Primo fecerunt ipsam totam mundam. . . . Secundo fecerunt sibi serenam conscientiam. . . . Tertio in ipsa aqua lachry-marum submersa sunt omnia crimina eius." *Sermones Quadragesimales eximii Doctoris, Fratris Iacobi de Voragine, Ordinis Praedicatorum, quondam Archiepiscopi Ianuensis* (Venice: Iohannes Baptista Somaschus, 1571), 162–63.

contrition. There were, however, theologians and preachers in this period—when not all wrinkles had been ironed out of penitential theology—who continued to believe that perfect contrition, alone, was salvific.[54] It seems that Jacobus de Voragine was among them.

Confession[55]

Confession required contrition; consequently, the two notions became irrevocably associated in the minds of the preachers. The lack of a theological consensus about where the efficacy of contrition ceased and that of confession began further muddled the issue. Additionally, the two notions were entangled in shared metaphors: both concepts often employed aqueous imagery—water and tears—so that language itself constructed a link between the two penitential obligations. Nicolas d'Haqueville associated them when he observed that Mary Magdalen came to Christ and washed her inner self in the tears of contrition and the waters of confession.[56] He further advised that the penitent soul wash itself two times in those waters.[57] Then, taking up the language and imagery of II Kings 5:14, he urged lepers (i.e., sinners) to go to Elijah (i.e., Christ) to wash themselves in the water of the Jordan (i.e., confession).[58] Using similar imagery, Guy

[54] Tentler, *Sin and Confession,* 19.

[55] The literature on confession is vast; a good starting point is Lea, *A History,* vol. 1, 250–55, and vol. 2, 415–18; Amédée Teetaert, *La confession aux laïques dans l'église latine depuis le VIIIe jusqu'au XIVe siècle* (Paris: J. Gabalda, 1926); Michaud-Quantin, *Sommes de casuistique;* L. Braeckmans, *Confession et communion au moyen âge et au concile de trente* (Gembloux: J. Duculot, 1971); and Thomas Tentler, *Sin and Confession.* Recently, scholars, following Lea, have examined the sacrament as an instrument of social control in the Middle Ages; see Roberto Rusconi, "De la prédication à la confession: transmission et contrôle de modèles de comportement au XIIIe siècle," in *Faire Croire: Modalités de la diffusion et de la réception des messages religieux du XIIe au XVe siècle* (Collection de l'École Française de Rome, vol. 51) (Rome: l'École Française de Rome, 1981), 67–85; Alexander Murray, "Confession as a Historical Source in the Thirteenth Century," in *The Writing of History in the Middle Ages* (Essays presented to Richard William Southern), ed. R.H.C. Davis and J. M. Wallace-Hadrill (Oxford: Clarendon Press, 1981), 275–322; the essays by Nicole Bériou, "Autour de Latran IV (1215): La naissance de la confession moderne et sa diffusion"; Jacques Berlioz, "Images de la confession dans la prédication au début au XIVe siècle. L'exemple de l'Alphabetum Narrationum d'Arnold de Liège"; Hervé Martin, "Confession et contrôle social à la fin du moyen âge," collected in *Pratiques de la confession. Des pères du désert à Vatican II* (Paris: Cerf, 1983); and Alexander Murray, "Confession before 1215," *Transactions of the Royal Historical Society,* 6th series, 3 (1993): 51–81.

[56] "Et ad Christum venit et lavit se in interius lacrimis contritionis et aqua confessionis." MS BAV Vat. lat. 1251, f. 16r.

[57] "Sequitur lavit se duplici aqua debet anima penitens lavare se aqua contritionis et confessionis." Ibid., f. 16v.

[58] "Nahaman significat peccatorem quia leprosus erat. Hic debet venire ad Elyseum id est

d'Evreux produced two schematized Mary Magdalen sermons on the inter-related subjects of cleansing and purification.[59] Jacobus de Lausanne, in a long meditation on washing, confession, and contrition, invoked a memorable metaphor on how confession should be made, particularly when it involved mortal sin. He observed:

> Just as a servant does not wash her clothes well if she throws them folded and tangled into the water; on the contrary, it is necessary that she unfold them all, one by one. Likewise, when confessing one ought to explain one's mortal sins and scrub well in any confession.[60]

As this passage suggests, confession was a highly regulated ritual in terms of verbal and physical comportment. Most handbooks for preachers contained a section that detailed rules for the confessor and penitent to follow. Fra Jacopo Passavanti (d. 1357), prior of Santa Maria Novella, outlines a point of confessional etiquette, using Mary Magdalen as the model:

> To be the person who wants to confess well, one has to go to the feet of the priest sorrowfully and repentant of every sin. . . . What the malefactor must do before the judge who has to judge him, is to throw himself humbly at his feet, either sitting or kneeling, in such a manner that he is at his side rather than before him; and especially if that person who is confessing is a woman, she must not position herself in such a way that her face and eyes can meet those of her confessor. And this she must do for the sake of modesty and so that she can more securely and openly confesses her sins. Which example Saint Mary Magdalen gives us, and about whom Saint Luke says in the gospel, "standing behind his feet." She, coming to Christ, stood behind, to the side of his feet.[61]

Aside from the requisite physical contortions, other *summae confessorum* direct that confession take place in public in order to avoid the possibility

---

Christum salvatorem nostrum qui docet leprosos id est peccatores mundare se per confessionem hoc est aqua iordanis." Ibid.

[59] MS BAV Borgh. 66, f. 175v; *RLS* 2: 493 and ibid. ff. 176v–178r; *RLS* 2: 495–97. Confession was imaged in various ways. Hugh of Saint-Cher envisioned it as a purgative vomiting of poison, MS Angelica 1057, f. 168v. Servasanto da Faenza compared confession to a thorough broom-sweeping of the house, MS Antoniana 490, f. 104v, while Berthold of Regensburg visualized it as the extraction of a toxic element (in this case lead) from a wound, MS BAV Pal. lat. 138, f. 81v.

[60] "Sicut vero ancilla non bene lavat pannos suos si eos plicatos et involutos in aquam proiciat immo oportet quod explicet eos quoslibet singillatim. Sic confidens debet peccata mortalia explicare et qualibet confessione fricare." MS BAV Vat. lat. 1250 P. II, f. 69r.

[61] *Lo specchio di vera penitenzia*, ed. Maria Lenardon, (Florence: Fiorentina, 1925), 180–81. *Lo specchio* was originally a set of Lenten sermons delivered at Santa Maria Novella in 1354. At the behest of his eager audience, Passavanti transformed them into vernacular devotional readings.

of scandal, that the confessor not look directly at the penitent, that the penitent kneel before the confessor, and that women cover their heads.[62] The penitent was also supposed to muster requisite shame during confession. Domenico Cavalca invoked Augustine to explain that "sorrow exists with shame; because as Saint Augustine says, shame is a great part of satisfaction, the great reason for forgiveness."[63] Mary Magdalen, of course, exhibited shame in an exemplary fashion. The sign of her shame, according to Ugo da Prato Florido, was that she stood *behind* Christ, blushing inwardly. But Ugo's sermon is more than an essay on repentance, it also offers a glimpse into the behavior of the ordinary medieval Christian. The preacher discloses a persistent difficulty between confessor and penitent, a problem in the confessional;[64] namely, that penitents were not adequately ashamed of their sins. Ugo contrasted the Magdalen's admirable behavior with that of those who did not blush, or worse still, laughed during confession.[65]

It was necessary to feel shame at the sin, not at the conditions of confession or penance; a subtle but nonetheless important distinction. Aldobrandino Cavalcanti applauded the Magdalen for feeling ashamed of her sins, the sign of which was her position *behind* Christ at the Pharisee's banquet.[66] Humbert of Romans was equally concerned that his audience not feel ashamed of their status as penitents. He admonished his confraternity of penitents to instruct themselves in the lesson of the Magdalen, learning by her example. He preached that it was necessary for those who wanted to do praiseworthy penance in the midst of the world to put aside human modesty as did Mary Magdalen when she entered the festivities at the house of Simon the Pharisee, offering her tears without so much as a blush of shame (at the circumstances).[67]

Humbert's reference to the Magdalen's tears was, in fact, a reference to

---

[62] Tentler, *Sin and Confession*, 82–83.

[63] *Specchio de' peccati*, ed. Francesco del Furia (Florence: Tipografia all'Insegna di Dante, 1828), 86.

[64] The confessional was not a standard piece of church furniture until the seventeenth century.

[65] "Fuit digna erubescentia. Et hoc est quod sequitur stans retro. . . . Et est confusio adducens gratiam et gloriam. Hoc est in contra multos qui in nullo erubescunt sed rident dum confitentur." MS Vall. C. 80, f. 56v. Both Aldobrandino Cavalcanti, MS BAV Borgh. 175, f. 28v; *RLS* 1: 342, and Eudes de Châteauroux, edition by Bériou, "La Madeleine," 334, also mention the problem of laughter during confession.

[66] Luke 7:38. "Primum est exemplum pudoris de culpa commissa. Cuius signum est quia retro stetit. Unde *stans retro* etc. et merito quia multa magna et publica peccata commiserat." MS BAV Borgh. 175, f. 28r; *RLS* 1: 341.

[67] In *Ad fratres de poenitentia*, reprinted in Gerard Gilles Meersseman, *Dossier de l'ordre de la pénitence au XIIIe siècle* (Spicilegium Friburgense, vol. 7) (Fribourg: Editions Universitaires, 1961), 125–28.

her confession. Tears could be the sign (the signifier) of confession, or they could be the confession itself (the signified), depending on the author. Geoffrey of Vendôme remarked in a Magdalen sermon:

> We do not read that she spoke, but that she wept; and nevertheless we believe that she spoke in a better way, but with tears rather than words. In fact, speaking with tears is very fruitful in the sight of God. While the woman maintained silence with her mouth, tears did the work; and while her tongue was silent, her tears were confessing and supplicating better, in a more useful way. For this reason, while weeping the Holy Sinner kept quiet, lest he [the Lord] accuse her of saying too little about the evil she had done. In all cases, prayers expressed by tears are better than those expressed by words.[68]

Whether the Magdalen's confession was literally made through her tears or merely represented as such was not of much help to preachers who had to confront the difficulty that no historical record of her verbal confession existed. An effusion of tears was all well and good, but where was the text? The attendant difficulties of enforcing oral confession, and finding suitable textual models for it, were two of the problems preachers faced in the aftermath of the Fourth Lateran Council. For those who were being compelled to articulate their sins verbally, and to the confessors who had to sit in judgment, a textual model of confession was of paramount importance. Thus, for literal-minded preachers and their penitents, the question of the Magdalen's confession was indeed a vexed one. In the following passage, Aldobrandino Cavalcanti seems to be responding to an insistent penitent's question on the topic. We can almost succeed in hearing the question itself if we listen very closely to his response. He replies:

> These things are plain in the gospel where confession is not discussed, because it was not necessary for her. Because the priest who absolved her knew simply and clearly all her sins and all the circumstances, and he also saw sufficient contrition in her heart for destroying her sins. It is even possible that she said some words in which she confessed herself a sinner, though one does not read it in the gospels.[69]

The question, then, seems to have been, "Why do we not read about the Magdalen's confession in the gospels?" Aldobrandino's reply, though quite ingenious, disclosed the difficulty associated with using the Magdalen as a paradigm of confession. He argued that the Magdalen's verbal confession

---

[68] *Sermo IX, PL* 158, 271–72.

[69] "Ista patent in evangelio ubi de confessione non agitur quia non fuit ei necessaria cum sacerdos qui eam absolvit sciret omnia peccata eius nude et aperte et omnes circumstantias peccatorum et videret etiam contritionem cordis sufficientiem ad delenda eius peccata. Possibile est etiam ea aliqua verba dixisse in quibus fatebatur se esse peccatricem etsi non legatur in evangelio." MS BAV Borgh. 175, f. 28v.

would have been redundant because the Lord, her priest, looked into her heart and saw sufficient contrition there. Aldobrandino could not, however, in good conscience, escape the irritating fact that the gospels make no mention of a verbal confession, a speech act; so he had to concede that in all likelihood Mary Magdalen probably uttered a few words confessing herself a sinner, but that the evangelists, for reasons known only to themselves, did not bother to record them.[70]

This is how Bertrand de la Tour, in a Lenten sermon that doubled as a Magdalen sermon, coped with the situation:

> For although before the death of Christ and the institution of sacramental confession, heartfelt sorrow along with physical or even mental tears were enough for the remission of sins, just as it appears here in the case of the Magdalen and of Peter (Luke 22); nevertheless from the time after the death of the savior, when sacramental confession was established, heartfelt sorrow with tears does not suffice, but a verbal confession is necessarily required: an utterance made before him who has the power to bind and loose.[71]

His was an argument about how confession had changed over time. Pope Innocent III, who presided over the council in which sacramental confession was enshrined, was far more audacious in managing the difficulty of an absent confession. His style in regard to his sermons was every bit as imperious and peremptory as it was in his ecclesiastical politics. If the evangelists had not bothered to record Mary Magdalen's confession, then, in her stead, he would articulate what was in her heart:

> Lord, do not be angry with your servant because I rush in so indecorously, because I stand here shamelessly, because I am lamenting in the midst of such pleasures, because I am pouring out tears in the midst of the banquet dishes, because I am unhappy among the guests, because I am in the way of those reclining; I am not able to tolerate it any longer. I cannot defer any more. I cannot wait until after the banquet. Because necessity is urging, anxiety is increasing, the pain is disquieting, the horror is terrifying, the weight of sin is pressing upon me, the ropes of adversity are drawing tight around me, guilt is tormenting me, my conscience gnaws at me. I am, Lord, an unhappy

---

[70] The absence of a text of Saint Peter's confession created the same problems for theologians and preachers. See Abelard, *Ethics*, 101–5.

[71] "Quamvis enim ante mortem Christi et sacramentalis confessionis institutionem sufficerent ad istam peccati remissionem dolor cordi cum lachrymis corporalibus vel etiam mentalibus, sicut apparuit de ista magdalena hic et de petro. Luc. xxii. Ex quo tamen fuit instituta sacramentalis confessio post mortem salvatoris, non sufficiunt . . . ad peccati remissionem dolor cordis cum lachrymis, sed requiritur necessario verbalis confessio: peccati expressio facta coram illo qui potest solvere et ligare." *Sermo 217, Sermones Bertrandi de tempore et de sanctis. Una cum quadragesimali epistolari.* (Strasbourg: Georg Husner, ca. 1500), no pagination.

woman, a wretched woman: disgraceful in reputation, notorious in turpitude, foul in body, loathsome in mind, full of crimes, and burdened by sins. . . . I confess and I know that I am worthy only of embarrassment, destruction, damnation; but you Lord, have mercy on me, you who came for the sake of the wretched, you who came down to ease the way for sinners. I am indeed unworthy to be heard, but you, Lord, are worthy to hear, and so hear this un-worthy woman, because I do not know whatever more I can do except to show you my sorrow with tears.[72]

Most thirteenth- and fourteenth-century preachers, Aldobrandino Cav-alcanti among them, were not brazen enough to follow Innocent's lead; instead, they continued to struggle to overcome the difficulties imposed by the historical record.[73] Although Innocent's solution—a reconstituted confession—did not become a standard feature in sermons, it did find a place in literary history. In both Cavalca's *vita* and the Franciscan *Medita-tions on the Life of Christ,* Mary Magdalen makes long, lachrymose confes-sions.[74] Innocent's confession also anticipated a genre of literature that made Mary Magdalen's confession its centerpiece.[75] In a text dated circa

---

[72] "Noli, Domine, indignari ancillae tuae quod importuna me ingero, quod impudens adsto, quod inter delicias gemitus prodo, quod inter epulas lacrymas fundo, quod contristo convivas, quod impedio discumbentes; non possum amplius sustinere, non possum differre, non possum usque post convivium expectare, quia necessitas urget, anxietas angit, amaritudo conturbat, terret formido, moles peccatorum me premit, funes iniquitatum me constringunt, culpa me torquet, conscientia me mordet. Ego sum, Domine, infelix femina, misera mulier, turpis notitia, turpitudine nota, foetens corpore, foeta mente, plena sceleribus, onerata peccatis. . . . Confiteor et cognosco quod digna sum confusione, perditione, damnatione; sed tu, Domine, miserere, qui pro miseris advenisti, propitiare qui pro peccatoribus descendisti. Ego quidem indigna sum exaudiri; sed tu, Domine, dignus es audire, ideoque indignam exaudi, quia quidquid ultra possim ignoro nisi quod in conspectu tuo dolorem lacrymis manifesto." MS BAV Arch. Cap. S. Petri D. 211, ff. 79r–79v. This excerpt is from my forthcoming edition of this sermon. See chapter 2, n. 52.

[73] I am aware of only two other sermons that re-create the Magdalen's confession. The first is the sermon once attributed to Odo of Cluny, *PL* 133, 715; the second is Bernardino da Siena, *Sermo 66* in *Opera Omnia,* vol. 3 (1956), 421–22. The humanist hagiographer Boninus Mombritius also wrote a confession in his *vita* of the saint in *Sanctuarium seu vitae sanctorum,* 2 vols. (Hildesheim–New York: Georg Olms Verlag, 1978), 182.

[74] *Meditations on the Life of Christ: An Illustrated Manuscript of the Fourteenth Century* trans. Isa Ragusa, ed. Isa Ragusa and Rosalie B. Green (Princeton: Princeton University Press, 1961), 170–71; Iohannes de Caulibus, *Meditaciones vitae christi olim S. Bonaventuro attributae,* ed. M. Stallings-Taney, CCCM 153 (1997), 111–12; *The Life of Mary Magdalen* (London: John Lane, The Bodley Head, 1904), 39–40; *Vita di Maria Maddalena* in *Vite de' santi padri,* ed. Bartolomeo Sorio and A. Racheli (Milan: Ufficio generale di commissioni ed annunzi, n.d.), 336.

[75] *La confessione di Maria Magdalena* (Padua: Alberto di Stendal, c. 1474), 1. See also *La confessione di Maria Maddalena* (Venice and Treviso: Angelo Righettini, 1621) and *La rappresentazione et conversione di Santa Maria Maddalena* (Venice: Alessandro de' Vecchi, 1606).

1474, in the introductory paragraph, the editor/author of one such confession remarked the Magdalen's reverence and devotion and began her confession saying, "The holy confession now begins." What then follows is a seventeen-verse confession, written in the first person, in which "Mary Magdalen" confesses every sin conceivable under the fifteenth-century sun. The helpful editor/author returns in the last two paragraphs to inform us that "Mary Magdalen made this confession when she was on the mountain of La Baume."[76]

Ironically, the Magdalen, who had no verbal confession on the historical record, became so irrevocably linked with the sacrament that in her legends—both the pictorial and literary versions—she performs miracles on its behalf. In the first miracle, repeated by Remigio de' Girolami, a young man inventories all his sins on a register and presents it at the saint's altar. No sooner has he done so than they are expunged from the celestial account books. This scene is illustrated and captioned in the *Leggendario Ungherese* (Fig. 34).[77] The second confession miracle tells of a young soldier, a devotee of the Magdalen, who was killed in combat. His parents, mourning at his tomb, rebuked the saint for having let him die unshriven. Mary Magdalen responded immediately. She raised him from the grave, whereupon he asked for a priest, confessed, received last rites, and finally died in peace.[78] Although it is not a common visual motif, the scene is included in the *Leggendario Ungherese* (Fig. 35), and in the Cappella Pipino at San Pietro a Maiella in Naples, where Mary Magdalen is represented in a nun's habit (Fig. 36).[79]

The Eucharist, as we have seen, was available only to those who had confessed at least once during the year. Confession, according to the theologians, purified and prepared the penitent for holy communion. Cavalca describes how the Magdalen was present at the institution of this sacrament, and how her soul soared when she partook of the divine meal.

> When the Magdalen had tasted the bread of angels, she was rapt in such sweetness and devotion as none could estimate, and she was well-nigh beside herself, so much so that she seemed to be in Paradise. Afterwards Messer Jesus

---

[76] *La confessione,* 4.

[77] *Golden Legend,* vol. 1, 382. Remigio: "Item ponentem cedulam sub palla altaris." MS Flor. Naz. Conv. Sopp. D. 1. 937, f. 232r; *RLS* 5: 806. For the miniature, see MS BAV Vat. lat. 8541, f. 104r. For the legendary, see *Heiligenleben. Ungarisches Legendarium Cod. Vat. lat. 8541* (Facsimile edition and commentary) (Zurich: Belser, 1990), and chapter 11, n. 62.

[78] *Golden Legend,* vol. 1, 382. Peregrinus de Oppeln relates the whole miracle (and indeed most of the legend) in his first Magdalen sermon, MS BAV Pal. lat. 465, f. 156r.

[79] MS BAV Vat. lat. 8541, f. 104r. For the decoration and patronage of the Cappella Pipino, see Bologna, *I pittori,* 316. For further discussion of the chapel and this motif in particular, see chapter 11.

Figure 34. *Confession Miracle* (1333–43). Miniature from the *Leggendario Ungherese*, Biblioteca Apostolica Vaticana, Città del Vaticano. (Photo: Biblioteca Apostolica Vaticana)

Figure 35. *Confession Miracle* (1333–43). Miniature from the *Leggendario Ungherese*, Biblioteca Apostolica Vaticana, Città del Vaticano. (Photo: Biblioteca Apostolica Vaticana)

Figure 36. *Confession Miracle* (early 14th c.). Fresco from Cappella Pipino, S. Pietro a Maiella, Naples. (Photo: I.C.C.D., Rome)

gave them of the Chalice of His most Holy Blood. Then when it came to the Magdalen she . . . experienced great sweetness.[80]

According to legend the Magdalen also received final communion. Sometimes the event was localized at La Sainte-Baume, other times at the church in Aix-en-Provence where Maximin presided. Jacobus de Voragine reported in the *Golden Legend* that Mary Magdalen, "shedding tears of joy, received the Lord's Body and Blood from the bishop [Maximin]. Then she lay down full length before the steps of the altar, and her most holy soul migrated to the Lord."[81] The scene of the Magdalen's final communion was a common theme in medieval sermons. Peregrinus de Oppeln related it in the first of his Magdalen sermons, while Servasanto da Faenza recounted that "Mary Magdalen received the body and blood of the Lord from the bishop with a great inundation of tears. Then, having prostrated her slight body before the altar step, that most holy spirit migrated to the lord after her death."[82]

Fresco cycles inevitably included this episode in their narrative sequences.[83] At the church of San Domenico in Spoleto, an early fifteenth-century fresco depicts her final hour: Maximin offering communion, her reverence before the altar, and finally, in the upper corner, her soul (still hair-clad) being transported to heaven by two angels (Fig. 37).[84]

Scholars have pointed out that the communion of the Magdalen was a rather common motif in medieval painting, so common in fact that Mary Magdalen was one of the saints most often represented on eucharistic tabernacles. But this image did not appear by chance. What needs to be emphasized is that preachers, hagiographers, and artists collaborated in

---

[80] *The Life*, 159–61; *Vita*, 360. As is his custom, the narrator warns his readers: "Now it is not to be read in the gospels that Madonna, or any other women, were at this supper; but it delights me to think it was thus, especially because of this Blessed Sacrament. And why should it not be so, and why not as meet or more for her and the Magdalen as for the disciples?"

[81] *Golden Legend*, vol. 1, 381.

[82] Peregrinus: MS BAV Pal. lat. 465, f. 155r. Servasanto: "Corpus et sanguinem domini ab episcopo beata Maria Magdalena cum multa lacrimarum inundactione suspecit. Deinde toto corpuscolo ante altaris prostrata lapidem, san[c]tissima illa anima migravit ad dominum post eius exitum." MS Antoniana 490, f. 101r; not in *RLS*.

[83] Among the fresco cycles it is included in the Cappella della Maddalena, Basilica of San Francesco, Assisi; Cappella del Podestà, Bargello, Florence; Santa Maria Maddalena, Bolzano; Santa Maria Maddalena, Bergamo, and the Cappella della Maddalena, San Domenico, Spoleto. For a listing of the major late medieval fresco cycles of the *vitae magdalenae*, see chapter 2, n. 62. In other visual media it is represented in the Magdalen Master panel, the *Leggendario Ungherese*, the Stoclet predella, the German ecclesiastical vestment, and the Botticelli predella.

[84] There is almost no literature on the chapel; for now see Roberto Quirino, "Un argomento di pittura spoletina fra tre e quattrocento: Il Maestro dei Cavalari," *Esercizi: Arte, Musica, Spettacolo* 5 (1982): 20–33.

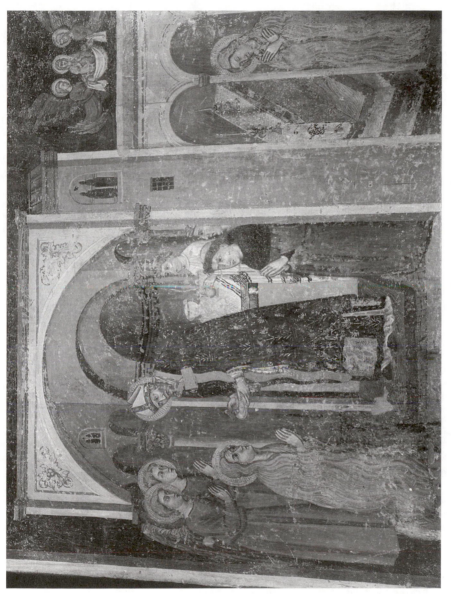

Figure 37. *Final Communion* (ca. 1400). Fresco from Cappella della Maddalena, Church of S. Domenico, Spoleto. (Photo: Hutzel Collection, by permission of the Getty Research Institute, Research Library)

making the symbol of the communicating Magdalen of legend a figure-head for eucharistic devotion in the later Middle Ages.[85]

Satisfaction

In his *Compendium theologicae veritatis,* Hugh of Ripelin, prior of the Dominican convent at Strasbourg,[86] put this case for satisfaction: although contrition expunges the *culpa,* satisfaction is still necessary to remit the *pena.*[87] He then elaborated the constituent parts of satisfaction:

> Satisfaction is composed of certain principal parts; namely prayer, fasting and almsgiving. Some of them, however, are reduced variously to such things as vigils, pilgrimages, and discipline. It must be said, therefore, that all works of mortifying the flesh are reduced to fasting, all spiritual works to prayer, and all works of mercy to almsgiving.[88]

Hugh categorizes the elements that composed the work of satisfaction under three principal headings: works of the spirit, represented by prayer; works of mercy, exemplified by almsgiving; and works of mortifying the flesh, symbolized by fasting. These works are familiar to us, having encountered them previously, albeit under a different rubric. In chapter 3 we saw that they composed a part of the active life as defined by Giordano da Pisa. We saw how Mary Magdalen made satisfaction for her sins through mystical prayer, almsgiving, and fasting. Hugh of Ripelin, however, mentions one work of satisfaction which we have yet to examine. As such, let us pause for a moment to take up the discipline.

Servasanto da Faenza, quoting Isaiah 22:12, remarked that the Lord called Mary Magdalen "to tears, to mourning, to baldness, and to sackcloth."[89] We know already that weeping and mourning were the signs of the Magdalen's contrition; Servasanto teaches us that sackcloth signified

---

[85] Bynum, *Holy Feast and Holy Fast: The Religious Significance of Food to Medieval Women* (Berkeley: University of California Press, 1987), 81. For a penetrating study of the symbolic meaning of the feast of *Corpus Domini,* see Miri Rubin, *Corpus Christi: The Eucharist in Late Medieval Culture* (Cambridge: Cambridge University Press, 1991). When the efficacy of the sacraments was reconfirmed during the Counter-Reformation the image of the communicating Magdalen became even more ubiquitous.

[86] This work was mistaken for Albert's own and was published in Albertus Magnus, *Opera Omnia,* ed. S.C.A. Borgnet, 38 vols. (Paris: Ludovicus Vivès, 1890–), vol. 34 (1905), 1–306.

[87] "Post remissionem culpe in contritione remanet debitum pene satisfactione." MS Balliol 230, f. 85r.

[88] "Satisfactionis quedam sunt partes principales; scilicet oratio, ieiunium, elemosina. Quedam vero varie que ad has reducuntur ut vigilie, peregrinaciones et discipline. Dicendum ergo quod omnia opera carnem affligentia reducuntur ad ieiunium; omnia vero opera spiritualia ad orationem; omnia autem opera misericordie ad elemosinam." Ibid., ff. 85r–85v.

[89] "Ad fletum et ad planctum et ad calvicium et ad cingulum sacci." MS Antoniana 435, f. 100v; not in *RLS.*

"how in her legend, she afflicted and macerated her body in penance."[90] Servasanto never did bother to explain how baldness pertained to Mary Magdalen; his image of sackcloth, however, is less opaque. The treasury of Saint John Lateran in Rome still preserves a reliquary that claims to contain a piece of the hairshirt that mortified Mary Magdalen's flesh.[91]

But sackcloth was only the beginning of the story. The *Thesaurus Novus,* in a sermon on the Magdalen, narrated how the saint became a spiritual martyr because of "the effusion of blood and daily affliction of her body."[92] This rather laconic remark only hints at the penitential practices in which the Magdalen was believed to have engaged. For a full description, we must turn to Domenico Cavalca's garrulous narrative of the saint's life. What we find is rather shocking. Cavalca narrates how, after her conversion, Mary Magdalen was so full of remorse for her past sins that

> she scratched her face until the blood came . . . and she cried: "Now, what revenge can I have upon this face, with which I have so much offended the God in me and in others?" And she put her hands to her hair and tore it out, and tried to bare her head, and she struck her eyes and her face with her fists; and taking a stone she struck herself, on her breast and where she thought it would not kill her; and she struck her feet, her legs, and her arms, and she clawed herself until the blood came. And she took her girdle with clasps, that she usually wore through vanity, and unclothing herself till she was quite uncovered, she beat herself with it from head to foot until the blood flowed, and she cried: "Take the reward, O my body, of the vain pleasures thou has frequented."[93]

Cavalca continues the narrative relating that she beat herself so severely—until she was bruised, bleeding, and almost unconscious; nevertheless, she resolved that every night "she would discipline her body till the blood flowed, as much as she could bear, asking mercy of God."[94] She then consoled herself reading the penitential psalms. Her choice of devotional reading material was apposite. Peter Damian, a great promoter of self-flagellation as a penitential exercise, had calculated that 3,000 lashes equaled the recitation of 20 psalters, which in turn remitted a year's penance.[95]

Although Cavalca spares his readers the details of the Magdalen's daily self-mortifications, he does describe two further episodes in which she was moved to flog her body. The first was in sympathy with the scourging Christ suffered at the pillar. Cavalca narrates that "she unclothed herself

---

[90] "Scilicet qualiter afflixerit et maceraverit corpus suum per penitenciam dicitur in legenda sua." Ibid.

[91] X. Barbier de Montault, "Sainte Marie-Madeleine d'après les monuments de Rome," *Revue de l'Art Chrétien,* 2d series, 12 (1880): 118.

[92] "Sanguinis effusio et quotidiana corporis afflictio." *Sermo 105, Sermones Thesauri,* unpaginated.

[93] *The Life,* 47–48; *Vita,* 338.

[94] *The Life,* 52; *Vita,* 339.

[95] *De ordine eremitarum, PL* 145, 332.

and struck herself from head to foot with such fervor that the blood flowed to the ground," all the while crying out, "How can I bear to think that Thou wast scourged for my sins."[96] The second episode was the night of the crucifixion. Unable to sleep, "she lacerated herself with the discipline . . . until the blood flowed" and accused herself of being Christ's murderer. "It was not the Jews who did this to my Master; rather it was thy sins, thou brazen sinner, for they could have done nothing, had it not been His will to save thy soul from the hell thou has deserved."[97]

Although the Magdalen as *battuta* does not appear as a subject in painting until the Catholic Reformation, we can obtain a sense of how it would have been represented in medieval iconography when we turn to the thirteenth-century *de modo orandi* (Fig. 38).[98] Here the miniaturist depicts Saint Dominic kneeling before a crucifix. Stripped to the waist, he is captured in the act of bloodying himself with an iron chain. Presumably medieval notions of decorum prevented artists from representing the Magdalen's female body likewise.

We cannot know whether such graphic stories of the Magdalen's penitential practices inspired Margaret of Cortona to cut up her face or Elena of Udine to load her shoes with stones as punishment for having danced too much in her youth; what we can know with certainty is that Italian *disciplinati* companies, whose *raison d'être* was to perform the discipline, often took Mary Magdalen as their patron saint.[99] Companies in Lucca, Viterbo, Rome, Bergamo, and Borgo Sansepolcro all put themselves under the Magdalen's protection.[100]

[96] *The Life,* 241–42; *Vita,* 375.

[97] *The Life,* 279; *Vita,* 382.

[98] MS BAV Ross. 3, f. 7r. For bibliography on this manuscript and its images, see chapter 2, n. 5.

[99] For Margaret, see Haskins, *Mary Magdalen,* 186; for Elena, see Simone da Roma, O.E.S.A., *Libro over legenda della Beata Helena da Udene,* ed. Andrea Tilatti (Tavagnacco [UD]: Casamassima, 1988), 135–37.

[100] The best introduction in English to the flagellant movement is John Henderson, "The Flagellant Movement and Flagellant Confraternities in Central Italy, 1260–1400," in *Religious Motivation: Biographical and Sociological Problems for the Church Historian,* ed. Derek Baker (*Ecclesiastical History Society,* vol. 15) (Oxford: Basil Blackwell, 1978), 147–60. For *Lucca* (1359), see Salvatore Andreucci, "La compagnia dei disciplinati di S. Francesco e S. Maria Maddalena in Lucca," *Bollettino della r. deputazione di storia patria per l'Umbria* (*BRDU*) 68/2 (1971): 233–40. For *Viterbo* (1315) and *Rome* (mid-15th c.), see Gennaro Maria Monti, *Le confraternite medievali dell'alta e media Italia,* 2 vols. (Venice: La Nuova Editrice, 1927), vol. 1, 210, 216. For *Bergamo* (1336), see Guido Tammi, who published the vernacular statutes, "Lo statuto dei disciplini di S. Maria Maddalena di Bergamo. Dal codice sigma 3,2 della Biblioteca Civica di Bergamo," in *Il movimento dei disciplinati nel settimo centenario dal suo inizio (Perugia—1260)* (Convegno internazionale: Perugia, 25–28 Sept. 1960) in *BRDU* 59 (1962): appendix, 257–68, and Lester K. Little et al. who published the Latin version in *Liberty, Charity, Fraternity: Lay Religious Confraternities at Bergamo in the*

Figure 38. *Saint Dominic's Discipline* (ca. 1280). Miniature from *De modo orandi*, Biblioteca Apostolica Vaticana, Città del Vaticano. (Photo: Biblioteca Apostolica Vaticana)

In Bergamo, the congregation of flagellants, which also included women, was ordered to gather on the feasts of the Virgin, the Magdalen, and all the apostles, dress themselves in their white hooded robes, and process through the city streets whipping themselves in the memory of the passion of Jesus Christ.[101] The statutes also ordained that the *battuti* bow and behave reverently whenever they found themselves in front of pictures or statues of Jesus, the Virgin Mary, and Mary Magdalen.[102] By the late fourteenth century, the *battuti bianchi* appear to have been a thriving congregation; they were rich enough to decorate their church with an elaborate fresco cycle illustrating the life of their patroness.[103] In one of the fres-

---

Age of the Commune (Northampton, MA, and Bergamo: Smith College and Pierluigi Lubrina, 1988), 191–204. For *Borgo Sansepolcro,* see James R. Banker, *Death in the Community: Memorialization and Confraternities in an Italian Commune in the Late Middle Ages* (Athens, GA: University of Georgia Press, 1988), 151.

[101] Little, *Liberty,* 196, 204. Women were admitted to the confraternity so long as they obtained permission from their husbands, fathers, or brothers. It is difficult to say whether or not they were permitted to take part in the rites of discipline.

[102] Ibid., 197.

[103] For the cycle, see *Pittura a Bergamo dal romanico al neoclassicismo,* ed. Mina Gregori (Milan: Silvana Ed. d'Arte, 1991), 9, 74, 226, and *I pittori bergamaschi dal XIII al XIX secolo,* 13 vols. (Bergamo: Bolis, 1975–92), *Le origini,* vol. 1 (1975), ed. Miklós Boskovits, 408–

coes Mary Magdalen is shown protecting her company of *battuti,* as does the Madonna della Misericordia (Fig. 48).

In 1345, the flagellants of Borgo Sansepolcro, whose confraternity had been in existence since 1302, began constructing a church known as "the church of the flagellants of Saint Mary Magdalen."[104] By 1349, documents show that they had twenty-seven members. In 1375 the brotherhood commissioned a processional banner from Spinello Aretino depicting the enthroned Magdalen wearing a scarlet mantle. In one hand she holds a crucifix, in the other her alabaster of oils. She is surrounded by a host of eight angels playing musical instruments. At her feet kneel four hooded *disciplinati,* whose robes are cut out at the back to reveal the spot where they ritually scourged their flesh. The vase insignia sewn onto the shoulder of their robes discloses their patron's identity (Fig. 39).[105]

Flagellant companies regarded their disciplinary practices not only as a means of participating in Christ's suffering; they also believed that by ritually beating their bodies either in congregation or in procession they could assume and then expiate the manifold sins of society.

Absolution

Satisfaction completed, we have arrived with Mary Magdalen at the final stage of the penitential obligation, absolution. Preachers formulated, or better, visualized the act of the Magdalen's absolution for their audiences in various ways. We shall examine two of them here. One of the most common ways to represent it was as the kiss of peace or reconciliation, a gesture that would have been familiar to most everyone in faction-riven medieval Italy. Here is how Luca da Bitonto envisioned the Magdalen's absolution:

> For [just as] enemies were accustomed to kiss each other when they came for peace, so indeed was it the case for this sinner who had waged war on the Lord who, now coming to make peace, gave kisses to the feet of Christ.[106]

Martin of Troppau represented the Magdalen's absolution similarly, further illuminating the significance of the gesture:

---

14. I am grateful to Lester Little for these references. Chapter 2, fig. 10 is a fresco from the *disciplinati* church in Bergamo.

[104] Banker, *Death in the Community,* 151.

[105] The banner is now in the Metropolitan Museum of Art, New York. The reverse side of the banner shows the flagellation of Christ. His face and upper torso have been removed and are now in the collection of the Camposanto Teutonico in Vatican City. See Federico Zeri, *Italian Paintings: A Catalogue of the Collection of the Metropolitan Museum of Art: Florentine School* (New York: Metropolitan Museum of Art, 1971), 42–46.

[106] "Nam homines inimici consueverunt cum veniunt ad pacem se invicem obsculari. Ista vero peccatrix quia domino gueram fecerat nunc ad pacem veniens Christi pedibus obscula dabat." MS Casanat. 17, f. 66v; not in *RLS.*

Figure 39. *Mary Magdalen as Patron Saint* (ca. 1375). Processional banner of the Disciplinati Company of S. Maria Maddalena of Borgo Sansepolcro by Spinello Aretino. The Metropolitan Museum of Art, New York. (Photo: The Metropolitan Museum of Art)

The kiss is the sign of perfect reconciliation. For however great the sinner is when he returns, [the Lord] forgives not part, but the entire sin. The symbol of which is Mary Magdalen, who had many sins, and to whom He said: "Your faith has saved you. Go in peace."[107]

Employing a different approach, Jordanus of Quedlinburg used the metaphor of the Magdalen's unguents to illustrate the workings of absolution. He suggested that the Magdalen's alabaster contained a compound composed of one part contrition, one part confession, and one part satisfaction. The mixture of these three oils produced no therapeutic results until it was completed by a fourth and final ingredient: the oil of divine mercy, which only the savior could provide. The penitential recipe, then, was completed when the Lord absolved Mary Magdalen of all her sins.[108]

Martin of Troppau continued the culinary motif. "I don't know how many dishes there were at the Pharisee's, but it must be presumed that they were many and that they were good," he preached. The Magdalen also contributed to this feast. Her contribution, however, was not prepared from corporeal food, but rather "prepared from penance and weeping about sins."[109] Giovanni da San Gimignano also used such alimentary imagery, suggesting that the Lord found Mary Magdalen's meal more pleasing and more flavorful than the corporeal dishes he was served. For Giovanni, absolution occurred at the moment when Christ consumed the spiritual repast served up by the penitent: "For just as carnal food is incorporated into the human being through the conversion of nature, so the sinner is incorporated into the mystical body, that is Christ and his members, by penitential conversion."[110] It is a graphic metaphor: Christ absolves the

[107] "Osculum enim est signum perfecte reconciliationis. Quantuscumque enim peccator fuerit cum redierit, non partem offense sed totum dimittit. In signum cuius Maria Magdalena que multa peccata habuit penitenti dixit. Fides tua te salvam fecit. Vade in pace." *Sermo 57, Sermones Martini Ordinis Praedicatorum penitentiarii domini pape de tempore et de sanctis super epistolas et evangelia cum promptuario exemplorum* (Strasbourg, 1488), no pagination. See also Giovanni da San Gimignano: "Obscula ergo Magdalene signabantur pacem et reconciliationem cum Christo." MS BAV, Barb. lat. 513, f. 101r; *RLS* 3: 378, and the Augustinian friar Gregorio da Cremona: "Reversa est beata Magdalena de via perditionis ad viam reconciliationis." MS Assisi 539, f. 238v; not in *RLS.*

[108] "Sed ex his tribus non bene conficitur unguentum nisi apponatur oleum misericordie divine, sine qua omnis penitentia est inefficax. Admixto autem oleo optimum unguentum efficitur. Et tale fuit unguentum Marie Magdalene que omnes partes penitentie perfectissime implevit, assistente sibi misericordia salvatoris." *Sermo 258, Opus postillarum et sermonum Iordani de Tempore* (Strasbourg, 1483), no pagination.

[109] "Quot autem pharisei convivio fercula fuerint nescio. Praesumendum tamen quod multa et bona. . . . istud convivium praeparatum ex penitentia et planctu peccatorum et est convivium dei." *Sermo 245, Sermones Martini Ordinis Praedicatorum,* no pagination.

[110] "Ipsa refecit eum cibo spirituali qui erat ei magis gratus et magis sapidus. Nam sicut cibus corporalis incorporatur homini per conversionem naturae, sic peccator incorporatur corpori Christi mistico id est Christo et membris eius per conversionem penitenciae." MS BAV Barb. lat. 513, f. 100r; *RLS* 3: 378.

sinner when he eats the meal made from penitential ingredients. Through the process of digestion, the sinner is reintegrated into his mystical body, the Christian community.

Jacobus de Voragine extended the banqueting conceit. He suggested that

> first, [the Magdalen] served up *contrition* which was demonstrated by the many tears that she shed. Second, she served up *confession,* for she confessed her sins publicly in a certain way, when among the guests she offered up tears. She served up *satisfaction* because, as Gregory says, she converted her multitude of accumulated sins to virtue.[111]

And absolution? Jacobus concludes the sermon by suggesting that Christ's absolution is represented in an act of reciprocity: he offered up a meal to Mary Magdalen by forgiving her sins, bestowing grace, and conferring eternal salvation and peace.[112] This meal, in which both the Magdalen and Christ participated—preparing and eating symbolic food—is the literary counterpart of the Thomistic notion of absolution. It will be recalled that for Aquinas and his followers, absolution was a collaboration between the contrite penitent and the priest. Jacobus, a contemporary of Thomas, and indeed a member of the same order, animated vividly the official Dominican position on absolution.

Hope

Given the purgative results of absolution, there was good reason for the average sinner to be optimistic about the possibility of salvation. This lesson was learned above all by the example of Mary Magdalen, the *beata peccatrix,* who through great penance became a great saint. Eudes de Châteauroux declared that Mary Magdalen symbolized instruction for sinners:

> For through her example, she is instruction for us. She teaches what we sinners ought to do. She did not despair, she did not presume, she did not deny her sins, she did not ignore them, but rather with bitter laments and tears, having cast off all human shame she sought forgiveness.[113]

---

[111] "In hac namque coena spirituali Magdalena posuit tres partes. Primo posuit contritionem quae apparuit per tantas lachrymas quas effudit. Secundo posuit confessionem, peccata enim publice quodammodo, confessa fuit quando inter convivantes lacrymas obtulit. Tertio satisfactione, quia sicut dicit Gregorius: convertit ad virtutum cumulum numerum criminum." *Sermones Aurei,* 255–56.

[112] "Christus autem alias tres partes posuit, scilicet peccati remissionem cum dixit: 'Remittuntur ei peccata multa.' Gratiae collatione cum subiunxit: 'Quoniam dilexit multum.' Et aeternam salvationem cum dixit: 'Fides tua salvam te fecit, vade in pace.'" Ibid., 256.

[113] Cited in Bériou, "La Madeleine," 332.

At bottom, the ultimate meaning of the Magdalen in the late Middle Ages was a message of hope.[114] Indeed, I would like to argue that Mary Magdalen became the primary symbol of hope in the late medieval period. Following Gregory the Great, popes and preachers alike represented her as such.[115] Innocent III told his audience of sinners that "you should not despair but turn your attention to Mary Magdalen."[116] The fourteenth-century Franciscan preacher Pietro da Padova called the saint a *speculum spei*, a mirror of hope. The anonymous Franciscan from Marseilles said she offered the hope of forgiveness for herself and others. And Jean de La Rochelle preached that "because of her example sinners should not despair."[117] Nicolas d'Haqueville interpreted the Magdalen's frequent position at Christ's feet as symbolic of hope (distancing herself would have signaled despair), while Jacobus de Voragine maintained that the Magdalen abided in hope, the sign of which was that she *stood* behind Jesus at the Pharisee's; if she had despaired she would have fallen.[118] Bertrand de la Tour, preaching a Magdalen sermon from the text of Isaiah 55:13, explicated the prophetic words in this way: "He [Isaiah] predicted the penance of the Magdalen, giving in her the example to sinners of not despairing."[119]

In another sermon, Bertrand reminded his listeners that hope was necessary for salvation; the Lord did not look kindly on those who despaired of his mercy:

> For hope and confidence of forgiveness are required necessarily on the part of the sinner. For God does not forgive the sins of those who are despairing and of those saying with Cain (Gen. 4:13): "My punishment is more than I can bear." Because of this Christ said to that paralyzed man (Matt. 9:2): "Believe, son, and your sins will be forgiven."[120]

---

[114] For the theology of hope, see J.-G. Bougerol, *La théologie de l'espérance aux XIIe et XIIIe siècles,* 2 vols. (Paris: Études Augustiniennes, 1985).

[115] *Hom. 25, Homiliarum in evangelia, PL* 76, 1196.

[116] "Nec sic utique desperes sed Mariam Magdalenam respicias." MS BAV Arch. Cap. S. Petri D. 211, f. 78r.

[117] MS Antoniana 435, f. 74r; *RLS* 4: 59. For Pietro, see Clément Schmitt, "Pierre de Padoue," *DS* 12 (1986), 1631. Anonymous of Marseilles: "Maria Magdalena ut pre esset peccatoribus ne desperarent." MS BAV Borgh. 138, f. 146r; *RLS* 9: 97. Jean de La Rochelle: "Illius exemplo non debent peccatores desperare." MS Angelica 823, f. 154r.

[118] Nicolas d'Haqueville, MS BAV Vat. lat. 1251, f. 16r. Jacobus de Voragine: "Habuit spem quod notatur cum dicitur: 'Stans retro.' Spes enim facit stare, cum desperatio facit cadere." *Sermones Aurei,* 258.

[119] "Praedicit penitentiam Magdalene dantis in ea peccatoribus exemplum non desperandi." MS Nap. Naz. VIII. A. 36, ff. 72v–73r; *RLS* 1: 897.

[120] "Spes enim et confidentia requiruntur necessario ex parte peccatoris ad istam remissionem. Non enim remittit deus desperanti peccata et dicenti cum Cayn Gen. iiii. Maior est iniquitas mea quam ut veniam merear propter hoc dixit Christus illi paralytico: sicut ha-

François de Meyronnes observed that Mary Magdalen was not only an example of hope for sinners, she was also their advocate. She was, he suggested, an "advocate chosen for sinners just as a queen intercedes with the king for the poor."[121] Thomas Aquinas was thinking along the same lines when he referred to the saint as the "holy intercessor and advocate of sinners."[122]

Hope sprung eternal in hymns and lauds honoring the Magdalen as well; it was "among the constant features of the hymns."[123] A fifteenth-century hymn sung:

Happy Maria,
hope of forgiveness,
model of penance,
mirror of conversion
who pleased the Lord for us.[124]

The theme of hope was taken up by painters of the late medieval period as well. In the latter half of the thirteenth century, a panel painting was produced in Florence in which the saint, clothed in nothing but her long mane of hair, gazes out beyond her frame, beckoning the spectator to stop and read the message inscribed on her scroll: "Ne desperetis vos qui peccare soletis. Exemploque me vos reparate Deo." (Do not despair those of you who are accustomed to sin. By my example return yourselves to God.) (Fig. 40).[125] Her message is hortatory and aimed at a "notionally present spec-

---

betur Matt .ix. Confide fili remittuntur tibi peccata tua." *Sermo 217, Sermones Bertrandi,* no pagination.

[121] "Advocata eligenda pro peccatoribus sicut regina pro pauperibus apud regem intercedit." *Sermones de laudibus sanctorum* (Venice: Pelegrinus de Pasqualibus, 1493), 78.

[122] *Sermo 8, Sermones festivi* in *Opera Omnia* (Parma: P. Fiaccadori, 1864), vol. 15, 220.

[123] "*Peccatrix quondam femina:* A Survey of the Mary Magdalen Hymns," *Traditio* 19 (1963): 117.

[124] Cited in Szövérffy, "*Peccatrix,*" 117. The "cantinella" from Marseilles also sung the message of hope. Assuming the Magdalen's voice it urged:

Ne vous désespérez point pêcheurs.
Sortez de la mauvaise voie,
Ayez douleur de (vos) péchés,
Pleurez, comme je faisais,
Et vous obtiendrez (votre) pardon.

Bernard Laluque, *Marseille fut-elle evangelisée par une femme?* (Marseilles: Le Comité du Vieux Marseille, 1986), 370.

[125] The Florentine artist is known only as the Magdalen Master. Nothing is known about the painting's provenance. In the eighteenth century it hung in the Servite convent of Santissima Annunziata in Florence, but no earlier documentation for the painting exists. It is now in the Galleria dell' Accademia in Florence. For the development of its iconography, see George Kaftal, *Iconography of the Saints in Tuscan Painting* (Florence: Sansoni, 1965);

Figure 40. *Symbol of Hope* (ca. 1280). The hermit-saint carries a scroll that reads: "Ne desperetis vos qui peccare soletis exemploque meo vos reparate Deo." ("Do not despair those of you who are accustomed to sin, and in keeping with my example, return yourselves to God.") Panel painting by the Magdalen Master, Galleria dell'Accademia, Florence. (Photo: Soprintendenza per i beni artistici e storici delle provincie di Firenze e Pistoia)

tator"—those of us accustomed to sinning. Now Mary Magdalen herself preaches the message of hope.

Scholars have long argued that many works of art produced in this period demand a reciprocal relation with their audience: "that the subject is only completed by the presence of the spectator."[126] This observation is particularly apt for this panel painting, which quite clearly demands its audience's attention. Who was the intended audience? Unhappily, since its precise provenance is unknown, so is its intended audience. But let us not despair; evidently it was seen enough for it contents to be copied, a reliable index for gauging medieval admiration. My research has turned up four more later Florentine examples. The first, a triptych, attributed to Andrea Orcagna, shows a Madonna and child flanked by Saint Ansanus (patron saint of Siena) and Mary Magdalen, who carries her pot of oils, wears a red gown (rather than just her flowing hair), and carries the inscribed scroll urging sinners not to despair. It was commissioned by Tommaso Baronci and hung in the chapel of Saint Ansanus in the church of Santa Maria Maggiore in Florence (Fig. 41).[127] The second example comes from the same church; this time the haggard saint, clothed in her mane of hair and carrying the sinners' banner, is frescoed onto one of the piers (Fig. 42). A third example, another fresco, at the Vallombrosan church of Santa Trìnita in Florence, represents the Magdalen in her cave receiving final communion. Above her head flutters a banderole on which her message of hope is inscribed (Fig. 43).[128] The final example, the commission of which has not been established, but which has been attributed to the workshop of Bernardo Daddi, depicts the hirsute Magdalen in the company of three other saints. Of the four saints, she is the only one to speak directly to the audience exhorting her beholders with the by now familiar words: "Do not despair those of you who are accustomed to sin. By my example return

---

Magdalen LaRow, *The Iconography of Mary Magdalen: The Evolution of a Western Tradition until 1300* (Ph.D. diss., New York University, 1982); and D. Russo, "Entre le Christ et Marie: la Madeleine dans l'art italien des XIIIe–XVe siècles," in Duperray, *Marie Madeleine,* 173–90. Though I have searched, I have been unsuccessful in finding a textual precedent for her scroll.

[126] John Shearman, *Only Connect . . . Art and the Spectator in the Italian Renaissance* (The A. W. Mellon Lectures in the Fine Arts, 1988. The National Gallery of Art, Washington, D.C., Bollingen Series XXXV.37) (Princeton: Princeton University Press, 1992), 261, 33. Millard Meiss, *Painting in Florence and Siena after the Black Death* (Princeton: Princeton University Press, 1951), chapter 5, esp. 123.

[127] It is now in the Archiepiscopal museum in Utrecht. See H. W. van Os and Marian Prakken, *The Florentine Paintings in Holland: 1300–1500* (Florence: Netherlands Institute for Art History, 1974), 27.

[128] The fresco is in the Cappella di San Benedetto and has been variously attributed as "scuola giottesca" and to Cenni di Francesco di ser Cenni. See Marilena Mosco, *La Maddalena tra sacro e profano* (Milan: Mondadori, 1986), 31.

Figure 41. *Symbol of Hope* (1350). Triptych of the Madonna flanked by Mary Magdalen and Saint Ansanus. Mary Magdalen carries a scroll inscribed with her message of hope. (See Fig. 40.) Painted for Tommaso Baronci and attributed to Andrea di Cione (Orcagna), ex Church of S. Maria Maggiore, Florence. Now in the Archiepiscopal Museum, Utrecht. (Photo: I.C.C.D., Rome)

Figure 42. *Symbol of Hope* (14th c.). The hermit-saint holds a scroll inscribed with her message of hope. (See Fig. 40.) Fresco from the Church S. Maria Maggiore, Florence. (Photo: Fratelli Alinari, Rome)

Figure 43. *Symbol of Hope* (14th c.). The hermit-saint receives communion while above her head flutters a banderole inscribed with her message of hope. Fresco attributed to Cenni di Francesco di ser Cenni from the Church of S. Trìnita, Florence. (Photo: Author)

yourselves to God."[129] Clearly, the Magdalen anticipated a response to her message. What she expected was that sinners would follow her along the *via penitentiae,* the way of penance.

Preachers often envisioned two paths to salvation: Mary Magdalen represented the way of penance, the Virgin Mary, the way of innocence. In the late twelfth century, the Parisian master Peter Comestor concluded that the way of the Virgin was more difficult. For "there are many more in the Church who have corrected their faults than there are those who never knew sin. More are justified than just. Many, therefore, learn by the Magdalen's example."[130] Giovanni da San Gimignano suggested that the Magdalen was the example of penance for all sinners, just as the Virgin Mary was the way for the just. And taking the metaphor to poetical heights he proposed: "And these two Marys are just like two eyes in the head of the Church. For one is the right eye directing the way of innocence, the other is like the left, directing the way of penance."[131]

Satisfying as binary conceptualization may be, it nevertheless has a tendency to obscure complexity. In this case, the oppositional framework misleads by presenting only two-thirds of the equation, merely alluding to the unspoken possibility of a third way, the *via perditionis,* the way of perdition, the way of Eve.[132] Indeed, before the new emphasis on penance, and its figurehead Mary Magdalen, it was difficult to imagine more than two ways. Ephrem the Syrian had declared: Mary was the bright eye illuminating the world, while Eve, the other eye, was blind and dark.[133] When we move from binary categories to a model of greater complexity, imagining

---

[129] Richard Offner, *A Critical and Historical Corpus of Florentine Painting* (New York: Institute of Fine Art, 1930–), Sec. III, vol. 5 (1947), fig. 26, 126. The other saints are Julian the Hospitaller, Michael, and Martha. Offner suggests that the presence of Saint Julian, patron of Florentine innkeepers, may indicate the altar or church for which it was made. Judith Oliver has pointed out to me that she has found yet another example of this image of the Magdalen in the Codex Gisle, a manuscript made in 1300 by the nun Gisela for the convent of Rulle, a house of Cistercian nuns in Westphalia. For discussion of this manuscript, see Judith Oliver, "Worship of the Word: Some Gothic *Nonnenbücher* in Their Devotional Context," in *Women and the Book: Assessing the Visual Evidence,* ed. Lesley Smith and Jane H. M. Taylor (Toronto: University of Toronto Press, 1996), 106–22.

[130] *PL* 171, 677. Migne erroneously attributed these sermons to Hildebert de Lavardin.

[131] "Et istae Mariae sunt sicut duo oculi in capite ecclesiae. Una quidem ut oculus dexter derigens per viam innocentie, alia ut sinister derigens, per viam poenitentie." MS BAV Barb. lat. 513, f. 97v; *RLS* 3: 337. Bonaventura also made the comparison between innocence and penance, although he used Saints Catherine and Cecilia instead of the Virgin Mary as examples of the way of innocence. See *de quinque festitatibus pueri Jesu* in *S. Bonaventurae S.R.E. Episcopi Cardinalis Opera Omnia,* ed. PP. Collegii S. Bonventurae, 10 vols. (Quaracchi: Typ. Collegii S. Bonaventurae), vol. 8 (1898), 90.

[132] The phrase "via perditionis" is from Gregorio da Cremona. See MS Assisi 539, f. 238v.

[133] Cited by Hilda Graef, *Mary: A History of Doctrine and Devotion,* 2 vols. (New York: Sheed and Ward, 1963–65), vol. 1, 59–60.

three beams emanating from one source, one strong and brilliant, the next one a bit less bright, and the third one dark and ineffective, we better approach how thinkers of the later Middle Ages conceived of this female trinity. Indeed, the way of penance was a *via media,* a third way, a road between innocence and perdition.[134]

In previous chapters we have seen how the Magdalen's pre-conversion life often conjured comparisons with the sinful Eve; equally her post-conversion life of penance was so efficacious that it made amends not only for her own mistakes, but also for those of her accursed fore-mother. Suggestively, all roads led back to the garden. Eve once knew the pleasures of paradise, but because of her calamitous sin, expulsion from Eden soon followed. Her sin was not merely a private matter between herself and an angry God, it had lethal consequences for the entire human race. Theologians such as Augustine argued that it stained all of humanity, passing as it did to subsequent generations through the act of sexual intercourse. The cruel irony was that humanity's curse was contained in its seed: the very source of life was defiled at its origin by the mark of perdition.

For the most part, theologians regarded the Virgin Mary as the second Eve whose virgin birth of Christ atoned for the devastating sin of the first woman. Frequently represented as the *hortus conclusus*—the unbreached garden of untrammeled innocence (an image borrowed from the *Song of Songs* 4:12)—Mary's fecund virginity was credited with having restored life where, due to Eve, death and destruction had reigned.[135] Christ's virgin birth through Mary had regained for humanity the possibility of paradise lost.

It must be remembered, however, that Mary Magdalen shared the role of *redemptrix* with the Virgin Mary in salvation history. Augustine had claimed in an Easter homily that just as "humanity's fall was occasioned by womankind, humanity's restoration was accomplished through womankind, since a virgin brought forth Christ and a woman announced that he had risen from the dead."[136] In John 20: 1–18, the Magdalen went to the sepulcher to anoint the body of her crucified Lord on Easter morning. She found the tomb empty and began a desperate search for him. Scriptural exegetes such as Alain de Lille explicated the lover of the *Canticles* (3:1–3) looking for her beloved as the prefiguration of the Magdalen in

[134] Jacques Dalarun, *Lapsus Linguae: La Légende de Claire de Rimini* (Biblioteca di *Medioevo Latino,* vol. 6) (Spoleto: Centro Italiano di studi sull'alto medioevo, 1994), 333, suggests in regard to married women: "Madeleine est la porte entrouverte qui leur permet de trouver place dans un plan de salut."

[135] For the Virgin and the exegetical tradition of the *Canticles,* see E. Ann Matter, *The Voice of My Beloved: The Song of Songs in Western Medieval Christianity* (Philadelphia: University of Pennsylvania Press, 1990), 151–77.

[136] *Sermo 232, SC* 116 (1966), 262.

the garden, searching for the Lord.[137] It was, moreover, in the garden that she received her commission from Christ, whom moments earlier she had mistaken for the gardener. It was a gift of grace for Mary Magdalen, who, since her conversion, had vigilantly guarded her chastity, making of herself a sealed garden.[138] By maintaining her purity, preachers argued, the Magdalen was transformed from *terra inculta,* a desolated and deserted land, into a garden abounding in delights.

Indeed, the friars often preached Magdalen sermons on the theme of "the wasteland made into a garden of delights" (Ezech. 36:35),[139] representing her pre-conversion life as a miserable and unyielding plot of earth. In contrast was her post-conversion state: a lush and flourishing garden, not unlike the paradisiacal garden evoked in the canticles. Here is Iohannes de Biblia on the subject:

> Beloved Mary Magdalen once was like a wasteland deserted by God, all care withdrawn . . . that is, she became a dwelling place for the devil, occupied entirely by the brambles of sin. Afterwards a zealous lord occupied her land. After the passing of winter, spring arrived during which, cultivating the land diligently, he cleared it, replenished it with new plants, and applied his care. Bursting into flower it became a garden. In the following summer he guided the abundant fruit to ripen. Thus she was transformed into a garden of pleasures just as if she were a sort of paradise of delights.[140]

It is extraordinarily evocative imagery, more so in the original than in translation, because the Latin, through the feminine pronoun, is able to evoke both the histories of the saint and the land simultaneously. The entire sermon elaborates the conceit of the turning of the seasons and its effects on the land. More expedient, however, was the care of the Gardener, the Lord, Jesus Christ.

The fourteenth-century Augustinian friar Gregorio da Cremona's Mag-

---

[137] Matter, *Voice,* 167.

[138] An anonymous Franciscan explained her chastity thus: "Blessed Magdalen maintained her chastity which liberated her heart and body from all sordidness, and the sign of this was because after she converted and did penance for her sins she stood in the company of the blessed Virgin." In the edition of Bériou, "La Madeleine," 339.

[139] "Terra inculta illa facta est ut ortus voluptatis." See Iohannes de Biblia, MS BAV Borgh. 24, ff. 57r–61r; Remigio de' Girolami, MS Flor. Naz. Conv. Sopp. D. 1. 937, ff. 229v–230r; *RLS* 5: 803, and Gregorio da Cremona, MS Assisi 539, ff. 236v–238r.

[140] "Dilectissima Maria Magdalena olim fuit velut terra inculta, a deo deserta, et omni sublata custodia . . . id est demonum erat habitatio facta et vepribus viciorum totaliter occupata postmodum vero çelatus dominus terram suam. Post transitum hyemis ver adduxit quo diligenter ipsam excolens purgavit et bonis plantationibus eam replens custodiam suam apposuit. Quae prorumpens in flores ortus effecta fuit. Estate vero succendente fructus uberes ad maturitatem perduxit. Sic que in ortum voluptatis conversa velut quidam paradisus deliciarum extitit." MS BAV Borgh. 24, f. 57v; cf. ibid., ff. 61v–62r; *RLS* 3: 91.

dalen sermon, based on the same text, specifies the elements necessary to transform a barren piece of earth into a fruitful garden:

> But note that agriculture consists of four things. It is in clearing, enclosing or guarding, cultivating and watering. The first is the confession of sins, the second the guarding of the senses, the third is the frequency of works, and the fourth the effusion of tears.[141]

Mary Magdalen's penitential regime thus merged imperceptibly with agricultural practice, transforming the barren *terra inculta* into a fertile and luxuriant garden, redolent of apples and lilies and spices, all the paradisiacal scents and flavors evoked in the canticles.[142] Mary Magdalen recaptured this fertile garden—the *hortus conclusus*—through enclosure, the heroic preservation of her chastity. Most likely it was for this reason that even Cathar preachers held out Mary Magdalen as an example of hope for their female auditors.[143]

The Magdalen's post-conversion chastity was a subject dear to the hearts and minds of many medieval preachers who regarded it as *almost* on a par with the virginal state. François de Meyronnes argued that the Magdalen was glorified by the quadruple crown, one tier of which was the virgin's floral coronet which the saint received for her great purity of mind and body. He preached: "The third is the floral crown which is given to virgins, not because she was a virgin: but after her conversion she maintained the highest purity of body and mind."[144] François was cautious: he gave her the virgin's crown, but did not admit her to the ranks of virgins. Nor did Giordano da Pisa, although he preached that Mary Magdalen was more chaste than all the other virgins. She was not a virgin of the flesh, however, only of the mind.[145] It is my suspicion that arguments such as these grew

---

[141] "Sed nota quod agricultura consistit in quartum. Est enim purgandus, claudendus sive custodiendus, excolendus et irrigandus. Primum facit confessio peccatorum, secundum custodia sensuum, tertium frequentia operum, quartum effusio lacrimarum." MS Assisi 539, f. 237v. For Gregorio, see D. Gutiérrez, "Grégoire de Crémone," *DHGE* 21 (1986), 1495–96.

[142] "(Can. v) Veniat dilectus meus in ortum suum et comedat fructum pomorum suorum; scilicet poma redolentia sunt superne suavitatis fragrantia quibus reficitur anima delicata. . . . (Can. vi) Dilectus meus descendit in ortum suum ad aureolam aromatum ut pascatur in ortis et lilia colligat." MS Assisi 539, ff. 237r–238r.

[143] Peter Biller, "The Common Woman in the Western Church in the Thirteenth and Early Fourteenth Centuries," in *Women in the Church,* ed. W. J. Sheils and Diana Wood (Oxford: Basil Blackwell, 1990), 150.

[144] "Et dicitur quod habuit quadruplicem coronam . . . Tertio coronam floream que datur virginibus non quod esset virgo: sed post conversionem suam puritatem altissimam mentis et corporis habuit." *Sermones de laudibus,* 79.

[145] *Prediche del Beato Fra Giordano,* vol. 2, 46. The passage is drawn from a sermon for the feast of Saint Matthew.

out of a question that preachers must have been asked time and again by members of their congregations. To wit: "Why is Mary Magdalen found at the head of the virgins in the litany of the saints?" Eudes de Châteauroux responded it was because "she was an apostle, she was a martyr of compassion, and preacher of the truth." He furthermore preached that though the Magdalen did not regain bodily wholeness, nevertheless her humility, patience, and love earned her the same crown as the virgins. Moreover, she was destined as an example to those who had maintained their bodies intact, lest they scorn those who had known the flesh.[146] François, Giordano, and Eudes each made subtle but important distinctions between virginity of the body and virginity of the mind. In chapter 10 we will see how such subtleties fared among the preachers' auditors.

Another way of conceiving of the Magdalen's penitential transformation was to formulate it in Pauline terms (Rom. 9:21–23). Friar Ludovicus preached that the Lord transformed the Magdalen from a ruined vessel, a vessel of wrath, a vessel of effrontery, into a vase of glory.[147] Whether conceived of as a vase of glory or as a lush and bounteous enclosed garden, breathing new life into the Pauline maxim "ubi abundavit delictum superabundavit gratia" (Rom 5:20), a phrase inevitably found in sermons on the saint, there was no doubt about the efficacy of the Magdalen's penance. It purified and readied her to accept Christ. This formulation helps to illuminate a curious motif in medieval art, the Magdalen as Christ-bearer. Marilena Mosco argues that this image was an assimilation of the Magdalen to the Virgin, a Byzantine-type *Cristophora*.[148] Only a vessel cleansed of all sin would have been appropriate to transport the Christ, as the Magdalen does in these images.

In a related motif, Jacques de Vitry preached that sinners ought not to despair because, "When Christ contracted marriage with this sinner, she gave birth to as many souls as she had converted to penance by her exam-

---

[146] In the edition of Bériou, "La Madeleine," 336.

[147] "Qui vas perditum vas ire vas contumelie transtulit et transformuit in vas glorie." MS Marc. lat. fondo antico, 91 (1775), f. 16v. Iohannes de Biblia cites the antiphon that used this formulation: "Unde de ea cantatur." MS BAV Borgh. 24, f. 63v. See also Iohannes de Castello, MS Assisi 470, f. 494v.

[148] *La Maddalena*, 31. Paolo Veneziano made two of these images. The first is in the Worcester Museum of Art and reproduced in Mosco, *La Maddalena*, 32, fig. 3; the second, in a triptych now in the Galleria Nazionale, Parma. It is reproduced in Lucia Fornari Schianchi, *La Galleria Nazionale di Parma* (Parma: Artegrafica Silva, n.d.). The saint was visualized similarly by the "Sienese Master of the Magdalen Legend," in the Abbey church of Hautecombe (Savoie). See Millard Meiss, "Notes on Three Linked Sienese Styles," *Art Bulletin* 45 (1963): 47–48, fig. 6. In all three, the hirsute Magdalen is borne aloft by angels and holds (or wears) an image of Christ's face on her chest. There is yet one more image, a wing of an Ambrogio Lorenzetti triptych (now in the Pinacoteca Nazionale, Siena), in which the Magdalen fully clothed, wears the Christ image, almost as a medallion.

ple."[149] Hers were the children conceived in penitential purity and reared in hope, not unlike the *convertite* to whom Ranulphe de la Houblonnière preached in 1273. Among other things, he told them not to despair.[150]

The narrative of the Magdalen's recovery of the fruits of the garden of paradise, lost through the wickedness of Eve, but reborn in the pure womb of the Virgin Mary, was an edifying tale. Ultimately it was a message suffused in hope: if one followed the way of penance, illuminated by the example of Mary Magdalen, one could, like the saint, find a glorious end in heaven. The next section examines how ever hopeful penitents invoked and emulated the Magdalen in pursuit of salvation.

[149] Edition in Lauwers, "*Noli me tangere,*" 261.

[150] Nicole Bériou, *La prédication de Ranulphe de la Houblonnière. Sermons aux clercs et aux simples gens à Paris au XIIIe,* 2 vols. (Paris: Études Augustiniennes, 1987), vol. 2, 139.

PART FOUR

Responses

EIGHT

Responses to the Scriptural Saint

O ne night in the Provençal jail of Millau an incarcerated thief by the name of Jacobus heard the church bells begin to toll ominously. The meaning of the refrain was all too clear to the prisoner: someone had been condemned to die in the gallows the following day. Awaiting sentencing himself and shackled in a prison tower, Jacobus became convinced that the church bells tolled for him, portending his own death sentence. In desperation he implored Saint Mary Magdalen for help. "Because he had heard that the Magdalen sought forgiveness with God for her sins, having made a mental vow, he turned to her for intercession so that just as she had obtained forgiveness for her own sins, she would thus seek forgiveness for his."[1] Jacobus had heard (doubtless in a sermon) that the Magdalen, like himself, had been a great sinner but that her sins had been forgiven. As such he cast in his lot with the *beata peccatrix* deciding to appeal to the mercy of the patron saint of penitent sinners for aid. His tearful petition was answered when, after a number of false starts, his shackles and chains miraculously burst apart allowing him to make an undetected escape. Soon after his divinely assisted deliverance, a grateful Jacobus made pilgrimages to both of Mary Magdalen's provençal shrines at Saint-Maximin and La Sainte-Baume to give proper thanks for his timely salvation.[2]

This edifying story, along with eighty-five others, comprises the register of Mary Magdalen's miracles, redacted circa 1315 by Jean Gobi the Elder, Dominican prior of the royal convent of Saint-Maximin from 1304 to 1328.[3] Gobi kept the book as a public record, an advertisement of sorts

---

[1] "Iohannes Gobi senior OP *Liber miraculorum b. Mariae Magdalenae*," ed. Jacqueline Sclafer, *AFP* 63 (1993): 113–206, no. 4, 141–43.

[2] Ibid., 142–43.

[3] The manuscript, although copied by Faillon, disappeared in 1887. It resurfaced a few years ago and was bought by the Bibliothèque Nationale in 1990 (Paris, B.N., nouv. acq. lat. 2672). For a complete manuscript description, history, and edition, see "Iohannes Gobi," ed.

for the sanctuary over which he presided, and to whose fortunes the convent was closely tied. But his book is more than propaganda intended to drum up business for a pilgrimage center. It contains priceless information about popular religious experience and practice[4] in that it describes the types of miracles effected, vows sworn, rituals performed, therapeutic cures obtained, and ex votos offered up in gratitude by pilgrims who had made the journey to the saint's tomb in Provence.[5] Most important for our purposes, however, the miracle register also provides precious evidence of the reception of Mary Magdalen by the laity and their ensuing devotion, the focus of the four chapters in this section.

Fr. Montagnes, the first modern scholar to work systematically on Gobi's miracle catalog, has remarked that it completes the cycle of Dominican preaching at Saint-Maximin dedicated to the Magdalen. It is "in effect the preaching of the guardians of the sanctuary . . . offering at once the expression and the result of their sermons."[6] Indeed, I would push this analysis further to suggest that the book is a collaborative effort between Gobi and the pilgrims. Although the final narrative account of the miracle register was inevitably shaped by the learned hand of the prior, it was still the pilgrims who provided the raw data. It was they who invoked the aid of the saint, they who made vows, they who benefited from the saint's miracles, they who came to the sanctuary, they who performed rituals before the saint's relics, and they who in thanksgiving left behind ex votos for grace received. Ultimately, then, the pilgrims' devotion to the saint was the fruit

---

J. Sclafer, 113–206. *Number of miracles:* The miracles are numbered 1–84; no. 41 is repeated twice and no. 60 contains two miracles.

[4] I use the word "popular" advisedly, merely for lack of a better descriptive vocabulary. The conception of popular religion that seeks to make sharp distinctions between elite and popular religion, or lay and clerical religion, has rightly had its share of critics. See Natalie Z. Davis, "Some Tasks and Themes in the Study of Popular Religion," in *The Pursuit of Holiness in Late Medieval and Renaissance Religion (Studies in Medieval and Renaissance Thought),* ed. C. Trinkhaus and H. Oberman (Leiden: E. J. Brill, 1974), 307–36; J.-C. Schmitt, "'Religion populaire' et 'culture folklorique,'" *Annales E.S.C.* 31 (1976): 941–53; Leonard Boyle, O.P., "Popular Piety in the Middle Ages: What Is Popular?" *Florilegium* 4 (1982): 184–93; and John Van Engen, "The Christian Middle Ages as an Historiographical Problem," *AHR* 91 (1988): 519–52.

[5] Fr. Bernard Montagnes has made a study of such aspects of Gobi's book in "Saint-Maximin, foyer d'une création hagiographique. Le *Liber miraculorum beate Marie Magdalene* (1315)," in *Marie-Madeleine dans la mystique,* 49–69. Montagnes's work was based on Faillon's copy of the text. By a strange coincidence the Bibliothèque Nationale bought the missing manuscript from a Paris bookseller at about the same time Montagnes's essay was published. Analysis of this miracle collection is central to Raymond Clemens, *The Establishment of the Cult of Mary Magdalen in Provence, 1279–1543* (Ph.D. diss., Columbia University, 1997).

[6] Montagnes seems to back away from this proposition at the conclusion of his essay. See "Saint-Maximin," 61.

of the friars' preaching and the miracle register its written record. From such a vantage point, we must now shift our attention away from the friars and their sermons to the prisoner Jacobus and others like him in order to examine audience response to the preachers' representation of Mary Magdalen. It is the task of the following four chapters to examine how the public received the multilayered meaning of the Magdalen preached by the friars. I maintain that although we may often find the friars' mirror of Mary Magdalen reflected back from the public unchanged, just as frequently we find a subtly modified Magdalen, suggesting a creative interchange between audience and image. In the event, I would like to argue that the friars' audience actively responded to, imaginatively shaped, and resourcefully used representations of the saint for their own purposes and toward their own ends.

Scholars have reiterated frequently that Mary Magdalen was an important model for female piety and devotion in the Middle Ages.[7] What needs emphasizing, however, is that she was an equally important model for men; thus, in what follows, although I center my discussion on female devotion to the Magdalen, it is always with an eye on concomitant male veneration. Clearly, this perspective provides a more complete view of medieval society's response to the saint; further, it allows for a gender analysis which asks whether men and women responded differently to the friars' preaching on the saint. Ultimately we shall be looking at both male and female responses, attempting to disclose what Mary Magdalen meant to those who invoked her intercessory powers, commissioned her image, dedicated churches in her name, or used her as a metaphor in their writings. In the pages that follow we shall examine audience reception, interpretation, and, where it exists, outright rejection and resistance to the images of Mary Magdalen received from the friars' preaching.

The Pre-Conversion Sinner: Vanity and *Luxuria*

When we turn to the Gregorian composite saint the Middle Ages knew as Mary Magdalen and proceed chronologically according to her biography as presented in the gospels, the first image of the Magdalen we encounter is that of Luke's tearful sinner who makes her dramatic conversion at the feet of the Lord. As we have already seen in chapters 5 and 6, by the later medieval period the Magdalen's pre-conversion life was represented as one suffused in sin; she herself had become the living embodiment of worldly

---

[7] See, for example, Haskins, *Mary Magdalen*, 177, following Bynum, *Holy Feast*, 94, and Dyan Elliott, *Spiritual Marriage: Sexual Abstinence in Medieval Wedlock* (Princeton: Princeton University Press, 1993), 234.

vanity and *luxuria*. We have seen that preachers and moralists harnessed this image in an effort to control women; but did their audiences do likewise? If not, how then did the public receive this aspect of the saint and to what ends was this image employed?

Appropriately, the Magdalen as the symbol of worldly vanity and *luxuria* is the aspect of the saint whom the purveyors of vanities embraced as their protector. In the Middle Ages Mary Magdalen became the patron saint of perfumers, apothecaries, glovers, hairdressers, cosmetic makers, and similar tradespeople.[8] In Bologna she was the patron saint of the drapers guild.[9] We have seen in an earlier chapter how she was also the patron saint to *convertite,* those women who had once been enslaved by the bonds of *luxuria*. By recourse to medieval notions of correspondence and analogy, the luxury trades took Mary Magdalen as their patron.

Such a mode of congruent reasoning also informed thinking about 22 July, Mary Magdalen's feast-day. The biographer of Diana d'Andalò (d. 1236), a Bolognese noblewoman and founder of one of the first Dominican convents of nuns in Italy, makes sense out of Diana's conversion by relating it to the feast-day on which it happened. Forced to live according to her family's noble station, Diana draped her body in luxurious purple silk and adorned herself in gold, silver, and precious stones until

> One day, on the feast of Saint Mary Magdalen, she announced that she wanted to visit the monastery called Ronzano. So she went to the house there with immense pomp and honor, with a great throng of ladies attending her. When she arrived there, she went alone into the sisters' dormitory, and suddenly asked for the habit, and was given it.

Worldly Diana appositely cast aside her vanities on the feast-day of Mary Magdalen; noble citizens of the Kingdom of Naples were compelled to do so when, in 1290, a sumptuary law regulating luxury goods went into effect in the *Regno* on the feast-day of the saint.[10] The rhythms of sacred chronology, in this case the feast-day of Mary Magdalen, clearly structured Diana's conversion experience as well as the Neapolitan law-making process. It may also be, as Natalie Davis suggests, that the "festive frame" accounts for why Thomas Manny killed his lascivious wife on 22 July 1529. Although he committed the murder in "hot anger," nonetheless when Manny later recalled the crime for the official court record he made sense

---

[8] Sebastiani, *Tra/Sfigurazione,* 151. Sebastiani points out that Mary Magdalen became the patron saint to glove makers because gloves were perfumed until the seventeenth century.

[9] See Haskins, *Mary Magdalen,* 135.

[10] For Diana d'Andalò, see *Early Dominicans: Selected Writings,* ed. Simon Tugwell, O.P. (New York: Paulist Press, 1982), 396. Giuseppe Del Giudice, *Una legge suntuaria inedita del 1290* (Naples: Tipografia della Regia Università, 1887).

out of it by noting that Mary Magdalen's feast-day was the appropriate time to kill a whore. Significantly, the preachers' image of the whorish pre-conversion Magdalen not only helped Thomas Manny justify his crime but also shaped the narrative of the pardon tale that he recounted to the court reconstructing the events of that day.[11]

When we advert to the intertwined theme of vanity and *luxuria* as it was construed in literary discussions of the Magdalen, we find that there are subtle differences in the way the image was interpreted and employed in the writings of men and women.

Confessors and hagiographers of the later medieval period (frequently one and the same) found the image of the luxury-suffused Magdalen irresistible.[12] Frequently they cast their female subjects as Magdalens, a favored method of contrasting the dramatic differences between pre- and post-conversion life. Fra Girolamo di Giovanni did so when he described the pre-conversion life of Beata Villana delle Botti (d. 1361).[13] This is his description of Villana's descent into worldliness after her marriage:

> Having celebrated her marriage according to the custom of the times, by divine permission Villana's mind began to indulge in the marital embrace such that almost all the fervor she had in her former life grew luke warm, and she was more concerned with pleasing the world than pleasing the Lord. Just as a second Magdalen aspiring to greater magnificence of life, she strove to pamper her lovely body (once content in ashes and hair cloth) in soft clothing, jewels and gold.[14]

According to Fra Girolamo, after her marriage Villana became a *secunda Magdalena,* indifferent to spiritual things, concerned only with worldly pleasures, her attentions especially focused on sartorial satisfactions. One day, however, when Villana, attired in shimmering purple and golden neck-

---

[11] N. Davis *Fiction in the Archives: Pardon Tales and Their Tellers in Sixteenth-Century France* (Stanford: Stanford University Press, 1987), 2–3, 29–30.

[12] Questions posed by historians of gender have recently led to fruitful discussion about the role of confessors/hagiographers in constructing female sanctity. It has become clear that male representations of female piety do not always correspond to that of the female voice on the same topic. For contributions to this burgeoning field, see the bibliography listed in my introduction, n. 23.

[13] For Villana, see Stefano Orlandi, O.P., *La Beata Villana terziaria domenicana fiorentina del sec. XIV* (Florence: Il Rosario, 1955), which in addition to the Latin and Italian *vitae* gives a useful précis of her life in its historical context. According to Orlandi, the *vita* was written about 1420. For Villana, see also Anna Benvenuti Papi, "La Famiglia, Territorio Negato," in *In castro poenitentiae,* 171–203. This essay was originally published as "Il modello familiare nell'agiografia fiorentina tra Duecento e Quattrocento. Sviluppo di una negazione (Da Umiliana dei Cerchi a Villana delle Botti)," *Nuova DWF* 16 (1981): 80–107.

[14] Orlandi, *La Beata Villana,* 78.

laces, was admiring herself in front of the mirror she caught sight of a hideously deformed spirit lurking within her soul.[15] This epiphany caused her so much distress that she burst into tears, cast off her jewel encrusted dress, and ran to the church of Santa Maria Novella where in repentance she flung herself at the feet of the nearest Dominican priest she could find.[16] Clearly Fra Girolamo's narrative modeling of Villana's penitential conversion followed the outlines of the paradigmatic conversion of Luke's sinner at the feet of the Lord. In transforming their potential saints into Magdalens, the Dominicans were rivaled only by their Franciscan counterparts. Fra Giunta Bevegnati, confessor and hagiographer of Margaret of Cortona (d. 1297), regarded his charge as another Magdalen.[17] Margaret had led a worldly life steeped in sin before the tragic death of her lover, the catalyst for her conversion. This, combined with her exemplary post-conversion life as a pious *pinzochera*, convinced Fra Giunta that indeed she was a second Magdalen. Margaret experienced a number of visions further sharpening the comparison between the two penitents. In her visions, as related by Fra Giunta, Christ often summoned the example of the Magdalen to give comfort to the anxious Margaret. In one, the Lord reminded her that Mary Magdalen had ignored the murmuring against her, scorned her jewels, and followed him, just as Margaret herself should continue to do.[18]

Both Villana and Margaret had lived worldly lives before their conversions but such was not the case with Catherine of Siena (d. 1380), the most celebrated tertiary of the Middle Ages.[19] Catherine was a virgin, knowing little of the wages of sin, facts Raymond of Capua, her confessor, did not fail to italicize in her *vita*. The absence of biographical affinities between Catherine and Mary Magdalen did not hinder Raymond from improbably shaping the virgin Catherine in the image of the sinner Magdalen. He nar-

---

[15] Ibid., 79.

[16] Ibid.

[17] AASS, Feb., vol. 3 (Antwerp, 1658), 298–357. For Mary Magdalen, see par. 284, 356. Bibliography on Margaret is growing exponentially; a good place to start is Anna Benvenuti Papi's "Cristomimesi al femminile," in *In castro poenitentiae,* 141–68, originally published as "'Margarita filia Jerusalem:' Santa Margherita da Cortona e il superamento mistico della crociata," in *Toscana e Terrasanta nel medioevo,* ed. Franco Cardini (Florence: Alinea, 1982), 117–37, and Fortunato Iozzelli, "I miracoli nella 'legenda' di S. Margherita da Cortona," *AFH* 86 (1993): 217–76.

[18] AASS, Feb., vol. 3, par. 102, 320.

[19] The basic source for Catherine is Raymond of Capua's *Legenda Maior* in AASS, April, vol. 3 (Antwerp, 1675), 851–978. I quote the translation by George Lamb, *The Life of St. Catherine of Siena* (London: Harvill Press, 1960). Bibliography on Catherine is enormous; a good starting point in English is the recent work of Karen Scott, "St. Catherine of Siena, *Apostola,*" *Church History* 61/1 (1992): 34–46, and "Urban Spaces, Women's Networks, and the Lay Apostolate in the Siena of Catherine Benincasa," in *Creative Women,* 105–19.

rated how Catherine's sister, Bonaventura, had tried to lure the young saint away from her austere penitential practices. But God, ever displeased with those who try to impede his servants, struck Bonaventura down. Raymond describes Catherine's reaction thus:

> On her sister's death the holy virgin, now seeing clearly the vanity of the world, turned to her Eternal Bridegroom with greater fervor and desire, and acknowledging her culpability and upbraiding herself, prostrated [herself] with Mary Magdalen at the feet of her Lord, [giving] . . . herself to tears.[20]

Thus Raymond's Catherine, who had not even succumbed to her sister's cajolery, but who had merely perceived the vanity of her age, tearfully prostrated herself with the Magdalen at the Lord's feet asking his forgiveness.

Raymond wrapped Catherine's encounter with vanity in Magdalenian motifs, but what did Catherine, when speaking in her voice, make of the Magdalen's vanity and her subsequent rejection of it? To answer, we must turn to Catherine's own vernacular letters.[21] In one letter written to a prostitute in Perugia, Catherine sounds like any other medieval preacher denouncing the evils of the oldest profession. She begins by scolding the woman, borrowing directly from the friars' metaphorical vocabulary:

> It seems that you are behaving like a pig wallowing in mud when you immerse yourself in the muck of the world. You have made yourself a servant and slave of sin; you have mistaken the devil for the Lord, serving him day and night.[22]

She then urges the woman to confess her sins, promising that the Lord will have mercy on her. Borrowing the leprosy metaphor from the friars' lexicon, but suffusing it in her own distinctive blood-soaked imagery, she exhorts: "You will see that he has made a bath of blood to wash away the leprosy of your mortal sin and the impurity in which you have remained for so long. You will not repel your sweet Lord." And finally: "Learn from that

---

[20] AASS, 30 April, vol. 3, 864–65; Lamb, *St. Catherine,* 40.

[21] According to Raymond, Catherine dictated her voluminous correspondence since she never learned to write either Italian or Latin. For the social significance of her letters, see Karen Scott, "'Io Catarina:' Ecclesiastical Politics and Oral Culture in the Letters of Catherine of Siena," in *Dear Sister: Medieval Women and the Epistolary Genre,* ed. Karen Cherewatuk and Ulrike Wiethaus (Philadelphia: University of Pennsylvania Press, 1993), 87–121. The edition I have used is *Lettere di S. Caterina da Siena,* ed. Niccolò Tommaseo, 4 vols. (Florence: G. Barbèra, 1860). The critical edition, containing only six years of her correspondence, is *S. Caterina da Siena, Epistolario,* ed. Eugenio Dupré Theseider (Rome: Tipografia del Senato, 1940). Suzanne Noffke has translated this volume into English as *The Letters of Catherine of Siena* (Medieval & Renaissance Texts & Studies, vol. 52) (Binghamton, NY: Center for Medieval and Early Renaissance Studies, 1988), vol. 1 (of projected 4). Where they exist I use her translations, otherwise the translations are my own.

[22] *Le lettere,* vol. 4, ep. 276, 16.

sweet and *innamorata Maddalena* who as soon as she had seen her sin and understood her state of damnation, immediately ... went in search of forgiveness."[23]

Umiltà of Faenza (d. 1310), founder of an order of Vallombrosan nuns and noted author of sermons, also employed the imagery of pollution when writing about the Magdalen's sinful life which was washed away by her purifying tears.[24] For Catherine Christ's blood was the purifying agent, for Umiltà it was tears:

> She was freed and delivered from the domination of sins, cleansed of all leprosy that contaminated her, cured of all disease that plagued her, revived from the serpent's poison and every corruption that had despoiled her; and in regard to all the blessings stripped from her, she was restored one hundred times over.[25]

Both women, then, drew from the contemporary metaphorical well when they employed the language of pollution in discussing the wickedness of Mary Magdalen's pre-conversion life; yet they were not entirely dependent on the preachers' vision of female vanity and its renunciation. It will be recalled that the preachers' greatest fear about vanity was that it led irrevocably to the mortal sin of *luxuria*. Female *luxuria*, they preached, engendered poverty, usury, prostitution, sodomy, and the entrapment and downfall of innocent men. For these reasons—for the common good—the friars appealed to the social consciences of women to repent.

Women, however, in meditating on the Magdalen's foresworn vanity, agreed entirely that vanity should be renounced, but not necessarily for the reasons the preachers posited. Their reasons centered on personal salvation rather than the commonweal. Catherine of Siena provides ample testimony. In one letter, Catherine encourages Monna Bartolomea of Lucca to follow the lessons of her teacher Mary Magdalen. She writes:

> She no longer turned to prestige or grandeur or her own vanities. She took no more pleasure or delight in the world. She did not think or worry about

---

[23] Ibid., 19. For the significance of blood imagery in Catherine's writing, see Bynum, *Holy Feast*, 65, 177–80.

[24] The main source for Umiltà's life is the *vita* in AASS, May, vol. 5 (Antwerp, 1685), 203–22. Elizabeth Petroff has translated it in *Consolation of the Blessed* (New York: Alta Gaia Society, 1979), 121–65. Although she deems it anonymous, Don Biagio, Umiltà's spiritual director, is the author.

[25] *Sermo Tertius* in *Sermones S. Humilitatis de Faventia Abbatissae Ordinis Vallisumbrosae nunc primum in lucem editi,* ed. D. Torello Sala (Florence: Officina Calasantiana, 1884), 150. There is a recent critical edition of the sermons: *I sermoni di Umiltà da Faenza*, ed. Adele Simonetti (Spoleto: Centro italiano di studi sull'alto medioevo, 1995). On the sermons, see Adele Simonetti, "I sermoni di Umiltà da Faenza: storia della tradizione," *Studi medievali*, 3d series, 32 (1991): 303–8.

anything but how she could follow Christ. No sooner had she set her affection on him and come to know herself than she embraced him and took the path of lowliness. For God's sake she despised herself, for she saw that there is no other way to follow or to please him. She realized that she was the lowliest of all people. She was no more self-conscious than a drunken woman, whether alone or with others. Otherwise she would never have been among those soldiers of Pilate, nor would she have gone and stayed alone at the tomb. Love kept her from thinking, "What will it look like? Will people speak ill of me because I am rich and beautiful?" Her thoughts were not here, but only on how she might find and follow her Master. She, then, is the companion I am giving to you. I want you to follow her because she knew the way so well that she has been made our teacher.[26]

For Catherine of Siena, concerns about status, appearances, and vanity—"What will it look like? Will people speak ill of me because I am rich and beautiful?"—were impediments to taking up the cross and following the Lord. Catherine's was an evangelical message in the spirit of Matt. 19:21. She suggested discarding the vanities of the world, despising oneself, and choosing the path of lowliness. She wrote to Monna Agnesa about the "beloved Magdalen in whom so much ardent love burned, that she cared for no created thing."[27] Contrary to the preachers who worried about vanity's link to *luxuria*, Catherine was more concerned about its connection to pride, the first of the deadly sins. Therefore her teachings stressed the virtue of humility, pride's antithesis. As such, when discussing the Magdalen, Catherine dwelt on her exemplary humility, the virtue that expunged all of pride's consequences. According to Catherine, it was only self-hatred (or humiliation of self) that allowed love of the Lord to flourish.[28]

Mary Magdalen, a regular presence in the visionary life of Francesca Bussa de' Ponziani (d. 1440) (known familiarly as Francesca Romana),[29] more than once admonished the impending saint to deny herself in order

---

[26] *Le lettere,* vol. 2, ep. 165, 452–57. The translation is Noffke's, given as *Letter 59* in *The Letters,* vol. 1, 183–86.

[27] *Le lettere,* vol. 1, ep. 61, 264–68.

[28] Ibid., vol. 2, ep. 165, 456.

[29] Her official *vita* and collection of visions written by her confessor, Giovanni Mattiotti, is found in AASS, March, vol. 2 (Antwerp, 1668), 88–216, and in a new edition by Alessandra Bartolomei Romagnoli, *Santa Francesca Romana. Edizione critica dei trattati latini di Giovanni Mattiotti* (Vatican City: Libreria Editrice Vaticana, 1994). For Francesca Romana, see Anna Esposito, "S. Francesca e le comunità religiose femminili a Roma nel secolo XV," in *Culto dei santi, istituzioni e classi sociali in età preindustriale,* ed. Sofia Boesch Gajano and Lucia Sebastiani (L'Aquila and Rome: L. U. Japadre, 1984), 537–62, now translated as "St. Francesca and the Female Religious Communities of Fifteenth-Century Rome," in *Women and Religion,* 197–218, and Katherine Gill, "Open Monasteries for Women in Late Medieval and Early Modern Italy: Two Roman Examples," in *The Crannied Wall,* 15–47.

to follow Christ. Sounding very much like Catherine's advice to Monna Bartolomea, the Magdalen counseled Francesca that "the soul must regard itself as a vile thing [and] hate itself."[30] Humility and self-abasement were the path to the heights of divine love according to the Magdalen of Francesca's visions: "Don't sink into your weakness but descend out of yourself through profound humility letting the bestowal of his love be the reason. And as low as you allow yourself to descend so much higher will you ascend."[31]

Umiltà of Faenza took self-loathing to such an extreme that she regarded herself as no better than a lowly little dog, her imagery recalling Mary Magdalen at the Lord's feet at the banquet of Simon the Pharisee: "Receive me even under the table, as if I were a little dog, and give me crumbs, so that I might live from the things which fall from the hands of sweet Christ."[32]

For women, then, the Magdalen's renunciation of vanity was clearly an act to be emulated but not necessarily for the reasons the friars preached. Specifically, women did not reject the vanities of the world because they believed that it would save innocent men from falling victim to their feminine wiles, or because it would save civil society from the evils of usury and sodomy; women renounced vanity and championed the virtues of humility as a means toward attaining personal salvation. Yet I suspect there was something more at stake as well: in renouncing the trappings of vanity, women also fashioned an implicit critique of the society in which they lived. Many of the women who repudiated their worldly possessions came from the privileged classes that forced such objects upon them as distinguishing signs of their class standing and status. Diana d'Andalò is a case in point. Although she had converted to Christ, she nevertheless continued to wear her rich brocades and jewels—signs indicative of her noble status—over the hairshirt that she wore next to her skin. Presumably she did so as not to alarm her family that she was about to embark upon the religious life that would have inevitably thwarted any social ambitions they may have had for her. In renouncing her lavish ways on the feast-day of Mary Magdalen, Diana rejected not only her own worldly concerns but also the social norms of medieval society that hypocritically expected women to represent their class standing in splendor but condemned them continually for doing so.

Luke's Sinner: The Penitent

From the Magdalen's follies and indiscretions we turn to images of her conversion at the Lord's feet, the penitential aspect of the saint. In chapter 7

[30] *Visio XXII* in *Santa Francesca Romana,* ed. Romagnoli, 487.
[31] *Visio LV* in ibid., 630–31.
[32] *Sermo Quintus* in *Sermones,* 147–48.

we examined the reformulation of penitential theology and the increased importance given to penance in later medieval society. Mary Magdalen, as we noted earlier, became a figurehead of sorts for the new emphasis on penitential practice. Because of her great penance, the *beata peccatrix* was transformed into the Lord's advocate for repentant sinners. Her penance and the absolution it achieved became a conduit by which lay people approached the Lord asking for forgiveness. Often such an approach was made through hymns and prayers. One such penitential prayer found its way into an anonymous merchant's commonplace book that was assembled between 1311 and 1331. Jostling alongside practical material treating weights and measures, business conditions around the Mediterranean, and a history of Venice, there is a small amount of devotional material including this entry on Mary Magdalen:

> This is a beautiful prayer to milady St. Mary Magdalen. "God save thee St. Mary Magdalen, of the grace of milord Jesus Christ you are full, you wept, and shed tears; with your tears you washed the feet of our lord, Jesus Christ; with your hair you dried them. In the Holy Sepulcher you sought him, in the guise of a gardener you found him, at his feet you threw yourself. You asked of him, sweet lady and holy Mary Magdalen, that if our Lord Jesus would succor you, you would give thanks for your merited blessings, and thus I pray that you pity me in our sins, and . . . give me this grace that I ask of you." Say three Paternosters, three Marys for your soul, and then ask grace that you may bear tribulation and trials in God.[33]

It is a revealing glimpse into lay religious devotion of the later Middle Ages. Our Venetian merchant was clearly a devotee of the penitent Magdalen because he believed that she was the Lord's advocate for repentant sinners, among whom he evidently counted himself.

But the holy sinner was more than just an advocate. She was also a model of penitential comportment. Lay people, since at least the time of Gregory the Great, had been encouraged to model their own penitential behavior on the Magdalen's.[34] We have already encountered the prisoner Jacobus who appealed to the sinner-saint for mercy; other prisoners and sinners, hoping for the same forgiveness that the Magdalen had obtained from the Lord, made themselves over in her penitential image. Jean Gobi's miracle collection recounts how yet another condemned prisoner turned toward the Magdalen in contrition "recognizing his crimes with great sadness and tears." Supplicating and commending himself humbly, "just as she had done when she sought forgiveness for her sins with the Lord," he vowed

[33] *Merchant Culture in Fourteenth-Century Venice: The Zibaldone da Canal*, trans. John E. Dotson (Medieval & Renaissance Texts & Studies, vol. 98) (Binghamton, NY: Medieval & Renaissance Texts & Studies, 1994), 170.

[34] For Gregory, see *Hom. 33, XL Homiliarum in Evangelia, PL 76*, 1245.

that should he escape from prison he would amend his way of life. That night a beautiful woman appeared to her penitential supplicant in a dream and assisted his escape.[35]

Lest we think that only incarcerated sinners invoked the aid of and modeled themselves upon the penitential saint, Gobi includes the story of a blind woman who petitioned the penitent-sinner at Christ's feet. Adhering to medieval notions of correspondence, she petitioned the lachrymose Magdalen with tears hoping that the saint's intercession would restore her eyesight. Jean Gobi narrated:

> When she had entirely lost her vision she turned the eyes of her mind to God with great devotion and to the one who had bathed his feet with the tears of her eyes. [The supplicant was] asking and praying that she, who had shed tears [and] had obtained forgiveness for her sins from God, would seek grace for her so that her sight, perhaps lost on account of sin, would be restored because of Mary Magdalen's merits.[36]

In the event, through the intervention of the penitent saint, the woman's eyesight was indeed restored.

The model of the penitent at Christ's feet was not gender-specific. Men seemed equally comfortable in casting themselves as well as others of their sex as penitent Magdalens. Perhaps it was Jerome who had first set the tone when he described himself as the penitent who had wept at Christ's feet and dried them with his hair.[37] The hagiographer of the Franciscan John of La Verna recounted that "the blessed Christ gently showed him his most holy feet, where Brother John wept so many tears that he seemed almost another Magdalen, beseeching that the Lord not scrutinize his sins."[38] The

---

[35] "Iohannes Gobi," no. 3, 140. Montagnes rejects Pierre-André Sigal's suggestion that Mary Magdalen "specialized" in liberating prisoners on the grounds that only 10.6% of her miracles are of this type. (He breaks down the other major categories of miracles thus: 25.9% are performed for the dying or in peril of death; 23.5% are for the blind, or those with impaired vision; and 12.9% are for those physically handicapped.) See his "Saint-Maximin," 56. Although Montagnes's numbers speak for themselves, the fact still remains that Mary Magdalen was popularly associated with freeing prisoners. Of the five miracles Jacobus de Voragine lists in the *Golden Legend,* one narrates the liberation of a prisoner, vol. 1, 383. In Salimbene's account of La Sainte-Baume and its saint, the *only* miracle story he narrates is how the Magdalen saved one of her devotees from the gallows, dating the event in 1283. See *Cronica,* vol. 2, 763–64. See my discussion of this miracle in chapter 11. Finally, of the four miniatures depicting miracles in the *Leggendario Ungherese,* one represents a prison release: MS Vat. lat. 8541, f. 104r. It is the only visual representation of this type of miracle known to me. It is worth noting that many saints effected this sort of miracle; it was the specialty, for example, of Saint Leonard.

[36] "Iohannes Gobi," no. 12, 151–52.

[37] *Letter 22* (To Eustochium), *CCEL* 54 (1910), 143–210.

[38] AASS, Aug., vol. 2 (Antwerp, 1735), par. 15, 472.

early fifteenth-century document known as "Instructions for a Devout and Literate Layman" instructs the male reader that after entering church, "with Mary Magdalen throw yourself at the feet of the most sweet Jesus, and wash them with your tears and anoint them and kiss them; and if not with your eyes and mouth, at least do this in your heart. Do not climb up to the cross, but in your heart say with the publican: 'Lord be merciful to me a sinner.'"[39]

Patrons and artists were also devoted to this aspect of the saint. It is noteworthy that Mary Magdalen's conversion at Christ's feet at the banquet of Simon the Pharisee is the biblical episode most often depicted of the saint, outstripping even the *noli me tangere* as the most represented scriptural motif in the visual cycles of her life. The honor of being chosen as the risen Christ's first witness was a privilege to be admired rather than imitated. But everyone could potentially emulate the Magdalen's penitential conversion, unquestionably presented as a model for imitation.[40]

Many penitents took up the challenge: they flung themselves at the feet of the Lord in the hopes of obtaining absolution as Mary Magdalen had done. Margaret of Cortona's hopes were realized. Fra Giunta narrated that one day after confession she heard Christ say to her: "And I, daughter, absolve you of all your sins in thought, speech, and deed which you committed from your birth until now." Ever the stickler for detail, anxious Margaret further beseeched the Lord: "Grant to me, that I may hear in spirit, what you deigned to say to blessed Mary Magdalen after her absolution: 'Go in peace.'"[41] John of La Verna also received Magdalenian consolation from the Lord. His hagiographer observed that, having prostrated himself at the feet of the Lord, "he received so much grace there . . . that he was calmed and consoled just as the Magdalen had been."[42]

When Villana delle Botti renounced her worldly possessions, her next act, as we have seen, was to prostrate herself in penance at the feet of her Dominican confessor. It was an act modeled on the Magdalen's peniten-

---

[39] W. A. Pantin, "Instructions for a Devout and Literate Layman," in *Medieval Learning and Literature: Essays Presented to Richard William Hunt*, ed. J.J.G. Alexander and M. T. Gibson (Oxford: Clarendon Press, 1976), 399.

[40] For a complete listing of visual cycles of her life in diverse media, see chap. 2, n. 62. The conversion scene is found in the fresco cycles at S. Lorenzo Maggiore (Naples); S. Francesco (Assisi); Cappella del Podestà Bargello (Florence); S. Croce (Florence); S. Pietro a Maiella (Naples); S. Maria Maddalena (Bolzano); S. Domenico (Spoleto); S. Maria del Belverde (Cetona); S. Maria Maddalena (Cusiano); and S. Maria (Pontresina), representing ten out of thirteen fresco cycles. In other media: the Magdalen Master panel, the Botticelli predella, the Stoclet predella, and the German devotional book, MS British Library Add. 15682, f. 10r. The *Leggendario Ungherese* does not include the scene as the miniatures based on biblical episodes have been lost.

[41] AASS, Feb., vol. 6, par. 195, 338.

[42] Ibid., Aug., vol. 2, par. 15, 472.

tial conversion at Christ's feet. Significantly, both male and female penitents threw themselves metaphorically at the Lord's feet in order to obtain absolution for their sins. Raymond of Capua reported that whenever Catherine discerned any evil in her soul, she reprimanded herself thus: "Know yourself and lament your sins at the Lord's feet, until you are worthy to hear with the Magdalen, 'your sins are forgiven.'"[43]

Presumably such sentiments inspired the Perugian testator Simonetta di Forteguerra in 1282 to bequeath to the local order of Friars of Penance her block of houses at Porta Sole. Her will stipulated explicitly that the friars were to use her bequest in order to construct a church in honor of Saint Mary Magdalen. Perhaps Simonetta hoped that such a pious act of charity made specifically to the Friars of Penance, in the name of Mary Magdalen, would help her to attain forgiveness for her sins.[44]

Ultimately, Mary Magdalen's penitential conversion was meant to be admired and imitated. It was also a didactic lesson. The fourteenth-century pilgrimage badge sold by the Dominican custodians of her shrine at Saint-Maximin bears such witness: it depicts a prostrate Mary Magdalen at Jesus' feet. Conversion and penance was the message that the Dominicans of Saint-Maximin wished pilgrims to take home, reflect on, and imitate.[45]

The Disciple

As we have seen in an earlier chapter, the friars, particularly the Franciscans, identified so deeply with the image of the faithful Magdalen who persevered beneath the cross that they often placed themselves beside her, or even in her stead in religious painting. But it was not only friars who commissioned these images. In 1363 one ser Daniel d. Francisci Ciccoli of Assisi provided specific instructions for his burial in the basilica of San Francesco. He bequeathed over one hundred pounds so that an image of Christ on the Cross flanked by the Virgin Mary and John the Evangelist could be painted on a pier near the door. He further instructed that Francis and Mary Magdalen be painted at the foot of the Cross.[46]

The Magdalen's great love and devotion for the Lord, especially at the foot of the cross, was yet another aspect of the saint that was greatly esteemed by audiences. When others displayed similar emotions they were

---

[43] Ibid., April, vol. 3, par. 12, 855.

[44] Cited in G. Casagrande, *Religiosità*, 166–67.

[45] M. E. Hucher, "Des ensignes de pélerinage," *Bulletin Monumental,* 2d series, 19 (1853): 506, also reproduced in Clemens, *The Establishment,* 210, fig. 1.

[46] In Cesare Cenci, O.F.M., *Documentazione di vita assisana 1300–1448,* 3 vols. (Spicilegium Bonaventurianum, vols. 10–12) (Grottaferrata: Collegium S. Bonaventurae ad Claras Aquas, 1974–75), vol. 1, 145–46.

frequently declared to be "second Magdalens." Such was the case with Lady Jacopa, a rich Roman widow and early follower of Francis of Assisi. The *Speculum perfectionis,* an account of the early Franciscans, cast Lady Jacopa as the Magdalen to Francis's Christ. The anonymous author observed: "She seems almost another Magdalen, always full of tears and devotion on account of her love for God."[47]

It did not go unnoticed by writers of the later Middle Ages that Mary Magdalen's love and devotion for the Lord fueled her fidelity and perseverance at the time of his passion. Almost every medieval author who ever put pen to page in regard to the Magdalen commented on her extraordinary perseverance. In 1405, Christine de Pisan wrote of Mary Magdalen and the other loyal female disciples at the cross thus:

> What strong faith and deep love those women possess who did not forsake the Son of God who had been abandoned and deserted by all His Apostles. God has never reproached the love of women as weakness, as some men contend, for He placed the spark of fervent love in the hearts of the blessed Magdalen and of other ladies, indeed His approval of this love is clearly to be seen.[48]

The distraught Magdalen's impassioned search for the Lord at daybreak on Easter morning was also characterized as perseverance. Catherine of Siena wrote of Mary Magdalen that "she had the virtue of perseverance. You showed this, dearest Magdalen, when you were seeking your beloved Master after not finding him in the place where you had laid him. So, oh Magdalen, love, you were beside yourself."[49] One of Catherine's compatriots, Giovanni Colombini (d. ca. 1367), founder of the Gesuati in Siena, used similar language and metaphor to describe this lesson: "She went searching for her beloved spouse as if drunk and half mad."[50] Fra Giunta described Margaret of Cortona similarly. His *nova Magdalena,* after having had a vision of Christ on the cross, believed that his body had been stolen. She was "drunk with sorrow, and in tears and a loud voice, she incessantly asked everyone whom she saw about her crucified Lord."[51] As was her penance, the Magdalen's passion for and fidelity to the Lord were both to be admired and imitated by her devotees.

[47] *Speculum perfectionis (minus),* ed. Marino Bigaroni, O.F.M. (Biblioteca Francescana, vol. 3) (Assisi: Ed. Porziuncola, 1983), 34.

[48] *The Book of the City of Ladies,* trans. Earl Jeffrey Richards (New York: Persea Books, 1982), 219.

[49] *Le lettere,* vol. 1, ep. 61, 265–66; *Letter 2* in Noffke, *The Letters,* 42.

[50] *Ep.* 71, in *Le lettere del B. Giovanni Colombini da Siena,* ed. Adolfo Bartoli (Lucca: Tip. Balatresi, 1856), 182. For Giovanni, see A. M. Piazzoni, "Colombini, Giovanni," in *DBI* 27 (1982), 149–53.

[51] AASS, Feb., vol. 3, par. 86, 316.

First Witness

Eventually of course Mary Magdalen found Christ in the garden, where, according to John 20: 16–17, she became the first witness to his resurrection. The visual analogue to this gospel passage is the *noli me tangere*. It usually represents a Magdalen who, having just recognized her master, kneels and reaches beseechingly toward a Christ who is generally shown turning toward her, his right arm outstretched, signaling that she should "touch me not; for I am not yet ascended to my Father." Fraught with ambiguity as is the *noli me tangere* scene, it should not be forgotten that it ultimately commemorates Mary Magdalen as the first witness of the resurrection, one of the central tenets of the Christian faith. Patrons and artists clearly viewed it as one of the most important episodes in her life as it is included in just about all visual cycles representing her *vita*.[52]

This aspect of the saint was no less important to ordinary people who were devoted to her. Perceval, a blind man from Liguria, called on the intercessory powers of the first witness to restore his sight. His reasoning through correspondences suggested that he supplicate the saint because she was the first to have *seen* the risen Christ. He made a pilgrimage to her shrine at Saint-Maximin, located the altar in which her relics lay encased, and positioned himself in front of them with great devotion and resolute hope. His prayers were answered when he opened his eyes and discovered his vision had been restored. Seized with great joy he cried out spontaneously: "I see everything! I see everything! Blessed Mary Magdalen has restored my sight."[53]

Perceval may have venerated the Magdalen as first witness of the resurrection but this aspect of the saint was not without its critics. As we have already seen, a venerable tradition carried on by preachers, in spite of the gospel evidence to the contrary, still accorded the honor of first witness to the Virgin Mary. Interestingly, some women followed suit, notwithstanding their own devotion to Mary Magdalen. Despite having taken the Magdalen as one of her patron saints, Francesca Romana maintained the position that the Virgin Mary was first to witness the risen Christ. In one of her visions she explained that the Virgin "felt the resurrection of her most holy son in her mind," after which he appeared to her and sat with her explaining how the prophecies about him had now been fulfilled.[54] Birgitta of

---

[52] For a listing of the visual cycles, see chapter 2, n. 62. Usually the absence of the scene from the *vita Magdalenae* can be explained by the fact that it has been lost (as in S. Lorenzo Maggiore) or that it has already been included in a *vita Christi* cycle in the same church (as at Bolzano).

[53] "Iohannes Gobi," no. 31, 164–65.

[54] *Visio LIX* in *Santa Francesca Romana*, ed. Romagnoli, 644–45. This account probably draws on the popular tradition represented by Domenico Cavalca and Giovanni de Caulibus discussed in chapter 2.

Sweden was of the same opinion. Even though she had made the pilgrimage to Provence—proof of her devotion to the Magdalen—she nonetheless claimed in her *sermo angelicus,* that although scripture says otherwise, "one must believe without doubt that the Virgin knew before all the others that indeed Jesus had shown himself to her first."[55] Margery Kempe, that indefatigable pilgrim of fifteenth-century England, affirmed similarly. On her pilgrimage to Jerusalem "she visited the chapel where our blessed Lord appeared to his blessed mother before all others on Easter Day." Upon reaching the site, just as the devotional books instructed, she imagined herself into the life of Christ:

> And that day she was with our Lady in a chapel where our Lord Jesus Christ appeared to her and said, "*Salve, sancta parens.*" And then this creature thought in her soul that our Lady said, "Are you my sweet son, Jesus?" And he said, "Yes, my blessed mother, I am your son, Jesus." Then he took up his blessed mother and kissed her very sweetly. And then this creature thought that she saw our Lady feeling and searching all over our Lord's body, and his hands and his feet, to see if there were any soreness or any pain. And she heard our Lord say to his mother, "Dear mother, my pain is all gone, and now I shall live for ever more. And mother, so shall your pain and your sorrow be turned into very great joy. Mother, ask what you will, and I shall tell you." And when he had allowed his mother to ask what she wished and had answered her questions, then he said, "Mother by your leave, I must go and speak with Mary Magdalen."[56]

Significantly, Francesca, Birgitta, and Margery were all mothers themselves. Devoted as each was in her own way to Mary Magdalen it must have been inconceivable to them that Jesus could have shown himself first to anyone but his mother. Thus devotion to this aspect of the saint was by no means accepted by everyone, scriptural evidence notwithstanding.

Ultimately the analysis of audience response undertaken in this chapter has yielded some rather surprising results. We have seen that the penitent saint

[55] The main source of Birgitta's life is AASS, Oct., vol. 4 (Brussels, 1780), 368–560. For her pilgrimage, 398. *Sermo angelicus,* in *Opera Minora II,* ed. Sten Eklund (Stockholm: Almquist & Wiksells, 1972), 129. My thanks to Stephan Borgehammar for supplying me with this text.

[56] *The Book of Margery Kempe,* trans. B. A. Windeatt (New York: Penguin Books, 1985; repr., 1994), 237. For Margery, see Clarissa W. Atkinson, *Mystic and Pilgrim: The Book and the World of Margery Kempe* (Ithaca, NY: Cornell University Press, 1983). Margery was a great consumer of devotional writings, and this scene is clearly influenced by a similar scene in the *Meditations on the Life of Christ.* Margery's view on the matter of the first witness may have been further influenced by Birgitta of Sweden, whose *vita* and writings she knew well.

was a popular aspect of the Magdalen's persona with both sexes. Both men and women called on the intercessory powers of the Magdalen in her role as advocate for sinners. They also did as the preachers suggested and made Magdalens of themselves when metaphorically (or sometimes in visions) they flung themselves at the feet of Christ hoping for forgiveness of their sins. But we have also seen that not all scriptural aspects of Mary Magdalen's persona were received with universal enthusiasm by the preachers' audiences. In response to what was preached about vanity and *luxuria,* we have found that while women certainly agreed that such sins should be renounced, they thought so not because their renunciation would save the souls of innocent men, or civil society, as the friars preached, but because to do so was to embrace humility, a step toward personal salvation. Further, we have seen that Mary Magdalen as first witness of the resurrection was a contested aspect of the saint. Mothers in particular seem to have maintained, contrary to scripture and along with some preachers, that the Virgin Mary—not the Magdalen—was the first to see her son on Easter morning. Maintaining such convictions reveals that audiences shaped their own responses to preaching and devotional reading. Thus it should be clear by now that medieval people were no mere passive auditors of the preachers' sermons. They actively and creatively constructed their own responses to the preached Magdalen. Examination of popular religious devotion reveals that the laity admired and imitated the Magdalen, but not always in strict fidelity to what had been written or preached about her.

NINE

Responses to the
Legendary Saint[1]

*I*n the last chapter we examined audience response to the scriptural saint; the present chapter analyzes how the friars' audiences responded to the two predominant aspects of the Magdalen of legend: the *apostola* of Marseilles and the hermit of La Sainte-Baume.

I have chosen to postpone until now discussion of audience response to Mary Magdalen as herald of the resurrection—an image authorized by scripture not by legend—because by the later Middle Ages, medieval authors inevitably associated her biblical role as herald of the good news with her legendary evangelization in Provence. Thus it would be a disservice to late medieval habits of thinking to consider one aspect of the saint without the other since by the twelfth century the two aspects had become so intimately intertwined.

Herald of the Resurrection

Devotion to the Magdalen as herald of the resurrection can be tracked in cycles of manuscript miniatures (mostly psalters) representing the *vita Christi*, the life of Christ. Many women commissioned or were the recipients of books that often included at least one image commemorating Mary Magdalen as *apostolorum apostola*. The *St. Albans Psalter* (1120–30), made possibly for Christina of Markyate, shows Mary Magdalen, right index finger elevated in the preaching gesture, announcing the good news to the other disciples (Fig. 1).[2] Another twelfth-century manuscript, *The Gospel*

---

[1] Some of the material contained in this chapter has been previously published in "Maria Magdalena: Apostolorum Apostola," in *Women Preachers and Prophets*, 57–96.

[2] MS Hildesheim, Dombibliothek, St. God. 1. For the psalter, see Otto Pächt, C. R. Dodwell, and Francis Wormald, *The St. Albans Psalter (Albani Psalter)* (London: The Warburg Institute, 1960), 5. For the dating of the MS, see R. M. Thomson quoted in *The Life of Christina of Markyate*, ed. C. H. Talbot (Oxford: Clarendon Press, 1959; repr. 1987), v.

Book of Henry the Lion, also represents this scene but this time through the lens of an Easter trope. Seven apostles greet Mary Magdalen and (on their scroll) ask, "Tell us Mary, what did you see on the way?" She answers (also by means of a scroll), "I saw the sepulcher of the living Christ and the glory of the risen one" (Fig. 44).[3] A third manuscript featuring this scene is the *Ingeborg Psalter* (ca. 1190s), so called because it belonged to the unfortunate Queen Ingeborg, forsaken wife of Philip Augustus. The psalter miniature shows an abbreviated scene of Mary Magdalen again using a scroll to bear the news that she has seen the risen Christ. It is accompanied by a French caption identifying the event.[4] Yet another manuscript, known as the *Queen Mary Psalter* (ca. 1310–20), shows the Magdalen preaching to five apostles. It has been suggested that this book was made for the devotional reading of Queen Isabella, wife of Edward II of England (Fig. 45).[5]

A final English manuscript of approximately the same date is the *Saint John's College Miscellany.* It merits closer attention as this book contains a cycle of miniatures that attempts to represent the conflicting gospel accounts of the events of Easter morning. The manuscript contains three scenes of the Magdalen heralding the good news to the apostles. In the first scene, Mary Magdalen, striking the orator's position, reports the empty tomb to Peter and John. (The adjoining scene shows the male disciples at the tomb verifying what the Magdalen had told them.) In the second miniature she executes the *computio digitorum,* another preaching gesture, this time before the twelve (Fig. 46). An accompanying French caption explains how Mary Magdalen came to the disciples to announce that she had seen and spoken with Christ, but the disciples did not want to believe her. The final representation of this scene is of the three Marys recounting to the disciples that they had seen the risen Christ. Its caption reiterates the message of the second: the disciples were unable to bring themselves to be-

---

[3] MS Wolfenbüttel, Herzog August Bibliothek: Cod. Guelf. 105 Noviss. 2°, f. 171r. The trope is from Wipo of St. Gall's *Victimae paschali,* written in the eleventh century. By the twelfth century it had been incorporated into the Easter drama, *Visitatio sepulchri.* See Karl Young, *The Drama of the Medieval Church,* 2 vols. (Oxford: Clarendon Press, 1933), vol. 2, 273–306. For the *Gospel Book of Henry the Lion,* see Franz Jansen, *Die Helmarschausner Buchmalerei zur Zeit Heinrichs des Löwen* (Hildesheim-Leipzig: August Lax, 1933).

[4] MS Chantilly, Musée Condé 1695. The most complete study of this manuscript, including black-and-white illustrations, is Florens Deuchler, *Der Ingeborgpsalter* (Berlin: Walter de Gruyter & Co., 1967), 60–61, and fig. XXVI.

[5] MS British Library, Royal 2 B VII, f. 301r. For the psalter, see George Warner, *Queen Mary's Psalter: Miniatures and Drawings by an English Artist of the Fourteenth Century* (London: Trustees of the British Museum, 1912), and for the intended audience, see Anne Rudloff Stanton, "From Eve to Bathsheba and Beyond: Motherhood in the Queen Mary Psalter," in *Women and the Book: Assessing the Visual Evidence,* ed. Jane H. M. Taylor and Lesley Smith (Toronto: University of Toronto Press, 1996), 185–86.

Figure 44. *Apostolorum Apostola* (12th c.). Mary Magdalen announces the good news to the apostles. On their scroll they inquire: "Tell us, Mary, what did you see on the way?" She answers: "I saw the sepulcher of the living Christ and the glory of the risen one." Miniature from the *Gospel Book of Henry the Lion*, Herzog August Bibliothek, Wolfenbüttel. (Photo: Herzog August Bibliothek)

Figure 45. *Apostolorum Apostola* (ca. 1310–20). Mary Magdalen strikes the preaching position and announces the Lord's resurrection to a group of apostles. Miniature from the *Queen Mary Psalter*, British Library, London. (Photo: The British Library)

lieve the women.[6] The book, then, presents a paradoxical response to the Easter gospel passages: on the one hand, by means of reiteration, the images laud Mary Magdalen as herald of the resurrection; on the other hand, the didactic French captions report that the other disciples did not believe her message. It presents an ambiguous message to the reader: the three images record the important role a woman played in the events of Easter morning, while the captions undercut the power of the images by reporting that female speech was dismissed by the male disciples.

As is well known, women's speech was considered problematic and therefore fair game for moralists and satirists of the Middle Ages. The example of Mary Magdalen *apostola,* however, stood in stark contrast to the grossly caricatured garrulous and gossipy woman who inhabited much of medieval discourse.[7] The image of the *apostola* served as an antidote to

[6] MS Cambridge, St. John's College, K21, ff. 55v, 56v, 57v. For a description of the manuscript, see M. R. James, *A Descriptive Catalogue of Manuscripts in the Library of St. John's College, Cambridge* (Cambridge: Cambridge University Press, 1922), 302–10. A contemporary French example of this scene is found in the lectionary of S. Chapelle (BN MS lat. 8892, f. 9r). On this motif, see Magdalen LaRow, *The Iconography of Mary Magdalen: The Evolution of a Western Tradition until 1300* (Ph.D. diss., New York University, 1982), 219, 221, 224. She notes four instances of this scene in the eleventh century, eight in the twelfth century (four of which are MS illuminations), and fourteen in the thirteenth century, half of which are miniatures.

[7] Christine de Pisan sums up and rebuts the female stereotype thus: "Some foolish preachers teach that God first appeared to a woman because He knew well that she did not

Figure 46. *Apostolorum Apostola* (early 14th c.). Mary Magdalen makes a point (*computio digitorum*) announcing the good news to the apostles. Miniature from a miscellany in St. John's College Library. (Photo: St. John's College, Cambridge University)

such gendered constructs and even provided a counterargument against them. Robert of Sorbon (d. 1274) told his audience that because the Mag-

know how to keep quiet so that this way the news of His resurrection would be spread more rapidly. [But they are] fools who said this. It is not enough for them to attack women. They impute even to Jesus Christ such blasphemy, as if to say that He wished to reveal this great perfection and dignity through a vice. I do not know how a man could dare to say this, even in jest, as God should not be brought in on such joking matters." *The City of Ladies*, 29.

dalen was the *predicatrix* (preacher) of the Lord's resurrection, men should not disdain women's words.[8] As a woman who earned her livelihood from crafting words, Christine de Pisan could not have agreed more. She drew inspiration from the Magdalen's scriptural role and used it as a defense of women's speech. In her *Book of the City of Ladies* she maintained:

> If women's language had been so blameworthy and of such small authority, as some men argue, our lord Jesus Christ would never have deigned to wish that so worthy a mystery as His most gracious resurrection be first announced by a woman, just as He commanded the blessed Magdalen, to whom He first appeared on Easter, to report and announce it to His apostles and to Peter. Blessed God, may you be praised, who, among the other infinite boons and favors which You have bestowed upon the feminine sex, desired that woman carry such lofty and worthy news.[9]

Christine's defense of women's speech using the exemplar of Mary Magdalen was not *sui generis;* rather, it came as an eloquent and powerful summation of the sentiments of those women and men who like her were devoted to Mary Magdalen precisely because Christ had bestowed on her the unique honor of heralding the good news of his resurrection.

Apostolorum Apostola

It will be recalled from the discussion in chapter 2 that the title *apostolorum apostola* (apostle of the apostles) emerged in the twelfth century to describe Mary Magdalen's privileged role of announcing Christ's resurrection to the other apostles. Soon thereafter it was used to refer to her apostolate in Provence, the stuff of legends of the same period. As such, by the later medieval period the title *apostola* could invoke simultaneously both the image of the scriptural herald and the legendary evangelist of Marseilles.

Such is the case with a miniature recently published by Susan Haskins. Here, in the donor page of the psalter of Jutta Tersina of Liechtenfels (ca. 1200), Jutta herself is shown kneeling at the feet of Mary Magdalen over whom the words *Sancta Maria Magdalena apostolorum apostola* are inscribed.[10] It is a lovely example of female devotion to Mary Magdalen, *apostola*. Since there are no disciples present, and this is not one in a series of miniatures devoted to the *vita Christi*, I suspect both aspects of the Magdalen's apostolate are being offered to and by the donor for veneration.

Dedication to the apostolic aspect of the saint took different forms in the

---

[8] Cited in Bériou, "La Madeleine," 279n. 33.
[9] *The City of Ladies*, 28.
[10] *Mary Magdalen*, 220–21, fig. 43, 452n. 78.

later Middle Ages. In the thirteenth century, Jutta Tersina had her image immortalized at the foot of the *apostola*, while in the fourteenth century two Tuscans commended her apostolate in their writings. The Florentine moralist Franco Sacchetti (d. 1400) showed his devotion to the apostolic Magdalen by praising her in one of his expositions on the gospels as the "disciple and apostle of Christ, who listened to the teaching of the savior as no other woman, and who went to Marseilles to preach, there converting the Duke and the Duchess and the other pagans."[11] A female contemporary of Sacchetti's was no less impressed by the Magdalen's apostolate in Provence. In a letter to Monna Agnesa Malavolti, Catherine of Siena lauded "that *innamorata* apostle Magdalen . . . who preached in the city of Marseilles."[12]

In mid-fifteenth-century England, devotion to the apostolic Magdalen manifested itself in diverse cultural forms. Isabel Bourchier, countess of Eu, commissioned the Austin friar Osbern Bokenham to write a life of Mary Magdalen for her personal devotional reading. In the *vita* itself the loquacious friar provides a precious glimpse into the circumstances of the countess's commission and her devotion to the saint:

> "I have," she said, "for a long time had a special devotion of pure affection to that holy woman who is called 'apostle of the apostles'; I mean blessed Mary Magdalen, whom Christ made pure and clean from sin, as the writers say. I desire to have her life made in English, and if you would undertake this work for my sake and for reverence of her, I would ask you to do it."[13]

Countess Isabel, like Jutta Tersina, was dedicated to the apostolic Magdalen, "that holy woman who is called apostle of the apostles." Her longtime devotion to the saint eventually culminated in the commissioning of Bokenham circa 1445 to make an English verse translation of the saint's life for personal meditation.[14]

---

[11] Franco Sacchetti, "Dalle sposizioni di vangeli," in *Opere*, ed. Aldo Borlenghi (Milan: Rizzoli, 1957), 889.

[12] *Le lettere*, vol. 1, ep. 61, 265–66; *Letter 2* in Noffke, *The Letters*, 42.

[13] Osbern Bokenham, "Mary Magdalen's Life," in *A Legend of Holy Women*, trans. Sheila Delany (Notre Dame: University of Notre Dame Press, 1992), 102.

[14] The countess of Eu was not the only fifteenth-century English lady accustomed to meditate on the life of Saint Mary Magdalen for the sake of devotion. In her household ordinances of 1485–95, Cecily of York's reading (or listening) habits were described thus: at dinner she listened to (or read) Walter Hilton, (Pseudo) Bonaventura, the *Golden Legend*, or saints' lives such as "the life of Saint Mary Magdalen, the life of Saint Catherine of Siena, or the Revelations of Saint Birgitta of Sweden." *Orders and Rules of the Princess Cecill, Mother of King Edward IV*, in *A Collection of Ordinances and Regulations for the Government of the Royal Household made in divers reigns. From King Edward III, to King William and Queen Mary* (Society of Antiquaries of London) (London: J. Nichols, 1790), 37, cited in Anne Clark Bartlett, *Male Authors, Female Readers: Representation and Subjectivity in Middle English Devotional Literature* (Ithaca, NY: Cornell University Press, 1995), 11.

Men, also, venerated the apostolic aspect of the saint. Three years after the countess of Eu commissioned a *vita* of Mary Magdalen, William Waynflete, bishop of Winchester and Lord Chancellor of England under Henry VI, founded a great institution of teaching and learning in the name of his patron saint, Mary Magdalen, the "glorious apostoless." That institution, founded in 1448, was first called Magdalene Hall; ten years later it became Magdalene College, Oxford.[15] It seems that Waynflete chose Mary Magdalen as his patron saint because his first mastership was at the hospital of Saint Mary Magdalen located outside the city of Winchester. He remained loyal to her throughout his life. Her image was inscribed in his episcopal seal, and she was the titular of the chapel in Winchester Cathedral where he was ultimately entombed.[16]

By the fifteenth century, the apostolic aspect of the saint was being packaged for consumption for faithful pilgrims who had made the journey to Provence to worship at Saint-Maximin or La Sainte-Baume. The industrious monks of Saint Victor and the church of Saint Lazarus, both in Marseilles, claimed to have relics of the Magdalen's provençal apostolate. Saint Victor boasted of having a crypt where Mary Magdalen had lived and done penance during her active days of evangelization; the church of Saint Lazarus claimed that it possessed the pagan altar where the saint had preached when she first reached the port of Marseilles.[17] The pilgrimage diary of Jerome Münzer, a German doctor who had made the journey to Provence in 1494–95, discloses in ample detail the Marseilles pilgrimage trade of which devotion to the apostolic Magdalen was central:

> We saw, in the monastery of Saint Victor . . . in a deep crypt under the choir, the place of penitence of the blessed Magdalen (before she withdrew to her hermitage) and we saw the table of stone on which she used to eat. In the morning, ascending to the citadel of the city, we saw the ancient collegiate church of Saint Lazarus, where after having heard mass, we saw the head and body of the bishop Saint Lazarus, whom Christ had resurrected. . . . We saw likewise the spot where the blessed Magdalen had preached to the pagans. How she came to be there in the first place is very clearly recounted in her legend.[18]

Testimonies such as these bear eloquent witness to the fact that many lay people were devoted to the apostolic aspect of the Magdalen, believing the

[15] Magdalene College, Cambridge, was founded in 1427 as a hospice for Benedictine monks. See chap. 4, n. 10.

[16] Virginia Davis, *William Waynflete: Bishop and Educationalist* (Woodbridge: Boydell Press, 1993), 13.

[17] Clemens, *The Establishment*, 250.

[18] E. Déprez, "Jérôme Münzer et son voyage dans le Midi de la France en 1494–1495," *Annales du Midi* 48 (1936): 67, cited in Clemens, *The Establishment*, 253 (my translation).

contemporary legends about her mission in Provence, and admiring her the more so for having evangelized the region so effectively. After all, the legends claimed that she had converted not only the city of Marseilles but also the ruler and his consort, as well as the neighboring city of Aix.

There is little doubt that depictions of Mary Magdalen's apostolate in Provence were offered up by preachers, hagiographers, and shrine-keepers for admiration rather than imitation. Be that as it may, we must ask whether representations of the Magdalen's apostolate nonetheless inspired medieval women to imitate Mary Magdalen and take up their own missions in the world. In a word the answer is yes: Mary Magdalen, *apostolorum apostola,* was invoked to justify the apostolates of heterodox and orthodox women alike.

As is well known, the English religious movement known as Lollardy, which subscribed to the teachings of Wycliffe and ran afoul of British ecclesiastical authorities in the late fourteenth century, was committed to the idea of lay preaching. In theory, at least, Lollards believed that both men and women were able to ascend the pulpit.[19] At his trial in 1381, Walter Brut, an educated lay Lollard, maintained not only that women had the authority to preach but that they also had the power to grant absolution. In the academic treatise condemning his propositions, Brut's convictions are enumerated then refuted. One of Brut's arguments in defense of women's public preaching reads thus: "It is confirmed, for we read that blessed Mary Magdalen preached publicly in Marcilia and in the area around about, which through her preaching she converted to Christ. Because of this she is called the 'Apostle of Apostles.'"[20]

Lollards, then, justified women's preaching by invoking the example of Mary Magdalen's public apostolate in Marseilles. Waldensians may have done similarly, but the only evidence for such a supposition comes not from them, but from one of their fiercest opponents. Recall that the Dominican inquisitor Moneta da Cremona fulminated against Waldensian women who defended their preaching by recourse to the example of Mary Magdalen.[21]

The Lollards and the Waldensians were heretical groups that championed the Magdalen's preaching, but it was not just the heterodox who turned to the Magdalen's example to defend their actions; we have evidence from "semi-orthodox" sources that the apostolic Magdalen was proposed among such groups as a model for women to emulate.

The "Sister Catherine" treatise, written in the first half of the fourteenth century, possibly in Strasbourg, is one such source. The anonymous text,

---

[19] On this question, see Shannon McSheffrey, *Gender and Heresy: Women and Men in Lollard Communities, 1420–1530* (Philadelphia: University of Pennsylvania Press, 1995).

[20] The documents relating to the trial are translated in Alcuin Blamires et al., *Women Defamed and Women Defended,* 250–60.

[21] See chapter 2, n. 27.

often associated with the Brethren of the Free Spirit, is a dramatic dialogue narrating a number of encounters between a spiritual advisor, a friar, and his spiritual daughter, a beguine. In the first four books the woman implores her confessor to help her find the road to salvation; she then follows the way of the Holy Spirit and achieves mystical union with God. In the sixth book, the penultimate and most lengthy book, the enlightened beguine and her confessor exchange roles. He becomes her disciple while she becomes his spiritual guide. The example of Mary Magdalen predominates throughout this book serving "to provide both a model and a warrant for the daughter's role reversal."[22] In one passage the beguine explains the Magdalen's apostolate to her spiritual son thus:

> You must understand it like this. Mary thought that all people should know what she knew. . . . This is verified by the fact that she went to all the places where she could proclaim that her creator had risen from his death and that he was both true God and human being. [She] preached the Christian faith as the apostles did and carried out everything a strong man should carry out. You have probably heard it said how Mary Magdalen converted a king and many nonbelievers.[23]

In her final commentary on the Magdalen's preaching the beguine argues:

> She did everything the apostles did in a perfect life. She went into all the lands in which she could preach Christianity and reveal the truth. You must know that Mary Magdalen accomplished more in a shorter time than any of the apostles.[24]

In both passages the author explicitly compares Mary Magdalen's apostolate with those of the male apostles, who are then found wanting. In the first passage the author commends the Magdalen for having succeeded at doing man's work; in the second, the saint is praised for having surpassed the male apostles in such labors. It is not unrelated that the beguine had done likewise when she herself had surpassed her male confessor in spiritual knowledge.

Another "semi-orthodox" writer who appealed to the authority of the apostolic Magdalen to justify her actions was Alijt Bake (d. 1455), prioress of Windesheim convent of Galilea in Ghent. Her autobiography, an *apologia* of sorts for her life as an activist religious reformer, includes a roster of

---

[22] Introduction to the "Sister Catherine Treatise," trans. Elvira Borgstädt, in *Meister Eckhart: Teacher and Preacher,* ed. Bernard McGinn (New York: Paulist Press, 1986), 13. For commentary on this treatise, see Barbara Newman, "Gnostics, Free Spirits, and 'Meister Eckhart's Daughter,'" in *From Virile Woman to Womanchrist* (Philadelphia: University of Pennsylvania Press, 1994), 172–81.

[23] "Sister Catherine Treatise," 372–73.

[24] Ibid., 380.

saints whom she used to vindicate her deeds. Alijt included Mary Magdalen among them and wrote of her that "together with the apostles she was sent into external service. For she started to preach and became a holy apostle." Alijt's own apostolate did not end in triumph: upon the publication of her autobiography and shortly after her death, the Windesheim chapter sanctioned her writings and those of other women who dared to write on theological or religious issues. The Windesheim officials evidently regarded women's speech in any form—oral or written—as a danger. They would have argued that Mary Magdalen's apostolate was to be admired not imitated.[25]

Another female activist who regarded Mary Magdalen as a model was Maria de Santo Domingo, an illiterate peasant woman of central Castile, who was a celebrated visionary and prophet in early sixteenth-century Spain. She was also a persuasive preacher. Her confessor Friar Antonio de la Peña reported that she "says admirable things that serve to edify souls, and in such a way that those who listen to her find themselves shedding tears and feeling the most sweet devotion and compunction and repentance in their breasts."[26] A recent historian of the *beata* has suggested that Maria was well aware of Mary Magdalen's legendary apostolate in Provence, praising the saint to the Lord and asking him to "grant me that wisdom and those tears You bestowed on Your precious Magdalen."[27] As Alijt's activism had done in the previous century, Maria's active public ministry eventually provoked suspicion in some quarters. In 1509–10 she was brought to trial by a group of Dominican officials who charged her with fraudulent sanctity and immorality. In the event she was exonerated of all charges, but presumably her trial served as a warning for other women considering a public ministry.

Both Alijt of Windesheim and Maria of Santo Domingo cited the Magdalen as an apostolic exemplar but they also mentioned Catherine of Siena as an activist model. Significantly, in her own day, Catherine modeled her active ministry in the world on that of Mary Magdalen.[28] Raymond of Capua reports that Catherine was plagued by anxieties before undertaking a life of public service, although that is indeed what she had wanted from the start, as Jesus in one of her visions reminded her. "Do you not re-

[25] Anneke B. Mulder-Bakker, "Lame Margaret of Magdeburg: The Social Function of a Medieval Recluse," *Journal of Medieval History* 22/2 (1996): 155–56. I thank Dr. Mulder-Bakker for bringing Alijt Bake to my attention.

[26] Cited in Jodi Bilinkoff, "Establishing Authority: A Peasant Visionary and Her Audience in Early Sixteenth-Century Spain," *Studia Mystica* 18 (1997): 48.

[27] Ibid., 51.

[28] Catherine was also the model for other "living saints"; see Gabriella Zarri, "Living Saints: A Typology of Female Sanctity in the Early Sixteenth Century," in *Women and Religion*, 219–303.

member that the zeal for souls which I planted and watered in your soul in the days of your infancy grew to such an extent that you planned to disguise yourself as a man and enter the Order of Preachers and go off into foreign parts, and so be more useful to yourself and other souls?"[29] But Catherine, knowing that her sex would be a hindrance to her, was not easily placated. She entreated the Lord: "How can I, wretched and frail as I am, be of use to souls? My sex, as you know, is against it in many ways, both because it is not highly considered by men, and also because it is not good, for decency's sake, for a woman to mix with men."[30] The Lord's response seems to have assuaged her tormented soul:

> You must know that in these latter days there has been such an upsurge of pride, especially in the case of men who imagine themselves to be learned or wise, that my justice cannot endure them any longer, without delivering a just chastisement upon them that will bring them to confusion. . . . To confound their arrogance, I will raise up women ignorant and frail by nature but endowed with strength and divine wisdom. . . . Therefore, be bravely obedient when in the future I send you out amongst people. Wherever you may find yourself I shall not forsake you, or fail to visit you, as is my custom, and direct you in all that you are to do.[31]

Revealingly, both Catherine's critique of female weakness and Jesus' justification for electing Catherine to minister to souls—to confound the pride of men with the example of a weak and ignorant woman—were reasons medieval preachers had proposed in explaining the Magdalen's apostolate. Raymond, a member of the Friars Preacher, would have been well aware that in defending Catherine he was employing the same arguments used in defense of the Magdalen's public ministry.

But what I have just described is Raymond's understanding of Catherine's mission. Did Catherine herself appeal to the example of the Magdalen to justify her apostolate? In a letter to Monna Agnesa she refers to the Magdalen as her *maestra,* and she invokes the saint who "runs and embraces the cross," the cross being Catherine's metaphor for apostolic ministry, as she makes plain on a separate occasion when referring to the apostles at Pentecost who "climbed into the pulpit of the holy cross."[32] As we have already seen, in the same letter to Monna Agnesa she lauds "that *in-*

---

[29] AASS, 30 April, vol. 3, par. 121, 883; Lamb, *St. Catherine,* 108.

[30] Ibid.

[31] Ibid., par. 122, 883; ibid., 109.

[32] *Maestra: Le lettere,* vol. 2, ep. 165, 456–57; *Cross:* vol. 1, ep. 61, 265–66. Karen Scott has argued that Catherine's own mission as *apostola* was at least partially shaped by recourse to the Magdalen's apostolic career. See "St. Catherine of Siena, 'Apostola,'" 42, and "'Io Catarina,'" 111–12. *Pulpit:* cited in Scott, ibid., 111.

namorata apostle Magdalen . . . who preached in the city of Marseilles."[33] And finally, in a letter of 1376 to Raymond, Catherine described a vision in which Christ gave her the cross and asked her to "tell them, I announce to you a great joy."[34] The Iohannine commission to Mary Magdalen resounds throughout the words she chose to describe her vision.

Following in the footsteps of Mary Magdalen, Catherine of Siena became a renowned preacher and was acclaimed as such. Fittingly, Aldo Manuzio, an early printer of Catherine's letters, in 1500 articulated his wish that they "would spread throughout the world like solemn preachers," contributing to ecclesiastical and individual reform.[35]

Ultimately preachers and hagiographers may have presented the apostolic Mary Magdalen to their audiences to admire; evidence suggests that some women may have done otherwise, when in imitation of the *apostolorum apostola* they took up the cross of active ministries in the world.

The Contemplative

Just as the image of the herald of the resurrection became almost inseparable from the image of the *apostola* in the later Middle Ages, so the aspect of the contemplative Mary of Bethany tended to merge with that of the contemplative hermit of La Sainte-Baume. As such, I have deferred discussion of audience response to that aspect of the saint until now.

The contemplative Magdalen of scripture, though a stock image of medieval sermons, was not among the saint's most popularly venerated aspects. Nor, as we saw in chapter 4, was it among the most popular visual motifs associated with the saint. Jean Gobi's miracle register reports only one case in which the saint's contemplative aspect was invoked at her shrine. A man from Barjols, as a result of a grave illness, had entirely lost his hearing. Unable to leave his home he beseeched Mary Magdalen who "sat at the feet of the lord *hearing* attentively his every word" to intervene for him. He vowed that should his hearing be restored he would light out for Saint-Maximin as soon as possible to present the saint with a pound of wax in the shape of a head. When his prayers were answered he fulfilled his vow by making a pilgrimage to the saint's sanctuary and tendering the gift of wax that he had promised.[36]

Contemplative foundations made in the name of the saint seem to have found eager patrons among the laity. In chapter 4 we noted the rise of

---

[33] *Le lettere,* vol. 1, ep. 61, 265–66; *Letter 2* in Noffke, *The Letters,* 42.
[34] *Epistolario,* vol. 1, ep. 65, 275.
[35] Cited by Zarri, "Living Saints," 282n. 95.
[36] "Iohannes Gobi," no. 34, 166–67.

monastic foundations for contemplatives dedicated to Mary Magdalen such as the one founded in 1334 by Monna di Rufo Petroio in San Gimignano.[37] Of course not everyone could afford to found or endow a convent in honor of the saint; nonetheless people found ways to support their contemplative Magdalens. In Orvieto, for example, the archival records reveal that Santa Maria Maddalena, the oldest female Augustinian monastic community (which began as a convent of eleven sisters), received many pious bequests. The commune itself provided them with support in the form of alms and gifts of wax, but so did devout citizens. The testament of domina Angela, wife of Guido Magaloctus, for example, left money to the mendicant churches in Orvieto including "20 solidi for the building fund of the monastery of Santa Maria Maddalena."[38]

Contemplative nuns also received alms for services rendered on the feast-day of Mary Magdalen. In 1400 the Dominican nuns of San Domenico in Pisa were contracted by Manno degli Agli, a colleague of the merchant of Prato, Francesco di Marco Datini, to say prayers for his soul at five appointed occasions during the year: one of those dates was "lo di di santa maria Maddalena."[39]

I suspect that the contemplative of Bethany was not so popular with audiences because it competed with her legendary aspect as a contemplative hermit. As such, when people wanted to appeal to the contemplative nature of the saint it was generally the hermit of La Saint-Baume that they invoked or represented visually, as we shall see. But sometimes the two personae converged, as in this passage written by the Poor Clare Camilla Battista da Varano in 1488. Meditating on Jesus' sorrows, she wrote: "He wanted to make and did make of her a mirror, an example, the standard of the blessed contemplative life—for she remained in solitude unrecognized by the world for thirty-three years, where she tasted and felt the ultimate effects of love, as far as one is able to taste and feel them in this mortal life."[40]

In later medieval thinking scripture shaded imperceptibly into legend to

[37] See chap. 4, n. 23.

[38] For the foundation, see Gutiérrez, *The Augustinians,* 203. The commune, for example, gave alms—25 lib. den.—on 23 December 1341 (item 2.2.85) and made a perpetual annual gift of wax on 26 July 1337 (item 2.2.81) to the nuns of the convent on the feast-day of their patron saint. See *Chiese e conventi degli ordini mendicanti in Umbria nei secoli XIII–XIV. Archivi di Orvieto,* ed. Marilena Rossi Caponeri and Lucio Riccetti (Perugia: Editrice Umbra Cooperativa, 1987), 40, 37. For the individual gift, one of many pious donations made to the convent, see item 4.1.6, ibid., 104.

[39] Cited in Ann M. Roberts, "Chiara Gambacorta of Pisa as Patroness of the Arts," in *Creative Women,* 152n. 49.

[40] *I dolori mentali di Gesù nella sua passione,* in Beata Camilla Battista da Varano (Clarissa di Camerino), *Le opere spirituali,* ed. Giacomo Boccanera (Jesi: Scuola Tipografica Francescana, 1958), 159.

create the contemplative recluse of La Sainte-Baume. Devotion to Mary of Bethany almost inevitably signified devotion first and foremost to the recluse who lived out her life as a solitary in the desert wilderness.

The Hermit of La Sainte-Baume

The contemplative ascetic tucked away in her provençal cave fired the imaginations of medieval people from all stations of life. Count Niccolo' della Corvaia, a nobleman perhaps from the Orvietan Monaldeschi family, counted himself among the devotees of the hermit-saint. In 1367, the same year that he became a Franciscan tertiary, he erected a hermitage in the forest of Cetona near Siena. That hermitage housed an oratorio dedicated to the Magdalen, which in the early years of the Quattrocento was frescoed by Andrea di Giovanni. Of the six scenes of her life, two picture her eremitical existence at La Sainte-Baume.[41]

Women patrons too showed their devotion to the eremitical Magdalen by contracting for devotional images of the hermit-saint. In 1307 a female confraternity in Urbania (probably associated with the Franciscans) commissioned a painting from Giuliano da Rimini of an enthroned Madonna and child around whose feet the likenesses of the female confraternity members are memorialized (Fig. 22).[42] On the far left, in the top register, Saint Francis is shown on the mountain of La Verna receiving the stigmata (Fig. 23), while on the far right, his counterpart Mary Magdalen is depicted in contemplative prayer in her cave in La Sainte-Baume (Fig. 24). The presence of John the Evangelist and John the Baptist in the same upper register points to the intermingling of the themes of contemplation and eremitism. But given the depictions of Francis's mountain, the Magdalen's cave, to say nothing of John the Baptist's position in the place of honor at the Virgin Mary's right shoulder, I would suggest that it is asceticism and eremitism that this altarpiece commissioned by women proclaims.[43]

In an earlier chapter we saw that when Mary Magdalen was associated with John the Baptist, the duo evoked asceticism and prophecy. In one of Birgitta of Sweden's revelations, Christ told her that there were three saints

[41] For the oratorio and frescoes, see Enzo Carli, *Gli affreschi di Belverde* (Florence: Edam, 1977).

[42] Female confraternities are few, but they do exist. Surprisingly little work has been done on them. For an overview of the literature and sources in Umbria, see Giovanna Casagrande, "Women in Confraternities between the Middle Ages and the Modern Age. Research in Umbria," *Confraternitas* 5/2 (1994): 3–13.

[43] Four female saints make up the lower register. They are (*l–r*) Clare, Catherine, Agnes, and Lucy. The painting is in the Isabella Stewart Gardner Museum in Boston. See Philip Hendy, *The Isabella Stewart Gardner Museum: Catalogue of the Exhibited Paintings and Drawings* (Boston: Trustees of the Museum, 1931), 175–78.

who pleased him more than all the rest: "Mary, my mother, John the Baptist, and Mary Magdalen."[44] John the Baptist and Mary Magdalen were also among the patron saints Christ singled out for Margaret of Cortona during one of her frequent visions.[45] Late medieval holy women, most of whom came from strongly urbanized backgrounds, dreamt of the solitary life of the desert penitents that the Baptist and the Magdalen represented.[46] But deserts, as Christ told Margaret of Cortona, were not suited to the times; consequently, she and other pious women had to make their own retreats in the midst of urban space. They did so in diverse ways. Margaret internalized her desert. Verdiana of Castelfiorentino (d. 1241) immured herself in a church wall. Umiliana de' Cerchi (d. 1246) locked herself away in the tower of her family's palazzo in Florence. Other women lived a vicarious desert existence by contemplating images of the desert saint. Around 1455 Annalena Anghiari, one of Sant'Antonino's spiritual daughters and founder of a group of tertiary Dominicans in Florence, commissioned a *sacra conversazione* from Filippo Lippi in which the eremitical Magdalen and that other famous desert penitent, Saint Jerome, adore the baby Jesus.[47]

Both women and men admired the reclusive Magdalen's asceticism, particularly her admirable regime of fasting. At the grotto of La Sainte-Baume, where she spent the last reclusive years of her life, Mary Magdalen, according to legend, abstained from earthly food for thirty-three years. Such behavior may have inspired a Cistercian monk called Arnold to take his penitential practice of fasting to such an extreme that eventually he fell so ill with stomach ailments that his very life was threatened. Caesarius of Heisterbach, however, reports his miraculous healing. Lying in his sickbed one night, Mary Magdalen appeared to him and laid her hand on his troubled stomach. The next day he awoke cured by her sacred touch.[48]

Women, too, most notably Catherine of Siena, imitated the Magdalen's miraculous fasting. Catherine's inedia was so extreme that her biographer, Raymond of Capua, was forced to defend it against "professional scandalmongers [who] said that it was all a pretense on Catherine's part to make

---

[44] Birgitta of Sweden, *Revelaciones, Book IV,* ed. Hans Aili (Stockholm: Kungl. Vitterhets Historie Och Antikvitets Akademien, 1992), 307. Thanks to Stephan Borghammer for sending me this text.

[45] AASS, Feb., vol. 3, par. 151, 350. For more on Margaret of Cortona's Magdalen devotion, see chaps. 4 and 10.

[46] Vauchez, *La sainteté en occident,* 229–32.

[47] The altarpiece, known as the *Pala di Annalena,* is now in the Uffizi. See Sarah Wilk, "The Cult," 695. For the penitent Jerome, see Eugene F. Rice Jr., *Saint Jerome in the Renaissance* (Baltimore: Johns Hopkins University Press, 1985).

[48] Caesarius of Heisterbach, *Dialogus Miraculorum,* 2 vols., ed. Joseph Strange (Cologne: J. M. Heberle, 1851), vol. 2, 149. To my knowledge this is her only therapeutic cure of stomach problems.

herself seem important."[49] In his first reference to the Magdalen's abstinence he tells his readers that "Mary Magdalen—and she alone—fasted for
thirty-three years, hidden away in a rock—and I think personally that it was
for this reason that the Lord . . . gave the Magdalen to [Catherine] . . . as
her mother and teacher."[50] He elaborates this theme when discussing how
Catherine regarded the Magdalen as a mother:

> As Mary Magdalen spent thirty-three years—a period of time which equals
> the savior's own age—in her cave in continual contemplation without taking
> any food, so from the time of this vision until the time she was thirty-three,
> when she died, Catherine devoted herself with such fervor to the contempla-
> tion of the Most High that, feeling no need of food, she found nourishment
> for her mind with the abundance of graces she received.[51]

Despite the ridicule of a few "scandalmongers," total abstinence from
food was widely regarded as a sign of sanctity in the later Middle Ages. As
the accounts of inedia demonstrate, it was frequently associated with host
miracles in which women lived on nothing but the eucharist, frequently
delivered by angelic means. Mary Magdalen, the legendary recluse, provided a model for such asceticism and its attendant supernatural phenom-
ena. Legends narrated that she received daily angelic nourishment at the
seven canonical hours. Her fasting and heavenly meals evidently inspired
others. Umiliana de' Cerchi once experienced an angelic feeding while
praying at the hour of terce. Having eaten nothing all week, an angel appeared to her carrying half a loaf of bread. It was white and fragrant and
without doubt, prepared with divine assistance.[52] Agnes Blannbekin (d.
1315), a Viennese beguine, prayed to be more like the Magdalen and, one
day, after saying the *Pater Noster,* she received the host in her mouth by no
human hands.[53] Another Agnes, this one the saint of Montepulciano (d.
1317), also experienced angelic communion. Her hagiographer, Raymond
of Capua, narrated how she received the eucharist from angelic hands.
He explicitly compares Agnes's angelic communion with that of the
Magdalen's.[54]

But imitation of the eremitical Magdalen did not stop with fasting and

---

[49] Ibid., par. 172, 896; Lamb, *St. Catherine,* 158.

[50] Ibid., par. 64, 868–69; ibid., 56.

[51] Ibid., par. 184, 899; ibid., 168.

[52] AASS, May, vol. 4, par. 29, 393.

[53] Cited in Peter Dinzelbacher, "Rifiuto dei ruoli, risveglio religioso ed esperienza mistica
delle donne nel medioevo," in *Movimento religioso e mistica femminile nel medioevo,* ed. Marco
Vannini, trans. Giovanna Fozzer (Milan: Edizioni Paoline, 1993), 76.

[54] Her life is found in AASS, April, vol. 2 (Antwerp, 1675), 791–817. The reference to
Mary Magdalen is found in Raymond of Capua, *Sant'Agnese da Montepulciano,* ed. Uga
Boscaglia. (Siena: Ed. Cantagalli, 1983), 69.

celestial nourishment—women also emulated the Magdalen's para-mysti-cal levitation. We have already seen how Margaret of Cortona levitated in mystical ecstasy, probably in imitation of Mary Magdalen. So did Cather-ine of Siena, according to both of her biographers. Raymond reports that

> as Mary Magdalen was taken up into the air by the angels seven times a day so that she could listen to the mysteries of God, so Catherine was for most of the time taken out of the world of the senses by the power of the Spirit, to contemplate heavenly things and praise the Lord with the Angels. The result was that her body was frequently lifted into the air, as many people, both men and women, claim to have seen.[55]

Tommaso Caffarini testified similarly maintaining that frequently Cath-erine's spirit soared upward pulling her body up along with it: "She was al-most as if another Magdalen suspended on high from the earth."[56]

Not everyone of course could or wanted to imitate the Magdalen's ec-static mysticism. For many it was quite enough to invoke the assistance of the ascetical saint or visit the grotto of La Saint-Baume where she lived out the last years of her life in mystical reclusion. The miracle register of Jean Gobi narrates how some imprisoned merchants from Marseilles called on the voluntary recluse to release them from captivity, vowing that if she did so, they would visit her grotto, "the place where she had done penance and incarcerated herself" for the love of the Lord Jesus Christ. The saint saw to it that her supplicants were liberated and in time the merchants made a penitential pilgrimage to La Sainte-Baume, flagellating themselves as they had vowed to do when they had first petitioned her intercession.[57]

Another ex-prisoner by the name of Jacobus, for whom the Magdalen had intervened, also made the pilgrimage to La Sainte-Baume to give thanks to the saint for his miraculous escape. He was so grateful for his lib-eration that he remained there for some time serving the sanctuary with the friars.[58] Gobi's miracle catalog shows two other petitioners who made the journey to the Magdalen's desert retreat: a canon from Valence and a leper called Jacobus from Amalfi.[59] Gobi's record indicates that the sanc-tuary's clientele was mostly local, one of the few exceptions being the un-fortunate Jacobus, the leper, from southern Italy.

Even though her relics were believed to be at Saint-Maximin, La Sainte-

---

[55] AASS, 30 April, vol. 3, par. 184, 899; Lamb, *St. Catherine,* 168.

[56] Tommaso d'Antonio Nacci-Caffarini, *Leggenda minore di S. Caterina da Siena* (Bo-logna: Gaetano Romagnoli, 1868), 47.

[57] "Iohannes Gobi," no. 8, 147.

[58] Ibid., no. 4, 143.

[59] Ibid., no. 52, 179–80; no. 82, 200.

Baume, the grotto where she reputedly spent the last thirty-three years of her life in penance and mystical contemplation, became an important provençal pilgrimage destination. It was already well-established by 1283, the date of Salimbene's pilgrimage there. He gives this detailed description of the sanctuary and the locals who frequented it:

> The cave of Saint Mary Magdalen, in which she did penance for thirty years is fifteen miles from Marseilles. I slept there one night immediately after her feast. It is in the highest rocky mountain, and if I remember well, it is indeed enormous in my opinion because it holds a thousand people; . . . and outside there is a certain church near the cave where certain priests live. . . . And the mountain is so high above ground level that, in my judgement and if I re-member well, three of Bologna's Asinelli towers could not reach the peak. . . . And because that region is still secluded, so uninhabitable and deserted, for this reason women and noble ladies of Marseilles go there out of devotion. They ride out on asses laden with bread and wine, turtle-doves and fish, and other edibles they desire.[60]

Salimbene's detailed account makes the ladies' excursions sound a bit more like a picnic in the countryside than a penitential pilgrimage; never-theless his report provides an important amendment to Gobi's information about the shrine's clientele. Other than male pilgrims fulfilling vows, local women seem to have journeyed to the cave as a regular part of their devo-tional lives.

For the thirteenth and fourteenth centuries we must depend on the re-ports of literate friars to gain a glimpse of the physical layout, clientele, and devotions made at the provençal grotto; by the fifteenth century, pilgrims were writing their own eyewitness accounts of what they had seen at La Sainte-Baume. John van der Saren, a Carthusian monk who made the jour-ney to Provence in 1469, described the chapels, the guest house, and the church that now made up the complex chiseled into the mountainside at La Sainte-Baume; he also mentioned the chapel atop the mountain com-memorating the spot where tradition maintained that Mary Magdalen had been elevated seven times daily into the ether by a host of angels.[61]

La Sainte-Baume attracted ordinary pilgrims and luminaries alike. One of the latter was Petrarch whose first visit to the shrine was made most likely in the year 1338. He made subsequent visits in 1347 and 1353. At La Sainte-Baume the poet was inspired to write his *Carmen de Beata Maria Magdalena,* a poem in praise of the Magdalen, which he left at the grotto as a memento on one of his visits. The poem treats three themes by now

---

[60] *Cronica,* vol. 2, 762.
[61] Cited in Clemens, *The Establishment,* 270–71.

quite familiar: Mary Magdalen's conversion, her fidelity at the cross, and her eremitical retreat from the world.[62]

This chapter has examined audience response to the preachers' legendary Magdalen. As in the previous chapter evaluating response to scriptural aspects of Mary Magdalen's persona, analysis in this chapter has generated some rather unexpected results.

We have seen that although preachers and hagiographers offered the model of the apostolic Magdalen for admiration rather than imitation, evidence suggests that women were not always aware of or did not always heed this learned distinction. We have cases of both heterodox and orthodox women who took up the cross of active ministries in the world, following in the footsteps of Mary Magdalen, *apostolorum apostola.*

We have also found that Mary the contemplative of Bethany, though a popular image in sermons, was not received with overwhelming enthusiasm by the laity, at least not so far as our sources reveal. The contemplative of Bethany was not so popularly venerated because her legendary aspect as a contemplative hermit provided an alternative outlet for such devotion. If people wanted to appeal to the contemplative nature of the saint they petitioned the recluse of La Sainte-Baume who was no mere novice at contemplation—she was a master whose mystical trances were accompanied by supernatural events. Women, many of them urban dwellers, were particularly attracted to this image of the saint and modeled themselves on the reclusive eremite. Both local women and men, our sources have disclosed, frequented the sanctuary of La Sainte-Baume.

Ultimately women seem to have modeled themselves more closely on the legendary aspects of the Magdalen than men. Men seem to have been more content to admire rather than imitate the legendary saint. This was clearly the case in 1489 when a pious Florentine auditor recorded some notes from a Magdalen sermon he had heard delivered at the church of San Lorenzo. They were notes for pious reflection on the saint rather than guidelines for imitation of her deeds.[63]

[62] For the poem and a commentary, see Joseph Gibaldi, "Petrarch and the Baroque Magdalene Tradition," *The Hebrew University Studies in Literature* 3/1 (1975): 1–19, and Eve Duperray, "Le Carmen de *Beata Maria Magdalena:* Marie-Madeleine dans l'oeuvre de François Pétrarque: image emblématique de la Belle Laure," in *Marie Madeleine,* ed. Duperray, 273–88.

[63] See n. IX, a *reportatio* (of sorts) of a sermon given by Mariano da Genazzano, O.E.S.A. at San Lorenzo 10 April 1489, in Zelina Zafarana, "Per la storia religiosa nel Quattrocento. Una raccolta privata di prediche," now collected in *Da Gregorio VII a Bernardino da Siena. Saggi di storia medievale,* ed. O. Capitani, C. Leonardi, et al. (Quaderni del Centro per il

In this and the previous chapter we have analyzed popular response to the scriptural and the legendary saint. In the next we examine creative responses to the Magdalen that may have been inspired by the friars' preaching and hagiography, but in the event, I would argue, were the result of a creative interchange between the needs and desires of the laity and the image of the saint received in the preaching of the friars.

---

collegamento degli studi medievali e umanistici nell'Università di Perugia) (Florence: La Nuova Italia, 1987), 279–377, particularly 283 and 312–16.

TEN

In the Shadow
of the Virgin

*P*reachers often envisioned the Virgin Mary and Mary Magdalen as two complementary paths to salvation. The Virgin Mary represented the way of innocence, the Magdalen the way of penance. Basing his understanding on *Genesis* 1:16, Friar Ludovicus imagined their salvific alliance thus:

> There are two great lights in the heavens. The more powerful light is the Virgin Mary standing at the head of the innocents lest they become too proud. The less powerful light, as at night, is Mary Magdalen leading the sinners lest they despair.[1]

The Franciscan preacher's formulation maintained two separate but corresponding paths to salvation; this chapter suggests that the friars' audiences, often for very personal reasons, were eager to find the confluence of the two paths. That is, it shows how members of the preachers' audiences interpreted the symbol of the holy sinner in the light of his or her own desires. The ultimate result was to produce a Mary Magdalen that still retained her own attributes but who now more and more began to resemble the Virgin Mary. By the later Middle Ages Mary Magdalen was considered both a virgin and invoked as mother.

Virginity Reconstituted

It will be recalled from the discussion in chapter 7 that preachers suggested that Mary Magdalen's great penance converted her metaphorically from a

---

[1] "Duo luminaria magna in firmamento celi luminare maius, id est beata virgo innocentibus ne superbirent. Luminare minus ut nocti id est Magdalena ut prae esset peccatoribus ne despererent." MS Marc. lat. fondo antico 91 (1775), f. 16r; *RLS* 4:15.

desolated wasteland to a lush and bounteous garden suffused in the aromatic perfumes of paradise. By vigilantly maintaining her chastity after her conversion she had made of herself a *hortus conclusus*—an enclosed garden—on the model of the Virgin Mary. It was for this reason that she earned the floral wreath, the crown traditionally reserved for virgins. It was, moreover, the reason preachers most often cited to explain Mary Magdalen's privileged position in the litany at the head of the virginal choir. The Dominican preacher Tommaso Agni da Lentini judged Mary Magdalen's relative position among the saints thus: she superseded the virgins in the catalog of saints, was equal to the apostles on account of her title apostle of the apostles, but subordinate to the Virgin Mary because the Virgin was without peer.[2] Lentini's Franciscan counterpart, Friar Ludovicus, made a similar argument when he preached:

> One should not be surprised at how much [Mary Magdalen] was honored before all the others in heaven as she was honored likewise on earth. On earth she was the apostle of the apostles . . . [In heaven] the holy church decided to put her in front of all the virgins in the litany.[3]

In what follows I would like to suggest that sermons such as these inspired penitent matrons distressed about the loss of their virginity, and its implications for salvation, to look to the example of the Magdalen to justify their claims to the virginal crown. The loss of virginity weighed far more heavily on the consciences of women than men. Lost virginity and its obstruction to celestial glory was, it appears, uppermost in the minds of many *pinzochere,* most of whom were married, had been married, or had experienced carnal relations.[4] They were not mad to dwell on its loss. According to received wisdom based on the parable of the sower (Matt. 13:8, 23), the married woman could only collect a thirtyfold reward of blessings, while widows obtained a sixtyfold reward. Only virgins attained the hundredfold fruit. Married women, then, had less of an opportunity of sanctifying themselves than others.[5] As such, they turned to the model of Mary Magdalen, who had been neither married nor widowed, and who, furthermore, was believed to have been no virgin, to justify their claims to the virgins' prize.[6]

[2] "Unde praefertur virginibus cathalogo sanctorum. Conparatur apostolis quia apostola apostolorum et beate virgini in mediatate subicitur illa enim beata inparatrix hec beata peccatrix. Gn. 1. fecit deus duo magna luminaria et sic patent omnia." MS BAV Vat. lat. 4691, f. 118v; not in *RLS.*

[3] "Non est mirum quantus prae aliis honoretur in celis que prae aliis honorabatur in terris. In terris ipsa fuit apostolorum apostola . . . Ecclesia etiam sancta in letaniis eam praeponere consuevit omnibus virginibus." Ibid.

[4] This theme is treated in Dyan Elliott, *Spiritual Marriage,* 208–45.

[5] Jacques Dalarun, *Lapsus Linguae: La légende de Claire de Rimini* (Biblioteca di medioevo latino, vol. 6) (Spoleto: Centro italiano di studi sull'alto medioevo, 1994), 255.

[6] It will be recalled that one legend identified Mary Magdalen as the betrothed of John

After all, if Mary Magdalen's great penance and post-conversion chastity had been so efficacious that she was now to be found among the chorus of virgins, perhaps penitent matrons too could imitate her and aspire to the virgins' floral wreath. Hagiography reveals that the Magdalen's apotheosis among the virgins provided comfort for many women troubled over the apparently irretrievable loss of their virginity. Her glorification in heaven provided hope that lost virginity was not an insurmountable obstacle in the quest for salvation and heavenly glorification.

The case of Margaret of Cortona is instructive. One of her visions—revealingly experienced on the feast-day of the virgin-martyr Catherine of Alexandria—lays bare the mental anguish she suffered over her lost virginity. Fra Giunta recounts that while Margaret was taking communion at the altar, she heard Christ's comforting voice: "Daughter, I will place you with the seraphim where the virgins aflame with love are found." The stunned Margaret replied, "Lord, how is this possible if I was so great a sinner?" To which the Lord answered, "Daughter your many punishments will purify your soul of every impurity . . . your contrition will restore your virginal purity." Margaret, ever wary, even at the promise of such great consolation, turned to Christ and posed yet another question, this one disclosing all her anxieties about personal salvation: "Lord have you also put the Magdalen in celestial glory among the virgins?" To which the Lord replied reassuringly, "With the exception of the Virgin Mary and the martyr Catherine, no one in the chorus of virgins is greater than the Magdalen."[7]

Presumably Margaret's guilt-ridden conscience was somewhat appeased upon hearing from the Lord that penance would restore her to a condition of virginal purity just as it had done for Mary Magdalen. The Magdalen's glorification among the virgins seems to have provided inspiration not just for Margaret of Cortona's claim to a place in the heavenly choir of virgins, but for other apprehensive matrons as well. I have already cited (without comment) Umiltà of Faenza's remark granting Mary Magdalen the reward of one hundredfold blessings on account of her penitential tears.[8] Now it should be noted that she bestowed on the Magdalen the reward traditionally reserved for virgins.

Umiltà of Faenza and other matrons envisioned Mary Magdalen among the chorus of crowned virgins. On 12 February 1433 the Roman matron Francesca Romana envisioned a great purgatorial fire of divine charity where many souls were purifying themselves. There she encoun-

---

the Evangelist, the couple for whom the marriage feast at Cana was celebrated. Most authors, like Jacobus de Voragine, adamantly rejected this tale.

[7] AASS, Feb., vol. 3, par. 72, 313.

[8] See chapter 8, n. 25.

tered Mary Magdalen and Saint Agnes who guided and encouraged her to approach the fire, where she could more readily see the congregation of virgins.[9] On another occasion Francesca envisioned the entire litany of saints: when she came to the virgins, she saw Mary Magdalen leading their number.[10]

Tellingly, when hagiographers described their anxious penitents' celestial glorification (as told to them by the women themselves or other female visionaries), Mary Magdalen was reassuringly standing at their sides. At Beata Villana's apotheosis (reported by a female relative who had prayed to see the glory bestowed on the saint in heaven), she was greeted by a crowd of women led by Mary Magdalen. After making her way through a heavenly host, Villana was finally presented to the Lord, whereupon he promptly and symbolically changed her name, transforming her from something rude and churlish (Villana) to a precious pearl (Margherita). He then ordered that she descend to earth in the company of the Magdalen to reveal to her friends the glory that she had received.[11] Given Mary Magdalen's presence at her side it can be inferred that the name change indicated a change in sexual status as well. Villana the matron had been transformed into Margherita, a pearl, whose shining whiteness signified the purity of virginity.

Vito da Cortona, hagiographer of Umiliana de' Cerchi, tells a story constituted of strikingly similar components about his *beata*.[12] This one begins during her lifetime, when in 1241, after the death of her husband, Umiliana returned to her father's house, not an usual turn of events for widows in medieval Florence. What happened next, however, is extraordinary: she claimed the tower of the family palazzo as her own private desert retreat. The tower, of course, can be read symbolically. On the historico-literal level, towers were important to the landscape of every Italian commune. Towers symbolized a given family's wealth, military might, and political power: they were, in essence, the family's stronghold. But there was also a mystical meaning of the tower: because it was walled-in and enclosed,

---

[9] *Visio XXII* in *Santa Francesca Romana*, ed. Romagnoli, 487.

[10] *Visio XI*, in ibid., 433–35.

[11] Orlandi, *La Beata Villana*, 88–90.

[12] The source for Umiliana's life is her *vita* by Vito da Cortona in AASS, May, vol. 4 (Antwerp, 1685), 385–418, probably written the year of her death. There is a *volgarizzamento* made in 1300–1350 known as *Leggenda della Beata Umiliana de' Cerchi*, ed. Domenico Moreni (Florence: Magheri, 1827). Anna Benvenuti Papi has done the most significant work on Umiliana; see her "Cerchi, Umiliana dei," in *DBI* 23 (1979), 692–96, and "Umiliana dei Cerchi: nascita di un culto nella Firenze del Dugento," *Studi Francescani* 77 (1980): 87–117, now collected as "Una Santa Vedova," in *In castro poenitentiae*, 59–98. See also Elizabeth Petroff, "Transforming the World: The Serpent-Dragon and the Virgin Saint," in *Body and Soul: Essays on Medieval Women and Mysticism* (Oxford: Oxford University Press, 1994), 97–109.

in the medieval symbolic vocabulary the tower was emblematic of virginity or chastity. It was the symbol of the Virgin Mary as well as the attribute of the virgin-martyr Barbara. Its function as a stronghold and its symbolic association with virginity doubtless informed Umiliana's decision to make of the family tower her own desert hermitage.

Stronghold though it was, Umiliana's tower did not protect her entirely from temptation and evil. She was besieged by serpents which, she believed, threatened her spiritual life, to say nothing of her bodily integrity. On one occasion, one fearful creature even wrapped itself around her body while she slept, causing her thereafter to take the precaution of using a belt to secure the hem of her dress firmly around her ankles whenever she lay down. This, she hoped, would impede the serpent from slithering up beneath her dress and winding itself around her naked body as she slept. Eventually Umiliana triumphed over the beast when, cursing it in the name of God, she hurled it from a window of her tower.[13]

It would seem that in ridding the tower of sexualized vipers Umiliana was purifying herself of any lingering pollution caused, she believed, by sexual activity in her marriage. When she purged the tower of the poison of the vipers she also purified herself. Sanctifying her tower, refusing to remarry, and steadfastly maintaining her chastity restored Umiliana to a virginal state, as her *vita* goes on to say. Her vigilance in guarding her chastity was rewarded in heaven. As Villana would do, Umiliana, on Mary Magdalen's feast-day, appeared in the company of the saint to a pious woman rapt in prayer.[14] On another occasion Umiliana made an appearance to a certain holy woman who noted that her long blond tresses more resembled golden thread than actual hair (a Magdalenian attribute, it will be recalled); furthermore, she was crowned with a double diadem. The first coronet was the *corona virginea,* the virgin's wreath; the second, the wreath of chastity. When asked why she had received the virgin's crown Umiliana responded, "The Lord did this for me because of the sorrow I perpetually carry in my heart for my lost virginity which was due to marriage."[15]

Another anxious matron who brooded over her lost virginity and its implications for personal salvation was Margery Kempe, mother of fourteen children. In her autobiography she reported a conversation in which she worried over the issue in the Lord's presence: "Because I am no virgin, lack of virginity is now great sorrow to me. I think I wish I had been killed as soon as I was taken from the font, so that I should never have displeased you." To which the Lord replied soothingly: "I have told you before that you are a singular lover of God, and therefore you shall have a singular love

[13] AASS, May, vol. 4, par. 21, 391.

[14] Ibid., par. 58, 400.

[15] Ibid., par. 60, 400–401.

in heaven, a singular reward and a singular honor. And because you are a maiden in your soul, I shall take you by the one hand in heaven, and my mother by the other, and so you shall dance in heaven with other holy maidens and virgins, for I may call you my dearly bought and my own beloved darling."[16] Significantly, the Lord of Margery's visions maintained that she was yet a maiden in her soul.

I have suggested in the foregoing pages that women, often uncloistered religious women—frequently matrons—responded enthusiastically to the preachers' image of the *beata peccatrix,* the sinner sanctified through penance. The Magdalen's glorification at the head of the chorus of virgins—her virginity restored—was a condition to which they themselves aspired. The notion of restored virginity—the reconstitution of the vase of glory from a vessel of sin—was, as we have seen, a great part of the message of hope contained in the friars' sermons. Women responded enthusiastically to this image and used it in turn to create sacred space for themselves in the heavenly choir of virgins. Not content to receive a mere thirtyfold celestial reward, their due according to convention, they represented themselves along with Mary Magdalen as recuperated virgins and claimed the hundredfold reward.

Even virgins such as Clare of Montefalco (d. 1308) defended the Magdalen's right to such celestial rewards. Clare's hagiographer Berengario di S. Africano recounted that one day a heretic challenged Clare's orthodoxy with this cunning question: "Since the Magdalen is greater in merit than is Agnes, what pleases the Lord more: the virginity of Agnes or the corruption of the Magdalen?" The savvy Clare evaded his trap by arguing that because the Magdalen had so much contrition about her sins, to say nothing of her devotion, ardent love, and other virtues, "she was able to supersede in merit [even] the virgin Agnes."[17]

One scholar, basing her argument on hagiographical material, has suggested that the meaning of virginity changed considerably from the early Middle Ages to the later medieval period. In essence, a shift occurred after the thirteenth century that moved the definition away from a purely physiological explanation to "interpret virginity in moral and psychological terms."[18] My research supports such a formulation, but I would add that such a transition was aided immeasurably by the new emphasis on penitential practice and the example of Mary Magdalen. The Magdalenian

---

[16] *The Book of Margery Kempe,* ed. B. A. Windeatt, 86, 88.

[17] Berengario di S. Africano, *Vita di S. Chiara di Montefalco,* in *Archivio storico per le Marche e per l'Umbria* 1 (1884): 557–625, and 2 (1885): 193–226, particularly 207–8. For Clare, see the essays by G. Casagrande and S. Nessi contained in *S. Chiara da Montefalco e il suo tempo.*

[18] Clarissa W. Atkinson, "'Precious Balsam in a Fragile Glass': The Ideology of Virginity in the Later Middle Ages," *Journal of Family History* (summer 1983): 131.

model of restored purity gave hope and provided a model for many matrons who might otherwise have despaired about their chances for personal
salvation.

We have traveled light years from the views of certain patristic authors
who regarded an unchaste gaze as enough to compromise a woman's virginity.[19] Late medieval women provided a sensible response to such views:
If a gaze or an impure thought was potent enough to imperil bodily integrity, then purity of mind was mighty enough to restore lost virginity.
Eventually, though, the notion of the Magdalen's restored virginity seems
to have provoked a debate among theologians that forced a distinction between spiritual and corporal virginity. Perhaps it was views such as the one
expressed in the fourteenth-century "Sister Catherine Treatise" that
pushed the issue into theological consideration. That treatise took the position that

> Mary Magdalen had neither husband nor child. That is the first thing. I will
> explain it to you still better. I am sure you are aware of the fact that like loves
> like naturally. You know that Christ would never have loved Mary Magdalen
> so sincerely if she had not been a pure maiden, nor would he have been so in-
> timate with her, nor would Mary Magdalen have been able to love Christ as
> much as she did if she had not been a pure human being.[20]

The author of the "Sister Catherine Treatise" seems to have believed that
Mary Magdalen was a virgin, both in body and soul. At about the time the
treatise was written moralists and theologians began asking whether virginity depended on bodily integrity alone.[21]

We have already seen that Giordano da Pisa and François de Meyronnes
participated in this debate in their sermons. Giordano preached that
though Mary Magdalen was not a virgin of the flesh, she was virgin of the
mind. François maintained that the Magdalen had earned the floral wreath
not because she was a virgin per se, but because after her conversion she
maintained unparalleled purity of body and mind. Recall also that François
had crowned the Magdalen with the quadruple aureola, one coronet of

---

[19] Brigitte Cazelles writes: "Inspired by a deep distrust of the body, a number of Church
Fathers posited that, in order to be, purity should neither be seen nor described. In their view,
a virgin ceases to be a virgin when she becomes the object of sensual love (Cyprian; third
century); when she endures unchaste gazing (John Chrysostom; fourth century); and when
she is submitted to the adultery of the eyes (Novatian; third century). Tertullian goes even
further when he declares that "every public exposure of a virgin is [to her] a suffering of rape."
Cited in Petroff, *Body and Soul*, 163–64.

[20] "Sister Catherine Treatise," in *Meister Eckhart*, 380.

[21] For a scholastic treatment of the subject, see Alexander of Hales, Sententiarum Lib. IV,
distinctio XXXIII. 3: *Quod autem castitas virginalis* in *Glossa in Quatuor Libros Sententiarum
Petri Lombardi*, ed. PP. Collegii S. Bonaventurae, 4 vols. (Quaracchi: Typographia Collegii
S. Bonaventurae, 1957), 520–34.

which was the virgins' floral wreath. Of course, the usual way to invoke the aureola was as a triple honor deriving from excellent deeds. It was envisioned thus in a miniature we have already seen (Fig. 7) in which Mary Magdalen wears the triple crown composed of a gold circlet for the learned, a red one for martyrs, and a blue one for virgins. In this image the Magdalen wears the virgins' crown and, in a departure from the conventions of medieval color symbolism, she wears blue rather than her customary red garments. It shall suffice to remark that blue, a color often made from precious lapis lazuli, was normally the color reserved for the Virgin Mary's mantle in medieval painting.[22]

Female concerns about personal salvation pressured those in more learned circles to reconsider and clarify the meaning of virginity in the later Middle Ages. It was not merely an academic exercise; rather, the debate was driven by matrons anxious about their celestial rewards. The case of the Magdalen provided the terms for discussion. The matter is exemplified in a letter written by the Dominican Antonino Pierozzi (d. 1459) to Diodata Adimari, one of the many women the bishop of Florence served as spiritual counselor. In this letter he is evidently responding to questions his correspondent had posed about the Magdalen's virginity:

> Some people have such affection [for Mary Magdalen] that they say that she was a virgin in body, but not of the mind, through her evil desires and wretched thoughts. Virginity lost either licitly through marriage, or illicitly outside of marriage cannot be regained bodily; nor is the crown reserved for it. One can regain mental virginity through true penance, and so the crown is reserved for it. And since Mary Magdalen did perfect penance, she regained virginity along with its crown.[23]

Although Antonino was himself a great devotee of Mary Magdalen, he concluded nonetheless that her penance restored her purity in mind only.

By the end of the Middle Ages the question of the Magdalen's recovered virginity had provoked new ways of thinking about the nature and meaning of virginity. Now one distinguished between bodily virginity which could never be restored, and mental virginity, which through true penance could be recuperated. Although apprehensive matrons had thrust the issue of virginity and its celestial fruits into the forefront of academic debate, we should not forget the power of another female figure who stood at the sidelines, silently pressuring this debate. The Virgin Mary was the

---

[22] See chap. 7, nn. 144–45 for the preaching of Giordano da Pisa and François de Meyronnes. See chap. 2, n. 66 for the MS miniature.

[23] *Lettere di santi e beati fiorentini,* ed. Antommaria Biscioni (Florence: Francesco Moucke, 1736), 224–25. Many of the letters in this collection were written to Diodata. For Antonino, see A. d'Addario, "Antonino Pierozzi," in *DBI* 3 (1961), 523–32. For his devotion to the Magdalen, see Wilk, "The Cult of Mary Magdalen," 691–98.

most imposing female figure on the late medieval landscape and her attributes shaped the construction of all other female saints. Even the figure of the sinner-saint could not resist such pressure; consequently Mary Magdalen was transformed into a holy virgin, at least in the mind. In the next section we shall see how motherhood, another of the Virgin's venerated attributes, came to be grafted onto the Magdalen's persona.

Mater Magdalena

One anthropological theory holds that "to communicate with divinity, or the supernatural, a person must direct her life toward this pursuit. For a woman to devote her attention to spiritual concerns, she must not be hindered by physical fertility but comes to develop instead the potential of symbolic motherhood."[24] These words are germane to any consideration of the Magdalen's symbolic representation as mother. They aid in understanding how an unlikely candidate such as Mary Magdalen, neither a mother in scripture nor in legend, came to be regarded symbolically as both a mother-figure and a saint who specialized in issues related to motherhood. The symbolic reversals which characterized so much of medieval thought also contributed to the Magdalen's figurative motherhood. It will be recalled that the friars frequently preached the counterintuitive proposition that promiscuity yielded sterility, while virginity produced abundant fruit. Such a conceit serves not only to illuminate how the Magdalen, once metaphorically sterile but now abundantly fertile, became the patron saint of vintners and gardeners, but also a maternal saint, along the lines of the Virgin Mary.[25] By the thirteenth century the reconstituted virginal Magdalen was endowed with generative, nutritive, and protective qualities.

These qualities are best illustrated in the Marseilles-miracle which took its most familiar shape in Jacobus de Voragine's *Golden Legend,* though it had already been attached to the saint's *vita* since the twelfth century.[26] That miracle story, one of the central events of Mary Magdalen's *vita,* comprising approximately one-third of the entire legend, recounts how the Magdalen converted the pagan ruler of Provence and his wife to Chris-

[24] J. Hoch-Smith and A. Spring, eds., *Women in Ritual and Symbolic Roles* (New York: Plenum Press, 1978), 15.

[25] For vintners and gardeners, see Marjorie Malvern, *Venus in Sackcloth: The Magdalen's Origins and Metamorphosis* (Carbondale, IL.: Southern Illinois University Press, 1975), 76.

[26] BHL 5457–58. Following Hans Hansel, Saxer believes this miracle to have been modeled on a romance of Apollonius of Tyre, widely diffused in the Middle Ages. He has reiterated this view most recently in "Philippe Cabassole et son *Libellus hystorialis Marie beatissime Magdalene,*" in *L'Etat Angevin: pouvoir, culture et société entre XIIIe et XIVe siècle* (Collection de l'École française de Rome n. 245) (Rome: l'École française de Rome, 1998), 202.

tianity.[27] She appeared to them on three separate occasions while they slept. Each time she chastened them for indulging their wicked ways while Christ's saints suffered. After her third nocturnal visit, they decide at last to convert to the new faith on the condition that Mary Magdalen intercede with the Lord to grant them a son. This she does and the ruler's wife finally conceives a child. Curious to learn more about their new religion the grateful couple decide to make a pilgrimage to Rome. They set out by ship, but on the way are caught in such a violent storm that the mother-to-be unexpectedly goes into labor. She delivers the child but dies in childbirth. Despite the ruler's imprecations, the superstitious crew, anxious to get rid of the body, abandons the dead woman, infant at her breast, on a desert island. The ruler continues the journey, arriving in Rome where Saint Peter spends two years showing him the holy places and instructing him in the faith. On the return voyage to Provence, the ship passes by the island where mother and child had previously been left for dead. The ruler begs the crew to pull ashore where he miraculously finds his son alive, healthy, and amusing himself by the seashore. Following the child, he finds his wife's lifeless body whereupon he immediately cries out to Mary Magdalen to restore her to life. No sooner has he uttered the words than his wife awakens and tells him that she too has just returned from a pilgrimage to the holy places guided by Mary Magdalen herself.

The essential elements of this miracle point to Mary Magdalen's maternal qualities and her patronage of concerns relating to motherhood. First, in her generative mode, Mary Magdalen as intercessor brought about a fertility miracle allowing the royal couple to conceive a child. Second, in her protective role, she did "midwife's service," delivering the child safely.[28] By virtue of her nutritive capacities, she effected a lactation miracle that allowed the newborn to nurse at his dead mother's breast. And finally, again in her protective mode, for two years she looked after the mother and child until they were rescued.

This tale was broadcast to an even wider audience when preachers such as Remigio de' Girolami and Peregrinus de Oppeln began to repeat the story in their sermons, and when it was frescoed onto church walls.[29] This episode of her *vita* was a favorite with artists and their patrons and was represented in varying degrees of complexity. It is the most represented miracle story in the visual cycles of Mary Magdalen's life. Of the thirteen late medieval fresco cycles of the *vita Magdalenae,* only three—San Domenico Maggiore (Naples), San Lorenzo Maggiore (Naples), and Sant' Antonio

---

[27] I discuss a different aspect of this miracle in chapter 6.

[28] *Golden Legend,* 379.

[29] For Remigio, see MS Flor. Naz. Conv. Sopp. D. 1. 937, f. 229v; *RLS* 5: 802. For Peregrinus, see MS BAV Pal. lat. 465, ff. 155v–156r; *RLS* 4: 147.

di Ranverso (Buttigliera Alta)—lack any reference to this episode.[30] By contrast, the church of Santa Maria at Pontresina dedicates eight of the seventeen episodes that make up the visual narrative of her life to representing this miracle. In the oratorio dedicated to the Magdalen at the Franciscan hermitage of Santa Maria del Belverde in Cetona (Tuscany), two of the six early Quattrocento frescoes which make up her *vita* picture this miracle. The first shows the abandonment of the dead mother and her baby, the second their rescue (Fig. 47).[31] From the thirteenth until well into the eighteenth century, a "cantinella," three verses of which commemorate the miracle, was recited during an Easter procession that went from La Vielle Major to the chapel built on the sight of her preaching campaign in Marseilles.[32]

The Marseilles miracle, promoting the maternal aspect of Mary Magdalen, was disseminated widely by the success of the *Golden Legend* and its attendant cultural forms, inspiring others to beseech the saint for similar favors. Jean Gobi's book of miracles narrates how, after twelve years, a certain couple still unable to conceive a child began to pray and supplicate

[30] The absence of this scene at San Lorenzo Maggiore and Sant'Antonio di Ranverso can be explained by the fact that these cycles have been badly damaged and many scenes have been lost. In the case of San Domenico Maggiore, there were only three scenes to begin with, one of which has been lost. The two remaining scenes are the *noli me tangere* and Mary Magdalen in her hermitage. Given the placement of the lost scene, I suspect that it was a biblical scene, probably her conversion at the house of the Pharisee.

[31] On the cycle, see Enzo Carli, *Gli affreschi di Belverde* (Florence: Edam, 1977). This hermitage was founded near Cetona in 1367 by count Niccolo' della Corvaia, a noble Orvietan, perhaps from the family Monaldeschi della Corvaia. In the year that he founded the hermitage he became a Franciscan tertiary.

[32] The "cantinella" was recited in Provençal. It has been reconstructed and translated by J. T. Bory and reprinted in LaLuque, *Marseille,* 365–70. Here are the pertinent verses:

A celui qui commandait à Marseille
Elle promit qu'il aurait un enfant
S'il croyait en son bon Seigneur
(Et son erreur il abjurait)
Et suivait ses commandements.

Le roi bien ressentit joie et frayeur
Quand il vit que vivait encore
La reine qu'avec grande tristesse
Il avait laissée morte
Et qu'il trouva un enfant souriant.

A Madeleine et au Créateur
Le roi très sincèrement rendit grâce
Et sa crainte en Dieu augmente
Car il était le premier à croire
Et fit croire grand nombre d'autres personnes.

Figure 47. *Marseilles Miracle* (early 15th c.). The ruler of Marseilles finds his wife and child alive on a deserted island thanks to the intervention of Mary Magdalen. Fresco by Andrea di Giovanni from the Oratorio of Mary Magdalen, Hermitage Church of S. Maria del Belverde, Cetona. (Photo: Author)

Mary Magdalen with candles in the hope that she would intervene and deliver them a child. Soon their prayers were answered and a son was born. The couple's happiness was short lived, however; after three months, the child grew perilously ill. The distraught mother again petitioned the Magdalen, only this time with reference to her legendary miracle in which she saved the royal couple's infant from death:

> Supplicating with endless sighs and gifts so that she who had resuscitated the wife of the Prince of Provence from death and also protected his abandoned son by her prayers. . . . She promised that if the saint liberated her son from the danger of death she and her child would present themselves at Saint-Maximin with fitting service.[33]

Happily the Magdalen intervened, the son was saved, and mother and child eventually came to the saint's sanctuary in Provence to give thanks.

The Marseilles miracle may have been the Magdalen's most famous ma-

---

[33] "Iohannes Gobi," no. 79, 196.

ternal miracle; it was not, however, her only effort in favor of expectant mothers. Jacobus de Voragine relates yet another miracle in which Mary Magdalen came to the aid of an impending mother. A pregnant woman in imminent danger from shipwreck invoked the aid of Mary Magdalen to save her from drowning. She vowed that if she lived and bore a son she would give him as an oblate to the saint's monastery. While the rest of the passengers drowned, Mary Magdalen came to her aid holding the expectant mother's chin above the water and guiding her safely to shore. In the fullness of time the woman gave birth to a son and fulfilled her vow to the saint.[34]

Other expectant mothers called on the intervention of Mary Magdalen in a very different manner: through dolls made in the saint's image. Mary Magdalen nuptial dolls were yet another link to the saint's association with fertility and motherhood. Notarial documents have recorded the presence of these curious dolls in the trousseaux of early modern Italian women. In 1499, Giovanni Buongirolami's wife entered her marriage with a "Saint Mary Magdalen dressed in red satin with pearls," whose "magical function" was to aid in giving birth to a beautiful child, the theory being that a baby would resemble that which a woman contemplated during her pregnancy.[35]

Another curious object, this one from late medieval Britain, is also affiliated with Mary Magdalen's newly found link with fertility, generation, and child protection. This was the childbirth girdle, a standard feature of parturition in England from the time of the Druids until well into the nineteenth century. It was believed that wearing such a girdle or belt would ensure safe delivery and prevent miscarriages. Many of these girdles were endowed with supernatural powers as was the one enshrined at the Cathedral of Saint Peter in Westminster. According to popular belief it belonged to the Virgin Mary. (Another one of her belts was in the care of the Carmelites, yet another one of red silk was in the custody of a convent at Bruton.) These relics could be summoned and were dispatched to women as they went into labor. Perhaps in an effort to conform more closely with the Virgin Mary's generative powers, a birthing girdle was also attributed to Mary Magdalen that was "sent also with great reverence to women travailing."[36]

Thus barren women, expectant mothers, women *in partu*, and distressed mothers implored Mary Magdalen's maternal intervention. One of the

---

[34] *Golden Legend*, 382.

[35] Christiane Klapisch-Zuber, *Women, Family, and Ritual in Renaissance Italy*, trans. Lydia Cochrane (Chicago: University of Chicago Press, 1985), 312, 317.

[36] *Medieval Woman's Guide to Health: The First Gynecological Handbook*, ed. and trans. Beryl Rowland (Kent, OH: Kent State University Press, 1981), 32–33.

consequences of petitioning the Magdalen in cases of infertility and for the protection of the unborn, infants, and mothers, was the improbable development of maternal Magdalen imagery. Implausible as it seems, Mother Magdalen became a popular motif—both literary and visual—among those who venerated her in the later Middle Ages.

Our first example (Fig. 13) comes from the giottesque Magdalen chapel commissioned by Bishop Teobaldo Pontano in the lower church of San Francesco at Assisi, completed about 1312. Very little is known about the bishop so it is all but impossible to discover with any degree of certainty the motives for his devotion to Mary Magdalen. But we can speculate. First and most obvious is that he was a Franciscan; Franciscan veneration of the saint was common, as we have seen. The second reason is that before his assignment to Assisi in 1296, he spent twelve years as bishop at Castellammare di Stabia and then Terracina, important cities in the *Regno*.[37] The *mezzogiorno* (south) was, at that time, ruled by another Magdalen devotee, the Angevin king, Charles II, who had discovered the saint's relics in Provence in 1279.[38] Teobaldo's various episcopates coincided with Charles's escalating devotion to his patron saint, expressed in his building program in her honor throughout the *Regno,* a factor possibly contributing to the bishop's own affection for the Magdalen. In any event, Teobaldo's sincere devotion to the saint was expressed in the chapel he commissioned in her honor, as well as in one of the two donor portraits decorating the walls. As is customary in this genre of painting, he is shown in smaller scale, and reverently posed in genuflection. Mary Magdalen, attired in scarlet, her cloak trimmed in glittering brocade, literally towers over him. The two, however, make strong eye contact: he looks up at the saint devotedly, she gazes down affectionately at her spiritual son. Significantly, rather than clasping his hands in an act of prayer, as is conventional in such portraits, he clutches the saint's hand as if he were a small child grasping for that of his mother, italicizing the maternal aspect of the saint.[39] It is instructive to compare this donor portrait with the second one he had made for the same

[37] Lorraine C. Schwartz, *The Fresco Decoration,* 197.

[38] Angevin devotion to the Magdalen is examined in chapter 11.

[39] The only other image of this sort known to me also comes from Assisi. It decorates a reliquary diptych of gilded glass dating circa 1320–30, a gift of J. Pierpont Morgan to the Metropolitan Museum of Art (#17.190.922). Each panel of the diptych contains two images. The upper right compartment shows a crucifix flanked by the Virgin Mary and Saint John; the lower right portrays Saint Agnes and a lamb. The upper left depicts a Madonna and child while the lower left shows a voluminous Mary Magdalen (crowned and nimbed) who holds the outstretched hand of a friar. By the second quarter of the fourteenth century Assisi had become a major center for the production of gilded glass. The decorator of this reliquary clearly modeled his Magdalen and friar on Teobaldo's donor portrait in the Magdalen chapel in the basilica, a likely location of the workshop itself.

chapel (Fig. 12). In the latter, as we have already seen, Pontano represents himself in his episcopal regalia with Saint Rufino, the first bishop of Assisi. In that fresco, Pontano kneels at the feet of Rufino in reverent prayer, a much more standard image for a donor portrait.[40] As a Franciscan he represented himself with the maternal Mary Magdalen; as a bishop he depicted himself with Rufino, the figure of male ecclesiastical authority.

In chapter 7 we noted that *disciplinati* companies throughout Italy often made the Magdalen their protector. It is worth noting here that the *battuti* in Bergamo represented themselves wrapped in the protective cloaks of both the Virgin Mary and Mary Magdalen. The *Madonna della Misericordia* is of course a familiar medieval aspect of the Virgin Mary emphasizing her protective maternal qualities. As does a mother hen, she shelters her spiritual brood under her outstretched wings. At the church of Santa Maria Maddalena in Bergamo, Mary Magdalen in imitation of the Virgin, becomes a solicitous mother and folds her penitents protectively into her ample wing-like cloak (Fig. 48).[41]

Gherardesca da Pisa (d. 1269) received the twin consolation of having been mothered by both the Virgin Mary and Mary Magdalen. One day, after having done battle against a demon, at the request of the Virgin, Mary Magdalen intervened to wrap the battered Gherardesca in her protective mantle. When the *beata* arrived home, the Magdalen, playing the part of a solicitous mother, stripped her of her tattered and bloody garments while the Virgin gave her fresh clothing and the kiss of peace.[42] In this account, both saints joined together to offer the *beata* maternal consolation.

The maternal aspect of the Magdalen is celebrated in Francesca Romana's visions and in their pictorial representation. Possibly to memorialize the commencement of Francesca's cause for canonization, three panel paintings were commissioned to glorify her visions. In one dating from the

[40] At roughly the same time, another bishop, this one a Dominican, had a donor portrait made of himself kneeling in the presence of a half-length Mary Magdalen. Simone Martini shows Trasmondo Monaldeschi in a more customary manner: the bishop of Orvieto is depicted in miniature, scarcely bigger than the Magdalen's right hand, his own hands crossed over his chest indicating a reverential bow. The Magdalen presents him to the Virgin Mary who occupies the central panel of this polyptych. When compared to other contemporary donor portraits, the distinctive maternal theme of Teobaldo Pontano's iconography becomes readily apparent. Simone Martini's donor portrait of Trasmondo is reproduced in Haskins, *Mary Magdalen*, 149, fig. 20. Trasmondo's dedication to Mary Magdalen is further documented in Orvieto: he paid for the celebration of a daily mass in her honor, a mass which he himself frequently sang. Joanna Cannon, "Dominican Patronage of the Arts in Central Italy: The Provincia Romana, c. 1220–1320" (Ph.D. diss., University of London, 1980), 147, quoted in Haskins, ibid., 428–29n. 29.

[41] For the frescoes, see *I pittori bergamaschi [dal XIII al XIX secolo]. Le origini*, ed. M. Boskovits (Bergamo: Edizioni Bolis, 1992), 408.

[42] Gherardesca's *vita* is in AASS, May, vol. 7 (Antwerp, 1688), 164–80. It has been translated by Elizabeth Petroff, in *Consolation of the Blessed*, 85–120; see 109–11.

Figure 48. *The Magdalen of Mercy* (mid-14th c.). Mary Magdalen protects her company of flagellants in Bergamo in her mantle. Fresco ex Disciplinati Church of S. Maria Maddalena, Bergamo. (Photo: Herziana)

mid-Quattrocento, Francesca is shown being received under the mantle of the Virgin (aided by Saint Paul), while her congregation of veiled oblates is shown being presented, gathered, and protected in another cloak held by Saints Benedict and Mary Magdalen (Fig. 49).[43]

[43] For the panel now in the Metropolitan Museum of Art, see George Kaftal, "Three Scenes from the Legend of Santa Francesca Romana," *Walters Art Gallery Journal* 11 (1948): 50–61, and George Szabó, *The Robert Lehman Collection* (New York: Metropolitan Museum of Art, 1975), 64–65. Saint Benedict's presence can be explained as Francesca's congregation followed the Benedictine Rule.

Figure 49. *Santa Francesca Romana and Her Patron Saints* (ca. 1445). Mary Magdalen and Saint Benedict protect and present Francesca's Oblates of Tor de' Specchi. Roman painter, panel painting. The Robert Lehman Collection, The Metropolitan Museum of Art, New York. (Photo: The Metropolitan Museum of Art)

The maternal Magdalen is also present in Raymond of Capua's *vita* of Catherine of Siena. Raymond narrated how Christ, in a vision, gave Mary Magdalen to Catherine as a mother:

"Sweetest daughter, for your greater comfort I give you Mary Magdalen for your mother. Turn to her in absolute confidence; I entrust her with a special care of you." The virgin gratefully accepted this offer, commended herself with great humility and veneration to the Magdalen, and begged her earnestly and passionately to take care of her now that she had been entrusted to her by the Lord. From that moment the virgin felt entirely at one with the Magdalen and always referred to her as her mother.[44]

Raymond revealed a further nuance of the mother-daughter relationship when he suggested that

it was therefore highly fitting that Almighty God should in His providence have given the virgin to Mary Magdalen as her daughter, and Mary Magdalen to the virgin as her mother; for it was proper for penitent to be united with penitent, lover with lover, contemplative with contemplative.[45]

Significantly, Raymond referred frequently to Catherine herself as his mother, a habit he felt obligated to explain in her *vita*. "We all involuntarily called the virgin "Mother"; because to us she was indeed a mother, who by day, without tears or fuss, brought us to birth through the womb of her mind until Christ was formed in us, and fed us with the bread of her life-giving holy doctrine."[46] It is not by coincidence that Raymond associates Catherine's generative and nutritive aspects with her virginity. Giovanni Colombini makes similar use of maternal imagery when discussing the Magdalen. His celebrated conversion while reading the life of Mary of Egypt is too renowned to be recounted again here; less famous, however, is his fervent dedication to that other sinner-saint, Mary Magdalen. In one letter he refers to "Magdalen, my mother"; while in another to suor Bartolomea he advises: "Love our mama Mary Magdalen." On yet another occasion he reminded her that "aflame with [Jesus'] sweet love you are always his true spouse and lover, just as was our sweet mother Mary Magdalen."[47] Devotion to Mary Magdalen seems to have run in the Colombini family. His daughter Agnola, upon her profession as a nun, changed her name to Suor Maddalena.[48]

---

[44] AASS, 30 April, vol. 3, par. 183, 899; Lamb, *Saint Catherine*, 168.

[45] Ibid., 899–900; ibid., 169.

[46] Ibid., par. 30, 928; ibid., 270–71.

[47] *Le lettere del B. Giovanni Colombini da Siena*, ed. Adolfo Bartoli (Lucca: Balatresi, 1856), ep. 51, 155; ep. 67, 177; ep. 66, 173.

[48] See Feo Belcari, *The Life of B. Giovanni Colombini* (trans. from 1541 and 1832 editions) (London: R. Washbourne, 1874), 93.

"Her Name Remade"

By the fourteenth century, the spiritual children of the Magdalen began to honor her by taking her name. It is not insignificant that the Christian name Maddalena begins to show up with regularity in this period. Maria Maddalena d'Agnolo Gaddi; Maddalena Bonsignori, a Bolognese legal scholar; Maddalena Scrovegni, the humanist scholar of the eminent Paduan family; Maddalena de' Medici, daughter of Lorenzo; and Saint Maria Maddalena de' Pazzi are some of the most well known Magdalens of the late medieval–early modern period. The name was even immortalized in Boccaccio's *Decameron*.[49]

Less celebrated Magdalens were also to be found by the later Middle Ages. At the Dominican convent of Camporegio near Siena the name Magdalen appears in the rolls of the dead as early as 1340, when on 25 May, Magdalena, "our tertiary, daughter of Talomey, was buried."[50] By the fifteenth century, in a thirteen-year period between 1417 and 1430, Camporegio recorded the death of eight Magdalens each of whom was in some way associated with the monastery. One of them was a sister of penance, the others were wives or daughters of the *popolo grasso,* those whose families were wealthy enough to have maintained tombs in the church or convent.[51]

Magdalen was a popular name among those women associated with third orders. A notarial document of 11 May 1448, concerning a small group of Dominican tertiaries in Rome, names the seven women who belonged to the community of Santa Cecilia. Two of the seven were called Maddalena.[52] Magdalens also turned up with regularity among professed fe-

---

[49] Maria Maddalena d'Agnolo Gaddi, presumably the daughter of the painter, owned a copy of Cavalca's *Specchio de' peccati,* inscribed with these words: "Questo libro e di Maria Maddalena d'Agnolo Gaddi." The manuscript is now in the Laurenziana. See Domenico Cavalca, *Specchio de' peccati,* ed. Francesco del Furia (Florence: Tipografia all'Insegna di Dante, 1828), xvii–xix. For information on the other Magdalens, see *The Annotated Index of Medieval Women,* ed. Anne Echols and Marty Williams (New York: M. Wiener, 1992), 292–93. Day IV: 3, *The Decameron,* trans. G. H. McWilliam (New York: Penguin Books, 1972; 1995, 2d ed.).

[50] *I necrologi di San Domenico in Camporegio,* ed. M.-H. Laurent, in *Fontes vitae S. Catharinae Senensis historici,* ed. M.-H. Laurent and Franciscus Valli (Florence: Sansoni, 1937), vol. 20, 56. The Latin is "vestita nostra." In the fourteenth century only two other Magdalens appear in the necrology. The first was in 1383, when Sister Magdalena of Arezzo, of the monastery Saint Ursula, was buried in the church "with the friars." The second was Domina Magdalena, wife of Nicolas Cristoforo Buonaventura, who was buried in her husband's tomb in 1398.

[51] The sister of penance was Domina Magdalena, "once the wife of Francesco Ventura, who for a long time wore the habit of penance of Saint Dominic." She died in 1417. The other Magdalens were the wives or daughters of perfumers, dyers, doctors, stationers, and the like. Ibid.

[52] Cited in Anna Esposito, "Female Religious Communities," 209.

male religious. To take the example of the convent of Monteluce, a Clarissan convent in Perugia, the necrology reveals two consecutive years in which nuns took the name Magdalen upon profession. In 1449 the noblewoman Ghirardescha of Florence took the veil and the name Sister Magdalena. (Two years later she became the abbess of the monastery.) In 1450, a young woman called Andrea Perone da Peroscia, upon making her profession at Monteluce, changed her name to Sister Magdalena.[53] Other sisters arrived with their religious names already in place. Sister Maria Maddalena of Mantua (d. 1472), born into the noble Coppini family, was named by her father who had heard a Mary Magdalen sermon preached on the day of his daughter's birth. It so moved him to compunction that he returned home and named his newly born daughter Maddalena.[54]

Yet it was not only female religious who called themselves or were named after the saint. The laity became enamored of the name as well. David Herlihy has noted that from about 1300 the culture of naming in Tuscany underwent a transformation: by the fourteenth century there was a marked tendency "to adopt or impose the names of saints."[55] His study of the Catasto of 1427 shows that of the 17 leading female names, 15 refer to saints. Of those 15, 9 are male saints' names feminized. Of the 6 remaining names, 4 refer directly to female saints. Those 4 female saints' names most favored by Tuscans were Caterina, Margherita, Lucia, and Maddalena.[56] Herlihy's study further shows that wealth and status did not much affect name choices. We have already noted there was a Maddalena among the Medici progeny; perhaps it is worth noting that in a court case predating Maddalena de' Medici's birth by ten years, a slave of Niccolò di Gentile degli Albizzi was sent to prison. The slave's name was Madelena.[57] In late medieval Florence, at least, the name Maddalena was not appropriated by any one class.

Why was the name Maddalena among the female names most favored by late medieval Tuscans? Certainly much of the credit must go to the hagiographers and friars whose preaching on the saint disseminated her legend, instilling veneration among people of all stations of life.[58] Those peo-

---

[53] *Memoriale di Monteluce. Cronaca del monastero delle clarisse di Perugia dal 1448 al 1838,* ed. Ugolino Nicolini (S. Maria degli Angeli: Edizioni Porziuncola, 1983), 10, 12.

[54] G. Michele Piò, *Delle vite degli huomini illustri di S. Domenico. Libri Quatro. Ove compendiosamente si tratta de i santi, beati, & beate, & altri di segnalata bontà dell'Ordine de' Predicatori* (Bologna: Sebastiano Bonomi, 1620), 439. Maria was added to her name when she entered the monastery of San Vincenzo.

[55] David Herlihy, "Tuscan Names, 1200–1530," *Renaissance Quarterly* 41 (1988): 577.

[56] Ibid., 574n. 37.

[57] Gene Brucker, *The Society of Renaissance Florence: A Documentary Study* (New York: Harper Torchbooks, 1971), 167–68. She was remanded to the Stinche on 23 March 1463.

[58] Herlihy, ibid., 581.

ple who named their daughters Maddalena were no doubt seeking spiritual benefits and the saint's protection. But that explanation is not entirely adequate. As Herlihy explains: there was a "desire not to cultivate the most powerful patrons, but to replicate experiences, to recapture a *fortuna,* [which] best explains the new, most popular Tuscan names."[59] Those who made their children namesakes of the Magdalen presumably identified with a particular aspect of her life or persona. It is perhaps revealing that the name Mary was not among Tuscany's most popular female names. The Virgin Mary's experiences were admirable, but hardly imitable; the friars offered the Magdalen as an everywoman, whose experiences, whose *bona fortuna,* could perhaps be replicated by a namesake.

This chapter has examined two little-studied aspects of Magdalen devotion in the later medieval period: her recuperated virginity and her motherhood. I have suggested that the power and prestige of the cult of the Virgin Mary exerted pressure on other female saints to conform to her likeness. Mary Magdalen was no exception. Consequently, the Magdalen now found herself at the head of the celestial choir of virgins in the litany of saints, and again among the virginal saints as naming practices in Tuscany reveal. Moreover, she was also to be found supporting anxious matrons in their claims to the virgin's floral wreath. The pressure from the cult of the Virgin Mary also influenced the development of the Magdalen's maternal aspects. Her recuperated virginity signaled fertility; as such, she was invoked as mother, and called upon to intervene in cases of conception, gestation, labor, and delivery, to say nothing of protecting newborn children and expectant mothers. The themes of Mary Magdalen's virginity and motherhood were not topics on which either her *vitae* or sermons had dwelt at great length. Rather, it was the desires of those who listened to the sermons that recast the saint in the image of the Virgin Mary elaborating her virginal and maternal aspects. As a reconstituted virgin, Mary Magdalen now assisted matrons in reaching for the virgin's crown. As a mother she was invoked to protect and defend her spiritual children. The next chapter examines the devotion of some of her most ardent spiritual children, the members of the Angevin dynasty of Provence and southern Italy.

[59] Ibid., 580.

ELEVEN

The House of Anjou: A Royal Response

On the anniversary of the death of Charles II, King of Sicily and Jerusalem, Duke of Apulia, Prince of Capua, and Count of Provence, Forcalquier, and Piedmont, the Dominican friar Giovanni Regina da Napoli (d. ca. 1350) preached a memorial sermon commemorating the virtues of the king.[1] Giovanni found the *curriculum vitae* of the pious Charles praiseworthy indeed; he was particularly impressed by the late king's devotion to Saint Mary Magdalen. In his sermon he observed that Charles's remarkable relationship with the saint was summed up at his death in this extraordinary sign:

> There was a visible sign on the fifth of May (namely, the day of the saint's translation) because on that day the above-cited Charles died and his soul was transported from this present misery to the blessed life . . . on account of which Mary Magdalen was truly able to say to him: "As a mother loves her only son thus she loved you." (I Kings)[2]

---

[1] For bibliography on the Angevins, see chapter 1, nn. 75, 77. The title is the one that Charles's chancery was using for official correspondence a year and half before the king's death. See his letter to the Cassianites regarding La Sainte-Baume dated 5 December 1307, printed in Faillon, *Monuments*, vol. II, 847–48. In 1306, Charles united the county of Piedmont to Forcalquier and henceforth added the rank of count of Piedmont to his title. As Charles II ceded the island of Sicily to the Aragonese in the peace established at Caltabellotta in 1302, I refer to the Angevins as rulers of the Kingdom of Naples, though contemporaries continued to refer to them as rulers of Sicily. The Angevins' Italian possessions are known also as the *Regno* and the *mezzogiorno*.

[2] "Et evidenti signo quia eadem die, quinta madii qua scilicet talis translatio facta fuit supradictus rex Karolus obiit et eius anima de presentia miseria ad vitam beatam in re vel in certa spe translata fuit propter quod beata Maria Magdalena ei vere dicere potuit id est *Reges* primo, 'Sicut mater amat unicum filium suum ita te diligebat.'" MS Nap. Naz. VIII. AA 11, ff. 24r–24v; *RLS* 3: 35. David d'Avray has published other excerpts from this and other memorial sermons on Charles in *Death and the Prince: Memorial Preaching Before 1350* (Oxford: Clarendon Press, 1994), 105, 123, 148–49, 187–88. I thank him for sending me

Charles II died on 5 May 1309. On the same day twenty-nine years earlier, Charles, then Prince of Salerno, had presided over the translation of Mary Magdalen's relics at her tomb at Saint-Maximin. According to Giovanni Regina da Napoli, Charles's death on May 5 was no mere coincidence: it was the final seal authenticating Mary Magdalen's great love for her spiritual son. This chapter brings together for the first time not only the evidence of Charles II's devotion to the Magdalen, but also that of his court and his heirs. It shows first how the members of the House of Anjou associated themselves with Mary Magdalen and how they demonstrated their devotion to the saint. It then argues that many of those who wished to ally themselves with the Angevin dynasty, the new rulers of southern Italy,[3] did so by venerating their patron saint. Piety was imbued by politics in the *Regno*: devotion to Saint Mary Magdalen frequently signaled allegiance to the Angevin monarchs.

Charles II

If ever a saint had a dedicated spiritual son, it was Mary Magdalen's Charles II who spent the last thirty years of his life erecting physical signs of his devotion to the saint throughout the county of Provence and the Kingdom of Naples. We do not know how or why Charles developed such affection for the saint, but I would suggest two obvious sources of transmission. The first is from his mother Beatrice, heiress to the county of Provence. When Charles was born in 1254, legends had long been in circulation relating Mary Magdalen's apostolate in southern Gaul. Perhaps Beatrice traced her family back to the legendary ruler of Provence converted by Mary Magdalen, thus emphasizing to her son her family's link to apostolic Christianity. If his affection for the apostle of Provence began at his mother's knee, it is more than likely that it was further cultivated by the Dominican friars with whom Charles was particularly close. Dominican hagiographers had been disseminating the provençal aspect of her legend since the first quarter of the thirteenth century; it is probable that his fondness for the saint increased under the tutelage of Dominican hagiography and preaching.

None of this, however, explains why Charles decided, despite all evidence to the contrary, that Mary Magdalen's relics still remained in

---

the pertinent passages of his text. For Giovanni, see T. Kaeppeli, "Note sugli scrittori domenicani di nome Giovanni di Napoli," *AFP* 10 (1940): 48–76.

[3] Charles I of Anjou defeated the Hohenstaufen forces at Benevento in 1266. Angevin rule of southern Italy is reckoned from that date.

Provence. According to contemporary sources her relics had been transported to Vézelay in the early Middle Ages and remained there still. Nonetheless, after having made some inquiries and completed some research, Prince Charles concluded otherwise, and at the end of 1279 led an archeological excavation to unearth her relics, which he believed were still buried at Saint-Maximin.[4]

In chapter 1 I suggested that given Charles I's preoccupation with empire-building, to say nothing of his indifference to matters religious, it fell to his son to find a saintly protector for the parvenu Angevin dynasty and their rapidly expanding empire. Mary Magdalen was the perfect choice: she was an intimate of the Lord's, she had evangelized the family's comital territory of Provence (and possibly converted his mother's ancestors), and if the prince was right, her relics still remained in Provence, where by tradition she could be invoked to protect the region and its inhabitants so long as she was venerated with the proper respect due a saint of her stature.

In the event, Charles of Salerno's intuition about the whereabouts of Mary Magdalen's relics proved well founded, for in December of 1279 her body was miraculously rediscovered at Saint-Maximin. According to Philippe Cabassole (not an eyewitness to the events), the eager prince could not be refrained from participating in the excavation. Indeed, he dug so fervently with his bare hands that he soon drenched himself with sweat, so much so that perspiration poured from his brow, not in drops but in rivulets.[5] In May of the next year, according to Bernard Gui, the saint's relics were solemnly displayed before a crowd that included prelates, churchmen, nobles, and a congregation of the local populace, after which the body was divided and translated into suitably precious reliquaries.[6]

Though the war of the Sicilian Vespers—the rebellion against Angevin rule in southern Italy, supported by the crown of Aragon—broke out in 1282, Charles, now appointed vicar of the *Regno* in his father's absence, still managed to make his first public act of devotion to Mary Magdalen on Italian soil the very next year. In a ceremony on 6 January 1283, in the presence of the Dominican Gerardo Bianchi, bishop of Sabina and apostolic legate to the Kingdom of Naples, the Prince of Salerno placed a stone in the foundation of San Domenico, initiating a rebuilding campaign for the Neapolitan church. Having endowed a certain sum for its enlargement

---

[4] For "inquiries and research," see the first bull of Boniface VIII regarding Mary Magdalen's relics cited at n. 20 below.

[5] *Libellus hystorialis Marie beatissime Magdalene* quoted in Faillon, *Monuments,* vol. 2, 792. For commentary on Cabassole's "little book," see Victor Saxer, "Philippe Cabassole et son *Libellus hystorialis Marie beatissime Magdalene.* Préliminaires à une édition du *Libellus,*" in *L'État Angevin,* 193–204.

[6] *Flores chronicorum seu catalogus pontificum Romanorum,* cited in Faillon, ibid., 779.

and refurbishment, Charles seems to have stipulated that the church's dedication be changed to honor his patron, Saint Mary Magdalen.[7]

In the same year, the Franciscan chronicler Salimbene reported a miracle in which the prince of Salerno took great interest. It bears rehearsing in brief. It seems that one day a butcher was on his way home from venerating Mary Magdalen's relics at Saint-Maximin when he was accosted by an acquaintance who asked what he had been doing. When the butcher made his devotion to the saint's relics known, his friend scoffed at his naivete telling him that "he had not kissed her shin bone, but the arm of some ass or pack animal which the clerics show to simplefolk for the purpose of enriching themselves." Rising to defend Mary Magdalen's honor, the butcher entered into a duel in which he accidentally killed his acquaintance. Convicted of murder, he was sentenced to die in the gallows. However, on the night before he was to be hanged, Mary Magdalen appeared to him in a vision and assured him that he would not be injured. When he was strung up the next day in front of a great crowd gathered for the spectacle, a white dove descended from the heavens and dissolved the chain by which he was hanging, delivering him ever so gently to the ground. A miracle was declared and Mary Magdalen was praised. "When he had heard about these things, [Charles] wanted to see and hear them from the man himself." The butcher was summoned, and appeared before the prince, who invited him to remain permanently with the court. The Magdalen's champion, however, declined the offer. He told the Angevin prince that nothing, not even dominion over the whole world, could persuade him from finishing out his days in the service of Mary Magdalen at Saint-Maximin.[8] Though Charles was probably disappointed at this reply, ultimately he must have been quite pleased with the butcher's story which served not only to verify the authenticity of the relics that he himself had discovered at Saint-Maximin, but also testified quite splendidly to their miraculous powers.

In 1284, any further plans Charles may have had for honoring his patron saint had to be postponed. Despite his councilor Gerardo Bianchi's sage advice, Charles led an attack on the Aragonese fleet that had recently blockaded the port of Naples. On 5 June 1284 the prince of Salerno was

---

[7] See Jürgen Krüger, *S. Lorenzo Maggiore in Neapel* (Werl-Westfalen: Dietrich-Coelde, 1985), 169, who published an excerpt of the episcopal bull of Andrew of Sora commemorating the event. It is generally agreed by scholars that construction of the church did not commence until 1289, after Charles had been released from prison. For a recent discussion of this church in relation to the building style of Charles II, see Caroline Bruzelius, "Charles I, Charles II, and the Development of an Angevin Style in the Kingdom of Sicily," in *L'État Angevin*, 99–114.

[8] Salimbene, *Cronica*, vol. 2, 761. Clemens has found three later versions of this miracle; see *The Establishment*, 86n. 44.

captured by the admiral of the Aragonese navy, and remanded to Catalonia where he was held prisoner for four years.[9] Within six months of his incarceration, his father King Charles I died at Foggia and Robert of Artois, the king's brother, and Gerardo Bianchi, the king's advisor and apostolic legate, were named co-regents to govern the *Regno* in the imprisoned heir's stead. The treaty of Canfranc negotiating the prince's release was finally signed in October 1288; Nicolas IV crowned Charles II King of Sicily and Jerusalem in Rieti on 29 May 1289.

Not much more than a year after his coronation, Charles was in Sulmona, where he was accustomed to pass the summer months. In 1290 he founded a Franciscan church there dedicated to Mary Magdalen. He was the first of Angevin royalty to donate relics to this foundation: he made the Franciscans a gift of a silver cross that contained a fragment of the true cross.[10]

While he was consolidating the rule of his kingdom, there was a five-year hiatus in Charles II's campaign to honor Mary Magdalen; in 1295, however, he returned to his cause in earnest.[11] In January of that year Charles II and his son Charles Martel participated in the ceremony installing Boniface VIII as pope in Rome. It was not insignificant that the new pope had been elected at Naples, the capital of the Angevin empire. As vassals of the papacy, the king and prince performed the subservient office of leading the white palfrey the new pontiff rode to Saint Peter's basilica. But the Angevins' servility to the papacy was not long-lived; less than three months later, the servant of the servants of God was serving his Angevin masters. In a bull dated 3 April 1295 Boniface VIII authenticated Mary Magdalen's relics, which Charles II had rediscovered at Saint-Maximin eighteen years earlier. In addition, he approved the plans for building a new basilica in the saint's honor at Saint-Maximin, as well as the construction of a royal convent of Dominican friars to care for the site.[12]

---

[9] While imprisoned in Barcelona the Dominican Pierre de Lamanon served as his spiritual advisor. See Bernard Montagnes, "La légende dominicaine de Marie-Madeleine à Saint-Maximin," in *Mémoires de l'Académie de Vaucluse,* 7th series, 6 (1985): 82n. 41.

[10] Matteo Camera, *Annali delle due Sicilie: dall'origine e fondazione della monarchia fino a tutto il regno dell'augusto sovrano Carlo III Borbone,* 2 vols. (Naples: Dalla Stamperia e Cartiere del Fibreno, 1806), vol. 2, 19. For the relic, see P. Piccirilli, *Monumenti architettonici sulmonesi (dal XIV al XVI secolo)* (Lanciano: Rocco Carabba, 1887; repr. 1976), 18.

[11] It should be noted that in 1294 and again in 1306 Charles made gifts to the convent of Dominican nuns of Sant'Anna in Nocera. Charles was of course partial to the Dominican Order, but it could not have hurt the nuns' cause that they too showed devotion to Saint Mary Magdalen: their oldest chapel was dedicated to the saint. See Gerardo Ruggiero, "Il monastero di Sant'Anna di Nocera: dalla fondazione al Concilio di Trento," in *Memorie Domenicane,* n.s., 20 (1989): 66–67 and 81–86.

[12] Faillon reprints all the bulls of Boniface VIII regarding Saint-Maximin in *Monuments,* vol. 2, 813–32.

Not content to have his patron saint honored in Provence alone, Charles desired that the Magdalen's praises be sung throughout his Italian territories in the *Regno*. Consequently, in the year between 1295 and 1296, when completing San Lorenzo Maggiore, a Franciscan church begun by his father in the capital of Naples, Charles commissioned a giottesque fresco cycle depicting the life of Mary Magdalen to decorate the chapel dedicated to the saint.[13] The king completed the century by commissioning restoration of a Magdalen chapel at the church of San Domenico in Manfredonia, which was dedicated by the archbishop of the city in his royal presence in 1299. The Angevin monarch's coat of arms, still visible above the church's portal, bears witness to his patronage.[14]

From the beginning of the fourteenth century until his death in 1309, Charles II accelerated his Italian building program honoring Mary Magdalen. In 1301 he endowed the Augustinian friars at Sant'Agostino alla Zecca in Naples with a block of houses in the city of Termoli, and seventeen ounces of gold, stipulating that "we are providing [funding] in order to construct the fabric of the church which in that place from now on [will] honor the blessed Mary Magdalen."[15]

After the peace of Caltabellotta (1302) was established, Charles lavished most of his devotion to Mary Magdalen on the Dominican Order. At Brindisi in 1304, he founded a Dominican convent in the name of his patron saint.[16] Four years later on 10 June 1308 Charles's account register records a payment to Pietro Cavallini. The Roman painter was in Naples working at the Dominican church of San Domenico Maggiore painting an abbreviated fresco cycle depicting three scenes from the life of Mary Magdalen in the Brancaccio chapel.[17] Fittingly, in the last year of his life, Charles made a final bequest to the Dominicans in favor of Mary Magdalen. Though he had already given the Order of Preachers of L'Aquila the *palazzo angioino* in 1300, in 1309 he dedicated the first stone of their church honoring his patron saint.[18] In addition to building and decorating Magdalen churches, monasteries, and chapels, Charles also gave alms

---

[13] For the decoration and attribution of the patron, see Bologna, *I pittori*, 94–97.

[14] Nicola de Feudis, "S. Domenico e la cappella de la 'Maddalena,'" in *Storia ed arte in Manfredonia* (Foggia: la Capitanata, 1967), 1–7, esp. 6. See also Gerardo Cioffari, *Storia dei Domenicani in Puglia (1221–1350)* (Bari: Edizioni Levante, 1986), 63.

[15] See Camera, *Annali,* vol. 2, 65, citing the destroyed Angevin registers of 8 August 1301: Reg. an. 1301 Arc. B. mazz. 45 num. 20; 3 October 1301: Reg. an. 1301 Lit. I. fol. 146v and Reg. an. 1302. E. fol. 176v. See also Krüger, *S. Lorenzo Maggiore*, 164.

[16] Camera, *Annali,* vol. 2, 113. See also Cioffari, *Storia dei Domenicani,* 64. See Bruzelius, "Charles I, Charles II" for Charles II's style of architecture "perhaps of Dominican inspiration," 105.

[17] For the chapel decoration, see Bologna, *I pittori*, 115–43.

[18] Luigi Lopez, *L'Aquila: le memorie, i monumenti, il dialetto* (L'Aquila: G. Tazzi, 1988), 151.

for the charitable work done at the leper hospital of Santa Maria Maddalena de' Leprosi in Aversa.[19]

During the course of his lifetime Charles II's devotion to Mary Magdalen manifested itself mainly in the construction of monastic and ecclesiastical buildings that bore the name of the saint. His devotion to her did not go unnoticed. One of the first to acclaim it was Boniface VIII in his bull of 1295 approving the establishment of the Dominican Order at Saint-Maximin. In it he extols the king for his

> exceptional devotion to Saint Mary Magdalen widely known by the facts, chiefly through the evidence of service you deigned to show, in that once while there was uncertainty about the place where her body had been buried you devoted your efficacious zeal to inquiring about it and discovering it, and at last, having found it, you had her buried in the above-cited church with great devotion and reverence in the presence of the clergy and the people convened from those parts.[20]

The Dominican Order was the primary beneficiary of Charles II's building campaign made in the name of Mary Magdalen.[21] In return for such generous patronage, after his death they became the principal publicists of his singular relationship with the saint. Ptolomy of Lucca, Bernard Gui, and Francesco Pipino, all members of the Friars Preacher, were some of the earliest chroniclers to commemorate the prince of Salerno's discovery of Mary Magdalen's relics at Saint-Maximin.[22]

But chroniclers were not alone in publicizing Charles II's connection to the saint. The Angevin king did his part in ensuring that his name and the saint's would always be mentioned in the same breath. After the completion of an elaborate reliquary in 1283, three years after the elevation of Mary Magdalen's relics at Saint-Maximin, Charles had the skull of the saint transferred to a golden head fitted with a crystal face through which the faithful could view the rather macabre relic.[23] The head reliquary was

---

[19] Camera, *Annali*, vol. 2, 184.

[20] *Bullarium Ordinis FF. Praedicatorum*, ed. Thomas Ripoll, 8 vols. (Rome: Hieronymus Mainardus, 1729–40), vol. 2 (1730), 40.

[21] In general the Dominicans of the *Regno* were the beneficiaries of Charles's largesse. In November of 1294 he made the gift of one gold florin a week to the following convents: San Pietro Martire and Santa Maria Maddalena, both in Naples; and others in Benevento, Gaeta, Sessa, Capua, Aversa, Somma, Salerno, Foggia, Manfredonia, Trani, Monopoli, Brindisi, Venosa, Sulmona, Penne, Chieti, Atri, and Ortona. See Cioffari, *Storia dei Domenicani*, 73.

[22] All cited in Faillon, *Monuments*, vol. 2, 775–84. Jean Gobi's register also publicized Charles II's discovery of the Magdalen's relics at Saint-Maximin in an account of one of the saint's miracles. After hearing of the Angevin prince's elevation of the relics in 1280, a man from Corsica, suffering paralysis of his limbs, decided to make the pilgrimage to Saint-Maximin. See "Iohannes Gobi," no. 41, 171–72.

[23] An engraving of the reliquary is reproduced in Faillon, *Monuments*, vol. 1, 909–10.

crowned by a royal diadem encrusted with jewels, pearls, and other precious gemstones, which Charles I had sent with orders that it sit atop the saint's head. Verses commemorating the extraordinary relationship between Mary Magdalen and Charles II were inscribed on the reliquary itself. They read in part:

> In the year 1283
> The prince of Salerno,
> from kindness and out of love for the Lord
> displayed her in gold,
> decorated with a sacred crown.
> Therefore, Mary, be our pious patron
> protecting him while living and in death.[24]

Now even Mary Magdalen's relics bore the imprint of Charles's royal devotion. As if that were not enough, the office for the translation of the saint's relics, which Charles himself had instituted, sang the praises of both the prince and the saint. One of the antiphons for nocturns sang first of the Magdalen who rose up from dust, then of "Charles of Provence, prince and crown, lover of clemency, glory of the country, who merited this gift."[25]

By the time of his death in 1309, Charles's publicity machine had become so adroit at disseminating the royal cult that it continued to do so long after the king himself had passed from the scene. We have already seen how fourteenth-century memorial sermons such as the one by Giovanni Regina da Napoli continued to publicize the king's close ties to the saint; by the fifteenth century Charles's devotion to the Magdalen entered the realm of legend. It will be recalled from chapter 1 that the Dominicans of Saint-Maximin, anxious to fabricate a foundation legend that drew equally from the wells of royalty and divinity, began circulating a tale circa 1458 that explained precisely how Charles had come to discover Saint Mary Magdalen's relics in Provence.[26] It seems that Mary Magdalen had come to him in a vision, and in return for liberating him from prison, Charles was commissioned to discover her relics at Saint-Maximin. Afterwards he would honor them properly by building a new basilica, instituting a new feast, and constructing a new convent to house the Dominicans whom she had selected as guardians of her shrine. Thus, almost two centuries after the prince had discovered the saint's relics in Provence, the explanation for

---

[24] Ibid., 907–10. In addition to the head, Charles also commissioned a silver arm reliquary mentioned frequently in Gobi's miracle register. Charles also had a tabernacle-type reliquary fabricated that enclosed a crystal vase containing what remained of the saint's hair.

[25] *Analecta hymnica*, vol. 13 (1892), 199.

[26] For an edition and the dating, see B. Montagues, *La légende dominicaine*, in *Marie Madeleine et l'ordre des Prêcheurs* (Marseilles: Atelier Sainte-Catherine, 1984).

why he had done so was finally supplied.[27] This legend was transmitted far and wide by Silvestro Mazzolini da Prierio (d. 1527), an Italian Dominican, who having made the pilgrimage to Saint-Maximin in 1497, included it in his sermon collection, *Aurea rosa*, a best-seller of the earlier sixteenth century.[28] Thus, in time, Charles II's devotion to his patron saint became the stuff out of which legends were made.

Curiae Familiares

As guardians of Mary Magdalen's provençal shrine and recipients of Charles II's largesse, the Dominicans had an obvious stake in promoting veneration to the saint. Others in Charles's court, though their devotion was in all probability genuine, nonetheless may have had similar motives for making public displays of their devotion to Mary Magdalen. Given the proximity of sanctity to politics in the later Middle Ages, indeed there was no better way to show loyalty to the king than to show reverence for his heavenly protector. Thus many noble Neapolitan families flew the Angevin flag by associating themselves with the dynasty's patron saint.

Loyalty to Charles II, demonstrated by reverence to Mary Magdalen, probably explains a frescoed Magdalen in the Minutolo chapel dedicated to Saints Peter and Anastasia in the cathedral of Naples.[29] Filippo Minutolo, canon and deacon of the cathedral, along with his family, had been early allies of the Angevin dynasty. Indeed, by 1271 Filippo was known in the Angevin registers as *consilarius* and *familiaris*. Thus it was no surprise, as one scholar has pointed out, that when the archbishopric of Naples fell vacant, that a member of a noble Neapolitan family loyal to the Angevin cause was appointed to fill the episcopal see. In 1288, the year Charles II was released from prison, Filippo ascended the archbishop's throne in the capital city. His episcopal tenure in fact coincided with the rebuilding of the cathedral begun by Charles II circa 1294. It was there, in the cathedral, that Filippo constructed a new family chapel, and there that he stipulated that he be entombed.[30] In the Minutolo chapel, in a deep and nar-

---

[27] It will be recalled, however, that the legend, satisfying though it may be, does not hold up to critical scrutiny. The legend says that the vision occurred while Charles was held captive in Barcelona, which would have been in 1284–88. He discovered her relics in 1279.

[28] Montagnes, *La Légende Dominicaine*, 75 deemed the *Aurea rosa* a "best-seller." A more extended treatment of Silvestro's work concludes this chapter.

[29] In what follows I am indebted to the analysis of Giuliana Vitale, "Nobiltà napoletana della prima età angioina: Elite burocratica e famiglia," in *L'État Angevin*, 562–65.

[30] On the chapel decoration, see Bologna, *I pittori*, 79–90, and Evelina Borea, "I ritrovati affreschi medievali della Cappella Minutolo nel Duomo di Napoli," *Bollettino d'Arte*, 4th series, 47 (1962): 11–23. The Magdalen is illustrated in fig. 12. The Minutolo chapel holds a celebrated place in literary history as it was one of the settings for Boccaccio's tale of Andreuccio da Perugia (Day II:5) in *The Decameron*.

row niche embedded in the entrance wall, a hair-clad Magdalen, hands raised to the chest in a gesture beckoning the spectator's attention, stands vigil over Filippo's celebrated tomb. This was a commission, it has been suggested, "clearly not without political meaning." The inclusion of a Magdalen in the Minutolo chapel signaled the family's allegiance to the Angevin dynasty.[31]

Homage to Charles II by way of reverence to Mary Magdalen also explains the presence of a thirteenth-century Neapolitan fresco cycle depicting scenes from the life of Mary Magdalen in the Cappella Pipino in the church of San Pietro a Maiella. The namesake of the chapel is Giovanni Pipino da Barletta (d. 1316) who, in 1300, led Charles II's crusade against the Arab colony at Lucera.[32] Flushed with victory, Giovanni Pipino seems to have given thanks for his martial success by becoming an ecclesiastical benefactor. In 1300 he founded the church of San Bartolomeo in Lucera on the spot where he had been thrown from his horse.[33] In the early fourteenth century he seems to have provided the funding for the construction of the Neapolitan church of San Pietro a Maiella. The titular saint was Pietro del Morrone, the hermit who became Pope Celestine V, widely regarded as an Angevin puppet. As in the case of Filippo Minutolo, Giovanni Pipino showed devotion to his sovereign by exhibiting reverence for Charles's patron saint in his family chapel. Thus the Pipino chapel, which safeguarded Giovanni's tomb, was frescoed with scenes from the life of Mary Magdalen.[34] The scenes include her conversion in the house of the Pharisee, the *noli me tangere*, her preaching in Marseilles, and the Marseilles miracle. Significantly, it also includes an episode from the *Golden Legend* not commonly represented in visual cycles of her life.[35] It depicts her miraculous resurrection of a knight killed in battle. Jacobus de Voragine gives no details about how the knight was killed, but the fresco in the Pipino chapel adds a few revealing details. In this visual rendering of the miracle, the unhorsed knight and his steed have both been killed and then brought back to life through the intercession of Mary Magdalen (Fig. 36). It would seem that Giovanni Pipino's recent brush with death in Lucera under similar circumstances informed his selection of Magdalenian iconography in his chapel.

[31] Vitale, "Nobiltà," 564.

[32] Bologna suggests that the chapel's patron is Giovanni Pipino, count of Altamura, lord of Bari, and chamberlain of Robert the Wise (Charles II's son), *I pittori*, 313–14. This is not conventional wisdom, however; I disagree with this attribution for reasons listed below. Caroline Bruzelius groups the church of San Pietro a Maiella with Charles II's building projects, effectively discounting Bologna's suggestion. See "Charles I, Charles II," 101.

[33] *Puglia* (TCI) (Milan: A Garzanti, 1978; 4th ed.), 240–41.

[34] For the chapel decoration, see Bologna, *I pittori*, 313–17.

[35] It is represented only in the *Leggendario Ungherese* (Fig. 35) and possibly in the cycle at Pontresina. The latter, however, is so damaged that any secure attribution of the subject is impossible.

Pipino's chapel, therefore, was a testimonial both to his earthly patron, Charles II, and his heavenly patron, Mary Magdalen.

Another example of loyalty to Charles II as expressed through devotion to his patron saint is to be found in the Brancaccio chapel.[36] We have already noted a payment made in 1308 by Charles II to Pietro Cavallini who was working at San Domenico Maggiore, the same church that in 1283 the young prince had tried to rededicate to Mary Magdalen. Cavallini was in Naples to decorate the Brancaccio family chapel in that church, the patron of which was Cardinal Landolfo Brancaccio (d. 1312), yet another of the king's men. In 1294 he was elected Cardinal of Sant'Angelo by Celestine V. It was no state secret that Charles II influenced most of the old pontiff's appointments. Brancaccio's career was further tied to Angevin interests when, in 1295, Boniface VIII named him apostolic legate to the Kingdom of Naples.[37] Landolfo made his sign of obeisance to the king by including three scenes from the life of Mary Magdalen in his family chapel dedicated to Saint Andrew, the expense of which was defrayed by none other than Charles II.[38]

A final act of political piety on the part of the Neapolitan nobility occurred in 1309, the year of Charles II's death. In that year the knight Matteo Caracciolo founded the church of Santa Maria Maddalena near Tripergole in the area of Pozzuoli, just outside Naples.[39] Significantly, in the years between 1300 and 1304 in that very same area, Charles II had founded a hospital dedicated to Saint Martha, Mary's sister. The hospital's mission was to care for the infirmities of the poor. Treatment included baths in purified water known to have therapeutic effects. Charles continued to show interest in the hospital even after his death: one of the provisions of his will stipulated that the unfinished hospital be completed.[40] It is more than likely that Matteo Caracciolo had the church of Mary Magdalen constructed in the same region so that the grateful poor, who had taken the cure at Charles II's hospital of Saint Martha, could give thanks for benefits received at the church of Saint Mary Magdalen. The Caracciolo knight paid homage to his lord by linking the sisters of Bethany in sister institutions, a point that would not have been lost on the Angevin king.

Discussion of what I am calling political piety has thus far centered on

---

[36] See Vitale, "Nobiltà," 565.

[37] For Landolfo, see I. Walter, "Brancaccio, Landolfo," in *DBI* 13 (1971), 784–85. In 1299, he was reappointed apostolic legate to the *Regno*, a responsibility that he shared with none other than Gerardo Bianchi.

[38] The two surviving scenes are a *noli me tangere* and an eremitical Magdalen (Fig. 19). I assume the lost scene, given its placement, was Mary Magdalen's conversion in the house of the Pharisee.

[39] Camera, *Annali*, vol. 2, 173.

[40] For the hospital mentioned in Charles's testament, see ibid., 177.

Naples, the Angevin's capital city. But this notion also serves to explain certain acts of Magdalen devotion in central Italy as well. Julian Gardner has recently suggested that the Magdalen altar, dedicated in 1297 in the Roman basilica of Saint John Lateran, can be read as a testament to the strength of the Angevin-papal relationship in the later thirteenth century.[41] The altar was dedicated by none other than Gerardo Bianchi of Parma (d. 1302), apostolic legate to Naples and royal councilor to the Angevin court.[42] (It will be recalled that Bianchi was so esteemed in the *Regno* that he was made vice-regent of the realm during the interregnum that preceded the coronation of Charles II.) The dedicatory inscription of the altar is noteworthy, for it discretely discloses the intimacy of the Angevin-papal compact. It reads:

> In the name of God amen. In the year 1297 the altar of the chapter was consecrated by order of Boniface VIII, by Lord Gerardo of Parma, Bishop of Sabina, to honor the Lord and Blessed Mary Magdalen. The body of the saint, minus head and arm, is buried in the altar along with relics of many other saints.[43]

It will be remembered that by 1293 Charles II had translated both Mary Magdalen's head and arm to extravagant made-to-order reliquaries preserved at Saint-Maximin. It will also be recalled that in April of 1295 Boniface had authenticated the saint's relics at Saint-Maximin. Later that same year he (implicitly) reconfirmed their authenticity when he granted an indulgence to pilgrims visiting them on her feast-day, on the anniversary of her translation, or during the octave of either of these two feasts. As intimates of Charles II, surely both Boniface VIII and Bianchi had the provençal relics in mind when the altar inscription was written. The final sentence of the inscription conspicuously noting the absence of Mary Magdalen's head and arm in the new altar, I would suggest, tacitly refers to the head and arm relics already famously associated with Charles II's munificence at Saint-Maximin. The Lateran altar, then, stands both as Gerardo's personal monument to the saint and as a discreet homage to his years of Angevin service. When he died in 1302 the Dominican cardinal was entombed in front of his Magdalen altar. We may assume that Charles II, a pallbearer at Gerardo's funeral, though no doubt saddened at the death of

---

[41] Julian Gardner, "Seated Kings, Sea-Faring Saints and Heraldry: Some Themes in Angevin Iconography" in *L'État Angevin,* 115–26.

[42] For Gerardo, see Peter Herde, "Bianchi, Gerardo," in *DBI* 10 (1968), 96–101.

[43] For the Latin inscription, see Saxer, *Le culte,* 215n. 143, who notes that Bianchi's altar was a refurbishment of an altar dedicated to the saint dating back to the pontificate of Honorius III. Saxer posits that the relics it contained were brought back as booty from the Crusade of 1204.

a trusted councilor, must have been gratified to see that Magdalen devotion was now officially instated in Saint John Lateran, the most prominent basilica of thirteenth-century Rome. Charles II's ardor for the saint had begun to take root outside the borders of the *Regno*.

Charles's affection for Mary Magdalen may also have informed the patronage of the giottesque Magdalen chapel at Assisi completed circa 1312. It will be recalled that its patron was Teobaldo Pontano, Franciscan bishop of Assisi, who had previously served in Charles II's *Regno*, first as bishop of Castellammare di Stabia, and subsequently at Terracina. In 1296 Boniface VIII assigned him to the bishopric of Assisi.[44] Given the lavish iconographical program in the chapel, there is no doubt that the bishop was devoted to Mary Magdalen (Fig. 13). But the origins of that devotion remain unclear. It is certainly possible that Charles II's devotion to the saint may have inspired or deepened Pontano's own reverence for Mary Magdalen; or, on the other hand, Charles's devotion to the saint expressed primarily through his patronage of the Dominican order, may have provoked the Franciscan bishop into a bit of friendly competition. Perhaps Pontano's Magdalen chapel, constructed in the very bowels of Franciscan spirituality, should be read as a Franciscan response to what was fast becoming Dominican domination of the cult of the saint. In establishing his Magdalen chapel in Assisi the bishop was both indicating his Angevin allegiances and, at the same time, impressing a Franciscan seal on Magdalen devotion. Either way, it is still probable that the Magdalen chapel in Assisi, in the words of one leading art historian, was a "prominent example of the dissemination of what had now effectively become an Angevin cult."[45]

Revealingly, despite the fact that the "Angevin cult" flourished among Charles II's *familiares* in Naples, and indeed by the late thirteenth century began to move beyond the borders of the *Regno*, particularly into Guelf

[44] For discussion of Teobaldo and the iconography of his chapel see chapter 10. Lorraine Schwartz has observed a strange emblem in the chapel, possibly indicating a definitive link with the Angevin dynasty. In the fresco of the "Arrival in Marseilles" is a "curious little figure consisting of a crenelated turret surmounted by two banners, each of which bears the symbol of the commune of Assisi. Suspended beneath the turret are two inverted crowns." Schwartz speculates that one of the inverted crowns refers to the abdication of Saint Louis of Toulouse, Charles II's son, who refused the Angevin crown in order to become a Franciscan friar. Louis died in 1297, his body was translated to the Franciscan church in Marseilles, and that same year Assisi concluded a treaty of alliance with Naples. Given this conjunction of people and events, it is a plausible scenario that through the curious emblem Bishop Pontano was signaling an Angevin affiliation in the "Arrival in Marseilles" fresco in his Magdalen chapel at Assisi. See Schwartz, *The Fresco Decoration*, 193–98. It should also be remembered that the decoration of the chapel and Louis's cause for canonization were almost contemporaneous. For Angevin involvement in Louis's case see chap. 1, n. 79.

[45] Gardner, "Seated Kings," 123.

strongholds in Umbria and Tuscany, it never really did take root in the rough and tumble world of those living outside the rarified atmosphere of the noble court circle. Though Charles had attempted to name many foundations throughout the *mezzogiorno* in favor of his patron saint, it is no doubt significant that a number of his Mary Magdalen dedications never adhered. In Naples, the Neapolitans did not respond to the new titular saint of San Domenico; they persisted in calling the church San Domenico, as indeed they do today.[46] Again in Naples, Sant'Agostino remained Sant'Agostino alla Zecca, despite Charles's attempt to rededicate it. He had no better luck in the Abruzzo: neither San Francesco in Sulmona nor San Domenico in L'Aquila seem to have retained their dedications to the Magdalen for long. Unlike Tuscany, where, as we have seen, the name Maddalena became one of the four most popular female names by the fourteenth century, it does not seem to have had the same success in the Kingdom of Naples.[47] Perhaps these signs may be read as popular resistance to an unpopular dynasty. The noble families of Naples had good reason to devote themselves to the Angevin saint. In showing devotion to Mary Magdalen they were showing loyalty to the new rulers of the *mezzogiorno*, and were usually handsomely rewarded for their pains. The plain people of the *Regno*, bitter over taxation policies and resentful of their new French overlords, had little to gain. Therefore they showed no such allegiance to the royal cult. Since the time of the Sicilian Vespers they had resisted the foreign rule of the French. As such, I would interpret popular indifference to the cult of the Magdalen as part and parcel of resistance, or better, outright rejection of the sovereignty of the House of Anjou in southern Italy.

The Angevin Dynasty

Despite popular resistance, devotion to Mary Magdalen was not interred with Charles II; his heirs continued to honor what had now become an Angevin cult. Robert the Wise (d. 1343), heir to the Angevin throne, showed his devotion to the Magdalen (and to his father) through patronage and sermons.

It has recently been suggested that Robert may have been the guiding

[46] An eighteenth-century description of the church relates: "Benché detto serenissimo Re facesse intitolare la detta chiesa col nome di S. Maria Magdalena, questo titolo però non lo ritenne, ma perserverò sempre col nome di Chiesa di S. Domenico, stante l'uso già fatto antecedentemente di chiamarla così." ASN, Mon. Sopp. San Domenico Maggiore, fasc. 25, f. 8.

[47] For example, there are no Magdalens listed in the published necrology of the convent of Santa Patrizia in Naples. See Anna Maria Facchiano, *Monasteri femminili e nobiltà tra medioevo ed età moderna: Il necrologio di S. Patrizia, sec. XII–XVI* (Salerno: Ed. Studi Storici meridionali, 1992); cf. the Tuscan and Umbrian necrologies, chapter 10, nn. 50–53.

force behind the giottesque Magdalen chapel in the Palazzo del Podestà in Florence (now known as the Bargello), a very good suggestion indeed.[48] In the later medieval period the palace housed the office of the podestà, the foreign civil magistrate who administrated the city of Florence. Trials were conducted there and those who received the death penalty were brought to spend their final evening in the Magdalen chapel to repent, confess, and receive last rights before justice was served the following morning.

The palazzo itself was expanded and refurbished in the 1260s, but it was not until 1296 that direct Angevin influence can be discerned. In that year a new door was added to the south wall of the palace over which the arms of King Charles II were surmounted. During Robert's *signoria* in Florence (1313–22), the palace was again remodeled, this time including the eastern wing that housed the Magdalen Chapel. At the end of his tenure, in 1322, funds were allocated for the decoration of this chapel.[49] Given Angevin interests in this building, and Guelf concerns to please their Angevin allies, it seems quite probable that Robert was indeed the *de facto* patron of this chapel, suggesting its dedication and iconographical program.[50] Indeed, Robert's image even appears in the chapel; he is amongst the blessed in Paradise. It appears, then, that the Magdalen Chapel in the Palazzo del Podestà in Tuscany is yet another example of the politics through which the Angevin cult of the Magdalen was disseminated in central Italy. The *parte guelfa*, which controlled the funding for the construction and decoration of the palazzo, clearly had an interest in pleasing their Angevin associates; as such, they seem to have agreed to honor the patron saint of their *signori* alongside Florence's own patron saint, John the Baptist, in the chapel of the communal palace that housed both Angevin and Florentine interests. The tendency noted earlier of pairing the Magdalen with the Baptist, Florence's patron saint, may be rooted in the Guelf-Angevin political alliance, partly explaining the Magdalen's popularity in Tuscany.[51]

In a famous backhanded compliment, Dante (whose image was also rep-

[48] In what follows I am indebted to Janis Elliott's analysis in "The Judgement of the Commune: The Frescoes of the Magdalen Chapel in Florence," *Zeitschrift für Kunstgeschichte* 61(1998):509–19.

[49] The eight episodes from the *vita Magdalenae* represented in the chapel are as follows: Conversion at the house of the Pharisee; the Raising of Lazarus; Mary Magdalen at the empty sepulcher; *Noli me tangere;* the eremitical Magdalen at prayer; angelic communion; final communion/assumption of the saint's soul to paradise; and the Marseilles miracle.

[50] Charles, Duke of Calabria, Robert's son, resided in the palazzo during his *signoria* of Florence, Elliott, ibid., 517.

[51] As Elliott astutely points out, the terms of their seigneurial contract gave the Angevins control over most of the important communal offices of Florence anyway. Ibid., 516–17. For my discussion of the pairing of John the Baptist and Mary Magdalen, see chap. 4, nn. 54–55.

resented in the podestà's Magdalen chapel) declared Robert of Anjou "a king made for sermons."[52] It was an epithet not without truth. Robert wrote quite a number of sermons: two hundred and sixty-six of them are extant.[53] Among them are three devoted to the feast-day of Mary Magdalen. One might suppose, given his family's intimate connection to the Magdalen, that his sermons on the saint might in some way reflect that deep devotion. They do not. They are as dry, pedantic, and formulaic as the rest of his sermons; one could never guess from their content that his father had discovered Mary Magdalen's relics in Provence or indeed that he himself was a patron of her shrine at Saint-Maximin.[54] The sermons are so concerned with showing off his mastery of the genre and his erudition— in one sermon he cites Chrysostom, Augustine, Ambrose, Cassiodorus, Gregory the Great, Anselm, and even Avicenna—that he loses all sight of his personal devotion to the saint.[55]

Robert's first sermon on Mary Magdalen is essentially an essay on the debilities of women. Its first sentence (after the gospel quotation) reads: "Woman naturally runs into adversity on account of her frivolous temperament." A few lines later he quotes Chrysostom approvingly: "The female sex is negligent and weak."[56] Perhaps Robert's sermon was informed by the problem of prostitution that continued to plague his capital, the port city of Naples. In 1314 he decreed that all "intemperate women living scandalously for sale by disgraceful prostitution" be expelled from the Piazza San Gennaro a Diaconia.[57] It will be recalled that preachers and moralists frequently argued that prostitution was the fate awaiting those women, weak by nature, who did not submit themselves to male guardianship or better, to a life of penance.[58]

Eventually, Robert was able to offer those "intemperate women living scandalously for sale" a life removed from the streets and dedicated to penance. In 1342 his Majorcan queen, Sancia (d. 1345), founded a con-

[52] *Paradiso*, VIII, 145–48.

[53] On Robert's sermons, see Jean-Paul Boyer, "*Ecce rex tuus.* Le roi et le royaume dans les sermons de Robert de Naples," *Revue Mabillon* 67 (1995): 101–36, and id., "Prédication et état napolitain dans la première moitié du XIVe siècle," in *L'État Angevin,* 131, for the number of extant sermons.

[54] Faillon, *Monuments,* vol. 1, 934–54 gathers together all the evidence of Robert's patronage of Saint-Maximin and La Sainte-Baume.

[55] Marc. lat. Cl. III. 76 (2101), ff. 89–90; *RLS* 5: 227. Of course, if using impersonal model sermons as exemplars, Robert would not have striven to personalize his own.

[56] "Mulier est naturaliter incurrens inadvertentiam ex levitate, ideo defectus proprios non cogitant. . . . Sexus enim mulieris incautus et mollis est ut dixit Chrysostom super Mattheum." MS Marc. lat. Cl. 76 (2101), f. 89.

[57] Camera, *Annali,* vol. 2, 228–29.

[58] See chapters 6–7.

vent for repentant prostitutes under the protection of Saint Mary Magdalen.[59] As we have seen, its mission was so successful that that same year she founded another establishment for *convertite*, this one dedicated to that other prostitute-saint, Saint Mary of Egypt.[60] Both convents were affiliated with the Franciscan Order. Sancia's affection for the Franciscans is well known and well documented. Her court was a haven for Franciscan Spirituals, among them her brother; she founded Franciscan convents, among them Santa Chiara in Naples, and she probably commissioned art destined for those convents, among them four panels by the master known as the Master of the Franciscan Tempera. The panels illustrate Sancia's ardor for the Minorites, but they also witness her devotion to Mary Magdalen. The saint is featured in two of the four paintings. In the first, a Virgin and child are flanked by the Magdalen and Saint Clare. The iconography is novel in two respects: first, it is one of the few examples where Mary Magdalen is paired with Clare rather than Francis, and second, because the kneeling Clare is represented as a *battuta*. The back of her habit is cut away to reveal bloodied flesh; in her right hand she holds a scourge. The hermit-Magdalen, on the other hand, is genuflecting, her hands crossed over her chest in a position of reverence. In the second panel, Sancia represents herself along with Robert in a donor portrait, in the company of Mary Magdalen at the foot of the cross (Fig. 50). Given the subject matter, it would seem that these panels were meant for Sancia's convent of Santa Chiara. She made Magdalen gifts to other Franciscan foundations as well. To the Franciscan convent of Santa Maria Maddalena that Charles II had founded in Sulmona, Sancia gave a silver tabernacle containing a finger of the saint.[61]

[59] It is possible that Sancia was already devoted to Mary Magdalen even before her marriage into the Angevin dynasty. It has been observed that many of Sancia's dedications follow those established by her family, the royal house of Majorca. For example, her mother, Esclaramonde of Foix, was the royal patron of the convent of Sainte-Madeleine in Perpignan. See Caroline Bruzelius, "Queen Sancia of Mallorca and the Convent Church of Sta. Chiara in Naples," *Memoirs of the American Academy in Rome* 40 (1995): 82. This convent was a house for repentant prostitutes; see Leah Lydia Otis, "Prostitution in Late Medieval Perpignan," 149. One of the chapels in the royal palace at Perpignan was also dedicated to Mary Magdalen.

[60] Camera, *Annali*, vol. 2, 491. For discussion of Sancia's Neapolitan foundation for repentant prostitutes, see chapter 6.

[61] For Sancia and the Franciscan Order, see Ronald Musto, "Queen Sancia of Naples (1286–1345) and the Spiritual Franciscans," in *Women of the Medieval World: Essays in Honor of John H. Mundy,* ed. J. Kirshner and S. F. Wemple (Oxford: Basil Blackwell, 1985), 179–214, and Bruzelius, "Queen Sancia of Mallorca." For the four panels, now in a private collection, see Bologna, *I pittori,* 235–45, plates XVII–XX. Bologna dates them ca. 1336 and argues that they reflect the Franciscan Spiritual environment of the Neapolitan court. The other odd detail about the panel featuring Clare and the Magdalen is that they each hold

Figure 50. *Mary Magdalen and the Angevin Monarchs, Sancia and Robert, at the Foot of the Cross.* (ca. 1336) Panel painting, Master of the Franciscan Tempera. Private Collection. (Photo: Herziana)

Giovanna I (d. 1382), granddaughter of Robert the Wise and heir to the Angevin throne, continued Sancia's patronage of the Magdalens of Naples. At the age of nineteen, during her first pregnancy, which apparently was not without its difficulties, like other expectant mothers of her time, she sought the aid of the penitent saint promising that if her suffering was relieved she would endow the Magdalen's Neapolitan *convertite* with one hundred measures of salt annually. Her petition was granted; her reg-

---

rosaries, which may be later over-painting. For the relic in Sulmona, see Piccirilli, *Monumenti,* 18. Some attribute the gift to Queen Maria Arpád, wife of Charles II.

ister of 1347 records the gift made according to a vow sworn during her pregnancy.[62]

This was not the only vow that Giovanna, finding herself in dire circumstances, made to Mary Magdalen. On another occasion, perhaps in 1355, when crossing from Naples to Provence by sea, the queen's ship was caught in a terrible storm. Giovanna vowed that if she survived she would donate nine hundred gold florins to the basilica of Saint Mary Magdalen at Saint-Maximin. The storm blew over, Giovanna survived, and when she again turned to affairs of the realm, she ordered her factors to fulfill the contents of the vow she had made at sea. Apparently they postponed payment to the sanctuary, since in a charter dated 1369 Giovanna again demands that the obligations of her vow be disbursed to the shrine.[63]

Aboard that endangered ship was another of Mary Magdalen's suppliants, Philippe Cabassole (d. 1372), a native Provençal and royal chancellor to the Angevin queen. And that day he too made a vow to the saint. Philippe's vow was recorded in his *Book of the History of Blessed Mary Magdalen*, completed in 1355.[64] In it he recounts how he and two hundred

---

[62] Matteo Camera, *Elucubrazioni storico-diplomatiche su Giovanna I a Regina di Napoli e Carlo III di Durazzo* (Salerno: Tipografia Nazionale, 1889), 39, quoting Reg. an. 1347, lit. F. fol. 155. Scholars suggest that the *Leggendario Ungherese* was made for Giovanna's first husband, Andrew of Hungary, who came to Naples in 1333. It seems that the book was a gift representing "the hagiographic pantheon" of the Hungarian branch of the Angevin family. See most recently Gábor Klaniczay et al., "'Vinum vetus in utres novos.' Conclusioni sull'edizione CD del Leggendario ungherese angioino," in *L'État Angevin*, 304.

The penitent Magdalen seems to have been close to Giovanna's heart; it is an image that she used even in her official correspondence. In supplicating Pope Innocent VI to grant a papal dispensation for the marriage of her sister Maria to Philip of Taranto she compared herself and her husband to "Peter and the Magdalen [who] cured the wounds of sinners with their penitent tears." See Camera, ibid., 201–2.

[63] Faillon, *Monuments*, vol. 2, 981–84, prints the entire charter. Though he was never able to claim the crown of Sicily he had inherited from Giovanna II (d. 1435), René of Anjou (d. 1480) continued the Angevin tradition of dedication to Mary Magdalen on French soil. We have already seen that he gave to the cathedral in Angers the font which he believed Mary Magdalen had used to baptize the pagan rulers of Provence. He also donated an urn which he had been assured Christ had used at the marriage feast of Cana to change water into wine, and which had been transported to Provence by Mary Magdalen. Moreover, out of devotion to the *secretaria et sola apostola Jesu Christi*, René built a reproduction of La Sainte-Baume called "La Baumette" under the cliff of Chanzé and gave the gabelle of Yères to her provençal shrines. Among his artistic commissions honoring the saint was his assent to Francesco Laurana's *Lazarus Altar* (1477) at La Vieille Major in Marseilles and two reliquaries to hold bits of the saint's hair. He also donated the reliquary to hold the holy ampule (see n. 79 below) to Saint-Maximin (Clemens, *The Establishment*, 274). A. Lecoy de la Marche, *Le Roi René: sa vie, son administration, ses travaux artistique et littéraires*, 2 vols. (Paris: Librairie de Firmon-Didot, 1875), vol. 1: 435, 547; vol. 2: 47–48, 76, 115, 138–39, 376 and Jacques Levron, *Le Bon Roi Réne* (N.p.: Arthaud, 1972), 153–56.

[64] For commentary on the *libellus*, see Saxer, "Philippe Cabassole," in *L'État Angevin*, 193–204.

and fifty other passengers, having been caught in the storm for many days, recited psalms, the litany of the saints, and other prayers in the hopes of forestalling a shipwreck. But it was not until he made a vow to make a pilgrimage to Mary Magdalen's shrine at Saint-Maximin that immediately "the south-west wind from Africa blew in causing the seas to calm down."[65]

Philippe's *libellus* is interesting on a number of different levels, not least of which is that it stands in a long line of Angevin propaganda linking the House of Anjou and the early Christian saint. Saxer has pointed to a particularly revealing passage in this regard:

> In the year of the Incarnation, 1279, December 9th, when Nicolas III brought the see of Peter to its apostolic heights, when Rudolph, king of the Romans, held the reins of the Empire, when Philip . . . son of the glorious king and blessed confessor Saint Louis ruled, and when from that same side of the family, Charles II presided happily over the realm of Jerusalem and Sicily, as well as the county of Provence and who was father of the blessed Louis, bishop of Toulouse, from the noble line of France, and who was the only one of all the kings of the earth granted the celestial vision.[66]

Philippe Cabassole, publicizing his Angevin patrons, places Charles II squarely in the midst of the illustrious stars of the thirteenth-century firmament: Pope Nicolas and King Rudolph; Philip the Fair and Saint Louis IX, members of the Capetian royal family from which the cadet branch—the Angevins—had sprung; and Saint Louis, bishop of Toulouse (d. 1297), Charles II's eldest son who was canonized in 1317. In one artful passage Philippe managed to evoke the entire family tree in which Charles was not only the nephew of a saint, but the father of one, too. Though not himself a saint, Charles II was the only one out of all those saints and meritorious kings to have received a divine vision. As chancellor of the Kingdom of Naples, Philippe Cabassole had learned well the art of atomizing the Angevin family tree with the odor of sanctity.

Philippe's *libellus* was clearly intended to serve on one level as a piece of dynastic propaganda for his Angevin patrons. But it must be remembered that Philippe was first and foremost himself a Provençal. Thus, when in mortal danger, it was not as chancellor of the *Regno* or as Angevin publicist that he called on Mary Magdalen's assistance, it was as a citizen of Provence beseeching his local protector. In that capacity Philippe was the beneficiary of three of the Magdalen's miracles. His *libellus* reports that because of vows he had sworn, the Magdalen intervened to protect him on two occasions, both when he was in danger of shipwreck. The third mira-

---

[65] Cited in ibid., 199. Clemens dates this miracle to 1346, *The Establishment*, 262.
[66] Cited in Saxer, "Philippe Cabassole," 197.

cle of which he was a beneficiary was when, upon another vow, the saint intervened to protect the life of his brother.[67]

Philippe Cabassole was not the only native Provençal to call on the aid of Saint Mary Magdalen. Jean Gobi's miracle register reveals that in fact most of the miracles recorded at the saint's shrine in Saint-Maximin were performed on behalf of citizens of Provence.[68] This is congruent with the miraculous activity of most medieval shrines: vows were sworn by the local populace to their local saint, and consequently, the saint produced miracles on their behalf. Indeed, the first miracle in Gobi's catalog reveals this pattern: some Provençal soldiers, held captive by the Genoese, petitioned the Magdalen as "special patron of all who are from the above-cited county of Provence, which has her body in that same place."[69] After 1279, Mary Magdalen became the protector of Provence for the simple reason that her relics were believed to be "in that same place."

Relics

Charles II, Provençals, and the Dominican caretakers of Saint-Maximin all believed that their shrine contained the body of Saint Mary Magdalen. Be that as it may, by the end of the Middle Ages bits of the saint's body turned up in reliquaries throughout much of western Europe. If we can use the multiplication of relics as a guide to the popularity of a saint, then Mary Magdalen was a very popular saint indeed by the later medieval period. Salimbene reported that in his day Vézelay, Saint-Maximin, and Senigallia (near Ancona) all claimed to have Mary Magdalen's body, a notion the friar denounced as an absurdity.[70] Little did he know that there were at least two more bodies claiming to belong to the saint. As we have seen, the Magdalen altar in Saint John Lateran in Rome claimed one, while the church of Saint Lazarus in Constantinople claimed another, this one having been translated from her tomb in Ephesus.[71]

[67] For a description of these miracles and their dates, see Clemens, *The Establishment*, 261–62.

[68] Significantly, only two of the eighty-six miracles cataloged by Gobi were effected for those in the Angevin's Italian territories: nos. 23 and 82. In no. 23 a blind man from Piedmont came to Saint-Maximin to kiss the arm of Mary Magdalen, while in no. 82 a leper called Jacobus from Amalfi, who had had no success at the therapeutic baths of Pozzuoli in the *Regno,* came to Saint-Maximin in search of a cure. See "Iohannes Gobi," no. 23, 159–60; no. 82, 198–200.

[69] Ibid., no. 1, 137–38.

[70] *Cronica,* vol. 2, 761. For wise words on the veneration of relics in the West, see Peter Brown, *The Cult of the Saints: Its Rise and Function in Latin Christianity* (Chicago: University of Chicago Press, 1981).

[71] Gregory of Tours provides sixth-century evidence of the Ephesus tradition. See his

Various other body parts were venerated throughout Europe. Despite the fame of Saint-Maximin's head reliquary, Abbeville also claimed to have Mary Magdalen's skull, while the Dominican nuns of Aix had possessed her jaw since 1281, when Charles II had bestowed it on them. Though Saint-Maximin had an arm reliquary, Cologne claimed two arms of the saint. There was another in Sicily, yet another in Hainault, a sixth in Marseilles, a seventh in Venice, and an eighth one in Fécamp, the one out of which Hugh of Lincoln famously took a bite.[72] Fingers turned up frequently. The canons at Exeter Cathedral had claimed a digit since the eleventh century. Queen Sancia of Naples gave the Franciscans in Sulmona another one encased in a silver reliquary. Saint Martha in Tarascon, Saint Victor in Marseilles, and San Marco in Venice all claimed to possess fingers.[73] Unsurprisingly, countless churches claimed locks of her abundant supply of hair.[74]

Aside from body parts, relics of the Magdalen's penitence were also popular. As early as 1200, "La Nunziatella" outside Rome claimed to have a fragment of the cave where Mary Magdalen did penance. The treasury of Saint John Lateran still has a reliquary containing a piece of her hair shirt. Santa Croce in Gerusalemme in Rome claimed to have the stone slab where Jesus reclined when he forgave her sins.[75]

Understandably, relics emphasizing Mary Magdalen's intimate relation

---

Glory of the Martyrs, trans. Raymond van Dam (Liverpool: Liverpool University Press, 1988), 47. The body from Ephesus was translated at the end of the ninth century by the Byzantine emperor Leo VI. It was interred along with Lazarus's relics in a church dedicated to him in Constantinople. See Haskins, *Mary Magdalen,* 108. These might have been the relics that ended up in Rome, as Saxer suggests, or the ones de Plancy reports Montserrat claimed. See J.A.S. Collin de Plancy, *Dictionnaire critique des reliques et des images miraculeuses,* 3 vols. (Paris: Guien et Compagnie, 1821), vol. 2, 139, who is not entirely reliable. He reports that Santa Maria di Constantinopoli in Naples also claimed the Magdalen's relics. I find no trace of such a claim in the literature on the church, which in any event is a sixteenth-century foundation.

[72] For the relics at Saint-Maximin, see Victor Saxer, "Les ossements dits de sainte Marie-Madeleine conservés a Saint Maximin-la-Saint-Baume," *Provence Historique* 27 (1977): 257–311. For the jaw at Aix which was ultimately reunited with the skull at Saint-Maximin, see Clemens, *The Establishment,* 73–74, 232. For Abbeville, Cologne, Sicily, and Hainault, see Faillon, *Monuments,* vol. 1, 903–5. For Marseilles, see de Plancy, *Dictionnaire critique,* vol. 2, 140; for Fécamp and Venice, see Haskins, *Mary Magdalen,* 104, 465n. 119. The listing of relics in these pages does not pretend to be complete; it is meant only as an indicator of their ubiquity.

[73] For Exeter, see Malvern, *Venus in Sackcloth,* 79; for Sulmona, see n. 61; for Tarascon, Marseilles, and San Marco, see de Plancy, *Dictionnaire critique,* 140.

[74] Among them in Rome alone: Santa Maria in Trastevere, San Lorenzo fuori le mura, and Santa Barbara. See X. Barbier de Montault, "Sainte Marie-Madeleine d'après les monuments de Rome," *Revue de l'art chrétien,* 2d series, 12 (1880): 116–26.

[75] For Rome, see ibid., 119.

to Christ also proliferated in the Middle Ages. Since the eleventh century, La Trinité de Vendôme was renowned for its *sainte larme*, "Christ's teardrop, captured and placed by an angel into a container of angelic fabrication and given to the Magdalen after the resurrection of Lazarus."[76] Vézelay had an arm reliquary into which Saint Louis had thoughtfully put some passion relics, commemorating that Christ received Mary Magdalen with such familiarity that he allowed her to touch him.[77] The celebrated *noli me tangere* relic at Saint-Maximin also commemorated touch. It was an uncorrupted piece of skin on Mary Magdalen's forehead that Christ had touched when he forbade her to touch him after the resurrection.[78] Saint-Maximin also possessed the holy ampule, a reliquary that held bits of blood-soaked stones from Golgotha that the Magdalen had brought with her to Gaul. In an annual miracle, the blood liquified on Good Friday.[79] The Frari in Venice, in 1479, received from the commander of the Venetian navy a vial containing a precious mixture of Christ's blood and some of the Magdalen's spikenard, a relic he had obtained in Constantinople. At the church of Saint Victor in Marseilles, medieval pilgrims were treated to the sight of Mary Magdalen's alabaster vase, the veritable emblem of the saint.[80]

Catholic belief maintains that a saint's virtues inhabit all of his or her relics, regardless of their fragmented or partial condition. Accordingly, bits and pieces of saints were (and still are) supplicated to perform miracles. But relics were not always what they appeared to be, as a fourteenth-century story well illustrates. It seems that the monks at Vézelay had given the Dominicans at Lausanne a precious piece of the Magdalen. The relic quickly became quite famous on account of the miraculous cures it was thought to

---

[76] Meredith Parsons Lillich, *The Armor of Light: Stained Glass in Western France, 1250–1325* (Berkeley: University of California Press, 1994), 228–29. I am grateful to Bill Jordan for this reference.

[77] Victor Saxer, *Le dossier vézelien de Marie-Madeleine. Invention et translation des reliques en 1265–1267. Contribution à histoire du culte de la sainte à l'apogée du Moyen Age* (*Subsidia hagiographica*, n. 57) (Brussels: Société des Bollandistes, 1975), 109.

[78] Faillon, *Monuments*, vol. 1, 882–83. La Madeleine in Paris claimed a piece of this relic as early as 1491. The relic was removed from the skull in 1789 and placed in a separate reliquary which can yet be seen on her feast-day. Michel Moncault, *La basilique Sainte-Marie-Madeleine et le couvent royal* (Aix-en-Provence: Edisud, 1985), 38. Philippe Cabassole seems to have been the first to describe this relic. See Clemens, *The Establishment*, 104.

[79] Victor Saxer, "La relique de Saint-Maximin (Var) dite *la sainte ampoule*," *Revue d'histoire ecclesiastique* 79/1 (1984): 87–96.

[80] Venice: Haskins, *Mary Magdalen*, 278. Marseilles: Ibid., 218, where she further relates that Saint Sever in Les Landes claimed some of the Magdalen's unguents. Helen Meredith Garth reports that in one of the apocryphal infancy gospels the Magdalen's alabastron was believed to hold the holy foreskin. See Garth, *Saint Mary Magdalene in Mediaeval Literature* (Baltimore: Johns Hopkins Press, 1950), 31.

effect. One day a man possessed by a demon presented himself at the shrine hoping to be cured of his affliction. The friar-sacristan brought out the relic and began to exorcise the demon by swearing on the Magdalen's virtue contained in the relic. No sooner had he begun than the demon called out, saying, "Brother, what are you saying? What are you saying? Mind what you are saying!" Unfazed, the friar continued the exorcism. Finally, the irritated demon called out again: "Clearly, friar, you do not know what you are saying, or what you are talking about; I am telling you that you are truly lying, because that is not the body or relic of Mary Magdalen, and for that reason I am not leaving this man of yours!"[81] The moral of the story, of course, was that the only true and therefore efficacious relics of Saint Mary Magdalen were those at her sanctuary in Saint-Maximin. Tellingly, this story was told by two of the great Angevin publicists for the provençal shrine: Jean Gobi the Elder and Philippe Cabassole.

The last of the late medieval-early modern publicists of the Angevin-Magdalen alliance was the Italian Dominican Silvestro Mazzolini da Prierio (d. 1527).[82] In the summer of 1497 Silvestro journeyed to Provence to fulfill a vow that he had made to the saint. He left two accounts of his pilgrimage: the first is his vernacular life of Mary Magdalen published in 1500, the second is contained in his *Aurea Rosa,* a widely disseminated preacher's handbook first published in 1503.[83] Like the ordinary pilgrim, Silvestro saw the usual sites and relics associated with Mary Magdalen's provençal sojourn, but unlike the ordinary pilgrim he requested to see and was permitted to read the manuscript text of the *Dominican Legend,* which he refers to as the *cronica.*[84] Silvestro freely incorporated most of the *cronica* into his own pilgrimage account. He recounts Charles's incarceration in Barcelona, and how Mary Magdalen miraculously released him from prison. He also relates how the saint directed the prince to Saint-Maximin

[81] "Iohannes Gobi," no. 84, 201–3.

[82] For Silvestro, known also as Prierias, see Michael Tavuzzi, *Prierias: The Life and Works of Silvestro Mazzolini da Prierio, 1456–1527* (Durham, NC: Duke University Press, 1997). He is best known as Martin Luther's literary adversary.

[83] *Vita de la seraphina e ferventissima amatrice de Jesu Christo salvatore sancta Maria Magdalena* (Bologna: Giovanantonio de' Benedetti, 1500). It was published again in Bologna in 1501 and a third time in Florence in 1592. It was also included in the Milan, 1519 edition of his *Opere vulgare.* Silvestro dedicated the Italian version of the *vita* to the countess Adriana da Thiene of Vicenza. *Aurea Rosa idest preclarissima expositio super evangelia totius anni de tempore et de sanctis tum secundum Ordinem predicatorum quam secundum Curia continens Flores et Rosas omnium expositionum Sanctorum doctorum Antiq. Preclarissimi et excellentissimi Sacre Theologie Doctoris Magistri Silvestri de Prierio pedemontani Sacri Ordinis Fratrum predicatorum de observantia* (Bologna: Benedetto di Ettore, 1503). I use the Bologna, 1524 edition.

[84] *Aurea Rosa,* 172.

in order that he discover her relics there, which Silvestro describes at length and confirms that he saw with his own eyes. Being a Dominican friar, Silvestro was also concerned to establish the Order of Preachers' connection to these miraculous events so he reports how Mary Magdalen directed the Angevin prince to bestow both Saint-Maximin and La Sainte-Baume on the Dominican Order by quoting the saint's instructions to Charles: "You will hand over to my brothers, the Preachers, the places where I died and where I did penance since I was both a preacher and an apostle."[85]

These are the familiar ingredients of the *Dominican Legend,* the mid-fifteenth-century narrative composed by the friar-custodians of Mary Magdalen's sanctuaries in Provence. The legend, it will be recalled, was mainly concerned with the divinely ordained Angevin-Dominican relationship in southern France. But Silvestro Mazzolini was an Italian Dominican who had spent time in the Kingdom of Naples and that experience structured his pilgrimage narrative, setting it apart from the *Dominican Legend.*[86] His account adds a necessary corrective to the provençal *Dominican Legend* as it weaves the neglected Italian threads of Charles II's devotion into the narrative fabric. Silvestro shows his readers Charles's affection for Mary Magdalen as it was expressed through patronage of the Dominican Order in the *Regno.* The friar makes a point of telling his readers that Charles founded twelve monasteries in the *mezzogiorno* for the order, many of which were dedicated to honor the Magdalen. But Silvestro's most persuasive evidence corroborating Charles II's intimate relationship with the Italian Dominicans was the silent witness of the monarch's heart, willed to them by Charles himself. The friars of Naples, the capital of the *Regno* and the metaphorical heart of the Angevin body politic, claimed the physical heart of Charles II, King of Sicily and Jerusalem, Duke of Apulia, Prince of Capua, and Count of Provence, Forcalquier, and Piedmont. Silvestro reports that "it is still conserved today in an ivory pyx in the convent of San Domenico in Naples which I inspected with my own eyes in 1495."[87] Five hundred years later the friars still preserve the heart of Charles II at San Domenico Maggiore, the Neapolitan church which in 1283 the Angevin prince had rededicated to honor his patron saint Mary Magdalen. It was the first of his many Magdalen dedications on Italian soil, and one of many that did not endure, spurned by the determination of popular will.

Given the phenomenal success of Silvestro's *Aurea Rosa*—published nineteen times in the sixteen century alone—the names of Charles II and

---

[85] Ibid.

[86] Silvestro spent the years 1494–95 in Naples on a mission to reform the Dominican convents of the *Regno*. Tavuzzi, *Prierias,* 27.

[87] *Aurea Rosa,* 173.

Mary Magdalen continued to be invoked together centuries after the Angevin monarch's death.[88] No doubt Charles would have been delighted to learn that subsequent centuries continued to remember his relationship with Mary Magdalen, just as he would have been pleased to learn of his provençal sanctuary's continued success.[89] But despite all his efforts to plant Magdalen devotion in the *mezzogiorno,* the royal cult of the Magdalen never fully took root in southern Italian soil. It remained a hothouse flower cultivated and tended by those whose interests were allied with Angevin concerns. Just as the plain people of the *Regno* never warmed to the foreign rule of the House of Anjou, so too they remained indifferent to Mary Magdalen, the Angevin patron saint. But where Guelf sympathies were strongest, particularly in central Italy, aided by the preaching of the friars, the royal cult of Mary Magdalen flourished throughout the Middle Ages.

[88] For the nineteen editions, see Tavuzzi, *Prierias,* 45 and his appendix, n. 16 which lists all of them. Madeleine Boxler has shown Silvestro's influence on what she calls the "Nürnberger Maria Magdalena-Legende," of the early sixteenth century. See Boxler, '*Ich bin ein predigerin und appostlorin*' (Bern: Peter Lang, 1996), 190–209, appendix, 579–84.

[89] By the fourteenth century both La Sainte-Baume and Saint-Maximin had become such successful pilgrimage sites that King Robert had to restore the pilgrims' hostel and increase the number of priests to celebrate mass for the visitors. In 1354, his successor, Queen Giovanna, had to deal with one of the frequent results of a successful venture: litigation, in this case a lawsuit concerning the right to sell pilgrim's badges at the shrine. The badges, it should be noted, bore the Angevin coat of arms. Faillon, *Monuments,* vol. 1, 942 and 971. For an image of the badge, see M. E. Hucher, "Des enseignes de pélerinage," *Bulletin Monumental,* 2d series, 19 (1853): 506.

"In Memory of Her":
From Legend to History

Although as many Latin as Greek doctors maintain that this
Mary is not the sister of Lazarus, Augustine, nonetheless,
in his *de consensu evangelistarum,* believed that she was the
same woman based on the text of John 11:2 where he says
(about the sister of Lazarus) "Mary was the sister of Lazarus,
who was ill, and was the one who anointed the Lord and dried
[his feet] with her hair." Thus it is clear because she
performed a similar act for him which Luke 7: 37–38
commemorates. Also in the last chapter of Mark 9, it is written
that "he appeared first to Mary Magdalen from whom he had
ejected seven devils." Gregory holds this opinion as does the
whole Roman church. . . . Beyond this, one should believe the
Latin tradition more than the Greek because she preached
among them in the region of Marseilles.
(Bernardino da Siena)[1]

As Bernardino's tortured explanation demonstrates, medieval preachers were aware that the figure of Mary Magdalen, composed of three
parts Gregorian fiat and one part legend, was not universally accepted. Like
Bernardino, many preachers, including Ubertino da Casale, Luca da
Bitonto, and Giovanni da San Gimignano, noted this difficulty in their sermons.[2] Iohannes de Biblia, for example, preached that neither Saint Ambrose nor Saint Bernard had assimilated Mary Magdalen to the unnamed
peccatrix of scripture, even though Gregory and Augustine had done so.[3]

---

[1] *Opera Omnia,* vol. 3 (1956), 419–20.

[2] *Arbor vitae,* Bk. 3, chap. 22, unpaginated; MS Casanat. 17, f. 66r; not in *RLS* and MS
BAV Barb. lat. 513, f. 97v; *RLS* 3: 377.

[3] "Notandum tamen quod Ambrosius et Bernardus dicunt hanc peccatricem non fuisse

In spotlighting the Church fathers' disagreement about Mary Magdalen's identity, preachers probably contributed to escalating doubts about the veracity of the composite saint.

By the later Middle Ages those seeds of doubt began to germinate among the laity. In Florence, Diodata Adimari was so vexed by the question that she wrote to her spiritual advisor, Antonino Pierozzi, to ask his view on the matter. In his epistolary reply he advised:

> About the first doubt: whether the female sinner is Mary Magdalen, sister of Lazarus and Martha, rich and honored nobles; or another woman whose name the evangelists do not plainly mention . . . I believe, along with Saint Gregory and Saint Augustine, that she is the same woman, first a great sinner, and then the great lover of Christ.[4]

The Gregorian composite saint had begun to unravel. As much as he was assuaging Diodata's doubts, Antonino appears to have been reassuring himself about the authenticity of the Gregorian saint. He was right to do so: within two generations of his death, in 1517, Jacques Lefèvre d'Étaples published a tract attacking Gregory the Great's Magdalen. A Dominican scholar trained in the new humanist techniques of textual criticism, Lefèvre brought these rigorous methods to bear on the tripartite Magdalen, arguing that there was no historical or scholarly basis for the Gregorian conflation of gospel figures.[5] Although the Sorbonne censured him and John Fisher, Bishop of Rochester, attacked his thesis, Lefèvre's view added fuel to the Protestant fire which burned in readiness to consume the cult of the saints. Luther's distaste for the saints is legendary, as is that of his followers. They made no exception for the *beata peccatrix*. Zwingli regarded the Magdalen as a prime example of the absurdity of Catholic teaching on saintly intercession, while Calvin, following Lefèvre, criticized the Gregorian conflation of scriptural characters. He added his own critique of the provençal legends for good measure and expressed characteristic scorn for her reduplicated relics.[6]

Theologians of the Catholic Reformation first responded to the attacks

---

Mariam Magdalenam sed aliam. Gregorius vero in omelia hodierna et Augustinus secundum *de consensu evangelistarum* dicunt hanc illam fuisse." MS BAV Borgh. 24, f. 61v; *RLS* 3: 91.

[4] *Lettere di santi e beati fiorentini,* ed. Antommaria Biscioni (Florence: Francesco Moucke, 1736), 224.

[5] Jacobus Faber Stapulensis, *De Maria Magdalena, et triduo Christi disceptatio* (Paris: Henri Estienne, 1517). See Anselm Hufstader, "Lefèvre d'Étaples and the Magdalen," in *Studies in the Renaissance* 16 (1969): 31–60, and Eugene Rice, "The Humanist Idea of Christian Antiquity: Lefèvre d'Étaples and His Circle," *Studies in the Renaissance* 9 (1962): 126–60.

[6] For Zwingli and Calvin, see Haskins, *Mary Magdalen,* 249. In the thirteenth century Salimbene had already criticized the fact that three different cities claimed her relics. *Cronica,* ed. Giuseppe Scalia, 2 vols. (Bari: Giuseppe Laterza & Figli, 1966), vol. 2, 761.

of the Protestant reformers by retrenching: the Council of Trent reaffirmed the efficacy of the sacraments and the cult of the saints. Inevitably, though, the Protestant assaults, and the Catholic response to them, reshaped the persona of Mary Magdalen. Where once the figure of the Magdalen was inscribed with multiple symbolic meanings, now the saint's efficacious penance, one of the five sacraments under siege by the Protestants, was emphasized above all else. Her role as *apostola,* legendary as it was deemed to be, dropped out of sight altogether as Trent worked to excise all representations of the saints that were based on legend rather than history.[7] Significantly, however, her great penance continued to be visualized at La Sainte-Baume, even though that too had its origins in legend. Clearly her example as a heroic penitent was too important to be lost to the besieged Church just because it lacked a historical pedigree. Nor should the powerful attraction to this ambiguous image be discounted. The medieval Magdalen's nakedness, which simultaneously evoked both innocence and sexuality, was too alluring to be discarded. But by the early modern period Mary Magdalen's nakedness revealed no sign of innocence reclaimed. Artists of the period made titillating portraits, sometimes even prurient ones, of the naked and ecstatic penitent luxuriating in her grotto at La Sainte-Baume.[8]

Though the Tridentine reformers attempted to expunge legendary elements from the *vitae* of the saints, their efforts were far from complete. A historically accurate cult of the saints would have to wait until 1969, when the Roman calendar was reformed.[9] In that reform, hagiographical scholarship, particularly the work of the Bollandists, was marshaled to test the historicity of figures such as Saints Christopher, Margaret, and Catherine of Alexandria, martyrs whose cults flourished throughout the Middle Ages. Such exacting scholarship was merciless on these legendary saints. As no evidence could be found to document their historical existence, their feast-days were summarily expunged from the Roman calendar.

Saint Mary Magdalen's stature suffered similarly in that reform. Four hundred and fifty-two years after Lefèvre attacked the Gregorian saint the Roman Catholic church decided to dismantle the composite Magdalen. As of 1969 it was decreed that she was to be venerated only as a disciple, the

---

[7] For the implications of the Tridentine decrees on images, see Odile Delenda, "Sainte Marie-Madeleine et l'application du décret Tridentin (1563) sur les *Saintes-Images*" in *Marie Madeleine,* ed. Duperray, 191–210.

[8] I am thinking of Titian's seductively naked penitent, a panel made ca. 1531–35, now in the Pitti Palace in Florence. It (and others of this genre) is reproduced in color as fig. 68, 193 in *La Maddalena fra sacro et profano,* ed. Mosco.

[9] Sacred Congregation of Rites, *Roman Calendar* (Washington, D.C.: United States Catholic Conference, 1970). The decree of the congregation and the apostolic letter of Pope Paul VI, lay out the principles of this reform. See also *Roman Calendar: Text and Commentary* (Washington, D.C.: United States Catholic Conference, 1976).

revised title inscribed after her name in the new calendar. In an earlier calendar reform her feast-day, which in the Middle Ages had been celebrated
by a duplex, the most elaborate of all liturgies reserved for the most important saints, was reduced to a memorial, a simple remembrance. Now
Mary Magdalen was to be remembered merely as one of many of Christ's
disciples, a pale shadow of the complexity of her symbolic significance in
the Middle Ages.

In the later medieval period a sermon on the saint could demonstrate
how Mary Magdalen exemplified the apostolic life, the life of action and
contemplation lived by the mendicant friars. At the same time it could provide a platform for the friars to denounce the follies of women and the effects of the sin of *luxuria* on society. It could also be the occasion on which
prostitutes were prevailed upon to convert. But most of all a Magdalen sermon was the vehicle by which preachers called people to penance and offered them the hope of salvation.

Notwithstanding all of this symbolic work, the receptive audiences of the
friars, acting on their own needs and desires, put the saint to work toward
their own ends. The Angevin dynasty and their allies took her as their protector, while others emphasized her maternal qualities and transformed her
into a patron of childbirth and motherhood. Apprehensive matrons, anxious over their lost virginity and its implications for salvation, used her glorification in heaven to argue for their own one hundredfold celestial reward. The laity of the later Middle Ages were nothing if not creative
consumers in the rich symbolic economy of the medieval world.

In applying the principle of historicity to the cult of the saints, we have
no doubt gained in historical accuracy, and that indeed is an important contribution to knowledge and scholarship. But the gains should not obscure
the losses. We must not forget that it is our own age that officially memo-
rializes Saint Mary Magdalen as a disciple; it was the "Dark Ages" that honored her as a preacher and apostle of the apostles.

Bibliography of Works Cited

UNPUBLISHED PRIMARY SOURCES

Manuscripts

ASSISI (Sacro Convento)
MS Assisi 452
MS Assisi 460
MS Assisi 461
MS Assisi 466
MS Assisi 470
MS Assisi 527
MS Assisi 529
MS Assisi 539
MS Assisi 682

CAMBRIDGE (St. John's College Library)
MS St. John's MS K.21

FLORENCE (Biblioteca Nazionale Centrale)
MS Flor. Naz. Conv. Sopp. A. 4. 857
MS Flor. Naz. Conv. Sopp. D. 1. 937
MS Flor. Naz. Conv. Sopp. E. 6. 1046
MS Flor. Naz. Conv. Sopp. G. 1. 516
MS Flor. Naz. Conv. Sopp. G. 4. 936
MS Flor. Naz. Conv. Sopp. G. 7. 1464

LONDON (British Library)
MS British Library Add. 15682
MS British Library Add. Royal 2 B VII

NAPLES (Biblioteca Nazionale Vittorio Emanuele III)
MS Nap. Naz. VIII. AA. 11
MS Nap. Naz. VIII. A. 36

OXFORD (Balliol College)
MS Balliol 230

PADUA (Biblioteca Antoniana)
MS Antoniana 208
MS Antoniana 435
MS Antoniana 466
MS Antoniana 490

ROME
(Archivum Generale Ordinis Praedicatorum)
MS AGOP XIV. 33
MS AGOP XIV. 35

(Biblioteca Angelica)
MS Angelica 158
MS Angelica 715
MS Angelica 812
MS Angelica 819
MS Angelica 823
MS Angelica 1057

(Biblioteca Casanatense)
MS Casanatense 1
MS Casanatense 17

(Biblioteca Vallicelliana)
MS Vallicelliana C. 80

VATICAN CITY (Biblioteca Apostolica Vaticana)
MS BAV Arch. Cap. S. Petri D. 211
MS BAV Arch. Cap. S. Petri D. 213
MS BAV Arch. Cap. S. Petri G. 48
MS BAV Barb. lat. 513
MS BAV Barb. lat. 2300
MS BAV Borgh. 24
MS BAV Borgh. 66
MS BAV Borgh. 138
MS BAV Borgh. 175
MS BAV Borgh. 343
MS BAV Chig. C. IV. 99
MS BAV Pal. lat. 138
MS BAV Pal. lat. 441
MS BAV Pal. lat. 465
MS BAV Ross. 3
MS BAV Vat. lat. 634
MS BAV Vat. lat. 963
MS BAV Vat. lat. 1198
MS BAV Vat. lat. 1250 P. II
MS BAV Vat. lat. 1251
MS BAV Vat. lat. 1255
MS BAV Vat. lat. 1261
MS BAV Vat. lat. 4691
MS BAV Vat. lat. 6005
MS BAV Vat. lat. 8541

VENICE (Biblioteca Nazionale Marciana)
MS Marc. lat. Cl. III. 76 (2101)
MS Marc. lat. fondo antico 91 (1775)

Archives

ASF, Diplomatico normale, San Gimignano, agostiniane, pergamene
ASN, Mon. Sopp. San Domenico Maggiore, fasc. 25
ASN, Mon. Sopp. Santa Maria Maddalena, fasc. 4421, 4442, 4445

PUBLISHED PRIMARY SOURCES

Vitae from the *Acta Sanctorum* (Antwerp, 1643–)

Agnes of Montepulciano. April, vol. 2: 791–817
Birgitta of Sweden. October, vol. 4: 368–560
Catherine of Siena. April, vol. 3: 851–978
Francesca Romana. March, vol. 2: 88–216
Gherardesca da Pisa. May, vol. 7: 164–80
John of La Verna. August, vol. 2: 453–74
Margaret of Cortona. February, vol. 3: 298–357
Mary Magdalen. July, vol. 5: 187–225
Umiliana de' Cerchi. May, vol. 4: 385–418
Umiltà da Faenza. May, vol. 5: 203–22

Decime

Aemilia. Le decime dei secoli XIII–XIV. Ed. Angelo Mercati, Emilio Nasalli-Rocca, and Pietro Sella (*Studi e Testi,* vol. 60). Vatican City, 1933.

Aprutium-Molisium. Le decime dei secoli XIII–XIV. Ed. Pietro Sella (*Studi e Testi.* Vol. 69). Vatican City, 1936.

Apulia, Lucania, Calabria. Rationes decimarum. Ed. Domenico Vendola (*Studi e Testi.* Vol. 84). Vatican City, 1939.

Latium. Rationes decimarum Italiae nei secoli XIII e XIV. Ed. Giulio Battelli (*Studi e Testi.* Vol. 128). Vatican City, 1946.

Lombardia et Pedemontium. Rationes decimarum Italiae nei secoli XIII e XIV. Ed. Maurizio Rosada (*Studi e Testi.* Vol. 324). Vatican City, 1990.

Tuscia I. La decima degli anni 1274–1280. Ed. Pietro Guido (*Studi e Testi.* Vol. 58). Vatican City, 1942.

Tuscia II. Le decime degli anni 1295–1304. Ed. Martino Giusti and Pietro Guido (*Studi e Testi.* Vol. 98). Vatican City, 1942.

Umbria I. Rationes decimarum Italie nei secoli XIII e XIV. Ed. Pietro Sella (*Studi e Testi.* Vols. 161–62). Vatican City, 1952.

Other

Abelard, Peter. *Sermo 13 (In die Paschae). PL* 178: 484–89.

———. *Ethics.* Ed. D. E. Luscombe. Oxford: Oxford University Press, 1971.

Alberto da Padova. *Evangelia totius anni dominicalia.* Turin: Antonius Ranotus, 1529.

Alexander of Hales. *Glossa in Quatuor Libros Sententiarum Petri Lombardi.* Ed. PP. Collegii S. Bonaventurae. 4 vols. Quaracchi: Typographia Collegii S. Bonaventurae, 1957.

Ambrose of Milan. *Expositio evangelii secundam Lucam,* Lib. X. *CSEL* 32 (1902), 454–528.

———. *De spiritu sancto,* Lib. III. *CSEL* 79 (1964), 149–222.

Analecta hymnica medii aevi. Ed. Guido Maria Dreves. 55 vols. Leipzig: Fues's Verlag, 1886–1922.

Anthony of Padua. *S. Antonii Pat. Sermones dominicales et in solemnitatibus quos mss. saeculi XIII codicibus qui Patavii servantur.* Ed. Antonius Maria Locatelli. Padua: Societas S. Antonii Patavini, 1895.

Aquinas, Thomas. *Summa Theologiae.* Ed. Blackfriars. 60 vols. London: McGraw-Hill Book Co., 1964–.

———. *Sermones festivi.* In *Opera Omnia.* Vol. 15. Parma: P. Fiaccadori, 1864.

Augustine of Hippo. *Sermo 232.* In *Sermons pour la Pâque. SC* 116 (1966), 260–79.

Bartholomew of Trent. *Epilogus in gesta sanctorum.* In *Bartolomeo da Trento. Domenicano e agiografo medievale.* Ed. Domenico Gobbi. Trent: Grafiche Artigianelli, 1990.

Belcari, Feo. *The Life of B. Giovanni Colombini.* London: R. Washbourne, 1874.

Berengario di S. Africano. *Vita di S. Chiara di Montefalco.* In *Archivio storico per le Marche e per l'Umbria* 1 (1884): 557–625, and 2 (1885): 193–226.

Bernard of Clairvaux. *Sermo 75. PL* 183: 1144–50.

Bernardino da Siena. *Le prediche volgari* (Quaresimale Firenze 1424). Ed. Ciro Cannarozzi, O.F.M. 2 vols. Pistoia: Cav. Alberto Pacinotti & Co., 1934.

———. *Le prediche volgari.* Ed. Piero Bargellini. Milan: Rizzoli & Co., 1936.

———. *Le prediche volgari* (Quaresimale Firenze 1425). Ed. Ciro Cannarozzi, O.F.M. 3 vols. Florence: Libreria Editrice Fiorentina, 1940.

———. *S. Bernardini Senensis Opera Omnia.* 9 vols. Quaracchi: Collegium S. Bonaventurae, 1950–65.

———. *Le prediche volgari* (Predicazione, Siena 1425). Ed. Ciro Cannarozzi, O.F.M. 2 vols. Florence: E. Rinaldi, 1958.

———. *Prediche volgari sul Campo di Siena 1427.* Ed. Carlo Delcorno. Milan: Rusconi, 1989.

———. *Prediche della settimana santa. Firenze 1425.* Ed. Marco Bartoli. Milan: Figlie di San Paolo, 1995.

Bersuire, Pierre. *Reductorium moralis.* Venice: Apud Haeredem Hieronymi Scoti, 1575.

Bertrand de la Tour. *Sermones Bertrandi de tempore et de sanctis. Una cum quadragesimali epistolari.* Strasbourg: Georg Husner (ca. 1500).

Bevegnati, Giunta. *Leggenda della vita e dei miracoli di Santa Margherita da Cortona.* Trans. E. Mariani. Vicenza: L.I.E.F., 1978.

Biblia sacra cum glossa interlineari ordinaria. Venice, 1588.

Birgitta of Sweden. *Opera Minora II.* Ed. Sten Eklund. Stockholm: Almquist & Wiksells, 1972.

———. *Revelaciones* (Book IV). Ed. Hans Aili. Stockholm: Kungl. Vitterhets Historie Och Antikvitets Akademien, 1992.

Boccaccio, Giovanni. *The Decameron.* Trans. G.H.M. McWilliam. New York: Penguin Books, 1995; 2d ed.

Bokenham, Osbern. "Mary Magdalen's Life," 101–24. In *A Legend of Holy Women.* Trans. Sheila Delany. Notre Dame, IN: University of Notre Dame Press, 1992.

Bonaventura. *Commentarius in evangelium S. Lucae,* vol. 7 (1895). In *S. Bonaventurae S.R.E. Episcopi Cardinalis Opera Omnia.* Ed. PP. Collegii S. Bonventurae. 10 vols. Quaracchi: Typ. Collegii S. Bonaventurae, 1882–1902.

———. *Sermones de tempore ac de sanctis complectens.* In *Sancti Bonaventurae ex ordine Minorum S.R.E. Episcopi Card. Albanen. eximii Ecclesiae Doctoris Operum Tomus. III.* Rome: Typographia Vaticana, 1596.

———. *De quinque festitatibus pueri Jesu,* vol. 8 (1898). In *S. Bonaventurae S.R.E. Episcopi Cardinalis Opera Omnia.* Ed. PP. Collegii S. Bonventurae. 10 vols. Quaracchi: Typ. Collegii S. Bonaventurae, 1898–1902.

———. *Bonaventure: The Soul's Journey into God, The Tree of Life, The Life of St. Francis.* Trans. Ewert Cousins. New York: Paulist Press, 1978.

Bullarium Franciscanum sive Romanorum Pontificum Constitutiones, epistolae, diplomata tribus ordinibus minorum, clarissarum, poenitentium a seraphico patriarcha Sancto Francisco institutis ab earum originibus ad nostra usque tempora concessa. Ed. Conrad Eubel, O.F.M. Rome: Typus Vaticanis, 1902.

Bullarium Ordinis FF. Praedicatorum. Ed. Thomas Ripoll. 8 vols. Rome: Hieronymus Mainardus, 1729–40.

Caesarius of Heisterbach. *Dialogus Miraculorum.* Ed. Joseph Strange. 2 vols. Cologne: J. M. Heberle, 1851.

Caffarini, Tommaso d'Antonio Nacci. *Leggenda minore di S. Caterina da Siena.* Bologna: Gaetano Romagnoli, 1868.

Camilla Battista da Varano. *Le opere spirituali.* Ed. Giacomo Boccanera. Jesi: Scuola Tipografica Francescana, 1958.

Caterina da Siena. *Le lettere di S. Caterina da Siena.* Ed. Niccolò Tommaseo. 4 vols. Florence: G. Barbèra, 1860.

———. *S. Caterina da Siena: Epistolario.* Ed. Eugenio Dupré Theseider. Rome: Tipografia del Senato, 1940.

———. *The Letters of St. Catherine of Siena.* Trans. Suzanne Noffke, O.P. (Medieval & Renaissance Texts & Studies, vol. 52). Binghamton, NY: Center for Medieval and Early Renaissance Studies, 1988.

Cavalca, Domenico. *I frutti della lingua.* Ed. G. Bottari. Rome: Antonio de' Rossi, 1754.

———. *The Life of Saint Mary Magdalen. Translated from the Italian of an Unknown Fourteenth Century Writer.* Trans. Valentina Hawtrey. London: John Lane, The Bodley Head, 1904.

———. *Specchio de' peccati.* Ed. Francesco del Furia. Florence: Tipografia all'Insegna di Dante, 1828.

———. *Vite de' santi padri.* Ed. Bartolomeo Sorio and A. Racheli. Milan: l'Ufficio generale di commissioni ed annunzi, n.d.

———. *Volgarizzamento del dialogo di San Gregorio e dell'epistola di S. Girolamo ad Eustochio.* Ed. G. Bottari. Milano: G. Silvestri, 1840.

Chiese e conventi degli ordini mendicanti in Umbria nei secoli XIII–XIV. Archivi di Orvieto. Ed. Marilena Rossi Caponeri and Lucio Riccetti. Perugia: Editrice Umbra Cooperativa, 1987.

Christine de Pisan. *The Book of the City of Ladies.* Trans. Earl Jeffrey Richards. New York: Persea Books, 1982.

Chronica XXIV generalium ordinis minorum. In *Analecta Franciscana* 3 (1897).

Chronica Fratris Nicolai Glassberger O.F.M., obs. In *Analecta Franciscana* 2 (1887).

Colombini, Giovanni. *Le lettere del B. Giovanni Colombini da Siena*. Ed. Adolfo Bartoli. Lucca: Balatresi, 1856.

Conciliorum oecumenicorum decreta. Ed. G. Alberigo, C. Leonardi, et al. (Centro di Documentazione Istituto per le Scienze Religiose—Bologna). Rome: Herder, 1962.

La confessione di Maria Magdalena. Padua: Alberto di Stendal, ca. 1474.

La confessione di Maria Maddalena. Venice and Treviso: Angelo Righettini, 1621.

Conversione di Maria Maddalena e resurrezione di Lazzaro. In *Le sacre rappresentazioni italiane. Raccolta di testi dal secolo XIII al secolo XVI*. N.p.: Bompiani, 1942.

Corpus iuris canonici. Ed. Aemilius Friedberg. 2 vols. Graz: Akademische Druck- und Verlagsanstalt, 1959.

Cronica antiqua conventus sanctae Catharinae de Pisis. Ed. Francesco Bonaini. In *Archivio storico italiano*, ser. I, 6/2 (1845): 399–593.

Cross, J. E. "Mary Magdalen in the *Old English Martyrology:* The Earliest Extant 'Narrat Josephus' Variant of Her Legend." *Speculum* 53 (1978): 16–25.

Damian, Peter. *De laude lacrymarum*. *PL* 145: 307–9.

———. *De ordine eremitarum*. *PL* 145: 327–32.

Dante Alighieri. *The Divine Comedy*. Ed. Charles S. Singleton (Italian Text, Trans., Commentary) Bollingen Series LXXX. Princeton: Princeton University Press, 1975.

De Bartholomaeis, Vincenzo. *Laude drammatiche e rappresentazioni sacre*. 3 vols. Florence: Felice le Monnier, 1943.

Decrees of the Ecumenical Councils. Trans. Norman Tanner. 2 vols. Washington, D.C.: Sheed and Ward, 1990.

Del Giudice, Giuseppe. *Una legge suntuaria inedita del 1290*. Naples: Tipografia della Regia Università, 1887.

Deuchler, Florens. *Der Ingeborgpsalter*. Berlin: Walter de Gruyter & Co, 1967.

Documentazione di vita assisana, 1300–1448. Ed. Cesare Cenci, O.F.M. (Spicilegium Bonaventurianum, vols. 10–12). 3 vols. Grottaferrata: Collegium S. Bonaventurae ad Claras Aquas, 1974.

Dominican Legend. In *Marie Madeleine et l'ordre des prêcheurs*. Ed. Bernard Montagnes, O. P. Marseilles: Atelier Sainte-Catherine, 1984.

Eadmer of Canterbury. *De quatuor virtutibus*. *PL* 159: 579–86.

Eudes de Châteauroux. *Sermones*. Ed. Johannes Baptista Pitra. In *Analecta novissima. Spicilegii solesmensis altera continuatio*. 2 vols. Frascati: Typus Tusculanus, 1883.

Filangieri, R. et al. *I registri della cancelleria angioina, recostruiti da Riccardo Filangieri con la collaborazione degli archivisti napoletani*. Naples: Accademia Pontaniana, 1950–.

Francis of Assisi. *De religiosa habitione in eremo*. In *Opuscula S. Francisci et scripta S. Clarae Assisiensium*. Ed. Ioannes M. Boccali, O.F.M. and Luciano Canonici, O.F.M. (Biblioteca Francescana, Chiesa Nuova, vol. 1). Assisi: Edizioni Porziuncola, 1978.

François de Meyronnes. *Sermones de laudibus sanctorum*. Venice: Pelegrinus de Pasqualibus, 1493.

Geoffrey of Vendôme. *Sermo IX (In festivate b. Mariae Magdalenae)*. *PL* 157: 270–74.

Giacomo della Marca. *Sermones dominicales*. Ed. Renato Lioi. 4 vols. Falconera M.: Biblioteca Francescana, 1978.

Giordano da Pisa. *Prediche sulla Genesi recitate in Firenze nel 1304*. Ed. Domenico Moreni. Florence: Magheri, 1830.

———. *La vita attiva e contemplativa predica di frate Giordano*. Ed. P. Zanotti. Verona: Tipografo Vescovile, 1831.

———. *Prediche del Beato Fra Giordano da Rivalto dell'ordine dei Predicatori. Recitate in Firenze dal MCCCIII al MCCCVI*. Ed. Domenico Moreni. 2 vols. Florence: Magheri, 1831.

———. *Quaresimale fiorentino 1305–1306*. Ed. Carlo Delcorno. Florence: Sansoni, 1974.

Girolamo di Giovanni. *La Beata Villana terziaria domenicana fiorentina del sec. XIV*. Ed. Stefano Orlandi, O.P. Florence: Il Rosario, 1955.

Gobi, Iohannes. *Liber miraculorum b. Mariae Magdalenae*. Ed. Jacqueline Sclafer. *AFP* 63 (1993): 137–206.

Gregory of Tours. *Glory of the Martyrs*. Trans. Raymond van Dam (Translated Texts for Historians. Latin Series III). Liverpool: Liverpool University Press, 1988.

Gregory the Great. *Homilia 25*. In *XL Homiliarum in Evangelia*. *PL* 76: 1188–96.

———. *Homilia 33*. In *XL Homiliarum in Evangelia*. *PL* 76: 1238–46.

———. *Homilia 3*. In *Homiliarum in Ezechielem prophetam*. *PL* 76: 806–14.

———. *Liber VI* (Cap. XXXVII). In *Moralium libri sive expositio in librum B. Job*. *PL* 75: 760–66.

———. *Ep. 22*. In *Registrum epistularum libri I–VII, Reg. II*. *CCSL* 140 (1982), 472–74.

Heiligenleben. Ungarisches Legendarium Cod. Vat. lat. 8541 (Facsimile edition and commentary). Zurich: Belser, 1990.

Holy Women of Byzantium: Ten Saints' Lives in English Translation. Ed. Alice-Mary Talbot. Washington, D.C.: Dumbarton Oaks, 1996.

Honorius III. *Sermones*. In *Opera Omnia Honorii III*. Ed. C.-A. Horoy, vol. 1. 2 vols. In *Medii Aevi biblioteca patristica seu eiusdem temporis patrologia ab anno MCCXVI usque ad concilium tridentini tempora*. Series Prima. Paris: La Bibliothèque Ecclésiastique, 1879.

Honorius Augustodunensis. *De Sancta Maria Magdalena*. In *Speculum ecclesiae*. *PL* 172: 979–82.

Hugh of Cluny. *Commonitorium ad successores suos pro sanctimonialibus Marciniacensibus*. *PL* 159: 949–52.

Hugh of Saint-Cher. *Prima pars huius operis continens textum biblie cum postilla domini hugonis cardinalis librorum infra signatorum*. 7 vols. Basel: Johann Amerbach, 1498–1502.

Humbert of Romans. *De modo prompte cudendi sermones*. In *De eruditione praedicatorum*. Ed. Marguerin de La Bigne. In *Maxima bibliotheca veterum patrum*. Vol. 25. Lyons: Anissonius, 1677.

———. *De persona praedicatoris*. In *De eruditione praedicatorum*. Ed. Joachim Joseph Berthier, O.P. In *Opera de vita regularis*. 2 vols. Rome: Typ. A. Befani, 1888–89.

Humbert of Romans. *Ad fratres de poenitentia.* In Gerard Gilles Meersseman. *Dossier de l'ordre de la pénitence au XIIIe siècle* (Spicilegium Friburgense, vol. 7). Fribourg: Editions Universitaires, 1961.

———. *De Maria Magdalena.* In *Liber de eruditione predicatorum.* Ed. Simon Tugwell, O.P. Oxford: Oxford University Press, forthcoming.

Innocent III. *Ep. 112.* In *Die Register Innocenz' III (Pontifikatsjahr 1198–99).* Ed. O. Hageneder and A. Haidacher, vol. 1, 169–70. Graz-Cologne: Hermann Böhlaus Nachf., 1964.

———. *Ep. 132 (141).* In *Die Register Innocenz' III. (Pontifikatsjahr, 1199–1200)* Ed. O. Hageneder, W. Maleszek, A. Strnad, vol. 2, 271–75. Rome-Vienna: Verlag der Oesterreichischen Akademie der Wissenschaften, 1979.

———. *Sermones.* In *Opera Omnia. PL* 217: 309–688.

———. *Sermo de Maria Magdalena.* Ed. Barthélemy Hauréau, vol. 1, 161–80. *Notices et extraits de quelques manuscrits latins de la Bibliothèque Nationale.* Paris: C. Klincksieck, 1890.

———. *Sermo de Maria Magdalena.* Ed. Katherine Ludwig Jansen. In "A Forgotten Sermon of Innocent III." Forthcoming.

———. *Sermo in resurrectione domini.* Ed. John C. Moore. In "The Sermons in Innocent III." *Römische Historische Mitteilungen* 36 (1994): 81–142.

———. *Tertius sermo in die sancto paschae.* Ed. Francesco Segna. Rome: Typ. Iuvenum Artificum a S. Josepho, 1903.

Iozzelli, Fortunato. "I miracoli nella 'legenda' di S. Margherita da Cortona." *AFH* 86 (1993): 217–76.

Isidore of Seville. *Isidori hispalensis episcopi etymologiarum sive originum.* Ed. W. M. Lindsay. 2 vols. Oxford: Clarendon Press, 1911.

Jacobus de Voragine. *Legenda aurea vulgo historia lombardica dicta.* Ed. Th. Graesse. Leipzig: Carolus Ramming, 1850; 2d ed.

———. *Sermones Quadragesimales eximii doctoris, fratris Iacobi de Voragine, ordinis praedicatorum, quondam archiepiscopi ianuensis.* Venice: Iohannes Baptista Somaschus, 1571.

———. *Sermones Aurei de praecipuis sanctorum festis quae in ecclesia celebrantur, a vetustate et in numeris prope mendis repurgati.* Mainz: Petrus Cholinus, 1616.

———. *Golden Legend.* Trans. William Granger Ryan. 2 vols. Princeton: Princeton University Press, 1993.

Jacques de Vitry. *The Historia Occidentalis of Jacques de Vitry.* Ed. John Frederick Hinnebusch, O.P. (Spicilegium Friburgense, vol. 17). Fribourg: The University Press Fribourg, 1972.

Jean de Mailly. *Abbreviatio in gestis et miraculis sanctorum.* Trans. Antoine Dondaine, O.P. as *Gestes et miracles des saints (Bibliothèque d'Histoire Dominicaine,* vol. 1). Paris: Cerf, 1947.

———. *The Life of St. Dominic.* In *Early Dominicans: Selected Writings,* ed. Simon Tugwell, O.P., 53–60. New York: Paulist Press, 1982.

Jerome. *Commentariorum in Sophoniam prophetam.* In *Commentarii in prophetas minores. CCSL* 76 (1970): 655–711.

———. *Epistola XXII (ad Eustochium). CCEL* 54 (1910), 143–210.

———. *Epistola CXXVII (ad Principiam). CCEL* 56 (1918), 145–56.

———. *Liber interpretationis hebraicorum nominum.* In *S. Hieronymi presbyteri opera (Pars I: Opera Exegetica). CCSL* 72 (1959), 1–161.

Jordanus of Quedlinburg. *Opus postillarum et sermonum Iordani de tempore*. Strasbourg, 1483.

Kempe, Margery. *The Book of Margery Kempe*. Ed. B. A. Windeatt. New York: Penguin, 1985; repr. 1994.

Laude cortonesi dal secolo XIII al XV (Biblioteca della rivista di storia e letteratura religiosa. Studi e testi, vol. 5). Ed. Giorgio Varanini et al. Florence: Leo S. Olschki, 1981.

Legenda trium sociorum. Trans. Nesta de Robeck. In *St. Francis of Assisi: Writings and Early Biographies: English Omnibus of the Sources for the Life of St. Francis*. Ed. Marion A. Habig. Chicago: Franciscan Herald Press, 1983; 4th rev. ed.

La légende dominicaine. Ed. Bernard Montagnes. In *Marie-Madeleine et l'ordre des Prêcheurs*. Marseilles: Atelier Sainte-Catherine, 1984.

Il libro di Lazero & Martha & Magdalena. Florence: Francesco Buonaccorsi, 1490.

The Life of Christina of Markyate. Ed. C. H. Talbot. Oxford: Clarendon Press, 1959; repr. 1987.

The Life of Cola di Rienzo. Trans. John Wright. Toronto: Pontifical Institute of Mediaeval Studies, 1975.

The Life of Saint Mary Magdalen and her Sister Martha. Trans. David Mycoff (Cistercian Studies Series 108). Kalamazoo, MI: Cistercian Publications, 1989.

Martin of Troppau. *Sermones Martini Ordinis Praedicatorum penitentiarii domini pape de tempore et de sanctis super epistolas et evangelia cum promptuario exemplorum*. Strasbourg, 1488.

Medieval Woman's Guide to Health: The First Gynecological Handbook. Ed. and trans. Beryl Rowland. Kent, OH: Kent State University Press, 1981.

Meditaciones vitae Christi olim S. Bonaventuro attributae. Ed. M. Stallings-Taney. *CCCM* 153 (1997).

Meditations on the Life of Christ: An Illustrated Manuscript of the Fourteenth Century. Trans. and ed. Isa Ragusa and Rosalie B. Green. Princeton: Princeton University Press, 1961.

Memoriale di Monteluce. Cronaca del monastero delle clarisse di Perugia dal 1448 al 1838. Ed. Ugolino Nicolini. S. Maria degli Angeli (Assisi): Edizioni Porziuncola, 1983.

Merchant Culture in Fourteenth-Century Venice: The Zibaldone da Canal. Trans. John E. Dotson (Medieval & Renaissance Texts & Studies, vol. 98). Binghamton, NY: Medieval & Renaissance Texts & Studies, 1994.

Misrahi, Jean. "A Vita Sanctae Mariae Magdalenae (BHL 5456) in an Eleventh-Century Manuscript." *Speculum* 18 (1943): 335–39.

Mombritius, Boninus. *Sanctuarium seu vitae sanctorum*. 2 vols. Hildesheim–New York: Georg Olms Verlag, 1978.

The Nag Hammadi Library in English. Ed. James M. Robinson. New York: Harper San Francisco, 1990; 3d rev. ed.

I necrologi di San Domenico in Camporegio. Ed. M.-H. Laurent. In *Fontes vitae S. Catharinae Senensis Historici*. Ed. M.-H. Laurent and Franciscus Valli, vol. 20. Florence: Sansoni, 1937.

Nicolas de Hanappes. *Exempla sacrae scripturae ordinata secundum alphabetum*. N.p., 1473.

Odo of Cluny (once attributed to). *Sermo II (In veneratione Sanctae Mariae Magdalenae)*. *PL* 133: 713–21.

Oratione devotissima di Santa Margarita con i sette gaudi di Santa Maria Maddalena. N.p., n.d.

Passavanti, Jacopo. *Lo specchio di vera penitenzia.* Ed. Maria Lenardon. Florence: Fiorentina, 1925.

Peter Comestor (attributed to Hildebert de Lavardin). *In festo sanctae Magdalenae sermo unicus. PL* 171: 671–78.

Petry, Ray C. *No Uncertain Sound: Sermons that Shaped the Pulpit Tradition.* Philadelphia: Westminster Press, 1948.

Peyraut, Guillaume. (Published under) Guillaume d'Auvergne. *Opera Omnia.* 2 vols. Paris-Orlèans: Ludovicus Billaine and F. Hotot, 1674.

Pierozzi, Antonino. *Lettere.* In *Lettere di santi e beati fiorentini.* Ed. Antommaria Biscioni. Florence: Francesco Moucke, 1736.

Pietro de' Natali. *Catalogus sanctorum.* Venice: Nicolaus de Frankfordia, 1516.

Pistis Sophia. Ed. Carl Schmidt. In *Nag Hammadi Studies,* trans. Violet Macdermot. Vol. 9. Leiden: E. J. Brill, 1978.

Pseudo-Antony of Padua. *Sancti Francisci assisiatis, minorum patriarchae nec non S. Antonii Paduani, eiusdem ordinis, Opera Omnia.* Ed. Iohannes de la Haye. Pedepontus (Stadt am Hof): Ioannes Gastl, 1739.

Pseudo-Augustine. *Sermo XXXV* (Ad Iudices). In *Sermones ad fratres in eremo commorantes. PL* 40: 1297–98.

Rabanus Maurus (once attributed to). *De vita Beatae Mariae Magdalenae et sororis eius Sanctae Marthae. PL* 112: 1431–1508.

Racconti esemplari di predicatori del Due e Trecento. Ed. Giorgio Varanini and Guido Baldassarri. 3 vols. Rome: Salerno Ed., 1993.

La rappresentazione et conversione di Santa Maria Maddalena. Venice: Alessandro de' Vecchi, 1606.

Raymond of Capua. *Sant'Agnese da Montepulciano.* Ed. Uga Boscaglia. Siena: Edizioni Cantagalli, 1983.

Rigaud, Eudes. *The Register of Eudes of Rouen.* Trans. Sydney M. Brown, ed. Jeremiah F. O'Sullivan. New York: Columbia University Press, 1964.

Sacchetti, Franco. *Dalle sposizioni di vangeli.* In *Opere.* Ed. Aldo Borlenghi. Milan: Rizzoli, 1957.

Sacre rappresentazioni dei secoli XIV, XV e XVI. Ed. Alessandro d'Ancona. 3 vols. Florence: Successori le Monnier, 1872.

The St. Albans Psalter (Albani Psalter). Ed. Otto Pächt, C. R. Dodwell, and Francis Wormald. London: The Warburg Institute, 1960.

St. Francis of Assisi: Writings and Early Biographies: English Omnibus of the Sources for the Life of St. Francis. Ed. Marion A. Habig. Chicago: Franciscan Herald Press, 1983; 4th rev. ed.

Salimbene de Adam. *Cronica.* Ed. Giuseppe Scalia. 2 vols. Bari: Giuseppe Laterza & Figli, 1966.

———. *The Chronicle of Salimbene de Adam.* Trans. Joseph L. Baird, Giuseppe Baglivi, and John Robert Kane (Medieval & Renaissance Texts & Studies, vol. 40). Binghamton, NY: Medieval & Renaissance Texts & Studies, 1986.

Santa Francesca Romana. Edizione critica dei trattati latini di Giovanni Mattiotti. Ed. Alessandra Bartolomei Romagnoli. Vatican City: Libreria Editrice Vaticana, 1994.

Savonarola, Girolamo. *Edizione nazionale delle opere di Giralomo Savonarola*. 24 vols. Rome: A. Belardetti, 1955–.

Sermones thesauri novi de sanctis. Strasbourg: Martinus Flach, 1488.

Sette gaudi di Santa Maria Maddalena. N.p., n.d.

Silvestro Mazzolini da Prierio. *Aurea Rosa idest preclarissima expositio super evangelia totius anni de tempore et de sanctis tum secundum Ordinem predicatorum quam secundum Curia continens Flores et Rosas omnium expositionum Sanctorum doctorum Antiq. Preclarissimi et excellentissimi Sacre Theologie Doctoris Magistri Silvestri de Prierio pedemontani Sacri Ordinis Fratrum predicatorum de observantia*. Bologna, 1524.

———. *Vita de la seraphina e ferventissima amatrice de Jesu Christo salvatore sancta Maria Magdalena*. In *Opere vulgare*. Milan, 1519.

Simone da Roma, O.E.S.A. *Libro over legenda della Beata Helena da Udene*. Ed. Andrea Tilatti. Tavagnacco (UD): Casamassima, 1988.

Sister Catherine Treatise. Trans. Elvira Borgstädt. In *Meister Eckhart: Teacher and Preacher,* ed. Bernard McGinn, 349–87. New York: Paulist Press, 1986.

Speculum perfectionis (minus). Ed. Marino Bigaroni, O.F.M. (Biblioteca Francescana, vol. 3). Assisi: Ed. Porziuncola, 1983.

Stapulensis, Jacobus Faber. *De Maria Magdalena, et triduo Christi disceptatio*. Paris: Henri Estienne, 1517.

Stephen de Bourbon. *Le traité des sept dons du saint esprit*. Ed. A. Lecoy de la Marche. In *Anecdotes historiques, légendes et apologues tirés du recueil inédit de E. de Bourbon*. Paris: Librairie Renouard, H. Loones, 1877.

Tertullian. *De cultu feminarum*. Trans. "The Apparel of Women." In *Disciplinary, Moral and Ascetical Works*. Trans. Edwin A. Quain (The Fathers of the Church, vol. 40). New York: The Fathers of the Church, 1959.

Thomas of Celano. *Vita prima*. Trans. Placid Hermann. In *St. Francis of Assisi: Writings and Early Biographies: English Omnibus of the Sources for the Life of St. Francis*. Ed. Marion A. Habig. Chicago: Franciscan Herald Press, 1983; 4th rev. ed.

Ubertino da Casale. *Arbor vitae crucifixae*. Venice: De Bonettis de Papa, 1485.

Ugo da Prato Florido. *Sermones de sanctis per annum*. Paris: O. Petit, 1542.

Umiltà da Faenza. *Sermones S. Humilitatis de Faventia Abbatissae Ordinis Vallisumbrosae nunc primum in lucem editi*. Ed. D. Torello Sala. Florence: Officina Calasantiana, 1884.

———. *I sermoni di Umiltà da Faenza*. Ed. Adele Simonetti. Spoleto: Centro italiano di studi sull'alto medioevo, 1995.

Van Dijk, Stephen. *The Ordinal of the Papal Court from Innocent III to Boniface VIII and Related Documents*. Completed by Joan Hazelden Walker (Spicilegium Friburgense, vol. 22). Fribourg: The University Press, 1975.

Vincent of Beauvais. *Speculum Historiale* (Bk. 4 of *Speculum Maioris*). Graz: Akademische Druck- und Verlagsanstalt, 1965; repr. of Douai, 1624.

Vita del povero et humile servo de Dio Francesco. Ed. Marino Bigaroni (Biblioteca Francescana, Chiesa Nuova, vol. 4). Assisi: Edizioni Porziuncola, 1985.

Vito da Cortona. *Leggenda della Beata Umiliana de' Cerchi*. Ed. Domenico Moreni. Florence: Magheri, 1827.

Warner, George. *Queen Mary's Psalter. Miniatures and Drawings by an English Artist of the Fourteenth Century*. London: Trustees of the British Museum, 1912.

Women Defamed and Women Defended: An Anthology of Medieval Texts. Ed. Alcuin Blamires, Karen Pratt, and C. W. Marx. Oxford: Clarendon Press, 1992.

SECONDARY SOURCES

Abbate, G. "Il *Liber Epilogorum* di fra Bartolomeo da Trento." In *Miscellanea Pio Paschini* I, 269–92. Rome: Facultas Theologica Pontificii Athenaei Lateranensis, 1948–49.

Adnes, Pierre. "Larmes." In *DS* 9 (1976), 287–303.

———. "Pénitence." In *DS* 12.1 (1984), 943–1010.

Amann, Émile. "Pénitence-Repentir." In *DTC* 12 (1933), 722–48.

Andreucci, Salvatore. "La compagnia dei disciplinati di S. Francesco e S. Maria Maddalena in Lucca." *Bollettino della r. deputazione di storia patria per l'Umbria* 68/2 (1971): 233–40.

Andrews, Frances. *The Early Humiliati: The Development of an Order c. 1176–1270.* Cambridge: Cambridge University Press, forthcoming.

Arquillière, H. X. "Jacques de Viterbo." In *DTC* 6 (1947), 305–9.

Atkinson, Clarissa. *Mystic and Pilgrim: The Book and World of Margery Kempe.* Ithaca, NY: Cornell University Press, 1983.

———. "'Precious Balsam in a Fragile Glass:' The Ideology of Virginity in the Later Middle Ages." *Journal of Family History* Summer (1983): 131–43.

Bacchi, G. "Il monastero di 'S. Elisabetta delle Convertite' di Firenze." *Bollettino Storico Agostiniano* 7/5 (1931): 145–47; *BSA* 7/9 (1931): 234–38; *BSA* 8/4 (1932): 150–52; and *BSA* 8/6 (1932): 182–83.

Bakhtin, Mikhail, M. *The Dialogic Imagination.* Ed. Michael Holquist. Trans. Caryl Emerson and Michael Holquist. Austin: University of Texas Press, 1981.

Baldwin, John W. *Masters, Preachers and Merchants: The Social Views of Peter the Chanter and His Circle.* 2 vols. Princeton: Princeton University Press, 1970.

Banker, James R. *Death in the Community: Memorialization and Confraternities in an Italian Commune in the Late Middle Ages.* Athens, GA: University of Georgia Press, 1988.

Banta, Frank G. "Berthold von Regensburg." Vol. 1, 817–23. In *Die deutsche Literatur des Mittelalters, Verfasserlexikon.* 8 vols. Berlin: Walter de Gruyter, 1978–.

Bartlett, Anne Clark. *Male Authors, Female Readers: Representation and Subjectivity in Middle English Devotional Literature.* Ithaca, NY: Cornell University Press, 1995.

Bataillon, Louis-Jacques. *La prédication au XIIIe siècle en France et Italie. Etudes et documents.* Aldershot, England: Variorum, 1993.

Battistero di Parma. 2 vols. Milan: Franco Maria Ricci, 1992–93.

Beaulieu, Marie-Anne Polo de. "La condamnation des soins de beauté par les prédicateurs du Moyen Age (XIIIème–XVème siècles)." In *Les soins de beauté. Moyen Age début des temps Modernes* (Actes du IIIe Colloque International, Grasse [26–28 April 1985]), 297–310. Nice: Centre d'Études Médiévales de Nice, 1987.

Bell, David N. *What Nuns Read: Books and Libraries in Medieval English Nunneries.* Kalamazoo, MI: Cistercian Publications, 1995.

Benson, Robert L., and Giles Constable, ed. *Renaissance and Renewal in the Twelfth Century.* Cambridge, MA: Harvard University Press, 1982.

Benvenuti Papi, Anna. "Cerchi, Umiliana dei." In *DBI* 23 (1979), 692–96.

———. *'In castro poenitentiae': santità e società femminile nell'Italia medievale.* Rome: Herder, 1990.

———. "Mendicant Friars and Female Pinzochere in Tuscany: From Social Marginality to Models of Sanctity." In *Women and Religion,* ed. Bornstein and Rusconi, 84–103.

Bériou, Nicole. "Autour de Latran IV (1215): La naissance de la confession moderne et sa diffusion." In *Pratiques de la confession. Des pères du désert à Vatican II,* 73–93. Paris: Cerf, 1983.

———. *La prédication de Ranulphe de la Houblonnière. Sermons aux clercs et aux simples gens à Paris au XIIIe.* 2 vols. Paris: Études Augustiniennes, 1987.

———, and François-Olivier Touati. *Voluntate Dei leprosus: les lépreux entre conversion et exclusion aux XIIème et XIIIème siècles.* Spoleto: Centro italiano di studi sull'alto medioevo, 1991.

———. "La Madeleine dans les sermons parisiens du XIIIe siècle." *MEFRM* 104/1 (1992): 269–340.

———. "The Right of Women to Give Religious Instruction in the Thirteenth Century." In *Women Preachers and Prophets,* 134–45.

———, and D. L. d'Avray. *Modern Questions about Medieval Sermons. Essays on Marriage, Death, History and Sanctity* (Biblioteca di Medioevo Latino, 11). Spoleto: Centro italiano di studi sull'alto medioevo, 1995.

Berlioz, Jacques. "Images de la confession dans la prédication au début au XIVe siècle. L'exemple de l'*Alphabetum Narrationum* d'Arnold de Liège." In *Pratiques de la confession. Des pères du désert à Vatican II,* 95–115. Paris: Cerf, 1983.

Bezzi, Quirino. "Gli affreschi di Giovanni e Battista Baschenis di Averaria nella chiesa di S. Maria Maddalena di Cusiano." *Studi Trentini* 49 (1970): 358–71.

Bilinkoff, Jodi. "Establishing Authority: A Peasant Visionary and Her Audience in Early Sixteenth-Century Spain." *Studia Mystica* 18 (1997): 36–58.

Biller, Peter. "The Common Woman in the Western Church in the Thirteenth and Early Fourteenth Centuries." In *Women in the Church,* ed. W. J. Sheils and Diana Wood, 127–57. Oxford: Basil Blackwell, 1990.

Binns, Alison. *Dedications of Monastic Houses in England and Wales, 1066–1216.* Woodbridge, England: Boydell Press, 1989.

Blamires, Alcuin, and C. W. Marx. "Woman Not to Preach: A Disputation in British Library MS Harley 31." *Journal of Medieval Latin* 3 (1993): 34–63.

———. "Women and Preaching in Medieval Orthodoxy, Heresy and Saints' Lives." *Viator* 26 (1995): 135–52.

Bloomfield, Morton. *The Seven Deadly Sins: An Introduction to the History of a Religious Concept with Special Reference to English Literature.* East Lansing, MI: Michigan State College Press, 1952.

Boesch Gajano, Sofia, and Odile Redon. "La *Legenda Maior* di Raimondo da Capua, costruzione di una santa." In *Atti del simposio internazionale Caterin-iano-Bernardiniano* (Siena 17–20 April 1980), ed. Domenico Maffei and Paolo Nardi, 15–35. Siena: Accademia Senese degli Intronati, 1982.

Bologna, Ferdinando. *I pittori alla corte angioina di Napoli 1266–1414.* Rome: Ugo Bozzi, 1969.

Bolton, Brenda. "Mulieres Sanctae." *Studies in Church History* 10 (1973): 77–95.

Bolton, Brenda. "Vitae Matrum: A Further Aspect of the Frauenfrage." In *Medieval Women,* ed. Derek Baker, 253–73. Oxford: Basil Blackwell, 1978.

———. *Innocent III: Studies on Papal Authority and Pastoral Care.* Aldershot, England: Variorum, 1995.

Bonniwell, William R. *A History of the Dominican Liturgy 1215–1945.* New York: Joseph F. Wagner, 1945; 2d ed.

Borea, Evelina. "I ritrovati affreschi medievali della Cappella Minutolo nel Duomo di Napoli." *Bollettino d'Arte,* 4th series, 47 (1962): 11–23.

Bornstein, Daniel E. *The Bianchi of 1399: Popular Devotion in Late Medieval Italy.* Ithaca, NY: Cornell University Press, 1993.

Børresen, Kari Elisabeth. *Subordination and Equivalence: The Nature and Role of Woman in Augustine and Thomas Aquinas.* Trans. Charles H. Talbot. Washington, D.C.: University Press of America, 1981.

Bougerol, J.-G. *La théologie de l'espérance aux XIIe et XIIIe siècles.* 2 vols. Paris: Études Augustiniennes, 1985.

Boureau, Alain. *La Legende Dorée: Le système narratif de Jacques de Voragine (†1298).* Paris: Cerf, 1984.

Bovon, Françoise. "Le privilège pascal de Marie-Madeleine." In *Révélations et Écritures: Nouveau Testament et littérature apocryphe chrétienne,* 215–230. Geneva: Éditions Labor et Fides, 1993.

Boxler, M. *"Ich bin ein Predigerin und Appostlorin." Die deutschen Maria Magdalena-Legenden des Mittelalters (1300–1550).* (Deutsche Literatur von den Anfängen bis 1700, 22) Berne: Peter Lang, 1996.

Boyd, Catherine. *A Cistercian Nunnery in Mediaeval Italy: The Story of Rifreddo in Saluzzo, 1220–1300.* Cambridge: Harvard University Press, 1943.

Boyer, Jean-Paul. *"Ecce rex tuus.* Le roi et le royaume dans les sermons de Robert de Naples." *Revue Mabillon* 67 (1995): 101–36.

———. "Prédication et état napolitain dans la première moitié du XIVe siècle." In *L'État Angevin,* 126–57.

Boyle, Leonard E. "The Summa for Confessors as a Genre and Its Religious Intent." In *The Pursuit of Holiness in Late Medieval and Renaissance Religion (Studies in Medieval and Renaissance Thought),* ed. Charles Trinkhaus and Heiko A. Oberman, 126–30. Leiden: E. J. Brill, 1974.

———. "Popular Piety in the Middle Ages: What Is Popular?" *Florilegium* 4 (1982): 184–93.

Bracaloni, Leone. "Origine, evoluzione ed affermazione della Corona Francescana Mariana." *Studi Francescani* (1932): 257–95.

Brady, Ignace. "Jean de La Rochelle." In *DS* 8 (1974), 599–602.

Braeckmans, L. *Confession et communion au moyen âge et au concile de trente.* Gembloux: J. Duculot, 1971.

Brett, Edward Tracy. *Humbert of Romans: His Life and Views of Thirteenth Century Society.* Toronto: Pontifical Institute of Medieval Studies, 1984.

Brody, Saul N. *The Disease of the Soul: Leprosy in Medieval Literature.* Ithaca, NY: Cornell University Press, 1974.

Brooke, Christopher N. L. "The Dedications of Cambridge Colleges and Their Chapels." In *Medieval Cambridge: Essays on the Pre-Reformation University,* ed. Patrick Zutshi, 7–20. Woodbridge: Boydell Press, 1993.

Brown, Peter. *The Cult of the Saints: Its Rise and Function in Latin Christianity.* Chicago: University of Chicago Press, 1981.

———. *The Body and Society: Men, Women, and Sexual Renunciation in Early Christianity.* New York: Columbia University Press, 1988.

Brucker, Gene. *The Society of Renaissance Florence: A Documentary Study.* New York: Harper Torchbooks, 1971.

Brundage, James A. "Prostitution in the Medieval Canon Law." *Signs* 1/4 (1976): 825–45.

———. "Sumptuary Laws and Prostitution in Late Medieval Italy." *Journal of Medieval History* 13 (1987): 343–55.

Bruzelius, Caroline. "Queen Sancia of Mallorca and the Convent Church of Sta. Chiara in Naples." *Memoirs of the American Academy in Rome* 40 (1995): 69–100.

———. "Charles I, Charles II, and the Development of an Angevin Style in the Kingdom of Sicily." In *L'État Angevin,* 99–114.

Buc, Philippe. "Vox Clamantis in Deserto? Pierre le Chantre et la prédication laïque." *Revue Mabillon,* n.s. 4, 65 (1993): 5–47.

Buckley, Jorunn Jacobsen. "'The Holy Spirit is a Double Name': Holy Spirit, Mary, and Sophia in the *Gospel of Philip.*" In *Images of the Feminine in Gnosticism,* ed. Karen King, 211–27. Philadelphia: Fortress Press, 1988.

Budge, E. A. Wallis. *Coptic Apocrypha in the Dialect of Upper Egypt.* Oxford: Horace Hart, 1913.

———. *Miscellaneous Coptic Texts in the Dialect of Upper Egypt.* Oxford: Oxford University Press, 1915.

Burke, Peter. *Popular Culture in Early Modern Europe.* New York: New York University Press, 1978.

———. *The Historical Anthropology of Early Modern Italy.* Cambridge: Cambridge University Press, 1987.

Butler, Dom Cuthbert. *Western Mysticism: The Teaching of Augustine, Gregory and Bernard on Contemplation and the Contemplative Life.* New York: Harper Torchbooks, 1966; 2d rev. ed.

Bynum, Caroline Walker. *Jesus as Mother: Studies in Spirituality of the High Middle Ages.* Berkeley: University of California Press, 1982.

———. *Holy Feast, Holy Fast: The Religious Significance of Food to Medieval Women.* Berkeley: University of California Press, 1987.

———. "Women's Stories, Women's Symbols: A Critique of Victor Turner's Theory of Liminality." In *Fragmentation and Redemption: Essays on Gender and the Human Body in Medieval Religion,* 27–51. New York: Zone Books, 1991.

Cadden, Joan. *Meanings of Sex Differences in the Middle Ages: Medicine, Science, and Culture.* Cambridge: Cambridge University Press, 1993.

Callaey, Frédégard. *L'idéalisme franciscain spirituel au XIVe siècle. Étude sur Ubertin de Casale.* Louvain: Bureau du Recueil, 1911.

Callman, Ellen. "Thebaid Studies." *Antichità Viva* 14 (1975): 3–22.

Camera, Matteo. *Annali delle due Sicilie: dall'origine e fondazione della monarchia fino a tutto il regno dell'augusto sovrano Carlo III. Borbone.* 2 vols. Naples: Dalla Stamperia e Cartiere del Fibreno, 1806.

Camera, Matteo. *Elucubrazioni storico-diplomatiche su Giovanna Ia Regina di Napoli e Carlo III di Durazzo.* Salerno: Tipografia Nazionale, 1889.

Cannon, Joanna. "Simone Martini, The Dominicans and the Early Sienese Polyptych." *Journal of the Warburg and Courtauld Institutes* 45 (1982): 69–93.

Caplan, H. "The Four Senses of Scriptural Interpretation and the Medieval Theory of Preaching." *Speculum* 4 (1929): 282–90.

Carli, Enzo. *Il Museo di Pisa.* Pisa: Pacini, 1974.

———. *Gli affreschi di Belverde.* Florence: Edam, 1977.

Casagrande, Carla, and Silvana Vecchio. *I peccati della lingua: Disciplina ed etica della parola nella cultura medievale.* Rome: Istituto della Enciclopedia Italiana, 1987.

Casagrande, Carla. "The Protected Woman." Trans. Clarissa Botsford. In *Silences of the Middle Ages,* ed. Christiane Klapisch-Zuber, 70–104. *A History of Women in the West.* Vol. 2. Cambridge, MA: Belknap Press of Harvard University Press, 1992.

Casagrande, Giovanna. "Movimenti religiosi umbri e Chiara da Montefalco." In *S. Chiara da Montefalco e il suo tempo,* ed. Claudio Leonardi and Enrico Menestò, 53–70 (Quaderni del centro per il collegamento degli studi medievali e umanistici nell'Università di Perugia, vol. 12). Florence: La Nuova Italia Editrice, 1985.

———. "Women in Confraternities between the Middle Ages and the Modern Age. Research in Umbria." *Confraternitas* 5/2 (1994): 3–13.

———. *Religiosità penitenziale e città al tempo dei comuni.* Rome: Istituto Storico dei Cappuccini, 1995.

Castelnuovo, Enrico. "Appunti per la storia della pittura gotica in Piemonte." *Arte Antica e Moderna* 13–16 (1961): 97–111.

Cheney, C. R. "Rules for the Observance of Feast-Days in Medieval England." *Bulletin of the Institute of Historical Research* 34 (1961): 117–47.

Chenu, M.-D. *Nature, Man and Society in the Twelfth Century: Essays on New Theological Perspectives in the Latin West.* Ed. and Trans. Jerome Taylor and Lester K. Little. Chicago: University of Chicago Press, 1968.

Cioffari, Gerardo. *Storia dei Domenicani in Puglia (1221–1350).* Bari: Edizioni Levante, 1986.

Clanchy, M. T. *From Memory to Written Record: England 1066–1307.* Oxford: Blackwell, 1993; 2d ed.

Clay, Rotha Mary. *The Medieval Hospitals of England.* London: Frank Cass & Co., 1906; repr. 1966.

Clemens, Raymond. *The Establishment of the Cult of Mary Magdalen in Provence, 1279–1543.* Ph.D. diss., Columbia University, 1997.

Coakley, John. "Gender and Authority of Friars: The Significance of Holy Women for Thirteenth-Century Franciscans and Dominicans." *Church History* 60 (1991): 445–60.

———. "Friars as Confidants of Holy Women in Medieval Dominican Hagiography." In *Images of Sainthood in Medieval Europe,* ed. Renate Blumenfeld-Kosinski and Timea Szell, 222–46. Ithaca, NY: Cornell University Press, 1991.

———. "Friars, Sanctity, and Gender: Mendicant Encounters with Saints, 1250–1325." In *Medieval Masculinities: Regarding Men in the Middle Ages,* ed. Clare A. Lees, 91–110. Minneapolis, MN: University of Minnesota Press, 1994.

Cohen, Sherrill. *The Evolution of Women's Asylums since 1500. From Refuges for Ex-*

Prostitutes to Shelters for Battered Women. Oxford: Oxford University Press, 1992.

Cohn, Samuel K. Jr. *Death and Property in Siena, 1205–1800: Strategies for the Afterlife*. Baltimore: Johns Hopkins University Press, 1988.

————. *The Cult of Remembrance and the Black Death: Six Renaissance Cities in Central Italy*. Baltimore: Johns Hopkins University Press, 1992.

Il complesso monumentale di Santa Croce. Ed. Umberto Baldini and Bruno Nardini. Florence: Nardini Editore, 1983.

Constable, Giles. "The Interpretation of Mary and Martha." In *Three Studies in Medieval Religious and Social Thought*, 3–141. Cambridge: Cambridge University Press, 1995.

Couchman, Jane. "Action and Passio: The Iconography of the Scene of Christ at the Home of Mary and Martha." *Studi Medievali*, 3d series, 26/2 (1985): 711–19.

Le couvent royal de Saint-Maximin. Ed. Jacques Paul. In *Mémoire Dominicaine* 8 (1996).

Cowdrey, H.E.J. "The Papacy, the Patarenes and the Church of Milan." *Transactions of the Royal Historical Society*, 5th series, 18 (1968): 25–48.

The Crannied Wall: Women, Religion, and the Arts in Early Modern Europe. Ed. Craig Monson. Ann Arbor, MI: University of Michigan Press, 1992.

Creative Women in Medieval and Early Modern Italy: A Religious and Artistic Renaissance. Ed. E. Ann Matter and John Coakley. Philadelphia: University of Pennsylvania Press, 1994.

Cuesta, A. Martínez. "Maddalene." In *DIP* 5 (1978), 801–12.

Culto dei santi, istituzioni e classi sociali in età preindustriale. Ed. Sofia Boesch Gajano and Lucia Sebastiani. L'Aquila and Rome: L. U. Japadre, 1984.

d'Addario, A. "Antonino Pierozzi." In *DBI* 3 (1961), 523–32.

Dalarun, Jacques. "Robert d'Arbrissel et les Femmes." *Annales E.S.C.* 39/5 (1984): 1140–60.

————. "La Madeleine dans l'Ouest de la France au tournant des XIe–XIIe siècles." *MEFRM* 104/1 (1992): 71–119.

————. *Lapsus Linguae: La légende de Claire de Rimini* (Biblioteca di Medioevo Latino, vol. 6). Spoleto: Centro italiano di studi sull'alto medioevo, 1994.

d'Amsterdam, Baudouin. "Guibert de Tournai." In *DS* 6 (1965), 1139–46.

Davis, Charles T. "Remigio de' Girolami O.P. (d. 1319) lector of S. Maria Novella in Florence." In *Le scuole degli ordini mendicanti (secoli XIII–XIV)*, 283–304. (Convegni del Centro di studi sulla spiritualità medievale XVII). Todi: Accademia Tudertina, 1978.

Davis, Natalie Zemon. "Some Tasks and Themes in the Study of Popular Religion." In *The Pursuit of Holiness in Late Medieval and Renaissance Religion (Studies in Medieval and Renaissance Thought)*, ed. C. Trinkhaus and H. Oberman, 307–36. Leiden: E. J. Brill, 1974.

————. *Fiction in the Archives: Pardon Tales and Their Tellers in Sixteenth-Century France*. Stanford: Stanford University Press, 1987.

Davis, Virginia. *William Waynflete: Bishop and Educationalist*. Woodbridge: Boydell Press, 1993.

d'Avray, D. L. *The Preaching of the Friars: Sermons Diffused from Paris before 1300*. Oxford: Oxford University Press, 1985.

d'Avray, D. L. *Death and the Prince: Memorial Preaching before 1350*. Oxford: Clarendon Press, 1994.

———. "Katherine of Alexandria and Mass Communication in Germany: Woman as Intellectual." In N. Bériou and D. L. d'Avray, *Modern Questions about Medieval Sermons. Essays on Marriage, Death, History and Sanctity*, 401–8. (Biblioteca di Medioevo Latino, 11). Spoleto: Centro italiano di studi sull'alto medioevo, 1995.

de Feudis, Nicola. "S. Domenico e la cappella de la 'Maddalena.'" In *Storia ed arte in Manfredonia*, 1–7. Foggia: la Capitanata, 1967.

Delaruelle, E. "Dévotion populaire et hérésie au Moyen Age." In *Hérésies et sociétés dans l'Europe pré-industrielle 11e–18e siècles*, ed. Jacques Le Goff, 147–55. Paris: Mouton & Co., 1968.

Delcorno, Carlo. *La predicazione nell'età comunale*. Florence: Sansoni, 1974.

———. *Giordano da Pisa e l'antica predicazione volgare*. Florence: Leo S. Olschki, 1975.

———. "Origini della predicazione francescana." In *Francesco d'Assisi e francescanesimo dal 1216 al 1226*, 127–60. (Atti dei convegni della società internazionale di Studi Francescani, vol. 6). Assisi: Typografia Porziuncola, 1977.

———. "Cavalca, Domenico." In *DBI* 22 (1979), 577–86.

———. "Il racconto agiografico nella predicazione dei secoli XIII–XV." In *Agiografia nell'occidente cristiano secoli XIII–XV*, 79–114 (Atti dei Convegni Lincei 48). Rome: Accademia Nazionale dei Lincei, 1980.

———. "Rassegna di studi sulla predicazione medievale e umanistica (1970–80)." In *Lettere Italiane* 33/2 (1981): 235–76.

———. "La *Legenda Aurea* e la narrativa dei Predicatori." In *Jacopo da Varagine*, 27–49 (Atti del I Convegno di Studi [1985]). Ed. Giovanni Farris and Benedetto Tino Delfino. Varazze: Centro Studi Jacopo da Varagine, 1987.

———. "Le *Vitae patrum* nella letteratura religiosa medievale (secc. XIII–XV)." *Lettere Italiane* 2 (1991): 187–207.

Delenda. Odile. "Sainte Marie-Madeleine et l'application du décret Tridentin (1563) sur les *Saintes-Images*." In *Marie Madeleine*, Ed. Duperray, 191–210.

Delhaye, Philippe. "Guillaume Peyraut." In *DS* 6 (1967), 1229–34.

del Punta, F., S. Donati, and C. Luna. "Egidio Romano." In *DBI* 42 (1993), 319–41.

Deremble, Colette. "Les premiers cycles d'images consacrées à Marie Madeleine." *MEFRM* 104/1 (1992): 187–208.

Dinzelbacher, Peter. "Rifiuto dei ruoli, risveglio religioso ed esperienza mistica delle donne nel medioevo." Ed. Marco Vannini, trans. Giovanna Fozzer. In *Movimento religioso e mistica femminile nel medioevo*, 31–89. Milan: Edizioni Paoline, 1993.

Dondaine, A. "Le dominicain français Jean de Mailly et la Légende Dorée." *Archives d'histoire dominicaine* 1 (1946): 53–102.

Dono, A. *Storia dell'affresco in Alatri*. Rome: Istituto Poligrafico e Zecca dello Stato, 1980.

Dorn, Erhard. *Der Sündige Heilige in der Legende des Mittelalters*. Munich: Wilhelm Fink, 1967.

Douglas, Mary. *Purity and Danger: An Analysis of the Concepts of Pollution and Taboo*. London: Ark Paperbacks, 1985; repr.

Duby, Georges. *The Three Orders: Feudal Society Imagined*. Trans. Arthur Goldhammer. Chicago: University of Chicago Press, 1980.

Duchesne, L. "La légende de Sainte Marie-Madeleine." *Annales du Midi* 5 (1893): 1–33. Reprinted in *Fastes épiscopaux de l'ancienne Gaule*. Paris: Albert Fontemoing, 1907.

Dunabin, Jean. *Charles I of Anjou: Power, Kingship and State-Making in Thirteenth-Century Europe*. London: Longman, 1998.

Duperray, Eve, ed. *Marie Madeleine dans la mystique, les arts et les lettres* (Actes du Colloque International Avignon 20–21–22 juillet 1988). Paris: Beauchesne, 1989.

———. "Le Carmen de *Beata Maria Magdalena:* Marie-Madeleine dans l'oeuvre de François Pétrarque: image emblématique de la Belle Laure." In *Marie Madeleine,* ed. Duperray, 273–88.

Duval, André. "Martin de Troppau." In *DS* 10 (1980), 964–65.

———. "Nicolas de Hanappes." In *DS* 11 (1982), 283–84.

Early Dominicans: Selected Writings. Ed. Simon Tugwell. New York: Paulist Press, 1982.

Echols, Anne, and Marty Williams. *The Annotated Index of Medieval Women*. New York: M. Wiener, 1992.

Eliade, Mircea. *Images and Symbols: Studies in Religious Symbolism*. Trans. Philip Mairet. New York: Sheed and Ward, 1961.

Elkins, Sharon. *Holy Women of Twelfth-Century England*. Chapel Hill, NC: University of North Carolina Press, 1988.

Elliott, Alison Goddard. *Roads to Paradise: Reading the Lives of the Early Saints*. Hanover, NH: University Press of New England, 1987.

Elliott, Dyan. *Spiritual Marriage: Sexual Abstinence in Medieval Wedlock*. Princeton: Princeton University Press, 1993.

Elliott, Janis. "The Judgement of the Commune: The Frescoes of the Magdalen Chapel in Florence," *Zeitschrift für Kunstgeschichte* 61 (1998): 509–19.

Elliott, J. K. *The Apocryphal New Testament*. Oxford: Oxford University Press, 1993.

Eremitismo nel francescanesimo medievale (Atti del XVII convegno della Società Internazionale di Studi Francescani, Assisi, 12–14 ottobre 1989). Perugia: Università degli Studi di Perugia, Centro di Studi Francescani, 1991.

Esposito, Anna. "St. Francesca and the Female Religious Communities of Fifteenth-Century Rome." In *Women and Religion,* ed. Bornstein and Rusconi, 197–218.

L'État Angevin: Pouvoir, culture et société entre XIIIe et XIVe siècle (Collection de l'École Française de Rome, 245). Rome: l'École Française de Rome, 1998.

Facchiano, Anna Maria. *Monasteri femminili e nobiltà tra Medioevo ed età moderna: Il necrologio di S. Patrizia, sec. XII–XVI*. Salerno: Ed. Studi Storici meridionali, 1992.

Faillon, E.-M. *Monuments inédits sur l'apostolat de Sainte Marie-Madeleine en Provence et sur les autres apôtres de cette contrée, Saint Lazare, Saint Maximin, Sainte Marthe*. 2 vols. Paris: J.-P. Migne, 1859.

Farmer, Sharon. *Communities of Saint Martin: Legend and Ritual in Medieval Tours*. Ithaca, NY: Cornell University Press, 1991.

Feuillas, Michel. "La controverse Magdalénienne au milieu du XVIIe siècle. Ripostes provençales à Jean de Launoy." In *Marie Madeleine dans la mystique, les arts et les lettres,* ed. Eve Duperray, 89–109.

Fiorenza, Elisabeth Schüssler. "Feminist Theology as a Critical Theology of Liberation." *Theological Studies* 36 (1975): 605–26.

———. *In Memory of Her: A Feminist Theological Reconstruction of Christian Origins.* New York: Crossroad, 1983.

Fleith, Barbara. "Legenda aurea: destination, utilisateurs, propagation. L'histoire de la diffusion du légendier au XIIIe siècle." In *Raccolte di vite di sante dal XIII al XVIII secolo,* ed. Sofia Boesch Gajano, 41–48. Fasano di Brindisi: Schena, 1990.

Frugoni, Chiara. "Altri luoghi, cercando il paradiso (Il ciclo di Buffalmacco nel Camposanto di Pisa e la committenza domenicana)." *Annali della Scuola Normale Superiore di Pisa* (Classe di Lettere e Filosofia), ser. III, vol. XVIII/4 (1988): 1557–1643.

Gamboso, V. "I sermoni festivi di Servasanto da Faenza nel codice 490 dell'Antoniana." *Il Santo* 13/1 (1973): 3–88.

Garancini, Gianfranco. "Persona, peccato, penitenza. Studi sulla disciplina penitenziale nell'alto medio evo." *Rivista di storia del diritto italiano* 47 (1974): 19–87.

Gardner, Julian. "Seated Kings, Sea-Faring Saints and Heraldry: Some Themes in Angevin Iconography." In *L'État Angevin,* 115–26.

Garth, Helen Meredith. *Saint Mary Magdalene in Mediaeval Literature.* Baltimore: Johns Hopkins Press, 1950.

Gavitt, Philip. *Charity and Children in Renaissance Florence: The Ospedale degli Innocenti 1410–1536.* Ann Arbor, MI: University of Michigan, 1990.

Geary, Patrick J. *Furta Sacra: Thefts of Relics in the Central Middle Ages.* Princeton: Princeton University Press, 1978.

———. *Living with the Dead in the Middle Ages.* Ithaca, NY: Cornell University Press, 1994.

Giannelli, Ciro. "Témoignages patristiques grecs en faveur d'une apparition du Christ ressuscité à la Vierge Marie," *Révue des Études Byzantines (Mélanges Martin Jugie)* 11 (1953): 106–19.

Gibaldi, Joseph. "Petrarch and the Baroque Magdalene Tradition." *The Hebrew University Studies in Literature* 3/1 (1975): 1–19.

Gilchrist, Roberta. *Gender and Material Culture: The Archeology of Religious Women.* New York: Routledge, 1994.

———. *Contemplation and Action: The Other Monasticism.* London: Leicester University Press, 1995.

Gill, Katherine. "Open Monasteries for Women in Late Medieval and Early Modern Italy: Two Roman Examples." In *The Crannied Wall,* ed. Craig A. Monson, 15–47.

———. "Women and the Production of Religious Literature in the Vernacular, 1300–1500," in *Creative Women,* 64–104.

———. "*Scandala:* Controversies Concerning Clausura and Women's Religious Communities in Late Medieval Italy." In *Christendom and its Discontents: Exclusion, Persecution and Rebellion, 1000–1500,* ed. Scott Waugh and Peter D. Diehl, 177–203. Cambridge: Cambridge University Press, 1996.

Goffen, Rona. *Piety and Patronage in Renaissance Venice: Bellini, Titian and the Franciscans*. New Haven: Yale University Press, 1986.

Gondras, Alexandre-Jean. "Matthieu d'Aquasparta." In *DS* 10 (1980), 799–802.

Goodich, Michael, E. *Violence and Miracle in the Fourteenth Century: Private Grief and Public Salvation*. Chicago: University of Chicago Press, 1995.

Goyens, J. "Bertrand de la Tour." In *DHGE* 8 (1935), 1084.

Graef, Hilda. *Mary: A History of Doctrine and Devotion*. 2 vols. New York: Sheed and Ward, 1963–65.

Gregori, Mina. *Giovanni da Milano in Santa Croce*. Valmorea: Comune di Valmorea, 1980.

———, ed. *Pittura a Bergamo dal romanico al neoclassicismo*. Milan: Silvana Ed. d'Arte, 1991.

Grundmann, Herbert. *Religious Movements in the Middle Ages*. Trans. Steven Rowan. Notre Dame, IN: University of Notre Dame Press, 1995.

Guarnieri, Romana. "Pinzochere." In *DIP* 6 (1980), 1721–49.

Guerrieri, Francesco. *La chiesa dello spedale del Ponte Petrino*. Prato, n.d.

Guillaume, Paul-Marie. "Marie-Madeleine." In *DS* 10 (1980), 559–75.

Gutiérrez, David. "Grégoire de Crémone." In *DHGE* 21 (1986), 1495–96.

———. *The Augustinians in the Middle Ages, 1256–1356* (History of the Order of St. Augustine, vol. 1). Villanova, PA: Augustinian Historical Institute, 1984.

Hansel, Hans. *Die Maria-Magdalena-Legende. Eine Quellen Untersuchung. (Greifswalder Beiträge zur Literatur und Stilforschung*. Vol. 16/1) Greifswald: Hans Dallmeyer, 1937.

Haskins, Susan. *Mary Magdalen: Myth and Metaphor*. London: HarperCollins, 1993.

Heerinckx, Jacobus. "Vita activa et vita contemplativa secundum S. Antonium Patavinum." *Apostolicum* 1 (1932): 2–8.

Henderson, John. "The Flagellant Movement and Flagellant Confraternities in Central Italy, 1260–1400." In *Religious Motivation: Biographical and Sociological Problems for the Church Historian*, ed. Derek Baker, 147–60 (Ecclesiastical History Society, vol. 15). Oxford: Basil Blackwell, 1978.

———. *Piety and Charity in Late Medieval Florence*. Oxford: Oxford University Press, 1994.

Hendy, Philip. *The Isabella Stewart Gardner Museum: Catalogue of the Exhibited Paintings and Drawings*. Boston: Trustees of the Museum, 1931.

Herde, Peter. "Bianchi, Gerardo." In *DBI* 10 (1968), 96–101.

———. *Karl I von Anjou*. Stuttgart: W. Kohlhammer, 1979.

Herlihy, David, and Christiane Klapisch-Zuber. *Tuscans and Their Families: A Study of the Florentine Catasto of 1427*. New Haven: Yale University Press, 1985.

———. "Tuscan Names, 1200–1530." *Renaissance Quarterly* 41 (1988): 561–82.

Hinnebusch, William, A. *The History of the Dominican Order*. 2 vols. Staten Island, NY: Alba House, 1966–73.

Hood, William. "St. Dominic's Manners of Praying: Gestures in Fra Angelico's Cell Frescoes at S. Marco." *Art Bulletin* 68 (1986): 195–206.

———. *Fra Angelico at San Marco*. New Haven: Yale University Press, 1993.

Hucher, M. E. "Des enseignes de pélerinages," *Bulletin Monumental*, 2d series, 19 (1853): 505–16.

Huelsen, Christian. *Le chiese di Roma nel medio evo.* Florence: Leo S. Olschki, 1927.

Hufstader, Anselm. "Lefèvre d'Étaples and the Magdalen." *Studies in the Renaissance* 16 (1969): 31–60.

Hughes, Diane Owen. "Sumptuary Law and Social Relations in Renaissance Italy." In *Disputes and Settlements: Law and Human Relations in the West,* ed. John Bossy, 69–99. Cambridge: Cambridge University Press, 1983.

———. "Distinguishing Signs: Ear-rings, Jews, and Franciscan Rhetoric in the Italian Renaissance City." *Past and Present* 112 (1986): 3–59.

———. "Regulating Women's Fashion." In *Silences of the Middle Ages,* ed. Christiane Klapisch-Zuber, 136–58. *A History of Women in the West.* Vol. 2. Cambridge, MA: Belknap Press of Harvard University Press, 1992.

Iogna-Prat, Dominique. "*Bienheureuse polysémie.* La Madeleine du *Sermo in veneratione Sanctae Mariae Magdalenae* attribué à Odon de Cluny (Xe siècle)." In *Marie Madeleine,* ed. Duperray, 21–31.

———. "La Madeleine du *Sermo in veneratione Sanctae Mariae Magdalenae* attribué à Odon de Cluny." *MEFRM* 104/1 (1992): 37–67 (expanded version).

Izbicki, Thomas M. "Pyres of Vanities: Mendicant Preaching on the Vanity of Women and Its Lay Audience." In *De ore Domini: Preacher and Word in the Middle Ages,* ed. Thomas L. Amos et al., 211–34. (Studies in Medieval Culture, vol. 27). Kalamazoo, MI: Medieval Institute Publications, 1989.

Jacquart, Danielle, and Claude Thomasset. *Sexuality and Medicine in the Middle Ages.* Trans. Matthew Adamson. Princeton: Princeton University Press, 1988.

James, Montague Rhodes. *A Descriptive Catalogue of Manuscripts in the Library of St. John's College, Cambridge.* Cambridge: Cambridge University Press, 1922.

———. *The Apocryphal New Testament.* Oxford: Clarendon Press, 1924.

Jansen, Franz. *Die Helmarshausner Buchmalerei zur Zeit Heinrichs des Löwen.* Hildesheim-Leipzig: August Lax, 1933.

Jansen, Katherine Ludwig. "Mary Magdalen and the Mendicants: The Preaching of Penance in the Late Middle Ages." *Journal of Medieval History* 21/1 (1995): 1–25.

———. "Maria Magdalena: Apostolorum Apostola." In *Women Preachers and Prophets,* 57–96.

———. "Innocent III and the Literature of Confession." In *Innocent III: Urbs et Orbis.* Forthcoming.

Janssen, Marga. *Maria Magdalena in der abendländischen Kunst. Ikonographie der Heiligen von den Anfängen bis ins 16. Jahrhundert.* Inaugural diss., Freiburg im Breisgau, 1961.

———. "Maria Magdalena." In *Lexikon der christlichen Ikonographie,* vol. 7 (1974), 516–41. 8 vols. Rome: Herder, 1968–76.

Johnson, Penelope. *Equal in Monastic Profession: Religious Women in Medieval France.* Chicago: University of Chicago Press, 1991.

Jordan, Édouard. *Les origines de la domination angevine en Italie.* Paris: A. Picard, 1909.

Jordan, William C. *Louis IX and the Challenge of the Crusade: A Study in Rulership.* Princeton: Princeton University Press, 1979.

Jotischky, Andrew. "Gerard of Nazareth, Mary Magdalene and Latin Relations with the Greek Orthodox," *Levant* 29 (1997): 217–25.

Jungmann, Josef A. *The Mass of the Roman Rite.* 2 vols. New York: Benziger, 1950–55.

Kaeppeli, T. "Note sugli scrittori domenicani di nome Giovanni di Napoli." *AFP* 10 (1940): 48–76.

Kaftal, George. "Three Scenes from the Legend of Santa Francesca Romana." *Walters Art Gallery Journal* 11 (1948): 50–61.

———. *Iconography of the Saints.* 4 vols. Florence: Sansoni, 1965–86.

Karras, Ruth Mazo. "Holy Harlots: Prostitute Saints in Medieval Legend." *Journal of the History of Sexuality* 1/1 (1990): 3–32.

———. *Common Women: Prostitution and Sexuality in Medieval England.* Oxford: Oxford University Press, 1996.

Katzenellenbogen, Adolf. *Allegories of the Virtues and Vices in Medieval Art: From Early Christian Times to the Thirteenth Century.* Trans. Alan J. P. Crick. New York: W. W. Norton and Co., 1964.

Kieckhefer, Richard. *Unquiet Souls: Fourteenth-Century Saints and Their Religious Milieu.* Chicago: University of Chicago Press, 1984.

Kienzle, Beverly Mayne. "The Prostitute-Preacher: Patterns of Polemic against Medieval Waldensian Women Preachers." In *Women Preachers and Prophets*, 99–113.

King, Karen. "Prophetic Power and Women's Authority: The Case of the *Gospel of Mary* (Magdalene)." In *Women Preachers and Prophets*, 21–41.

Klaniczay, Gábor. *The Uses of Supernatural Power: The Transformation of Popular Religion in Medieval and Early-Modern Europe.* Trans. Susan Singerman. Princeton: Princeton University Press, 1990.

——— et al. "'Vinum vetus in utres novos.' Conclusioni sull'edizione CD del Leggendario ungherese angioino." In *L'État Angevin*, 301–15.

Klapisch-Zuber, Christiane. *Women, Family, and Ritual in Renaissance Italy.* Trans. Lydia Cochrane. Chicago: University of Chicago Press, 1985.

Krüger, Jürgen. *S. Lorenzo Maggiore in Neapel. Eine Franziskanerkirche zwischen Ordensideal und Herrschaftsarchitektur.* Werl-Westfalen: Dietrich-Coelde, 1985.

Ladurie, Emmanuel Le Roy. *Montaillou: The Promised Land of Error.* Trans. Barbara Bray. New York: Vintage, 1979.

Laluque, Bernard. *Marseille fut-elle evangelisée par une femme?* Marseilles: Le Comité du Vieux Marseille, 1986.

Landes, Richard. *Relics, Apocalypse, and the Deceits of History: Ademar of Chabannes, 989–1034.* Cambridge, MA: Harvard University Press, 1995.

LaRow, Magdalen. *The Iconography of Mary Magdalen: The Evolution of a Western Tradition until 1300.* Ph.D. diss., New York University, 1982.

Laurent, M-H. *Le culte de S. Louis d'Anjou à Marseille au XIVe siècle* (Temi e Testi, 2). Rome: Ed. di Storia e Letteratura, 1954.

Lauwers, Michel. "*Noli me tangere:* Marie Madeleine, Marie d'Oignies et les pénitentes du XIIIe siècle." In *MEFRM* 104/1 (1992): 209–68.

Lea, Henry Charles. *A History of Auricular Confession and Indulgences in the Latin Church.* 3 vols. Philadelphia: Lea Bros. & Co., 1896.

Lebreton, Marie-Madeleine. "Eudes de Châteauroux." *DS* 4 (1960), 1675–78.

Lecoy de la Marche, A. *La chaire française au Moyen Age spécialement au XIIIe siècle.* Paris: Librairie Renouard, 1886.

Lecoy de la Marche, A. *Le Roi Réne: sa vie, son administration, ses travaux artistique et littéraires.* 2 vols. Paris: Librairie de Firmon-Didot, 1875.

Le Goff, Jacques. *The Birth of Purgatory.* Trans. Arthur Goldhammer. Chicago: University of Chicago Press, 1984.

———. *St. Louis* (Paris: Gallimard, 1996).

Léonard, Emile-Guillaume. *Les Angevins de Naples.* Paris: Presses Universitaires de France, 1954.

Lesnick, Daniel R. *Preaching in Medieval Florence: The Social World of Franciscan and Dominican Spirituality.* Athens, GA: University of Georgia Press, 1989.

Levron, Jacques. *Le bon roi René.* N.p.: Arthaud, 1972.

Lightbown, Ronald. *Sandro Botticelli.* 2 vols. London: Paul Elek, 1978.

Lillich, Meredith Parsons. *The Armor of Light: Stained Glass in Western France, 1250–1325.* Berkeley: University of California Press, 1994.

Little, Lester K. *Religious Poverty and the Profit Economy in Medieval Europe.* Ithaca, NY: Cornell University Press, 1978.

——— et al. *Liberty, Charity, Fraternity: Lay Religious Confraternities at Bergamo in the Age of the Commune.* Northampton, MA, and Bergamo: Smith College and Pierluigi Lubrina, 1988.

Lobrichon, Guy. "Le dossier magdalénien aux XIe–XIIe siècle." *MEFRM* 104/1 (1992): 163–80.

Longère, Jean. *La prédication médiévale.* Paris: Études Augustiniennes, 1983.

Lopez, Luigi. *L'Aquila: le memorie, i monumenti, il dialetto.* L'Aquila: G. Tazzi, 1988.

Luchs, Alison. *Cestello: A Cistercian Church of the Florentine Renaissance.* New York: Garland, 1977.

Maccarrone, Michele. *Studi su Innocenzo III* (Italia Sacra, vol. XVII). Padua: Antenore, 1972.

Macey, Patrick. "*Infiamma il mio cor:* Savonarolan *Laude* by and for Dominican Nuns in Tuscany." In *The Crannied Wall,* ed. Craig A. Monson, 161–89.

La Maddalena tra sacro e profano. Ed. Marilena Mosco. Milan: Mondadori, 1986.

La Madeleine (VIIIe–XIIIe siècle). MEFRM 104/1 (1992).

Maisch, Ingrid. *Maria Magdalena zwischen Verachtung und Verehrung: das Bild einer Frau im Spiegel der Jahrhunderte.* Freiburg: Herder, 1996.

Malvern, Marjorie. *Venus in Sackcloth. The Magdalen's Origins and Metamorphoses.* Carbondale, IL: Southern Illinois University Press, 1975.

Mangenot, E. "Hughes de Saint-Cher. In *DTC* 7.1 (1922), 219–39.

Mannowsky, W. *Der Danziger Paramentenschatz: kirchliche Gewänder und Stickereien aus der Marienkirche.* Berlin: Brandussche Verlagsbuchhandlung, 1932.

Mansfield, Mary Claire. *Public Penance in Northern France in the Thirteenth Century.* Ph.D. diss., University of California, Berkeley, 1989.

———. *The Humiliation of Sinners: Public Penance in Thirteenth-Century France.* Ithaca, NY: Cornell University Press, 1995.

Marchesani, Carlo, and Giorgio Sperati. *Ospedali genovesi nel medioevo* (Atti della Società Ligure di Storia Patria, n.s., 21 (95)-Fasc. I). Genoa: Società Ligure di Storia Patria, 1981.

Marjanen, Antti. *The Woman Jesus Loved: Mary Magdalene in the Nag Hammadi Library and Related Documents.* Leiden: E. J. Brill, 1996.

Martin, Hervé. "Confession et contrôle social à la fin du moyen âge." In *Pratiques de la confession. Des pères du désert à Vatican II*, 117–36. Paris: Cerf, 1983.

———. *Le métier de prédicateur en France septentrionale à la fin du Moyen Age 1350–1520*. Paris: Cerf, 1988.

Mason, Mary Elizabeth. *Active Life and Contemplative Life: A Study of the Concepts from Plato to the Present*. Milwaukee, WI: Marquette University Press, 1961.

Matter, E. Ann. "Innocent III and the Keys to the Kingdom of Heaven." In *Women Priests: A Catholic Commentary on the Vatican Declaration*, ed. Leonard and Arlene Swidler, 145–51. New York: Paulist Press, 1977.

———. *The Voice of My Beloved: The Song of Songs in Western Medieval Christianity*. Philadelphia: University of Pennsylvania Press, 1990.

Mayor, A. Hyatt. *Prints and People: A Social History of Printed Pictures*. New York: Metropolitan Museum of Art, 1971.

Mazzi, Maria Serena. *Prostitute e lenoni nella Firenze del Quattrocento*. Milan: Mondadori, 1991.

McDonnell, Ernest W. *The Beguines and Beghards in Medieval Culture, with Special Emphasis on the Belgian Scene*. New Brunswick, NJ: Rutgers University Press, 1954.

McSheffrey, Shannon. *Gender and Heresy: Women and Men in Lollard Communities, 1420–1530*. Philadelphia: University of Pennsylvania Press, 1995.

Meersseman, Gilles Gérard. *Ordo fraternitatis: Confraternite e pietà dei laici nel Medioevo* (Italia Sacra, 24–26). Rome: Herder, 1977.

Meiss, Millard. *Painting in Florence and Siena after the Black Death: The Arts, Religion, and Society in the Mid-Fourteenth Century*. Princeton: Princeton University Press, 1951.

———. "Notes on Three Linked Sienese Styles." *Art Bulletin* 45 (1963): 47–48.

Metz, René. "Recherches sur la condition de la femme selon Gratien." In *Studia Gratiana* (*Collectanea Stephan Kuttner*, II) 12 (1967): 379–96.

Michaud-Quantin, Pierre. *Sommes de casuistique et manuels de confession au moyen âge (XII–XVI siècles)* (Analecta Mediaevalia Namurcensia, 13). Louvain: Nauwelaerts, 1962.

Michel, A. "Pénitence du IVe concile du Latran à la réforme." *DTC* 12 (1933), 947–1050.

Ministeri, B. "Agostino d'Ancona (Agostino Triumfo)." *DBI* 1 (1960), 475–78.

Monasticon Italiae I: Roma e Lazio. Ed. Filippo Caraffa. (Centro Storico Benedettino Italiano) Cesena: Badia di Santa Maria del Monte, 1981.

Monasticon Italiae III: Puglia e Basilicata. Ed. Giovanni Lundardi, Hubert Houben, and Giovanni Spinelli. (Centro Storico Benedettino Italiano) Cesena: Badia di Santa Maria del Monte, 1986.

Moncault, Michel. *La basilique Sainte-Marie-Madeleine et le couvent royal*. Aix-en-Provence: Edisud, 1985.

Montagnes, Bernard. "Saint-Maximin, foyer d'une création hagiographique. Le *Liber miraculorum beate Marie Magdalene*. (1315)." In *Marie-Madeleine*, ed. Duperray, 49–69.

———. "La légende dominicaine de Marie-Madeleine à Saint-Maximin." *Mémoires de l'Académie de Vaucluse*, 7th series, 6 (1985): 73–86.

Montault, X. Barbier de. "Sainte Marie-Madeleine d'après les monuments de Rome." *Revue de l'art chrétien*, 2d series, 12 (1880): 116–26.

Monti, Gennaro Maria. *Le confraternite medievali dell'alta e media Italia*. 2 vols. Venice: La Nuova Editrice, 1927.

———. *La dominazione angioina in Piemonte*. Turin: Casale Monf., 1930.

Mooney, Catherine M. *Women's Visions, Men's Words: The Portrayal of Holy Women and Men in Fourteenth-Century Italian Hagiography*. Ph.D. diss., Yale University, 1991.

———. "The Authorial Role of Brother A. in the Composition of Angela of Foligno's Revelations." In *Creative Women*, ed. E. Ann Matter and John Coakley, 34–63.

Moore, R. I. *The Formation of a Persecuting Society: Power and Deviance in Western Europe, 950–1250*. Oxford: Blackwell, 1987.

Moorman, John. *A History of the Franciscan Order from Its Origins to the Year 1517*. Oxford: Clarendon Press, 1968.

———. *Medieval Franciscan Houses*. St. Bonaventure, NY: Franciscan Institute, 1983.

Mortier, Daniel-Antonin. *Histoire des maîtres généraux de l'ordre des frères prêcheurs*. 7 vols. Paris: Alphonse Picard et fils, 1903–14.

Mulder-Bakker, Anneke B. "Lame Margaret of Magdeburg: The Social Function of a Medieval Recluse." *Journal of Medieval History* 22/2 (1996): 155–69.

Murray, Alexander. "Confession as a Historical Source in the Thirteenth Century." In *The Writing of History in the Middle Ages: Essays Presented to Richard William Southern*, ed. R.H.C. Davis and J. M. Wallace-Hadrill, 275–322. Oxford: Clarendon Press, 1981.

———. "Confession before 1215." *Transactions of the Royal Historical Society*, 6th series, 3 (1993): 51–81.

Murray, Robert. *Symbols of Church and Kingdom*. Cambridge: Cambridge University Press, 1975.

Musto, Ronald. "Queen Sancia of Naples (1286–1345) and the Spiritual Franciscans." In *Women of the Medieval World: Essays in Honor of John H. Mundy*, ed. J. Kirshner and S. F. Wemple, 179–214. Oxford: Basil Blackwell, 1985.

Nessi, Silvestro. "Le *religiosae mulieres*." In *Il processo di canonizzazione di Chiara da Montefalco*, ed. Enrico Menestò, 546–55. Florence: La Nuova Italia Editrice, 1984.

———. "Chiara da Montefalco, Angela da Foligno, e Iacopone da Todi." In *S. Chiara da Montefalco e il suo tempo*, ed. Claudio Leonardi and Enrico Menestò, 3–51. Florence: La Nuova Italia Editrice, 1985.

Newman, Barbara. "Gnostics, Free Spirits, and 'Meister Eckhart's Daughter.'" In *From Virile Woman to Womanchrist*, 172–81. Philadelphia: University of Pennsylvania Press, 1994.

Nitschke, A. "Carlo II d'Angiò." In *DBI* 20 (1977), 227–35.

Norman, Diana. "The Case of the *Beata* Simona: Iconography, Hagiography and Misogyny in Three Paintings by Taddeo di Bartolo." *Art History* 18 (1995): 154–84.

Novelli, Leandro. "Due documenti inediti relativi alle monache benedettine dette 'Santucce.'" *Benedictina* 22 (1975): 189–253.

Noye, Irénée. "Miséricorde (oeuvre de)." In *DS* 10 (1980), 1327–49.

Nuti, Ruggero. "Lo spedale del Ponte Petrino e la sua chiesa." *Archivio Storico Pratese,* 5(4) an. 10, fasc. IV, 152–58; 5(5) an. 11, fasc. I, 17–25; 5(5) an. 11, fasc. II, 81–88.

Ocker, Christopher. *Johannes Klenkok: A Friar's Life, c. 1310–1374.* Philadelphia: American Philosophical Society, 1993.

Offner, Richard, with Klara Steinweg. *A Critical and Historical Corpus of Florentine Painting.* New York: College of Fine Arts, New York University, 1930–; repr. Florence: Giunti Gruppo Editoriale.

Oliver, Judith. "Worship of the Word: Some Gothic *Nonnenbücher* in Their Devotional Context." In *Women and the Book: Assessing the Visual Evidence,* ed. Lesley Smith and Jane H. M. Taylor, 106–22. Toronto: University of Toronto Press, 1996.

Origo, Iris. *The Merchant of Prato: Francesco di Marco Datini.* New York: Knopf, 1957.

Ortenberg, Veronica. "Le culte de Sainte Marie Madeleine dans l'Angleterre Anglo-Saxonne." In *MEFRM* 104/1 (1992): 13–35.

Otis, Leah Lydia. *Prostitution in Medieval Society. The History of an Urban Institution in Languedoc.* Chicago: University of Chicago Press, 1985.

———. "Prostitution and Repentance in Late Medieval Perpignan." In *Women of the Medieval World,* ed. J. Kirshner and S. F. Wemple, 137–60. Oxford: Basil Blackwell, 1985.

Pagels, Elaine. *The Gnostic Gospels.* New York: Random House, 1979.

Pansier, P. *L'oeuvre des repenties à Avignon du XIIIe au XVIIIe siècle.* Paris and Avignon: Honoré Champion and J. Roumanille, 1910.

Pantin, W. A. "Instructions for a Devout and Literate Layman." In *Medieval Learning and Literature: Essays Presented to Richard William Hunt,* ed. J.J.G. Alexander and M. T. Gibson, 398–400. Oxford: Clarendon Press, 1976.

Paravicini Bagliani, A. "Cavalcanti, Aldobrandino." In *DBI* 22 (1979), 601–3.

Parkes, M. B. "The Literacy of the Laity." In *The Medieval World,* ed. David Daiches and Anthony Thorlby, 555–77. London: Aldus Books, 1973.

Pavan, E. "Police des moeurs, société et politique à Venise à la fin du moyen âge." *Revue historique* 264 (1980): 241–88.

Péano, Pierre. "Luc de Bitonto." In *DS* 9 (1976), 1121–22.

———. "Nicolas d'Hacqueville." In *DS* 11 (1982), 283.

Pellegrini, Luigi. *Insediamenti francescani nell'Italia del duecento.* Rome: Ed. Laurentianum, 1984.

Petroff, Elizabeth. *Consolation of the Blessed.* New York: Alta Gaia Society, 1979.

———. *Body and Soul: Essays on Medieval Women and Mysticism.* Oxford: Oxford University Press, 1994.

Piazzoni, A. M. "Colombini, Giovanni." In *DBI* 27 (1982), 149–53.

Piccirilli, P. *Monumenti architettonici sulmonesi (dal XIV al XVI secolo).* Lanciano: Rocco Carabba, 1887; repr. 1976.

Pilosu, Mario. *La donna, la lussuria e la chiesa nel Medioevo.* Genoa: ECIG, 1989.

Pinto-Mathieu, E. *Marie-Madeleine dans la littérature du Moyen-Age.* Paris: Beauchesne, 1997.

Piò, Michele G. *Delle vite degli huomini illustri di S. Domenico. Libri Quatro. Ove compendiosamente si tratta de i santi, beati, & beate, & altri di segnalata bontà dell'Ordine de' Predicatori.* Bologna: Sebastiano Bonomi, 1620.

I pittori bergamaschi dal XIII al XIX secolo. 13 vols. Bergamo: Bolis, 1975–92.

Plancy, J.A.S. Collin de. *Dictionnaire critique des reliques et des images mirculeuses.* 3 vols. Paris: Guien et Compagnie, 1821.

Poggi, Giovanni. *Il Duomo di Firenze.* Berlin: Bruno Cassirer, 1909.

Politi, Marco. "Giovanni Paolo II corregge i Vangeli. 'Fu Maria la prima a vedere Cristo risorto.'" *La Repubblica,* 22 May 1997, 1 and 25.

Pomeroy, Sarah B. *Goddesses, Whores, Wives, and Slaves: Women in Classical Antiquity.* New York: Schocken Books, 1975.

Poncelet, A. "Le légendier de Pierre Calo." *Analecta Bollandiana* 29 (1910): 5–116.

Pope-Hennessy, John. *Donatello Sculptor.* New York: Abbeville, 1993.

Poschmann, Bernard. *Penance and the Anointing of the Sick.* Trans. Francis Courtney, S.J. New York: Herder and Herder, 1964.

Powell, James M. "*Pastor Bonus:* Some Evidence of Honorius III's Use of the Sermons of Pope Innocent III." *Speculum* 52/3 (1977): 522–37.

Quetif, Jacobus, and Jacobus Echard. *Scriptores Ordinis Praedicatorum.* 3 vols. Paris: J.-B.-C. Ballard & N. Simant, 1719–1934.

Quirino, Roberto. "Un argomento di pittura spoletina fra tre e quattrocentro: Il Maestro dei Cavalari." *Esercizi: Arte, Musica, Spettacolo* 5 (1982): 20–33.

Raguin, Virginia Chieffo. *Stained Glass in Thirteenth-Century Burgundy.* Princeton: Princeton University Press, 1982.

Rayez, André. "Hugues de Prato." In *DS* 7.1 (1969), 893–94.

Reames, Sherry. *The Legenda Aurea: A Reexamination of Its Paradoxical History.* Madison, WI: University of Wisconsin Press, 1985.

Rech, Clara. *Terracina e il Medioevo.* Terracina: Quasar, 1989.

Ricci, Carla. *Mary Magdalen and Many Others: Women Who Followed Jesus.* Minneapolis, MN: Fortress Press, 1994.

Rice, Eugene. "The Humanist Idea of Christian Antiquity: Lefèvre d'Étaples and His Circle." *Studies in the Renaissance* 9 (1962): 126–60.

———. *Saint Jerome in the Renaissance.* Baltimore: Johns Hopkins University Press, 1985.

Richardson, Ernest C. *Materials for a Life of Jacopo da Varagine.* New York: H. W. Wilson, 1935.

Roberts, Ann M. "Chiara Gambacorta of Pisa as Patroness of the Arts." In *Creative Women,* 120–54.

Le roi René en son temps (1382–1481). Aix-en-Provence: Musée Granet-Palais de Malte, 1981.

Rossiaud, Jacques. *Medieval Prostitution.* Trans. Lydia G. Cochrane. Oxford: Basil Blackwell, 1988.

Rossman, Heribert. "François de Meyronnes." In *DS* 10 (1980), 1155–61.

Rubin, Miri. *Corpus Christi: The Eucharist in Late Medieval Culture.* Cambridge: Cambridge University Press, 1991.

Ruggiero, Gerardo. "Il monastero di Sant'Anna di Nocera: dalla fondazione al Concilio di Trento." *Memorie Domenicane,* n.s., 20 (1989): 5–166.

Runciman, Steven. *The Sicilian Vespers: A History of the Mediterranean World in the Later Thirteenth Century.* Cambridge: Cambridge University Press, 1958; Canto ed., 1992.

Rusconi, Roberto. "De la prédication à la confession: transmission et contrôle de modèles de comportment au XIIIe siècle." In *Faire Croire: Modalités de la diffusion et de la réception des messages religieux du XIIe au XVe siècle,* 67–85 (Collection de l'Ecole Française de Rome, 51). Rome: l'École Française de Rome, 1981.

———. "*Forma apostolorum:* L'immagine del predicatore nei movimenti religiosi francesi ed italiani dei secc. XII e XIII." *Cristianesimo nella storia* 6 (1985): 513–42.

———. "Women Religious In Late Medieval Italy: New Sources and Directions." In *Women and Religion,* 305–26.

———. "Women's Sermons at the End of the Middle Ages: Texts from the Blessed and Images of the Saints." In *Women Preachers,* 173–95.

Russo, Daniel. "Saint François, le Franciscains et les représentations du Christ sur la croix en Ombrie au XIIIe siècle. Recherches sur la formation d'une image et sur une sensibilité au Moyen Age." *MEFRM* 96/2 (1984): 647–717.

———. "Entre le Christ et Marie: la Madeleine dans l'art italien des XIIIe–XVe siècles." In *Marie Madeleine,* ed. Duperray, 173–90.

Sabatelli, G. "Antonio da Padova, santo." In *DBI* 3 (1961), 561–68.

Santa Chiara da Montefalco e il suo tempo. Ed. Claudio Leonardi and Enrico Menestò (Quaderni del "Centro per il collegamento degli studi medievali e umanistici nell'Università di Perugia, 12). Florence: La Nuova Italia, 1985.

Sapegno, Natalino. "Il Pucci, il Sacchetti e la letteratura borghese." In *Il Trecento,* vol. 5, 404–16. In *Storia letteraria d'Italia.* 9 vols. Padua: La Nuova Libreria Editrice, 1981; 4th rev. ed.

Saxer, Victor. "La vie de sainte Marie-Madeleine" attribuée au pseudo-Raban Maur, oeuvre claravalienne du XIIe siècle." In *Mélanges Saint Bernard* (XXIVe Congrès de l'Association bourguignonne de Sociétés savantes [VIIIe centenaire de la mort de S. Bernard]), 408–21. Dijon: Marlier, 1953.

———. "Un manuscrit décembré du sermon d'Eudes de Cluny sur Ste. Marie-Madeleine." *Scriptorium* 8 (1954): 119–23.

———. "Les saintes Marie Madeleine et Marie de Béthanie dans la tradition liturgique et homilétique orientale." *Revue des sciences religieuses* 32 (1958): 1–37.

———. *Le culte de Marie-Madeleine en occident des origines à la fin du moyen-âge.* 2 vols. (Cahiers d'archéologie et d'histoire, 3) Auxerre-Paris: Publications de la Société des Fouilles Archéologiques et des Monuments Historiques de l'Yonne-Librairie Clavreuil, 1959.

———. "Maria Maddalena." In *BS* 8 (1967), 1078–1107.

———. *Le dossier vézelien de Marie-Madeleine. Invention et translation des reliques en 1265–1267. Contribution à histoire du culte de la sainte à l'apogée du Moyen Age.* (*Subsidia hagiographica,* n. 57) Brussels: Société des Bollandistes, 1975.

———. "Les ossements dits de sainte Marie-Madeleine conservés a Saint Maximin-la-Sainte-Baume." *Provence Historique* 27 (1977): 257–311.

———. "La relique de Saint-Maximin (Var) dite *la sainte ampoule.*" *Revue d'histoire ecclésiastique* 79/1 (1984): 87–96.

Saxer, Victor. "Le culte et la tradition de Sainte Marie-Madeleine en Provence." *Mémoires de l'Académie de Vaucluse,* 7th series, 6 (1985): 41–51.

———. "Les origines du culte de Sainte Marie Madeleine en Occident." In *Marie Madeleine,* ed. Duperray, 33–47.

———. "Philippe Cabassole et son *Libellus hystorialis Marie beatissime Magdalene.* Préliminaires à une édition du *Libellus.*" In *L'État Angevin,* 193–204.

Schianchi, Lucia Fornari. *La Galleria Nazionale di Parma.* Parma: Artegrafica Silva, n.d.

Schmitt, Clément. "Pierre de Padoue." In *DS* 12 (1986), 1631.

Schmitt, J.-C. "'Religion populaire' et 'culture folklorique.'" *Annales E.S.C.* 31 (1976): 941–53.

———. *Mort d'une hérésie: L'Église et les clercs face aux béguines et aux béghards du Rhin supérieur du XIVe au XVe siècle.* Paris: Mouton, 1978.

———. "Entre le texte et l'image: les gestes de la prière de Saint Dominique." In *Persons in Groups: Social Behavior as Identity Formation in Medieval and Renaissance Europe,* ed. R. Trexler, 195–220. Binghamton, NY: Medieval and Renaissance Texts and Studies, 1985.

Schneyer, Johannes Baptist. *Geschichte der katholischen Predigt.* Freiburg im Breisgau: Seelsorge, 1969.

———. *Repertorium der lateinischen Sermones des Mittelalters für die Zeit von 1150–1350* (Beiträge zur Geschichte der Philosophie und Theologie des Mittelalters 43). 11 vols. Münster-Westfalen: Aschendorffsche, 1969–90.

Schwartz, Lorraine C. *The Fresco Decoration of the Magdalen Chapel in the Basilica of St. Francis at Assisi.* Ph.D. diss., University of Indiana, 1980.

———. "Patronage and Franciscan Iconography in the Magdalen Chapel at Assisi." *The Burlington Magazine* 133 (1991): 32–36.

Sclafer, Jacqueline. "Iohannes Gobi Senior OP, *Liber miraculorum b. Mariae Magdalenae.*" *AFP* 63 (1993): 113–206.

Scott, Karen. "St. Catherine of Siena, *Apostola.*" *Church History* 61/1 (1992): 34–46.

———. "*Io Catarina:* Ecclesiastical Politics and Oral Culture in the Letters of Catherine of Siena." In *Dear Sister: Medieval Women and the Epistolary Genre,* ed. Karen Cherewatuk and Ulrike Wiethaus, 87–121. Philadelphia: University of Pennsylvania Press, 1993.

———. "Urban Spaces, Women's Networks, and the Lay Apostolate in the Siena of Catherine Benincasa." In *Creative Women,* 105–19.

Scuppa, Giuseppe. *I sermoni di Innocenzo III.* Tesi di laurea, Pontificia Universitas Lateranensis, 1961.

Sebastiani, Lilia. *Tra/Sfigurazione: Il personaggio evangelico di Maria di Magdala e il mito della peccatrice redenta nella tradizione occidentale.* Brescia: Queriniana, 1992.

Sensi, Mario. "Anchoresses and Penitents in Thirteenth- and Fourteenth-Century Umbria." In *Women and Religion,* 56–83.

Shapley, Fern Rusk. *Paintings from the Samuel H. Kress Collection: Italian Schools.* 3 vols. London: Phaidon Press, 1966.

Shearman, John. *Only Connect . . . Art and the Spectator in the Italian Renaissance* (The A. W. Mellon Lectures in the Fine Arts, 1988. The National Gallery of Art,

Washington, D.C., Bollingen Series XXXV.37). Princeton: Princeton University Press, 1992.

Sheingorn, Pamela. *The Book of Saint Foy.* Philadelphia: University of Pennsylvania, 1995.

Sigal, Pierre-André. *Les marcheurs de Dieu, pèlerinages et pèlerins au Moyen Age.* Paris: A. Colin, 1974.

Simon, André. *L'ordre des pénitentes de Ste Marie-Madeleine en Allemagne au XIIIme siècle* (Thèse présentée à la faculté de théologie de l'université de Fribourg, Suisse pour obtenir le grade de docteur en théologie). Fribourg: Imprimerie et Librairie de l'oeuvre de Saint-Paul, 1918.

Simonetti, Adele. "I sermoni di Umiltà da Faenza: storia della tradizione." *Studi medievali,* 3d series, 32 (1991): 303–8.

Simons, Walter. "The Beguine Movement in Southern Low Countries: A Reassessment." *Bulletin de l'Institut historique belge de Rome* 59 (1989): 63–105.

Slim, H. Colin. "Music and Dancing with Mary Magdalen in a Laura Vestalis." In *The Crannied Wall,* ed. Craig A. Monson, 139–60.

Spiegel, Gabrielle M. "The Cult of St. Denis and Capetian Kingship." In *Saints and Their Cults,* ed. S. Wilson, 141–68.

Spitzig, Joseph A. *Sacramental Penance in the Twelfth and Thirteenth Centuries.* Washington, D.C.: Catholic University of America Press, 1947.

Stampfer, Helmut. *La chiesa di Santa Maddalena presso Bolzano.* Bolzano, 1988.

Stanton, Anne Rudloff. "From Eve to Bathsheba and Beyond: Motherhood in the Queen Mary Psalter." In *Women and the Book: Assessing the Visual Evidence,* ed. Lesley Smith and Jane H. M. Taylor, 172–89. Toronto: University of Toronto Press, 1996.

Steinburg, Ronald M. *Fra Girolamo Savonarola, Florentine Art, and Renaissance Historiography.* Athens, OH: Ohio University Press, 1977.

Stock, Brian. *The Implications of Literacy: Written Language and Models of Interpretation in the Eleventh and Twelfth Centuries.* Princeton: Princeton University Press, 1983.

Strayer, Joseph. *The Albigensian Crusade.* Ann Arbor, MI: University of Michigan Press, 1992.

Sulle tracce degli Umiliati. Ed. Maria Pia Alberzoni et al. Milan: Vita e Pensiero, 1997.

Sullivan, Ruth Wilkins. "Mary Magdalen Anointing Christ's Head: A Rare Devotional Image." *Arte Cristiana* 78 (1990): 307–24.

Sumption, Jonathan. *Pilgrimage: An Image of Mediaeval Religion.* Totowa, NJ: Rowan and Littlefield, 1975.

Supino, I. B. *Giotto.* 2 vols. Florence: Istituto di Edizioni Artistiche, 1920.

Szabó, George. *The Robert Lehman Collection.* New York: Metropolitan Museum of Art, 1975.

Szövérffy, Joseph. "*Peccatrix quondam femina:* A Survey of the Mary Magdalen Hymns." *Traditio* 19 (1963): 79–146.

Tagliabue, M. "Francesca Romana nella storiografia: fonti, studi, biografie." In *Una santa tutta Romana: Saggi e ricerche nel VI centenario della nascità di Francesca Bussa dei Ponziani (1384–1984),* ed. Giorgio Picasso, 199–264. Abbazia di Monte Oliveto Maggiore: Edizioni: "L'Ulivo," 1984.

Tammi, Guido. "Lo statuto dei disciplini di S. Maria Maddalena di Bergamo. Dal codice sigma 3,2 della Biblioteca Civica di Bergamo." In *Il Movimento dei disciplinati nel settimo centenario dal suo inizio (Perugia—1260)* (Convegno internazionale: Perugia, 25–28 Sept. 1960). *BRDU* 59 (1962): 257–68 (appendix).

Tavuzzi, Michael. *Prierias: The Life and Works of Silvestro Mazzolini da Prierio, 1456–1527.* Durham, NC: Duke University Press, 1997.

Teetaert, Amédée. *La confession aux laïques dans l'église latine depuis le VIIIe jusqu'au XIVe siècle.* Paris: J. Gabalda, 1926.

Tentler, Thomas. *Sin and Confession on the Eve of the Reformation.* Princeton: Princeton University Press, 1977.

Thompson, Augustine. *Revival Preachers and Politics in Thirteenth-Century Italy: The Great Devotion of 1233.* Oxford: Clarendon Press, 1992.

Thompson, Sally. *Women Religious: The Founding of English Nunneries after the Norman Conquest.* Oxford: Clarendon Press, 1991.

Tombu, Jeanne. "Un triptyque du maitre de la légende de Marie-Madeleine." *Gazette des Beaux Arts* 15/1 (1927): 299–311.

Trexler, Richard. *Public Life in Renaissance Florence.* New York: Academic Press, 1980.

———. "La prostitution florentine au XVe siècle: patronages et clientèles." *Annales E.S.C.* 6 (1981): 983–1015.

———. "*Correre la Terre:* Collective Insults in the Late Middle Ages." *MEFRM* 96 (1984): 845–902.

Turner, Victor. *The Ritual Process: Structure and Anti-Structure.* Chicago: Aldine, 1969.

Van Engen, John. "The Christian Middle Ages as an Historiographical Problem," *AHR* 91 (1988): 519–52.

Van Marle, Raimond. *The Development of the Italian Schools of Painting.* 28 vols. The Hague: Martinus Nijhoff, 1924–38.

Van Os, H. W., and Marian Prakken. *The Florentine Paintings in Holland: 1300–1500.* Florence: Netherlands Institute for Art History, 1974.

Vauchez, André. "*Beata Stirps:* Sainteté et lignage en occident aux XIIIe et XIVe siècles." In *Famille et parenté dans l'occident médiéval* (Collection de l'École Française de Rome 30 [1977]), ed. Georges Duby and Jacques Le Goff, 397–401.

———. *La sainteté en occident aux derniers siècles du Moyen Age d'après les procès de canonisation et les documents hagiographiques.* (Bibliothèque des Écoles Française d'Athénes et de Rome, fasc. 241) Rome: l'École Française de Rome, 1981.

———. "Pénitents au moyen âge." In *DS* 12 (1984), 1010–23.

———. "Homebon de Crémon (†1197), marchand et saint." In *Les laïcs au Moyen Age. Pratiques et expériences religieuses.* Paris: Cerf, 1987.

———. *The Laity in the Middle Ages.* Trans. Margery J. Schneider. Notre Dame, IN: University of Notre Dame Press, 1993.

———. *Sainthood in the Later Middle Ages.* Trans. Jean Birrell. Cambridge: Cambridge University Press, 1997.

Vavalà, Evelyn Sandburg. *La croce dipinta italiana e l'iconografia della passione.* Verona: Apollo, 1929; Rome, 1980; 2d ed.

Venarde, Bruce L. *Women's Monasticism and Medieval Society: Nunneries in France and England, 890–1215.* Ithaca, NY: Cornell University Press, 1997.

Vicaire, M.-H. *L'imitation des apôtres: moines, chanoines et mendiants IVe–XIIIe siècles*. Paris: Cerf, 1963.

———. *Saint Dominic and His Times*. Trans. Kathleen Pond. Green Bay, WI: Alt Publishing, 1964.

Vitale, Giuliana. "Nobiltà napoletana della prima età angioina: Elite burocratica e famiglia." In *L'État Angevin*, 562–65.

Vogel, Cyrille. *Le pécheur et la pénitence au moyen âge*. Paris: Cerf, 1969; 2d ed., 1982.

Volbach, Wolfgang Fritz. *Il Trecento Firenze e Siena*. Trans. Francesca Pomarici (Catalogo della Pinacoteca Vaticana). 4 vols. Vatican City: Libreria Editrice Vaticana, 1987.

Volpato, Antonio. "Il tema agiografico della triplice aureola nei secoli XIII–XV." In *Culto dei santi*, ed. Sofia Boesch Gajano and Lucia Sebastiani, 509–26.

———. "*Corona aurea* e *corona aureola:* ordini e meriti nella ecclesiologia medioevale." *Bollettino dell'Istituto Storico Italiano per il Medio Evo* 91 (1984): 115–82.

Walter, I. "Brancaccio, Landolfo." In *DBI* 13 (1971), 784–85.

Ward, Benedicta. *Harlots of the Desert: A Study of Repentance in Early Monastic Sources*. Kalamazoo, MI: Cistercian Publications, 1987.

Warner, Marina. *Alone of All Her Sex: The Myth and the Cult of the Virgin Mary*. New York: Vintage Books, 1983.

Warren, Ann K. *Anchorites and Their Patrons in Medieval England*. Berkeley: University of California Press, 1985.

Watkins, Oscar D. *A History of Penance*. 2 vols. London: Longmans, Green, Co., 1920.

Weinstein, Donald. *Savonarola and Florence: Prophecy and Patriotism in the Renaissance*. Princeton: Princeton University Press, 1970.

———, and Rudolph M. Bell. *Saints and Society: The Two Worlds of Western Christendom, 1000–1700*. Chicago: University of Chicago Press, 1982.

Weissman, Ronald F. E. *Ritual Brotherhood in Renaissance Florence*. New York: Academic Press, 1982.

White, Lynn Townsend, Jr. *Latin Monasticism in Norman Sicily*. Cambridge, MA: Medieval Academy of America, 1938.

Wilk, Sarah. "The Cult of Mary Magdalen in Fifteenth-Century Florence and Its Iconography." *Studi Medievali*, 3d series, 26 (1985) II: 685–98.

Wilson, Stephen. ed. *Saints and Their Cults: Studies in Religious Sociology, Folklore and History*. Cambridge: Cambridge University Press, 1983.

Wire, Antoinette Clark. *Corinthian Women Prophets: A Reconstruction through Paul's Rhetoric*. Minneapolis, MN: Fortress Press, 1990.

Witherington III, Ben. *Women and the Genesis of Christianity*. Cambridge: Cambridge University Press, 1990.

Women and Religion in Medieval and Renaissance Italy. Ed. Daniel Bornstein and Roberto Rusconi. Trans. Margery J. Schneider. Chicago: University of Chicago Press, 1996.

Women in Ritual and Symbolic Roles. Ed. Judith Hoch-Smith and Anita Spring. New York: Plenum Press, 1978.

Women Preachers and Prophets through Two Millennia of Christianity. Ed. Beverly Mayne Kienzle and Pamela J. Walker. Berkeley: University of California Press, 1998.

Worstbrock, F. J. "Siboto." In *Die deutsche Literatur des Mittelalters,* vol. 8 (1992), 1138–40. 8 vols. Berlin: Walter de Gruyter, 1978–.

Young, Karl. *The Drama of the Medieval Church.* 2 vols. Oxford: Clarendon Press, 1933; repr. 1951.

Zafarana, Zelina. *Da Gregorio VII a Bernardino da Siena: Saggi di storia medievale.* Ed. O. Capitani, C. Leonardi, et al. (Quaderni del Centro per il collegamento degli studi medievali e umanistici nell'Università di Perugia). Florence: La Nuova Italia, 1987.

Zarri, Gabriella. "I monasteri femminili a Bologna tra il XIII e il XVII secolo." *Atti e Memorie. n.s. Deputazione di storia patria per le province di Romagna* 24 (1973): 133–224.

———. "Living Saints: A Typology of Female Sanctity in the Early Sixteenth Century." In *Women and Religion,* 219–303.

Zeri, Federico. *Italian Paintings: A Catalogue of the Collection of the Metropolitan Museum of Art: Florentine School.* New York: Metropolitan Museum of Art, 1971.

Index

Note: Mary Magdalen is abbreviated as "MM." Churches, confraternities, convents, and hospitals dedicated to Saint Mary Magdalen are abbreviated as "SMM." Medieval persons are generally but not always listed under their first names. Visual material is listed under the city in which it is now located.